THE LIFE OF JOHN STUART MILL

By

MICHAEL ST. JOHN PACKE

With a Preface by

PROFESSOR F. A. HAYEK

ILLUSTRATED

CAPRICORN BOOKS, NEW YORK

MARTIN SECKER & WARBURG LTD.
7 John Street, Bloomsbury, London, W.C.1
Published by Arrangement with Michael St. John Packe

CAPRICORN BOOKS EDITION 1970

To

KATHRYN WHARTON PACKE

PRINTED IN THE UNITED STATES OF AMERICA

CONTENTS

		page
Preface, by Professor F. A. Hayek		v
Author's Acknowledgements		vii
Note on Sources		ix
Book One	Tabula Rasa	1
Book Two	Friends of the Species	113
Book Three	"A verra foolish piece o' friendliness"	155
Book Four	The London and Westminster Review	189
Book Five	Cause and Effect	249
Book Six	The Hoped-for Heaven	341
Book Seven	The Saint of Rationalism	395
Notes		511
Bibliography		532
Index		543

ILLUSTRATIONS

JOHN STUART MILL *Page* 2
(from a photograph in the possession of the *Picture Post* Library)

JEREMY BENTHAM 112
(from an engraving by J. Posselwhite after the portrait by J. Watts)

JAMES MILL 114
(from a photograph in the possession of the *Picture Post* Library)

HARRIET TAYLOR (*née* HARDY) 156
(from a miniature in the British Library of Political and Economic Science)

JOHN STUART MILL 156
(from a cameo, *c.* 1840, aet. 34)

JOHN TAYLOR 188
(from a miniature in the British Library of Political and Economic Science)

"A CHELSEA INTERIOR" 190
(from the painting by Robert Tait, *c.* 1857–58. Reproduced by kind permission of the Marquess of Northampton)

JOHN STERLING 248
(from an engraving, after a painting by B. de la Cour in 1830)

JOHN STUART MILL and HELEN TAYLOR 250
(from a photograph in the possession of the *Picture Post* Library)

JOHN STUART MILL 342
(from the portrait by G. F. Watts, in 1873, in the National Portrait Gallery)

PREFACE

THERE are few other eminent figures in the intellectual life of the nineteenth century about whom some unusual facts are so widely known, and yet of whose whole character and personality we know so little, as John Stuart Mill. Perhaps in no other instance can we see how misleading an impression even the most honest of autobiographies can give. Mill's account of his own life is of course a document of such psychological interest that its very popularity was bound to discourage others from attempting to draw a fuller picture. This alone, however, does not adequately explain why, for eighty years after his death, no satisfactory biography of Mill has been available. In many ways, the unique value of his own description of his intellectual development has increased rather than diminished the need for a more comprehensive account of the setting against which it ought to be seen.

Until recently, the material on which such a picture could be based was not available. For fifty years Mill's papers had been closely guarded, first by his step-daughter and later by her niece. When the latter died, they were offered for public auction, and were widely dispersed over two continents, at a time when Mill's reputation was passing through that eclipse which, a generation or two after a man's death, most reputations seem to suffer. Only during the last twenty years, as interest in the nineteenth century gradually revived, did it become apparent how much information could be brought to light by patient search. Most of the dispersed material has since been traced, much of it collected together, and some of the more important documents have been published.

The time was therefore just about ripe when a few years ago Mr. Packe set out on a new attempt to write Mill's life. It has been my privilege to watch his progress during part of the period, and occasionally to help on particular points when I happened to be specially familiar with the material. Yet even though I had seen a good deal of the new information, it was something of a surprise to me to see how complete and rounded a picture Mr. Packe has been able to draw by carefully fitting together all the evidence. Hitherto, we have had occasional glimpses of the human being concealed behind what was, it must be admitted, a somewhat forbidding appearance: now, for the first time, Mr. Packe has resurrected a whole personality with all its failings and achievements. Though the emphasis of the book is on John Stuart Mill the man, rather than on the philosopher and economist, the nature of his influence upon the intellectual life of his time stands out all the more clearly against the background of his whole life. There may still be details to be filled in here and there; but on the whole I feel that Mr. Packe has given us the definitive biography of Mill for which we have so long been waiting.

F. A. Hayek

AUTHOR'S ACKNOWLEDGEMENTS

THE main sources of original information about John Stuart Mill are the Mill-Taylor Collection, in the British Library of Political and Economic Science; the John Stuart Mill Collection, in Yale University Library; and the Keynes Library, at King's College, Cambridge. My first acknowledgements must be to the Librarians and Faculties of those Institutions, for friendly facilities accorded to me in their Reading Rooms, and for permission to quote from their indispensable documents. I am also indebted to the National Library of Scotland, and to Miss Anna J. Mill, and the Librarian of Mount Holyoke College, Mass., for allowing me to quote from further manuscripts. Mrs. Edna Gemmell, of South Africa, a grand-daughter of Mill's youngest sister Mary Colman, and Mrs. Helen Sutherland of Adelaide, a descendant of Harriet Taylor's brother Arthur Hardy, have kindly provided me with interesting family material; as has also Mr. F. W. Rycroft, the present owner of Birksgate, formerly the Yorkshire home of the Hardys. For access to a great number of printed books, I must thank the Director of the Reading Room at the British Museum, and his efficient staff.

As regards the Illustrations, I should like to thank the Marquess of Northampton for his kind permission to reproduce Robert Tait's painting of the Carlyles in their house in Cheyne Row, "A Chelsea Interior"; the National Portrait Gallery, for a print of the Watts portrait of Mill; the British Library of Political and Economic Science, for the use of the miniatures of John and Harriet Taylor; and the *Picture Post* Library for the engraving of Jeremy Bentham, for the photograph of Mill here presented as a Frontispiece, and for the photograph of Mill with Helen Taylor.

In addition, I have many debts of a personal kind. Here, first and foremost, I must try to give some account of what I owe my wife (and, I trust, more precisely than did John Stuart Mill). She has carried out a fair share of the research. She has prepared the Index. She has typed, and retyped, from my deplorable handwriting many times. During the fashioning of the book, she has given unflagging encouragement: she has started many lines of thought, and has made many careful suggestions for its improvement. To Professor F. A. Hayek, late of the London School of Economics and now at the University of Chicago, I owe far more than he has indicated in the Preface. Indeed, without his many years of fruitful research, neither this nor any other full biography of Mill could have been written: while his constant interest and timely advice have exceeded anything I could have hoped. Mr. Francis E. Mineka, of Cornell University, has freely given me many pieces of information hitherto unknown to me, especially in the earlier period of Mill's life. John R. W. Smail, of Harvard, has also taken great trouble with the manuscript, and has made many valuable suggestions.

Many others have assisted less directly. To all, I would express my cordial thanks. It is their support which has enabled me to finish what has sometimes seemed a rash and presumptuous undertaking. An undertaking justified only by the belief that Mill's ideals were never more required than at the present time, and that consequently Mill himself would welcome any honest effort, however many its shortcomings, to bring him once again before the public.

NOTE ON SOURCES

THE sources of quotations are given in detail at the end of the book: there is also a bibliography. I have thought it convenient to include in the text such notes as contain matters of fact, and are therefore likely to be of interest to the general reader. They are accordingly printed at the bottom of the appropriate pages, and are signalled in the text by an asterisk. Small raised numbers in the text refer to the notes at the end of the book. Square brackets in quotations indicate the author's interpolations.

I should explain that, principally in the sources but occasionally in the text, certain authorities which are quoted frequently are referred to by abbreviations. They are as follows:

MT Coll. The Mill-Taylor Collection in the British Library of Political and Economic Science (e.g. MT Coll 27/3 = Mill-Taylor Collection, Vol. 27, folio 3).

Yale The John Stuart Mill Collection in Yale University Library.

King's The Keynes Library, at King's College, Cambridge.

Elliot, *Letters* *The Letters of John Stuart Mill*, Ed. Hugh S. R. Elliot, Longmans Green & Co., 2 vols. London, 1910.

Bain, *James Mill* *James Mill, a Biography*, by Alexander Bain, Longmans Green & Co., London, 1882.

Bain, *JSM* *John Stuart Mill, a Criticism*, by Alexander Bain, Longmans Green & Co., London, 1882.

Hayek *John Stuart Mill and Harriet Taylor*, by F. A. Hayek, Routledge and Kegan Paul, London, 1951.

NOTE ON SOURCES

A.C. *Letters of Thomas Carlyle to John Stuart Mill, John Sterling, and Robert Browning*, Ed. Alexander Carlyle, T. Fisher Unwin Ltd., London, 1923.

Lévy-Bruhl *Lettres inédites de John Stuart Mill à Auguste Comte*, L. Lévy-Bruhl, Alcan, Paris, 1889.

d'Eichthal *John Stuart Mill, Correspondance Inédite avec Gustave d'Eichthal*, Eugène d'Eichthal, Alcan, Paris, 1898.

Amberley Papers *The Amberley Papers*, Ed. Bertrand and Patricia Russell, 2 vols. Hogarth Press, London, 1937.

All references to the *Autobiography* of John Stuart Mill (with certain specified exceptions) are to the John Jacob Coss Edition, published by Columbia University Press, New York, 1944.

BOOK ONE

TABULA RASA

1806–1830
aet. 0–24

Picture Post Library

JOHN STUART MILL

I

LIFE was ungracious in the hamlet of Northwater Bridge during the last quarter of the eighteenth century. There were only two reasons for there being such a place, and neither of them, it appears, was a sufficient one. The first was the presence of the bridge. It had been built during the reign of Queen Elizabeth across the shallow, racing river which, rising to the westward among the two-thousand-foot domes of the black Grampians, and pouring across five miles of misty plain, emptied itself into the sea just north of Montrose. Over the three-arched bridge of stone and down the middle of the plain the traffic rolled and rumbled between the North of Scotland and the South.

The second reason was the Earl of Kintore, who owned, along with other comfortable slices of Forfar, the entire district or parish of Logie Pert. This estate he rented to a number of small farmers, the most desirable tenement being that at Northwater Bridge, where the farmhouse could be used as an inn and posthouse for the passing traffic. Barclay, the tenant, profited from this, and was able to build a dozen or more cottages of clay and thatch, which in turn he rented to his labourers, or to the tradesmen, the blacksmith, wright, mason, carrier, and grocer, who were attracted to the small community by his deployment of capital.

The latest house to be completed was occupied, in about 1773, by a shoemaker, called James Milne, who had come from Edinburgh. His resources were not great, yet for a time he prospered gently. He was able to hire a man or two to work for him until such time as the children he proposed to breed should have grown sufficiently to help him make of it, in the accustomed manner, a family concern in which the profit was not diminished by the payment of outside labour. With this intention he had, a year earlier, acquired a wife, a girl of seventeen, a servant girl in Edinburgh, named Isobel Fenton, whom he now installed as mistress of the cottage. The cottage had two doors and three windows. It had to provide a workshop for the cobbling as well as a crèche for the firstborn, also called James, who duly made his appearance in the spring of 1773, and was followed at two-yearly intervals by a brother William and a sister May.

As the family grew up, the girl wife grew into a woman. Running contrary to her husband's planned economy, she imposed her own decided personality upon that industrious artisan. She was haughty. In 1745, her father had followed the banner of Lord Ogilvie into the field for the Pretender, along with the other warm-blooded farmers and residents of Forfarshire. Like them he had escaped the cut of Cumberland's steel only to sink into ruin as a result of ravages upon his land and property. Thus, as she had been a servant girl by accident and not by birth, Isobel now became a drudge from necessity but not by nature. Her eldest son must be restored to the position which was his by heritage. For her part, she was prepared to slave for it; his father and brother and sister must be prepared to slave for it as well. The purpose of the family henceforth would no longer be to build up a decent village business; but instead, by their own sacrifice, to launch upon the world a boy properly fitted and equipped, who should regain the honourable station which was rightfully theirs. Fortunately, the eldest son was born blue-eyed; he was also strong, and showed indubitable promise.

The mother of James Mill began her campaign with small departures which had the effect of making her heartily unpopular. She changed the family name from the locally undistinguished Milne to the less common Mill. She aggravated her neighbours by supposing that her son would be called "*Mr.*" and his wife "*Mrs. Mill*", since among the common people it was not usual for a wife to take her husband's name. Worse, she scorned the staple porridge. "If you give me porridge, I'll die, but give me tea and I'll live," she is reputed to have said on her sick-bed to her husband: and tea was well beyond the family budget. She cultivated a friendship with their landlords, the Barclays, who were among the most well-to-do of the thousand-odd souls in the whole parish of Logie Pert. So well did she succeed that the Barclays came to treat her with a marked distinction. When she came to tea with them, they always took out their best set of china.

As soon as he was able to walk the two miles there and back, James Mill was sent to the parish school. And before he was seven, Mr. Peters, the parish minister, who made a habit of keeping in close touch with the schoolmaster, became aware that a boy of remarkable ability had, in some curious way, sprung from amongst the mud cottages of Northwater Bridge. Doubtless he was even more pleased to hear that the boy came from honest, hard-working, god-fearing stock. God-fearing they were, too: nothing had ever been said against James Milne the father, except that he had a troublesome habit of abstractedly whistling between his teeth; and even this he had never been heard to do on Sundays. Should the boy's promise be maintained, it would be a pleasure for the minister to reward such parents by advancing their son into the Church, as well as his duty to secure new talent which might otherwise easily flow into impious channels.

Meanwhile young James proceeded at the proper age to Montrose Academy, where he was lodged in the town at a cost of half-a-crown a week to his parents. At the week-ends he walked home in order to save them further expense. Across the longest of their three rooms his mother hung a canvas curtain, closing off the end containing the gable window and the fireplace. This pampered corner now became his study. His brother William was at work for his father: his mother did the housework: May, his sister, did the shoe-binding for the shop, as well as tending the cow, which was for years the principal insurance of the household against starvation. But James Mill worked at his books, by order, all the time.

At last the family gained its reward. Sir John and Lady Jane Stuart, who every year moved from Edinburgh to spend the summer in their mansion of Fettercairn, not far from Logie Pert, decided that the time had come to take some steps to educate their only daughter, prior to projecting her into Edinburgh society. As Lady Jane Stuart was a principal contributor to a fund for training suitable young men for the Church, she asked her minister to name one as a tutor. He in turn asked Mr. Peters, who promptly mentioned his special protégé. Young James Mill, now seventeen, created a favourable impression by his handsome appearance, his reserved manner, and his clear grasp of knowledge. He was sent to the great University of Edinburgh, and was provided with lodgings and with his tuition fees. In return, it was required only that he should study for the Ministry, devote his spare time to teaching the beautiful and noble girl three years younger than himself, and spend his summer vacations with the family at Fettercairn. These not uncongenial tasks he fulfilled unexceptionably. His young charge, when taken from his care at the age of eighteen, was so well versed in all the graces, that on her début in Edinburgh she rocked the heart of Sir Walter Scott into a romantic passion. She then married the son of a banker, bore him a son who afterwards became a Professor of Natural Philosophy, and died.

Her tutor, however, lived. The magic touch of patronage had lifted him clean into a life with a richer prospect. As was his way, he wasted no time in wondering, but applied his natural talents to better his good fortune. At Montrose Academy his field of acquaintance had been limited enough, bringing him the intimacy only of Joseph Hume, later in life his devoted follower. But here in Edinburgh the embryonic great crowded and jostled in profusion. Thomas Thomson, the famous chemist, was his classmate and his lifelong friend. Jeffrey, who became editor of the *Edinburgh Review* before he was promoted to be Lord Advocate of Scotland, was his contemporary. Henry Brougham, a Lord Chancellor in waiting, the most brilliant and ambitious of his generation, here began the association with Mill which helped to carry the Great Reform Bill. Amongst all these probable young men, James took his place as an equal, and the acquaintanceships thus started were never relinquished until some further good had come of them.

His Latin was already far enough advanced to make it unnecessary for him to go to further courses, but his Greek and Logic he swallowed in great gobbets. Whenever he was able he would listen spellbound to the lectures on Moral Philosophy delivered with exquisite eloquence and modulation by Dugald Stewart, successor to Reid and Brown, latest chieftain of the Scottish school of Common Sense. Having completed his general course, he entered upon his special training in Divinity, which occupied him for four winters. His private reading at this time seems somewhat free for a discreet aspirant to the clergy. It included a preponderance of Plato, backed by Fénelon and Rousseau; a heavy mass of Psychology (or Mental Philosophy as it was then called), a smattering of Voltaire, and the sceptical works of David Hume. Nevertheless, he satisfactorily completed his various homilies and dissertations on the Gospels, and in 1798 he was licensed as a Preacher.

While waiting for a living, Mill, in accordance with the usual practice, rode from one parish to the next whenever the resident minister was away or sick, carrying in his saddle-bag his batch of sermons. Soon enough his good friend Mr. Peters made occasion for him to preach in his native Logie Pert. His devoted mother, now racked with a consumptive cough, but with all her dreams so far fulfilled, listened to him from behind the stair, not daring to sit out in her own pew. Everybody admired his poise, his shapely leg, his resonant voice which rose and fell and went ringing through the church. But the abstruseness of his argument, his immaculate reasoning, his accent now bereft of all its homely idiom, were too much for his humble peasant congregation. They could not understand a word he said. "I've heard him preach," said one of them, "and no great han' he made o't."

Perhaps on this account, or perhaps because the influence of his loyal patron Sir John Stuart weighed less with the Almighty than he had supposed, Mill was still without a living as he neared his thirtieth birthday. Worse, the family which had abandoned everything for his success, now shrank under a succession of ruinous blows and virtually disintegrated. His mother, prematurely old, succumbed to consumption. His brother William, stay of the business, followed her. His father became paralysed and could not work. The business went bankrupt. The cow had to be sold. Only his sister May remained, and she was an idle girl: only May, that is, and the journeyman who worked for them, and whose exiguous fortunes were bound up in their affairs.

James Mill was a man of resolution: but what could he do? He had no money. The Church, for which he was eligible, had passed him by: for the other gentlemanly professions of medicine and the law he was not qualified. Fortunately, from the general wreck his own self-confidence was spared. He was endowed with a fine brain in a comely body. He had had as good an education as Scotland could provide, probably better than any other in the kingdom, and he had made the most of it. He was well equipped to make a living as a literary privateer, if only he could find his opportunity. There was none to be had in Scotland, where progress moved slowly, cautiously, penuriously from rank to rank, until stopped by the impenetrable wall of puritanical conservatism. He must go to a fatter land, where his hungry tribe had room to move, need not prey unproductively upon each other; where the virtues of a dominant will, a body inured to hardship and a mind to toil, might hope to gain a share of the wealth which daily flowed so comfortably from fool to rogue. Early in 1802, Sir John Stuart, who had to attend the opening of Parliament, obligingly gave him a seat to London in his post-chaise.

Mill's optimism was redoubled by his first impressions of the London scene. The bustle of the choking streets persuaded him that fortunes were being made; the cosmopolitan shipping on the Thames was so many thousand tons of further evidence; and in the Park he might encounter figures of fame at any time. One Sunday as he walked along, two gentlemen rode up behind him, deep in quiet conversation: Pitt and Addington. He stared, and Pitt stared back. A little further on he saw the Prince of Wales on horseback, and then the Princess of Wales, poor creature, in an open chaise. He went freely to the House of Commons to listen to debates. He paid deep attention to the speeches of Pitt, Fox, and Sheridan, but was astonished by the mediocrity of the rest. He presented his introduction to his countryman Dr. Bisset, and was greatly impressed that a man of no genius and of knowledge inferior to his own should be able to earn six or seven hundred a year by his pen alone. "It will be devilish hard", he wrote, "if a man, good for anything, cannot keep himself alive on these terms."[1]

After only six months' grubbing, he was accepted for the editorial staff of the *Anti-Jacobin Review*, and took permanent rooms at 33 Surrey Street. Within the year, he persuaded the publisher Baldwin to launch an entirely new periodical called the *Literary Journal* with himself as editor. Two years later he was also editing a newspaper, the *St. James's Chronicle*. These successes brought him an income of about £500 a year. His first concern on acquiring ready cash was, naturally, to retrieve as far as possible the wreckage of his parents' home. The stock in trade was all sold up; and under the friendly supervision of David Barclay and Mr. Peters, many of the debts were paid off from the proceeds. Those that remained Mill paid himself, and also made sufficient provision for his crippled father to maintain him till his death a few years later. His sister May, whose alternatives would seem to have been dim, very sensibly married the journeyman, and set him about the task of starting again the ruined trade of shoemaker. That accomplished, James Mill turned his back upon his origins so successfully that his famous son, who certainly had every opportunity of knowing anything that his father considered of interest, was unable in later life to give any account of their early circumstances.*

Mill next began to look round for a wife. With his prospects much improved he was able, on 5 June 1805, to marry the daughter of a strikingly handsome Yorkshire widow who kept a prosperous establishment for lunatics in Hoxton. His bride, Harriet Burrow, was an extremely pretty girl of twenty-three, with a small, fine figure and an acquiline type of beauty which gained for her her only immortality by reproducing itself in her eldest son. Along with these natural advantages she brought with her a dowry of £400, a quantity of family plate and furniture (emblems of security not known in Logie Pert), and a house, 12 Rodney Terrace, Pentonville, which Mrs. Burrow bought for them in return for a rent of £50 per annum.[2] Here, on 20 May 1806, a son was born. And out of deference to the man whose patronage had made possible the realization of Isobel Fenton's ambitions, he was named John Stuart Mill.

II

With all his duties honourably discharged, with his name now not unknown in the cloudy world of literary enterprise, a household decently provided, and no other burden than "a healthy, fair-complexioned, bright-eyed, sweetly-smiling babe"[3], James Mill had certainly got the beginning which he craved. As editor of two separate organs and manager of one, he might have felt some

* When Barclay came to London, he had dinner with the Mills. According to Bain, while young John Mill and his mother were in the room "not a word was said of Scotland; but the moment they left the room, Mill burst out in eager enquiry after everybody in Logie Pert". Bain, *James Mill*, p. 110.

confidence, particularly as this was the foundation period of the great political reviews; but he still felt insecure. Although some of them might make their way by unpredictable chance, periodicals of all sorts came and went, and editors were tossed from one to the other, without becoming visibly better off. Some more substantial achievement, something to bring him permanently before the literary eye, was an essential part of his scheme. Accordingly he relinquished his editorships and invested his talents for a three-year term in a *History of India*. That he had never been to India he regarded as his principal qualification for undertaking such a project, since he would be the better able to take an objective view of the whole vast field. At all events, it had never before been attempted, and undeniably had the virtue of solidity. But by taking twelve years instead of three it upset his calculations, and for a time impoverished his swelling household.

Meanwhile, his journalism remained extraordinarily circumspect for one who had grown up in the stormy period of the French Revolution, lived to see England changed from an agricultural to a manufacturing nation, and had digested so much philosophy of a sceptical leaning. Yet the strange fact is, that although he never in his life doubted the truth of his opinions, and was so soon to become the trenchant apostle of reform, he had, up to his thirty-fifth birthday, made no recorded utterance whatever of a political nature. Until the year 1808, his story of success had been as blameless to conservative ears as that of Dick Whittington. He had written very little, and only in papers of such irreproachable loyalty as the *Eclectic* or the *Anti-Jacobin Review*: while what he said breathed respect for the wealthy and admiration for the great. If he mentioned the name of Malthus it was with sentimental horror. And in taking to task an author who had blasphemously denied the value of the Old Testament, he wrote, "These books comprise the extraordinary code of laws communicated by a benevolent divinity to man."[4]

Nor did his eagerness to conform allow him to stop short of action. A year or so before Trafalgar, it had dawned upon the English people, as from time to time it does, that they were about to be invaded. As is customary, this unwholesome possibility, once fully grasped, evoked considerable indignation and patriotic fervour: everybody joined the Volunteers, and Mill among them, although he could ill afford the two-and-twenty guineas it cost him for his uniform. When the King inspected a parade of the 30,000 defenders of London in Hyde Park, he paused in front of Mill, who was standing loyally in the line of his Scottish regiment. George III, who seldom trusted anyone, was fond of Scotsmen, because Lord Bute had been one, and because he believed them to have a long tradition of fighting for the King, especially if he were unpopular. So now he paused to study them. "A very pretty corps, a very pretty corps *indeed*—all Scotsmen, my Lord, all Scotsmen?" he confirmed contentedly.[5]

These manifestations of conformity on the part of Mill were the result not of sentiment so much as of necessity. Church and State had been till now his bread and butter, so to speak. It was by the ministry and through patronage that he had been raised from the depths of hopeless poverty. It may be that he felt less joy in his new station than resentment for his old, less gratitude to his benefactors than contempt for their claims to privilege, less pride in his achievement than passion at the system which made deference rather than ability the condition of success. He may have felt all this: indeed, his subsequent behaviour would be almost inexplicable if he did not. None the less, the long arm of aristocratic orthodoxy, if once affronted, could certainly stop his further progress, and could very likely unmake what it had made. It would be unwise for him to shout too loud till he was out of reach. So for thirty-five years he kept quiet, until he met a man who had not only seen the abuses of the social order as clearly as himself, but who had dared for many years to point them out.

Jeremy Bentham was benevolent enough to suppose that injustice could not be a deliberate policy; naïve enough to think that abuses continued not because they were lucrative but because they were unseen; and conceited enough to hope that as soon as they were illuminated by his unique genius, they would be gratefully corrected. He had therefore felt no qualms about pronouncing his opinions as fast as they came to him and as forcefully as he could. Now, at the age of sixty, if he was for the first time beginning to doubt the soundness of his premises, the main point was that he was alive and kicking. Authority at first had gasped, then laughed; hesitated, when the force of his common sense proved unanswerable; and finally, when his international reputation reached an overwhelming pitch, accepted and consulted him. Nobody had ever attempted to lock him up.

This was a revelation to James Mill. He quickly learnt that under the massive protection of Bentham's influence he could act without fear of his overlords, who he now saw were not competent to suppress the truth. For Bentham too there was fresh knowledge. From what Mill told him, he at last perceived that it was no mere matter of exposing the wiles of lawyers to a duped and outraged nation. The whole fabric of society, it now seemed to him, was thoroughly corrupt, and sinister interests lay behind every discriminative anomaly in the constitution. While he struck furiously at King and clergy, nobleman and pander—at anyone who stood on the side of keeping things as they were—the cool craft of his associate unerringly directed his raging, and still more the attention of his influential followers, to each momentary weakness in the machinery of privileged government. Though so different in temperament that their relations were on occasion inharmonious, each was indispensable to the other. Their impact generated an intellectual fire which burnt all through the century, and from which, in certain winds, the embers still emit a glow.

The intimacy once begun ripened with the utmost urgency. As a matter of habit, Mill walked several times a week across London from his house near King's Cross to Westminster, to talk with Bentham late into the night; leaving his wife at home with the infant John Stuart, and her new-born daughter Wilhelmina Forbes. Bentham was currently working on a scathing criticism of the law reform proposed for Scotland: in 1808 Mill hustled the pamphlet into print, and adorned it with a glowing appreciation in the *Annual Review*. Recently, Mill had become a contributor to the great new quarterly of the Whigs, the *Edinburgh Review*, by the mediation of Henry Brougham with their college contemporary, Jeffrey, who was its editor. It was paying him good money—about thirty shillings a page for some hundred pages a year [6]—and kept his home in funds while he slaved unremunerated at the *History of India*. But now he made his articles the vehicle of his new enthusiasm for Bentham. Jeffrey soon complained of their monotony; and even dared to hack and prune at one of them so stringently that it read more as a censure than a hymn of praise.* This liberty made Mill so angry that he not long after severed the connection, fees and all.

The effect on Jeremy Bentham was even more apparent. Hitherto he had taken no interest in affairs. A year before, in 1807, the mob of Westminster, exalted to the limit of political excitement, had

* Review of Dumont's French translation of Bentham's *Principles of the Penal Code*.

surged and swayed outside his door, acclaiming the triumph of Sir Francis Burdett, whose cause they had carried at the hustings. Bentham had barely noticed the tumult, had not bothered to look out to see the Royal Guard fingering the ball ammunition with which they had been issued. Now, however, he plunged incontinently straight at the dangerous heart of reactionary repression.

Among the devious means the government employed to prevent the inconvenience of popular journalism, the most useful was the law of libel. For libel came not before a public but a special jury, carefully selected to enable the judge to sentence a defendant, if he deemed it necessary, to seven years' transportation. This system Bentham vigorously exposed, in a pamphlet baldly called *The Elements of the Art of Packing*. The risk attaching to such a publication was extreme, and although Mill's own printer Baldwin reluctantly took it on, his spirit failed him half-way through, and his type-setting faltered to an intimidated stop. Mill was indignant. The way with flagrant wrong, he now believed, was to defy it. Of course the pamphlet must be published, he told Baldwin, and as soon as possible; he himself would herald it with a slashing article, which he perhaps optimistically intended to insert between the respectable covers of the *Edinburgh Review*. But the printer was stubborn: even if the title were changed to the milder *Perils of the Press*, still he would not print it. Advice was taken from Bentham's friend, Sir Samuel Romilly, who was legally eminent. On reading the pamphlet he became extremely agitated. Even a friendly Attorney General, he reported, might be forced to prosecute such imprudence; there could be no doubt of the attitude of the present one.

Fortunately, Romilly had his way: the pamphlet was privately circulated, but was not published till a later date when reprisals were less certain. Shortly afterwards, William Cobbett was sent down for two years and fined £1000 for criticizing flogging in the army in his *Political Register*. And all the brilliance of Brougham's forensic skill, though several times successful, could not at last save Leigh Hunt and his brother John, whose newspaper the *Examiner* was suspected of radical views, from the same heavy penalty for describing the Prince Regent as a "fat Adonais of fifty". Bentham visited the Hunts in prison, and sympathetically whiled away their time at battledore and shuttlecock. As for justice, he added in his pamphlet, the practice of appointing barristers to be judges was as sensible as choosing a procuress for mistress of a girls' school. Unabashed, he soon produced his *Plan of Parliamentary Reform*, also tactfully delayed by his friends, although its tenets were adopted later as the political programme of the Radicals.

Though neither Mill nor Bentham seemed to fear that their new activities might be violently curtailed, they naturally desired to see their cause assumed by a young disciple, willing and worthy to carry it forward after they were dead. For this purpose, they found close to hand Mill's hopeful-eyed young son of three.

James Mill, from his hard experience, knew ability as the only art by which a boy of moderate parentage could hope for fame and fortune, and his stern sense of duty alone would have determined him, as a father, to give John Stuart the surest grounding he could provide. In addition, his own interests tended towards the science of the mind which, save for the expositions of Locke and Hartley, had scarcely begun to be examined even as a field of speculation, in the English tongue. Characteristically, he reached conclusions which were sharp, swift, and final. Characteristically, he never dreamed that they were wrong or incomplete. He would not have believed that a century later men would devote their lives to studying a mountain of research upon one aspect of the subject, and would be happy to achieve in it a tenth part of the assurance he felt for the whole. "If I had time to write a book," he once told Francis Place, "I would make the human mind as plain as the road from Charing Cross to St. Paul's."[7] He did eventually write a book, the *Analysis of the Human Mind*; he also wrote the article on *Education* for the supplement to the fifth edition of the *Encyclopaedia Britannica*. Having the courage of his convictions, and genuinely intending to do the best he could for his son, he could do no other than teach him according to his lights. At the same time, he was sure that such an education applied to an individual thoroughly under his control, would be not only an interesting experiment, but a triumphant vindication of his views.

According to James Mill's theory, all minds started as much alike as all stomachs or all hands or any other physical organs. They were all blank sheets, forced to record every experience which the senses introduced to them: and, in the event of a repeated sequence of experiences, to recall the order in which they came about, so that the last events in the sequence could be predicted from the first with such certainty that they could be said to have been caused by them. Thus, minds differed only in so far as they recorded different chains of experiences, and from them formed different habits of association. As every new experience either confirmed, altered or added to all that had gone before, it became a part of the composition of the mind itself, and the mind never ceased to change and grow throughout its life. But as it grew older, it became more crowded, and the effect of each experience grew less; whereas when it was young, the force of each new impression upon the comparatively unsullied sheet was very powerful. Whoever had power to regulate the sequence and the strength of the experiences which flowed in upon a young mind, decided the habits of association it would form, and to that extent determined both the character and the ability of the later man. This process of regulation was what was known as education, and the variety of its applications was as wide as the endless variety of mankind.

The sovereign rulers of men's actions, Mill had learnt from Bentham, were the pursuit of pleasure and the avoidance of pain. The educator should, therefore, by a judicious use of the pleasures and pains at his disposal, not only build up a chain of associations which would induce the child to act as he desired, but also encourage it to develop by experience a knowledge of what caused what; a faculty of reason, enabling it to ensure that its actions were those likely to produce ultimately pleasurable results. For these purposes, he thought, it was necessary to insist in education that consequences were as they would be generally throughout life. Painful or restrictive punishments were to be avoided whenever they would attribute to an action consequences which did not prove to be inevitably connected with it. On the other hand, it was wrong to give a child what it wanted simply to stop its crying, for crying would not in the future achieve that end.

It was, Mill felt, quite easy to persuade a child that it would be happier if everyone around it was happy, and so make it endeavour in its own interest to practise habitual unselfishness: but it was equally easy to make it selfish, by letting it glean from experience that the happiness of others could only be promoted at the expense of its own. Similarly, he thought it essential to avoid any expressions of disgust over differences of prejudice, of colour, race or creed; otherwise the child would anticipate evil consequences from agents who did not necessarily cause them, such as negroes, Jacobins, and Roman Catholics.

In short, all that an educator need hope to do was to help a child to reason accurately: for that granted, it would act unerringly towards its own final happiness, which was good, and would avoid evil, which was definable as a miscalculation of chances. Finally, since "the first sensations experienced produce the greatest effects", it was necessary on the intellectual side to prevent a child from cluttering its youthful brain with idle emotions, dreams or recreations. It should be tied down to the strict development of its faculties: anything which did not assist the main course of character and reason would only cloud the vision and dissipate the clarity of mind. From these premises James Mill set out to educate his son. With Helvétius, he believed that "l'éducation peut tout".

Jeremy Bentham, the exponent of much of this theory, endorsed it all. And in addition he had other reasons of his own for being concerned in John Mill's education. He had a most pressing need for young assistants to take intimate care both of his life and works. For his life was a lonely one. All his attempts to provide himself with a life companion in the conventional manner had miscarried. During his youthful visits to Bowood, the country seat of his patron Lord Lansdowne, he had passed his time at falling unsuccessfully in love with all the ladies of the house, whom he courted with a clumsy jocularity, while playing chess with them or giving them lessons on the harpsichord. Hopeful to the last, at the age of eighty he wrote again to one of them, recalling to her memory the far-off days when she had "presented him, in ceremony, with the flower in the green lane" [8] To the end of his life he could not hear of Bowood without tears swimming in his eyes, and he was forced to exclaim, "Take me forward, I entreat you, to the future—do not let me go back to the past."[9]

In 1792, when, by his father's death, he had come into a long-delayed sufficiency of £600 a year, he had settled in Queen Square Place, a prim, ancestral building with a deep umbrageous garden, at the end of a blind passage; a kind of oasis in the heart of Westminster. Here for a time he was saved from loneliness by the company of his brother Samuel, who fully shared both his enthusiasm and his ingenuity. But when Samuel married, and became preoccupied with construction for the Navy, Jeremy was left alone in his shady hermitage.* Into this void had come James Mill. He, certainly, provided enough of intellectual contest, but he was not a cosy man. Moreover,

* His only intimate friend at this period was his French editor, Dumont, who enlivened his solitude with the excitement of an occasional quarrel.

it was clearly his intention to galvanize the recluse, driving out everything irrelevant to his political purposes. Gone were the days of Bentham's fortune-making enterprises, of peculiar half-commercial projects like the "FRIGIDARIUM" he had built in 1799, with the assistance of a young scientist, under a mound in a well-shaded corner of his garden. Henceforth Mill would never let him out of harness. Bentham was doubtful whether even his sturdy health could stand the augmenting strain. Long years of lucubration had given him pains in the eyes, and he feared constantly that, like Milton's, his work would finish in a night of blindness. Sometimes he longed to escape with the self-styled potentates who came to him for their Constitutions, to the bright republics which they hoped to build; with adventurous Aaron Burr to Mexico, or with General Miranda to Venezuela.

The pressure of new work required, at the very least, someone to read to him, write for him, check his utterances by research, and arrange them for publication, a task for which he had no capacity and James Mill had no time. Nor was it at all an easy task. His "shop", as he called his study, was a jungle of books and papers, spilling over the desk of his own design on to the organ where he would sit and improvise. Because he never looked where he was writing, his manuscript was shocking: nor was his meaning clarified by his peculiar views on language, from which he demanded stark economy. "Prose", he said, "is when all the lines except the last go on to the end. Poetry is when some of them fall short of it." Consequently, his sentences were framed in a breathless telegraphic form, bereft of prepositions but full of obscurely urgent import. When he could find no word appropriate to his purpose he had no hesitation in inventing one: of these, "international", "minimize", and "maximize" are some which, having been accepted by the language, no longer sound so outlandish as they did when he first used them. When starting to compose a work, he took a large sheet of widely ruled paper, and on it drew up an exhaustive classification of his subject under various heads. On each head he wrote his opinion separately, without reference to the others, and then left the resulting maze of near contradiction and repetition for someone else to put in order. Odd thoughts occurring to him as he went along he scribbled down on slips of paper, and pinned to a green curtain at his elbow, whence they were later to be detached and fitted into convenient openings in his argument.

Of this system, named sometimes "The Porphyrian Tree", and sometimes "the dichotomous or bifurcate method", Bentham was inordinately proud. But to find student clerks, or "reprobates" as he called them, equal to its subtleties was seldom an easy matter. For a time he had John Colls, a milk-and-water lad, sent to him to get training for the law: though treated like the others, benignly if bizarrely, he ended recreant, became a parson, and eventually wrote a book called *Utilitarianism Unmasked*, giving a gruesome and imaginative account of the last hours of the famous infidel. Later, Bentham was adopted by the pompous Radical, John Bowring, a would-be Boswell who jealously sought to exclude all other influences, even the formidable James Mill himself, and duly produced what Leslie Stephen justly calls "the worst biography in the language". Bowring also was, at various times, a hymn writer, a mighty linguist, Governor of Hong Kong, Hawaiian minister to Europe, and a Knight.[10] But he and the other spiteful mediocrity were no more than a vague nightmare of the future, when Bentham first clapped eyes on the curly head of John Stuart Mill.

Wishing both to attract and to improve the boy, Bentham cast his memory back over his own upbringing. Through a dim emotional mist he mused upon the valuable effects of wholesome surroundings on a child. He remembered the excursions from his home in Houndsditch to his mother's house at Browning Hill, in beautiful country, and within hearing of the bells of Boghurst Church. "Dear to me beyond expression", he recalled fondly, "when first it greeted my ears, was the sound of those three bells; one a little cracked, another much cracked, and the third so cracked as to be almost mute."[11] He decided upon a course which he continued almost without intermission for ten years: he would arrange every summer to have the Mill family come to stay with him for a long vacation in the country. In this way, not only would the boy be able to enjoy the civilizing influences of the rural scene, but Bentham would be able to keep a watch on his development. It would also be convenient to have John's father near at hand for their mutual labours.

Accordingly, in July 1809 Bentham invited them for a visit to Barrow Green, a magnificent mansion, commanding a splendid view of the Oxted hills, with an avenue of chestnuts which he called the "cloisters", and a seven-acre lake. This pretentious residence he had rented at a bargain rate from a widow fallen on hard times, who acted as housekeeper and possessed the solitary virtue of baking bread as good as his mother had made. The Mills set out with alacrity in a post-chaise, leaving the "brat" (Wilhelmina Forbes, aged one) in the care of her maternal aunts. That John Mill was already devoted to his benefactor is plain from James Mill's letter of acceptance:

> "When I received your letter on Monday, John, who is so desirous to be your inmate, was in the room, and observed me smiling as I read it. This excited his curiosity to know what it was about. I said it was Mr. Bentham asking us to go to Barrow Green. He desired to read that. I gave it to him to see what he would say, when he began, as if reading—'Why have you not come to Barrow Green, and brought John with you?'" [12]

From this letter it is apparent that John's education dated in earnest from this visit. He was now three, and evidently not yet expected to read English. From his own account, before he was much older he was reading Greek. Certainly, Bentham would have considered an introduction to the classics to be overdue. When he himself was three, his father, normally a parsimonious man, had gone so far as to outlay two and eightpence to provide him with Latin grammars. At the same age, as a diminutive visitor at a country house, Bentham had dismayed his elders by deserting them during a walk because their conversation bored him. Enquiring for him anxiously on their return, they learned that he had gone straight home, called for a footman to bring lights, and reach him down a folio of Rapin from the dusty library shelves, and was still comfortably buried in historical researches.

Not that Bentham wished to see his own experience repeated in all respects. For the formal education of the time he had a profound contempt. Westminster, where he was not even provided with a bed to himself, had been his special hell. At Oxford, his tutor was "a morose and gloomy personage, sour and repulsive—a sort of Protestant monk". He heartily endorsed James Mill's opinion that an academic education was greatly overrated, and that a close supervision of the boy in his own home was both cheaper and of far more value. There is much in favour of this view. Gibbon, ten years Bentham's senior, spoke of his time at Oxford as "the fourteen months the most idle and unprofitable of my whole life". Much later, Byron shortly said of Trinity College, Cambridge "the place is the devil". Shelley, after being pelted with hard tennis balls at Eton, was expelled from Oxford for militant atheism. Whereas, of those who were privately schooled, the younger Pitt was a classical scholar before he was ten and at twenty-two became Prime Minister. Macaulay, before he was eight, compiled a compendium of universal history, and a romance in three cantos in the style of Scott. Tennyson, at twelve, wrote an epic poem of six thousand lines. And across the Atlantic there was some concern because Emerson at three was backward in his reading.

The introduction of John Mill to Greek at three was accomplished by a method then unknown. A number of common words were written out on cards, together with their English meaning; and these he was required to recognize, by comparing them with the actual articles they represented. Having mastered that, a copy of *Aesop's Fables* was produced, and he proceeded at once to translate them. No attention was for some years wasted on the intricacies of Grammar, which could only have confused his infant brain. He read, simply by identifying the Greek words he had learnt, and applying their general meaning. Nor was the subject matter at first of any concern. The exercise was purely in reading Greek and transposing it simultaneously into English. In this way, *Aesop's Fables* finished, he began Herodotus; read right through it, and moved on to Xenophon. But his natural curiosity soon made him wish to know the meaning of what he read. This tendency, he later felt, might well have been encouraged had Plato's dialogues been replaced in his seven-year-old reading, by something he had a chance of understanding.

With John fairly launched in Greek, his father set aside an extra portion of the evenings to teaching the elements of arithmetic, lessons which the boy like many another heartily disliked. Apart from reading and writing, which were taken for granted, Greek and Arithmetic were the only subjects he was made to learn until he was eight.

This early start put a greater strain upon the father than upon the son. Having heard John construe, and set him down to further preparation, James Mill would turn at once to make up time on his own labours, either the *History of India*, or the article he was currently writing to earn the family living. They sat on two sides of the table in the crowded living-room, with Wilhelmina Forbes howling in one corner, and the third-born Clara Esther in another. As there were then no Greek-to-English lexicons, John had to ask his father for the meaning of every word he did not know. And the real miracle is that, despite the incessant interruptions, the family was supported and several volumes of the history written, without James Mill becoming even more impatient than he was.

Bentham meanwhile tried to bring the Mill family to his town as well as to his country doorstep, in order to watch developments more closely. At the bottom of his garden was an old stone building which it was his pleasure to display. When he had a guest, he would trot down alongside of him, and on reaching it, would suddenly shriek out, "On your marrow bones, sir", brandishing Dapple, his heavy walking-stick, over the shoulders of his astonished companion. The latter, in an attitude of enforced genuflection, would then be made to read out loud a tablet, bearing the legend, "Sacred to Milton, Prince of Poets". In this little house of Milton's, Bentham persuaded James Mill to set up his family abode, and during the summer of 1810 they moved there instead of making their usual visit to Barrow Green. It soon transpired that the cottage was too dark and damp for the health of Mrs. Mill and the children, and they had to move out again almost immediately. As they were unable to regain their lease at Pentonville, they had to take a house at Newington Green, further away from Westminster than ever.

This was disappointing: all the same, Bentham was able to contribute vitally to John Mill's education, by making available the resources of his ample library, and so providing him with the means of knowledge for lack of which his own childhood had been severely handicapped. For many years both father and son had free access to any books they needed: when they were at length able to afford their own, the process became mutual. For the present, the concession was of the greatest value to John Mill. It did not, it is true, provide him with the playthings he so badly needed, but it did enable him to beguile in private reading the spare hours carefully allotted to him.

Since children's books had not yet become a specialized function of the publisher's art, such fairy stories as there were often propounded morals rightly considered more than questionable by John's father. As for Bentham, he had been so terrified at an early age by tales of bugbears and hobgoblins, that all his life he had to have one of his assistants sleeping in the same room with him—an uncomfortable duty since, as he himself observed, "if a Bentham does not snore, he is not legitimate".[13] So, instead of wasting time with fairy tales, small John was encouraged to read true accounts of resourceful, energetic men who overcame their difficulties; of Drake and Cook; Philip of Macedon and Frederick the Great. For amusement, he was allowed *Don Quixote* and the *Arabian Nights*; and, as with other boys, *Robinson Crusoe* was his pre-eminent favourite. Stirring histories also were encouraged, and he was early excited by heroic achievements, like the defence of the Knights of Malta against the Turks, and of the Netherlanders against the Catholic power of Spain. He liked to make notes on slips of paper as he read. From these he told the stories to his father, as he accompanied him on his constitutional walks before breakfast in the country lanes round Newington Green. He had a proper relish for the lurid light of wars and battles. As a youthful partisan, he supported his national side in the American War of Independence, until the voice of his father's reason pointed out that the right in this case was on the side of the rebels and victors.

In July 1812 James Mill fell ill of the then universal gout. Although he was evidently not *in extremis*, Bentham wrote to sympathize, prudently foreseeing the worst. Ignoring the other major inconveniences of his friend's demise, such as the complete lack of provision for his wife and family of small children who, with the recent addition of Harriet Isabella, now numbered four, Bentham went straight for the darling project which most concerned them both. "If you will appoint me guardian to Mr. John Stuart Mill, I will, in the event of his father's being disposed of elsewhere, take him to Q.S.P. and there or elsewhere, by whipping or otherwise, do whatsoever may seem most necessary and proper, for teaching him to make all proper distinctions, such as between the Devil and the Holy Ghost, and how to make Codes and Encylopaedias, and whatsoever else may be proper to be made, so long as I remain an inhabitant of this vale of tears."[14] To which James Mill replied at once: "I am not going to die, notwithstanding your zeal to come in for a legacy. However, if I were to die any time before this poor boy is a man, one of the things that would pinch me most sorely, would be, the being obliged to leave his mind unmade to the degree of excellence of which I hope to make it. But another thing is, that the only prospect which would lessen that pain, would be the leaving him in your hands. I therefore take your offer quite seriously, and stipulate, merely, that it shall be made as good as possible; and then we may perhaps leave him a successor worthy of both of us."[15]

The reference to whipping was, of course, one of Bentham's cumbrous jokes. He did not believe in it. He himself had never been chastised, but it had been a remarkable escape in the Westminster of his day, and he had lived in a constant state of dread. As for James Mill, force played no part in his theory of education, and the sharpest punishment he inflicted on any of his children was the biting sarcasm of his tongue: in this, at a time when the whack-happy Dr. Keate was the *dernier cri* at Eton, they must be considered fortunate. John Mill was taught by reason, and reason was his God. That the system was achieving the intended end was plain, as his mind was already turning into the desired channels of argumentative and literary skill. At five he was able to engage Lady Spencer, wife of the First Lord of the Admiralty, in an animated comparison of Wellington and Marlborough. At six and a half he compiled from his own reading, in his sprawling hand, a History of Rome in fifteen hundred words.

His eighth year, 1814, was a memorable one. As in most normal children at that age, the pulse of his learning quickened, and under the hothouse conditions of his mental growth, in the next four years he was able to add Latin, Algebra, and Geometry to his curriculum of Arithmetic and Greek. The experiment successfully tried with Greek was tried again with Latin: he began reading Cicero straight away, and by the time he was twelve had chewed convincingly on Ovid, Livy, Virgil, Horace, Lucretius, Tacitus, and Juvenal. In Mathematics he soon outran the rather superficial knowledge of his father, who could not spare the time necessary to keep ahead of him. So James Mill left him to solve his own problems in this field, merely exhorting him irritably from time to time to get on faster, as he galloped through trigonometry, conic sections and the differential calculus, towards the study and the application of higher mathematics. As in the other subjects, it is not John's age that astounds, but the speed at which, once started, he was able to advance.

By way of introducing him to poetry, his father used a method still uncustomary at the present day. While John was struggling with an early passage of the Iliad, he drew his attention to Pope's translation. Young John became devoted to it. He read it many times, and tried to improve upon it himself: he also swung with relish into the wide acres of Greek poetry. He was not required to waste his time in the useless composition of classical verses; instead, he was encouraged to write English verse; because, said his father, who always gave a reason for what he made him do, some things were more forcibly expressed in metre than in prose, and poetry generally cut more ice in the world at large. As for his plain composition, during this period he wrote several more histories including a voluminous review of the Roman government, all of which he later destroyed. They were for his own amusement only, and his father sensibly did not demand to see them. Mitford's *Greece* had now become the favourite of John's private reading; he took due care to allow for the Tory prejudices of the author, who tended to whitewash despots and decry democracy too strongly for the liking of James Mill. Chemistry by now was one of his delights, and would have become more so had he had as his instructor Bentham, who loved to dabble in experiments, and never tired of describing the greatest raree-show he ever saw, the dramatic ascent of Lunardi, one of the earlier gas balloonists. But instead John had James Mill, who in everything was over-satisfied with abstractions, and not enough given to demonstrations. He kept his son from all the stinks and bangs so dear to other boys, confining him to the dull theoretic treatises.

The monitorial system, the ability to pass on knowledge and to supervise the work of others, was another lively precept in John's education. Accordingly, when he was still eight, and just beginning Latin, he was compelled to teach his sister Wilhelmina, and shared responsibility with her for the tremulous answers she made to questions on Latin grammar put to her by her father. This process intensified year by year as the younger children came of age for teaching, and as the number of subjects taken by the elder ones increased.

In writing of all of this forty years later, when under another influence entirely, John Mill forgot, in his dignified security, the narrow edge of his early circumstances, and how much his father had achieved for him. From the pages of his *Autobiography* his childhood emerges as a weary drudgery; his home cheerless, godless, silent, and afraid.

The teaching of the younger children seemed a tremendous burden. He gave it no credit for his own success, not noticing that his later ability to assume the leadership of any group with which he was associated could be attributed in part to the experience he then so hardly gained. Moreover, he had not been the only one to be considered. James Mill, amidst his other labours, had been hard put to it to find time for teaching, and where there was no money for books the hire of a tutor was out of the question. By making the plenty which he gave the one serve also for the many, he avoided the error his own mother had made in sacrificing the interests of the younger children to the advancement of the eldest son. It is impossible to believe that one so violent for the cause of women's education as John Mill had become by the time he wrote his *Autobiography*, could have wished to deny it to his own sisters: and there was no means by which they could have been taught, if not by him.

Never satisfied that with the right upbringing he would not have been a poet, he reproached his father for being unpoetic—while admitting in passing that by him he was introduced to Milton, Goldsmith, Burns, Grey, Cowper, Beattie, Spenser, Scott, Dryden, Campbell, and Pope—a not inconsiderable list. And if his father, being old-fashioned, had little regard for Wordsworth, Coleridge, Byron, and Shelley, those contemporary poets surely were rightly left for the voracious appetite of youth to discover for itself.

Again, finding himself uncertain and insufficient in religious outlook, he once more blamed his father, representing himself as a rare example of one who had not exactly thrown off religious belief, but who had never had it. His father, he said, confided to him his own advancing disbelief in the doctrinal tenets of the time—original sin, eternal damnation, and the morality of the Old Testament. But no pressure was put upon him. James Mill was no inveterate atheist: when he met Bentham he was still a church-goer; and even after that, his doubts, or rather his indignation, mounted slowly, finally reaching agnosticism only in 1816, when John was ten.[16] If the boy was not taught to pray, he was certainly not taught to despise conscience; and his outward observances in his early youth were far more formal than he has let it be supposed. His mother and her family were averagely religious folk. All the children were baptized, and the daughters at least went regularly to church.* It was indisputably John Mill himself who observed chattily to his maiden aunt, on the way back from one of these attendances, that "the two greatest books were Homer and the Bible".

* Many years later John's sister Harriet recalled, "My grandmother (Mrs. Burrow) was a truly excellent and religious woman and taught us to pray, etc. I remember her giving me *6d.* for learning my catechism! My father never interfered and as quite children we girls used to go to church." Harriet Mill to the Rev. J. Crompton, 26 October 1873. MS. letter, King's.

If therefore he grew up irreligious and unpoetic, the fault was at least to some extent his own. He resentfully piled his own shortcomings on his father's shoulders. He criticized his education from the standard not of necessity but of perfection.

III

Bentham, in 1814, at last remunerated by the Government to the tune of £23,000 for the abandonment of his model prison The Panopticon, and enriched by a successful flutter in the socialist Robert Owen's venture at New Lanark, made it his first concern to remove the Mills from their bursting impecunity at Newington Green. He made them his neighbours at 1 Queen Square, Westminster, himself paying half the rent, or £50 a year. Next, remembering the scale of life at Bowood, and being dissatisfied with Barrow Green, he indulged another of his bachelor's whims by renting Ford Abbey, near Chard in Somerset. This colossal pile, sunk amongst green hills and approached by inaccessible roads, had a south front of three hundred feet, in which the designs of Norman builders mingled indiscriminately with Gothic and Tudor work, finished off in the domestic style by Inigo Jones. There were two ornamental lakes, and deer in the park whose ears he could fondle. All this he acquired cheaply at £400 a year. He moved in immediately, bringing three servants with him and engaging two more locally. He also employed three male attendants, one a sort of footman. He soon fell out with the farmer who rented the park, and planted a row of hornbeams all round the upper part of the property, to keep him out of view. Here Bentham spent the better part of the next four years, until in 1818 his losses in an unfortunate speculation in a Devonshire marble pit compelled him to abandon all magnificence, and to return to his hermitage in Queen Square Place.

He was joined, soon after his arrival at Ford Abbey, by the Mills, who stayed with him rather more than six months in the year, bringing with them their humble maid of all work. John had never seen anything like it. The spacious park swept back, up to a wooded crest seven or eight hundred feet high. Here he could wander, guided by the sound of ornamental waterfalls, through open forests of beech and fir, across the rides laid out to give the most entrancing views of the estate, until he came into the quarter mile of chestnuts leading back to the house, which was guarded by a giant cedar of Lebanon standing on a sweep of close-cut cobweb-glistening lawn. The house, an uncompromising mass, towered up beyond a gravel path thirty feet wide. Behind it lay the outbuildings and kitchen garden, then fields leading down to the muddy river Axe, and in the distance, on a rising slope, the little town of Chard.

Inside the house, John was surprised to find many staircases, each leading to a different style of decoration. One led to a room in which the bed was made of plush, and the looking-glass was lined with nun's lace from the works at Honiton. Another, to a great saloon fifty feet long and thirty feet high, lit by majestic casements opening on a balcony overlooking the park. Attached to this was a small library, and beyond it, numerous rooms, one all Chinese, another hung in silk. A little further was the nursery, so long empty that now the astonished farmer called his sons to hear the unfamiliar sound of child voices in the dark old abbey. Down some steps, the east wing, once a dormitory, ran off sideways in a long corridor known as the Monk's Walk: here were the servants' rooms. The lower portion of this wing was a length of Gothic cloister, used by Bentham for his "vibrations", as he aptly called his regular digestive trots. The east wing was a draughty, gloomy quarter of the house. But Bentham stoutly professed a disbelief in ghosts, on the grounds that he could not believe in ghostly clothes, and yet had never heard of anyone who saw a naked one. The Mills of course had no time for such things.

The ground floor of the house contained a private chapel; and beyond the Tudor gateway, a huge banqueting hall with a vaulted ceiling studded with golden stars. Then a square dining-room, with a gorgeous allegory of cherubs and virgins painted on the ceiling, and at the extreme west end the drawing-room. Above, were the eight bedrooms used by the family. They made less than one quarter of the upper floor of the house, although, as John Mill quickly reported to an envious acquaintance, they were "as many as all the rooms in your house, and considerably larger".[17] Indeed, the place was so large that the patient biographer Alexander Bain, who later made a pilgrimage there, was much puzzled why Bentham and Mill and all the children worked in the same room. "In summer, when heating was not required," he said, "they might easily have had a room apiece."[18]

Yet so it was, as Bentham himself recalls. "In that saloon we used to sit and work—Mill in one place—I in another. This was in the summer. In the cold weather we adjourned to the drawing-room, where the tapestry was, and we had means of warmin."[19] Perhaps the tapestries were the explanation. They were everywhere about the house, telling their graceful enigmatic legends; but the finest of all, cartooned with scenes from Raphael, were in the drawing-room and the saloon, shedding their affluent lustre upon the designers of democracy. Rather than miss their grandeur, Bentham endured their inconveniences, and good-naturedly built a wall of books to protect himself from the stare of antiquaries who came to see them. Yet for all his love of splendour, he never was a toady: when Alexander, Czar of all the Russias, sent him a diamond ring, he returned the parcel with the seal intact, indicating that what he really wanted was to codify the Russian law.

To all these generous surroundings, John Mill later accorded a great influence on his development. He was doubly fortunate to have them at the very period when otherwise his life would have been one of real poverty. His father, still plodding dourly in the morass of Indian history, was earning only a possible £150 a year by articles. When he came to Ford Abbey he left behind him debts which Francis Place, the energetic tailor of Charing Cross, defrayed by loans amounting to £300 (later on repaid). In this plight James Mill welcomed the board and shelter so long afforded by the abbey, especially as the friends who had recently acclaimed the appearance of the fifth child, James Bentham Mill, were soon to congratulate the family hoarsely on yet another happy occasion. But it offended his sensibility that Bentham should in addition still be paying half the rent of his London house, and this circumstance led to a quarrel with his benefactor soon after their new establishment opened. Happily, the problem of the rent was quickly solved: Dr. Thomson, an old friend of Mill's, got married and came in to share the London house, thereby relieving Bentham of his part of the burden. The arrangement was satisfactory on all sides: all was soon mended. And by the time Thomson left to take up a professorship in Glasgow in October 1817, Mill's financial siege was over.

Bentham's work during the four years at Ford Abbey was characterized by a mounting vehemence. At first, he was harmlessly engaged on his *Chrestomathia*; a detailed scheme for universal education. Teaching, so far as there had been any for poorer people in the eighteenth century, had been the exclusive function of the Church. When therefore a young Quaker, Joseph Lancaster, opened a non-denominational school in London, the whole wrath of the established Church descended on him. Southey and Coleridge in the *Quarterly* thundered at the *Edinburgh Review*, which had taken his part as a Scot and a Whig and a Dissenter. The pulpit of St. Paul's quaked with indignation. Lancaster was joined by another Quaker, William Allen, by other non-conformists, and by Burdett, Place and Mill, but their own dissensions prevented the foundation of the second school which they proposed. None the less, in 1813 they formed themselves into the British and Foreign School Society, with the noble object of providing primary and secondary schools, based on the monitorial system, indiscriminate in membership and unclerical in teaching, all over London at an annual cost of five shillings a head. Mill brought the scheme to Bentham: he, hot from his successful investment in New Lanark, received it with enthusiasm. A pattern school was to be built at once on a site he offered in his garden. Shares of £10 each were to be issued. At Ford Abbey, he immediately started to sketch out the whole curriculum, enumerating in minutest detail the true principles of tuition: the classroom, for example, was to be circular, with concentric benches raised in banks, easily overseen by a single master seated in the middle on a revolving chair.

While writing the curriculum, Bentham became so incensed at the entrenched proscriptive power of the Church that he began to call it "Juggernaut" or "Jug" for short, and swung straight into his *Church-of-Englandism*, a violent indictment of its unchristianity. When he heard that his old friend General Miranda, who on his way to liberate Venezuela had been betrayed to the Inquisition and flung into a Spanish gaol, had died there unshriven and accursed after languishing four years, his anger spread to embrace Catholicism, and he compiled a further book, *Not Paul but Jesus*. In this he asserted that St. Paul, far from bearing a divine mandate, was an ambitious mountebank who had constructed a clerical edifice on principles of asceticism and intolerance directly opposed to those of Christ as stated in the Gospels, and that Paul, in fact, was Antichrist.

Such outbursts of militant impiety could not fail to make an impression on the quick young mind of John Mill, who was in close contact with them between the ages of eight and twelve. But for the present he worked away quietly at his prescribed studies, and there was much else to keep him occupied. In 1817, when he was eleven, and the *History of India* was coming off the press, his father's activities reached fever pitch: he was now rising at four in the morning and working until midnight for months on end, and even so was unable to accept the lucrative offers of further articles for the Encyclopaedia showered upon him by Napier, the editor. In these circumstances, he was forced to add to his son's labours by turning him to service, and John was employed to read back the manuscript to his father while he was correcting galley-proofs. The boy felt a delectable new importance in this exercise, acquiring on the side a knowledge of the Indian continent which was of great use to him later on.

Life was not unsociable at Ford Abbey. Bentham was on good terms with all his neighbours, and used his great banqueting hall for giving occasional dances; for although he hated dancing, he enjoyed the music well enough. More frequently, he used the room for exercising his whole household at his favourite battledore and shuttlecock, a game he took immensely seriously, resenting the increasing tendency to treat it as a childish pastime. "No shuttlecocks but these tawdry ones," he grumbled on opening a package sent from London; "all glitter, no worth; just like the age, and a startling exemplification, and a conclusive proof of the degeneracy. Pointed epigrams, yes; but pointed shuttlecocks never were, nor ever will be, good for anything."[20]

In addition to these diversions, there was a continuous stream of guests, people from all walks of life, all concerned with one or other of Bentham's varied interests, all in some way notable. His brother Samuel and his family were among the first: then came Joseph Hume, James Mill's school-friend, now a Member of Parliament and in process of conversion to the radical faith; and Sir Samuel Romilly, the great law reformer, whose main purposes were closely knit with Bentham's own. In 1817 Mill's follower and creditor Francis Place arrived, who, it was hoped, would edit Bentham's famous *Rationale of Evidence*, a task so complex that it had already been abandoned by James Mill, but was deemed too urgent to be left until the coming of age of John. In the end Place never did accomplish it, nor indeed were his capacities ever equal to it; but in the meantime, always eager to improve himself, he joined freely in the Mill academy, learnt Latin, and became steeped in Benthamism.

Place, a fair-minded, level-headed, hard-working tailor of nearly fifty, was the prototype of that nineteenth-century prodigy, the self-educated leader of the working class. Starting life in the Benefit Society of the breeches makers, he soon found himself elected leader of a strike. The strike was easily broken; the men were unable to regain their jobs anywhere in the trade, and Place spent eight months in extreme misery, living in one room where he and his young wife watched their child die of under-nourishment and small-pox. But even that could not distract him from his self-taught studies. He next joined the notorious Corresponding Society just after its founder and secretary, Thomas Hardy, had been arrested for high treason. Place became chairman, and was remarkable for his moderation: when the society was finally raided, its members were just voting to join the Volunteers against the threatened French invasion.

At the same time Place had worked his way up to master-tailor and acquired a thriving business at Charing Cross. Being for the first time reasonably secure himself, he turned his efforts to the education of his fellows. Collecting a large number of books, he opened a poor man's library in the back premises of his shop, which became a kind of rendezvous for all parties interested in Reform. During the Westminster election of 1810, he acted skilfully as people's general in the organized ructions attendant upon Burdett's committal to the Tower. While Burdett was being arrested in the act of reading Magna Carta to his son from an enormous scroll; and while his little daughter, lost in the mob outside, answered a gruff enquiry about her name with a brave "Clara Burdett-for-ever, Sir", Place added a sinister touch to the drama by looming about the cellars of Burdett's house with kegs of gunpowder, urging death sooner than submission. He met James Mill during the Lancaster school controversy, and rapidly formed a deep regard for the man who, two years his junior, and starting from a similar depth of poverty, had far surpassed him in self-improvement. Mill, quickly grasping the value of his influence with the London crowd, took great pains to curb his raving about natural rights, and to make him an enlightened Radical.[21] Place, too, was a memorable man for an eleven-year-old boy to meet.

A letter from Place to his wife gives a clear description of the daily life at Ford Abbey:

"Mill is up between five and six. He and John compare his proofs. Willie and Clara are in the saloon before seven, and as soon as the proofs are done with, John goes to the farther end of the room to teach his sisters. Then he turns to geometry till breakfast at nine. Mr. Bentham rises soon after seven and gets to work about eight. After breakfast, Mill hears Willie and Clara and John at their lessons, under a broad balcony. All the lessons and readings are performed aloud, and occupy full three hours, say till one o'clock.

From nine to twelve Mr. Bentham continues working: from twelve to one he performs upon an organ in the saloon.

At one we all three walk in the lanes and fields for an hour. At two all go to work again till dinner at six, when Mrs. Mill, Mill, Bentham, I and Colls dine together. We have soup or fish, or both, meat, pudding, generally fruit, viz: melons, strawberries, gooseberries, currants, grapes; no wine. The first day I came, wine was put upon the table; but as I took none, none has since made its appearance. After dinner Mill and I take a sharp walk for two hours, say, till a quarter past eight, then one of us alternately walks with Mr. Bentham for an hour; then comes tea, at which we read the periodical publications, and eleven o'clock comes but too soon and we all go to bed.

Mrs. Mill marches in great style round the green in front of the house for about half an hour before breakfast and again after dinner with all the children, till their bedtime. Mrs. Mill is both good-natured and good-tempered, two capital qualities in a woman; she is, however, not a little vain of her person, and would be thought to be still a girl."[22]

Place did not greatly care for Mrs. Mill, whom he suspected of unworthy bourgeois pretensions. It is fairly certain that he was influenced in this by the attitude of her husband, whose feeling towards her was bitterly expressed between the lines of his letter congratulating Dr. Thomson on his marriage. "I am satisfied", James Mill wrote, "that you will have made a good choice, both because I know you are not easily deceived in persons, and because you are past that hey-day of the blood when the solid qualities are apt to be overlooked for the superficial. I am happy that she is an old acquaintance, because then people are more likely to know one another, and less likely to have any source of disappointment."[23] In Mill's own case, disappointment in his wife's intellect led him to treat her with scorn; while the hey-day of his blood impelled him to make her ruin her appearance in bearing him a succession of nine children over a period of twenty years. A prolonged experience of servitude seldom makes a happy mother or a pleasant home. John, her eldest son, in an early draft of his *Autobiography*, indicted her because her sensibilities were frozen:

> "That rarity in England, a really warm-hearted mother would in the first place have made my father a totally different being and in the second would have made the children grow up loving and being loved. But my mother with the very best intentions only knew how to pass her life in drudging for them. Whatever she could do for them she did, and they liked her because she was kind to them; but to make herself loved, looked up to, or even obeyed, required qualities which she unfortunately did not possess. I thus grew up in the absence of love and in the presence of fear; and many and indelible are the effects of this bringing up in the stunting of my moral growth."[24]

Eventually, however, John thought better of it, and in the *Autobiography* as published there was no mention of his mother at all. In truth, her shortcomings were largely the result of misery. Coming from a household where femininity had been the rule, she found herself a lonely woman in a society of eccentric males, resembling each other only in their utter self-absorption. And, having surrendered up her generous marriage portion, she had to wage a thankless struggle for respectability in an impoverished and overcrowded family. There was no choice but submission: no outlet for exasperation save in the flaunting of her tattered vanity.*

For the handling of the children, Place was full of admiration, having had a great number of his own.

> " . . . Since I have been here there has not been one single instance of crying among the children, who certainly give less trouble . . . than any I ever knew, notwithstanding they have a plentiful lack of manners, and as much impertinence, sometimes called impudence,

* John Mill's third sister Harriet, though she never saw the draft that he had written about their mother, came nearer than her brother to the truth: "Here was an instance of two persons, as husband and wife, living as far apart, under the same roof, as the north pole from the south; from no 'fault' of my poor mother most certainly; but how was a woman with a growing family and very small means (as in the early years of the marriage) to be anything but a German Hausfrau? How could she 'intellectually' become a companion for such a mind as my father?" (Letter to Rev. J. Crompton dated 26 October 1873, King's.) This defence of Mrs. Mill appears to refer to Bain's assessment of her, given in his *James Mill*, p. 59. That Bain's was the generally accepted view at the time is confirmed by Mrs. Grote's remarks to Lady Amberley: "He married a stupid woman, 'a housemaid of a woman', and left off caring for her and treated her as his squah but was always faithful to her." (*Amberley Papers*, Vol. I, p. 421.)

as any children need have. . . . They have a hard time of it, learning their lessons every morning from eleven to one; and learning again in the afternoon—learning too, with a precision unknown to others. . . . [James Mill] is beyond comparison the most diligent fellow I ever knew or heard of: almost any other man would tire or give up teaching, but not so he; three hours every day, frequently more, are devoted to the children, and there is not a moment's relaxation. His method is by far the best I have ever witnessed, and is infinitely precise; but he is excessively severe. No fault, however trivial, escapes his notice; none goes without reprehension or punishment of some sort. Lessons have not been well said this morning by Willie and Clara; there they are now, three o'clock, plodding over their books, their dinner, which they knew went up at one, brought down again; and John, who dines with them, has his books also, for having permitted them to pass when they could not say, and no dinner will any of them get until six o'clock. This has happened once before since I came. The fault today is a mistake in one word."

And, again to his wife, Place wrote:

"John is truly a prodigy, a most wonderful fellow; and when his Logic, his Languages, his Mathematics, his Philosophy shall be combined with a general knowledge of mankind and the affairs of the world, he will be a truly astonishing man; but he will probably be morose and selfish. Mill sees this; and I am operating upon him to counteract these propensities, so far as to give him a bias towards the management of his temper, and to produce an extensive consideration of the reasonings and habits of others, when the time shall come for him to observe and practise these things."

These unbecoming tendencies were later strenuously denied by John Mill himself.* The impression of conceit, he thought, must have come from his being encouraged to give his opinion fearlessly on matters beyond his age to grown-ups whom he respected only so far as they deserved. Place, certainly, was a proud man who might well have been irritated by flat contradictions from a boy of eleven, especially when the reasons given were always thorough, and the corrections always right.

In ability, John Mill vainly claimed he was no more than average, and in contrast to Place's generally accepted portrait of a dismally precocious child, it is refreshing to come upon new evidence in a letter written at this time by the boy himself to his maternal grandmother. The handwriting is tidy and laboriously rounded: neither in execution nor in content is it at all beyond his age:

* In the *Autobiography*.

"Ford Abbey
Oct 27th 1817

"Dear Grandmother,

I write to you now, as both my Sisters are writing, and there is not likely to be another parcel going to town for a great while.

I have very little news to tell you: Willie has informed you of the accident which has happened to James's eye. Willie, Harriet, and Clara, have begun music: and you learn from Willie's and Clara's letters this also. Willie and Clara are ready to begin the first lesson: Harriet has not yet finished the treble notes.

The rainy weather has at length set in here, after an exceedingly dry autumn. I am however very glad to say, that no rain now can do any injury to the crop, which is almost all in.

We are still learning to write. How much Willie and Clara have improved, you will know by reading their letters.

I hope that all my aunts and uncles are very well. I did not know that I had a new little cousin, till Willie saw it in the paper. I believe my Mother has written you a very long letter: and I suppose that she has told you all the little news that we have; so that I have very little to tell you: moreover, I had only two days notice to write four letters: or else I would probably have written more.

We are all in very good health, except little Jane, who has got a little cough. I had lately the tooth-ache very bad. I hope that you are also in very good health.

Since we were here, there has been a groping in the pond for eels. Mr. Bragg's two sons went into the mud (after almost all the water had been let out) and groped with their hands for eels. Those caught were, many of them, very large ones. A number of trout, caught in the river, were afterwards put in that pond.

All of us send our love to you and all our other relations, and our good friends I am

Your affectionate Grandson

John Stuart Mill"[25]

Admittedly, on first opening the *Autobiography*, the mind boggles at the long list of even longer names of Greek and Latin authors cited as his daily fare. But the names must not be taken to mean more than they are worth. For instance, John's sisters certainly made no claim to erudition; in fact, in later life they were under the impression that their own education had been somewhat sketchy. Yet here is how John described the progress of the two eldest, two years later, when one was eleven and the other nine: "I believe my sister Willie was reading Cornelius Nepos when you saw her." As he was writing to Sir Samuel Bentham, whom they had not seen for five years, that must have been when she was six. He goes on:

> "She has since that time read some of Caesar; almost all Phaedrus, all the Catiline and part of the Jugurtha of Sallust, and two plays of Terence; she has read the first, and part of the second book of Lucretius, and is now reading the Eclogues of Virgil.
>
> Clara has begun Latin also. After going through the grammar, she read some of the Cornelius Nepos and Caesar, almost as much as Willie of Sallust, and is now reading Ovid. They are both tolerably good arithmeticians; they have gone as far as the extraction of the cube root. They are reading the Roman Antiquities and the Greek Mythology, and are translating English into Latin from Mair's *Introduction to Latin Syntax*."[26]

The Mills left Ford Abbey for the last time in January 1818 and returned to Queen Square, Westminster. Their financial difficulties were now and for ever ended. The *History of India* was an immediate success, swelling generously the emoluments of the Encyclopaedia articles. Moreover, despite its harsh strictures on the government of India by the East India Company, and its saturation in radical sociology, it revealed so deep a knowledge of Indian affairs that James Mill was enabled to apply for a subordinate place in the India House itself. Suitable canvassing by his friends drew the attention of Canning, then President of the India Board, to his claims, and in May 1819 he was appointed an Assistant to the Examiner of India Correspondence—a job worth £800 a year, requiring office attendance from 10 to 4, and bearing, for one of Mill's capacity, the certainty of rapid promotion. Within four years he had risen to second place in the department, and in 1830 became Chief Examiner at a salary fixed shortly before his death at £2000. As it was his function to supervise all despatches and instructions sent out to the executives in India, he was virtually head of the Indian administration, holding a position equivalent to Under-Secretary of State. But he did not permit his new responsibility to interfere in any way with his other activities.

On their return from the country, his instruction of his son entered a new phase. The boy, at twelve, was well beyond him in mathematics, and could understand both Greek and Latin as easily as English. The gates of knowledge stood open to him: it remained for him to go inside and gather for himself. He was set to reading Logic; Hobbes, as well as the ancients. From Plato he learnt the Socratic method of enquiry, and so grew a good nose for a fallacious argument. His father did not omit to develop his rhetorical sense in passing. He made John read aloud to him, and constantly criticized his elocution. He drew John's attention to the skill with which Athenian orators insinuated their ideas into the minds of their hearers at the moment when a gradual and persuasive preparation had ripened them for an acceptance of the unpalatable. He also pressed him remorselessly with problems still beyond him, such as the syllogism, berating and taunting him for his incapacity, and never supplying him with the right answer until he was exhausted in trying to find it for himself. In this way he contrived to make the understanding precede the fact, and avoided parrot knowledge even in this whirlwind syllabus. Precise thoughts were all ten commandments to James Mill. He strictly catechized his son for remarking that something was true in theory but required correction in practice: if the theory were true, he said, the practice was so inevitably true as to require no demonstration. It was, John admitted, a severe school: but, he added placidly, "a pupil from whom nothing is ever demanded which he cannot do, never does all he can."[27]

IV

The next year it was Political Economy. This subject had always interested James Mill: his first known publication was a pamphlet on the impolicy of a subsidy on grain exports. David Ricardo, whom he met at Bentham's house in 1811, fanned his interest into a passion. Ricardo was a Jew of about his own age who had, on the Stock Exchange, amassed an enormous fortune in an amazingly short time. He had then very properly devoted himself to studying the largely uncharted sea of Economic Science. He started from Adam Smith and Malthus, at that time the only acknowledged experts, like them presuming a completely free economy. Complete absence of artificial stimulants and of any governmental meddling was the desire of every commercialist in those bountiful days of opportunity, nor was a planned economy of anything like the strictness of the present day considered possible, even in a bad dream. Ricardo took society as he found it, and, in the fashion of the eighteenth century, represented the findings of his analysis as universal truths inevitable in any stable society at any time. In consequence his principles were often erroneous, and, being entirely abstract, appeared to be inhumane. Frequently, like Malthus, he was accused of originating evils he only intended to point out.

Yet for James Mill and his associates Ricardo had a special value. For one thing, his arguments were logically appealing. For another, he provided a scientific background for a new political party of intellectual calibre, based for the first time upon economic instead of upon social theory. The doctrine of rent pointed plainly against the Tory landowner as a parasite upon society. The wage-fund theory showed the inability of the Whigs' almighty Parliament to interfere successfully with free industrial enterprise: when coupled with Malthusianism it also indicated that self-control and harder work, not agitation or philanthropy, were the only hopes for the working classes. Much that the Church had claimed as acts of Providence or grounds for charity now seemed to be inexorably controlled by material forces quite divorced from ethics. Ricardo chimed in neatly with Bentham's social formula that each man was the only proper judge of his own interest, the function of the government being no more than that of referee. His views in favour of free trade, sound currency, and liquidation of the national loans found much support from wise financiers in the City. All in all, Ricardo's hero was the capitalist, and his system was most likely to attract and bind together the rising industrialists, the most powerful body in the country still without political coherence.

James Mill and his friend J. R. M'Culloch incorporated the Ricardian theory into the body of their radical philosophy. A Ricardian Society was formed, and the whole doctrine was developed with such apostolic bigotry that M'Culloch, when challenged to account, in the light of Ricardo's identification of value with labour, for the increasing value of a cask of wine with age, did not hesitate to maintain that the process of fermentation was a form of labour. Ricardo, a shy, amiable man with a quick and gentle smile, became Mill's closest, possibly his only real friend; falling, over a period of years, completely under his influence. Mill sought, as he had done with Bentham, to make Ricardo realize the practical implications of his abstract principles, persuading him, against his natural reserve, to enlarge upon them in a treatise, duly published in 1817. Finding this treatise still too specialized for the general reader, Mill resolved to widen its scope himself, and once more called upon his son's assistance for the purpose. John was not only expected to make a complete summary of Ricardo's book for easy reference: he also accompanied his father on long walks in the country, listened as he expounded stage by stage the whole reach of Political Economy, reduced the utterances to writing on their return, and presented them the following morning in the form of minutes, permanently impressed on his own mind and no less useful to his father when he came to write his *Elements of Political Economy.** In addition, Ricardo was a frequent visitor at No. 1 Queen Square. He had an easy way with children, and took great interest in John, who soon adored him. They used to walk and talk together, or repair to Ricardo's house for man-to-man discussions on the latest state of the new science. Inevitably therefore John Mill's economics were preponderantly Ricardian. In 1819, having retired to a country house in Gloucestershire, Ricardo got himself elected to Parliament, again at the instance of James Mill. There he loyally swelled the agitation for reform: he also laid the highway of the movement which was to culminate in Peel's famous *volte face* over the Corn Laws. It is said that on his sudden death from a mastoid in 1823, James Mill for the only time in his life gave signs of an uncontrolled emotion.†

In 1820, when John was nearly fourteen, James Mill decided that his son had learnt all he could from lessons: the only thing left for him to learn was how to take his place with other human beings. In order to defy as utterly as he had done the age-group theory of education, it had been essential to preserve John from all contact whatever with other boys. The only two boys John mentions having met until this time, recoiled from him in horror at his lack of religious views. He played no games. Leslie Stephen, one of the most rugged of the late Victorians, felt that John would have been better for a game or two of cricket: it would have been of little value to him, for he had no dexterity. He was growing into a lanky boy, handsome enough and healthy, but awkward in his movements and apt to be forgetful both of his appearance and of his manners. He was not shy. Nor, although

* Published in 1821.

† In a letter to M'Culloch on 19 September 1823, James Mill gave a careful description of the full course of Ricardo's illness, which leaves no doubt as to the cause of death. (Bain, *James Mill*, p. 210.)

sharply dogmatic in his statements, did he think himself in any way superior. In his world there were no comparisons: it consisted entirely of principles, reasons, and conclusions. This state of things, his father knew, could not go on for ever. It was necessary to accustom him as gradually as possible to the fact of other people. Fortunately Bentham's brother Samuel had a family of children all somewhat older than John. Moreover, they now lived in France, and French was useful. In so far as the English rationalists respected any systematic culture other than their own, the French was certainly their choice. There, the impact of scientific scepticism in the eighteenth century had been more brilliant, just as the outbreak of the masses had been less gradual and more lurid: and now in the ashpiles of orthodoxy philosophers were pecking for new rules of human life. There was much to be learnt in France. It was arranged that John should go for a six months' visit.

Before he left, there was one more parental duty to perform. His father took him for a solemn walk in Hyde Park, and there, with th deepest sincerity, told him that on going into the world, there was something most important for him to know. If it should appear to him that he was, in some respects, ahead of other boys, he must attribute it not to any virtue in himself, but to his good fortune in having had a father to teach him so devotedly and so well.

John never forgot his astonishment at the suggestion that he might be ahead of other boys: it had always been his impression that he was miles behind. Looking back in later life, he admitted that he was indeed ahead, ahead to the extent of twenty-five years beyond his contemporaries. But he re-echoed his father's warning: what he had done, he said, could be done by any child, male or female, of ordinary intelligence with a similar upbringing. He was forced to this opinion not only by his genuine modesty, but by his loyal adherence to the theory of *tabula rasa*; for he could not accept for himself native abilities which he denied to the rest of the world.

Miss C. M. Cox, in a study of three hundred young geniuses, the three hundred names most famous since the Reformation, placed him in a class of his own at this age, with the prodigious I.Q. of 190. But this may be due to the relatively minute details available of his attainments. Professor Bain, on the other hand, a psychologist of an older school, thought that his achievement was remarkable, but not exceptional. John Mill himself believed that though the experiment achieved astonishing results in the intellectual part of his mind, it cramped at the same time other equally valuable facets of his nature. What James Mill or Bentham thought of their product we shall never know. It is possible to suppose that the wholeness of the later man was reached because of, not in spite of, his beginnings. That what he took to be, in the profound crisis of his youth which shortly followed, a deliberate rebellion in which he salved one half of his being by the curtailment of the other, was really inherent in his education: an inevitable *démarche*, adding gain to gain, but never letting drop an inch.

John left London on 15 May 1820, in the care of a Mr. Ensor, an Irish friend of his father's. He crossed by the packet from Dover, and on arrival in Paris on the 18th presented his father's introduction to M. Jean Baptiste Say, the distinguished French economist, and another admirer of Ricardo. Say's family took the young visitor in, and busied themselves in showing him the wonders of Paris: he noted them all, but displayed emotion only once, when he saw the Palais Royal, an "Immense building belonging to the profligate Duc d'Orleans, who, having ruined himself with debauchery, resolved to let the arcades of his palace to various tradesmen".[28] John delivered his various messages, played battledore and shuttlecock with the son of the house, caught a glimpse of the Comte de St. Simon slaving away at his evangelical socialism in suicidal poverty, was shown by Mme. Berthollet, wife of Bentham's scientific friend, round her beautiful garden, and after nine days took leave of the Says and Mr. Ensor amid general invitations to return.

He was now on his own for the first time in his life, with a four days' journey in a foreign land before him. Almost at once he made a blunder; he chose, in the decently empty diligence, to ride in the cabriolet, and his decision made him, as the places filled, the companion of vulgarity. At Orléans, an enormously fat butcher got in, squeezed him gustily into a corner, and blew the thick smoke of plug tobacco over him for two full days. The butcher got out at Limoges, but was replaced by a slut of a girl with a running sore on her face who revolted him even more. At last a vacancy occurred in the interior, and John, as passenger of longest standing, eagerly claimed it, only to see a woman, dewy-eyed and pleading, interpose herself. But John was not one to be swindled by foreigners merely for ignorance of their language, nor could feminine pretensions wheedle him into a gallant withdrawal. He knew his rights, and firmly stood by them. The *Maire* had to be called in to settle the dispute. Justice prevailed. And John, much satisfied, sat back in the comfortable upholstery to admire the country.

Brigadier General Sir Samuel Bentham had no less taste for magnificence than his elder brother. On retiring from the Admiralty in 1812, he had set his heart on acquiring an estate in the sunny south of France, where now, with his family, he occupied in some style a château overlooking the valley of the Garonne, between Montauban and Toulouse. Like Jeremy, he was a genial man, quick in the uptake, thorough, and benign. In him, too, an inventive genius was clearly marked, although in his case it expressed itself in mechanics rather than in jurisprudence. But unlike Jeremy he was a man of the world, widely travelled, and possessed of considerable martial prowess. As a young man, on a mineralogical expedition made in company with a single Russian officer, he had penetrated across the uncharted vastness of Siberia right up to the Chinese frontier, where he had seen many strange things, and witnessed savage tribal customs: the Roskolniks, for example, who, sooner than change their heathen faith for the orthodox Russian creed, performed orgies of appeasement to their gods, gashing themselves with knives and not infrequently burning themselves to death; and, by contrast, in another distant settlement, he was amazed to find the peasants peacefully playing cricket. A little later on he was appointed by Potemkin as naval engineer to the new arsenal then being built at Kherson on the Black Sea. While he was there, the Turkish fleet attacked the port, and by some mischance he found himself in sole command. Aided only by his labour battalion, a motley gang of all nations and all trades of whom none had ever fired a piece of ordnance, he immediately manned some old hulks lying in the harbour which he had resourcefully fitted out with cannon of his own design, recoil-absorbent guns firing explosive ammunition. With these he opened up upon the over-confident enemy. The self-recoiling guns kept up an unheard of rate of fire: the exploding shells tore gaping holes in the sides of the stateliest ships; in flame and confusion the entire Turkish fleet was sunk. For this resounding service the Empress Catherine personally presented Samuel with a gold-hilted sword and the rank of Brigadier General.[29]

A man of such experience and daring was rightly chosen as the very man to fill the gaps in John Mill's studious but by no means unimpressionable nature. He knew the boy quite well, and liked him. Seven years before, when Jeremy had taken the Mills, father and son, on a tour of Oxford and the cities of the south-west, they had stopped at Samuel's house in Gosport and he had shown them round the Portsmouth dockyards. A year later, they met again at Ford Abbey, where with his family he stayed for a few days just before he went to live in France. To Samuel, John seemed as good as every other boy, though rather bookish. To John, Sir Samuel seemed quite different from all his father's other friends. And Lady Bentham, too, was most unlike his mother. She was the daughter of an old friend of Jeremy's, Dr. Fordyce, the Scottish chemist who had made the gas for Lunardi's balloon ascent; knowledgeable, determined, and with the answers to immediate problems always at her call, nobody ever questioned that she should rule the household. After her husband's death she wrote a biography in defence of his remarkable but unrewarded achievements for the Navy. It was an exceptional book because, while entering fully into the technical detail of his inventions, she compressed their private lives to a total of twelve lines. Their son, George, was a good deal older than John, being now about twenty, and already a fervent botanist. The youngest of their three daughters was enough John's senior not to appear outrageously far behind in intellect.

This family, then, John Mill joined at breakfast on 2 June 1820. They were in process of moving from the château to an apartment in Toulouse, and immediately took him on a visit there, so that the diary which he sent regularly to his father to inform him of his progress at first recorded more sight-seeing than useful work. Indeed, the Benthams from the outset seemed to have determined deliberately to interrupt John's reading, using the confusion consequent upon their move as a means to that end. The books in the library were all packed up, a task in which he was expected to assist, and the door was locked against him. When he wished to read, they sent him out with one of the servants to see his proud little peasant holding and help him gather cherries from it. They saw to it there was nothing for him to study save a few simple French books—but with determination at last he made a start. He had come to learn French: so he began by memorizing a long French fable. When, four days later, the Benthams again dragged him away in the carriage to Montauban, he took a volume of Racine in his pocket. So he was able to improve his time by reading two plays during the journey, and a comedy of Voltaire on the return. No matter what the difficulties, he assured his father, he would not allow any time to be lost. The letter concluded with an animated discussion of the French elections, which he had had to hear about during the time he was unable to read.

He was so bewildered by his lack of books that he even began sleeping late, once not getting up till nine o'clock. One of the daughters pitying his plight gave him Legendre's Geometry. He dissected it eagerly, although its muddled thinking on Ratio took away a good deal of his opinion of its merits as an elementary work. The confusion in the house grew worse; a dog went mad and terrorized the servants. To John's orderly mind the Benthams seemed to live in a state of constant uproar. They were always interrupting him for other things. He was never left to himself. They took him to see peasant dances, and up into the hills to see the twilight beacons started on the *Veille de St. Jean.* "Mr. George" took him for walks and started his lifelong interest in botany. When the day of the move came at last, John set out ahead on foot, only to be picked up by the family in a char-a-banc. Then, to his horror, one of the girls passed him the reins to try his hand at driving.

Things got no better at Toulouse: after the château it felt cramped, and his room was a little hole where it took time for him to set up his shelves and arrange a library around himself. George made him go bathing in the Garonne before breakfast (Jeremy, who never learnt to swim, had once as a young man nearly drowned, and Samuel consequently insisted that everybody should be taught). One evening they all went to Franconi's circus, enjoyed it, and went again another time. Lady Bentham, saying John's trousers were too short and his waistcoat too long, sent him to a French tailor for a new suit requiring several fittings.

Tutors were provided for him, but all in subjects strange to him. French lessons he had in the house, five times a week. He was sent daily to a singing master who made him ape his grimaces, swallow his tongue and emit a tentative Do-ra-me. From eleven to twelve daily he spent an hour with Mlle. Boulet, a gentlewoman reduced by the Revolution, who taught him at the piano. Her exercises caused him to write in Latin to his sisters, advising them to suspend their music till he got home, as he now saw he had started them on the wrong lines. Fencing lessons were the next indignity; then riding, and finally the foppery of dancing. He hated these gentlemanly pursuits, but was made to continue, even though he was quite incapable of acquiring grace in the movements of his jerky, unaccustomed body.

Steadily the time left for his solitary mathematics, classics and logic was whittled down until he could no longer study all of them on the same day. Clinging desperately to his nine-hour standard, he got up ever earlier and went to bed later. Lovingly, like a miser, he counted the fragmentary periods, dividing them up minute by minute between subjects, switching abruptly from one to another, resenting even the moments lost in changing over books. Unconsciously he began to give precedence to his favourite mathematics. His father disapproved: in the circumstances, he informed John stiffly, he ought at least to distribute his time more fairly.

Gradually John succumbed: his father heard less about his Socratic dialogue, more about the population, the Departments and the rivers of France; less about the differential calculus, and more about Franconi's circus revisited. One day, when John went on a picnic in the forest of Bouconne and caught ten butterflies worth keeping, there was no time for study at all. The next, he went with a party to the house of the astronomer, M. Daubisson, gazed at his celestial charts and peered through his telescope, and found time only for a chapter or so of Voltaire. In August, lessons stopped, and the whole family left for a tour of the Pyrenees. John's diary, now written in French, became purely descriptive. The mountain scenery entranced him. He took in every detail of the villages, the hardiness of the people, their habits and their industries. And when they climbed *Le Pic du Midi de Bigorre*, and looked out towards the sunset in the west, his limited fund of poetry failed him. "Mais jamais je n'oublierai la vue du côté méridionale," and the diary ended altogether.

In September, Lady Bentham wrote to his father, giving a favourable account of his progress. Now that they had all been boxed up together for some weeks, she said, they had had more chance to observe John's peculiarities. She was glad to say he was distinctly teachable: "Upon all occasions his gentleness under reproof and thankfulness for correction are remarkable", and they "have been considerably successful in getting the better of his inactivity of mind and body" when deprived of his books. They were fond of him. As the family were about to enter the property they had just bought in Montpellier, might he not stay for another six months to take the excellent courses available at the local university? She felt they were just reaching a crucial stage in their efforts to fit him for the world at large. He still had to learn to brush his hair.[30]

Stay he did, and rode triumphantly to Montpellier through a mountain pass purpling with the hues of autumn. The University was only an excuse, and he learnt little there. But he was happy, and for the first time in his life felt strongly about his personal lot. In January he wrote gratefully to Sarah Austin, a friend and neighbour in Queen Square; with laced courtesy, in faultless French, and in a trim neat hand, he thanked her for undertaking to teach his sisters in his absence, thus removing the main objection to his longer stay abroad. If they were not sensible of the debt they owed her, he concluded heartily, he most surely was.[31] Behind the Benthams' new residence rose St. Loup, a mountain of unusual shape. John loved to climb it. When he returned to the stuffiness of Westminster in July, he had breathed for more than a year "the free and genial atmosphere of continental life".[32] Behind the candlepower of Logic he had glimpsed the snowcapped peaks, hidden by mist or gleaming in the sun. Within the graphs of Political Economy he saw swarthy sweaty folk, laughing and loving, suffering and dying, all to a tune of music unwritable and unknown. No slight learning in a boy of fifteen.

V

When John returned from France in July 1821 he joined his family at Marlow, where they had gone for a summer holiday. They were all waiting for him: there were now four of his brothers and sisters to be taught—Willie, Clara, Harriet, and the seven-year-old James, and whatever small part had been helpfully played by Sarah Austin in his absence, the main burden had fallen on his father, who had perforce confined himself to perfunctory instruction in Latin. The children for their part never regretted that their education lacked the thoroughness of John's, but they sadly missed the intervention of their wonderful brother between themselves and their father's mounting impatience. "*His* great want was 'temper'", wrote the middle sister Harriet,

> " . . . though I quite believe circumstances had made it what it was in our childhood, both because of the warm affection of his early friends, and because in the later years of his life he became much softened and treated the younger children very differently. . . . After he was in the India House *we* could only see him in an evening, when we were always in disgrace over the hated Latin. We were never shown how to learn but had difficult books given us which we were ordered to translate! My father could not teach us as he had done John by companionship; (how many of us would have lived through the same cramming I can only guess)."

John stepped quietly back into his old position, and his resumption of responsibility smoothed away most of the frayed contacts in his over-concentrated family. Harriet went on:

> "He at once wrote and pinned on the walls the way in which the hours of the day were to be passed by the four of us. . . . Any regular teaching we had was from him, and he carried some of us very far in mathematics and algebra. Indeed I have been told that he said I could have taken the Senior Wrangler's degree at Cambridge. I believe that mathematical training has been very useful to me."[33]

James Mill carefully scrutinized the boy who had so calmly eased his irritation. He was older in many ways: fourteen months was a long time in such a crowded childhood. Was he not also grown a little independent? He seemed to have learnt something new, something he had not been taught. Besides, he even seemed to have made a friend for himself while at Montpellier. Who was this young Balard the boy kept speaking of, kept writing to?* Was he suitable? A budding scientist, apparently; well, it might be worse, but it would have to be carefully watched. That was the trouble with

* Antoine Jerome Balard, 1802–1876. Distinguished French chemist and discoverer of Bromine. Writing to Comte in 1842, Mill said, "I am very glad to hear you are a native of Montpellier; it is another bond of sympathy, for I myself passed the happiest six months of my youth in that town, in the winter of 1820–1821. It was also there that for the first time I found a friend, that is to say a friend of my own choice, as opposed to those given me by family ties. This friend I have never seen since; for a long time we kept up a correspondence which finally ended a little by the fault of both of us, and I do not even know if he is still alive." (*Lettres Inédites de J. S. Mill à August Comte*, L. Lévy-Bruhl, Paris, 1899, p. 94.) In reply Comte assured him that Balard was alive, and had left his pharmacy at Montpellier for Paris, where he was doing well as a professor.

tabula rasa: since every experience helped to form decisive associations, you had not only to impress your own influence on the boy, you had to censor all the others. So far he had not done too badly: the two Benthams, Ricardo, Place—all remarkable men, able and active, old enough to stretch a young boy's intellect, and there would be others like them. No women. But now that John was moving on his own, travelling in France, walking freely about London, there was no telling what impressions he was picking up. There was no time to watch him everywhere.

Already there were dangerous symptoms. Why was he rushing round to Bentham's, pulling out every book he could find about the French Revolution, tearing through them with an eagerness that went beyond due diligence? For John had not been taught about the Revolution: he had only been taught that the French, in a lamentable lapse of reason inexorably punished by its consequences, "had put the King and Queen to death, guillotined many persons, one of whom was Lavoisier [their greatest scientist], and had ultimately fallen under the despotism of Bonaparte". He had learnt, of course, plenty about democracy: he had painfully learnt a body of rules by which, ideally, any society of men should be regulated so that each would count for one and for no more than one, and should be free to follow out his own advantage to the greater happiness of the whole. But what he had not learnt was that the rules could be applied. He had thought that, since the blaze of Athenian pavements at least, the pursuit of them had been a blinded earthbound struggle, each upward thrust being ruthlessly stamped out by the crass ignorance or sinister motives of superior power. Now, of a sudden, he discovered that these same principles were the dreams of men and not the ideas of scientists; that they had been patiently built up; "had borne all before them in France thirty years earlier, and had been the creed of a nation". The discovery astonished him, and disturbed him greatly.[34]

There were two things, his father thought, which must be done. The boy had been preserved from all knowledge of his origins so successfully that, for all he knew, he might have been born, as he had been brought up, in a kind of test-tube. It was time for him to know the idea behind it all, why he had been so carefully insulated, what his father had been trying to do. Fortunately he could now read French: James Mill set him down to study Condillac's system of psychology. More serious was John's display of enthusiasm, his obvious hunger for a cause. This meant that if the experiment were to succeed, if he were after all to be the proponent of Benthamism, the ultimate moment had come. The tide was full, and if once missed, might well be missed for ever. As a rite of initiation James Mill gave his son Dumont's edition of dear Mr. Bentham's greatest work, the *Traité de Législation.*

The book was taken deep. "Nature has placed mankind under the governance of two sovereign states, pain and pleasure. It is for them alone to point out what we ought to do, as well as to determine what we shall do. . . . In words a man may pretend to abjure their Empire; but in reality he will remain subject to it all the while", began the introduction. Within a few pages, by a deft enlargement, the concept of the greatest happiness of the greatest number struck the boy in overwhelming force as the only binding consideration in social organization. The duplicity of other reasoners, who, with their loose appeals to high-sounding generalizations like the "law of nature" or "the moral sense of man", justified decrepit institutions, was blindingly exposed. They were all swept away, to be replaced by a complete fabric of legislation based on the single criterion of common expediency. "When I laid down the last volume of the 'Traité', I had become a different being. The 'principle of utility' understood as Bentham understood it, and applied in the manner in which he applied it through these three volumes, fell exactly into its place as the keystone which held together the detached and fragmentary component parts of my knowledge and beliefs. It gave unity to my conception of things. I now had opinions; a creed, a doctrine, a philosophy: in one among the best senses of the word, a religion: the inculcation and diffusion of which could be made the principle outward purpose of a life. And I had a grand conception laid before me of changes to be effected in the condition of mankind through that doctrine."[35] He was to be a reformer of the world.

Having secured his mind, his father next turned to the question of his support. John's godfather Sir John Stuart had recently died, leaving £500 for the express purpose of sending him to Cambridge; but James Mill obstinately refused, despite the earnest entreaties of his friend Professor Townshend, of Trinity. John already knew more than he could learn at Cambridge, he insisted. The law, he felt, while being too often a means of fraudulent enrichment, combined the offer of high rewards with the opportunity of ample leisure: it was also a career well in line with the course of young John's studies, and with the mould in which he had been cast. To instruct him in the Roman law there was nearby an expert of unusual brilliance. In the winter after his return John began to take lessons from John Austin, the husband of Sarah who had taught his sisters while he was away. The Austins were new neighbours in Queen Square. He quickly became a favourite with their small daughter: "John Mill is ever my dearest child friend, he really doats on Lucie, and can do anything with her,"[36] her mother used to say. He accompanied her on expeditions into Bentham's garden where, like the other children, she was privileged to play. Sometimes, when not absorbed in high-pitched conversations with Lucie's father, Bentham himself came trotting out in his full rig, in his plain brown quaker-cut coat, old-fashioned knee-breeches and white woollen stockings, "list" shoes and merino-lined leather gloves, his white hair streaming from under his narrow-rimmed straw hat. Poking his stick "Dapple" at Sir John Langborn,[37] chieftain of his prancing army of plebeian cats, he would suddenly stop short and explain to them the ground-plan of the model Panopticon he had marked out with white tapes across the flower-beds. More often he had Austin walking with him, and that had a sobering effect upon the scene.

John Austin had begun as an army officer in Peninsular days, but had soon sent in his papers: whereon his father, a prosperous Ipswich miller, had shrewdly aimed him for the bar because, though in other ways timid, he was an exceptionally fine talker. During his training at Norwich he met Sarah, the youngest of the seven daughters of the John Taylors, an East Anglian family, who were cousins of almost everybody in the neighbourhood including the famous house of Martineau. Comfortable, numerous, intelligent, well-read, and devout in an inner-lighted way, they were also great humanitarians: at the fall of the Bastille the patriarch John Taylor had been moved to write a song with the refrain "Fall tyrants, fall! fall! fall! These are the days of liberty":[38] in this the family vociferously joined.

Besides sharing characteristics, Sarah, when John Austin proposed to her, was nineteen, decidedly good-looking, lively, and something of a flirt. To everyone's surprise she readily accepted him, despite his gloomy love-letter concluding, "and may God, above all, strengthen us to bear up under those privations and disappointments with which it is but too probable we are destined to contend".[39] She gave up dancing, and settled down to Jurisprudence. Deep in the inert mass of Austin's despondency she sensed the smouldering of genius; she resolved to bring it out, to defeat the cramped feeling of incompetence which forestalled achievement with elaboration, and made him ill with worry. For John Mill, his new acquaintances were of great value. Austin had much to teach him: he went a long way with Benthamism, and where it stopped he went beyond. With him the law was a passion of almost mystical force: in consequence he taught with a feeling for its deeper meaning and a reverence for its broad principles more genuine than his pupil would have hitherto thought possible.

In the summer of 1822 John went with the Austins to stay with their family in Norwich. While he was there a trivial mishap occurred of some symbolic interest. "I wish I had nothing else to tell you", he wrote in his letter to his father, after giving his usual account of himself and of his doings; "but I must inform you that I have lost my watch. It was lost while I was out of doors, but it is impossible that it should have been stolen from my pocket. It must therefore be my own fault. The loss itself (though I am conscious that I must remain without a watch till I can buy one for myself) is to me not great and much less so than my carelessness deserves. It must, however, vex you, and deservedly, from the bad sign which it affords of me."[40] James Mill must have been well satisfied with such a clean confession: and no doubt he was able to reply comfortably to Sir Samuel's musing enquiry, "how far your son continues to pursue his studies with the same extraordinary success which we witnessed, and what line of life he seems likely to take to".[41] His son was dutiful again, and the danger of the grand design foundering in revolt had for the present been averted. But for John it was humiliation. There was in his letter neither cringing nor defiance, only a desperate honesty; a detachment and admission of guilt, the more remorseless for being exactly logical. "I was so much accustomed", he wrote afterwards, "to be told what to do either in the form of direct command or of rebuke for not doing it that I acquired a habit of leaving my responsibility as a moral agent to rest on my father and my conscience never speaking to me except by his voice."[42] When years later at his father's death he received as an heirloom the watch which had belonged to his admired Ricardo, he hastily gave it to his brother Henry: nor was he ever again seen to wear anything but the plainest of silver watches.[43]

At Norwich he met Charles Austin, the younger brother of John, and not enough older than himself to be regarded as an adult.

Charles was a young man with a quick wit, and possessed more dazzle if less light than his scholastic brother. He was much taken with young Mill's ability, and at once proposed that he should make a visit to the Cambridge Union, of which he was then the ephemeral god. He planned no doubt, by showing him off to Macaulay, to the brothers Hyde and Charles Villiers, to Strutt, and to Romilly, the son of Bentham's friend, to gain the credit formerly conceded to great ladies who displayed the precocious talents of their nigger boys to the rest of the galaxy in their firmament. The Union at that time enjoyed an influence well beyond the confines of its rather crowded premises behind the Red Lion Inn. The University followed keenly the debates; and outside the University, the nation re-echoed the dangerous resolutions. For they loved to shock. To be new was fashionable, to be outrageous was sublime. Charles Austin had neatly extracted from his brother the most blasphemous conclusions of Benthamism, had added to them, and reproduced them to his approving audience in a shattering cascade of epigrams. He was marked out for success: sure enough, later on, when John Austin was still needily pondering the ins and outs of Jurisprudence, Charles as a barrister was earning £40,000 a year. John Mill was greatly excited at being chosen by this self-assured young man, and readily accepted the invitation. He went to Cambridge, and he spoke. His massive power in disputation, uttered from a flimsy body in the creaking tones of sixteen, stilled the brittle oratory of the adolescent giants. He left a great impression.

That winter back in London he recalled with admiration Charles Austin's saucy heterodoxy and the adulation of his Cambridge peers. Debating seemed to him an excellent sport, as well as a useful way of training the mind and clarifying the expression. His father had recently taken a prominent part in starting the important Political Economy Club devoted to the furtherance of Ricardo's principles, and even the great Malthus was not exempted by his sacred theory of population from attending its meetings and hearing the rest of his opinions acidly destroyed. He, John, would start his own society. He confided in Bentham's latest literary apprentice, and secured the old man's disused downstairs dining-room as a meeting place. For disputants, besides the amanuensis, he recruited William Eyton Tooke, the son of Thomas Tooke, the founder of the senior Political Economy Club, who brought with him a friend, William Ellis. To these he added another youth who caught his fancy, George John

Graham. As a flaunting banner he chose the title Utilitarian Society, culling the term from Galt's Scottish novel *The Annals of the Parish*, where it was used in an approbrious sense.* On this foundation the five young men, who all thought much alike, together with one or two others whom they initiated from time to time, met regularly every fortnight for over three years. They churned over the various aspects of their philosophy; and from the chilly notions of their seniors, they distilled the cheery vision of the redemption of mankind.

All this time John was reading steadily: logic, metaphysics, psychology, and political economy. Cause and effect and association of ideas brought him abreast of his father's *Analysis of the Human Mind*, begun in the summer of 1822 at Dorking in Surrey, where they spent the six weeks' holiday from the India House. It was time, his father saw, that he was harnessed to the discipline of literary argument. Towards Christmas the owner of the *Traveller* newspaper, Colonel Torrens, slipped into some heresy in speaking of Ricardo and found himself corrected in his own columns by a trite and querulous letter.† Condescending to the début of the son of an old friend, Torrens earnestly defended himself, giving his young antagonist the chance of the last word.

The new year 1823 saw the publication of three of John Mill's letters on a more vital topic in a more distinguished journal. Two years before, the *Morning Chronicle* had passed to John Black, an able reporter who had risen to be editor, and was endeavouring to make of it the voice of day-to-day radicalism long desired by Mill. Where the Whigs criticized the Constitution or the Established Church, he lashed out in detail at the police, the laws, the daily injustices of the courts. By browsing through bookstalls he had acquired gobbets of obscure information which, used appositely, lent his leading articles an air of having been composed by a large staff with ample leisure for research: whereas in fact it was almost entirely written, as well as edited and owned, by Black himself. He pandered to nobody; more than once he had dared to face and to argue down the whole of the Political Economy Club when he thought that their principles were heartless. Yet the spell of James

* John Mill was mistaken in supposing that he had discovered the word "Utilitarian". As long ago as 1802, Bentham had written to Dumont about the heading "*Benthamite*", "What sort of an animal is that?—As to religion . . . *Utilitarian* (Angl) *Utilitairien* (Gall) would be more 'propre'."

† Through the agency of his editor Coulson, another of Bentham's former secretaries.

Mill was so great that their friends could tell from the Monday-morning articles when the two had been together on the Sunday.[44]

Just now Black was fully enlisted in the cause of Richard Carlile who, although already in gaol, was nevertheless in trouble as usual. This time the government, unable to punish him in any other way for publishing the *Republican*, sank to the depths of calling up a huge fine outstanding from his previous conviction. For this his furniture and stock-in-trade were seized, and his sentence extended by a further three years. Next, the arm of justice turned on his accomplices, his wife and sister. The brave Duke of Wellington headed a public fund for their prosecution: his wife was given two years, his sister one year and a fine of £500, and nine of his shopmen were also sent to prison.

Carlile's journalism was not of a high class. It was too scurrilous to command much attention from the *Morning Chronicle*, and his ideas were too diffuse and hazy for the favour of the Radicals. He was full of the aerated notions of the rights of man which Bentham had sternly defined as "nonsense upon stilts". Personally, he got little sympathy; many of the Radicals felt that he had earned the due reward of folly. It was the freedom of the press which interested them.

This was expounded by young John in five trenchant letters, three of them published by Black, the remaining two being declined as over-vehement. Curiously, he seemed concerned not so much with mere restriction of the press, as with the danger to the cause of human progress of allowing an established opinion, safe in the comfortable support of the multitude of the nation, to squash out a single strident voice of opposition, however contrary or profane it might appear. Eighteen months later, writing on the same subject from the loftier level of the *Westminster Review*, instead of the scorn which his father poured upon the errors of the enemy, he launched towards them an emotional appeal: " . . . That Christians, Protestant Christians, whose reformers perished in the dungeon or at the stake as heretics, apostates, and blasphemers; Christians, whose religion breathes charity, liberty, and mercy in every line; that *they*, having gained the power to which so long they were the victims, should employ it in the self-same way, and strive to crush the opposition of opinion, or of passion even, by vindictive persecution, is most monstrous.*"[45]

* This article, though attributed to John Mill by Bain, is not included in Mill's usually accurate list of his own publications.

His youth would explain his rash belief that the smooth upholstery of his opponents could be pricked by conscience. His education taught him that where nothing could be proved an open mind must be maintained. Perhaps he had a personal interest, since Place was his friend and Carlile the friend of Place, to account for his indignation. But whence came his half-expressed belief in the rights of man, the implication that man had the same title to liberty as he had to air, the right he had to breathe? Not, certainly from his father. Romantic passions had no place in the role he was intended for. The philosophy he was to walk was like a tight-rope, not permitting expansive gestures or *pas de joie*.

Material security for life came to John in May 1823. His father's promotion to second place in the Examiner's office of the India House made a vacancy which the court of directors allotted to his son, "on a footing", James Mill contentedly wrote to his friend Professor Thomson, "on which he will in all probability be in the receipt of a larger income at an early age than he would be in any profession: and as he can still keep his hours as a student of law, his way to the legal profession is not barred, if he should afterwards prefer it."[46] As a junior clerk the remuneration was not great: for the first three years he received instead of salary, an annual gratuity of £30: he also had to work under the direct supervision of his father. But he soon learned that the required six hours were more than ample to despatch the work he had to do. His father's system of letting it accumulate through days or weeks before disposing of it in a gust he too found practical. So he had leisure in the office to interview his friends; and, as a day in the life of a Mill reckoned many more than six working hours, time for many other things outside.

The East India Company of those days comprised three divisions, the Secretary's, the Military Secretary's, and the Examiner's Offices: John Mill was in the latter, where the executive instructions were compiled. From the first he was excused the usual duties of indexing and record hunting, and was put straight on to writing despatches to the three Indian Presidencies on political subjects, relating mostly to the Native States and foreign potentates. The Company, though gradually being deprived of its powers, still flourished the flag of private enterprise on a magnificent building with Doric columns in Leadenhall Street in the City. John Mill, shining and respectable in the mantle of the civil service, used to walk to his work there, through the park. As a result of this innocent practice, within a few weeks he nearly ruined himself by being arrested on a charge of distributing obscene literature.

There are many reasons why the truth of this indiscreet adventure is difficult to extract. John Mill himself had shortly many reasons for forgetting it, and when in later life the illuminating correspondence returned to him by Francis Place went absent in the post, it was a matter of some concern to both of them. His enemies at his death, fearful that so great a heretic might join the marbled immemorables in Westminster Abbey, muckraked vigorously. His allies, true to the standards of the time, stoutly denied as best they could that such a thing had ever happened, and loyally obscured a lapse which would now be considered a deliberate virtue. The whole topic of birth control was so delicate that as late as 1898 Graham Wallas in his frank biography of Francis Place could only mention it obliquely.

Place had taken the Malthusian doctrine in its liberal sense, that population must be checked by moral restraint rather than by misery and vice.* But glancing from the teeming streets of London to the nineteen howling inhabitants of his own home, he realized sadly that moral restraint was not enough. The French manage these things better, a friend confidently assured him; he had been himself to Paris to find out; he had interviewed a number of people, mostly prostitutes and doctors, and returned with valuable news. The aid to moral restraint, it was revealed, was an obstruction of nature. The details were not entirely gentlemanly, but Place was a self-made man: he eagerly incorporated them into a book which he was writing called *Illustrations and Proofs of the Principle of Population.* As this was too abstruse for the reading eye of his public, he reduced the essentials to a pamphlet headed *To Married Working People.* This broadsheet he caused to be distributed freely far and wide. Great blocks of it were hidden under market stalls, and given away as wrappings for farthing candles. He was, as *The Bull Dog* sturdily denounced him, "the master spring that moves the whole infernal machine".

* "Between 1801–1831, the inhabitants of England, Wales, and Scotland rose from eleven to sixteen and a half millions." (G. M. Trevelyan, *Illustrated English Social History*, Vol. IV, p. 8.) At the time, this was naturally taken as evidence of an increasing birth-rate. In fact it was so taken until 1926, when G. Talbot Griffith showed that the birth-rate was declining steadily during the period, the increase in population being due to a very marked reduction in the death-rate.

John Mill, seventeen and neatly dressed on a summer morning, was not thinking about this as he swung healthily through St. James's Park on his way to the India House. Under a tree, a bundle caught his eye. Curious, he stopped and probed. It was a baby, blue, new-born and strangled, wrapped up in grimy rags, and left. He reported it some time later to the first watchman he encountered. Then, passing the Old Bailey, he saw bodies of criminals dangling, decorous in white smocks, grotesque, ungainly, hanging by the neck. Their hands were pinioned. Seven ages of man, and all unwanted. Shocked, he told Francis Place what he had seen. Place explained the alternative to misery and vice, and made it clear what he must do.

With an unknown friend, he sped through London with the tracts. Why bear children you cannot feed, cannot educate? Better not bear them at all. As the practical information concerned women principally, they strewed it in their way, down area steps where maids were scrubbing dumbly, at factory gates at the close of the sixteen-hour day. At last they were caught, and hailed away to Bow Street, where they were locked up till they could be brought before the magistrate. When he heard their names, and their offence, he was dumbfounded. Some say that overawed by their good standing he sent them home to their families. Others, that they were sent to prison but released on the intervention of their friends. The most likely version is that the magistrate remanded them to the Lord Mayor, the highest authority in the city. The Lord Mayor was amazed at the depravity of the leaflet, and asked them what they thought they were about. Mill told him, speaking, no doubt, fearlessly, accusingly, and at length. Not satisfied with this eloquent excuse, convinced that they had been attempting to corrupt the purity of English womanhood, the Lord Mayor gave them fourteen days; but on mulling over the question they had posed him about the appalling conditions in his brick-and-mortar empire, he thought better of it and released them, on surety for their good conduct, after a day or two. Years later, in the full panoply of public esteem, Mill found himself facing this same Lord Mayor across the table at a banquet. The Lord Mayor beamed civilly; "I have had the pleasure of sitting opposite you before, Mr. Mill", he said. Mill agreed tartly: he would have a happier memory of the occasion, he replied, if the Lord Mayor had been as quick then as he was now in perceiving opposites: for he would have been able to discriminate between an attempt to prevent infanticide and the promotion of obscenity.

The incident was carefully hushed up, and shortly afterwards Richard Carlile clouded over the issue. When Place visited him in prison and told him what had happened he pounced upon the pamphlet, made a candid summary of its salient advice, embellished it with salty observations and published the result as the leading article in his *Republican* under the headline "*What is Love?*" So that everyone concluded that he had been at the bottom of the whole affair. Nothing about Mill got into the papers, such rumours as there were being confined to a not very definite verse by the poet Thomas Moore, a professional lampoonist.

> "There are two Mr. M..ls, too, whom those who like reading
> What's vastly unreadable, call very clever;
> And whereas M..l senior makes war on *good* breeding
> M..l junior makes war on all *breeding* whatever."

This wretched doggerel was resurrected by the *Times* in its scathing obituary on the death of Mill.

At the time, John Mill was unrepentant. The close of the year saw an article of his in Wooler's illicit weekly *The Black Dwarf*, still maintaining stoutly the necessity of restricting population by whatever means. He did not feel aggrieved. When he was managing editor of the *London and Westminster Review* his assistant John Robertson doubtfully approached him with a favourable notice of the latest volume of poems by the satirical Thomas Moore, and was specially told to print it, since the earlier harmful lines about Mill and his father were no grounds for supressing any praises of Moore's verses to which they were otherwise entitled. But Mill learnt once and for all the lesson his father had always tried to teach him, the advantage of cool science over rash passion as a means of sociological improvements. Long afterwards, in 1868, one Haslam, an Irishman, felt it his duty to disseminate the same information in a more clinical style, and sent him a pamphlet for his advice; his reply was oracular and cautious: "I thank you for the pamphlet. Nothing can be more important than the question to which it relates, nor more laudable than the purpose it has in view. About the expediency of putting it into circulation in however quiet a manner you are the best judge. My opinion is that the morality of the matter lies wholly between married people themselves, and that such facts as those which the pamphlet communicates ought to be made known to them by their medical advisers. But we are very far from that point at present, and in the meantime everyone must act according to his own judgement of what is prudent and right."*

VI

By 1824 it was very definitely James Mill's intention to form a third political party. He had the programme, complete, however doctrinaire; he had the necessary men of ability; what he needed most, in those peaceful days when periodicals were the principal means of propaganda, was a devoted review. To that lack the failure of the Chrestomathic educational scheme could be attributed, and both he and Bentham saw it plainly. For a time, the *Morning Chronicle* had filled the gap, but that was only a daily, fit enough for squibs and letters of criticism, but too slim for serious proselytizing.

It was a most propitious time to found a party. As long ago as 1688, the Whigs, who were theoretically the people's champions, had achieved their political aim, a sovereign Parliament. Since then, so far as they were concerned, the state of affairs was perfect, and should continue as it was for ever. Their power was so complete that George III, endeavouring to restore the royal supremacy, had had to play the game according to their terms; he could not hope to

* The incident is admirably discussed by Norman E. Himes in an article called "John Stuart Mill's attitude toward neo-Malthusianism" in the *Economic Journal* (Economic History Series No. 4, Supplement), January 1929. And, although Himes did not know it at the time, his conclusions are confirmed by a letter of John Robertson's given in *The Amberley Papers* by Bertrand and Patricia Russell, 1937, Vol. II, p. 247. There is also a letter in the Mill-Taylor Collection (MT Coll. 8/35) indicating that a Dr. Drysdale, lecturing in Manchester in 1878, when told that Mill would have disapproved of birth control, replied, "If you had known the late J. S. Mill as well as I did, you would not have said so; Mr. Mill when a young man passed a night in prison, for distributing tracts upon the population question." Dr. Drysdale gave Professor Bain as his authority.

rule without a Parliament, he could only hope to rule Parliament by packing it, at great expense, with men of his own choice. It is true the Whigs resisted him, and even considered some sort of electoral reform to prevent him making their senate into a loft of royal vultures. But all the time they were mainly concerned for their exclusiveness. For nearly a century and a half the Whigs and Tories eyed each other with an urbane tolerance, convinced that whatever their differences they all were members of a grand debating club, the paragon and envy of the world; had not even foreigners, distinguished men like Montesquieu, admitted it? The standard of parliamentary oratory has never been so high as when Pitt and Fox and Burke thundered away across the house, and members luxuriating in their stately perorations drowsily bumbled the conclusions to the Latin tags.

The standard of actual government, on the other hand, has never been lower than during the closing years of the eighteenth century. Under the stress of war and impact of industrialism, conditions at the heart of the kingdom, in the country as well as in the towns, were steadily sinking towards savagery. The sturdy yokel of the speeches, the white-smocked, finger-tilting merry Englander with his Dresden shepherdess, lived in fact in a kind of pastoral wilderness; scratching together shelters of mud and straw, rooting about half naked in the frozen fields, uncertain whether he would die from plague, or in the jaws of the manorial mantraps; swiftly in the hands of the hangman, or slowly in the transportation hulks. From all such knowledge "the great oaks which shade a nation" kept aloof. When they went to the country, they went to calm magnificence: outside lay Grecian temples at the end of bosky colonnades; inside was the mellow choice of port or claret, quadrille or minuet. In town, their emblazoned carriages conveyed them from the gaming tables straight to the doors of the House, where the voice of the demagogue never marred their cultured deliberations. In so far as the people of England had a voice, it was shut outside, to express itself in the futile violence of the Luddites, or in the pathetic martyrdom of Peterloo.

When therefore the tide at last began to set towards Reform, the issue was less between Whig and Tory than between Parliament and people. There was, ready waiting, an incalculable weight of numbers to support any new party that would challenge the whole system at its root, the mounting arrogance and seclusion of parliamentary privilege. In 1820 John Wade's *Black Book or Corruption Unmasked*, a summary of radical grievances addressed to the unvoting middle classes, made the following assessment of the state of the representation:

"Relations to Peers	228
Lawyers	25
Officers in the Navy	15
Officers in the Army	80
Placemen & Pensioners	126
Miscellaneous (*a*)	186
Representatives of the People	0

(*a*) Principally bankers, a few merchants and traders, fox-hunters, men totally unknown, representatives of rotten boroughs, etc."

As with parties, so with the periodicals. In 1802 the *Edinburgh Review* was founded. It was intended for the class of aristocracy which was industrial rather than landowning, somewhat parvenu, but increasingly influential. It deplored, in the name of Liberty, governmental measures like the Corn Laws protecting the interests of the squirearchy against the free progress of successful enterprise. The *Edinburgh* was competently managed by the political acumen of Brougham, the business sense of Jeffrey, and the genuine wit of Sydney Smith. It made its mark to such effect that in 1809 the Tories were compelled to put out a rival organ solidly bound and beautifully printed to extol the old virtues of Church, State, and the common law. Atavism was ever a popular line, and the *Quarterly Review* also found a ready market. It paid its writers well, and attracted contributions from men as eminent as Lockhart, Scott, and Wilson, Southey, and Coleridge. After a few spasmodic brushes, these two reviews, like their respective parties, settled into a kind of convenient enmity. Each had its own dominion, and a running fight was mutually profitable. By 1820 the *Quarterly* was well enough established to turn its attack against the heresies of the contemporary poets. It had chewed up Keats and was opening its maw upon the tougher tenderloin of Shelley.

At this moment of negligent over-confidence, the new Radical Party struck. Bentham had often talked over with James Mill the possibility of inserting into the cavity between the two great quarterlies, a new review with a new object, aimed at the wide reading public of the middle classes who had so far been ignored in the discussions batted elegantly back and forth. Late in 1823 Jeremy had put up the money. Mill was prevented by his public office in the India House from becoming editor, but undertook instead to muster all the literary influence at his disposal, by this time a formidable list of names. John Austin, George Grote the historian, Albany Fonblanque the great columnist of the *Times* and later editor of the *Examiner*, W. J. Fox, a persuasive Unitarian minister; and on the younger side, his own son John with his associates, Charles Austin, Eyton Tooke, Graham, and Roebuck.

The first number of the *Westminster Review* in January 1824 was something of a literary bombshell. James Mill himself led off: with shrewd political insight he attacked the nearest enemy first, sailing not against the Tories but against the Whigs of the *Edinburgh Review*. When coupled with his article on "Government" in the *Encyclopaedia Britannica*, his tirade contained all the essentials of the political theory of the party of Philosophical Radicals who were his followers. He showed how the unfortunate *Edinburgh* existed not to correct the errors but to flatter the prejudices of its readers. Readers who included all those members of the sovereign Parliament not directly nominated by the two hundred families of the Tory aristocracy; readers who were influential clerics dissenting only from the most exclusive pretensions of the established church; readers politically excluded for the moment from the offices of highest legal dignity, Lord Chancellor or Lord Chief Justice, but none the less disposed to express full veneration for the Common Law and for the Matchless Constitution, the sources of their pliant livelihood. By analysing all that they had published he demonstrated how the Reviewers achieved their end. How by the judicious use of vague grandiloquent terms they trimmed between irreconcilable opinions, professing when the Tories were in office lofty apothegms like Liberty, threatening correction by the mob; and during a Whig predominance, stressing the value of settled government, of a stately progression restrained by continual reference to history and to precedent. How they maintained by these means a see-saw of alternate praise and censure, addressing one section of the upper classes, criticizing another, but never doubting that those classes were the only ones that mattered. The Whigs were utterly dismayed at this pungent and informed exposure by their former contributor. They had imagined for themselves a comfortable monopoly of all progressive sentiment; they had not heard of the third party, nor had they been warned about the *Westminster Review*. Their attention had been so dulled in anticipating the Wagnerian lunges of the *Quarterly* that at first they did not perceive even the direction of the sharp new attack, and for the present observed the silence of confusion. It took them five years to equip a satisfactory champion to reply.

Meanwhile, John Mill, who had filled his father's quiver for the great assault by reading through all back editions of the *Edinburgh*, followed up in the second number with a continuation of the argument into his special field of libel laws and freedom of the press. This first appearance as a fully-fledged reviewer he himself described as worthless, save for the experience he gained in composition. But certain excursions of his own about the position of women foreshadowed his later interest in that topic, an interest independently acquired as his father cared nothing for it. His article also marked the beginning of an association with the *Westminster* which continued, sometimes intimate and sometimes distant, all his life, and was at one period to turn him wholly into a practical journalist. For the present he was an enthusiastic and profuse contributor. For the first eighteen numbers he provided thirteen full articles, more than any other single writer, on subjects more or less polemical. Each showed a greater skill and greater power, culminating in a masterly appraisal of Scott's *Life of Napoleon* in 1828.*

In the fourth number, James Mill turned, as scheduled, the remains of his invective on the *Quarterly*. It was, he said, a periodical sustained largely by furnishing light amusement and social prattle to dandies and to literary loungers. For the rest, it did nothing but glorify the existing scheme of things by vacuous appeals to the emotions. In the next issue he gave some attention to a new work by one of its paladins, Southey's *Book of the Church*. "It is an old woman's story-book; containing tales about the changes of religion, and the lives of the workers of wonders, in Great Britain, from the time of the people who set up rocking stones, and venerated the mistletoe, to the time of those who sent our legitimate sovereign to count his beads at Rome."[47] "Southey", said Jeremy Bentham in a fit of passion, "is an ultra-servile sack-guzzler."

* For an excellent account of the *Westminster Review*, see G. L. Nesbitt, *Benthamite Reviewing*, 1934.

With such stuff as this, the *Westminster* soared for some time on easy feathers. The first number leapt at once to the unexpected circulation of 3000, a figure far below that of the actual readers, many of whom, being of the unwealthy classes, shared copies in the libraries of co-operative societies and other reading rooms.

Yet from the very first there had been dissensions between the promoters of the new review. When James Mill had refused the editorship, Jeremy had been induced to entrust it to Bowring, his other confidant, a man whose views in many points were distasteful to Mill, and whose insinuating efforts to gain for himself complete control over the life of the septuagenarian philosopher hardened the distaste into an implacable dislike. In such hands, thought the elder Mill, the *Westminster* was already doomed to certain failure; John Mill and the staff of younger writers thought alike with him. Their fears were sharpened by the resignation of the literary editor, Henry Southern, and the consequent assumption of full power by Bowring. Moreover, the funds were steadily dwindling, for despite its successful sales, the *Westminster* could not pay its way. Some of the writers, led by the two Mills, forwent their original payment of something over ten guineas a sheet,* and continued their contributions free; but even so the affairs soon came to crisis.

A convenient crisis, thought the Mills: in conference with Bowring they explained that they and their associates were prepared to keep the review in being, but that clearly it would be impossible for the finances to stand any longer the burden of a salaried editor. By this device, they were quite sure they could get rid of him, but Bowring was too quick for them. He secretly negotiated a deal whereby Colonel Perronet Thompson, a wealthy and orthodox Political Economist, assumed ownership of the review, retaining him as editor at the same emolument as before. He then wrote to the Mills to tell them of the new arrangement, adding that he hoped to be able to include in his next number articles by both of them for which he was able to offer generous terms. Far from consenting, they both for the time being ended all connection with the *Westminster*, and remained proof against all blandishments. When Bowring, seeing as he thought his chance to win them back, asked John to review a book on logic by his old comrade in the south of France,

* A publisher's sheet, comprising sixteen pages.

George Bentham—an invitation which he no doubt felt the young man could not easily refuse—this is the final answer he received:

"10 March 1828

"My dear Sir

Your letter which I received this morning, is a more good natured one than I fear mine was. I am much obliged to you for not being offended at my *taking huff* as I did, and I will now tell you exactly what I think of Mr. George Bentham's book—and what I am ready to say of it, if you think that it would be more satisfactory to Mr. Bentham than an entire omission.

I do not think that Mr. George Bentham's book affords any proof of want of talent—far from it—but many of haste, and want of due deliberation. His mistake was, as it seems to me, that of supposing that he was qualified to write on such a subject as Logic after two or three months study, or that so young a logician was capable of maintaining so high a ground as that of a critic upon Whately. The consequences of his mistake have been twofold: first of all, he has produced nothing but minute criticism, which even when most just, is particularly annoying to the person criticized when so much stress appears to be laid on it. . . . In the second place, Mr. George Bentham seems not to be aware, that Dr. Whately is a far greater master of the science than he is, and that the public will think the disproportion still greater than it is. It would therefore have been wiser in him not to have assumed the tone of undisputed and indisputable superiority over Whately which marks the greater part of his critique. To be entitled to do this, a writer should not only *be* superior, but *prove* himself to be superior, in knowledge of the subject, to the author whom he criticizes. He should let people see that if he differs from Whately it is not because Whately knows more than he but because he knows more than Whately.

I have put this more strongly, and enlarged upon it more fully, to you, than I should in the *Westminster Review*. But I should think it wrong, in noticing the book, not to say something of the sort.

Very truly yours,

J. S. Mill."[48]

VII

John Mill had been brought up on a definite plan, based on a psychological theory, intended to make him not merely a reasoning machine, but a machine that reasoned in a radical way. To that end he had been subjected to certain influences both intellectual and personal, and to that end he had been protected from all others. Up to his eighteenth birthday the experiment was a complete success. His mental activity was enormous, and he delighted in it; his corporal pleasures had been severely limited to what was necessary for his health. Any display of emotion had been ruthlessly stamped out. Like a machine, he had no ideas of his own, not even a conscience of his own, and his intellect was all the sharper for being narrow. His brothers and sisters apart, he knew scarcely anyone of his own age or younger. Except for Balard, whom he had not seen since he left Montpellier, he had never had a friend.

It was in 1824 that he met John Arthur Roebuck, who was to be very intimate with him for several years, for life his inveterate admirer, and in the end his greatest personal failure. Roebuck was born in Madras: while he was still quite young his father, a doctor, died; his mother married again, and the family migrated to Canada. At the time in question he had just returned to England, a young man of twenty-two, to make a career for himself at the bar, and had entered chambers at the Inns of Court. He is described by his latter-day friend and biographer as "a thin, slight figure, with clean-cut, thoughtful face, uttering curt· crisp sentences which from the first rang out incisively in clear telling tones".[49] He was also distinguished by a downright energy, and a man-of-the-world attitude contrasting oddly with a ceremonious respect for the proprieties, all characteristic of his colonial upbringing. One of his first actions on finding himself alone in London was to present at the India House his letter of introduction to Thomas Love Peacock, a friend of his mother's, who held the post immediately junior to James Mill. Peacock did well by the young man. He said, "I think I can introduce you to a young friend of mine in this house, who belongs to a disquisitive set of young men, and you may find his acquaintance agreeable and useful."

John Mill was then summoned, and after a few courtesies bore his charge away to his own room. "Mill and I", recorded Roebuck, "immediately entered into conversation, in which I laid myself entirely open, having, as I thought, nothing to conceal. Mill, I afterwards found, was cautious, and approached his own peculiar views with great precaution." Roebuck knew nothing of philosophy, but Mill thrust into his hand "a small octavo manuscript" setting out the purpose of the Utilitarian Society, then meeting periodically to read papers to each other at Bentham's house. He then hurried him off to the British Museum, where Roebuck was much amazed at the catholicity of his knowledge. Roebuck went to the next meeting of the society. "It met in a low, half-furnished desolate sort of room —I believe the dining-room of the house, not Mr. Bentham's dining-room. The place was lighted by a few tallow candles. A desk was drawn across the end of the room, at which desk sat the chairman, and some half-dozen young men sat in chairs round the room and formed the society. The essay was a critique for some review of an edition of a Greek author."[50] Roebuck became on the instant a fanatical admirer of Mill, and sought the companionship of another member, George John Graham, who admitted to having the same infatuation. The two walked home together, accompanied by an older, taciturn sort of man. Roebuck was astonished when they stopped in Charing Cross, and the silent man took his leave outside a small shop above which swung a creaking sign marked "Place, Tailor". "This", wrote Roebuck, "was my first experience in democracy."

The friendship of the trio ripened, and soon Mill on his way to the India House would pick up Graham, and Roebuck at his chambers, and they would walk together to the City. No theories of human nature ever seemed more simple and incontestable to men round about twenty than did theirs to them; nor did measures for the betterment of the race ever fly from one to the other with more sweeping clarity, spurring both narrator and listeners to further flashes of optimistic fancy, persuading them that what they dreamed was as good as done. They became inseparable. At the week-ends the other two joined Mill on his interminable walks out of London to the country: talking, talking, botanizing fitfully and talking more, they swung along, a band of intellectual musketeers. On these occasions Mill used to fill his pockets with wild violet seed, and in emphasis of his discourse scattered it to enrich the private hedgerows as they passed. In the summer, he invited his friends to spend the week-end with his parents in the country out at Croydon. They were both personable young men. Old Jeremy had taken a rapid liking to the newcomer Roebuck, and called him "my new tame puss", so John brought them home in pride and confidence. But his father, so long apprehensive of the day when he would begin to consort with other youths, in his anxiety set too high a standard. He did not think much of John's new friends: worse, he said as much, bluntly, to Roebuck, who answered back with his colonial doggedness. There was a row. The younger children remembered hearing their mother, her eyes grief-swollen, wail that "John is going to leave the house, all on account of Graham and Roebuck".[51] It was the guests, however, who left in dignity by the next passing coach. John stayed behind to confront his father. He then walked back to London, where he arrived still pale with anger and told them he had "vindicated his position". The bonds of friendship were redoubled, but they never again tempted the hospitality of James Mill.

Perhaps as the result of this episode, the Utilitarian Society disintegrated. It was replaced by a new society, which met, on the suggestion of Prescott, one of the members, in the City, at the house of his partner George Grote, far away from Queen Square Place. George Grote, at this time in his early thirties, was an amiable heir of a banking lineage. He was painstaking enough, but naturally easy-going, until his quiet city friend Ricardo introduced him to James Mill. Then, like all the others, he was dragged to the chariot of radical politics and made to pull in harness. A year later his good nature and possibly his fortune involved him with another powerful personality, and he was ripped away from Kant and Political Economy to attend a ceremony at the altar. The new Mrs. Grote was a high-powered woman, forcible, ambitious, and incurably loquacious. Sydney Smith maintained that she was the origin of the adjective grotesque. Another observer remembered her "piquant sauciness and masculine moods". After the shortest of skirmishes she sentenced her conquered mate to the plodding lifelong labour of compiling a history of Greece, a work which she felt was needed, and well suited to his patient talents. For herself, she launched a political drawing-room, and set out to build a career for their joint establishment.

She gladly received the young reformers who came seeking a haven for their studies in her house in Threadneedle Street. She took

them in, and made a point of getting to know them
they met for several years two mornings in every
past eight till ten, when they were due at their vari
rules of the new society were sternly systematic. I
text-book and provided themselves with copies, one of them read aloud a section. They then discussed it, following up every point suggested, and even every collateral speculation, until each member was individually satisfied with his own solution to the question. The cardinal rule was that no problem could be left unsolved, however intricate the knot, however opposed the conflict of personalities. Sometimes they argued for weeks on end over a single point before they agreed to move on to another section of the book. Thus exhaustively they dissected several standard works of Ricardian economics. That accomplished they moved on to Hobbes' logic and the latest treatise of Dr. Whately, in which study they were reinforced by the attendance of George Grote himself. Finally, they worked their way through the psychology of Hartley, and there by common consent they stopped. But two years later, in 1829, they reopened their meetings to subject James Mill's *Analysis of the Human Mind* to the same strict examination: so that the father, whose *Political Economy* had been the first, provided also the last course of their deliberations.

As a boy, John Mill had led no gangs, nor had he belonged to any team. And so his adolescent passion for founding societies was not easily quenched. It found a third expression in another enterprise, also dating from 1825, when the energetic wanderings of Roebuck brought him to a meeting of the Owenites, who weekly debated their visionary communism at a hall in Chancery Lane. Rooted firmly in the doctrine of the unselfish brotherhood of man, the Owenites flouted the rigid laws of Political Economy, denouncing them as perversions of human nature and as heartless immoralities. Roebuck was horrified: he defended his faith as best he could, and hurried back to Mill. These sentimentalities must not be allowed to pass, they felt: persuasive solicitations to an illusory Utopia could not go unchallenged in the market place. Debates were arranged: for three months the battle raged. On the one side was the solid battery of Ellis, Roebuck, and Mill, supported by the pyrotechnics of Charles Austin's wit. On the other, William Thompson, champion of the Owenites, was backed by the venerable Gale Jones, an elderly martyr of the libel laws, and by the unexcelled brilliance of Thirlwall, bishop and historian. The issue, as was expected, was indeterminate; but the argument was stimulating, and at M'Culloch's suggestion it was decided to form in London a replica of the Edinburgh Speculative Society. For whatever the truth might be, it was agreed, it was no bad thing to have it forcibly expressed.

The founder members met and drew up a plan. Besides Mill and Roebuck, they were the three Villiers brothers, Romilly, and Charles Austin—all part of the set of young men who had so eagerly listened to John Mill in Cambridge years previously, and who were now down from the University, setting about their careers of varying usefulness in London. Casting about for other allies, they soon roped in the most brilliant remaining member of their coterie, Thomas Babington Macaulay; also Henry Taylor, who was starting in the Colonial Office; Samuel Wilberforce, son of the great reformer and afterwards a high church Bishop of Oxford; Albany Fonblanque; and, when in vacation, nearly all the contemporary stars of the Oxford and Cambridge Unions, including Edward and Henry Lytton Bulwer and Richard Monckton Milnes, a rich young man who set the seal of cultured propriety on any society he thought it worth while gracing with his membership. Meetings were to be held fortnightly during the winter months at the Freemason's Tavern in Chancery Lane, a setting fashionably informal, and accessible to the many members coming from the Inns of Court and Fleet Street. The fame of the project grew: as the numbers swelled, ever more influential figures decided it would be unwise not to join. "That society," wrote James Mill to M'Culloch in August 1825, "which owes its origin chiefly to you and John, is in a most flourishing way —upwards of a hundred names, several members of Parliament, some Lords, all among the young men likely to have the leading influence in the affairs of the next fifty years of their country. The effects cannot but be important. Good principles and talents will be equally advanced."[52]

It had been planned to make a resounding start with a full clash of Tory and Liberal principles, a pitched battle striking Promethean sparks to soar up into the night sky above an expectant city; but as the opening date drew on, a grave shortcoming became obvious. Almost all the promising young men they had enrolled were Liberals of one breed or another: their differences, though many enough, were differences of method not of faith: without a tilting opponent of sufficient mettle the sonorous blows could not be struck. An orthodox

Tory, a man of dazzling brilliance, must be found to open the debate. At last someone suggested a name, a man of recent academic renown at Oxford and of legendary powers of oratory, and he after some pressure agreed to fill the bill.* The day arrived. The house was full. The whole battery of the liberal opposition keenly thumbed the notes containing their vehement points of view. The Oxford Orator took his place. He rose shakily to his feet: he was intimidated. He snuffled and choked, frizzled and cracked: the great orthodox principles, instead of being proudly flourished in the face of his assailants, were shamefully mumbled in a doubtful undertone. The liberal points of view were given no case to answer, no hooks on which to hang their eloquence: they went home angry and disappointed. All the élite shrugged, and went their way: the founder members of the Society were once more alone.

John Mill was most upset. He had hoped to create overnight a whole new factor in the intellectual life of London. He saw now that he had been over-confident. In a half-empty hall devoid of lustre he opened the second debate himself to a dispirited gathering of his associates. Henry Taylor wrote to his mother in December 1825: "Young Mill is to open the debate on Friday week with an attack upon the aristocracy as a pernicious class. He is about twenty years old, a great speaker, and considered to be a youth of very singular ability. Singular one can certainly tell him to be in a moment. I have only heard him speak a few words now and then when the rules of the Society were debated. He is an animated, determined-looking youth, and speaks, I am told, without hesitation, digression, ornament or emphasis, in a tone to me in the little I heard almost ridiculously simple and with very odd but very considerable effect."[53]

Thereafter he spoke in almost every meeting: so did the loyal Roebuck. Little by little they again built up the ground. The next

* The Oxford Orator was Donald Maclean, born on the island of Barbados, 1800. M.A., Balliol College, Oxford. Lincoln's Inn, 1827. D.C.L., 1844. M.P. for Oxford City, 1835–1847. Died 1874. Mill in his *Autobiography* says that he later became a Tory M.P., but withholds his name. I am indebted for the above information to F. E. Mineka of Cornell University.

Mr. Mineka has also provided me with a list of members of the London Debating Society as at 1 November 1826, a year after its inauguration, totalling 188. The Society, however, appears to have had rather a floating membership. Sir Henry Cole (*Fifty Years of Public Work*, London, 1884, p. 16) gives a summary of notable names in its hey-day a year or two later. Of these, two-thirds only are included in the original list.

year they were reinforced by further graduate blood from Cambridge, by Charles Buller, lusty and entertaining, and by Cockburn, a future Lord Chief Justice. The other side was kept up by two able Tory lawyers, Abraham Hayward and Sergeant Shee. They were no match for Mill and Roebuck: "Mill", it was later said, "went over Hayward as a ploughshare goes over a mouse."* However, he and Shee continued gamely. They were regular speakers, and resilient. Gradually, the society began to earn the fame its founders had formerly hoped to achieve without effort. Gradually, the élite came trailing back.

The Debating Society was only one of Mill's minor activities in 1825. There were many others, by far the most arduous being provided by Jeremy Bentham. His papers on the *Rationale of Judicial Evidence*, his longest, most technical, and most important work, had just been returned by the French translators, and he now made his claim on the services of John for the preparation of the English publication. It was a massive task which had lain waiting many years for someone with enough ability and industry to get it done. The great difficulties inseparable from the preparation of any of Bentham's treatises were in this case augmented, because in the interval he had seen fit to rewrite the whole thing twice, and now required John to make a synthesis of all three versions, incorporating as much as possible of the earlier two into the fabric of the third. In addition, John had not only to unroll the jargon into English, but to fill up any gaps which Bentham might have left in his complete analysis of the procedure of the English courts, and to answer in editorial notes the objections made by reviewers of Dumont's French edition to many of the more original of its doctrines. As a necessary preliminary, he studied on his own account all the best authorities past or present on the English Law of Evidence. He then

* It is supposed to have been the rankling memory of these encounters that drove Hayward, half a century later, to write his chilly obituary of Mill for the *Times*. This in turn involved him in a public controversy with Rev. Stopford Brooke, Hayward taking the opportunity to damage Mill's reputation further by hinting at the incident of the birth-control leaflets. He sent a letter containing this and other suggestions of immorality round to all the most influential figures of the day, apparently to stop Mill's friends from getting him buried in Westminster Abbey. He was so far successful that Mr. Gladstone, the Prime Minister, withdrew his support from the Mill memorial committee. But as Mill had left very clear directions for his burial, the Abbey was never in real danger. See *John Stuart Mill and Mr. Abraham Hayward, Q.C.*, W. D. Christie, 1873.

went to work: "it occupied nearly all my leisure for about a year",[54] he recorded, and the labour of bringing the five large volumes through the press took nearly as long again. The experience was not wholly without value to him: apart from a detailed knowledge of legal procedure he learnt to arrange and clarify an intricate mass of commentary, and acquired a new facility of style. As he had undertaken the work for love and not for advantage, these natural gains were the only ones he sought. So when in April 1827 the finished proofs, annotated, tidied up, methodically arranged, and adorned by a laudatory preface, appeared on Bentham's table, they bore only the name of Jeremy Bentham. He could barely credit the boy's lack of acumen, to labour at the work so long, and then omit to take his reward, the imponderable literary esteem to be derived from having his own name coupled with the master's in the front of an important book. He wrote him a note of some acerbity: "It is a matter of no small surprise to me to see the title page without your name to it. Nothing could be more clearly understood between us than it should be there."[55]

John's answer read: "I certainly did not understand you to have expressed any desire that my name should be in the title page. Nevertheless, if you positively require it, I am willing that it should be so, rather than that you should imagine I had taken less pains with the work under the idea of its being (so far as I am concerned) anonymous! But I confess I should greatly prefer that my name should be omitted—That the work should be benefited by it is out out of the question. I myself might be benefited. . . . But on the other hand . . . I should be very sorry to be suspected of wishing to obtain a reputation at a cheap rate by appearing before the public under the shelter of your name."

But Bentham did insist: "My dear John. Your name is of far too great importance to the work to be omitted in the title page." John's pride relented, and his name was duly printed. The book made a massive mark. Writing late in the century, Sir Henry James Sumner Maine, a reliable jurist and one certainly not likely to give praise to that quarter if it could be avoided, said, "I do not know a single law reform effected since Bentham's day which cannot be traced to his influence." The present correspondence ended with a pleasantry: "Dear John. Amen. If you know not what that means send to the booksellers for a Hebrew Dictionary. J. B. P.S. Name at the end of the Scriptures."

So, in the single year 1825 when he was nineteen, John Mill set out to edit Bentham, founded the Debating Society, discussed Political Economy three hours a week at Grote's house in Threadneedle Street, wound up the Utilitarian Society, contributed major articles to the *Westminster Review*, went for long country walks with Graham and Roebuck, carried out his mounting duties at the India House with conspicuous success, and continued to be solely responsible for the education of his brothers and sisters. He also found time to write an article to lead off the first number of the *Parliamentary History and Review*, a periodical sponsored by Mr. Marshall, a worthy Leeds manufacturer and friend of his father. To fill up the remaining cracks of leisure he decided to learn German: languages never bothered him, and he took a course of lessons with Sarah Austin, who was an expert, and began to address her from that time forward by the pet name "Mutterlein". The intellectual activities in this fantastic list were none of them of a transitory nature and all of them continued unabated into 1826. Retribution inevitably followed.

VIII

One evening in 1826 just as the year was dying John Mill looked up restlessly from the magic circle of his lamplit books. He was depressed. Away in the country the south wind trumpeted, driving before it close swathes of low damp cloud: the leaves fell sodden and heavy from the sweating trees, and stuck together. He was twenty. He felt old: his mental age already had the timelessness of the Sphinx; but he still did not feel independent, he felt cramped and incomplete. He had been busy enough these last five years, since he first read Bentham, ranting away with brittle zeal about the means of the betterment of the race. He had even felt a faint relish that the betterment of the race was not likely to be achieved in his lifetime, at any rate not in any final degree: for that gave him a guarantee of continued enthusiasm, a prospect of perpetual bridges to be forced, on a road bounded by a brightening but ever receding rainbow. He had been taught to seek his own happiness in the betterment of the race. The means of that betterment were never in doubt, they were before him all the time. So axiomatic had they seemed that he had gone on mechanically day by day pursuing them, without questioning that he was happy any more than he questioned that the aims were good. He had not had the time, nor yet, perhaps, the power, to stand outside himself and say, "Exactly, now, what are you trying to do?"

But now, he was not happy, he was depressed. Some part of his system missed its beat. He got up, looked out of the window: in the London streets steam rose from the shining flanks of cart-horses towards the foggy roofs, and the muffled draymen blew on their chilly hands and shook the reins. The grey was giving way to black, and with the night came the long tunnel of the English winter, and endless darkness, oppressive, cheerless, raw. He drew the curtain.

Long ago, in the Middle Ages, the monks had lived lives somewhat like his own. They too claimed salvation in a distant faith, and earned present tranquillity by eating up their energy in work. Yet every now and again, they fell into a distressing lassitude: their faith was sapped, their cells seemed narrow and abhorrent, and they had no stomach for their works. In this condition they were beyond care, hopeless, without belief: nothing was worth while; the whole of creation, life, death, and eternity, was all one to them, dreary, dead, and void. So serious were the effects of this malady and so frequent its incidence that it was naturally attributed to the mischief of some demon. It assumed a high place among the vices. Along with concupiscence and pride it was listed by the Pope as one of the deadly inner sins. It became a thing of terror. To escape its onslaught the monks avoided thought like a poisonous snake. They found a name for it; they called it *accidie.** The monks could have told John Mill what had gone wrong with him; they could have told him how to purge it out with prayer and flagellation; could have warned him what, if he went on fretting, would happen next. But his was a utilitarian cell immune from Catholic experience, and he was unaware of them.

So he went on with his gloomy self-analysis. He was alone. For

* See the article "Accidie" in *On the Margin*, by Aldous Huxley: George H. Doran, 1923.

making friends he had been given little opportunity, and those he had made were far behind him mentally. "If you should find yourself ahead of other boys"—he was quarter of a century ahead, that was just the trouble. He thought of Roebuck, and his boyish enthusiasms, Roebuck reading poetry, Roebuck tossing off sketches and water-colour landscapes with a laugh; there was a great difference between them. He thought of their little group, Roebuck, Graham, Tooke, together with himself, allies in certain ventures, never friends; somehow, since the aims themselves seemed insignificant, they all appeared absurd. His mother? He could not think about his mother. His father? Oh, his father, that great, astringent man. He saw him clearly as he had often seen him, winning over another important convert: "His perfect command over his great mental resources, the terseness and expressiveness of his language and the moral earnestness as well as intellectual force of his delivery, made him one of the most striking of all argumentative conversers: and he was full of anecdote, a hearty laugher, and, when with people whom he liked, a most lively and amusing companion."[56] He thought also of the reverse side of his father's nature. "At home", says Bain, "he did not care to restrain the irritability of his temperament. In his advancing years, as often happens, he courted the affection of the younger children, but their love for him was never wholly unmingled with fear, for, even in his most amiable moods, he was not to be trifled with. His entering the room where the family was assembled was observed by strangers to operate as an immediate damper."[57] One of the strangers was young Henry Solly: "His manner to me and other visitors was usually stately, simple, and courteous, and not unkind to his children, though he seemed to take little notice of them except of John; but accustomed as I was to my father's behaviour to my mother, and that of other gentlemen whom I had observed in similar relations, I could not help being rather pained at his manner occasionally to Mrs. Mill. She was a tall, handsome lady, sweet-tempered, with pleasant manners, fond of her children: but I think not much interested in what the elder ones and their father talked about."[58] No. He could not talk to his father. "I grew up with an instinct of closeness. I had no one to whom I desired to express everything which I felt, and the only person I was in communication with to whom I looked up, I had too much fear of to make the communication to him of any act or feeling ever a matter of frank impulse or spontaneous inclination."[59] He was alone.

That did not matter. He was used to that. Loneliness was a necessary symptom of greatness for anyone dedicated to noble aspirations. He turned back to his chair. He pictured again the anodyne, mankind perfected, intelligent, strong, and free, and heard in answer to his gull's cry invocation, the insensate roar of the turbulent ocean of humanity. He put the question to himself again, more formally: "Suppose that all your objects in life were realized: that all the changes in institutions and opinions which you are looking forward to, could be completely effected at this very instant: would this be a great joy and happiness to you?" To this direct question the rebellious fiend inside him which he preferred to call "an irrepressible self-consciousness", distinctly answered, "No!"[60]

He was dumbfounded. "At this my heart sank within me: the whole foundation on which my life was constructed fell down. All my happiness was to have been found in the continual pursuit of this end. The end had ceased to charm, and how could there ever again be any interest in the means? I seemed to have nothing left to live for." Soberly, he went to bed, to see what a good night's sleep would do.

It did nothing. The gloom of dull unechoing night was fastened on his soul. He put the question in another way. Leaving out himself, suppose the reformers should succeed, suppose Prometheus should be unbound, should be provided with his vote, his freedom of the press, would he then soar in all the possible dignity of man? To this again the demon answered "No!" For what he had seen was not Prometheus, but himself, and his own inability to soar.

He was utterly dejected. The world had become a senseless mass plunging through an unintelligible void without beginning and without end. Worst of all, he did not care a rap. He was suffering not only from loss of faith: he was suffering from lack of feeling. He did not care about his own condition, he did not care about his family: he did not care enough for anyone to be able to discuss his situation: and if by sudden tremors of the earth unseen thousands were to be crushed to death in fearful agony, still he did not care.

It was embarrassing and shameful. Mechanically he continued with his daily work, drafting out copious instructions to improve the lot of millions of Hindoos, when all the time he knew the fate of the Hindoos meant nothing to him. There was no escape. He went on with the Debating Society, lecturing on the benefits which would accrue from this or that reform, painting out the bright prospect for the future of the race. He saw with an envy near to loathing the shining zeal which lit the healthy faces of his friends as they went busily after perfection. In his own heart he knew he was a liar.

He could not feel at all. Desperately, he tried everything that might make him feel. He tried the moody food of music, Mozart and Weber, hitherto an unfailing balm. Now he could make nothing of it, except an arid nightmare, a recurring dread lest, since the number of notes and possible harmonies was mathematically limited, all of them should become exhausted and the creation of new music come to a final end. He turned to poetry. Byron, Prince of the Passions, could strike no spark from him. There was nothing there but the mirror of his own dreary grief, the hollow melancholy of satiety. Painfully, he applied his sovereign remedy. Analyse, Analyse, he had always thought: face up to your shady fears and by the time they are dissected they will have disappeared. But in this case analysis merely turned against itself. Analysis, he found on close inspection, was itself at the root of the trouble. His whole life had been spent in sharpening his power of analysis, and now analysis had whittled away all his feelings and emotions. Worse, it was now too late to acquire new habits of feeling. No pleasures were left to him save on the purely physical plane, and these he knew would soon die of their own surfeit. He could not feel, he never would feel. Everyone had told him that sympathy with other people and unwearying labour for the good of mankind at large were the surest sources of happiness. He did not doubt it for a minute, "but to know that a feeling would make me happy if I had it, did not give me the feeling". He could see well enough what needed doing in the world, and apart from this one flaw he could have done it. "I was left stranded at the commencement of my voyage, with a well-equipped ship and a rudder, but no sail; without any real desire for the ends which I had been so carefully fitted out to work for: no delight in virtue, or the general good, but also just as little in anything else."[61] The deficiency seemed to him permanent and fatal. Grim logic led him to a grim resolve. He decided to give himself a year to develop some sort of feelings, and after that, drastically to cut short a life so burdensome and useless as his was bound to be.

But with the spring came a dawn of better things. One day, he was gloomily reading the *Mémoires* of Marmontel, the recollections of a minor French playwright of the eighteenth century, who lived, like Rousseau, on the immense importance attached to the arts by the nobility of the period. At the beginning of his frank record of an unelevating life, Marmontel described his father's sudden death, the despair of his mother, the penury of the family, "and the sudden inspiration by which he, then a mere boy, felt and made them feel that he would be everything to them—would supply the place of all that they had lost." At this point Mill was shaken with compassion, and found tears pouring freely down his face. He was delighted. He must have feelings after all. The crisis was past. "I was no longer hopeless: I was not a stick or a stone. I had still, it seemed, some of the material out of which all worth of character, and all capacity for happiness, are made."[62] The sun shone, watery at first: the birds began to sing again; books gripped, and he was able to laugh among his friends.

It is the fault of Mill himself that this incident has become so surrounded with confusion. Describing it thirty years later in his *Autobiography*, he used a device of authorship to hang on this one hook the detail of his life for nearly four years, and what in general he considered to be the faults and results of his father's teaching. It is therefore difficult to determine how far he was setting out his opinions at the time of writing, and how far simply recording his experiences of 1826. For instance, he made repeated references to Coleridge, although he never read Coleridge until a good deal later; and he made cutting comments about the English national character which certainly sprang from a later period in his life. He seems, in fact, to have had no clear idea of what had happened to him. The burden of his account throughout was of his lack of feeling: the gloom itself was a vacuum of no feeling: the cure, a sudden ability to feel. And yet throughout he was in an agony of shame and despair which drove him to the edge of violence. Quite possibly, the very time when he says he had no feeling was the time when he was feeling most acutely and for the first time in his life.

Still, as he enshrined the whole in a lengthy chapter under the momentous heading "A Crisis in my Mental History", most commentators have attached a good deal of importance to it, and as his account was indefinite, they have naturally made their own interpretations according to their various proclivities. Bain and Leslie Stephen in their downright manner attribute the whole to overwork, a breakdown of his intellectual apparatus shockingly overburdened from his earliest youth. Others, of the religious school, have made great play with it, as the awakening of his soul. The most concise of these was an American lady, Mrs. S. E. Henshaw, who said it was "the last protest of his defrauded moral being before it should finally sink from inanition. What it needed was the bread of life. What it dumbly sought was God."[63] More recently, a psychological approach diagnosed a psychic trauma, a secret death-wish towards his father, which was released and exorcised on reading in Marmontel of a boy in similar circumstances whose father died, and who stepped into his place as head of the family.[64]

None of these explanations, his own included, is sufficient; but each of them, as Mill so frequently observed to be the case, contains an aspect of the truth from which the whole may be built up. In the first place, it was not so prolonged or recurrent a crisis as he himself made out. In its intense form, it lasted only from winter until spring, from November until March, the months, as Voltaire pointed out, of the east wind, when Englishmen hang themselves in dozens. The months when a black gloom settles over the entire nation, and even those strong enough to keep their health at least lose their good humour.[65] Nor was it a breakdown in any complete sense of the word: he went on with his normal work: none of his family or friends observed anything unusual about him: until he himself told of it, nobody knew there had been anything the matter with him. He was overworked, and lived a life as narrow as in any monastery. In consequence, in the depths of winter, the fearful lassitude of *accidie* descended on him. As for the psychological aspect, though the death-wish theory may be over-laboured, there is reason to suppose that he may have been obsessed at least by a compassion for his mother. His complete omission of all reference to her in the final draft of the *Autobiography*, his apparent scorn of her in later life, when coupled with his fanatical devotion to the cause of women in general and to one woman in particular, seem to indicate a conflict ending in sublimation.*

At the same time he was beginning to achieve a degree of independence from his father. A few months previously, in May, his gratuity of £30 a year was replaced by a regular salary of £100, and his work thenceforth was less directly supervised. His first action in his new affluence was to engage a French tutor for his sisters. A

* *Autobiography*, p. 73. Though it is true that, even before his breakdown, Mill had already taken exception to his father's proposal to exclude women from the vote on the grounds that their interest was safeguarded by their menfolk, his objection had been a rational and not an emotional one. He was arguing from Bentham's formula that every human being, whether man or woman, black or white, was the only proper judge of his own interest.

year or two before, he had overcome his fear sufficiently to stand up to his father over Roebuck; now, he was economically more free, and in every way a little less accountable. For the first time that great part of him which up to now had been obediently suppressed began to blossom. It was not so much a revolution as an enlargement.

He had been taught that happiness was the end of life. The lesson that he learnt from his malaise was not in any way alien to his father's teaching; it was a correction of his own misunderstanding. Happiness, he had thought, was a quarry that could be hunted to a kill in the performance of good works. He now saw it as a more elusive quality, vanishing in the seeking:

> "Ask yourself whether you are happy, and you cease to be so. The only chance is to treat, not happiness, but some end external to it, as the purpose of life. Let your self-consciousness, your scrutiny, your self-interrogation, exhaust themselves on that; and if otherwise fortunately circumstanced you will inhale happiness with the air you breathe, without dwelling on it or thinking about it, without either forestalling it in imagination, or putting it to flight by fatal questioning."[66]

In short, like the monks, he was returning to his faith and works and giving up analysis. His own ultimate happiness being no longer the automatic crown of virtue, he required some less theoretic, more impulsive guide to conduct. As a result, he exalted his feelings, so long subdued, beyond a proper balance. Time and again from this time forward he dragged his reason along behind his sympathies; time and again he acted extravagantly from his passions, and found a flawless chain of reasoning to justify it afterwards. So elemental did the tendency become that it invaded all his thought, and a subsequent logician, Jevons, was forced to the perplexing conclusion that "however it arose, Mill's mind was essentially illogical".[67] He remained as he had been before, a reformer of the world: but he now went after emotion like an addict after drugs.

He felt bitterly ashamed about an essay he had written in his unenlightened youth, cynically attacking all sentiment and emotion. He was doubly ashamed when he remembered how he had given it, not without pride, to Mrs. Grote of all people.* He found the poetry of Wordsworth, and gulped it down in hasty draughts. Wordsworth wrote of the country, and he loved the country; of mountains, and he recalled the scenes which had left him speechless in the Pyrenees;

* Later he got it back and destroyed it. (*Amberley Papers*, Vol. I, p. 421.)

Wordsworth, too, had taken refuge from a pressing world in sentimental botany:

> "Thanks to the human heart by which we live,
> Thanks to its tenderness, its joys, and fears,
> To me the meanest flower that blows can give
> Thoughts that do often lie too deep for tears."

Mill was greatly moved. "I long continued", he wrote defiantly, "to value Wordsworth less according to his intrinsic merits, than by the measure of what he had done for me. Compared with the greatest poets, he may be said to be the poet of unpoetical natures, possessed of quiet and contemplative tastes. But unpoetical natures are precisely those which require poetic cultivation."[68]

The declaration of his new enthusiasm led him into conflict with Roebuck. They remained allies in numerous enterprises, but when in the summer of 1828 Mill went with friends on a fortnight's ramble through Berkshire, Buckinghamshire, and Surrey, Roebuck was not of the party. From then, there was a barrier between them. Mill genuinely admired, and without envy, Roebuck's quick and easy sensibilities; his effortless appreciation of music, poetry, and the theatre, and his natural talent with a canvas. But it irritated him that one so gifted should be so little precious, should see no value in the cultivation of the feelings, and should wish to have them deadened instead of quickened. He made Roebuck read Wordsworth too. But Roebuck, the man of action, strongly admired the hated Byron, and had no time for all this stuff on "flowers and butterflies". Deeper issues were involved in their dispute over their favourite poets: Byron was the traditional hero-poet of the *Westminister Review*, "the only useful lord".[69] Mill's disdain of him must have seemed to Roebuck damning evidence of mounting heterodoxy. In the winter, they fought it out like gentlemen, in the Debating Society, where they appeared for the first time on opposite sides.

The same debate that saw the weakening of one friendship saw also the beginning of another. In the audience there was a newcomer called John Sterling. He had heard Mill speak before, but never on such a theme, or in such a mood. Instead of the dry, querulous chant, the remorseless rightness he expected, he heard a high emotion, an undecided pause, the promise of passion and a groping for expression. Wordsworth was a favourite with him too, and the speaker seemed to lay bare all his own feelings. He was amazed. That evening, not for the first or last time in his life, John Sterling revised his first opinion.

He and his firm friend Frederick Denison Maurice became regular attendants at the meetings, and soon transformed the intellectual climate by introducing the breath of Coleridge, under whose spell they lay.

Coleridge, then at the height of his prophetic powers, wielded tremendous influence. He was writing little: he was too much a spiritual vagrant, too greedily preoccupied with the rich lands of his discovery to spend much time describing them within the confines of the written word. But he talked, like any tramp: and young men, eager and adventurous like Maurice and Sterling, sat listening to him by the hour. As the story-teller ran along in his soft sweet voice, his hearers forgot him and forgot themselves. For he told of the white marble palaces of heart's desire, the lilting song of legend, the never quite obtainable view beyond the outlet of the soul, and the warm drone of summer evenings, all endlessly, easily, plainly, so that in the end impossibility was reality indeed, and reality a drained forgotten cask.

His effect varied a great deal with his hearers. Sterling wrote, "I was in his company about three hours, and of that time he spoke during two and three-quarters. It would have been delightful to listen as attentively, and certainly easy for him to speak just as well, for the next forty-eight hours." Dean Milman was more critical of Coleridge's discourse: "I used to be wicked enough to divide it into three parts: one third was admirable, beautiful in language, and exalted in thought; another third was sheer absolute nonsense; and of the remaining third I knew not whether it were sense or nonsense."[70] Mill, unlike most others, was bewitched less by the presence than by the written word. In April 1834 he wrote, "Few persons have exercised more influence over my thoughts and character than Coleridge has; not much by personal knowledge of him, though I have seen and conversed with him several times, but by his works, pieced together by what I have otherwise learned of his opinions."[71]

Everything about him was directly contrary to radical beliefs. While Radicals worked industriously, building up their man-made tower to heaven, he wasted time in sloth and lassitude, and said that heaven was already in the world, all but the seeing of it. Where they dealt in proofs, he dispensed faith. For him there was no truth at all in theory, and little in practice; truth could only be glimpsed from time to time by a blinding flash of intuition inaccessible to the world at large. Intuition was dogmatic, undemonstrable: as a philosophical approach the Radicals despised it. They trusted a chain of argument neatly built up by tested reasoning to uncontradictable conclusions. To conclusions reached suddenly and without evidence they attached the suspicions a schoolmaster feels when the answers to mathematical problems are set down without any method or working shown.

The very delicacy of his opposition to radicalism made it all the more dangerous. The general run of intuitionist defended Church, State, and the Aristocracy simply and for what they were—their country right or wrong. Not so Coleridge: his distinction between the apparent shadow and the spiritual substance enabled him to attack the existing framework of the institutions while exalting the possibility of what they might be made. None was ahead of him in deploring inhumanities and injustices, the slave ships, the child labour, the presumption of the rich, the complacency of the clergy. He was ahead of all in describing the spirit of the whole, the concept of broad and settled government and of peaceful unquestioning religious faith, of a gracious civility between the orders of society working together harmoniously towards a proud and placid destiny. His philosophy was cloudy, his thought as imponderable and various as the wind; his economics, on his few reluctant excursions into those fields, were outrageously misinformed. But his vision of a transformed society and a devoted church was so bright, and his power of portrayal so vivid, that by his influence working through the many important young men who came to listen and could never forget, he did in time create a large part of what he taught. The opposed movements of Christian Socialism and Oxford Mysticism alike derived from him. In the great battle of the century between authority and the individual, between tradition and science, he was the most significant of the patricians. He stated the highest case for his party, and stated it with immense and almost supernatural power. Although Carlyle, envious of his pre-eminence, furiously assailed his teaching as "transcendental moonshine", the treason failed, and Coleridge remains the venerable monarch of conservatism.

The impact of the Coleridgeans on the Debating Society was decisive. They became a third party between the Tories and the Radicals, subscribing much to each and all to neither, and stimulating the whole for a short time so that it blazed with fame and notoriety. But it could not last. Under the complication of a further point of view, the level of debate fell from protagonism of rival philosophies, to the more subtle sectarian differences involved in deciding means towards ends for all practical purposes the same. Mill had expected the Society to widen, not to shrink: in 1829 he left it to its fate, and eloped with the newcomers, Maurice, and John Sterling.

For Mill, Maurice was not of much interest; in later life, there remained between them a distant respect. "I believe he retains a feeling of kindness to me still",[72] wrote Maurice. For all that, their fundamental difference of opinion showed itself in a sort of grudging rancour. Maurice, commenting on Mill's article on Bentham, wrote to Sterling in 1838: "I have a very uncomfortable apprehension that the writer is the most plausible of all speculators, and has the fewest earnest convictions."[73] "I have always thought", said Mill in his *Autobiography*, "that there was more intellectual power wasted in Maurice than in any other of my contemporaries. Few of them certainly have had so much to waste."[74]

With Sterling it was another matter. Son of a restless father who wandered fruitlessly through the more outlandish corners of the British Isles before settling at last in London to become the famous Thunderer of the *Times*, Sterling was by nature as much of a vagrant as was Coleridge himself, although in a more terrestial sense. In his thirty-eight short years, only twice did his body remain in the same lodgings for more than two of them. He had an intellect not too acute, an urge for creative writing, an enthusiasm which, if locally disastrous, was also humanly engaging, particularly in a life so solidly dogged by misfortune as was his. To a beauty of speech and a sweetness of expression he added a devoted sincerity. He had the capacity to elevate his opponents without one whit reducing the strength of his own convictions. If he expressed little in writing, he was undeniably rich in person, and drew from Mill the loving observation that some few men benefit the world immeasurably by their mere existence, irrespective of what they do.

That they started from opposite poles of thought made for emphasis rather than for difference. Sterling's zeal was of the expansive sort, not condemning his adversaries but hoping always for conversion, greeting eagerly not only belief but disbelief, welcoming every crack in the lacquered face of a decided opinion. While Mill, in his new eclecticism, gave yards rather than feet away to gain something he could not define but which he knew to be more important than a lost contention. For years by circumstances they were separated, and not only by circumstances but by intervening personalities. Yet whenever they met it was as brothers, and they always found surprisingly that each had moved a little more towards the other. There was true sympathy between them. On his early but protracted deathbed Sterling wrote daily to his son, adverting in the midst of parental advice incessantly to Mill. "He is a friend of many years, and one of the truest and worthiest, uniting a warm, upright and really lofty soul with a still and even cold appearance, and with a head that reasons as a great Steam Engine works. You will be very fortunate if you ever come to know him well; and my intimacy with him has been one of the two great fortunes of my life—though hardly—I suppose were ever two creatures more unlike than he and I. I have often wondered that he ever put up with me at all. Yet I am sure he would cut his hand off tomorrow if he could see me recover from this illness."[75]

At first, the association was for Mill something of a flirtation with the enemy. To choose for himself a friend from the opposite camp was a wholly new and exciting experience, completing the destruction of his earlier rigidity and adding to the temporary fluidity of his mind. "If I am asked", he wrote, "what system of political philosophy I substituted for that which, as a philosophy, I had abandoned, I answer, no system: only a conviction that the true system was something much more complex and many-sided than I had previosuly had any idea of, and that its office was to supply, not a set of model institutions, but principles from which the institutions suitable to any given circumstances might be deduced. The influences of European, that is to say, Continental, thought, and especially those of the reaction of the nineteenth century against the eighteenth, were now streaming in upon me."[76] He clearly perceived Coleridge as his main and permanent adversary; but that did not prevent him from according Coleridge the due honours of his rank. With other young men he ascended Highgate Hill to sit at the feet of the master. Also, to his father's disgust, he read articles then appearing in the *Edinburgh* by Thomas Carlyle, a new artist of the mystic school, although for the moment they struck him as "nothing but insane rhapsody".

From these dangerous migrations he was soon diverted by a real emergency.

IX

Towards the end of 1828 his father's *Essay on Government* and other articles in the Encyclopaedia were printed as a separate volume, and the whole heart of radical thought was therefore fully expounded between two slim pasteboard covers. The Edinburgh Reviewers, still smarting under the effects of James Mill's sudden onslaught nearly five years previously, here saw their opportunity for retaliation. Indeed, the occasion for vengeance was all that they required, for a most powerful avenger was already at their side.

Thomas Babington Macaulay was one of the few of John Mill's acquaintances who successfully resisted the spell of conversion extended by both Mills, father and son. He was well within range. His father, Zachary, an ardent philanthropist prominent in the attack on slavery, had been for many years on close terms with James Mill and was an enthusiastic reader of his *Political Economy*: Thomas himself was still a friend of Charles Austin, and at his instigation had joined the London Debating Society as a founder member: moreover, his friendship had widened to include John and Sarah Austin, intimate friends of the Mills, and he made frequent visits to their house in Queen Square. Yet, he stood out stubbornly. He was, by very nature, an historian, and he would not lend support to any theory of politics which treated historical experience and the recorded behaviour of men to such scant respect as did the Radicals. It would not do, he felt, to sit down with a sheet of paper, say that every man always follows his own interest if unrestrained, and that therefore political systems will always be corrupt unless, by a system of penalties and rewards, the interests of the men in power can be made to conform to that of the community at large. It denied the whole historic progress of man from barbarism to parliament: armies of crusaders contradicted it; the ghosts of careful statesmen, Chatham, Walpole, Burghley, sonorously deplored; whole dungeons full of martyrs rose and shook their chains. He would, if necessary, forsake his friendships in order to beat out the heresy. He was a formidable antagonist. Words flowed from him in a tumultuous procession, so that the senses were numb to the sharpness of the axe he was grinding away below, until, striking fast and clean, he took the head off in a trice. Although only just emerging from a pinching poverty, he had an ambition to rise through Whig channels to political and declamatory fame. For him the Whig party was the current total of human achievement. He was a perfect Edinburgh Reviewer.

In the number for March 1829 he made his assault upon James Mill, his theory of Government, and his followers, the Utilitarians, "these smatterers, whose attainments just suffice to elevate them from the insignificance of dunces to the dignity of bores". From this challenging aperitif, he launched into the main attack:

> "We have here an elaborate treatise on Government, from which but for two or three passing allusions, it would not appear that the author was aware that any government actually existed among men. Certain propensities of human nature are assumed; and from these premises the whole science of politics is synthetically deduced! We can scarcely persuade ourselves that we are not reading a book written before the time of Bacon and Galileo.
>
> "What proposition is there respecting human nature which is absolutely and universally true? . . . that men always act from self interest. This truism the Utilitarians proclaim with as much pride as if it were new, and as much zeal as if it were important. . . . When we pass beyond those maxims which it is impossible to deny without a contradiction in terms, and which, therefore, do not enable us to advance a single step in practical knowledge, we do not believe it is possible to lay down a single general rule respecting the motives which influence human actions. There is nothing which may not, by association or by comparison, become an object either of desire or of aversion. The fear of death is generally considered as one of our strongest feelings. It is the most formidable sanction which legislators have been able to devise. Yet it is notorious that, as Lord Bacon has observed, there is no passion by which that fear has not been often overcome. Physical pain is indisputably an evil; yet it has been often endured and even welcomed. Innumerable martyrs have exulted in torments which made the spectators shudder: and to use a more homely illustration, there are few wives who do not desire to be mothers. . . . But, when the question is propounded generally about the whole species, the impossibility of answering is still more evident. Man differs from man; generation from generation; nation from nation. Education, station, sex, age, accidental associations, produce infinite shades of variety."

In passing, and more for argument than from conviction, he probed a great weakness in James Mill's proposed limitation of the right of voting:

"'One thing', says he, 'is pretty clear, that all those individuals whose interests are involved in those of other individuals, may be struck off without inconvenience. . . . In this light women may be regarded, the interest of almost all of whom is involved either in that of their fathers, or in that of their husbands.'

"If we were to content ourselves with saying, in answer to all the arguments in Mr. Mill's essay, that the interest of a king is involved in that of the community, we should be accused, and justly, of talking nonsense. Yet such an assertion would not, as far as we can perceive, be more unreasonable than that which Mr. Mill has here ventured to make. Without adducing one fact, without taking the trouble to perplex the question by one sophism, he placidly dogmatizes away the interest of one half of the human race. If there be a word of truth in history, women have always been, and still are, over the greater part of the globe, humble companions, playthings, captives, menials, beasts of burden. Except in a few happy and highly civilized communities, they are strictly in a state of personal slavery. Even in those countries where they are best treated, the laws are generally unfavourable to them, with respect to almost all the points in which they are most deeply interested."[77]

The *Westminster*, naturally, hastened to defend itself; and the battle continued through many more numbers on both sides, expostulating and explaining. It was all good journalism. There was nothing the public liked better than a serial controversy between the leading reviews, and the sharper the strictures the better they liked them. No relations were strained by the dispute; when Macaulay applied for a post in India, his cause was unexpectedly championed by James Mill; he got the job, and they became the best of friends.

John Mill, on the other hand, was seriously dismayed. He did not wish to be persuaded by Macaulay. The historical method of constructing politics from the analysis and comparison of past experience led to essential conservatism, and all too easily to a habit of worshipping anything that was old; a tendency evident in Macaulay himself, who, for all his parade of orderly progress and constitutional reform, was at bottom rooted in a profound and drowsy satisfaction with the world as it was and particularly with England as it was. Mill knew it well enough. "I am reading Macaulay's book", he wrote when the famous *History of England* first appeared in December 1848, ". . . I have no doubt like all his writings it will be and continue popular—it is exactly *au niveau* of the ideal of shallow people with a touch of the new ideas—and it is not sufficiently bad to induce anybody who knows better to take pains to lower people's estimation of it."[78] But if

Macaulay's emotion was histrionic and his motives insincere, nevertheless his quick intellect had in this case penetrated too near to the heart of John's own dissatisfaction with his father's theory for him to be able to gainsay it. There was much truth in what Macaulay wrote. The passage about the position of women struck him particularly hard: throughout his life, that question was so much a passion with him that he often made it the final issue, the test on which depended his acceptance or rejection of a philosophic system. In this case, it was the means of doubling the gap between his father and himself; and although he did not accept Macaulay on the strength of it, he incorporated unconsciously and without acknowledgement the two striking concepts—that the interests of women were no more identical with that of their husbands than the interests of subjects with their kings, and that the denial of rights to women was the enslavement of one half of the human race—almost word for word into the groundwork of all his future dissertations.

So, thought John Mill, both Macaulay and his father were wrong, though each achieved an element of truth. Having thrown off bigotry, he attempted for the first time to do what later became habitual with him; to form his own theory of politics, extracting what was sound from both of them, rejecting the unsound, and reconciling opposites. With his father, he agreed that the correct approach must be deductive, arguing from broad general rules of human conduct. Macaulay's plea for the historical method, building up political science from careful observation of what had happened in the past, was quite invalid since it demanded evidence more exact and accurate than any yet available. The human past was no laboratory. Cause and effect could not be proved with the necessary precision, until the raucous corridors of History had been swept and cleared of rumour, partiality and contradiction. Yet, while accepting the deductive process, he agreed with Macaulay that his father's general rules were too remote. His father had argued from laws of human nature which, even if true of the individual, were of little assistance to the study of mankind in the mass. In deriving political principles from psychological abstractions he had played one game by the rules of another to an unwarranted degree. What was now needed, Mill concluded, was a body of general rules more specifically related to society as a whole. So he began to chase that alluring Jack-a-lantern, a philosophy of history.

An influence was close at hand to urge him on his way. In May 1828, Eyton Tooke strolled in to the Debating Society with a young

Frenchman who had been dining with him, Gustave d'Eichthal. d'Eichthal was in England partly to collect material for a book he was to write; and more particularly, to spy out the ground for the transformation in human organization and in human nature believed by him, along with the other members of the Saint-Simonian sect of which he was a rapturous adherent, to be not only overdue but imminent.

Saint-Simonism became a revolutionary religion against the intentions of its founder, for there was very little extravagance in the original designs of the Comte de Saint-Simon. A patriot who fought with Lafayette under the American flag; an aristocrat imprisoned by the Terror; a speculating scientist ruined by ventures like his plan for cutting a canal across the isthmus of Panama; his main intention was to found a steady constitutional régime, to protect France against the twin extremes of her recent experience, the unmanageable fury of revolution and the despotism of Napoleon.

So far he was no more than the mirror of his times, for the decade of the eighteen-twenties was the golden age of liberal revolution. In England it was the time of the Cato Street Conspiracy. In Greece, of the defence of Missolonghi. In Italy, the Carbonari left their secret cells and boldly waved their tricolours of red and blue and black. In Spain, the army mutinied, and the people took their ruler captive for a season. Even in the musty intrigues of the Russian Imperial Court, the Decembrists were able to delay the full force of Czarist vengeance. The great enlightened despots of the eighteenth century had been succeeded by dynastic rulers who were for the most part truculent and vain, and were all acutely nervous of sharing the fate of Louis XVI. All over Europe, whole peoples rose against them in the cause of national freedom.

It was not at all a movement of the sans-culottes; nobody desired a repetition of the horrid excesses barely a quarter of a century old. Nor was there anything chauvinistic about the nationalism. The flag of patriotism was not yet stained; it was an invocation, not an obstacle, to the brotherhood of man; it was the flag of freedom, and freedom was a cause without a frontier. Liberalism was strictly reasonable in its aims. Instead of paunchy tyrants there were to be decent kings: instead of rule by capricious force there was to be strong government in the hands of able men, answerable in varying but always definite ways to the broad middle classes of the people. Instead of the present state of things, wherein the only hope was patronage and misery was the common lot, the new society would permit each to live fairly by his own effort, and, in achieving his own prosperity, to contribute to the welfare of the whole.

But in France, as is traditional, vitality and energetic logic magnified the passing mood of Europe. The sane objectives were abandoned in favour of visionary extremes. In the course of his studies the Comte de Saint-Simon happened to look into the Bible, and, inspired no doubt by his own pitiable poverty (he was driven in 1823 to attempted suicide), he became absorbed by an emotional concern for the condition of the poor. In his work *Le Nouveau Christianisme* he carried the Christian ethic into social theory, reaching the conclusion that the whole of society ought to be devoted exclusively to the amelioration of the existence of its poorest class. Some years before, he had become associated with Auguste Comte, a striking young man who, at the age of twenty, had decided to draw up a complete compendium of human knowledge and to finalize thought in an unsurpassable system of philosophy. Beyond a general agreement that everything needed changing there was little in common between the two. Saint-Simon exhorted; Comte dictated. One was mystic, the other materialist. One aimed at social equality, the other at sole authority. They soon quarrelled, and at Saint-Simon's death in 1825, Comte left the movement to pursue a more systematic train of thought of his own contrivance. Before that happened, the Saint-Simonians pounced upon the essentials of Comte's historical philosophy, compounded them with the evangelical precepts of their master, and produced a complete doctrine, religious, social, and economic, for the regeneration of humanity by the practice of brotherly love.

Made of ingredients basically hostile, it was an indigestible creed; but it was no less fanatical on that account. It certainly had all the virtues of originality. History was seen as an alternation of "critical" periods, marked by warlike selfishness and sceptical lack of faith, with "organic" periods of cooperation, progress and fertile religious sentiment. The long "critical" phase which had lasted since the Reformation was soon to burst into a new "organic" Saint-Simonian age of man. The existing social order was to be extensively recast. There was to be an ideal communism. Inheritance and private property would be abolished. The error of the Owenites would, however, be avoided; and instead of an ownership divided equally between all members of the community, regardless of their services, individual effort for the common good would be promoted. Each would be rewarded strictly according to his merits, and society would be ranged in classes determined entirely by deserts.

The classes would reflect the spiritual, mental, and physical functions of the individual man. In recognition of superior worth, the spiritual power would be supreme, with an organization and status borrowed *en bloc* from the mediaeval Catholic hierarchy. Feminine nature being essentially spiritual, ultimately a woman would be found of prodigious originality and power who would become the supreme symbol of the spiritual order, and she would pronounce the new relation of the sexes. In the meantime, a partnership of man and woman was to be assumed. Women were to be counted in all respects the free equals of men, subject to all the privileges and duties of the priestly order of which they were the *ex officio* members.

The Saint-Simonian theology was a pantheism similar to that of Coleridge and the German mystics. "All which surrounds us, inanimate objects, ourselves, our feelings, are a fragment of God."[79] In the womb of the Almighty, nothing died. The old Catholic dogma of the dualism of soul and body was entirely superseded: man was a divine unity within himself, and his flesh, instead of being mortified, was to be raised to its true dignity as the third estate of his microcosm. The new order was to embrace the whole of humanity without distinction of race or creed. Starting in Paris it was to blaze across France, England, and Germany: Europe was the first objective, after that, the world. Force would vanish from international affairs; in fact, there would be no international affairs. Henceforth there was to be only one relation public or private between human beings, the relation of brotherly love.

Gustave d'Eichthal, listening at the Debating Society, had no difficulty in perceiving Mill's ability. "What struck me most", he reported, "was the speech of a young man of great talent, M. Mill, who spoke last, and took up one after the other all the points touched on in the discussion, even those the furthest from the subject, giving his opinion on each in a few words with a measure, a good sense and a grasp of the matter altogether astonishing."[80] Eyton Tooke introduced them; and finding that the speaker's nature was as receptive as his intellect was powerful, d'Eichthal decided then and there that he had found the man to lead the Saint-Simonian crusade in England. On his return to Paris he set about the work of conversion, sending Mill a copy of Comte's *Système de politique positive*, and also the back numbers of *Le Producteur*, the original journal of the Saint-Simonians, discontinued since 1826.

Comte had a great power of conviction. His knack of dividing a subject into three components, and a second totally different subject into three other components which he then showed to be analogous to the first, was both distracting and persuasive. Mill was impressed but not deceived. He suspected Comte of a fault common to many French philosophers:

> ". . . of insisting on only one side of the question when really there are several, or of perceiving only one face of an object, from a single viewpoint, when there are several others equally essential to the true appreciation of that object. If I wished to instance cases of this fault in Comte's book, I could do so on every page, for it permeates the whole book and is, I think, the reason why Comte is able to give his ideas a tight and systematic form, so that they appear to be a sort of positive science."[81]

From the remainder of the Saint-Simonian theory, Mill picked out one or two points that pleased him. From their philosophy of history he gleaned two pregnant new ideas. First, that the human characteristics of his own era might only be the peculiarities of an age of transition, and not, as he had supposed, the perpetual attributes of human nature. This enabled him to believe, for the first time, in the progress of the species, and to "look forward, through the present age of loud disputes but generally weak convictions, to a future which shall unite the best qualities of the critical with the best qualities of the organic periods; unchecked liberty of thought, unbounded freedom of individual action in all modes not hurtful to others; but also, convictions as to what is right and wrong, useful and pernicious, deeply engraven on the feelings by early education and general unanimity of sentiment, and so firmly grounded . . . that they shall not, like all former and present creeds . . . require to be periodically thrown off and replaced by others."[82] Secondly, and in consequence of the first, the sobering historical reflection that "institutions which, considered in themselves, are incapable of producing anything but the most frightful evils (the Catholic Church for example) have none the less been, at some particular stage in the progress of the human mind, not only useful but absolutely indispensable, as the only means by which the mind has been able to advance to a higher grade in its development."[83] He admired the pioneering spirit of the Saint-Simonians; he welcomed their views on women; but he thought their social organization dangerously rigid and some of their economic proposals, especially the abolition of inheritance, downright heretical. Here would have ended his connection with them had it not been for the persistence of d'Eichthal, whom he really liked.

d'Eichthal was determined to convert both Mill and Eyton Tooke, who were at this time intimate enough to share his letters. "I feel compelled to transmit to you", he pleaded, "the sacred fire which has been kindled in myself."[84] When Mill told him that he and his friends were about to start a journal, he promptly wrote to say that it must be a Saint-Simonian journal, that Mill must become the leader of a group in London, that he must come to Paris to see the headquarters of the party, now numbering about forty, in their little mission in the *rue Taranne*.

At last Tooke wrote very frankly saying he had not the least intention of becoming a Saint-Simonian. They were narrow sectarians: the very words they used, the "School", the "Doctrine", "our Society", "our Master", "initiation", "conversion", showed them for what they were. He had, moreover, a fundamental objection to the creed. "You start always from the happiness of the whole human race, from the future progress of the whole human race, as if you were concerned only with the human race as a collective being, and lost sight of the individuals who compose it. . . . To pretend that men ought to concern themselves with the interests of the whole race, before striving to procure a living for their wives and children, is a palpable absurdity. . . . I myself am persuaded of an essential error at the heart of your doctrine."[85]

Within a few days of this downright, thoroughly English defence of the rights of the individual, Eyton Tooke, distraught by a love affair, slashed his throat and prematurely ended a promising career. d'Eichthal was profoundly shocked, and wrote at once to Mill. "I would like to be near you, I would like to clasp you in my arms; I would like to mix my tears with yours. . . . What news! Eyton dead! And by such a death!"[86] At the same time, he realized that with Tooke had gone the main influence against Mill's enrolment, and he redoubled his pressure. Mill stood firm. He maintained that the new order of society was "impracticable, and not desirable if it were practicable like that of Mr. Owen. . . . In France it may be otherwise, but . . . in England, the idea of beginning a moral reform by preaching an overall doctrine, is a notion which would never enter the head of anyone who had lived here long enough to know our people.

The English invariably mistrust the most evident truths if he who propounds them is suspected of having general ideas."[87] Accordingly, if d'Eichthal persisted in his purpose of coming to England, he would gladly receive him, but it must not be supposed that there was the least chance of his conversion, nor had he any intention of undertaking the publication of any journal in England for the propagation of Saint-Simonian views. It was never Mill's way to allow his various would-be spiritual fathers to exaggerate through over-enthusiasm the degree of his allegiance.

Nevertheless, he did what he could to help in minor ways. In February 1831 he consented to meet their envoys, Ms. Janski and Bontemps, though without abandoning an inch of his ground. Later that year, he gratefully acknowledged a complimentary copy of the organ of the sect, *Le Globe*, and provided d'Eichthal with a list of eminent names differing as widely in their outlook as the poet Southey, Dr. Arnold of Rugby, W. J. Fox, and Colonel Perronet Thompson. It might, he felt, be of advantage to the movement to send them each a copy. Finally, when d'Eichthal made his threatened appearance at the end of 1831 Mill gave him an introduction to Thomas Carlyle, another mystic recently arrived in London who was also attempting to recruit him as a disciple, in the hope no doubt that both having equally misunderstood his purpose they might find consolation in each other.* Wrote Mrs. Carlyle to her sister-in-law, "You may fancy how my heart beat when a card bearing the name of Gustave d'Eichthal was sent up the other day . . . He is a creature to love at first sight—so gentle and trustful and earnest-looking, ready to do and suffer all for his faith."[88]

Within a few months, Mill's caution was vindicated, for the crash came. Bazard, the leader of the movement, was supplanted by his colleague Enfantin, who wished to see the new society established at once in corporal form. He carried the sect off from Paris to his country estate at Menilmontant, where he established the sacerdotal hierarchy and presided over it in sole supremacy, adopting the title "Father of Humanity". Here for some months forty of them lived a life of rural communism, rewarding each other according to their merits, and

* Although Mill engineered the first meeting between Carlyle and d'Eichthal, the two had been in correspondence for some time. (See "Letters from Thomas Carlyle to the Socialists of 1830," in the *New Quarterly Review*, Vol. 2, 1909.) Carlyle even seems to have made an English translation of *Le Nouveau Christianisme*.

acting up to their faith in a mannner considered quite outlandish, by doing their own housework. As always, the profession of unusual views about property and the relation of the sexes was one thing, and their performance was another. They received unsavoury publicity: it was rumoured that their proceedings were orgiastic. They were prosecuted. They marched to their trial in a body, wearing beards and a peculiar uniform, singing a succession of hymns written and set to music by themselves. As counsel, Enfantin had two female adorers, of whom he took not the slightest notice, conducting his own defence. His address was frequently interrupted by rapt pauses "pour attendre des inspirations", and now and then he shot strange glances round the court, to show, as he said, the power of a look.[89] He was rewarded according to his merit by a year's imprisonment and a heavy fine, while the rest were variously sentenced or dispersed. Some of them, dissatisfied with their experiences, concluded that western womanhood was too inhibited to be capable of the free and equal comradeship to which their creed would elevate her, and organized an expedition to Constantinople in search of "la femme libre", the prototype of emancipated femininity. Others pursued activities regarded by Mill as even more extravagant: "One or two . . . have become disciples of Fourier, a sort of Robert Owen, who is to accomplish all things by means of cooperation and of rendering labour agreeable, and under whose system man is to acquire absolute power over the laws of physical nature; among other happy results the sea is to be changed into lemonade."[90] Gustave d'Eichthal avoided punishment, and for the time being retired to Italy.

Although Mill ridiculed the extreme conclusions of the Saint-Simonians, they produced in him results more drastic than he then recognized. During the years of his close association with d'Eichthal, their influence predominated in his literary activities. The first effect of their impact was a confused pause while he assimilated the fundamental changes in his outlook. In 1829 he deserted the London Debating Society in company with John Sterling, because its political objects of desire were no longer in accordance with his: it was also the only year during the whole of his journalistic career when he published nothing at all. Next came a period when the lure of France, lively ever since his fourteen months with Samuel Bentham, became a complete absorption. In 1830 his friend Fonblanque took over the editorship of the *Examiner* from Leigh and John Hunt, who, wearied of continual prosecutions, retired into private life. Under Fonblanque's wise guidance the stormy periodical settled down, and in course of time acquired the sort of reputation now enjoyed by the *New Statesman*. At his request, John Mill began to write for it, and with one or two exceptions all his many contributions dealt exclusively with the politics and culture of the French. He was indignant at the utter disregard of the English for the activities of their recent enemies across the channel, especially since it seemed to him as if the soil of France, cleaned and ploughed over by so many great convulsions, was of all countries in Europe the most fertile for the growth of new social ideas and institutions. He soon became recognized as the authority on contemporary French affairs, and from his articles it is plain that he was assiduously collecting his materials for the history of the French Revolution he had been contemplating for some time.

Finally in the winter and spring of 1831, a series of seven articles called "The Spirit of the Age" appeared in the *Examiner*, expressing his full adherence to the Comtist-Saint-Simonian philosophy of history, and relating it to the existing state of England, where, just before the Great Reform Bill, it was not hard to show the babble of voices, disunity, and lack of a firm faith characteristic of a dying critical epoch. He went on to present the future promise of an enlightened despotism by a scientific *corps d'élite* who, being the rulers naturally in tune with the dynamic of the age, would inaugurate plenty, peace, and the religion of humanity. Contained in this laborious nonsense, of which Mill himself was later much ashamed, there were two points of great importance. In deciding that the natural and desirable condition of mankind is to be ruled by and to obey the proper people, he rejected Bentham's basic principle that each man is the best judge of his own interest, and so ran counter to the whole edifice of political checks and balances his father had built upon it. It made no difference that John Mill's aristocracy was to be one of worth instead of birth, for Benthamism was rooted in a sturdy individualism suspicious of the motives of all rulers whatever, whereas he now presumed the possibility of power being used disinterestedly. Secondly, he became a revolutionary. In order that "man may achieve his destiny. . . . There must be a moral and social revolution, which shall, indeed, take away no men's lives or property, but which shall leave no man one fraction of unearned distinction or unearned importance."[91]

Now no young visionary worth his salt will long be satisfied with speculation; and, as might be expected, Mill's change from disquisitive radicalism to ideal humanism was accompanied by a desire for action. The first evidence was his new choice of friends. Clearly, there were no half measures about d'Eichthal, and Sterling was if anything still more militant. While at Cambridge, Sterling had joined a small society limited to a dozen members known as the Apostles whose discussions were subversive to the point of risk, and went far beyond the usual prerogative of undergraduates. In November 1827 young Monckton Milnes wrote his mother a letter which must have filled her with alarm: "A Mr. Sterling told us we were going to have a revolution, and 'he didn't care if his hand should be the first to lead the way'."[92] Worse was to follow in fulfilment of this promise.

Among the droves of liberal refugees exiled from their Continental homes by reactionary governments, and sheltering in England at that time, were a party of Spaniards driven out by Ferdinand VII. Their leader, General Torrijos, like Garibaldi after him, resolved to free his country by direct assault, and in this enterprise Sterling and his Apostles, now down from the university and at large in London, energetically encouraged him. Lieutenant Robert Boyd, a cousin of Sterling's and a wild Ulsterman late of the Indian Army, acquired a ship and set about repairing and victualling it for the expedition. Meanwhile, Sterling was busy making speeches on behalf of the conspirators, and on 31 March 1830 he wrote to John Mill asking whether he could obtain credit from some business house, perhaps that of Joseph Hume the distinguished Radical, or possibly that of Grote and Prescott, to finance the new Government of Spain until it should become established. Sterling himself, together with several other Apostles, Trench, Kemble, Alfred Tennyson, and Hallam, was determined to bear a musket in company with the rebels, and Mill did nothing to restrain him.

Mercifully, at the last moment Sterling fell incurably in love with Susan Barton, sister of another Apostle, and after profound heart-searchings decided in favour of home and beauty. The plot miscarried, and the ship was impounded. Torrijos, Boyd and their little army of fifty devotees set out for Gilbraltar by another route, accompanied by Trench, and Kemble; from there, having taken leave of their faithful Apostles, who were dissuaded by consular officials from going any further, they launched the invasion which was to rouse their compatriots against the tyrant. But the cruel and vindictive government, fully informed of their every movement by the secret police, had been watching them like cat and mouse. They were rounded up, and summarily executed by fusillade against the city walls of Malaga. Sterling, who in the meantime had married and become a father, was settled on a sugar plantation at St. Vincent in the West Indies when the terrible news eventually reached him. He was bitterly distressed. "I hear the sound of that musketry", he told his brother Anthony; "it is as if the bullets were tearing my own brain."[93]

Mill's own opportunity for action came, appropriately, in Paris. In July 1830 the monarchy of Charles X collapsed under its own inanity. The incompetent autocrat packed his bags and returned to comfortable exile at Holyrood Palace. His rascally minister Polignac was locked up, and his kinsman Louis Philippe, the Citizen King, stood as his successor in the Palais Royal waiting to shake hands with any of his subjects who felt so inclined.

These events stirred John Mill to the depths, for this was Revolution, and the arrogance of royal presumption had been painlessly discarded in favour of responsible government. Gathering up Roebuck and Graham, he hastened to the scene. "Bliss was it in that dawn to be alive", he must have felt. They gripped the hand of aged Lafayette, once more the champion of the hour. They took tickets for the opera, and, as the Citizen King shuffled into the royal box, they rose to their feet and called exuberantly for the Marseillaise, until the whole house joined them; then they cried "Debout! debout!", forcing the patient monarch to stand up with the rest of the audience while the national anthem was being played. So great was their ardour that they stayed for several weeks investigating eagerly the methods and intentions of the new régime. They met the Saint-Simonian leaders, Enfantin and Bazard, who seemed to them to be all that they expected: but nowhere else did they find a trace of the selfless idealism that inspired themselves. On the contrary, the members of the government seemed callous or even cynical. One of them could think only of the shape of the new cockade for the uniform of the National Guard. Another was busy changing the names of the streets; and most of the others were working out comfortable positions for themselves.[94] "At present", John wrote disgustedly to his father, "if I were to look only at the cowardice and imbecility of the existing generation of public men, with scarcely a singly exception, I should expect very little good."[95]

Back in England shortly afterwards, the current of events appeared to be rushing headlong to a far more violent climax. While cholera raged in London, Captain Swing and his insurgents ravaged in the south, burning down ricks, breaking threshing machines, destroying workhouses and ceremonially deporting the overseers, beating up the Irish labourers who were content to come in and work for the pitiful wages which, by the side of their own indigence, seemed abundance. Troops were called out. The Duke of Wellington attributed the whole trouble to the mischievous example of the French, while Lord Eldon alleged that most of the rioters were foreigners. On the orders of the Privy Council, the Archbishops of Canterbury and York directed special prayers to be read for the restoration of order, and for Grace for the simple and ignorant who had been led astray. Everyone was arrested and tried: in an atmosphere of terror and anxiety, 101 capital sentences were passed, of which nine were carried out: 457 men and boys were deported without reasonable hope of return, and 400 others were imprisoned.[96]

The distance that separated John Mill from his father at this stage of his development was never better demonstrated than in their reactions to the calamity which now looked imminent. Distinct though their difference had been since John's breakdown of four years before, and enlarged though it had been by Macaulay's penetrating criticism, in the face of revolution it widened to another plane. Whatever may be said of James Mill's radicalism, the one thing which most securely linked him to his favourite associates, Bentham, Brougham, Ricardo, M'Culloch, Grote and the others, was his dislike of violence. Nobody carried cleaner or more stiffly starched linen than James Mill: no one was more punctilious in manner, or more formal in expression, even in moments of irritation. When the *Morning Chronicle*, at the height of the Reform excitement, reported the speech of Attwood the Birmingham socialist, no Tory was more horrified than he. "The nonsense to which your Lordship alludes", he wrote to Brougham, "about the rights of the labourer to the whole produce of the country, wages, profits, and rent, all included, is the mad nonsense of our friend Hodgkins. . . . These opinions, if they were to spread, would be the subversion of civilized society; worse than the overwhelming deluge of Huns and Tartars."[97] *

Indeed, the spiteful aphorism about James Mill, attributed by Bowring, probably quite untruthfully, to Bentham, was not far off the mark. "His creed of politics", it went, "results less from love of the many, than from hatred of the few."[98] He relied even more than most

* Hodgkins was sub-editor to Black, and slipped in socialist propaganda whenever he could without Black's knowledge.

philosophers upon the security afforded by organized society to protect him while he upset it. Accordingly, all his efforts were towards the Reform Bill as the alternative to revolution, and fortunately he was in good trim for the purpose. Never before had so many normally divergent lines of English opinion united so wholeheartedly behind any constitutional measure. James Mill, by reason of his long influence on the works of Bentham, as well as of his own steady service for the cause during the last twenty years, stood at the conflux of many tributaries and currents, contrary and unruly though they often were, as they flowed towards the great sea of democratic progress.

First there was his own loyal party of Philosophical Radicals, whether in Parliament already, or waiting election to it when it was reformed. To these were added the valuable young men seconded to his cause by the influence of his son, nearly all the members of the Utilitarian and London Debating Societies. From the heights of public office, his mercurial school-fellow Brougham, and Burdett, the liberal squire of Mayfair, looked to him for their party line. The critical borough of Westminster, after years of turmoil, was largely in his sway. If he were not in complete accord with Macaulay and the Whigs of the *Edinburgh Review* on the one hand, or with Cobbett, the ranting orator Hunt, and the Socialists on the other, all of them were prepared to forgo their differences until the attainment of the common cause. In the newly founded London University, for whose emancipation from religious discrimination he had so fondly struggled, he had an entire academy behind him, and with it an immeasurable weight of non-conformist support. In the Press, Black of the *Morning Chronicle*, Perronet Thompson of the *Westminster* and Fonblanque of the *Examiner* would print anything he asked them. While in the dark uncharted alleyways of London, Place the Tailor martialled his army of unnumbered cockneys to parade the slogan "GO FOR GOLD—AND STOP THE DUKE", so that the national credit was threatened by a prolonged and crippling run on the bank.

Compared with the part his father played in the passing of the Bill, John Mill's share was no more than dutiful. He assisted, but his heart was not in it. The Reform Bill had come to be regarded as a universal medicine for all ills. He agreed with the genial warning of Sydney Smith against expecting too much from its results:

"There will be mistakes at first, as there are in all changes. All young ladies will imagine (as soon as this Bill is carried) that they will be instantly married. Schoolboys believe that Gerunds and Supines will be abolished, and that Currant Tarts must ultimately come down in price; the Corporal and Sergeant are sure of double pay; bad Poets will expect a demand for their Epics; Fools will be disappointed, as they always are; reasonable men, who know what to expect, will find that a very serious good has been obtained."[99]

John Mill, however, doubted whether the good would be great enough. In his present mood he came close to rejecting the possibility of any great improvement by constitutional means. Things had gone so far, he felt, the old machinery of society was so outworn, that it was incapable of any effective patching. In fact, he was more in favour of Revolution than Reform. In October 1831 he wrote Sterling a long letter discussing the probable effects of further delay in the passage of the Bill.

"If the ministers flinch or the Peers remain obstinate, I am firmly convinced that in six months a national convention, chosen by universal suffrage, will be sitting in London. Should this happen, I have not made up my mind what will be best to do: I incline to think it would be best to lie by and let the tempest blow over, if one could but get a shilling a day to live upon meanwhile; for until the whole of the existing institutions of society are levelled with the ground, there will be nothing for a wise man to do which the most pig-headed fool cannot do much better than he . . . If there were but a few dozens of persons safe (whom you and I could select) to be missionaries of the great truths in which alone there is any well-being for mankind individually or collectively, I should not care though a revolution were to exterminate every person in Great Britain and Ireland who has £500 a year. Many very amiable persons would perish, but what is the world the better for such amiable persons?[100]

All of this is highly incendiary stuff. The public expression of such views would, in the present day, very likely have resulted in the loss of civil rights, if not in actual confinement. By the standards of his time they would have branded him a Jacobin, and the modern significance of that term is Communist. Nor is the comparison a glib one, for the Saint-Simonians professed all the essentials of the Marxist philosophy. The cyclic view of history; the theory of the unregenerate ruling classes, from which it was an easy step to the class struggle; the inevitable Revolution; communal ownership of the means of production; world conversion; the rosy promise of an ultimate Utopia; the acceptance of a temporary dictatorship during an interim without set limits; the confusion of determinism and idealism, of what was bound to happen with what ought to happen—it was all there, and John Mill embraced it all, with the exception of the property clauses: being logical, he would have had to accept those also in the end, had he persisted in his course. As for his veneration for the fathers of the Revolution, they could, *mutatis mutandis*, have equally well been Russian as French. At the age of twenty-five he was an uncompromising intellectual red.

Nor was it all the fault of the Saint-Simonians: the root of the trouble went back to his mental breakdown, to his decision to exploit his feelings at the expense of his intelligence, and exalt the spiritual above the mental faculty. He saw his father as his own reason incarnate, as indeed, in so far as reason is formed by education, to some extent he was. In recoiling from him, he rejected the means of human improvement in favour of its ends; and wherever the ends are allowed to dictate the means, there tyranny will flourish. His apparent authoritarianism was soon to mislead Carlyle about his real outlook. Happily, the aberration of his ideas was quite short-lived; very soon he was to come under the dominating influence of his life, an influence that was to pluck him out of his dangerous floundering in opinions quite unsuited to his nature, and to lead him surely in the course of his true development for which he had sought so long, and sought in vain.

X

Early in 1831, James Mill, now at the head of the India Office, and a figure of some opulence as well as of public influence, took leave of Jeremy Bentham and the Austins, his neighbours in Queen Square, Westminster, and removed his large family, complete at last at nine, to a capacious villa in Vicarage Place, Church Street, Kensington, where they remained until his death. The previous summer he had also bought a cottage at Mickleham, near Dorking, and there every year they spent the summer, and sometimes an autumn vacation. John continued to live at home, although had he so wished his resources would have allowed him to take a separate establishment. The education of the younger children was still very much a part of his daily duties. During the Long Vacation of 1831, his next eldest brother, James Bentham, then a boy of about sixteen, brought with him to Dorking one of his friends at University College, Henry Solly. Solly records a tribute to John's ability as a teacher, besides a pleasant account of his contribution to the happiness of the household:

"I remember one evening receiving from him my first notions of geology; for finding me densely ignorant on the subject, but eager for information, he fetched a number of books, laid them flat a-top of one another, and showed me that if the strata of the crust of the earth had always remained in that position, we should never have been acquainted with anything but the upper layer. Then by tilting them up at one end so that the edges of each layer came successively to the surface, he made me see how we got each in turn, as we travel in various directions. . . . He was evidently very fond of his mother and sisters, and they of him; and he frequently manifested a sunny brightness and gaiety of heart and behaviour which were singularly fascinating. His three elder sisters, also, were very nice, unaffected, pleasant girls, rather handsome, especially the youngest of the three, and talked on interesting subjects."[101]

When in the following year Solly's father compelled him to leave the university and enter the family counting house in Leadenhall Street, John Mill consoled him with a cordial invitation to visit him whenever he liked in the Examiner's Office just across the way. At one of these friendly meetings, Solly asked him how he found time for all his literary activities, and Mill replied, "'I get so much time for that work because I can get through my India work quickly', adding with his singularly pleasant smile, 'and that's why I can afford time to talk to you.'"[102] At this period he had more time at his disposal than was usual. His literary work was confined to his articles in the *Examiner*. It is true that he was engaged in working out his views on Political Economy in a series of essays intended to form a synthesis with others written by his friend G. J. Graham; and also that he was beginning to arrange his thoughts on Logic.*

* Mill's five essays were written in 1830 and 1831, but Graham never completed his share of the bargain. The fifth, called the "Definition of Political Economy," was published in the *London and Westminster Review* in October 1836, and they all appeared as a book entitled *Essays on Some Unsettled Questions of Political Economy* in 1844, when the success of the *Logic* had established a demand for his writings.

But in neither case was it more than a preliminary clearance of the ground, a mere spare-time occupation, in no way so strenuous as the editorial labours on Bentham's *Rationale of Evidence* or his father's *Analysis of the Human Mind*, which in previous years had made such heavy demands upon him. His societies had all wound up, his tutorial duties were very much reduced, and for the first time in his life he had an opportunity to set out into the world of fashion and of literary drawing-rooms as an elegant, educated man about town.

Most of the entertaining for his immediate coterie was done by Sarah Austin and by the indefatigable Mrs. Grote in Threadneedle Street, or "Threddle" as she kittenishly called it. To their tea parties and soirées he stepped round as a matter of course. A little later on, the more glittering chandeliers of Mrs. Charles Buller, whose household joined the circle in Queen Square after the Mills had left it, revealed to him the world of wit and quality, of blue-blooded familiarities and of fashionable escapades, the world of the Villiers brothers, of Strutt, Greville, and Henry Taylor, of Richard Monckton Milnes, and Charles Buller, two more of Sterling's former Apostles. These were the days when literary lionizing was the vogue, and although nearly every author wrote with scorn and loathing of such functions, most of them attended scrupulously, and secretly probably enjoyed themselves. Mill was always welcome; for if to modern ears his contemporary writings, such articles as the "Currency Juggle", or "Corporation and Church Property", have a dry and forbidding sound, he was none the less an author in times when novels were considered idle rubbish by the intelligentsia, and important authorship was generally confined to sober, serious work.

Breakfast was the favourite time for gentlemen to meet and talk. To be summoned to the breakfast table of Samuel Rogers, and to listen to his wit and repartee, was a cherished honour; while the famous "Conversation Sharp", who lived not far from the Mill's summer cottage down at Mickleham, used to invite the father and son to similar repasts. It was customary for these meals to occupy the greater part of the day, not infrequently from ten o'clock till three: the mode of conversation was by monologue rather than by quick exchange, so that when two famous talkers were together, as on one occasion were Samuel Rogers and Sydney Smith, the party was usually a failure, as each one pinioned the soaring fancies of the other. To be able to go on and on without losing the attention of the company was considered the height of excellence. Smith, Macaulay, and later on

Carlyle, by common consent the finest talkers of the period, were all capable of continuing throughout these sessions without an interruption from start to finish.* John Mill was not held to be over-successful at this art, owing to his habit of hesitating in his speech to master his ideas, so that he gave "the appearance of being always working in his mind a proposition or a syllogism".[103] None the less, he was a popular guest, and Henry Taylor records his presence once or twice a week for breakfast at his house, where he met, besides other notables, the Poet Laureate, Southey, and his cherished Wordsworth.[104] In 1830 he was elected to the exclusive Athenaeum, of which his father was a founder member, just then moving into its new clubrooms.[105] With Taylor he went to call on Coleridge at Highgate.[106] And of an evening he would sometimes dine with Fonblanque.[107]

To complete the life of comparative leisure and easy social intercourse which he was living at this period, John Mill used to spend some part of his summer vacation from the India House touring England on foot with one or two companions, usually colleagues from the office. These excursions, which he kept up fairly regularly all through life, he recorded in diaries and notebooks. In July 1831, finding himself in the heart of Wordsworth's lake scenery, he made several pilgrimages to Grasmere and renewed with the poet he so much admired the acquaintance recently begun in London.[108] The following summer he toured the South of England and the New Forest with Henry Cole, and in September of that year explored the neighbourhood of Penzance, walking, botanizing and seeing the sights.† In his journal, he was by this time writing for another pair of eyes to read, and his painful struggle towards the poetic vein is a change from the incisive measure of his published prose, and carries a childish and untutored feeling:

> "Sunny seas are fine things, for the ocean is beautiful as well as sublime: but there is nothing really awe-striking but a gloomy sea. In a showery and gusty day when clouds dark as night conceal the greater part of the sea and you do not clearly distinguish how much is ocean and

* Sydney Smith, when asked what he thought of Macaulay's performance on one of these occasions, replied, "Unusually brilliant, some splendid flashes of silence". Mill said they always reminded him of a group of Frenchmen he had seen, one of them talking on and on, and the second so eager to butt in that an onlooker remarked excitedly, "If he spits, he's done." (Bain, *J. S. Mill*, p. 189.)

† Later Sir Henry Cole of Great Exhibition fame. First met Mill in the Debating Society 1826.

how much is cloud; when the sea is covered with dark streaks any one of which seems the horizon till you perceive another behind it; then you know the grandeur of the sea. It then seems to be indeed the boundary of the earth, boundless itself, for you do not as in a clear day see the apparent verge of it, but look forth into the darkness till you can see no further, and know not what frightful or what perilous thing that darkness may conceal from you. Vagueness is of the essence of the sublime: it is therefore that darkness is sublime, light only beautiful: and hence among other reasons it is that painting so rarely attains the sublime, since it can only act in light, and through light."[109]

Yet, in spite of his many distractions, John Mill was at this time the victim of a gnawing loneliness. Roebuck could not share his admiration for Wordsworth: Graham had only just returned from a five-year spell in India: Eyton Tooke, believing that a love affair with Henry Solly's sister was going wrong when in fact it was going right, had killed himself: Sterling, now a married man, was in the West Indies. There were no other intimates. On 15 April 1829 Mill had written to Sterling:

"I am now chiefly anxious to explain to you, more clearly than I fear I did, what I meant when I spoke to you of the comparative loneliness of my probable future lot. Do not suppose me to mean that I am conscious at present of any tendency to misanthropy—although among the very various states of mind, some of them extremely painful ones, through which I have passed during the last three years, something distantly approximating to misanthropy was one. At present I believe that my sympathies with society, which were never strong, are, on the whole, stronger than they ever were. By loneliness I mean the absence of that feeling which has accompanied me through the greater part of my life, that which one fellow-traveller, or one fellow-soldier has towards another—the feeling of being engaged in the pursuit of a common object, and of mutually cheering one another on, and helping one another in an arduous undertaking. This, which after all is one of the strongest ties of individual sympathy, is at present, so far as I am concerned, suspended at least, if not entirely broken off. There is now no human being (with whom I can associate on terms of equality) who acknowledges a common object with me, or with whom I can cooperate even in any practical undertaking, without feeling that I am only using a man, whose purposes are different, as an instrument for the furtherance of my own."[110]

Now, when a man in his early twenties, in all respects well-favoured, expresses sentiments in this vein, it can only mean that he is marriageable. John Mill was no bad match. The eldest son of a most respected family, his resources were ample and his prospects good (in 1830, his father's promotion to the top of the Examiner's office made him fifth, with an increase to his salary, which was already £600 a year): in addition, he was a minor star in the literary firmament, and attractive enough in person. "His manners", said Henry Taylor,[111] "were plain, neither graceful nor awkward; his features refined and regular; the eyes small relatively to the scale of the face, the jaw large, the nose straight and finely shaped, the lips thin and compressed, the forehead and head capacious; and both face and body seemed to represent outwardly the inflexibility of the inner man. He shook hands with you from the shoulder. Though for the most part painfully grave, he was as sensible as anybody to Charles Austin's or Charles Villier's sallies of wit, and his strong and well-knit body would heave for a few moments with half-uttered laughter." From his observations of his mother and sisters, coupled with the fruits of his own studies, he had already formed an uneasy feeling that the lot of women in society was not all that it should be—a valuable weakness in a man seeking a life companion.

His search for a wife was a knightly quest for an ideal. It was in his nature to mistake good for excellence, loyalty for nobleness, and enthusiasm for ability; but his basic standards were extremely high. Although from chivalry he might incline to tinted spectacles, he would never take to blinkers. No sultry Guinevere for him, nor Petrach's legendary Laura, nor Don Quixote's homely maid. The woman who won him must be a "higher nature", by which he meant "those characters who from the combination of natural and acquired advantages have the greatest capacity of feeling happiness and of bestowing it. Of bestowing it in two ways: as being beautiful to contemplate, and therefore the natural objects of admiration and love; and also as being fitted . . . by their qualities of mind and heart, to promote . . . the greatest possible happiness of all who are within the sphere of their influence."[112] It was not an easy standard to come up to.

In 1829, Fanny Kemble, sister of the Apostle, playing her first lead as Juliet, had nearly brought down Covent Garden. She was the rage of the town. Along with Maurice and Sterling and the other impressionable young men all more or less in love with her, John Mill had paid a visit, but left without more than thanking her courteously for a pleasant evening. About this time, too, it is said he thought of Eliza Flower, an elfin creature, musical and poetic. And in October 1830, while staying with his father at Buckenham Castle in

Norfolk, the seat of Alexander Baring,[113] he met the brilliant society hostess Lady Harriet Baring.* Of their encounter Greville says, "Two men were certainly in love with her, both distinguished in different ways. One was John Mill, who was sentimentally attached to her, and for a long time was devoted to her society. She was pleased and flattered by his devotion, but as she did not in the slightest degree return his passion, though she admired his abilities, he at last came to resent her indifference; and ended by estranging himself from her entirely, and proved the strength of his feeling by his obstinate refusal to continue even his acquaintance with her."[114] The truth is, that a month or two earlier another meeting had taken place at which the die was cast, and although Mill took some time to realize it, probably at first denied it wilfully, his soul was given over to a being from whose presence Lady Harriet Baring could only gracefully withdraw.

It was some time during that summer of 1830, just before their trip to Paris,† that John with his usual companions Graham and Roebuck was invited to a quiet dinner party at the house of Mr. John Taylor, a prosperous merchant in the City. What took place that evening, of what they conversed or how they looked and bore themselves; what sudden glance of private understanding kindled, in those polite circumstances, the spark of emotion which was to grow to such a furnace, still remains obscure. However it came about, the whole course of Mill's life and work was altered on the instant: "a passion sprang out of the bushes like a hundred Ashantees, and he was carried away captive".[115]

In many ways, the attachment was not unsuitable. The young lady, his own age but for a year or two, to look at was quite lovely. She was so slender that although only just above five feet, she gave the impression of a tall and willowy grace.‡ Her brown hair, high pale forehead and almond-rounded face were but a setting for a pair of

* Although the tradition is that Charles Buller introduced Mill to Lady Harriet Baring, and Charles Buller did not himself meet her until 1837, it is hard to believe that Mill can have behaved in the manner described by Greville so long after the events of the summer of 1830.

† Probably before, because Harriet Martineau, who was at the dinner party, appears to have left London some time during July. See *Harriet Martineau*, by Theodora Bosanquet, 1927. Mill was in Paris for most of August, and by the end of that month Harriet Taylor was staying in the country with her husband.

‡ In her passport issued in 1838, her description is 5 feet 1 inch tall, aged thirty, brown hair, high forehead, brown eyebrows, brown eyes, medium nose, and round chin. (MT Coll. Box III/68.)

enormous, deep-set eyes, whose dark depths blazed with feeling. She was vivacious as well as grave, serene as well as gay. She had more than an element of poetic fire, and at the same time a depth of philosophic calm. She was capable of a consuming violence either of love or of indignation, and her pride was majestic. A description of her at about this time says: "She was possessed of a beauty and grace quite unique of their kind. Tall and slight, with a slightly drooping figure, and movements of undulating grace. A small head, a swan-like throat, and a complexion like a pearl. Large dark eyes, not soft or sleepy, but with a look of quiet command in them. A low sweet voice with very distinct utterance emphasized the effect and enhanced the charm of her engrossing personality."[116] Thomas Carlyle, whose vivid personal sketches were always revealing, described her as he first saw her a few years later, and before he grew to hate her: "She is a living romance heroine, of the clearest insight, of the royalest volition, very interesting, of questionable destiny, not above five-and-twenty."[117]

Indeed, had her world been a stage, one would have felt even at this her first appearance that she was set apart from other players in all the garb and panoply of tragedy. There was, therefore, every reason in the world why the ardent Mill should carry off her gage. But there was also a contrary reason, a complicating circumstance that rendered it calamitous. It happened that the lady was his hostess: opposite her at table sat her solid, jovial husband; and upstairs, above the candle-light and the clinking glasses, her two children slumbered.

Picture Post Library

JEREMY BENTHAM

from an engraving by J. Posselwhite after the portrait by J. Watts.

BOOK TWO

FRIENDS OF THE SPECIES

1830–1834
aet. 24–28

Picture Post Library

JAMES MILL

I

HARRIET HARDY was born on the eighth of October 1807 at 8 Beckford Row, Walworth. Her mother, born Harriet Hurst, came from Cavalier stock, who at the time of the Civil War were prominent in the Royalist cause. Among other trophies, her descendants of the present day possess a portrait of King Charles I as a martyr with a crown of thorns, reputedly presented to their ancestor Sir Nicholas Crispe by Prince Rupert; a portrait which was given to Harriet herself by her mother, and for many years was proudly owned by her, hanging for some time in her daughter's bedroom. Her father, Thomas Hardy, was of a mellow lineage. According to a family tradition, the Hardys were descended from Clement Le Hardy who was Lieutenant Governor of the island of Jersey in 1488: if that is so, Harriet was connected, though very distantly, with Thomas Hardy the novelist and poet. In 1732 the Rev. John Hardy, curate of the village of Kirkburton, not far from Huddersfield in Yorkshire, bought the Tudor manor house of Birksgate in a wooded dale overlooking a small torrent at nearby Thunder Bridge. To this estate was later added the lands and manor of Shepley, and the whole passed to Harriet's father on the death of his uncle in 1836. He retired to live there, and until his death in 1849 he was an active magistrate; but when Harriet was born he was practising in his wife's purlieus of Walworth at the outset of his career as "surgeon and man-midwife", or in other words an early obstetrician. He had been for five years a member of the Royal College of Surgeons.[1]

Harriet was the middle child of seven, of whom five were boys.

Of her brothers, the eldest, who went into practice with his father, died of consumption while still in his twenties. Another went to live in Naples, and two others emigrated to Australia. The elder of these two, Alfred, became one of the first Crown Prosecutors for South Australia, and built what is still one of the largest houses in Adelaide, calling it after the family seat. The second, Arthur, is commemorated as the builder of the first two bridges over the river Torrens in Adelaide. The remaining brother, Edward, inherited the Yorkshire estate, but seems to have ruined himself by a calamitous marriage; first he let Birksgate and retired to Shepley; then a little later he had to sell off land; and finally Birksgate itself was sold by his successor in 1870.

Harriet's relations, then, were in various ways distinguished. As a family, they were well-born and intellectually active; they were also wilful, proud, and headstrong. Her father, according to her later correspondence where he is usually referred to as "the Governor", was a stern and stingy man. Caroline, her younger sister, lived at home with their mother, and there developed between the three women an emotional triangle which on occasion drove Harriet to the edge of exasperation. Matters were not improved by Caroline's marriage to Arthur Ley, a dissolute lawyer who knocked her about when she attempted to restrain his drinking, and was always suspected by Harriet of tangling up to his own advantage any family business that came his way. Only for Arthur, the youngest of the family, did she retain any lasting affection, and afterwards she wrote to him in a flurry of disgust "you are pretty nearly if not quite the only respectable relative I possess".[2]

Except for these rather unhappy developments, there is no information whatever about Harriet's early life. The next that is known is that she was married on 14 March 1826, when she was eighteen and a half, by the rector of Walworth, to John Taylor of Islington.[3] John Taylor was a prosperous fellow, a junior partner with his Uncle David in a long-established family firm of wholesale druggists, with premises in Mark Lane in the City.

How the marriage came about is not known: Islington and Walworth were both at that time salubrious country parishes, the one as far out of London to the north as was the other to the south, so there was no neighbourly contact in the matter. Both families were Unitarian, but the chapels attended by the Taylors at Hackney and later at South Place, Finsbury, were barely accessible to the Hardys at Walworth, and it is improbable that they could have encountered one another there. A surgeon, of course, would have constant recourse to druggists, and conceivably, if he were thrifty, to a wholesale druggist, so there may have been some professional contact. It is hinted that Harriet's father arranged the match as a way out of money troubles, though what he stood to gain from it is far from clear, as it would have been the bride's father who was expected to produce the jointure: nor is there the least evidence to suppose that he was in financial difficulties at that time. At all events, Harriet could not have arranged a marriage for herself. Being a minor, her father had to be present at the ceremony and give his formal and express consent. And as both parties were Dissenters, they had at that time no right at all to legal matrimony, and could be married in church only at the option of the rector, a concession requiring elaborate negotiations by both sets of parents. Probably, therefore, she simply followed her father's wishes; she had no reason to dread exchanging the bickering of her own home for the comfort and fond indulgence of John Taylor's.

After they were married they lived at 4 Christopher Street, Finsbury, where eighteen months later a son was born to Harriet, whom they called Herbert. A letter she wrote to her husband on 7 July 1828 from Ryde, Isle of Wight, where she was on holiday with the infant, is filled with the misty trivialities of maternal bliss, and with the sweet pangs of temporary separation:[4]

"My dearest John,

Though I knew that I must not send you another letter for some days, as I only wrote yesterday, yet I cannot bear to defer the pleasure of writing, even tho' you should not see it at present. I received your letter my dearest by Edward last night—every letter you send me the mere sight of your writing, gives me great pleasure but the happiness the delight I have received from this can scarcely be imagined—every question I asked you, all that I have said is answered in the very words I would have chosen. . . . I put it under my pillow that I might read it to our dear little one as soon as he awoke this morning. . . . Oh my dear John each hour that passes brings us nearer the day when we shall meet and I think from my present feelings that I shall never again consent to our parting. . . . I went this morning with the dogs a walk of 4 miles before breakfast as the weather is now too warm for afterwards. . . . I need not repeat the joy I shall feel when I perceive you on the boat for I know you will feel the same. Our little one is rather poorly again, but looks well and will soon be so as his tiresome tooth does appear to be coming through at last.—Adieu dearest till the happy moment comes—Adieu—

Harriet Taylor"

She was clearly very much in love. And indeed from every account of him, even in the trying conditions that ensued, John Taylor appears as a most amiable man. He was not, it is true, well-favoured personally, if his miniature is to be believed, being rather on the stocky side, with high cheek bones and a heavy jaw, and a forehead exceptionally squat. But if he was ugly, he was also completely honourable, genial and kindly. He adored Harriet, and spoiled her greatly, but did not fail in gentle firmness when she stepped too far across his fundamental judgements. He was eleven years older than she, but as he was not yet thirty when they married, can scarcely be said to have been too old for her. He was not unintelligent; in politics he was soundly liberal, and lived up to his beliefs. His hospitable doors were always open to the numerous patriots of all nations who were taking asylum in London from tyranny. He was a good host, and his principal fault was the agreeable one of a liking for good meals, in friendly company, and a bumper, or perhaps two, of wine. He would never have interfered with Harriet's activities, never would have forced her privacy: he would have given her gladly all she wanted, and so long as she was living happily under his roof he would have been content, for contentment was the mood most natural to him. Things, in fact, might have gone on quietly enough until the staid and durable affections of long association came to consolidate the marriage tie. Might have done, had not cross currents and counter influences already been at work.

II

The Taylors' house in Christopher Street was chosen for its handiness both to the place of business and to the South Place Unitarian Chapel, where John Taylor was a prominent member of the congregational council. In July 1827 he attended the dinner held in the London Tavern to celebrate the second anniversary of the founding of the British and Foreign Unitarian Association, making the main speech of the evening. Early the next year, when the minister fell ill, Taylor was much distressed, and took some pains to find a competent replacement for as long as might be necessary. The Chapel being therefore one of his keenest interests, it was not long before his young wife, also of non-conformist stock, made an appearance in that milieu; a milieu which was to have a deep effect upon her.

The various sects dissenting from the established Church of England were a social rather than a religious problem. Although, being sects, they hated one another cordially, there was a marked similarity about their composition. Reliance upon the inner light rather than upon the comfortable irresponsibility of dogma implies great sternness and an inexorable will; and a man so equipped is likely to achieve prosperity, for the better he does, the plainer it becomes to all the world that he is in favour with the Eternal Taskmaster. Thus it came about, if not that all Dissenters were rich business men, at least that a large number of rich business men happened to be Dissenters. And the Wesleyan mission to the working people notwithstanding, dissent continued generally to draw its influence from the commerical classes.

That they could be stubborn, ruthless and uncompromising; that their religious determinism was capable of a subversive political corollary, the Stuart kings had been made violently aware, and since the Restoration non-conformists had been officially discouraged by serious civil disabilities. But the restrictions tended to strengthen rather than to thin their ranks. Indeed, they even welcomed persecution, for it was one of their chief notions that virtue must overcome adversity; and as they needed a cross to bear in any case, it was considerate of the government to provide them with one so reasonably light.

They lived quietly for the most part in little warrens drawn all the closer by their outlawry, like that of the Quaker Foxes down at Falmouth or of Sarah Austin's family at Norwich. Pecuniarily speaking they possessed the township, and nobody who was not one of them could long be comfortable in the neighbourhood. They worked and worked, and praised the Lord; they washed their linen in private and in public did good deeds. If they sang, it was always hymns or other responsible songs: if they drank, it was from a closely watched decanter: and if they kissed with passion, the family sentence was always marriage. On Sundays, they did nothing at all but go to meeting house, where, to relieve the monotony of the day, they paid a great deal of attention to the preacher, demanding from him not words of calm morality or advice on scriptural topics, but an inspired peroration, a violent onslaught which would subdue and ravish their emotions, and provide a purge for the funds of sensibility stored up in them during the preceding week. A sermon such as they would get, for instance, from the redoubtable Rev. Joseph Irons, pastor of the chapel at Camberwell Grove, where Robert Browning used to go as a boy every week to be "ironed" as the family idiom had it. On one occasion, out of curiosity to see how far the ringing tones would reach, Browning approached the building from outside while the sermon was in progress, and from half-way down the street distinctly heard the well-known voice pronouncing, "I'm very sorry to say it, beloved brethren, but it is an undoubted fact that Roman Catholic and midnight assassin are synonymous terms".[5]

In contrast to the other principal sects, the Unitarians were almost entirely free from bigotry. They drew their membership to a large extent from the scientific professions. In consequence, they dwelt on a more highly intellectual level than the rest, and their outlook was very rational, individualistic, and unregimented. Intending to unite all brands of non-conformists, at first they had succeeded merely in producing a doctrine so attenuated that it was scarcely a religious system at all. In the eighteenth century they had taken for their guiding light Joseph Priestley, a chemist of permanent importance, and also the originator of the soda-water industry. A keen believer in the perfectibility of man, and the first proponent of the Greatest Happiness principle, he had added to their creed the humanistic tang which rendered it significant.

At the time of Harriet's marriage, the most prominent of the Unitarians was William Johnson Fox. Although not striking in appearance—he was a tubby little man of forty with a moon-like face, black hair, and piercing eyes—Fox had an almost miraculous gift for preaching, a soft melodious voice irresistibly compelling. To the level-headed Unitarian elders, who demanded good sense purveyed by powerful oratory, he seemed exactly suitable. They did not wish to rouse unseemly ecstasy in their congregation. They wanted a rapt attention, here and there an eye discreetly piped, and above all something that would fetch a brisk clatter in the collection plate. His success was so resounding that they had soon moved him from the Gravel Pit at Hackney to the new South Place Chapel they had built especially for him in Finsbury, where many of them lived.

Great preacher though he was, Fox's interests were more temporal than divine. Being aware that the written word penetrated far more widely than the spoken among the literate classes to whom the Unitarian faith appealed, he sought to extend his flock more as a journalist than as a priest. For some years he contributed faithfully to the existing Unitarian organ, the *Monthly Repository*. Then, as it was dowdy and parochial in flavour, he resolved to buy it, to introduce articles of more general interest by well-known writers, and so bring the Unitarian gospel into the homes of all well-read, broad-minded families. Soon after he reached Finsbury he began to cast about for possible contributors; and long before the *Monthly Repository* finally came into his hands in 1831, he had built up a small but very intimate circle of his personal devotees. Into this circle Harriet was introduced on her marriage in 1826, and she lived and moved among its members almost exclusively until she met Mill four years later.*

The most dependable of them from the literary point of view was Harriet Martineau, sister of James, the future Unitarian leader. Belonging to Fox's native city of Norwich, and to the same staunch Taylor-Martineau clan as Sarah Austin, she had much in common with Fox besides religious views. Like him she was a careerist. Totally deprived of hearing at the age of twelve; reduced to penury, and robbed, by an uncommon run of ill-fortune, of father, lover, and a brother all before she was twenty-four, she had nothing to live by but the facility of her pen. Setting out to be a writer, she started a new race of women, for she became the first female journalist writing frankly for her living under her own name. She had written for the *Repository* since 1821 when she was nineteen, and her first essays had been accepted. Although she did not settle finally in London until 1832, when her line of stories illustrating Political Economy was successfully established, undoubtedly she had been in South Place scores of times before that date. She was a violent feminist of the severer type: no fancy fripperies or free-love for her, only the stern course of duty. She was bitterly disliked by her own sex, amongst whom her frank treatment of the population problem produced a good deal of smutty comment.

To set beside her regular and useful industry, there were the virginal charm and enthusiasm of the Flower girls, whose part in furthering Fox's plans came to be all that he could wish. The

* For an admirable history of the *Monthly Repository*, see *The Dissidence of Dissent*, by F. E. Mineka, Chapel Hill, 1944.

daughters of his greatest friend, a fellow Unitarian, they were described by a close acquaintance as "two of the most beautiful women of their day"[6]: in addition, they were singularly gifted. They both contributed energetically to the *Monthly Repository*; Sarah by poems and articles identified by her pen name SY (Sallie); and Eliza, or Lizzie as she was known, who was a composer, by little tunes appropriate to the time of the year, which appeared as musical scores headed "Songs of the Months". Between them they produced most of the hymns used at the South Place Chapel, and sang them side by side in the choir.

Sarah was a tall, noble looking creature with a rich contralto voice. She married a fellow writer for the *Repository*, but never abandoned her daring ambition to go on the stage. She finally secured a part in a West End Theatre, earning good reviews in the *Spectator* and other critical periodicals, until the long-pursuing doom of consumption overtook her. Before her death she completed a full-length dramatic poem entitled "Vivia Perpetua", dealing with the sufferings of early Christian martyrs; and she finally achieved immortality by writing the hymn "Nearer, my God, to Thee".

A more tumultuous fate was held in store for her sister Lizzie. She too had the characteristic symptoms of consumption, the transparent complexion, the unnatural bloom and burning eyes; but in her case the psychological tendencies were more pronounced, and of the two she was the more like the traditional artistic victim. She was frail, and slim, highly imaginative, and excitable. To her intimates she sent continual letters, or rather fragments, which it is doubtful if they ever read: for not only did she, in the fashion of the time, turn the page sideways and write across her lines, but the whole was dashed off in a wide and frantic hand. Even if they could read what she had written, they would not have been much the wiser; for the intensity of her feelings and the flight of her fancy soared into expression quite regardless of her subject. Possessed by a fiercely emotional moral ardour, if she was not herself a female Shelley, she was certainly the dream of maidenhood he sought, an unbridled fairy creature of delight.

A valuable result of their work for the *Repository* was that a number of other members of Fox's congregation, friends of the young ladies like Margaret Gillies the miniature painter and Mary Gillies the novelist, became familiars. Chief in importance was young Robert Browning. His family had often gone from Camberwell to attend chapel at the Gravel Pit in Hackney, and from his early years he had been well acquainted both with the Foxes and the Flowers. Being of a precocious genius, he fell in love with Lizzie, and had proffered shyly to her, she being twenty-two at the time and he twelve, a little book of poems called "Incondita". Lizzie read them through, and made a copy of them which she showed to Fox, who praised the poems and so greatly encouraged the young author that Browning came to regard him as his literary father. Although Browning burnt Lizzie's copy of "Incondita" along with all the love letters and verses he had written for her when they were returned to him at her death, for her lifetime his devotion to her remained active. In 1833 she appeared as his ill-starred "Pauline", warmly heralded by Fox in the *Monthly Repository*; and a year later she was probably the muse of a rather maudlin sonnet which was printed for the first time in its columns, followed by "Johannes Agricola" and "Porphyria's Lover". Later still he desired her to set to music the lyrics of "Pippa Passes", but she declined.

Harriet Taylor rapidly grew intimate with Eliza, and, like all the personal encounters of that young woman, their friendship flowered exotically large. Soon they were corresponding copiously by letter and by note, in addition to meeting several times a week. In 1829 Benjamin Flower, the father, died leaving his orphaned daughters, aged by that time twenty-six and twenty-four, in the care of his trusted friend. The first effect of Fox's guardianship of these two rather larger than lifesize sisters was that, before long, Fox and Lizzie were in love. Though nothing came of it in the way of open cognizance till three years later, it is safe to assume that by the summer of 1830 the parsonage was humming with all the paraphernalia of love-notes and renunciations, heart-breaking sighs and meaning glances, passionate hopes, resigned despairs, quarrels and reconciliations, while in the shadows the drab figure of Mrs. Fox, a joyless wife of ten years' standing, shocked and uncertain what to do, pathetically shooed her three children along before her.

In her tribulation Lizzie turned to Harriet, whom she not only counted well up to her exacting standard in sensibility, but looked towards, although four years the younger of the two, as to a figure of command, a sure and sound adviser and a rock of strength:

"But as for my being so well off as not to want you, as never to have wanted you (for so your words translate) you know better than that—

you know how it was with me when I found you and how your smile fell like a ray over a troubled sky—pshaw to write this down but you know how I cling to you. . . ." *

Harriet responded with becoming zest, and the tone of Lizzie's letters grew powerfully charged:

". . . if it were not for fear of accidents and making Mr. Taylor jealous, I could say how 'I would I were a man' to have laid my heart at your feet while you were talking yesterday."[7]

In comparison with this exciting influence, it is not surprising that Harriet Taylor's home life, and the company of her phlegmatic husband, began to seem prosaic and dull. At the same time that Eliza was arousing her emotions, Fox was widening her mind. Her standard of education at her marriage was already high, and he eagerly absorbed her into the private staff he schooled with care as individuals and indoctrinated as a group. She found herself in an atmosphere busily intellectual and strongly feminist, through which Miss Martineau flitted imperiously with her ear-trumpet, making it a duty for a woman both to know and do a lot. Harriet Taylor had ample time to spare; she had a nurse for her baby and her husband's purse would reach to any number of domestics. So, as was intended and expected of her, she began to write.

Although nothing of hers actually reached cold print in the *Repository* before 1831, her personal papers are full of drafts and fragments of articles, reviews, moral stories with the Martineau touch, and snatches of poetry, and from the watermarks it is evident that some of them were written a year or more earlier. Her ode, "Written at Daybreak", for example, is watermarked 1827, and the final version is dated 1828 in her own hand. The most significant of these early papers is one on marriage: it makes up in spirit what it lacks in style, and it reflects the way her mind was turning. Fox, like Milton, became as a result of his own marital difficulties an outspoken champion of divorce, and wrote trenchant articles about it in his review, as did also "Junius Redivivus", who had had an unhappy marriage with a daughter of Francis Place. Quite possibly it was Harriet's task to ghost for them.

* MT Coll. 27/23. Although what remains of their correspondence is mostly a collection of Eliza's outbursts in the years 1831 and 1832 when they were flung together with especial violence by the coincident crises of their love affairs, it is certain that they knew each other long before, and there is no reason to suppose that the tone of their friendship altered very much.

At all events, she wrote uncompromisingly:

"No institution that could possibly be devised seems to me so entirely tending to encourage and create mere sensualism as that of marriage. In the first place it makes some mere animal inclination respectable and recognized in itself. . . . Marriage is the only contract ever heard of, of which a necessary condition in the contracting parties was, that one should be entirely ignorant of the nature and terms of the contract. For owing to the voting of chastity as the greatest virtue of women, the fact that a woman knew what she undertook would be considered just reason for preventing her undertaking it."[8]

A little later, she developed this theme in the draft of a letter*:

"Women are educated for one single object, to gain their living by marrying (some poor souls get it without church going in the same way —they do not seem to me a bit worse than their honoured sisters)—to be married is the object of their existence and that being gained they do really cease to exist as to anything worth calling life or any useful purpose. One observes very few marriages where there is real sympathy or enjoyment of companionship between the parties—The woman knows what her power is, and gains by it what she has been taught to consider 'proper' to her state.

. . . I have no doubt that when the whole community is really educated, though the present laws of marriage were to continue they would be perfectly disregarded, because no one would marry—The wisest and perhaps the quickest means to do away with its evils is to be found in promoting education—as it is the means of all good—but meanwhile it is hard that those who suffer most from its evils and who are always the best people, should be left without remedy: would not the best plan be divorce which could be attained by *any, without any reason assigned*, and at small expense, but which could only be pronounced after a long period?

. . . Whoever would take the benefit of a law of divorce must be those whose inclination is to separate, and who on earth would wish another to remain with them against their inclination? I should think no one . . ."[9]

Again, in a paper headed "Education of Women" of about the same date, there occurred this pithy comment:

"All that has yet been said respecting the social condition of women goes on the assumption of their inferiority. People do not complain of their state being degraded at all—they complain only that it is *too much* degraded."[10]

These sentiments, the thin raw melody for Mill's *Subjection of Women* published nearly forty years later, were in sharp contrast to the loving and submissive letter of the young wife written a few

* Probably to Mill.

years earlier. Exactly when the change began to happen is not clear, but it may have been in 1829. In July that year she was again on holiday, this time in a boarding-house in Ramsgate, where her husband addressed to her a letter full of anxious solicitude:

> "Papa told me that sea bathing will suit you on a warm day if you feel quite disposed for it and if you only just *dip* and out again; you must on no account remain in longer than just time enough to get *one dip*, and if you feel the *least cold* or shivering afterwards you must not repeat the bath.—Attend to all this and you have your husband's full permission to bathe.—Excuse this *Lordly* way of putting the affair, but *you know* it is his love and affection for his sweet girl that alone make him appear dictatorial."[11]

There was some excuse for this fond and admirable advice. He had consulted Harriet's father, the obstetrician, because he had just been made aware that she was now carrying his second child. But Harriet turned the page, and scribbled on the back in pencil:

"MERMAID'S SONG

In chrystal caves of Ocean's deep
I make my pearly home
The rocking surges soothe my sleep
With wild and plaintive moan.

Sometimes I roam where glist'ning sands
Reflect bright Hesper's ray
Or bend to distant sunny lands
My happy cheerful way."

Her thoughts, it seems, were wandering in the upper air, an air populated by ethereal spirits like Eliza Flower, too rarefied for the weightier John Taylor, to whom and to whose counsel she was no longer altogether attentive. Whether it was her mental and emotional awakening at the hands of her new friends that changed her mind, or whether some unfortunate clumsiness by John Taylor offended her, or whether it was both, we cannot tell. But it must be noted in passing that after the birth of the second son Algernon, or Haji as he was always known, she bore him a third child, a daughter, Helen, in July 1831, about a year after she met Mill; and that her most violent strictures against the institution of marriage seem to have been written at that time.

Some time in the spring or summer of 1830, as soon as she recovered from the birth of Haji, she went to Fox; and, according to Carlyle, who had it from Harriet Martineau, who knew the details, told him that she was worried by a number of philosophical problems, and had no one to discuss them frankly with: that her husband, while being all that was kind and good to her, was lacking in the intellectual and artistic tastes which would have made him a companion for her; in short, that she was bored by him.

At this, Fox made a curious decision. Instead of administering pastoral advice, instead of proffering spiritual cheer, he determined that Harriet should meet John Mill.

That Mill was an advanced Radical, rightly suspected of free-thinking tendencies, was not the most surprising feature of Fox's choice. During the first quarter of the century, the breach between the Dissenters and the Radicals had narrowed sharply as the former became more political in their interests and the latter more earnest and evangelical. On the common ground of education they had reached outright alliance during the Lancaster school controversy, an alliance signed and sealed with the opening of the undenominational University College in Gower Street in October 1828. James Mill was prominent on the council, and his son James Bentham Mill mixed indiscriminately with the other students of non-conformist or radical background. John Mill was a member of John Austin's brilliant post-graduate class in Jurisprudence.

More particularly, the Unitarians were becoming closely linked with the Utilitarians. In Joseph Priestley they had had a common origin. Both were essentially middle class in composition. Both were rationalistic, scientific, and, in so far as that permitted them to be, humane and full of optimism for the future of the race. Several of the regular *Westminster* reviewers, Henry Southern, Edwin Chadwick, and Dr. Southwood Smith, were also Unitarians; while the vulturine Bowring outdid even Sarah Flower as an inveterate hymn-writer, with his "Watchman, what of the night?", and a score of others. In an intellectual sense, the Unitarians might be described as Utilitarians in their Sunday best.

Yet the growing rapprochement was no sufficient reason to induce Fox to pitch upon John Mill. Certainly, Fox had known the Mills for several years. In 1824, the first article in the first number of the *Westminster Review* was written by him. Furthermore, the Mills had old acquaintance with the Taylors, for John Taylor's grandfather had lived next door to them at Newington Green. But there is no indication that any of them knew each other intimately.

Why, then, did Fox look outside the circle of his immediate flock, and go to an outsider, a comparative stranger, in search of consolation for a member of his congregation? It is difficult to see what inspiration he expected Mill to give to Harriet, which she could not have equally well obtained amongst her many talented compeers. Fox's young votary was beautiful, clever, passionate, and, by her own confession, a restless wife. How, in any worldly way, could he think it prudent to thrust her into association with John Mill, whom he knew as a young man, susceptible and unattached, of great intellect, secure position, and of excellent prospects? A young man, moreover, whom Carlyle was shortly to describe as "a slender, rather tall and elegant youth, with small clear Roman-nosed face, two small earnestly-smiling eyes; modest, remarkably gifted with precision of utterance, enthusiastic, yet lucid, calm."[12]

Perhaps he saw a chance of setting a handsome sprat to catch an exceptional mackerel; of gaining a coveted pen for his *Repository*. Turning his mild, persuasive face towards his anxious penitent, Fox assured her that he knew the very man to solve her difficulties, an able and most promising young thinker. When she looked doubtful, he kindly offered to make all the necessary arrangements. And so in due course it came about that Mill, escorted by Graham and Roebuck, went to dine with Harriet and John Taylor at their house. Also present were Fox himself, and the inevitable Harriet Martineau.

III

John Mill found that he had much in common with the Taylors. He was in close sympathy with John Taylor's enthusiasm for political refugees, and as he was also the accepted expert on French affairs he was a welcome visitor at the house in Christopher Street. For Harriet, he quickly formed a warmer sentiment than could be explained by a common interest in idealistic foreigners; and it is even probable that their frequent meetings on that account were to some extent a convenient excuse.

The urgency was caused in part by Mill's own state of mind. The great drawback of a logical way of thinking such as his, was that it argued as though everyone were alike. Dealing entirely with abstractions it left no room for personality: it was so much taken up with how to think that it allowed for no divergence in what was actually thought. Mill indeed had seen this shortcoming during his period of despair and self-analysis, and had since that time reached out deliberately towards anybody charged with force or passion, regardless of the purity of their disputative methods. His curiosity, his hunger for enthusiasm, grew so great that he was mistaken as a convert by everyone of forceful feelings with whom he came in contact; by Sterling, d'Eichthal, and Carlyle in turn; an error he encouraged by seeking always to endorse what he agreed with in them, and never damping them by stating disagreement. Having learnt to mistrust the habit of analysis, he permitted himself to be guided too much by his feelings. When he encountered Harriet, those which linked him to his other friends fell away before the overriding impulse of a craving for feminine comradeship and love. Plain affection was scarcely known to him in relation to women. His love for his mother, mangled in their chilly home, became an incoherent pity so intense, that all feeling being unbearable, he had no feeling left for her at all. His sisters were his pupils: between him and them stood the insuperable code of family duty which enclosed them all. He continued to live at home, continued to give the compliance and pleasantness demanded from him by the code. But privately he hated his father's house, removed everything of himself that was of any value, and slammed the door behind him.

With Harriet all this was different, for her society was not imposed but freely chosen. His view of her was not the twisted, stunted view he had of his own family, but a whole view suddenly come upon, and fresheningly unfamiliar. Her mind was expanding, reaching eagerly for knowledge and for the best ways to apply it. The atmosphere of her coterie was as a lumber room of liberalism, and she was busy sorting. Mill admired the sureness of her grip as she flung aside all that was vague or sentimental, saving out only those things with the hard bright lustre of vitality. There was, too, the sharpness of her wit, that now and then would leave him breathless at its point and daring; and its reverse side, the quick flash of anger in defence of her beliefs, not held tentatively as he held his, but jealously possessed as though she lived by them. This incisiveness, this appearance of being constantly embattled, was in vivid contrast to her femininity, to her fragile body, sloping shoulders, fine white throat, and huge dark eyes, and it delighted him. For even when she talked with greatest earnestness, and he listened solemnly and with attention, he was lapped about by her aura of delicacy, of repose, and of warm intuitive sympathy, the essence of her feminine nature. Over all her excitement, whether playful or intense, brooded the stillness of her dignity, drawing her together, adding balance to her liveliness. Looking at her, with her hair put up in a Greek knob with a few scattered curls coming out beneath the comb, his mind went singing off into the vision of Athenian days that was his heaven. Not that he consciously saw her as a woman. He was too fastidious for a physical approach. She was, rather, his companion spirit; and companion spirits are traditionally sexless. As he said in a letter a little later on:

> "But the women, of all I have known, who possessed the highest measure of what are considered feminine qualities, have combined with them more of the highest *masculine* qualities than I have ever seen in but one or two men, and those one or two men were also in many respects almost women. I suspect it is the second-rate people of the two sexes that are unlike. The first rate are alike in both—except—no, I do not think I can except anything—but then, in this respect, my position has been and is, what you say every human being's is in many respects, 'a peculiar one'."[13]

Harriet for her part found him serious but never quaint. She preferred serious men; they were less likely to treat her roguishly, and that was her especial horror. John Mill was known as a profound philosopher, and to have him, as at first he was, for a close friend of the family, would lend *ton* to her household. Moreover, to talk to him freely and at length was of itself the best part of her education: for her method of assimilation was by discussion rather than by reading, and until now she had never had anyone much to talk to save Lizzie, who was too fanciful, and her own husband, who was too mundane. Mill's expansion into many-sidedness had made him attractive to confide in. His knowledge was immense, and he never thought any opinion absurd. Where he could add to her thoughts from his experience, he did; and where he could not, he listened respectfully to what she told him. His fault, in fact, was to be over-tolerant at this stage. In the force of his reaction he had been carried far beyond the healthy catholicism of the youthful mind, and had come to a point of acquiescence which must if continued have destroyed his personal outlook.

Now Harriet was a good antidote for over-tolerance. She had not his wealth of intellectual background, and so, like most of those accustomed to protect their views, she waded into her opponents lustily, not bothering to save the grain of truth from them, or even to understand where they had gone wrong. It became her mission to rescue Mill from his fatuous amiability, and to put him back into the course of decision and judgement, outlined no longer by logical speculation but by the forthright statement of her own mind. She never overcame his habit of studying the opposing point of view: she came in fact to see its value as a weapon and to use it too, but only in order to press her own the more effectively. She was the more truly romantic of the two, he being only an uncomfortable wanderer lost in an alien field. She did not make him more romantic: rather she made him retire into his native rationalism, and justify the romantic standpoints which she gave him.

From the beginning, their recognition of each other was both rapid and complete, and quite soon, each one also had a confidant. Some time in the winter of 1830, while Sterling and Mill were both staying with the Bullers down in Cornwall, they went strolling on the beach, and Mill told his friend about the admirable new family who had become his intimates. They collected from the shingle the pretty, brittle shells left shining in the retreating water, and Mill gave them to his young friends, Harriet's little boys. Two years later, Sterling, walking alone on a West Indian shore, his heart quite broken by the fate of Torrijos, his health impaired, his house torn down over the heads of his wife and infant by a hurricane, still remembered the incident, and seeing the gleam of shells, once more stooped and gathered them.[14] In July 1831, while Mill was striding about at Ambleside in quest of Wordsworth, Harriet was down at Hastings with her husband awaiting the birth of Helen. Eliza Flower wrote constantly to amuse her with her prattle: she told a mocking little tale about the Benthamites, and then remembering suddenly how things stood, she ended apologetically, "pray laugh I did—only I suppose 'tis spoilt now".[15] In another of her letters at that time, Eliza asked about a review of Thomas Moore's *Letters and Journals of Lord Byron*, which had just appeared in the *Edinburgh Review*, "did you or Mill do it?" In fact they neither of them had, but it is clear Eliza thought that either or both together might have done.[16]

Their first contact was purely literary. Harriet, not yet aware of the august mouthpiece she was soon to gain, had a great ambition to become a writer like Harriet Martineau. Mill was a first-class teacher and advised her constantly, and in May 1832, soon after she had finished with the trials of childbirth, her work began to flow regularly into the *Monthly Repository*. At first book reviews, then poems, and finally articles.

Mill was most deeply excited by her poetic strain. In July, while rambling in the Isle of Wight, he recalled a landscape sketch in the *Repository*, which he evidently thought that she had secretly written, although it soon turned out that he was wrong, and that the article was, in fact, by Fox. Making his way to Sandown Bay, he stood enraptured looking out, and then confided in his journal:

> "To some it might appear less interesting than many other parts of the southern coast; but to me it was consecrated by the touch of genius: it had been the subject of one of the most beautiful sketches in our recent literature, which, though it appeared in a fugitive publication (the *Monthly Repository*) will, I trust, some time or other be reprinted, and will hold a distinguished place among the works of its author, *be* he even the person he is suspected to be."[17]

He could not keep away. Two days later he was staring at the bay from a different angle, once more fascinated by "the beauty of the scene, enhanced as it was to me by the charm which true poetry (whether metrical or not) gives to all which it has touched, endowing it with beauties not its own". *

Nor, perhaps, did Mill confine himself to admiration and encouragement. In November Harriet reviewed a book about the Revolution of 1830, which she wrongly imagined to have been translated by Sarah Austin. Certain passages sound strangely familiar in their sweep of prose and clearness of expression:

> "There can be no doubt that the state of things in France is again slowly tending towards a great moral or physical revolution. That the former may suffice, all friends of humanity must desire; but should that force of itself be insufficient to produce agreement between the spirit of the government and the spirit of the time, they will be no true friends

* By November 1833, Mill had been disabused about the authorship, but was still confident that Harriet could, and should, do something even better. He wrote to Fox, "I have the strongest wish, and some hope, that there will someday arrive a sketch of Paris in the manner of some of your local sketches—if there does, it will be the most beautiful thing ever written—she has spoken quite enough to me at different times, to show what it would be." (F. A. Hayek, *John Stuart Mill and Harriet Taylor*, p. 55.)

> of humanity who shall not welcome any power which, by means of some evil, may work the regeneration of the people who lead the political education of Europe."[18]

That, both in style and matter, is the work of the author of *The Spirit of the Age*.

Mill, meanwhile, continued to busy himself with his articles in the *Examiner*, preferring that his *protégée* should have full scope to make her own way in the *Repository*. In April 1832 Fox approached him with a direct request for an article which he gently turned aside. But towards the end of the year there came a change. Harriet's contributions began to decline in frequency, and soon altogether ceased, while Mill began to be a regular contributor above his own press-sign "Antiquus" or "A". His first article, on "Genius", was a powerful plea for originality, looking longingly back to the glories of Athenian democracy. The Greeks, he said, considered wisdom not as a private luxury to be indulged in a select salon or in a precious cloister, but as a quality essential to success, a practical weapon of daily life available to all. To this end the mind was instructed how to think, not what to think. Socrates, the greatest of all teachers, laid down no word of dogma; his teaching was by demonstration of a method, of the thrust and parry of a clear thinking mind. "Her philosophers were not formed, nor did they form their scholars, by placing a set of ready-made truths before them, and helping them to put them on." But that was the present practice. Modern education was all cram. In this way we could never progress or throw up genius, no matter how far we went in enlightening the masses. The question was whether "our mental light . . . has not lost in intensity at least a part of what it has gained in diffusion; whether our 'march of intellect' be not rather a march towards doing without intellect, and supplying our deficiency of giants by the united efforts of a constantly increasing multitude of dwarfs."[19]

This picture of democracy as a weary level of neutral mediocre colours could never have been derived from the young Radical so recently the advocate of votes for everyone and schools for all. Nor could the appeal for individuality have stemmed from the stern authoritarian who, only a year before, had told Sterling "it is good for man to be ruled: to submit both his body and mind to the guidance of a higher intelligence and virtue"; while the liberal concept of "making every man his own guide and sovereign-master, and letting him think for himself"[20] showed, he had said, a deplorable misunderstanding of the needs of human nature. The article on "Genius" was quite unlike anything that Mill had thought before. It was, on the other hand, a lucid expansion of a principle stated by Harriet in a paper written at this time though never published. "Whether it be religious conformity, Political conformity, moral conformity or Social conformity," she said, "no matter which the species, the spirit is the same: all kinds agree in this one point, of hostility to individual character. . . . What is called the opinion of Society is . . . a combination of the many weak, against the few strong: an association of the mentally listless to punish any manifestation of mental independence. The remedy is, to make all strong enough to stand alone; and whoever has once known the pleasure of self-dependence, will be in no danger of relapsing into subserviency."[21] Mill who had swung about so easily in the last few years had swung now for the last time. What her fragment on Marriage was to *The Subjection of Women*, this on Toleration was also to the *Liberty*. The question how to free the many without crushing the superior few rang out from time to time throughout their twenty-eight years of union, and at Harriet's death was examined with melancholy care in the book which Mill most felt was hers. Thus, the main outline of his two crusades was settled within two years of their meeting.

Another excursion made by Mill away from his accustomed beat was into the field of poetry, or rather of poetics. It began in January 1833 with a laborious essay called "What is Poetry?" This was followed in October by a second part, analysing two forms of poetic genius; the cultured or deliberate, where thought is clothed with emotion and imagery as is typically the case with Wordsworth: and the spontaneous, where emotion bubbles up luxuriantly as in the case of Shelley. Wordsworth was Mill's favourite, and Shelley Harriet's: her own poems have more than a trace of Shelley's phraseology, and it is to Shelley that Mill likened her at this time of their first acquaintance. Probably he had never studied Shelley till she brought him to it, and beyond all doubt this article was at her instigation. He said as much to Fox:

"I have nearly made up my mind to transfer to you the paper on Poetry which I thought of putting at the head of a review on Tennyson somewhere. I think I could make a better review of Tennyson, and with the same ideas too, in another way.

If you like the idea, and if you see *her* before Monday, will you mention it to her—you know it is hers—if she approves it shall be yours. I shall see her on Monday myself, and then I will speak of the matter to her."[22]

In March 1833, after a five years' absence, Browning reappeared in Fox's presence, and proudly gave him twelve copies of "Pauline", his first major poem. Fox gave it a rousing review in the *Repository*, and sent one of the copies off to Mill in the hope that he would give it a welcome in the more widely read *Examiner*. Browning was delighted. "I can only say that I am very proud to feel as grateful as I do", he wrote excitedly to Fox; "I shall never write a line without thinking of the source of my first praise."[23]

Mill duly wrote some friendly words. During a chat with Harriet, however, he could not refrain from indulging his new craft of critic, and he jotted down in pencil on the flyleaf of the book his real opinion of it. He did not like it. Whatever of beauty it contained was ruined for him by the author's Byronic treatment of his heroine. "All his aspirings and yearnings and regret point to other things, never to her; then he *pays her off* toward the end by a piece of flummery amounting to the modest request that she will love him and live with him and give herself up to him *without* his *loving* her—*moyennant quoi* he will think her and call her everything that is handsome, and he promises her that she shall find it mighty pleasant. . . . Bad luck to him! as the Irish say. . . . If he once could muster a hearty hatred of his selfishness it would go: as it is, he feels only the *lack* of good, not the positive evil. He feels not remorse, but only disappointment; a mind in that state can only be regenerated by some new passion, and I know not what to wish for him but that he may meet with a *real* Pauline."[24]

Having expressed his indignation, he returned the book to Fox, requesting him not to let the author see what he had said. He thought, of course, that Browning would read his other more favourable notice in the press: but, incredibly, he could not get it printed: it was too long for Fonblanque; Tait had already mentioned "Pauline" in the "Other Books". Worse, Fox disregarded his request, and Browning received intact the annotated copy, followed shortly by his entire first edition returned by the publishers in unbound sheets with the news that not a single copy had been sold.

It was of no avail that Harriet, taking a more lenient view than Mill of the churlish handling of "Pauline", had scribbled at various places in the margin admiring comments like "most beautiful", or "deeply true". Disaster was complete. Above Mill's observations the young poet wrote, "Robert Browning. 30 October 1833." And under that, "only this crab remains of the shapely Tree of Life in this

Fool's paradise of mine". For thirty-five years he refused to reprint it, and when finally compelled to do so for his collected poems, he wrote, "I acknowledge and retain it with extreme repugnance and purely of necessity."[25] *

Mill's next contribution to the *Monthly Repository* was a series of translations of the *Dialogues of Plato*, written some years before, probably after his depression of 1826, when he was attempting to rescue Greek humanism and the Socratic method of analysis from the ruins of his father's teaching. While writing his essay on "Genius" he dug them out, and they were greatly admired by Harriet who persuaded him to publish them. So he added to the plain translation a series of notes typical of his new frame of mind, insisting on the importance of the imagination and affections as a guide to virtue more effective than the intellect, and handed them over to Fox.[26] They appeared in the *Repository* at intervals during 1834 and 1835. Mill was surprised to find that they acquired a wider popularity than anything he had so far written, and that no doubt helped to confirm his belief in Harriet's judgement.

Nor were his activities on behalf of the *Repository* confined to writing for it. At different times, he canvassed both John Nichol, Professor of Astronomy at Glasgow University, and Carlyle, trying to persuade them to write for it or at least to read it regularly. He also continued to advertise it, and its "Songs of the Months" with words and music by the Flower girls, in the *Examiner*. In February 1834 Eliza Flower wrote to Harriet, "I did a foolish thing there this evening. He was writing to JSM but all at once he said 'do finish it for me'—and while I was writing he added 'tell him to give the songs a notice', and I did as I was bid—but afterwards I wished I had not—was that weak? most likely—for 'tis just I feel all over now—yet am I not thine beloved friend with true and strong love."[27] Mill added in his reply to Fox a postscript for her "The three beautiful children shall have justice done them ere the appearance of the third. The birth of the oldest was announced, and a good word spoken for the expected family. February is a beauty, but March is grand."[28]

* This document may still be seen in the Victoria and Albert Museum. It is widely believed now that Mill's criticism of Browning's first attempt at subjective poetry was instrumental in deciding Browning to write henceforth in the dramatic medium.

IV

That Mill should do his best for Fox was natural. Fox was, after all, the lover of Harriet's closest friend, and the four of them were by this time being drawn by the similarity of their predicament into the greatest intimacy. Within the pattern of Mill's contact with the *Repository* is woven the whole story, tormented, obscure and involved, of this most critical phase of the relationship. In May 1832, when the main block of Harriet's writings started to appear, he was still her admiring teacher and she his devoted student; but this situation so easily provocative of stronger feelings was abruptly altered. Instead of teaching her, he began to be taught himself: instead of his pupil, she became his oracle and his goddess. She, as before, continued to adore him as her Abelard: but to him she became more than Héloïse. Taken unawares by the rapid change in him, Harriet found her own steady consideration for him kindle and spread into an answering blaze. From this moment all other concerns were secondary; the world was blotted out, and they were finally in love.

They turned and twisted in the toils of their hopeless circumstances. They struck a lovers' bargain to examine separately and philosophically their ideas about the vital topics, marriage and divorce. Mill's essay started:

> "She to whom my life is devoted has wished for written exposition of my opinions on the subject which, of all connected with human Institutions, is nearest to her happiness. Such as that exposition can be made without *her* to suggest and decide, it is given in these pages: she, herself, has not refused to put into writing for *me*, what she has thought and felt on the same subject, and *there* I shall be taught, all perhaps which I have, and certainly all which I have not found out for myself."[29]

It was marvellous, when they exchanged their briefs, how closely they concurred. They were agreed upon, as Mill defined it, "the absurdity and immorality of a state of society and opinion in which a woman is at all dependent for her social position upon the fact of her being or not being married. Surely it is wrong, wrong in every way, and on every view of morality, even the vulgar view—that there should exist any motives to marriage except the happiness which two persons who love one another feel in associating their existence." They accepted Robert Owen's wide criterion of sexual morality: "*Chastity*, sexual intercourse *with* affection. *Prostitution*, sexual intercourse *without* affection." They perceived that "the indissolubility of marriage is the keystone of woman's present lot, and the whole comes down and must be reconstructed if that is removed." Harriet, as Mill anticipated, went even further than he did in her applications. Since all the valid difficulties about divorce were in consideration for the children, it must be made the woman's interest not to have children unless she could maintain them. She ought to be made the equal of men in all respects, responsibilities as well as rights. Then all laws whatever regarding marriage should be done away. Inclination, not dependency, should be the tie; and what was known as the law of divorce should be called instead the proof of affection.

What ought to be was very far from being what was. Divorce was an ecclesiastical concern. Adultery and brutality were the only grounds that counted: the children remained the property of the father: and divorced persons could remarry only by a special Act of Parliament. A legal solution of their problem was a day-dream. The position was very dangerous. Mill, facing a brilliant future as a moral philosopher, was more vulnerable than others to the touch of scandal. Like Auguste Comte and his Clothilde de Vaux, he might easily be exposed to ignominy and even ridicule, and he had none of the invincible egoism which enabled Comte to rise above it. Harriet had three small children to consider, of whom she was naturally fond and they of her. She was also fond of her worthy husband, and was grateful for his kindness; while he obviously adored her, and looked up to her with trust and confidence and admiration of her beauty, as though he could never accustom himself to his good fortune in being married to her. To do him any injury would be treacherous. Both she and Mill were highly responsible folk and, or so they thought themselves, sober and sensible to a degree. They tried very hard to solve the matter honestly. Mill, who was the light and life of his family circle, squarely answered the questions of his father, with whom he had not been on the best of terms for several years, and told him of his plight: but old James Mill, foreseeing the wreck of all his hopes, was sour. His radicalism was limited to mental jugglery and did not carry into everyday life or social intercourse, on which matters his views were strict and even Puritanical. He told John baldly that he was in love with another man's wife, an interference in the rights of property just as reprehensible, to his way of thinking, as coveting his ox or his ass. There was no understanding to be gathered there.

Harriet likewise went and told John Taylor that she wished him to understand she had found in Mill a being who reached more deeply into her heart than he could ever do, but that there was nothing guilty in it. Her affection for him was unimpaired, she said, as was shown by her readiness to confide frankly in him; and she asked him to trust her, and to take no notice of any gossip he might hear. Taylor was most upset, not so much at hearing she loved Mill, as at learning thus incidentally that she had never loved him. However, he advised her reasonably enough, as much for Mill's sake as for her own peace of mind and her duty to her household, to "renounce sight"; enduring for the moment the bitter-sweet pain of a broken love affair in order to achieve the lasting satisfaction of having done the best for all.

This she promised to try. Accordingly, when Mill returned at the beginning of August 1832 from a fortnight's walking with Henry Cole in the south of England, in vigorous health, bursting with news to tell her, and laden with flowers he had collected for her, he found a note forwarded by a go-between, most likely Lizzie Flower, to say that all was over and they must meet no more. His sorrow was overwhelming, but he managed a tragic and dignified reply in French, which reached her by the same means as hers had come:

> "Blessed be the hand which traced these characters! She writes to me —that is enough: although I do not pretend that it is not to say good-bye to me forever.
>
> She must not believe that I accept such a farewell. Her way and mine have separated, as she says. But they can, they ought to, meet again. At whatever time, in whatever place that may be so, she will find me always the same as I have been, as I am still.
>
> She shall be obeyed; no further letters of mine shall disturb her peace, or pour one extra drop into her cup of sorrows. She shall be obeyed, for the reasons which she gives,—she would have been, even if she had confined herself to telling me her wishes. To obey her is for me a necessity.
>
> She will not refuse, I trust, the offering of these little flowers, which I have brought for her from the depths of the New Forest. Give them to her, if necessary, as if they came from you." [30]

But, as with all good love stories, this estrangement was the beginning, not the end. The issue was not so simple as John Taylor saw it. During his eclipse, Mill did not loiter palely outside their doors, but flung himself into work as the sovereign remedy for his trial of the spirit. "Every man's work is the chief part of his life", he wrote to Carlyle, "and since my return to town it has been the whole of mine, except some little reading, which is also in the same sort work."[31] To Harriet, closely watching, the spectacle must have been profoundly moving, especially as the articles he tore off with such furious determination were quite indifferent, stilted, logical, and dull, more like the style he had so painfully outworn, and quite devoid of the easy power of which she knew him to be capable. Being herself in an embattled state where the sense of duty could be tipped to support her strongest inclinations, it seemed to her as if John Mill the writer would shrivel away to nothing all for need of her; and that alongside her debt to her husband and her family, she must set her responsibility to humanity for making or breaking the man who, she was sure, with her aid could do so much for its advance. From now on she assumed this burden equally with her others, and tried continually to reconcile the conflict between them for the possession of her person. Her task would have been impossible had either of the men she had to deal with been violent or unscrupulous: but fortunately Mill's nature was to behave as a Roman gentleman, while Taylor was of that easy-going stamp which when confronted with a crisis can rise suddenly to the heroic. Each gave the other much, and neither worried about his own indignity. And so, through the medium of their genuine love for her, and by the sheer power of her personality, she was able to maintain a balance between them.

She told John Taylor that his bid had failed, that she could not and would not put Mill off from her entirely. He was readmitted to the house within a month, and soon was corresponding as before with Taylor about the refugees, and with Harriet about their writings. Though with a difference. The terms on which she took Mill back were not that he should coach her any longer, but that she should be of help to him. She gave up her manful ambition to become a Harriet Martineau, and decided to express herself in a more feminine way through her effect on him. It was Mill, not she, who was to be the writer; his, not her, development that was important to the world. From now on, he ceased to write as though he were scratching footholds in a shifting sand of contradiction, towards conclusions as cheerless and inevitable as an obelisk. From now on, he wrote with a broader step and a wider eye, picking up things of unusual shape or glittering interest as he went along.

For a time after the upset everyone felt easier. At the end of September Mill went off to the Bullers in Cornwall, and walked for a fortnight in the neighbourhood before returning to the India House. In October, the Taylors went together for a carriage tour of North Wales; when they got back, they left their house in Finsbury and moved to a more spacious residence at 17 Kent Terrace, Regent's Park. Here Mill continued to call upon Harriet several times a week, probably by tacit arrangement with John Taylor, who went out to his club on most occasions, contenting himself with limiting their frequency. On 19 May 1833 Mill wrote to Fox:

> "I knew not that you were to be in K.T. on Wednesday, and I seldom go there without some special reasons on that day of the week—for as it cannot be right in present circumstances to be there *every* evening, none costs so little to give up as that in which there is a much shorter time and only in the presence of others."[32]

This rationed intercourse was quite insufficient for the volume of their love, and they supplemented it by a copious correspondence, made more urgent by the feeling that it was in some sense illicit, and rising in intensity whenever they were separated for a few days by illness or other accident. Little by little they began to search about for means of extra meetings. "As for *me*, I am going to K.T. today, despite its being Wednesday. However meet we must and soon too",[33] said Mill to Fox in June. Sometimes the arrangements had all the excitement of traditional intrigue:

> "Yes dear, I will meet you, in the chaise, somewhere between this and Southend.—The hour will depend on what your note says tomorrow. (That is supposing the chaise is to be had of which there is very little doubt).
>
> Bless you dearest! I did not write yesterday. I wish I had for you seem to have expected it. I have been well and quite happy since that delicious evening, and I may perhaps see thee today, but if not I shall not be disappointed—as for *sad* I feel since that evening as tho' I never shall be that again. I am *very* well in all respects, but more especially in spirit.
>
> Bless thee—tomorrow will be delightful and I am looking to it as the very greatest *treat*—
>
> dear, if you do not meet me on your road from Southend you will know that I could not have the chaise.
>
> Friday."[34] *

* This letter from Harriet to Mill is not dated and not signed. But it is in her handwriting, and seems to refer to this period.

John Taylor again tackled his wife about the situation, and demanded more strongly than before that she should give up seeing Mill. She again refused, and he then said, in that case it would be better for her not to live with him, as the present arrangement was most unsettling, and not a little degrading. Harriet was quite adamant: she would not give up Mill entirely, but short of that would do anything her husband asked. If it was his wish that she should leave him, she would go: although there was nothing in her friendship with Mill that could make that necessary. If John Taylor were insisting on it not for his own sake but because he thought it to be what she herself desired, she could only say that provided he left her at liberty to see her friend, she would much sooner stay with him, look after his house and the children, and help him in all the little ways she knew he so much needed. But Taylor did insist, and it was eventually decided that she should go off to Paris for six months to see how they felt in the cooler atmosphere of separation.

Each expected a different result from this experiment. Taylor was certain that as soon as she got away from home she would wish she were back, and would soon be willing to give up Mill and return to him. Harriet on the other hand was convinced that while she was away Taylor would miss her so much that he would soon be only too glad to have her back Mill or no Mill. While Mill, for his part, when he heard about it, concluded that the temporary separation was a politely gradual move towards a permanent break; that at the end of six months they would each be the more certain they were in the right, and Harriet would be no more ready to abandon her lover than Taylor would be to have her back unless she did so. There would be no agreement. And since it would be her husband who had put her off, not she who had run away, there could no longer be any objection to his living with her altogether, and crowning with the physical fact their deep-rooted mystical union of spirit.

As a first step towards this heart's desire, Mill's present course was plain. She was in trouble, and he must be at her side: she was to travel alone, and he must be there to look after her. He was unable to endure a six months' absence from her, and come what might he would go to Paris too. On 18 May he wrote to tell Carlyle, who was pressing him to spend his summer holiday with him up in Scotland, that he might not be able to get there after all. In July he repeated the warning, and on 5 September revealed the desperate truth:

"You have probably heard from Dr. Carlyle before this reaches you, that I shall not, after all, see you this autumn. There were about twenty chances to one that I should, but it is the twenty-first which has taken effect in reality. I was mistaken, too, when I said that if I went not to Craigenputtock I should go nowhere. I am going to Paris; the same cause which I then thought, if it operated at all, would operate to keep me here, now sends me there. It is a journey entirely of duty; nothing else, you will do me the justice to believe, would have kept me from Craigenputtock after what I have said and written so often; it is duty and duty connected with a person to whom of all persons alive I am under the greatest obligations. If I had not so short a vacation the two journeys would not be incompatible, but alas for him who must abide eleven months of the year at a desk in Leadenhall Street!"[35]

From this it seems as though Mill's uncertainty were due more to Harriet's own delay in deciding to go to Paris than to any objection she made to his determination to be with her wherever she might be. Perhaps, as is often the feminine way, she took a less tragic view of the affair, having a better notion than either of the men how it might be expected to turn out. As matters had been settled with John Taylor, it was all left to her. If she had had any real intention of forgetting Mill, she would never have permitted him to follow her. But, on the other hand, she never had any idea, as Mill hoped, of letting him elope with her anywhere or everywhere, leaving behind her children, and the ruins of all he might have been or done. If nothing was decided in six months, she would stay in Paris till it was; and in the meantime any reason for getting out of England in the darkening autumn of the year was, as it always was throughout her life, most welcome to her.

As the time approached for her departure, the implications of it loomed larger to John Mill. Believing what they were doing to be final, he feared, not indeed, for their future, nor for what might be said about him by his friends and enemies, but for his own state of mind, which was shaky and irresolute, opportunist, following events rather than directing them. He was possessed by doubts, gloomy and distrait. She could only watch, unable to interfere, unable to ask what worried him till he confessed it to her, distressed beyond measure that what ought to make him happy made him sorrowful and drear. At last he wrote it out, and set her free, and her love poured out on him in reliet and consolation:

"I am glad that you have said it—I am *happy* that you have—no one with any fineness and beauty of character but must feel compelled to say *all* to the being they really love, or rather with any ***permanent*** reservation it is not *love*—while there is reservation, however little of it, the love is just *so much* imperfect. There has never, *yet*, been entire confidence *around* us. The difference between you and me in that respect is, that I have always *yearned* to have *your* confidence with an intensity of wish which has *often*, for a time, swallowed up the naturally stronger feeling—the affection itself—you have not given it, not that you wished to reserve—but that you did not *need* to give—but not having that need of course you had no perception that I had and so you have discouraged confidence from me 'til the habit of *checking first thoughts* has become so strong that when in your presence timidity has become almost a *disease* of the nerves. It would be absurd, only it is so painful to notice in myself that every word I ever speak to you is detained a second before it is said 'til I'm quite sure I am not by implication asking for your confidence. It is but that the only being who has ever called forth all my faculties of affection is the only one in whose presence I ever felt constraint. . . .

If I did not know them to be false, how heartily I should scorn such expressions, 'I have ceased to will!' Then to wish? for does not wish with the power to fulfil constitute will?

It is false that 'your strength is not equal to the circumstances in which you have placed' yourself.—It is quite another thing to be guided by a judgement on which you can rely and which is better placed for judgement than yourself.

Would you let yourself 'drift with the tide whether it flow or ebb' if in one case every wave took you further from me? Would you not put what strength you have into resisting it? Would you not *wish* to resist it, would you not *will* to resist it? Tell me—for if you would not, how happens it that you will to love me or any?"[36]

Mill, responding to her rallying call, felt that he had been craven. He wrote to Fox next day:

". . . she is like herself: if she is ever out of spirits it is always something amiss in *me* that is the cause—it is so now—it is because she sees that what ought to be so much easier to me than to her is in reality more difficult—costs harder struggle—to part company with the opinion of the world, and with my former modes of doing good—however, thank Heaven, she does not doubt that I can do it.

Yes—I shall see you often, I hope, at Clapton when she is gone."[37]

Harriet left for Paris shortly afterwards, and for the next month Fox was the constant solace of Mill's loneliness and the only recipient of his confidence. After years of contumely and neglect, Mrs. Fox had retired to the upstairs portion of their house in order to avoid the spectacle of his affair with Eliza Flower: from there, in 1832, she directed him a letter of complaint demanding a separation, and this he answered formally, to the effect that their finances would not admit of separate establishments, and that they must continue to live under the same roof, but that all would be free to go on in their own way. Dissatisfied with his humiliating reply, his wife expressed her indignation to her friends and neighbours, with the result that by this time the whole of the South Place congregation was in uproar and was vigorously taking sides. The atmosphere in the house itself was fever-hot, and for Eliza's fervid temperament, insupportable. She had taken refuge more and more in the fellow-circumstances of Harriet, her clearer-minded friend; and, in reverse fashion, Mill grew into the habit of consulting Fox. He spent a few days at Dorking with his family, who must have been astonished by the sudden reserve of their usually expansive favourite; then, after providing Fox with a great budget of material for the review, he left for Paris on 10 October, fully certain of success, and asking merely that Fox be sure to send them the *Monthly Repository* for next month.

From what Mill said, Fox gathered when they went away that Harriet had parted from Taylor for ever, and that Mill would henceforth live with her; it was the course he had constantly advised for them. He was therefore surprised to hear from Mill in Paris of further doubts and indecisions; and very dismayed when on meeting Taylor he found him in a state of great exuberance, saying that Harriet had written him letters in the warmest tone, proving him right in thinking that in absence her affection for him would revive: that she had quite resolved to give up Mill, and was determined at the end of the six months either to return to him or to remain alone in Paris; and that he was shortly going over there himself to see if he could bring her back. Fox at once wrote anxiously to ask Mill for the facts. By the same post, a letter of more modest optimism arrived for Harriet from her husband, and she handed it to Mill for him to read. Mill then wrote to Fox in some indignation at his stupidity:

> "When the separation had actually taken place the result did as you say seem certain—not because we had willed to make it so, but because it seemed the necesssary consequence of the new circumstances if the feelings of all continued the same. This was the sole cause and I think cause enough for the hopefulness and happiness which I felt almost all the month and which must have made a false impression on you. I never felt sure of what was to be after the six months, but I felt an immense increase of the chances in my favour. When I came here, I *expected* to find her no more decided than she had always been about what would be the best for all, but *not* to find her as for the first time I did, doubtful about what would be best for our *own* happiness—under the influence

of that fact and of the painful feelings it excited, I wrote to you. *That* doubt, thank heaven, lasted but a short time—if I had delayed my letter two days longer I should never have sent it.

If Mr. Taylor feels as you believe he does, he has been very far from telling her 'all he feels'. . . . He is most entirely mistaken in all the facts. . . . Because her letters to Mr. Taylor express the strong affection she has always felt, and he is no longer seeing, every day, proof of her far stronger feeling for another, he thinks the affection has *come back*. He might have seen it quite as plainly before, only he refused to believe it. *I* have seen it, and felt its immense power over her, in moments of intense excitement with which I am sure he would believe it to be utterly incompatible.

Her affection for him, which has always been the principle, is now the sole obstacle to our being together—for the present there seems absolutely no prospect of that obstacle's being got over. She believes—and she knows him better than any of us can—that it would be the breaking up of his whole future life—*that* she is determined never to be the cause of, and I am as determined never to urge her to it, and convinced that if I did I should fail. Nothing could justify it but 'the most distinct perception' that it is not only 'necessary to the happiness of both', but the only means of saving both from insupportable unhappiness. . . . She will, if it is in human power to do so, make him understand the exact state of her feelings, and will as at present minded, give *him* the choice of every possible arrangement except entire giving up, with the strong wish that her remaining here may be his choice. . . . This seems but a poor result to come of so much suffering and so much effort, but for *us* even so the gain is great."[38]

At the end of this exhaustive explanation, Harriet added her own happy greeting:

"I had written to you dearest friends both, as you are, but now that I have seen that letter of yours, I cannot send mine. It is sad to be misunderstood by you—as I have been before—but it will not be always so—my own dear friends. O what a letter was that! but my head and my soul bless you both.

He tells you quite truly our state—all at least which he attempts to tell—but there is much more might be said—there has been so much more pain than I thought I was capable of, but also O how much more happiness. O this being seeming as 'tho' God had willed to show the type of the possible elevation of humanity. To be with him wholly is my ideal of the noblest fate: for all states of mind and feeling which are lofty and large and fine, he is the companion spirit and heart's desire—we are not alike in trifles only because I have so much more frivolity than he. Why do you not write to me my dearest Lizzie? (I never wrote that name before) if you wd say on the merest scrap what you are talking about what the next sermon is about where you walked to, and such like, how glad I should be! You must come here—it is a most beautiful paradise. O how happy we might all be in it. You will see it with me, bless you! won't you?"

A paradise it always was to Mill, and in the intervals of working out his personal destiny, he managed, during his six weeks' stay, to see a good deal of Paris. He rejoiced once more in the easy social friendliness, the free acceptance of new ideas that would be thought outrageous in England, and the lack of emphasis on income; but he was distressed to find Parisians still unusually lethargic. In the trough of revolution they were tired of inspiration; the well-to-do were as satisfied with their ample budget as the peasants with their precious bit of land, and there was a total lack of enthusiasm save for the railroad speculation mania they had copied from the English. He met a great number of people—Economists, Saint-Simonians and the like, and notably two Republican leaders he had long admired: Armand Carrel, editor of the *National*, a quiet, elegant, clean-shaven young man, standing out from a roomful of his colleagues, all swarthy and ferociously moustached as was then the fashion of the 'left'; and Godefroy Cavaignac, President of the revolutionary *Society of the Rights of Man*, a violent atheist, and "a man whose name is energy, who cannot ask you the commonest question but in so decided a manner that he makes you start".[39]

On 18 November he returned alone to London. In the meantime, Harriet, with the assistance of her brother Edward Hardy, who had visited her in Paris and had access to John Taylor, successfully cured her husband of his over-optimism. He was never able to deny her what she wanted very long, and the plan she proposed he accepted easily, even apologetically. She wrote to Mill:

"I had yesterday one of those letters from Mr. Taylor which make us admire and love him. He says that this plan and my letters have given him delight—that he has been selfish—but in future will think more for others and less for himself—but still he talks of this plan being good *for all*, by which he means *me*, as he says he is sure it will 'prevent after misery', and again he wishes for complete confidence. I have written exactly what I think without reserve."[40]

And so in due course she came back to Kent Terrace, and they went on exactly as before. This was not what Mill had expected, for as soon as he got back to the India House he had written to Carlyle that he would very likely have to go to Paris again the following summer; but she counselled him on the virtues of resignation, assuring him that her affection for her husband, although it must continue to exist in equal measure with her love for him, was an emotion of very inferior value:

> "I do not believe *affection* to be natural to human beings—it is an instinct of the lower animals for their young—but in humans it is a made up combination of feelings and assocations wh. will cease to exist when artificiality ceases to exist. Only passion is natural—that is temporary affection—but what we call affection will continue so long as there is dependence."[41]

United by the suffering they each had undergone, and by the nobleness each had achieved, the problem became impersonal to all three, and they grew comradely. They combined to give the benefit of their experience to their common friends Fox and Lizzie in their similar difficulties. These had not been made easier by the departure of the other Flower sister from the storm-tossed neighbourhood. Sallie, who had been writing faithfully for the *Repository* for some time, grew fascinated by another contributor unknown to her, who signed himself "Junius Redivivus". She drew Mill's attention to his worth, and Mill not only gave him a full appreciation in the *Repository* for April 1833, but in June put a friendly review of his book, *The Producing Man's Companion*, into *Tait's Magazine*. This brought about a meeting, and the end of anonymity. "Junius Redivivus" turned out to be one William Bridges Adams, a charitable non-conformist and a railway engineer. He invented, amongst other things, the fish-plate junction for two lengths of railway line, which made but little fortune for him although it is now in universal use. He and Sallie met in Harriet Taylor's drawing-room some time in the summer of 1833, and married early the next year.

Sallie gone, Mrs. Fox found the situation no longer tolerable, and made a formal complaint to the congregation of South Place about the conduct of the minister, her husband, and it became necessary for him to defend himself in open church. In this crisis, Mill, Harriet, and her husband, completely forgetful of their own dissension, rallied solidly behind their friend, pondering long and seriously what he best might do. Eliza was quite beside herself with anxiety and flung herself on Harriet:

> "O you—no not even you can imagine what the wretchedness of this state is—I mean when one *must* bear, and so quietly too! and one's whole existence is condensed into the mere effort of enduring—you say you couldn't stand it—sometimes I think 'twill sink me dead. . . . Will you come soon! I cannot write to you tonight, but you will come soon."[42]

Fox, who had been driven ill with worry, was rather in favour of ignoring the specific question of his adultery, on the grounds that it was no concern of the congregation, and for fear that they might call him to account for the views he had expressed in the *Repository* on the free relation of the sexes. Mill, who never doubted his innocence, assured him this would be a great mistake: he need not beg the question of his principles, but "we all think it of real importance that every public mention of the charge should be accompanied by mention of your denying it".[43] Harriet for her part went hurrying down to Walworth to see whether her father Thomas Hardy, another prominent Unitarian, would use his influence for Fox.

Their endeavours were successful. In the ferment of debate it was generally forgotten that the main issue was Fox's own behaviour; the matter became a battle over the claims of free love and fidelity, in which his party triumphed. But Fox imprudently spoilt his victory: he made a monetary settlement upon his wife, and, leaving her in the Clapton house, moved across to Bayswater. There, in January 1835 he opened a second establishment with Eliza in full domestic charge, to the scandal of old friends and neighbours including Harriet Martineau, who all railed against her shamelessness. Harriet and Mill were far from being shocked at all of this, blaming the hounds rather than the hares; but the settling of their various affairs removed the king-bolt from their intimacy, especially as Fox strongly disapproved the friendly compromise the Taylors had achieved. They remained in close touch, but gradually saw each other less and less.

V

In June 1834, at the height of the conflict over Fox, Mill became more and more dissatisfied with his own position. It seemed to him that the settlement was too much in favour of John Taylor, that the sound and fury of the previous winter had but landed them all back where they were before, and that Fox's solution of all or nothing was probably right, and should be taken up again. He wrote:

> "Our affairs have been gradually getting into a more and more unsatisfactory state—and are now in a state which, a very short time ago, would have made me quite miserable, but now I am altogether in a higher state than I was and better able to conquer evil and to bear it. I will tell you all about it some day—perhaps the first time we meet—but by that time perhaps the atmosphere will be clearer—adieu."[44]

Accordingly, he expressed his doubts to Harriet. So far from gaining the further union they had struggled for, the present situation was anomalous. She was neither his mistress in one sense, nor was she less than that in another: he could not take her out and flaunt her in the face of the world as he would like to do, but instead must visit her furtively, by leave and permission of her husband. Apart from anything else, the outward appearance of their present arrangement was frankly specious; he feared for its effect upon the multitudes incapable of understanding the high deliberation of their motives, who might take their example as a justification for incontinence. To this she replied cautiously, fighting him with the weapon she knew to be most effective, fighting for her love, and fighting, above all, for the precarious balance she had established:

> "Those words yesterday *were cold* and distancing, *very*, at *first* . . . but this comes and must come from the uncongenial circumstances—the circumstances which tend to elate or to despond do not come at the same time to both—and tho' such things in no degree *alter* one's mind, they *have* their effect in deciding which state of the mind shall be for the time uppermost—and always will have so long as it pleases heaven to endow us with a body and senses.
>
> *Yes*, dearest friend, things as they are now bring to me, besides *moments* of quite complete happiness, a *life* how infinitely to be preferred to all I ever knew! I never for an instant could wish that this had never been on my own account, and only on yours if you could think so—but why do I say *mine* and *yours*, what is good for one must be so for the other, and will be so always—*you* say so—and whatever of sadness there may sometimes be, is only the proof of how much happiness there *is* by proving the capacity for so much more.
>
> You say that what you think virtue, the 'wise and good' who have long known and respected you, would think vice—How can you think people wise, with such opposite notions? You say too that when those who profess different principles to the vulgar, *act* their principles, they make all worse whom they do not make better, and I understand you to believe that they would make many worse and few better in your own case—Is not this then the 'thinking with the wise and acting with the

foolish' principle? And does not this imply compromise and insincerity? *You* cannot mean that, for that is both base and weak—if made a rule and not an occasional hard necessity.

I was not *quite* wrong in thinking you feared opinion—I never supposed you dreaded the opinion of fools but only of those who are otherwise wise and good but have not your opinions about moralities."[45]

Fortunately John Taylor intervened. Sensing the inconvenience of cramped quarters for such strong emotions, he provided her with a small place in the country down at Keston Heath near Bromley in Kent.* For him it was a great easement after his prodigious flights into supernal ethics. There, and at Walton-on-Thames, where later on they took a more accessible retreat, she spent most of her time, with Helen as her diminutive chaperone; returning to Kent Terrace at frequent intervals, for the boys' school holidays, or for the family birthdays which were celebrated all together as an annual ceremony. There, her mother sometimes went from Walworth to stay with her. There, too, Mill was able to spend week-ends. While even her husband used to pay occasional friendly visits. For the lovers it was a shrine, referred to reverently in their letters:

"In the beautiful stillness of his lovely country, and with the fresh feeling of all the enjoyment it has been to him—and so soon after that which to him is such a quick-passing pleasure—he is perhaps feeling again, what he once said to me, that 'the less human the more lovely' I seemed to him—do you remember that my love? *I* have, because I felt that whatever such a feeling was, it was not love—and since how perfectly he has denied it—or that may not be exactly the feeling, but only his old 'vanity of vanities' may have come back? Neither one nor the other grieves *me*, but for his own dear sake—for me—I *am* loved

* It has been supposed that her first house was at Kingston-on-Thames. This appears to depend entirely on Carlyle's statement to C. E. Norton (See the *Letters of C. E. Norton*, ed. Sarah Norton, 1913, vol. I, pp. 496–7). But there is a letter to Harriet from her sister Caroline dated 11 August 1837 addressed to her at Keston Heath, Bromley, Kent. (MT Coll. 27/92.) Moreover, Carlyle himself, writing to Mill in the spring of 1838, said, "I pray you say for me, at Keston, all that is grateful and obliging; consider also how much there may be of regretful, in which, however, it is needless to indulge." (Alexander Carlyle, p. 165.) He was clearly refusing an invitation. Also, Harriet when writing to Mill about the *Autobiography* in February 1854 referred to their "lives at Kes—n and Wal—n" (Hayek, p. 196), although, as the word is not clear in MS., Professor Hayek assumed it to be Kis—n. Keston Heath would explain the references to the Common in the letters: neither Kingston nor Walton is near a Common. It would also explain Harriet's proposal to visit Lizzie and Sallie when they were at Sevenoaks (Hayek, p. 95), for Keston is quite close to Sevenoaks, while Kingston is over twice as far away.

as I desire to be—heart and soul take their rest in the peace of ample satisfaction after how much [illeg.] and care which of that kind has passed for ever. O this sureness of an everlasting spiritual home is itself the blessedness of the blessed, and to that being added . . . this exquisiteness which is and has been each instant since, and seems as if with no fresh food it would be enough for a long life's enjoyment."[46]

With everything thus agreeably concluded, it seemed that little remained to be done, but Mill was not quite satisfied. He was immeasurably conscious of his debt to Harriet, and also immeasurably proud of her beauty and attainments. Like anyone who has caught a goddess on the wing, he wished to show her to his friends, to witness her amusement and their envy. In the dark days of crisis, Fox had devised a Saturday scheme, whereby he and the Flower girls and Harriet and Mill used to meet occasionally to dissipate their worries by a half-day's chatter. Mill had been glad enough of that, at the time, for her sake more than his: she had "more frivolity" than he, and loved good company. Those bad days were gone: there was no reason now why they could not enter brighter halls, talk with the wits and beauties in salons calm and dillettante, instead of moving in the shadows. Now that John Taylor was party to the whole, no harm could come of it. They started going out together. As was frequently his fault, Mill overrated people: he entirely failed to sense the flood of scandal that opened at their approach and closed, frothing and gurgling, in their wake.

It was at Mrs. Buller's soirée the disaster happened. Most of the guests were already assembled, and stood talking, or swooped across to greet each other beneath the myriad diamonds glinting in the chandeliers, when the voice of the footman barked above the murmur, and John Mill stood in the spacious doorway with Harriet Taylor on his arm. There was a pause. She was blushing a little, and he over-attentive. It was true, then. Here and there a fan fluttered or a white glove flicked, and a half-audible titter ran swiftly round the room. Then good breeding intervened: their hostess galloped forward, the talk resumed, and that was all.

Roebuck, who was present, had long ago lived down the quarrel about Byron and Wordsworth. He was Member for Bath in the Reformed Parliament, and when a proposal for female suffrage was greeted in the House with ribald cheers, it was to him that Harriet appealed. Mill's letters spoke of him as one of the most promising of the Radicals. His *Pamphlets for the People*, published at three-halfpence, had done much to publicize their principles. And it was, Mill said, to his perpetual credit that he had put forward at this early date a suggestion for free national education. Their relations were as warm again as ever they had been, and Roebuck no doubt earnestly wished his friend would stick to his Wordsworth and let Byron go hang, for he made but a wan Don Juan:

> "My affection for Mill was so warm and so sincere that I was hurt by anything which brought ridicule upon him. I saw, or thought I saw, how mischievous might be this affair, and as we had become in all things like brothers, I determined, most unwisely, to speak to him on the subject.
>
> With this resolution I went to the India House next day, and then frankly told him what I thought might result from his connection with Mrs. Taylor. He received my warnings coldly, and after some time I took my leave, little thinking what effect my remonstrances had produced.
>
> The next day I again called at the India House, not with any intention of renewing the subject, but in accordance with a long-formed habit of constantly seeing and conversing with Mill. The moment I entered the room I saw that, as far as he was concerned, our friendship was at an end. His manner was not merely cold, but repulsive; and I, seeing how matters were, left him. His part of our friendship was rooted out, nay, destroyed, but mine was left untouched. . . ."[47]

Mill was possessed by a dry, icy fever: he could not imagine, while there was breath in his body, that an insult should drift in the air around her head. It reawakened all his old desire to cast loose from the world and escape with her for ever. Even though, he sadly reminded Harriet, two famous cases of women who had run off with their lovers had recently gone to show that such measures never prosper, he was prepared to face the risk, and should not care, if he became obscure and insignificant.* She hastened once more to defend her compromise:

* One of these cases may well have been that of George Sand and Alfred de Musset, who had set out for Italy at the end of 1833, only to have their alliance founder and break up within a year.

Both Harriet and Mill had a great respect for George Sand. In 1841 he wrote to G. H. Lewes, "I return Sand's letter which it was very pleasant to have an opportunity of reading. I have no right or claim to send any message to her but I should be willing she should know that there are other warm admirers of her writings and of herself even in this canting land—among whom I am neither the only nor the best." (*George Lewes and George Eliot*, A. T. Kitchel, 1933, p. 38.) Afterwards Mill sent her a copy of his *Political Economy* (Bain, p. 155). All this does much to dispose of C. E. Norton's unfounded notion that Mill disapproved of George Eliot (see *The Letters of C. E. Norton*, ed. Sarah Norton, 1913, vol. I, p. 499).

"I should without hesitation say 'let it be'. . . . I do not hesitate about the certainty of happiness, but I do hesitate about the rightfulness of, for my own pleasure, giving up *my* only earthly opportunity of 'usefulness'. *You* hesitate about your usefulness and that however greater in amount it may be, is certainly not like mine *marked out* as duty. I should spoil four lives and injure others. This is the only hesitation. When I am in health and spirits I see the possibilities of getting over this hesitation—when I am low and ill I see the improbabilities. Now I give pleasure around me, I make no one unhappy, and I am happy tho' not happiest myself. I think any systematic middle plan between this and all is impracticable. . . ."[48]

Next morning, seeing the danger to be mortal, she panicked into a gust of anger:

"Good heaven have you at last arrived at fearing to be '*obscure and insignificant*' What *can* I say to that but 'by all means pursue your brilliant and important career'. Am *I* one to choose to be the cause that the person I love feels himself reduced to 'obscure and insignificant'! Good God what has the love of two equals to do with making obscure and insignificant. If ever you *could* be obscure and insignificant you *are* so whatever happens and certainly . . . not one to brave the world. I never before (for years) knew you to have a mesquin feeling. . . . There seems to be a touch of Common Place vanity in that dread of being obscure and insignificant—you never will be that—still more surely *I* am not a person who in any event could give you cause to feel that *I* had made you so. Whatever you think I could never be either of those words."[49]

But the wound had gone too deep; it had reached the heart, and her lover could not be startled back even by those rare slaps of temper. From now on, he began progressively withdrawing from the world; and little by little his impenetrable reserve, like an unhealthy vapour rising from the ground, swirled up around them and concealed them in its cold embrace.

BOOK THREE

“A VERRA FOOLISH PIECE O' FRIENDLINESS”

1831–1835
aet. 25–28

HARRIET TAYLOR (*née* HARDY)

from a miniature in the British Library of Political and Economic Science.

JOHN STUART MILL

from a cameo, *c.* 1840, aet. 34.

I

"IT is a work of genius, dear",[1] sighed Jane Carlyle one day in 1831: the Man of Destiny growled ungratefully, stuffed into his pocket the biography of his first thirty-five years of life, and stumped out of the house. He was not always easy to live with. He was haunted, without any doubt at all, by the genius of depiction. And although the course it took with him was principally dramatic, that is only symptomatic of the poetic tendency in its most violent form: the last and strongest manifestation of the creative drive, before it bursts out from the mental into the physical forms of expression.

The pressure of this force within him was so great that its inevitable companion-spirit of frustration was also more pronounced in him than is usually the case, and he was subject, not indeed to an inferiority complex, but to a sense of inadequacy, an inability properly to give vent to his superiority. Thus he was first and foremost naturally splenetic, disposed to batter and abuse the words which were his tools of craftsmanship, gashing and hewing with them furiously, and never considering how, by a more disciplined use of them, he might give to the expression of his mind a more effective polish and coherence. Convinced that in his case the puny vehicle of language could never carry his titanic meaning, yet having at hand no other medium, he was half inarticulate and always rampant. And, which was more disastrous still, he was so oppressed by the enormous chaos of feeling already elbowing and shouting for release inside him, that he was incapable of intellectual study, incapable of absorbing any knowledge except as food for his immediate purpose, or of accepting the experience of others as a modification of his own, for fear of overcrowding his frantic brain and adding to the confusion it contained.

It would not be right to look to the circumstances of his early years as a cause of these eccentricities, for they were congenital. Indeed, no man ever changed less during the course of a life of eighty years than did Thomas Carlyle; he lived and died as he was born, and his character, being purely original, gave the lie more heartily to the associationist theory of psychology, which he detested, than anything he ever wrote against it. It is even questionable whether he learnt anything from experience at all. His philosophy, meaning in his case not a system of mind communicable to other people, but rather a comforting justification for his feeling as he did, was in all essentials complete by the time he reached maturity; and the half century remaining to him he could devote to re-emphasizing in parables of increasing violence, under the guise of history, what he had already said in other parables. His mentality was not progressive, and the whole of what he had to say was included fully and often several times over in any one of his major works. His Teufelsdrockh, who was himself, he pictured as being discovered, never born; or, to use another of his allegories, new life flies up fully feathered like the phoenix from the ashes of the old, and greatness emerges fully fashioned from the womb of destiny. Not, therefore, a growing and becoming, but a having and a holding was the essence of culture as Carlyle conceived it. Finality thus easily acquired made for concentration, and gave him an enormous force of personality: it also saved him from a great deal of cerebral agitation, and left him free to exploit his fancy, which was as luxurious as his reasoning was meagre.

Although his circumstances cannot be said to have determined his nature, none the less, they contributed largely to it. Born, like James Mill twenty years before him, of Scottish cottagers; and dedicated to learning as a pitiful, cherished mite of talent earned by some miracle of human endurance upon the fruitless moors: thrown upon the waters of society, so to speak, like a bottle with a message full of challenge and of mystery, he knew both the responsibility of his mission and the lessons of the edge of poverty. For both Carlyle and James Mill, there being no place in Scotland, and being too good for the galleys of emigration, there remained only to follow the caravan of ability to the south, the scornful decision not "to kick against the pricks, but smite where it is softer"; the comradeship of knowing, as only a gutter-cat can know, how to work, how to make a way, and how never to reveal its secret.

Like James Mill, Carlyle set off gallantly; and yet he did not turn his back upon his origins. What for James Mill was a private shame to be lived down and forgotten as he raised himself above it, was for Carlyle a grievance to be flung in the teeth of society, a bitter jest of which his own genius was the salt. Instead of helping his parents furtively, he acknowledged them: instead of abandoning his dialect as fast as possible, he wallowed in Scotticisms: instead of smoothing his hair and taming his neck to the convention of stiff white starch, he stuck to rough worsted and a pagan hairdress.

Except for that, their early histories were like enough to make Carlyle admire the older man. "I will tell you what", he remarked in his old age to one who was questioning him about John Mill, "his father, James Mill, a great, big, burly fellow whom I used to see at the India House, was essentially by far the greater man of the two." James Mill, in fact, was not above five foot eight, but for Carlyle size was the first requirement of the hero.

Next to poverty, the thing they had most in common was their puritan upbringing, and of this they each bore the scar throughout their lives. Each had an inveterate hatred of luxury and idleness, each thought frivolity a deadly sin: with each the favourite indulgence was thrift or mortification in one form or another; each could be genial when it suited him, or snap up advantage from acquaintanceship as if it were a providential stepping-stone. Above all, their common heritage was most plainly marked in what passed with them for humour. "Laughter", Carlyle once observed, "is the cipher-key of the whole man", and so perhaps it is. Sheer volume of sound apart, there was no difference either in quality or in cruelty between the thunderous mockery of Carlyle and the icy sarcasm of James Mill.

At this point the comparison breaks down. James Mill, with his intellect once stirred, threw puritanism to the winds and cleared himself as fast as possible of all except the least eradicable traces; while Carlyle, the more imaginative of the two, never escaped from the sternest and strongest of its bugbears. That, in part, was because of the more intensely pietistic treatment he had been subjected to. When his time came to go to the University to study for the ministry, his devout old mother, who was no scholar, taught herself to write, especially in order to be able to counteract by her letters the awful doubts and questionings that would confront him in unsponsored libraries and enlightened lecture rooms. For the time, all her best efforts were in vain and her worst fears fulfilled: her son Thomas was no match for the readings of Voltaire and the *Philosophes*, of Hartley and Hume, or for the teaching of their spiritual executors who composed the most brilliant faculty in the British Isles. There was no room here for half-measures or for contradictions. One by one his cherished preconceptions, held fondly until now from familiarity rather than conviction, were hauled up and remorselessly examined, reduced to vacancy, cashiered into absurdity, and torn away from him. Before long he was stripped quite naked; driven out, as he later put it, into "the howling deserts of infidelity".

He gave up all idea of the ministry. For a time he wandered helplessly, until his svelte and clever fellow townsman Edward Irving offered him a job as schoolmaster at the school which he had founded. As soon as Carlyle had saved a meagre pittance, he turned to the law as the only other learned profession open to him, and went back to Edinburgh to take his course. This too was a failure, and at the age of twenty-five he was in black despair. He was devoid of all belief: there seemed no object for him in life and no hope in death, no place in the world where he could fit. He was living in dingy lodgings and paying the rent from what he earned by casual tutoring. As a result of undernourishment and spiritual dissatisfaction he was crippled by dyspepsia; outside, a thick industrial smoke hung oppressively over the streets of "Auld Reekie", where discontent lurked dumbly, and cordons of troops tramped past in silent menace. Once, as a solace for his loneliness, he fell in love, only to see the girl packed off by her parents to marry a rich Englishman, without evident dissatisfaction on her part. To complete his discomfort, she wrote to him afterwards saying that no doubt he was a genius, but advising him with all good will that he would get on better if he would improve his manners.

In this state of despondency, he was as much exposed as was John Mill in 1826 to an onslaught of Accidie. Sure enough, the fiend soon leapt upon him; not indeed in the sunless depths of winter, but as he was going out of Edinburgh along Leith Walk to bathe away the exhaustion caused by three weeks' sleeplessness and the sultry summer sun. With due allowance for their differences of temperament and language, there is a marked resemblance in the course of the attack as he described it:

"To me the Universe was all void of Life, of Purpose, of Volition, even of Hostility: it was one huge, dead, immeasurable Steam-engine,

> rolling on, in its dread indifference, to grind me limb from limb. O the vast, gloomy, solitary Golgotha, and Mill of Death! Why was the Living banished thither companionless, conscious? Why if there is no Devil; nay, unless the Devil is your God?"[2]

But the reactions of the two men to the same gloomy doubts were very different. Where John Mill suffered all winter long, analysing his distress in lonely melancholy, Carlyle lashed out immediately, puffing up his own spirit to an overwhelming act of assertion and defiance. Where Mill blamed some inadequacy in himself, some incompleteness in his nature, Carlyle blamed influences beyond his own control, his philosophical teachers and the French sceptics who had broken down his faith. Mill's sorrow was his lack of feeling: Carlyle's grievance was the theft of his belief. Mill abandoned analysis and self-consciousness as prejudicial to the pursuit of happiness: Carlyle set up one part of himself as a permanent watchdog over his own fidelity. Mill looked forward to completing the gap in his equipment: Carlyle sought only to restore what he had been before, and to buttress it against further inroads with sandbags full of extra affirmations.

Thus, Mill looked forward cheerfully to continual self-improvement, saw duty as a royal road to happiness, and became sympathetic, tolerant and humane. But Carlyle, instead of unravelling the problem, cut through the knot of it, setting adrift his doubts and binding himself fast to the rigid masthead of belief. The loosening play of speculation became for him a deadly evil, and his critical faculties, deliberately stunted and deformed, sank away through atrophy into acquiescence. His constant preoccupation with the exclusion of opinions not agreeable to his own made him defiant, suspicious and eventually cruel. The necessity of his own rightness inverted his judgement, so that he magnified in others the shortcomings most obvious in himself, and at the same time despised the qualities he lacked with as much violence as he worshipped those he thought that he possessed. Praising tyranny, he became himself a tyrant, and like a tyrant could love only what was incapable of challenging him. For this reason, his highest sympathy was pity, and his pity was as invariably interwoven with condescension as his merriment was shot through with scorn.

Yet in transactions of this kind the Devil does not exact his payment till the end: in the beginning the wretched client is confirmed in his bargain by the relief of quick returns. So it was with Carlyle:

his judgement being suspended, the world became clothed in bright colours of belief or disbelief, and everything was simple.

His first decision was that he would marry Jane Baillie Welsh, a pretty, spirited girl of twenty-one with a faculty for writing, who had been introduced to him because she was interested in authors, by Edward Irving with whom she was in love. The only daughter of an ancient presbyterian house, she was, at least by Carlyle's standards, something of an heiress. Her father was dead, but her mother took an immediate dislike to Carlyle for his boorishness and his domineering manner. Jane herself demurred, but resistance was useless; from the very start the matter was a question not of why she should marry him, but of her reasons for not doing so. These, of which there were originally several, melted away in the most appalling manner before his patience and incredible persistence.

First, Irving married someone else. Next, again by Irving's intervention, Carlyle got the job of private tutor to the sons of Mr. and Mrs. Buller. This in a worldly way was of great value to him: his health improved with his diet, his appearance grew less uncouth, and from continual contact with the world of culture he even learnt to practise the first elements of social courtesy. When after two years his eldest pupil, Charles, was sent to Cambridge, Carlyle emerged with a greatly elevated *ton* and savings sufficient to give him temporary independence. As Jane had stipulated that he must become a real and established writer, he at once took lodgings in London and set about becoming one.

Having complied with her conditions, he was soon able to demand once more the favour which had become in the interval, mysteriously, his right. Direct refusal was a waste of breath. So strong was his position now, that he even began to question whether she was fit to be his wife, or whether, deceived by the easiness of her previous life and her ambition to be wedded to fame and fortune, she had overlooked the years of drudgery and rejection that not only would but ought to lie before them. As a proof of earnestness, she signed over all her fortune to her mother, and she also made a will bequeathing it to Carlyle on her mother's death. There was now no turning back. He went in to claim his prize, and she succumbed:

> "I am going to be a very meek-tempered wife. Indeed, I am begun to be meek-tempered already. My aunt tells me she could live for ever with me without quarrelling, I am so reasonable and equable in my humour."[3]

A little dagger of wit, a bantering irony, was all that she managed to save from her total defeat.

During the five years it took him to accomplish this first *tour de force*, Carlyle was busy working out his creed. At the time of his conversion in Leith Walk he had done no more than cast out his agony of doubt by determining, as a general attitude, to believe without cause shown. This, though it formed nine-tenths of his philosophy, was not enough. It remained to settle which of the multitudinous articles of faith available to man best suited his purpose as a solvent for his apocalyptic genius. France, he genuinely felt, as an entity had betrayed him, taken away his faith. He therefore turned to Germany, which shared with him Cassandra's fate of not being understood.

The English do not take easily to the philosophies of other peoples, and at the time of Carlyle's conversion little was known about the Germans. James Mill had heard of Kant, and said vaguely that he knew "what the man would be at". Coleridge had been there, and had left half his spirit to share their dreamy trail of cloud and mystery. Sarah Austin, who knew the language, was busily translating their works for whatever they would fetch. But that was almost all. The Germans were thought of as a small and struggling people, who under energetic leadership in the previous century had just gained what is now called self-determination, only to be slapped down again by Bonaparte, from which reverse they were once more emerging gamely.

Into this untouched granary of new ideas Carlyle plunged like a marauding pigeon. For the metaphysics he had little use, finding them sawdustish and too abstruse for his colourful imagination, and suspecting them of being contaminated by the deadly sin of speculation. But among their conclusions he pecked eagerly and at large, and found in them much that he desired to hear.

The whole object of the universe, he learned, is for the divine purpose to obtain expression in material form. This it does by splitting fragments off itself and lodging them in created mechanisms. So long as the fragments, or Beings, can maintain a free intuitive contact with each other and with the parent force, the whole natural order will roll along smoothly to its transcendent goal. But should the mechanisms, or minds wherein the fragments dwell, exceed their proper function of applying the inscrutable precepts to the material world, and try to find the precepts for themselves, disorder will prevail. The precious link to the infinite will be cut off, the divine plan will be disrupted, chaos and discord will ensue. Then, the immutable Purpose will resort to extraordinary means in order to restore the balance. A man will appear, furnished with a larger Being than the rest. His instructions will be clearer, fuller; and his will more dominant. It will be his mission to lead mankind back to proper harmony with the infinite, either by prophecy and exhortation, or, if that is not enough, by force.

The whole of this process, the faithful toil, the fall from grace, the arrival of the Hero, and the restoration of order, is history. It is cyclic and repetitive, not progressive. Except in relation to the cycle, there is no such thing as progress upon earth. If there is progress, it is not human but divine, and it is as ineluctable as the passage of the universe through space. Like the nature of the Godhead, the nature of the Hero, and the nature of man, it is a sacred mystery.

It is therefore incumbent upon every individual man, not to cultivate his Being, which is perfect as it is, but to keep clear the means of its activity, by subduing the mutinous lusts of his physical organism and avoiding the treacherous blandishments of reason: to be convinced that the task nearest to his hand was laid out, together with its requisite tools, as the purpose of his existence; and that it will bear its own reward, if not to him in this world, then to the order of things in general. Above all it is the duty of man to look out for the advent of the Hero, and if possible to spot him when he comes: this admittedly may be a matter of some difficulty, as his only credential is success. But at all events he is to be assisted as soon as recognized, and loyally supported in the execution of his special mission.

This philosophy greatly pleased Carlyle. It fitted neatly with certain aspects of Calvinism which, for the sake of his mother, he could never quite renounce. Bred to a sense of guilt, no enjoyment seemed honest to him unless it contained a greater part of suffering; and if he sought relief, it was not because he was drawn to it by pleasure, but because he was driven to it by pain. So he readily believed in the Eternal Taskmaster always at his elbow; a revengeful God always ready to strike him down, or on the other hand to give signs of his approval by material success. Add to this, that the present times were out of joint, that he knew himself as the bearer of tidings for their remedy, and it is easy to see what this poor fellow would be at.

He went to work to write about the Germans. Irving, who had

already found him his wife-to-be and his position with the Bullers, performed one further service before lapsing into frenzy. He gave Carlyle an introduction to the *London Magazine*, whose editors undertook to pay him sixteen guineas a sheet for a series of sketches of men of genius, of whom Schiller was to be the first. This was published in 1825 and earned Carlyle £100, but the series was discontinued on his return to Scotland. His greatest Hero of them all was Goethe, a strange choice, for although undoubtedly a poet of universal brilliance, he subscribed nothing to the transcendental philosophies surrounding him, and lived out a long life of philandering without making any pronouncements that were properly heroic, beyond the peripatetic observations of his Faust. Perhaps it was because in an age of materialism and unrest Goethe refused rationalism; or because he exchanged civilities with Bonaparte, an unquestionable Hero, who exclaimed of him, "There is a Man"; for masculinity as an attribute was so excessively important to Carlyle that it has led to a great deal of inconclusive argument about his own virility. In any case, he translated Goethe's *Wilhelm Meister*, and sent the author a copy which was gracefully acknowledged, and a correspondence was begun. When he left London and returned to Jane, the master sent him an autographed copy of his poems as a wedding present.

Part of Jane Carlyle's inheritance was a remote farm called Craigenputtock, and it was there that Carlyle intended they should make their home. He had, while in London, been distressed at the prevalence of hack-writing, of penny-a-liners who would sing any tune for their bread and butter, and whom he felt were mere prostitutes of the genuine mission of literature. On the distant farm it was his proposal to devote himself to serious writing, and at the same time to scrape a living from the soil: in this way he would both do the duty that lay nearest to him, and also prepare himself in the wilderness for his vocation as a prophet. This proposal Jane refused, on the ground that life would be too lonely; that Carlyle had no propensity for farming, and that he must, if he was to be a writer, be content at first to write for his living. She suggested instead that they should share a house with her mother. So for a time a compromise was struck, and they went to live in Edinburgh. Jane, who had her own ideas of how to make her husband a success, soon attracted the attention of Jeffrey, who was still the editor of the *Edinburgh Review*. He spotted talent in Carlyle's fumings, and saw his way to starting a new line of mysticism in the magazine, but after a few articles it became plain that public interest was slight. Carlyle's earnings, depleted by continual allocations to assist his brothers, were quite inadequate for city life, and by 1828 there was nothing for it but to retire, after all, to the wilds of Craigenputtock.

The house was "gaunt and hungry-looking": the landscape "unredeemed either by grace or grandeur, mere undulating hills of grass and heather, with peat bogs in the hollows between them".[4] At an elevation of 700 feet above the sea, mostly there was a raging gale, so that any trees with the hardihood to live were bowed penitently to one side. In the rare intervals between the storms, it was so still, Jane said, that one could hear the sheep munching quarter-of-a-mile away. Here Jane tried to keep house on a budget insufficient even for a well-trained Scotswoman. Her only assistant was a silent "Scotch Brownie" of a servant: the nearest cottage was more than a mile away. She had no children, and, apart from occasional shooting parties wandering on the moors, who looked in unbidden as if to a settlement in the middle of a desert, no visitors. Their only contact with the outside world was the weekly carrier, who on Wednesdays brought up their mail and groceries and other requirements from the market in Dumfries. The urbane Jeffrey was shocked at her condition: he remonstrated vainly with Carlyle, tried to secure his appointment as his successor on the *Edinburgh*, and to find a niche for him somewhere in the Civil Service—anything to improve his finances and bring them back to civilization. He even tried to give him an annuity of £100. But the man of destiny stood firm.

For his own part, Carlyle was satisfied enough. The very wildness, representing the dark primordial tumult that was raging in him, was an exhilaration; while solitude was the perfect condition for him to hear the still small genius of his intuition. He never ceased to extol the benefits of quiet. "Beware of speaking", he recorded in his notebook. "Speech is human, silence is divine." It was, however, a one-sided injunction, for one of the best judges in London, when asked about the greatest talkers of the day, replied without hesitation: "Carlyle first, and all the rest nowhere." As Jane wrote to his mother, "it is my husband's worst fault to me that I will not or cannot speak. Often when he has talked for an hour without answer, he will beg for some signs of life on my part, and the only sign I can give is a little kiss."[5] As for her, she had no grounds to make complaint. Had he not warned her forcefully enough that the soft sociability of her easy life had quite unfitted her for the rough paths of exile she would have to share with him?

For gardening, the climate was against him; nothing but docks seemed to flourish in those wind-tossed latitudes, and his interest turned more and more to literature. He desired to write a book, a major work, and to be done with piece-meal scribbling for a living. In this frame of mind he composed *Sartor Resartus* and, on its completion, the economic situation being compulsive, he stuffed the "work of genius" into his pocket, borrowed fifty pounds of journey money and an introduction to John Murray from Jeffrey, and set out for London to get it published.

II

It was not to be so easy. *Sartor Resartus* (The Tailor Retailored) was not the sort of contribution any publisher would want to take from any tyro author. It was absolutely without form, devoid of coherent exposition, and couched in a quite unprecedented jargon. It consisted of three parts, loosely strung together by unintelligible narrative. The first was an animadversion about clothes, gleaned from Swift's *Tale of a Tub*, and expanded into an article for a London review which had declined to take it. Next came a garbled autobiographical sketch up to the time of the author's conversion to mysticism in Leith Walk. And lastly a series of comments about things in general, seen from the angle of one vehemently influenced by German Calvinism. Originality it had beyond dispute; it created, as did all Carlyle's productions, an atmosphere of mystery and anticipation never quite fulfilled; and for those who screened it patiently it contained nuggets of rare insight and poetic vigour. But the prodigal distribution of capital letters, of italics, hyphens, dots and dashes, marks of exclamation and interrogation, was of itself enough to make any typesetter goggle helplessly. Murray's, who did not wish to offend the influential Jeffrey, shilly-shallied;

Longman's, who had it next, looked into it and blanched. After two years' hawking, *Fraser's Magazine* at last undertook to print it, and it came out as a serial, in small doses, over a period of ten months. Its appearance was greeted with indignation in some quarters and bewilderment in others. *The Sun*, a newspaper for which Mill occasionally wrote, called it "a heap of clotted nonsense". The *North American Reviewer*, whose tendency was to take its English literature seriously, cautiously observed: "After a careful survey of the whole ground, our belief is that no such persons as Professor Teufelsdrockh or Counsellor Heuschrecke ever existed."

Carlyle, who had hoped to get £200 for it, was disappointed but not cast down by his reverse; it was after all no more than an example of the disdain he had long predicted. He resolved to stay in London and see what contacts he could make which might in the future bring grist to his mill. In this connection there was one acquaintanceship he greatly wished to make. The main point of his philosophy of clothes was that the vestments of society, the Church, State, Aristocracy, and Body of Learning, were all worn out and rotten, and no longer bore resemblance to the pure ideals of which they were the outward manifestations. This being so, they were inexorably condemned by the order of things to sudden convulsion and wholesale overthrow, and would emerge reformed, renewed, once more aligned to the eternal purpose. While compiling this thesis, he had chanced to read, in the *Examiner*, a series of articles called "The Spirit of the Age" by an unknown hand, repeating in more reasoned language all his own notions of corruption and revolution, of the cyclic nature of history, and of the approach of the Saint-Simonian Golden Age. He not unnaturally concluded that there was another mystic abroad in England, and on enquiring about the articles on his arrival in London was surprised to hear they had been written by John Mill. He had heard of Mill as a Utilitarian and Radical, and had in fact berated him generously at intervals in *Sartor*, along with his father, in a series of identifiable puns:

> "Shall your Science proceed in the small chink-lighted, or even oil-lighted, underground workshop of Logic alone; and man's mind become an Arithmetical Mill, whereof Memory is the Hopper, and mere tables of Sines and Tangents, Codification, and Treatises of what you call Political Economy, are the Meal?"[6]

All this was now forgotten in the glorious news of Mill's conversion.

Charles Buller, who had a great affection for his old tutor, and as a Radical was a close intimate of Mill, was for the moment out of town. So it was left to Sarah Austin to effect the introduction; this she was well qualified to do, being at the heart of radical society and at the same time a keen student of German literature. Almost at once she gave a tea-party. Carlyle described it to his wife:

"Then off to the Austins, where I knew there would be green tea, which I had privately determined not to have. The Frau Austin herself was as loving as ever—a true Germanized spiritual *screamikin.* We were five of a party: her husband, a lean grey-headed painful-looking man, with large earnest timid eyes and a clanging metallic voice, that at great length set forth Utilitarianism *steeped* in German metaphysics not dissolved therein; a very worthy sort of limited man and professor of law. Secondly, a Frenchman, of no importance whatever, for he uttered not a word except some compliments in his own tongue. Thirdly, John Mill, 'Spirit-of-the-Age'. . . . This young Mill, I fancy and hope, is 'a *baying* you can love'. A slender, rather tall and elegant youth. . . . We had almost four hours of the best talk I have mingled in for long. The youth walked home with me almost to the door; seemed to profess, almost as plainly as modesty would allow, that he had been converted by the head of the Mystic School, to whom personally he testified very hearty-looking regard."[7]

Mill wrote to Sterling:

"Another acquaintance which I have recently made is that of Mr. Carlyle, whom I believe you are also acquainted with. I have long had a very keen relish for his articles in the *Edinburgh* and *Foreign Reviews,* which I formerly thought to be such consummate nonsense; and I think he improves upon a nearer acquaintance. He does not seem to me so entirely the reflection or shadow of the great German writers as I was inclined to consider him; although undoubtedly his mind has derived from their inspiration whatever breath of life there is in it. He seems to me as a man who has had his eyes unsealed. . . . He has by far the widest liberality and tolerance that I have met with in any one; and he differs from most men, who see as much as he does into the defects of the age, by a circumstance greatly to his advantage in my estimation, that he looks for a safe landing *before* and not *behind.* . . . He is a great hunter-out of acquaintances; he hunted me out, or rather hunted out the author of certain papers in the Examiner (the first, as he said, which he had ever seen in a newspaper, hinting that the age was not the best of all possible ages): and his acquaintance is the only substantial good I have yet derived from writing those papers, and a much greater one than I expected when I wrote them. He has also, through me, sought the acquaintance of Fonblanque (of the Examiner). . . ."[8]

Ten days later, they renewed their conversation. "Tuesday night John Mill came in and sate talking with me till near eleven—a fine clear enthusiast, who will one day come to something; yet to nothing poetical, I think: his fancy is not rich; furthermore, he cannot *laugh* with any compass. You will like Mill."[9] To prove it, Carlyle made haste to invite Mill round, on 6 October 1831, to meet Jane, who had just arrived from Scotland to join him for the winter in his lodgings at 4 Ampton Street.

Charles Buller was highly satisfied at the speed of their concordance: satisfied and not a little surprised. He had looked forward to their meeting with some apprehension, thinking perhaps that he could not imagine any two men whose temperaments and purposes were less alike. John Mill, at the height of his expansive phase, would take to anyone: Carlyle was not so much to be relied on. This, for example, is how he described another of his new acquaintances: "Heigh ho! Charles Lamb I sincerely believe to be in some considerable degree insane. A more pitiful, rickety, gasping, staggering, stammering Tomfool I do not know. He is witty by denying truisms and abjuring good manners. His speech wriggles hither and thither with an incessant painful fluctuation . . . Besides, he is now a confirmed, shameless drunkard; *asks* vehemently for gin and water in stranger's houses, tipples till he is utterly mad . . . "[10] But then, Mill was a better listener than Lamb, who had not in any degree the golden virtue of silence. Buller hastened to take things as he found them and, on his return to London, joined the group, making along with Mill what Jane described as "a pleasant forenoon call of seven hours and a half". Meanwhile, Mill had been able to do his new friend an invaluable service in his search for literary sponsors, by introducing him to Henry Taylor and his circle, the orbit of Wordsworth, Southey, and other luminaries.

There is some evidence that the Carlyles now intended to make their home in London, and were looking for a house,[11] but the death of Carlyle's father put an end to this and on 14 April 1832 they returned to Craigenputtock, whence Carlyle opened a correspondence with Mill which was to continue uninterrupted until their next meeting two years later. Carlyle was sure of Mill. The young man of twenty-five, eleven years his junior, was, he was certain, more than half way to mysticism. Mill was, without a doubt, in that same Centre of Indifference Carlyle himself had reached after his first conversion, and before his final revelation of the path that he must tread. Another few years would make all the difference. The factor he could not know about, of course, was Harriet Taylor. It was quite true that, at the time of their first meeting, Mill's mind was fully opened, inviting and receptive of whatever intellectual seed might blow upon it. It was not Carlyle's fault he did not know that he had been forestalled, and that his potent but belated sowing went ineffectively to waste. He could probably not have realized it had he known. The first physical requirement of a prophet is a disciple to do his bidding, and one so gifted as John Mill, one moreover so well placed in the literary world, was irresistibly attractive. There was a kind of compulsion about it: to Carlyle it was just as obvious that Mill was his disciple, as it had formerly been obvious that Jane would be his wife. Like Jane, Mill found himself, simply through the passage of time, mysteriously in guilt: like Jane, he had to make many material payments to ease his debt: but unlike Jane he never did surrender.

At first they started frankly, man to man. "You I look upon as an artist, and perhaps the only genuine one now living in this country"[12] Mill baldly wrote, and Carlyle replied by insisting that he come to Craigenputtock in order that they might become better acquainted in the silence of the moors. The demand was reiterated in subsequent letters until Mill, who was forced by another adventure closer to his heart to remain evasive about his future plans, found himself specifically pinned down to spend his next vacation there in August 1833. In March of that year he began to feel uneasy lest he should somehow be to blame for giving Carlyle a false idea of his adhesion, but all his attempts to open the subject were briskly brushed aside, and by the autumn two events had occurred to bring matters to a head. First, the decision that he would go to Paris with Harriet instead of visiting his expectant friend put him more than ever in the wrong. Secondly, Ralph Waldo Emerson, then on his first visit to Europe, had been sent to Mill by Gustave d'Eichthal, for an introduction to Carlyle, whom he especially wished to meet. Emerson duly arrived at Craigenputtock just as the Carlyles were finishing Sunday dinner. He was very impressionable, and an excellent listener. Moreover, he willingly undertook the agency of Carlyle's works in America, promising not only to see them properly published and not pirated, but also to remit prompt payment of the proceeds; and this he later accomplished so successfully that the first American edition of the *French Revolution* was sold out, and the payment of £50 for it received by Carlyle, before he had had a penny from his English publishers. Emerson therefore made a favourable impression on the prophet, and Mill, who had not found him "a very hopeful subject", was astounded to hear him described as "a most gentle, recommendable, amiable, whole-hearted man". He concluded that Carlyle was a far more broad-minded fellow than he ever had supposed, and regretted bitterly that he had not avoided the whole tiresome confusion by letting him meet Harriet in the first place. "If I had known you as well when you were in London as I do now, how many more persons should I have brought to see you! I now know that *any* human being is interesting to you. Since you were so much pleased with Emerson, I feel encouraged to try you with almost any person who has any sort of good in him."

It was too late for that, but it led Mill, on his return from Paris, to make a full confession of his sin in allowing Carlyle to mistake him for a disciple. He explained how, when they first met in London, he was "in a state of reaction from logical-utilitarian narrowness of the very narrowest kind", and had emerged into its direct opposite: in this condition, he had become "catholic and tolerant in an extreme degree, and thought one-sidedness almost the one great evil in human affairs, seeing it was the evil which had been the bane of my own teachers, and was also that of those who were warring against my teachers. I never indeed was tolerant of aught but earnest belief; but I saw, or seemed to see, so much of good and of truth in the positive part of the most opposite opinions and practices . . . that I scarcely felt myself called upon to *deny* anything but denial itself. I never made strongly prominent my differences with any sincere, truth-loving person. . . . I never, or rarely, felt myself called upon to come into *collision* with any one, except those to whom I felt myself altogether superior, and with whom, if I had any intellectual communion, it was not for the sake of *learning* but of *teaching*."[13] Recently he had come to see that this attitude was not really honest, and had done much, at least negatively, to give Carlyle and others a false opinion of him. "Whether if you knew me thoroughly I should stand higher, or lower, either in your esteem or in your affection, I know not, in some things you seem to think me *further* from you than I am, in others perhaps I am further from you than you know. On the whole I think if all were told I should stand lower. . . ."

As for their immediate differences, he continued, the first and most important was that, try as he would, he could not aspire to Carlyle's firm, unquestioning belief in God: for him there could be no more than a merely probable God, which to Carlyle must appear the same thing as, or even worse than, no God at all. Secondly, he was still, and was likely to remain, a Utilitarian, though not one of "the people called Utilitarians", who indulged in good works and soup-kitchen benevolence. While recognizing with Carlyle "the infinite nature of Duty", and the responsibility laid upon each individual to do with his utmost strength the task for which his faculties were best suited, he could not believe in the performance of duty as an end in itself, but only as a means to advancing the "good of the species" upon which conception Carlyle poured such unmitigated scorn.

These painful confidences moved Carlyle to great depths of parental indulgence. The poor good boy! His honest, innocent, self-examination was so like him, and so lovable. "At several of your revelations, and computings whether you would stand lower with me or higher (but you rather thought lower), a smile came over me, in which lay a greater kindness than it were good to put in words." All that was really wrong with Mill, he said, was that he was as yet consciously nothing of a Mystic, and for this, as Carlyle had always known, time was the anodyne. "Patience! Patience! Time will do wonders for us; Time which, as the Germans say, brings roses—if there be a stem."[14] The grounds of his belief were strengthened by the style of Mill's letters. These, as was the case with many people who corresponded with the sage at any length, were showing more and more unmistakable traces of his own peculiar dialect; latterly Germanisms were creeping in, and in one notable instance Mill for the only time in his life ended up by saying "Mit Glück und Heil". As a result, Mill's efforts to convince his would-be mentor of the serious degree of his dissent were utterly frustrated; instead, he found that their effect had been to bind them together more firmly in an even closer intimacy. Nothing more could be done for the moment: the attempt to explain about Harriet had to be abandoned. All must now wait upon Carlyle's return to London, which was becoming imminent. But before he came, Mill thought it prudent to write, reminding him again that he was greatly changed, more so than Carlyle could expect or understand until he had been brought abreast of "many incidents in the spiritual history" of his believed disciple.

During this long and intricate game of touch-and-go, Mill was allowed to be of service to his friend in many small practical ways. He was the link between Craigenputtock and the outside world, charged to bring in such news as was required in the retreat, and to execute many errands. He was to send Carlyle magazines—the *Examiner* and the *Monthly Repository*—and books, especially books.

He was to arrange for Carlyle's letters to be franked. He was to keep him informed about his London friends, the Austins and the Bullers. He was to provide thumbnail sketches of new personalities whose names had crossed Carlyle's path—Harriet Martineau, Grote, Roebuck, and John Sterling. He was to give a full account of the fate of the Saint-Simonians. He was to visit Carlyle's unfortunate friend Glen, who was in a mental breakdown. All these commissions he completed punctually and even thankfully. But there was one thing especially about John Mill that strongly interested Carlyle, and that was his knowledge of France.

Of that country Carlyle knew next to nothing. Since his revulsion from the *Philosophes* he had turned his back contemptuously upon the race, and his whole knowledge of them was confined to a fleeting glimpse of Paris in 1824, to a rough memory of Voltaire, and a list of prejudices he believed to be their faults. Mill, on the other hand, had made a methodical and thorough study of French history and culture, and had become in the world of English letters the solitary expert on French affairs. During their talks in London he had opened to Carlyle a whole new vault of human knowledge, and although at first Carlyle did not perceive its full significance, it provided him with matter for reflection.

When he got back to Craigenputtock he began to write an article on Diderot for Cochrane's *Foreign Quarterly Review*; for his experiences in London had convinced him that his desire to abandon periodicals in favour of writing books could not for the present be realized. He was, he said, very curious about France, and invited Mill to send him any books he might possess about recent conditions there, and particularly any readable history of the Revolution. Mill responded handsomely to his appeal and sent him a whole packet of books on France, including Thiers' *History of the Revolution*, which Carlyle found to be "a rather good book". His imagination was stirred to ask for more—anything about the prisoners during the Reign of Terror, about Danton, or the Assignats. He had at this time moved to Edinburgh for the winter, and as for the moment libraries were accessible, Mill, besides sending the books Carlyle could not obtain there, furnished him with a complete reading list for his own reference, covering specifically the aspects about which he had enquired. "On the whole," Mill said, "it is wonderful how little can be traced of the private and social life of that period."[15]

From this time forward, a grand, fiery, cloudy panorama began gradually to unfold itself in Carlyle's mind. Mill, of course, was the expert; and, of course, intended to write about the Revolution as soon as he had the opportunity. But if Mill should fail of his purpose? What more splendid, awe-inspiring spectacle had there ever been of the Wrath of God descending upon a frivolous and apostate people? What a punishment of the French for their many faults: what dire revenge upon the *Philosophes* for their presumption: above all, what a lurid warning to the remainder of mankind! "I should not have known what to make of this world at all if it had not been for the French Revolution",[16] he later used to say.

He began to think of settling in Paris for a time; and when, in September 1833, Mill announced that he was going there, the pang of disappointment was lessened for Carlyle by thought of all "the little practical things" Mill would be able to do for him, to fill the void of his ignorance. How much did it cost to live in Paris? Could one get into the libraries? Were men of literature easily accessible? What books, what men would tell him most of contemporary life and recent history? He needed a decent dictionary; as an afterthought he found he also needed maps of Paris and the Ile de France.

He had read Mill's article on Alison, a review of a very indifferent English work on the Revolution, flung off as a favour for Fox while his affairs with Harriet were in their most entangled and despairing state. This, Carlyle thought, as far as it went, was well: but Mill should expand and enlarge his knowledge of the subject into something more substantial, and as soon as possible. He added, "To me, it often seems as if the right *History* (that impossible thing I mean by History) of the French Revolution were the grand Poem of our Time; as if the man who *could* write the *truth* of that, were worth all the other writers and singers. If I were spared alive myself, and had means, why might not I too prepare the way for such a thing? I assure you the attempt often seems among my possibilities."[17] Mill, on the edge of departure for Paris, replied from his parents' cottage at Dorking. "It is highly probable I shall do it sometime if you do not, but besides the difficulty of doing it tolerably, there is the far greater difficulty in doing it so as to be read in England, until the time comes when one can speak of Christianity as it may be spoken of in France—as by far the greatest and best thing which has existed on this globe, but which is gone, never to return—without *saying out* one's whole belief on that point, it is impossible to write about the French Revolution in any way professing to tell the whole truth."[18] Thus, Carlyle obtained his mandate.

As a preliminary, he began to work on a storied scandal of the Bourbon court he had come across in reading the memoirs of Lamotte, and the indefatigable Mill was called upon once more to make detailed researches both in Paris and in London. *The Diamond Necklace*, as it was called, was finished before Christmas. Although it is one of the best mystery stories in the language, it was some time before it found a publisher, and it is scarcely heard of at the present day. That completed, Carlyle turned to his main purpose. It was plainly out of the question to undertake a task of such magnitude from Craigenputtock: it was necessary for him to have easier facilities for books, and closer touch with his adviser. Early in the New Year 1834 he began to turn his eyes once more to London.

There were other more pressing reasons why London beckoned him. Jeffrey had left the *Edinburgh Review*, and his successor, Macvey Napier, was disinclined to take Carlyle's work, a piece on Ebenezer Elliot, printed soon after the return to Craigenputtock, being the last. Since then, two articles on the death of Goethe in different magazines, the article on Diderot, *Fraser's* undertaking to publish *Sartor* as a serial, and their acceptance of "a half-mad production" called "Count Cagliosto," represented almost all Carlyle's achievement in the last two years. It was not enough to live on. Although Mill tactfully referred to his indiscriminate choice of periodicals as if it were a deliberate policy, the horrid truth was that Carlyle had to go far afield to place his work, and it became gradually more difficult to get it into print. This was no doubt partly due to the general preoccupation with politics for which he had no patience; but all the same, with further disbursements to his family, his bank roll was growing slim. "Think of *me*", he complained to Mill in October 1833, "and poor *Fraser's Magazine*! yet such is my *best* speaking-mechanism at this moment; for aught I know, it is my only one."[19]

On 22 December of that year Mill wrote to confirm a question of Carlyle's about the *Examiner* being in difficulties. It was only too true. Fonblanque, the editor-proprietor whom they both respected, had been far too prodigal in his private expenditure, and seemed likely to pull down the paper with him in his bankruptcy. To save him, it was necessary to raise £1000, and in this endeavour Mill was an active participant. It was hoped to raise the sum in subscriptions of £10: £600 had already been forthcoming, and the remainder was ultimately obtained. In parenthesis, Mill added a piece of news likely to be encouraging to Carlyle. There was a proposal among several leaders of the Radicals to take this opportunity to found their own Review. Mill wrote:

> "They would, I believe, make *me* editor if I would take it, but I cannot; hampered again! But this time it is of little consequence, for I hope they will have Mr. Fox, who will be quite as fit: if they will not have *him*, there *are* other candidates not *unfit* though not *so* fit. If this scheme goes on, I hope you will write *for* the review, or at least *in* it. As an organ of utterance it will be at least more congenial to you than *Fraser's Magazine*. It is true the prejudices of our utilitarians are at least as strong against some of your writings as those of any other person whatever, though the individual signature would smooth many difficulties. But such an article as that on Johnson they would have delighted in; that on Ebenezer Elliot and various others of yours would have suited them perfectly. In fact, I hardly know one of your *opinions*, as often as you do not feel yourself called upon to make a direct attack upon themselves, which they would have any difficulty in getting on with; and I expect no difficulty in getting a passport for any of *mine*, which, except in mere metaphysics, are quite as unlike theirs as yours are: what revolts them is the combination of opinions new and often strange to them, with a manner to them equally new and still more strange, and which prevents them not only from understanding your meaning but from desiring to understand it. I have never found one of them who, after taking the trouble to read enough of your writings to understand anything of your drift, did not recognize in them much more of what he deemed good than of what he deemed bad; it is true I have found few who would take the trouble, and some of those few would not have done so if they had not had *faith* (derived from my testimony) that it was worth while. I tell you this to let you know how the land lies."[20]

This surprisingly forceful yet always tactful invitation was as the arrival of tumblers at a tea-party: it aroused expectations. But Carlyle had his pride. The proposal was, he said, of true interest to him. He only wished he could enter fully into the project, share in its purpose and enthusiasm; that would be so much more agreeable than selling it an article now and then. He had little hope of it with the Radicals: their speculation was as barren as the Sahara sand, and he could not see why they required a new review when they already had the *Westminster*, *Tait's*, and the *Monthly Repository*. Nevertheless, he had several ideas for articles that might suit them. "My further contributions must depend on the treatment I experience; on the course matters take; and I need not assure you, the closer my connexion can grow the better pleased shall I be."[21] The pith of the matter he confided only to his journal: "Letter from Mill about a new Radical Review in which my co-operation is requested. Shall be ready to give it if they have any payment to offer."[22]

It even crossed his mind that they might make him editor. For that, he must be on the spot. London was the place for him, without a doubt. In the meantime, the post fell open of Astronomical Observer and Professor in the city of Edinburgh, and as a last alternative he wrote to suggest himself to Jeffrey. That he knew less of astronomy than bees know of botany never struck him as a disadvantage, and when his former benefactor declined his application decisively and even wrathfully, Carlyle regarded it as an unforgivable breach of friendship. That settled it. At his bidding, Jane wrote to Sarah Austin telling her to look round for a house for them, while he bade Mill to give her all assistance; and, on hearing all was satisfactorily arranged, in May 1834 the Carlyles left Craigenputtock for the last time.

III

As soon as he arrived in London, Carlyle hurried off to see the Austins, whom he found at a low ebb of their affairs. John Austin had been compelled by ill-health to abandon his course of lectures on Jurisprudence, and in 1832 they had had to leave Queen Square for less expensive quarters in Bayswater. At this time they were dependent for their living on the growing success of Sarah's translations from the German. In August 1833 the situation was improved by Austin's appointment to the Criminal Law Commission with its promise of £500 a year, and at this work he was now engaged, after recuperating at Boulogne. But his health remained bad: he was a victim of excruciating headaches, and his sense of incapacity was as oppressive as before.

As a relief from her exertions and from her husband's dreary pessimism, Sarah, now a handsome, vigorous woman of 39, had in the interval involved herself in a romance with Prince Puckler Muskau, a rogue of a German princeling who, having run through the fortune of one heiress and deserted her, had come to England some years previously to find another. He was charming, dashing, accomplished both as a horseman and a dueller; and although he returned to his mortgaged estates empty-handed as regards the heiress, he had collected a good deal of spicy information about the upper ranks of English society. He wrote a book, which Sarah read and asked his permission to translate; her version proved quite fruitful for them both. Although she had never seen Prince Puckler Muskau, she loved him desperately, and began a lengthy correspondence with him in language of the most ardent intimacy. There was no real harm in it: she kept her head, recalled her duty to her husband, to her daughter Lucie, and to the respectable traditions of the Taylor-Martineau family. She evaded all the attempts of her gallant to meet her either in London, Paris, or, most hopeful of all, on his own domains. But letters are letters. Their exposure would have caused an ignominious scandal. Her husband would have been finally unhinged, and the decent little practice as translator she was carefully building up would have been dashed to atoms. Her lover was a villain, an imposter: she was in the midst of imploring his compassion and his mercy, and was herself a wreck of anxiety and secretiveness, when Carlyle arrived.[23]

To cover her own traces, she greeted him with a volley of tattle, a "Niagara of gossip", omitting no detail of the affair of John Mill and Harriet Taylor, of how things stood, or of what other people thought about it, much to the astonishment and not a little to the disgust of her visitor. He did not know what to make of it. Later, he met Charles Buller, who was inclined to jest about it, and so concluded there was probably not much in it. All the same, he wisely kept quiet about so sensitive a subject, and in due course Mill introduced Harriet to him and to his wife: they received her with guarded admiration:

> "We have made, at least Jane has made, a most promising acquaintance of a Mrs. Taylor, a young beautiful reader of mine and 'dearest Friend' of Mill's, who for the present seems 'all that is noble' and what not. We shall see how that wears. We are to dine there on Tuesday and meet a new set of persons, said among other qualities, to be interested in *me*. The editor of the Fox Repository (Fox himself) is the main man I care for."[24]

This dinner party, which took place early in August 1834, was eventful, for during it Carlyle came to realize that Mill had no intention of inviting him, as he had hoped, to be editor of the proposed new radical review:

> "We dined with Mrs. (Platonica) Taylor and the Unitarian Fox one day. Mill was also of the party, and the husband—an obtuse, joyous-natured man, the pink of social hospitality. Fox is a little, thick-set, bushy-locked man of five and forty, with bright, sympathetic, thoughtful eyes, with a tendency to pot-belly and snuffiness. . . . Mrs. Taylor herself did not yield unmixed satisfaction, I think, or receive it. She affects, with a kind of sultana noble-mindedness, a certain girlish petulance, and felt that it did not wholly prosper. . . .
>
> Here too let me wind up the Radical-Periodical Editorship which your last letter naturally speculates upon. Mill I seem to discern has given it to this same Fox (who has just quitted his preachership and will, like myself, be out on the world); partly I should fancy by Mrs. Taylor's influence, partly as himself thinking him the safer man."[25]

He was utterly mistaken on this point. As a matter of fact it had been arranged that Mill himself was to be the editor, and that immediately disqualified Fox or any other personality of such significance from taking place beneath him. He never had the least idea of inviting Carlyle, who was if anything less qualified to direct a radical review than to be a Professor of Astronomy. Carlyle's vision was clouded by his desperate situation. At the age of thirty-nine he still had no book in circulation, no great demand for articles, and no prospect of other employment. It was some eighteen months since he had earned one penny by the craft of literature: between him and starvation stood only his dwindling savings of £200. He was continually thinking of emigrating to America. From the first Carlyle had been goaded by a prick of resentment against the fair creature who had stepped in between him and his disciple—had stepped in so quietly and carried off the quarry before he knew of it. And now, he began to think, her influence was working against his material interests.

Nevertheless, he could not deny a secret interest, a lurking admiration for her calm, fragile beauty; for her self-possession and for her effectiveness. Beyond that, he felt a keen and worldly curiosity about the exact nature of the relationship between the amorous philosopher and his muse. In his journal, he described how one afternoon he set out with Jane to go and call on Harriet: their carriage broke down in Regent's Park, and while they were waiting, Harriet herself came walking by, with her husband: "pale she, and passionate and sad-looking; really felt a kind of interest in her." Jane, too, sensed the force of her attraction: "There is a Mrs. Taylor whom I could really love, if it were safe and she were willing; but she is a dangerous looking woman and engrossed with a dangerous passion, and no useful relation can spring up between us."[26] Steeped as they were in the romantic plots and duels and boudoirs of the past, the Carlyles were already able to see in Harriet the *femme fatale*. When the delicate and not altogether dissociated affair of Fox and Eliza Flower burst into open scandal and social offence, all interest and attraction vapoured off before the furious flame of Carlyle's Puritanism. The inviolability of the marriage tie under every circumstance was cardinal to him. Once when his wife spoke up for a married woman who had gone off with her lover, he reduced her to tears by calling her "the advocate of whores"; and as for the equality of women, the dearest principle of all for Mill and Harriet both, he had explained his views to Jane before their marriage: "'The man should bear rule in the house, and not the woman.' This is an eternal axiom, the law of nature, which no mortal departs from unpunished. . . . I must not, and I cannot, live in a house of which I am not the head."[27] He was one of those for whom the perfect woman was still inferior to an average man, and the general run of them sirens, expert in deceit.

Accordingly, when he found that besides their own questionable situation Mill and Harriet were to some extent involved in this other more notorious case; that they were in an intimate web with sinners who not only expounded heresies but were fully ready to put them into practice, he concluded that his unfortunate friend had been seduced, spiritually if not bodily, and dashed off to his brother John, the recipient of most of his confidences, a full anathema:

"Mill and one of two of his set are on the whole the reasonablest people we have. However, we see them seldom, being far off, and Mill himself, who would be far the best of them all, is greatly occupied of late times with a set of quite opposite character, which the Austins and other friends mourn much and fear much over. It is the fairest Mrs. Taylor you have heard of: with whom, under her husband's very eyes, he is (Platonically) over head and ears in love. Round her came Fox the Socinian and a flight of really wretched-looking 'friends of the species', who (in writing and deed) struggle not in favour of duty being *done*, but against duty of any kind being required. . . . Jane and I often say 'Before all mortals beware of a friend of the species!' Most of these people are very indignant at marriage and the like, and frequently, indeed, are obliged to divorce their own wives, or be divorced; for though this world is already blooming (or is one day to do it) in everlasting 'happiness of the greatest number', these people's own *houses* (I always find) are little hells of improvidence, discord, and unreason. Mill is far above all that, and I think will not sink into it; however I do wish him fairly far from it, and though I cannot speak of it directly, would fain help him out: he is one of the best people I ever saw and—surprisingly attached to *me*, which is another merit."[28]

Carlyle's great error in regard to Mill was never to allow him any strength of purpose. In later life he repeatedly described him as "wire-drawn", "colourless", "aqueous", and other synonyms for weak. He never believed Mill to hold opinions conflicting with his own, however often he expressed them, and never imagined him to have the power or the right to love of his own free will. For as long as possible Carlyle clung to him simply by denying their differences, which had from the first moment been insuperable, and then in jealousy blamed them all upon the woman Mill loved better than himself. His genuine affection for the man was consumed in his hatred of the woman, for hate her he did from this time forward with all the hefty violence at his command.

Only in private, for the present. He was worldly-wise enough to know the fatal effects of letting Mill discern his change of feeling. Their Sunday walks continued regularly as the ringing of church bells, and once or twice a week Mill, with or without Harriet, would call on the Carlyles in Cheyne Row. When *Sartor Resartus*, regathered by *Fraser's* from the serial, appeared as a private pamphlet, the author inscribed a copy for each of them. The Carlyles continued to dine pleasurably at the Taylors'. When Carlyle was away in Scotland Mill hastened to visit Jane and kept her plied with letters, while Carlyle in return promised to call upon Harriet at Kent Terrace when he got back. They were all, for a long time yet, in the closest unity and apparent friendship. Mill was so keen to help with Carlyle's literary difficulties that in September 1834 he offered to print the misfortunate *Diamond Necklace* at his own expense, in order to be able to review it.

IV

One afternoon, early in 1835, when making one of his customary visits to the India House, Carlyle found John Sterling there, of whom he had often heard Mill speak, and whose novel *Arthur Coningsby* he had been induced to read by Mill's praises, to his mind rather extravagant. The introductions over, they at once launched into an argument about slavery, on which topic Sterling had strong views acquired partly from his friend Frederick Maurice, whose sister he had married, and partly from his own observation of the behaviour of the planters in the West Indies; while Carlyle held to the whip-cracking opinion. The meeting at Mill's office was repeated, and before long they were all on the best of terms.

John Sterling had come back from St. Vincent in September 1832 glowing with his conversion to the established church. It did not reduce his intimacy with Mill. On the contrary, fearing the quips of Charles Buller, and the more cruel mockery of other friends, it was to Mill of all people, who had "ground him to powder for excessive piety"[29] in the London Debating Society, that he turned for sympathy and for protection. They were readily forthcoming. In Bonn, where Sterling went to study the German philosophers, particularly Schelling, whom he believed to share the much revered ideas of Coleridge, he fell in with Archdeacon Hare, who removed his last religious doubts. They returned together to England, whereupon Sterling took orders and became Hare's curate at the parish of Hurstmonceaux in Sussex. By the time he met Carlyle in February 1835, ill-health had forced him to give up his curacy, and he was in process of moving his family to Bayswater, to the gruff satisfaction of his new friend. For Sterling was easily susceptible, patient, sympathetic, and immensely attractive in a slightly effeminate way: therefore, despite his orders and his undiminished faith, he was a far more promising candidate than the obdurate Mill for the still vacant discipleship of Carlyle.

"Have seen a good deal of that young Clergyman (singular *Clergy*man!) during these two weeks: a sanguine, light, loving man: of whom to me nothing but good seems likely to come. . . . He is off today; and will send me (bless him for the favour!) all the 'errors of style', faults, etc. he has to discover in Teufelsdrockh."[30] The result was a good-humoured correspondence, continuing until Sterling's death some eight years later, wherein both men were at their best, and Jane intervened at intervals with her sure, sharp wit. Sterling berated Carlyle affectionately for his paganism, his lack of a personal God, and for his barbaric style. On the last count he even made a slight impression. Criticism of Carlyle's style was widespread, and John Mill too discreetly indicated "it would often *tell* better on the reader if what were said in an abrupt, exclamatory, and interjectional manner were said in the ordinary grammatical mode of nominative and verb".[31]* "So many persons, almost everybody that speaks to me, objects to my style as 'too full of meaning'", groaned Carlyle. "Had it no other fault! I seldom read in any dud of a book, novel, or the like, where the writing seems to flow along like talk (certainly not 'too full') without a certain pain, a certain envy. Ten pages of that were easier than a sentence or paragraph of mine; and yet such is the result."[32]

From his own side of the friendship, Carlyle pressed gently and unremittingly towards his aim, making it his business to convert Sterling from Coleridge and his "transcendental moonshine", from the Church of England, from John Mill, and indeed from any influence other than his own. He succeeded so well that Sterling dropped "the Reverend", badge of orthodoxy, from his pen-name; came to admire Goethe whom he had previously hated; and began, like Mill, despite himself to write in Carlylese, once actually calling Carlyle "Poor fellow!", heroically reversing Carlyle's habitual epithet. They were genuinely fond of each other. From his death-bed, Sterling directed to Carlyle some stanzas of loving verse "written as if in star-fire and immortal tears".

* Or, as J. M. Robertson delightfully put it (*Modern Humanists Reconsidered*, 1927, p. 18) when Carlyle apostrophized Macaulay with "Flow on, thou shining river", the proper answer would have been, "Splash on, thou frothing cataract."

V

Meanwhile, the *French Revolution* was progressing. Mill, having given his friend his rights in this great enterprise, was as determined Carlyle should do justice to it as he was that it should succeed in bringing recognition to its author. He was constantly at hand with advice, with books, with information of all kinds. "Mill is very friendly", Carlyle gratefully reported in his journal. "He is the nearest approach to a real man that I find here—nay, as far as negativeness goes, he *is* that man, but unhappily not very satisfactory much farther. It is next to an impossibility that a London-born man should not be a stunted one."[33]

In February 1835 the first volume was completed, and Mill, anxious to get a clear view of the whole, proudly carried off the manuscript. Carlyle, low in spirits and exhausted by creation, with a sigh tore up his finished notes, drew out a clean sheet, and took up his pen again: "Vol. II, Book 1—The Feast of Pikes." His task lay heavy on him—"gloomy, huge, of almost boundless meaning".

On the dark evening of Friday 6 March Carlyle was sitting with Jane, resting after a long day of this toil. He was, for him, in a fairly placid mood: the room was cheerfully lit, and warm; silence, and blue smoke curling from his lusty pipe, all indicated ease. But over the way, at Kensington, at this same hour there was the opposite of ease. Drawers were opened, papers rummaged, clutching suspicion growing into truth. Servants were hectored, dustbins searched, the kitchen stove ransacked and a few charred sheets of paper seized. John Mill, no longer pensive and sedate, bounded from the house, hired a cab, and set off at best speed towards Kent Terrace. There, after a few whispers of despairing agony, Harriet joined him in the carriage: she could not, would not let him be alone at such a time. At No. 5 Great Cheyne Row Mill jumped down, leaving her sitting where she was. He ran up the steps, rapped staccato at the door: a hurried enquiry of the maid and he was on the stairs, in the familiar room, from which ease faded on his appearance like creases before an iron. He staggered, he could hardly stand: he was quite speechless, his face was wild and white. "Why, Mill, what ails ye, man?" exclaimed

Carlyle, rising to take him by the arm. He managed to speak to Jane, begged her to go down to Harriet: she glanced at Carlyle, and they were in accord. It had come then, at last, they thought; the elopement, and ruin and disgrace that they had feared. Quickly Jane ran down the stairs and into the waiting carriage; but from her companion in the darkness lit only by the glimmering of the giglamps, she could get nothing except quiverings and gasps. "Oh! you'll never speak to him again!" was all she heard, and as feminine consolations were impossible until she knew what was amiss, she hastened back to the two men and demanded information.

Mill was collapsed into a chair: her husband slowly folded up a fragment of a sheet of paper, lit it, and held it as it burnt. And then it all came out. Except for those poor scraps, the entire manuscript of the first volume of the *French Revolution* had, while in Mill's charge, been destroyed by fire. As was his habit, Mill had read much of it aloud to Harriet, and had discussed with her the observations he proposed to make upon it. In the meantime he had laid it out in his room at his father's house; and there, while clearing out old papers for kitchen use, he had swept it off to limbo. His sister was not likely to forget the search they made, nor the few shreds they eventually rescued.[34]

Outside, they heard the carriage with its silent occupant grind off into the night. Carlyle behaved royally. The loss to him was five months' solid writing, his last throw in the unrewarding game of literature. His notes were gone, and the mood uncapturable, for his system was to read till he was full of his subject, and then to write in a high fever of excitement. None the less, his immediate resolution was to start again, and his first thought was to relieve his friend's distress. For at least two hours he talked to his distracted visitor of other things, until Mill regained sufficient composure to enable him to leave. Next day they wrote each other letters:

"My dear Mill,

How are you? You left me last night with a look which I shall not soon forget. Is there anything that I could do or suffer to alleviate you? For I feel that your sorrow must be far sharper than mine: yours bound to be a *passive* one. . . .

I have ordered a *Biographie Universelle*, this morning;—and a better sort of paper. Thus, far from giving up the game, you see, I am risking another £10 on it. Courage, my Friend!

That I can never write *that* Volume again is indubitable: singular enough, the whole Earth could not get *it* back; but only a better or a worse one. There is the strangest dimness over it. A figure thrown into the melting-pot; but the metal . . . is there; the model also *is*, in my head. O my Friend, how easily might the bursting of some puny ligament or filament have abolished all light *there* too! . . .

Thanks to Mrs. Taylor for her kind sympathies. May God guide, and bless you both! That is my true prayer."[35]

Mill pleaded, as an act of friendship, to be permitted to make good what alone was reparable, the loss of time and labour; that was, he said, of income. That much was granted him. He sent £200, of which £100 was returned, and nothing would induce Carlyle to take more than the bare sum he had expended during the period of writing. Books Mill also sent, "brave cargoes of Books", all that Carlyle named, and all that he could think of: if he had not got them, he searched, and bought them specially. There were so many, that Carlyle only needed to go to the British Museum once or twice a week.

Thus, surrounded by new tools, Carlyle went to work: first, he completed the "Feast of Pikes", the second volume of the three. He wrote to Mill insisting that their misfortune be hushed up, save from his publisher and his immediate family who had a right to know of it in general terms. They were, he felt, drawn still closer together than before by their common calamity. He offered the new volume as soon as finished, provided Mill dared take it; but this offer Mill declined, feeling too sharply his unforgivable carelessness. "If, however, you would give me the pleasure of reading it", he added, "give it to Mrs. Taylor—in her custody no harm could come to it."[36] He saw no more of it until the whole was safely into print, when he received the first bound copy from the press, in order that he might complete his debt by sending it off with a welcome in his *Review*.

JOHN TAYLOR

from a miniature in the British Library of Political and Economic Science.

BOOK FOUR

THE LONDON AND WESTMINSTER REVIEW

1834–1840
aet. 28–34

"A CHELSEA INTERIOR"

From the painting by Robert Tait. Reproduced by kind permission of the Marquess of Northampton.

I

IN June 1834, Mill wrote excitedly to Fox:

"I have some news for you: Molesworth, without any suggestion or solicitation, has spontaneously offered to establish, at his own expense, the review we were talking of and making but one condition, viz: that substantially it shall be under my direction—he knows that I cannot on account of my position in the India House, be myself the editor, or be ostensibly connected with the review in any way, except as an occasional writer—but he will appoint his editor under the complete understanding that he is to be guided altogether by me.

This is a much more feasible scheme than the former one—because there will be but one person to satisfy, and he a man of decided movement principles, docile, and who will certainly be pleased with the thing if it is such as will please us. At the same time we must not allow him to throw away his money. We must see our way clearly to being able to carry it on before we announce it—a failure would be a disaster to the cause."[1]

The cause was in a promising position. Never in the history of their struggle to obtain control of Parliament from outside had the Radicals been better placed. When the Reformed Parliament met, the Tories were demoralized and few: the Whigs triumphant and secure. The Whigs soon showed, by the limited use they made of absolute power, that they were no real friends of the popular factions which had helped them to carry the Bill. In deference to their radical allies, they passed a law or two, much as bones are thrown to a dog. In response to Roebuck's plea for free and universal education, they made a miserly annuity of £20,000: although this was subsequently increased to £30,000, it was still, in 1845, less than a third of the sum devoted to the purpose by the single state of Massachusetts. They freed the conscience of Empire from the incubus of slavery, by paying twenty million pounds in compensation to plantation owners. They nationalized the Poor. They allowed Dissenters to get married properly, and made tithes less onerous. And, although it was not enforced, they yielded to Lord Ashley's Tory plea that women and children under eighteen should not be allowed to work in the factories more than twelve hours a day. That was all: in most respects it was less than a beginning. Their true temper was shown in 1837, when Lord John Russell announced that no further reform of Parliament was in the least desirable, and became hilariously known as Finality John.

The object of the Mills, who had foreseen this turn of events, was to force the hand of the Whigs, and this they seemed strong enough to do. From the new vote, all parties as they veered towards the left received proportionately more support. All the leading Radicals had been elected, Roebuck, Buller, Prescott, Warburton, Strutt, Romilly —about twenty out-and-out. There were also a number of independents, like Slingsby Duncombe, the "Dandy Demagogue" of Harrow and the Guards; Cobbett, and Attwood of Birmingham; joined later by Dr. Wakley, founder of the *Lancet*, and by Bowring. Of the Whigs, there were several who might go either way; some of them in or near the Cabinet, and others like Lytton Bulwer, uncertain where their interest lay. By the session of February 1835, the height of radical influence, the party mustered seventy or eighty, even without the Irish members, of whom there were rather more than a hundred, a restless and unsettling proportion in any institution, led by their "Liberator" Dan O'Connell. Although unpredictable, O'Connell was, as Irish politicians go, both moderate and consistent, and he had been for some time an associate of Bentham. As the Whig majority by then was only twenty-three, the Radicals were able for the first time to dictate to their hated masters.

From the first, their ability to gain their way was hampered by their own dissensions. The Radicals in Parliament were quite without cohesion. Their creed, insisting that every elected member was an individual plenipotentiary not to be bound by party platforms, automatically made it impossible for them to hold together. They were all vain men, and each one followed his private foible or animosity. Hume, the nominal leader, devoted his efforts to deploring the expense of Government. Cobbett, useless in debate, stormed away against the paper currency. Attwood, on the other hand, fought ardently for a circulation of paper under national control. Buller was humorous but dilatory, Bulwer tenuous. Burdett became a Tory: Hobhouse, his partner for Westminster, a Whig. Molesworth was fanatical against the Whigs. Roebuck, the wiry, rough-haired figure of a fearless man, fought a duel with Black of the *Morning Chronicle*. Grote, the banker, a timid man, contented himself by moving ceremoniously once a year a resolution for the secret ballot, and felt that little further could be done: he also thought that Roebuck went too far. When an electioneering dinner was arranged for the Middlesex members, Hume and Byng, it was denounced by Place and Roebuck: Hume blamed Roebuck: Place blamed Hume.[2] Everyone disliked Bowring, bald and cadaverous, glinting pompously behind his silver spectacles. When he rose to speak there was a general shuffle towards the lobbies. So it went on. "Some of them", wrote John Mill, "are full of crotchets, others fastidious and overloaded with petty scrupulosity; *none* have energy, except Roebuck and Buller; Roebuck has no judgement, Buller no persevering industry. Those two, however, will improve, and we shall hear more of them every year; all the others will remain as they are now. There is more hope in new converts like Clay and Gisborne, who at least speak their mind."[3] It was easy, in the circumstances, for Lord John Russell to parry their attacks. Whenever serious criticism arose, he promised a Royal Commission to go into the question. The Radicals were given places on these enquiries to keep them usefully occupied, and Melbourne was masterly at doing nothing about their findings.

Failing a leader, the only instrument for whipping these unruly elements into line was an authoritative periodical. Debarred from politics by the India House, both Mills had always seen it as their greatest possible contribution to the cause. That it was even more urgently required now, on the eve, as it appeared, of radical victory, than in the early days before Reform, was about the only remaining point of agreement between John Mill and his father.

There was no suitable organ in existence. The *Examiner* was in difficulties. The *Morning Chronicle* was only a daily. Fox's *Monthly Repository* and *Tait's Magazine* could not allow sufficient elaboration of radical grievances. In any of them, the best articles would be lost in a welter of indifferent stuff, instead of gaining their true weight by appearing all together in a review of homogeneous quality. As for the old *Westminster*, it had become completely barren since it was taken over by Bowring. For five difficult years, since 1830, it had been kept going by Colonel Perronet Thompson, an old war-horse of a Radical and formerly Governor of Sierra Leone, who had in his lifetime expended some £30,000 for the cause and had sacrificed his military preferment to it.[4] Under his direction the magazine had covered manfully every conceivable topic, from the question of fagging at Westminster School to the then much-debated problem of Marriage with a Deceased Wife's Sister. But as he was not only proprietor but editor and almost sole contributor as well, the contents had acquired a certain sameness. In order to fill it up, he had to devote more and more space to his favourite abuse, the Corn Laws, and to technical articles on his great object of enthusiasm, the Enharmonic Organ. This dryness and monotony must be avoided at all costs.

The project of a new review had been in John Mill's mind since the Reform Bill. On 17 January 1834, shortly after he mentioned it to Fox and to Carlyle, he wrote to Professor John Nichol, asking him to join the staff of potential contributors which Roebuck, Buller and he were gathering together.* The money necessary was to be raised in shares of £25 or more, to be taken up by the wealthier members of the party. It had been hoped to start that month, but one way or another the funds were not forthcoming, and the list of writers was too narrowly confined to orthodox Philosophical Radicals. There for a time the thing had stuck until now, in June, a wealthy young baronet had impulsively stepped forward and guaranteed the necessary £3,000, on the sole condition that Mill was to be in fact if not in name everything that meant control.

Mill's description of Sir William Molesworth as "docile" cannot be allowed to pass without a question. He was a most eager young man. The scion of a Cornish family, he became baronet and landlord at the age of thirteen. His mother sent him first to Edinburgh and then to Cambridge, where he made a lifelong friend of Thackeray, and spent the rest of his time hunting. In 1828 he challenged his

* John Stuart Mill to John Pringle Nichol, Professor of Astronomy in the University of Glasgow. See article by William Knight in the *Fortnightly Review*, Vol. 61, Jan.–June 1897. Their friendship resulted from discussions on Political Economy in *Tait's Magazine*. In Knight's article the letter is attributed to the year 1833, not 1834. This is almost certainly an error.

tutor to a duel with pistols, for which insubordination the Vice-Chancellor invited him to leave. Nothing daunted, he went on a grand tour of the Continent, pursued by the infuriated tutor. The duel took place at Calais in 1829, apparently without bloodshed. As soon as he reached the eligible age of twenty-one, Molesworth was elected unopposed to the Reformed Parliament for his native constituency of East Cornwall, ostensibly as a Whig. This brought him into contact with his neighbouring member, Charles Buller of Liskeard. Their friendship was marred only by a mutual fear, on the part of Molesworth that Buller in his levity would truckle to the Whigs; and of Buller, that Molesworth would cut short his career by over violence to them. Molesworth's resentment against the Whigs was as boundless as it was vociferous. As he expressed it to his mother, "There is but one opinion with regard to the present administration, they are the miserablest brutes that God Almighty ever put guts into."[5]

To anybody else than Mill, he would have seemed the opposite of "docile and modest as anyone could be";[6] but he worshipped Mill. He made it plain from the first that Mill's despotism over the Review was to be complete, not sparing even himself. In October 1834 he wrote to Mrs. Grote: "I have an article, Deo (John Mill) volente, for the Review, which is, I hope, prospering."[7] A little later he tore off an article about a book of Brougham's which seemed to him to be "the most infernal trash", only to have Mill reject it on the ground that its excessive violence would offend more potential Radicals than it would convert Whigs. Molesworth, although in a high pitch of excitement, and although he was after all the patron while Mill was merely his editor, was not at all rebellious. "I am rather out of humour with John for refusing my article on Lord Brougham",[8] was all he said.

II

Stacks of neat-cut paper and an exhilarating reek of printer's ink. The two young men set out to launch not only a great metropolitan magazine (it lasted well into the present century), but the official organ of a strong and rising political party which would, so they intended, in a year or two come into power.* The Review must be worthy of their ambitions. It would include several novel features. All pretence was to be discarded. Articles would appear as articles, instead of disguising themselves as book reviews. And, instead of sheltering behind anonymity and the editorial "we", as was the general practice of the time, each writer would have his own identifying mark, and would be individually responsible for what he said. It would thus become possible to state both sides of a subject in different articles in the same number, and the reader would be able, without interference from the editors, to form his own conclusion on the merits of the case. It was to come out quarterly. A normal edition would consist of 2000 copies, half of which would be bespoken, the rest selling in course of time.

Their assets were not equal to their optimism. Their editorial premises were non-existent. Their staff was very limited for such an undertaking. They had commissioned a bookseller and a printer for two years. All they further required besides themselves, they thought, was a good journalistic hack, and this for a time they found in Thomas Falconer, Roebuck's brother-in-law.

Enthusiasm amply made up for everything they lacked, and they soon could boast an imposing list of authors. On Christmas Day in 1834 Mill wrote to Fonblanque:

> "Will you allow me to remind you of our hopes of an article from you for the first number? and to say that I am ready to work for the Examiner to any extent that would be needful while you are about it.
>
> We have promises of support (as writers) from my father, Grote, John Austin, Bailey of Sheffield, Peacock, Fox, James Martineau of Liverpool, Nichol of Montrose, Cornewall Lewis, Buller, Roebuck,

* Mill, four years the elder, was at this time only twenty-eight.

Wilson, Strutt, Mrs. Austin—everybody in short whom we thought worth asking except Bulwer, and he has *almost* promised. But without you we should be weak in some very important departments—and there would not be sufficient relief to our heaviness and dulness."[9]

"John", wrote Molesworth, "is in such spirits that he says he would make it succeed single-handed. Old Mill will write, consequently we shall be 'spectable."[10] "Old Mill" was in a gingery mood, having just effectively satisfied his long-felt desire to "touch up Mackintosh before I die".[11] He had touched him up to such effect that, out of common decency to the dead, he had been forced to hold up publication of the book until the old philosopher had mouldered in his grave a year or two.

The leading article in the first number of the *London Review*, as it was called, in April 1835, was James Mill's "State of the Nation", a comparatively harmless reiteration of what he had always said, as related to the present state of politics. But the second number, in July 1835, began with his article on the Church; a rip-roaring onslaught upon every aspect of that august institution, from its ceremonies and doctrines to the character of its clergy, and more especially to the content of their sermons. His outspoken statement, at a time when the public was still accustomed to regard articles as the considered view of the whole editorial staff of a periodical, caused personal embarrassment to that body; particularly to Molesworth, who on the strength of it failed in his suit for Mrs. Buller's niece. It also damaged the circulation of the *Review* at its very outset; it drove away many who were liberal in outlook and would otherwise have become readers, and it left a permanent taint of atheism which was anything but "'spectable". It was perhaps with something of relief, therefore, that the management saw the impious author struck down almost on the spot by a haemorrhage of the lungs. He recovered sufficiently to make the journey down to Mickleham, but arrived there in a state of collapse, able to gasp out only "give me some marmalade and some milk", to the consternation of the family, who had nothing but cold meat to offer.[12]

John Mill's contributions during the first year of the *Review*, in contrast to his father's, were models of propriety. They began, in the first number, with an article on Sedgwick. This was his first published work of any importance on moral philosophy, and stated the grounds upon which the theory of Utility was to rest in future—grounds very much more subtle and profound than those used by

Bentham and his father; and also, being less dogmatic, more pregnable. Where they had been interested in clarifying general principles, chiefly in order to remove objections to specific social or legal reforms, he was trying to build a philosophic theory of permanent validity.

Professor Sedgwick was an eminent geologist nearly twice as old as Mill. He was also a divine, who once announced to a British Association meeting that if his science interfered with orthodox religion, he would dash it to the ground. In his discourse on the studies of Cambridge University, he had criticized the faculty of moral philosophy for relying too much in their teaching on the experiential school, as represented by Locke and Paley, instead of on the intuitive; and had developed his criticism into a sharp attack on the theory of Utility. Mill made fair mincemeat of him. He showed, first, that Sedgwick was wrong in regarding Paley as a representative of the theory of Utility. Utilitarians were those who, maintaining human happiness to be the end and test of morality, decided their actions by considering whether or not their probable consequences were conducive to that end. The test of actions as defined by Paley was by pain and pleasure, certainly: but not the pain and pleasure of mankind. It was the hope of heaven and the fear of hell. That was far removed from the theory of Utility, which did not admit the consideration of eternal punishment and reward as a valid factor in the argument. To obey a powerful superior for hope of gain or fear of lashes was at the best prudence, and in certain circumstances craven cowardice. There could only be morality where there was no duress.

Not only had Sedgwick mis-stated both Paley and the theory of Utility, continued Mill, but he had entirely failed in demolishing the only point they had in common. He had said no man was capable of foreseeing all the consequences of every individual action, and therefore depended on a sense of right and wrong taken on trust from God. Of course a man acted on his sense of right and wrong: the point was that it was not taken on trust from God, but formed by his own foresight, aided by what he had learned from the accumulated experience of mankind. And as for Utility being a debasing creed, a selfish computation of profit and loss directed by the appetite, that showed completest ignorance of the theory. The assumption at the root of Utilitarian calculation was that the happiness of the individual was merged in the common good. To say that men were not yet up to this was quite another matter: it demonstrated not the fault of the principle, but the improvement necessary in mankind.

For his next article, in the second number, Mill turned back to poetry. He had been reading two small volumes published in the last few years by a young poet, Alfred Tennyson. He, and more especially Harriet, had admired them, and the result was an article originally intended to supplement the one he had given Fox. He started by giving iron to the Keats-killers of the *Quarterly*: "Every new claim upon its admiration, unless forced upon it by the public voice, or recommended by some party interest, it welcomes, not with a friendly extension of the hand, but with a curl of the lip: the critic (as we figure him to ourselves) taking up the book, in trusting anticipation of pleasure, not from the book, but from the contemplation of his own cleverness in making it contemptible." Tennyson, Mill said, was already expert in the art of creating scenery in keeping with a state of mind. When his cultural discipline and reason had overhauled and tamed his imaginative power, he could scarcely fail to become a leading poet. Mill included plentiful quotations, among them the "Lady of Shalott" in its entirety, and extracts from the "Lotus Eaters". He always did this with books he liked, regarding it as excellent advertisement. His wholehearted appreciation, and his withering attack upon the adverse critics, was the first responsible praise bestowed upon the poet, and did much to gain him general recognition. It was Mill's atonement for his fiasco with young Browning.

His third article in October was something different again, a review of de Tocqueville's *Democracy in America*, the first volume of which had just appeared. While giving the book warm greeting, and printing generous extracts, this article was largely superseded by his review in the *Edinburgh* of the work as a whole on the publication of the second volume in 1840. In the latter article Mill examined fully the major adjustments to political theory which de Tocqueville's book entailed, and as these made permanent changes in his own philosophy they were of great importance.

Alexis de Tocqueville was a young French nobleman, whose aristocratic sympathies had been brought into conflict with intellectual liberalism. He had become convinced that the new phenomenon, Democracy, was neither a sickness contracted from mis-government, nor a curtain lifting to reveal Utopia, but simply a change in the spirit and framework of society. It occurred to him that instead of hysterically welcoming or deploring it, it would be of more service to the countries of western Europe which had somehow to accommodate it, and especially to his own, which was already in the throes of its arrival, if he were to examine and dissect it carefully and become acquainted with its true nature.

For this purpose, he turned to a living specimen which had been developing unnoticed for the last fifty years in almost clinical isolation. Beyond the damp mists hanging over the Atlantic, and beyond the great winds howling on the face of the swelling waters, the forest's edge was rolling back at a rate of seventeen miles a year. Far removed from the European turmoil of toppling thrones and raging philosophies, safe from adulteration by lingering traditions or outworn institutions, the society of the future was being hacked into its pure and physical form. de Tocqueville therefore arranged for the authorities to send him to America, nominally to observe the prison system there.

He arrived in 1831, when he was twenty-six, and during the nine months allowed for the completion of his task, toured through all the states east of the Mississippi. He then returned to France and produced one among the most remarkable books of the century. It was a full sociological study, embracing all aspects of American government; it was at once a quarry of minutest observation and a grand display of broad coherent trends. Apart from a native haughtiness the author could not quite conceal—as, for example, when he stated that political corruption being inevitable, he would sooner be cheated by gentlemen than by crude democrats—the work was wholly dispassionate. It was so levelly balanced that during the debate on the English Reform Bill of 1867, two speeches for and against the bill on two successive nights were both based on de Tocqueville.

The modern reader of *Democracy in America* is bound to wonder how so young a man could fasten in so short a time upon the permanent characteristics of Americans, or rather of Anglo-Americans, as he felt strictly speaking they should be designated. The very chapter headings remain provocative in the present day:

"The example of the Americans does not prove that a democratic people can have no aptitude and no taste for Science, Literature or Art."
"The trade of Literature."
"Of the taste for physical well-being in America."
"Why some Americans manifest a sort of fanatical spiritualism."

"Why the Americans are so restless in the midst of their prosperity."

"Why among Americans all honest callings are considered honourable."

"Why the Americans show so little sensitiveness in their own country and are so sensitive in Europe."

He also made a series of startling predictions, arrived at purely by a process of reasoning from his own observations. He foretold the abolition of slavery in the South, and the attempt by the South to break the Union; he also remarked that abolition would tend to increase the repugnance of the white population for the black. He foretold the emergence of America as the industrial emporium of the West, and as the greatest naval power in the world. He foresaw the general tendency in the world towards omnipotent central governments minutely inquisitive about personal affairs, and assuming more and more power to control private undertakings by special enactments. His conclusion, stated precisely and without hesitation, has all the solemnity of prophetic vision:

> "There are at the present time two great nations in the world, which started from different points, but seem to tend towards the same end. I allude to the Russians and the Americans. Both of them have grown up unnoticed; and while the attention of mankind was directed elsewhere, they have suddenly placed themselves in the front rank among the nations. . . .
>
> All other nations seem to have nearly reached their natural limits, and they have only to maintain their power; but these are still in the act of growth. . . . The Anglo-American relies upon personal interests to accomplish his ends and gives free scope to the unguided strength and common sense of the people; the Russian centres all the authority of society in a single man. The principle instrument of the former is freedom; of the latter, servitude. Their starting point is different and their courses are not the same; yet each of them seems marked out by the will of Heaven to sway the destinies of half the globe."

As soon as Mill had read the book he wrote to Aristide Guilbert, who was acting as Paris agent for the *Review*: "Tocqueville's book 'de la Démocratie en Amérique', is an admirable book. Can you tell me anything of Tocqueville? What is his history? And in what estimation is he held in France?"[13] The author for his part was delighted with Mill's appreciation. "Of all my reviewers", he wrote to Mill, "you are perhaps the only one who has thoroughly understood me; who has taken a general bird's-eye view of my ideas; who sees their ulterior aim, and yet has preserved a clear perception of the details. . . . I wanted this testimony to console me for all the false conclusions that are drawn from my book. I am constantly meeting people who want to persuade me of opinions that I proclaim, or who pretend to share with me opinions that I do not hold."[14] He came to England and was riotously fêted: Mrs. Grote especially found him a comely figure for lionizing: "a small and delicate looking young man—is a most engaging person. Full of intelligence and knowledge, free from boasting and self-sufficiency—of gentle manners, and handsome countenance. In conversing he displays a candid and unprejudiced mind—about thirty-two years of age, of a noble race in Normandy, and unmarried."[15] This last qualification de Tocqueville quickly spoiled by marrying an English girl. He promised Mill an article for the *Review* on the social condition of France; much to the jubilation of the latter, who was convinced that this, together with the contributions of Nisard then appearing, would greatly increase the following in France, and expended a considerable sum in commissions and advertisement on the strength of it.

The whole method of de Tocqueville's monumental work was much to the taste of Mill. It demonstrated what he had long believed, that human nature was as much subject to general laws as physical nature; that they could with patience be identified, and the inferences from them safely used as a means of prediction. It also proved what was not generally admitted, that democracy in action, so far from being anarchic, was a stable and effective social system. Both he and Harriet, moreover, must have warmly welcomed de Tocqueville's praise of the buxom, forthright women of America who received equal shares both of education and of hardship, and went through life as free partners in a common enterprise.

Mill was much perturbed at de Tocqueville's insistence on the possible tyranny that might be exerted by a majority under conditions of political equality. In America, where enormous distances made centralized government difficult, the danger was mitigated by the large part the people themselves played in public affairs, deriving from it both political education and a jealous regard for their local interests and customs. Even so, de Tocqueville thought, there was already evidence of a general political apathy. Sometimes, as in the case of lynching, there was no redress for breaches of the law by a majority; while those who troubled to come forward and take office were often inferior men pursuing private gain rather than the public good. In Europe, where the same degree of self-government did not exist, it was relatively certain that a democratically elected government would be permitted, through a sense of false security among the people, to establish a central control more drastic than any power wielded by a despot. "Such a power does not destroy, but it prevents existence", Mill exclaimed in horror; "it does not tyrannize, but it compresses, enervates, extinguishes and stupefies a people, till each nation is reduced to nothing better than a flock of timid and industrious animals, of which the government is the shepherd. . . . And no one will ever believe that a liberal, wise and energetic government can spring from the suffrages of a subservient people."

The apathy which de Tocqueville took to be the result of social equality, Mill maintained was also prevalent in England where there was no such equality. He attributed it to other causes: in America, to the preoccupation of the people in practical pursuits like the building of their houses; in England, to advancing civilization, to the worship of wealth and commercial success, and the increasing insignificance of the individual before the machine. So far from increasing the evil, democratic self-government would eventually cure it, through the educational and stimulative tendencies of personal participation. Democratic institutions were the best safeguard against the dangers of democracy.

Nevertheless, Mill thought, the danger indicated by de Tocqueville was a mortal one. It was not so much the central government he feared, as that a dull majority should come to dominate in matters of opinion and taste, to the eventual elimination of all originality on the grounds that it was eccentric. He conceived that in the last resort, independence of thought was the fundamental source of vigour in a people, and the only ultimate defence against tyranny. For, politically speaking, where there was no healthy contradiction there could only be dogmatism on the one hand and servility on the other: and he who could control opinion owned the world.

This idea, already foreshadowed in Harriet's *Toleration* and in the essay on "Genius", became fundamental in Mill's thought. In another article in the *Review,* he complained that civilization tends to curb the heroic spirit; to enervate intelligence, and concentrate effort on unworthy objects. "Thus it happens that in highly civilized countries, and particularly among ourselves, the energies of the middle classes are nearly extinct. . . . The few great minds which this country has produced have been formed in spite of nearly everything which could be done to stifle their growth."[16] Henceforth in his political theory, the restraints on corruption which had been the limit of his father's vision took second place to the development of self-reliance, and the protection of the widest possible variety of thought.

III

In the New Year 1836, with his father an invalid, John Mill was promoted at the India House with a salary increased to £800. At the same time his editorial work was putting an increasing strain on him, owing to the incapacity of his assistant Falconer. He was also turning out leading articles for the *Globe* and the *Morning Chronicle*, besides occasional contributions to other papers. He had his father's family duties to look after, and, as if that were not already enough, he was still engaged as a matter of course in teaching the youngest of his eight brothers and sisters, Mary and George.

Not surprisingly, he began to show definite signs of overwork. His thirty years of labour had a cumulative effect upon him, and now when his efforts reached their peak his powerful physique at last gave way. It has been alleged, curiously enough by those who elsewhere maintain that he was undersexed, that the breakdown in his health was due to sexual starvation and excitement in his relation to Harriet. It is certain that a large part of his despondency was due to plain exhaustion. For the rest, the vicissitudes of love may well have been responsible. In March, his father primly wrote to his brother James, who had just sailed for the Indian Civil Service: "John is still in rather a pining way; though, as he does not choose to tell the cause of his pining, he leaves other people to their conjectures."[17] To make more out of it than that is to push the evidence further than it will reach. Outwardly at any rate, the relationship had settled, during the two previous years, into a regular routine. Harriet divided her time between Kent Terrace and her country house at Keston; Mill saw plenty of her with the full consent of her husband, so that secrecy or concealment were no longer necessary except by their own choice. Their friends still had free access—it was at Harriet's house that Carlyle met Mazzini on his arrival in England—and in January 1836 George John Graham wrote to her about two casks of wine he had brought over at John Mill's request for the stocking of the Kent Terrace cellar.

Mill was in fact suffering from a general physical collapse, very much more serious than his mental crisis of a decade before, in that it left him with weakened lungs, a deranged stomach, and a nervous twitching of the right eye, complaints from which he suffered more or less for the remainder of his life. At the end of February, Carlyle accompanied him on a week-end cruise down the river from London to the Hicksons at Gravesend, but Mill needed longer rest. He was seized with violent pains in the head; on the first of April Jane Carlyle reported him as "dangerously ill",[18] and later in the month he was ordered off to Brighton.*

While he was there, his father, who had returned to Kensington and rallied somewhat during the spring, began to sink down towards death. John wrote anxiously to his brother Henry to know whether it would be of use to curtail his own cure: "As to my father, tell me as fully as you can how he is, both as to his illness itself, and as to spirits, and what you think would be pleasantest to him; not what he would wish or say out of kindness to me."[19] On these terms he evidently was not summoned. James Mill died, on 23 June, "as much of a bright reasoning man as he ever was—reconciled to his fate, brave, and calm". He was buried in Kensington church, and in memory of all that he had so unwearyingly done in his dry decided manner for the public good, the impressionable Molesworth was one of those most overcome with grief.

After the obsequies the Mills retired to Mickleham. John, in no fit state to face alone the pale gloom of a family bereavement, asked Carlyle, who had written a most moving letter of sympathy, to go there with him. Carlyle grumbled ungraciously about it to his brother: "Mill asks me to go with him, as far as Dorking in Surrey where they have a Countryhouse, on Saturday till Monday morning. It is very uncertain whether I will go. It costs some shillings of money, it wastes some hours of time: and small enjoyment reaped by it."[20] However, his sense of friendship prevailed, and go he did. It was an unfortunate visit from the start. They were to leave on

* By a young Doctor King, who soon afterwards married his sister Willie.

Saturday 16 July, and arranged to meet on the Dorking coach. Carlyle, always an excitable rather than an effective traveller, omitted to find out that there were two such coaches running on that morning, and so had to travel alone in one, while Mill and Horace Grant, their mutual friend from the India House, boarded the other.*

They returned to London on the Monday, parting at the "Elephant and Castle", where their paths diverged. While at Mickleham, Carlyle had behaved with suitably mournful tact; but when he got home he sent a most uncivil account of his outing to his "little lassie", who had retreated to her mother's house in Scotland to recuperate from the climactic tempests of the *French Revolution*:

> "The Mills have joined some 'old carpenters' shops' together and made a pleasant summer mansion (connected by shed-roofed passages), the little drawing-room door of glass looking out into a rose lawn, into green plains, and half a mile off to a most respectable wooded and open broad-shouldered green hill. They were as hospitable as they could be. I was led about, and made attentive to innumerable picturesquenesses, etc. etc., all that evening and next day. . . . There was little sorrow visible in their house, or rather none, nor any human feeling at all; but the strangest *unheimlich* kind of composure and acquiescence, as if all human spontaneity had taken refuge in invisible corners. Mill himself talked much, and not stupidly—far from that—but without emotion of any discernible kind. He seemed to me to be withering or withered into the miserablest metaphysical *scrae*,† body and mind, that I had almost ever met with in the world. His eyes go twinkling and jerking with wild lights and twitches; his head is bald, his face brown and dry—poor fellow after all. It seemed to me the strangest thing what this man could want with me, or I with such a man so *unheimlich* to me. What will become of it? Nothing evil; for there is and there was nothing dishonest in it. But I think I shall see less and less of him. Alas, poor fellow! It seems possible too that he may not be very long seeable: that is one way of its ending—to say nothing of my own chances."[21]

To this the "little lassie" replied with a stab of subtle—far too subtle—irony: "Poor Mill! He really seems to have loved and lived: his very intellect seems to be failing him in its strongest point: his implicit devotion and subjection to you."[22]

John Mill was clearly very ill. He wrote next to nothing during

* Horace Grant (1800–1859) was Mill's colleague in the Examiner's Office 1826–1845. Later notable as author of a series of books on education much in advance of their time (Bain, *James Mill*, p. 356.)

† *Scrae*—old shoe.

1836, and, apart from the article on "Civilization," his only contribution to the *Review* was his "Definition of Political Economy" written five years previously. Brighton having failed, it was decided that he should go abroad to see what the "free and genial" atmosphere of his beloved France could do for him. The India House granted him three months' leave of absence: his editorial duties had to be left in the incompetent hands of Falconer; and Molesworth undertook to write the political summaries that were a regular part of Mill's task. He set out from London on 30 July, accompanied by his brothers; Henry, who at sixteen was also seriously ill, and young George aged about twelve. Harriet, although in indifferent health herself, hastened over to take care of him: she passed through Boulogne two days before he started and awaited him in Paris. As she had brought with her all her three children and a nurse, they made a sizeable and assorted party, though not a cheerful one, since at least three of them were ailing. Young George, however, took great pleasure in an experience never enjoyed by his eldest brother at his age, a playfellow only a year or so his junior. With Herbert Taylor, he formed a friendship which was to endure for the rest of his short life, and in which Harriet's other son Haji also came to share.

The party travelled all together to Geneva and Lausanne. There Harriet and Mill took leave of their respective charges and the nurse, and went on to Nice in September. Henry reported home that Mill's head was still obstinately troublesome: "John wrote to us a very desponding letter, saying that if he had to go back without getting well, he could not again go to the India House, but must throw it up, and try if a year or two of leisure would do anything."[23] Carlyle, much concerned, enclosed a lot of sympathy and good advice in a letter of Horace Grant's. At the same time he could not resist writing to tell Sterling, who was at Bordeaux for his own health, his private opinion of their friend's persistent illness:

> "Mill, they say, writes from Nice: he is not going into Italy, owing to Cholera and quarantine: his health is a little, and but a little, improved. Mrs. Taylor, it is whispered, is with him, or near him. Is it not very strange, this pining away into dessication and nonentity, of our poor Mill, if it be so, as his friends all say, that this charmer is the cause of it? I have not seen any riddle of human life which I could so ill form a theory of. They are innocent, says Charity; they are guilty, says Scandal: then why in the name of wonder are they dying broken-hearted? One thing only, is painfully clear to me, that poor Mill is in a bad way."[24]

As it happened, they did go into Italy, but no further south than Genoa. Thence they returned to Switzerland via Milan and the Italian Lakes, reaching their family in Lausanne at the end of October. A few days later they were in Paris, and on the 12 November they returned to England. It was not a good time to come back, just as the long nights were drawing on and winter was beginning to spread out its chilly fingers. Mill, in his debilitated state was open to any infection there might be, and when London was gripped by its usual influenza epidemic both he and Harriet succumbed immediately, to the permanent damage of his lungs.

Nevertheless, Mill had to turn at once to the various duties occasioned by his father's death. He had been promoted again in the India Office and was now third Examiner with a salary of £1200 and Thomas Love Peacock as his chief—a post he held comfortably enough for twenty years before becoming, in his turn, Head Examiner. For the moment he deplored the extra work. There was also his father's estate to be cleared up and his family to be provided for. They had moved to a smaller house in Kensington Square, and in all domestic matters from the payment of the rent to Henry's tuition fees at London University, it was to John they turned. He was feeling no better as a result of his excursion, and his labours, so far from abating, were redoubled. "You may wonder that I have been so long in writing to you," he wrote to Sarah Austin in Malta, "though after all, I write first: but you would not wonder if you knew the endless drudgery I have had upon my hands, with arrears of India House business and private affairs, without counting review matters or any other writing."[25] Next day, writing to Nichol, he said the same again. It was the only occasion in his life when he complained of overwork.

IV

Early in 1836 the old *Westminster* was bought for £1000 by Molesworth from Colonel Perronet Thompson, who found that the new radical review had stolen away his market. The two were merged, and in April, for its fifth number, the *London* took on the title of *The London and Westminster Review*.

Mill was to a great extent responsible for this success. From the first he had been determined to avoid all narrowness and make the *London* as readable as possible. His own articles were extremely versatile, and he worked tirelessly to add to the regular staff of writers any others that were attractive, irrespective of their creed. He had bargained with Fox and Fonblanque, bartering his work in the *True Sun* and the *Examiner* in return for contributions. He had tactfully, though so far unsuccessfully, flattered Lytton Bulwer about his article on Sir Thomas Browne: "I did not know at the time that it was yours, and could not conceive what new accession had come to the *Edinburgh Review*. I first thought it might possibly be Macaulay's, but as I read on I felt it to be far too good for him."[26] He had approached John Sterling, who from the height of his orthodoxy had declined to become connected with the only periodical making, as he said, no distinction between right and wrong. He had appealed to Sarah Austin, and received warm and ready help:

> "My dearest John,
>
> Of course I shall do all I can—I hope I can finish the [?article?] for you—if not I will tell you my dear, and you shall help me—You did right to apply to me, I should have been jealous if you had not and miserable if you had sacrificed your rest when I could help you—I shall put aside all for this and with pleasure. It is a small earnest dearest John of what I should be glad to do for you if I could—and if you get any satisfaction from that I am more than rewarded. The time is short but I will try.
>
> Your Mutterlein."[27] *

Of all his friends, the one best calculated to disperse an atmosphere of sameness was Thomas Carlyle. Mill knew that Carlyle would be

* This letter may refer to an article on the "Translators of Faust", which appeared in July 1836.

glad of the money, for at the time of the burning of the *French Revolution*, he had been admitted into the fearful state of the "actual economic position".[28] Accordingly, he pressed continually for articles, at first without conspicuous success. Carlyle did not like the first number which Mill gave him, finding it hidebound and uninspiring. A review of the works of Hannah More he had been contemplating was abandoned because the necessary books were not delivered to him in time. Instead, he contributed a serio-comic fragment called the "Physiology of the Épicier", culled from the sidelines of his French researches.

In February 1836, Carlyle, who was thrifty with his works, suggested that Mill might like to take the still unpublished *Diamond Necklace*. Mill hesitated; suggested cutting and alterations which were refused, and finally sent it to John Sterling for an opinion. Sterling replied that it was not suitable for the *Review* because of "the capricious licentiousness of the grammar" and "the length to which the rhapsody is drawn out".[29] In the meantime the despised but faithful Fraser bought it for £50 and published it in his "cess-pool of a magazine".[30] It appeared in 1837 and was almost as scornfully received as *Sartor Resartus* had been before it. At Mill's earnest request, Carlyle undertook to provide in place of it some further by-products of his *French Revolution*. The first, the "Histoire Parlementaire," was easily accomplished, but required much alteration that had to wait Carlyle's pleasure. The second, on Mirabeau, was more of a struggle. After many groans, he bought himself an enormous white hat to ward off headaches, and observing his wife's injunction never to wear it in her presence, he began to write.

To his fury, while Mill was away in France, Falconer and his printer treated him cavalierly. Not only did they delay "Mirabeau" into the new year, pending, as he thought, quite unnecessary revision. They lost his amendments to it in the press, and, even worse, omitted to send him the twelve copies he had promised to Emerson in Boston. Emerson was doing a brisk trade as his American agent. He had sold out one edition of *Sartor* and had started on another before it had ever been printed as a book in England. He must not therefore be kept waiting. "I begin to be weary of the treatment I experience here",[31] Carlyle complained to Sterling.

These and other inefficiencies persuaded Mill on his return that the time had come for a complete change over in the management.

After the number for April 1837, Falconer was replaced by one John Robertson, and the bookseller Hooper of Pall Mall undertook production. Mill wrote to Sarah:

> "I send you the review, the last number to be brought out by Falconer—he and I have all along differed completely as to the management and the difference at last came to a crisis and he resigned. It is now in the hands of a man as efficient as he was inefficient, a man who seems made by nature to conduct the detail business of a review, and who (he is very young) promises, I think, to be fit for much better things too."[32]

He added, when apologizing to his Paris agent for the irregular arrival of the *Review*, "under the new management we have prospects of much greater pecuniary success than before—that is, we may hope to pay our expenses, which we have never yet done."[33]

John Robertson was yet another Scot. Brought up as a cooper's apprentice in Aberdeen, and trained for the Ministry, he had left to pursue a literary career in London. He came to Mill's notice as a fellow member of the Reform Club, and as a fellow writer for the *Morning Chronicle*, and he contributed articles above ordinary merit on Shakespeare and on Bacon to the *London and Westminster*. Professor Bain, who knew him well, was rather surprised at John Mill's enthusiastic estimate of his attainments, which he thought were of the slightest, while his industry was, to say the best of it, fitful. He was a lively young man, with an unfailing eye for a careless feminine ankle; hard-hitting to the point of rashness, ambitious, and possessed of an honest sense of humour. An association with Mill was for him the summit of success, and he was determined to make the most of it.[34] He was full of new devices for making the *Review* more saleable, some of them finding little favour with his superior. He proposed, for instance, that instead of printing contributions in a solid wad under a single title, they should be split up and made more intriguing by periodic headings. This, Mill felt, was likely to confuse the reader. He insisted on the old method being preserved at any rate in the case of his own articles, "for I don't like people not to see at once what they are about".[35] But Robertson's ideas were generally stimulating, and he was extremely facile in conversation and in composition. The very effort to curb and instruct his young enthusiasm was as a tonic to the jaded editor.[36]

The change in management of the *Review* caused an acerbation of the differences already becoming apparent in the radical camp. Falconer, who was Roebuck's brother-in-law, was not at all satisfied with his treatment, and when Mrs. Grote on her husband's behalf declined to furnish an article on Greek history, Molesworth took it as a piece of party feeling, and wrote a "flippant letter in mighty bad taste about our ceasing to write for the L & W".[37] Robertson made things worse. During the summer of 1837 he was in Boulogne and did not come into contact with the Grote coterie. But in September and October, while Mill, sadly bewailed by Harriet, was away on a walking tour in Wales, he was left in sole charge with "carte blanche about fill up matter".[38] His vigorous and roughshod methods caused much annoyance, especially as he was not quite a gentleman, and they were therefore considered an impertinence.

Such petty quarrels would have been of no significance, had they not been the outcome of other, deeper causes of dissension. From the first, there had been a major difference of aim and object between Mill and the remainder of the radical party. For them, sudden political importance had proved too heady. They had narrowed their ranks, and made themselves more exclusive than before. While they looked upon the *Review* as a means of reiterating the challenge of pure dogma, Mill saw it as a means of resolving discords, revealing unities, and kneading the whole amorphous lump of radical opinion into a potent political weapon. He told Fonblanque, "I have never had any other notion of practical policy since the Radicals were numerous enough to form a party, than that of resting on the *whole body* of Radical opinion, from the Whig-Radicals at one extreme to the more reasonable and practical of the working classes, and the Benthamites, on the other. I have been trying ever since the Reform Bill to stimulate, so far as I had an opportunity, all sections of the Parliamentary Radicals to organize such a system of policy: not saying to them—Adopt my views, do as I bid you; but Adopt *some* views, do *something*."[39]

The difference of approach was well exemplified in the attitude of Molesworth. At the time when his association with Mill began, the young baronet was one of the most rabid of the Whig-baiters. When the glorious news of the election for the session of February 1835 became public, he wrote triumphantly to his mother: "This is the commencement of a party which will one day or another bring destruction upon both Whigs and Tories."[40] Shortly afterwards he was able to announce progress in his campaign for embarrassing the

Melbourne ministry. "We have damaged the Whigs, and some of them had better look to their seats."[41] Not content with aggravating the Whigs in Parliament whenever possible, he carried his persecution into the social field. With John Temple Leader, one of the members for Westminster, he took a house in Eaton Square, installed an excellent cook, and opened a dining club for Radicals only, which in 1836 took the name of the Reform Club. For the Whigs, this was too much. Political licence was one thing; being blackballed from a club was quite another. After all, most of the Radical M.P.'s were returned as Whigs at least in name. The result was an angry interview between Molesworth and Parkes, and two senior members of the cabinet. At this stage, Mill—himself a member of the club as was also John Taylor—intervened. He pointed out to Molesworth that the best tactic for the new party was not to enrage the Whigs, but to court them and win them over. So great was his ascendancy over his colleague that Molesworth instantly reversed his policy. The Whigs were admitted to the Reform Club in such numbers that they entirely swamped the Radical founder members. And he became so affable an ambassador of goodwill that Sarah Austin wrote from Malta and complained to Mill, "He is too much a frequenter of dinners".[42] Mill hastened to his defence:

> "Roebuck and Charles Buller are now in very high reputation everywhere—those two in particular, and the party in general. It is all owing to Molesworth. You say he is too fond of going to dinners—it may seem so at a distance, but to us who are here it is plain that he did not go to one dinner too many—he went only when a demonstration was needed, and has produced an effect through the country which will be permanent. . . . I have been driving them [the Radicals] these four years to what they have now at last done most successfully."[43]

Mill's efforts to give a broad embracing character both to the radical party and to the *Review* received an added impetus upon his father's death. He had always revered his father. Immediately after the event, he had entered into a long correspondence with the Austins about the selection of a suitable epitaph, and some years later he leapt to arms to defend his father's memory from the slights slurred over it in Bowring's biography of Bentham.[44] But he had also feared him. So long as James Mill lived, the heretical humanism so offensive to the stricter Benthamites had been held in check. Now that he was gone, all that was changed. In November 1836 Mill wrote to Lytton Bulwer, whose work he was once more anxious to obtain:

> "As good may be drawn out of evil—the event which has deprived the world of the man of the greatest philosophical genius it possessed, and the review . . . of its most powerful writer, and the only one to whose opinion the editors were obliged to defer—that same event has made it far easier to do that in the hope of which alone I allowed myself to become connected with the review, namely, to soften the harder and sterner features of its Radicalism and Utilitarianism, both of which in the form in which they originally appeared in the *Westminster* were part of the inheritance of the eighteenth century . . . If you do not find the atmosphere of the *London and Westminster Review* more and more congenial to you it will not be my fault. . . . Your aid, to whatever degree afforded . . . would conduce, more than any other literary assistance I can think of, to render the Review what it is not now even in the slightest degree, an organ of real literary and social criticism."[45]

This purpose met with strong antagonism from Mill's old friends, and the gusting bone of it was his inclusion of Carlyle. "Mirabeau" produced a storm of censure. "I am quite persuaded the Review will cease to be the engine of propagating sound and sane doctrines on Ethics and Politics under J.M.", wrote Mrs. Grote to Roebuck. "Whether by getting hooks baited with carrion, he hopes to attract other sorts of fish than those *we* angle for, and thus render it a better investment, I really am not in a condition to judge. But, on the other hand, it is a matter of entire indifference to me so viewed. For my part I only wonder how the people contrive to keep improving, under the purveyance of the stuff and nonsense they are subjected to."[46] The Austins far away in Malta also voiced their disapproval: "Thank you for the *London Review*. I think it is a very good number. Mr. Lewis* and my husband are clamorous against poor Carlyle's article and say that you will ruin the review if you admit any more. I am afraid this is a very general opinion, though I grieve it should be so."[47]

"*Apropos* of your remark on Carlyle's article 'Mirabeau'", Mill firmly answered: " I am not at all surprised that Mr. Austin or that Lewis should dislike it, but it has been the most popular article we ever had in the review and I think has been extremely useful to us. Except Roebuck, Grote and Senior, I have met with nobody here,

* Sir George Cornewall Lewis, 1806–1863, John Austin's colleague on the Malta Commission, and a periodical contributor to the *Review*. He later became editor of the *Edinburgh Review*, and held important cabinet offices under Palmerston.

of any account, who disliked it: and these three dislike everything, the *style* of which is not humdrum."[48]

At the elections in July 1837 the country rallied chivalrously about the person of the girl-queen, and there was a Tory gain. The Whigs suffered heavily; the Radicals were ruined. Roebuck and Hume were both defeated; Grote got in by a mere six votes, and they returned only nine representatives in all. "I will tell you what *we* are coming to, Grote", observed Charles Buller ruefully; "in no very long time from this, you and I will have to 'tell' Molesworth."[49] In the face of catastrophe, all was at sixes and sevens. Roebuck, raging on the pavement, was all for joining the Tories in order to damage the Whigs. Mill, while not going quite to that length, was inclined to agree with him that a Tory majority for a short time was the only means of obtaining a favourable reaction. Molesworth was frankly sick of politics. And Grote, as usual, thought the only thing to do was to press for the ballot.

At such a time, Mill's trifling with the enemy seemed to the sterner Radicals worse than treason. But he was not to be deterred. The last sheets of the *French Revolution* had rumbled through the press, and neither his editorial discretion nor his sense of personal debt towards Carlyle permitted any doubt as to what he ought to do. In the *London and Westminster* for July 1837 he greeted it enthusiastically, soaring into lyricism as befitted the herald of a lasting fame.

> "This is not so much a history as an epic poem: and notwithstanding, or even in consequence of this, the truest of histories. It is the history of the French Revolution, and the poetry of it, both in one; and on the whole no work of greater genius, either historical or poetical, has been produced in this country for many years."

Other critics, awaiting the event, had been busy fitting out again their miserable harriers. The *Athenaeum* had already said "it is one thing to put forth a few pages of quaintness, neologism, and whimisical coxcombry; and another to carry such questionable qualities through three long volumes of uninspired persiflage and flippant pseudo-philosophy."[50] But at the appearance of Mill's eulogy the hunt drew off. The furore occasioned by the *French Revolution* was immediate. "Dickens carried a copy of it with him wherever he went. Southey read it six times over. Thackeray reviewed it enthusiastically.* Even Jeffrey generously admitted that Carlyle had succeeded upon lines on which he had himself foretold inevitable failure."

* In the *Times*.

Macaulay, Hallam, Brougham—"they with the rest were obliged to admit that there had arisen a new star, of baleful perhaps and ominous aspect, but a star of the first magnitude in English literature."[51]

Carlyle at first was greatly pleased and flattered. "No man, I think, need wish to be better reviewed", he wrote to Mill. "You have said openly of my poor Book what I durst not myself dream of it, but should have liked to dream had I dared. It is a courageous Article."[52] But later on he found that times had changed. He was no longer a prophet in the wilderness, he was a literary lion. His course of lectures on German Literature, arranged by Henry Taylor, Richard Monckton Milnes, Harriet Martineau and other friends, to save him from the backwoods of America, became a national event. The doors were jammed. What further need had he of Reviews or of Reviewers? Only money: for although he now had fame, he had not yet touched the wages of it. He had never liked Mill's magazine. A year before, he had written to Emerson: "As for Mill's *London Review* (for he is quasi-editor), I do not recommend it to you. Hide-bound Radicalism; a to me well-nigh insupportable thing! Open it not: a breath as of the Sahara and the Infinite Sterile comes from every page of it."[53] Now he was in a position to bargain. Robertson had asked him to write an article on Scott: he wrote to Mill as man to man:

> "I think I either ought to make some engagement of some permanence, we will say for a year; or not to intermeddle with the Periodical concern farther at all.
>
> The thing I want to ask you therefore is, contrasting honestly in your mind my capabilities with the wants of your Enterprise, what is the utmost amount of employment (I mean money-amount, at so much per page, or otherwise reckoned on what principle you liked) your Review could afford me, say, from this December 1837 till the same date of 1838? That is the first of all questions. . . . Farther, I should desire, indeed I should need, to have, if not my own choice of subjects, yet something very like that; also, I doubt if I could stand much *editing*. . . .
>
> And now, my dear Mill, I will beg only one other thing of you: that you meditate this question not as my friend but as the Manager of your own Review; this with all freedom and singleness of view. It is really much the same to me how you decide. . . ."[54]

The result of this letter he reported to his brother. "Mill called almost the next day, and at great length unfolded his pecuniary position with regard to that Review; which Molesworth, after spending some thousands on it, quits altogether in April next, leaving it in Mill's keeping; not in a very solvent state. Many of the Articles *Must* be gratis: from me an Article *every other No.* would be most acceptable, etc. etc. in short, it was quite quite clear that here lay no bread for me; hardly salt to my bread. Meanwhile poor Mill looked dolefully anxious that I should not desert him. In brief, I answered next day that I *would* do that *Scott*: . . . it will bring me in somewhat like fifty pounds; that is the only use of it."[55] Mill immediately sent Robertson scurrying off to find the requisite books which, if necessary, he himself would pay for.

As it happened, Molesworth left the *Review* not in the following April but at the end of 1837. It is not easy to say exactly how much money it had cost him. The only figures quoted are those given by Carlyle, and they are at best conjectural: in his *Reminiscences* he said it was £4000, but he told Emerson £3000. As a matter of fact it is most unlikely that Molesworth paid out anything much as a lump sum at the founding of the *Review*: he only had to guarantee to underwrite the losses. These at the rate of £100, stated by Robertson, per number for the eleven issues which he sponsored come to £1100, and in addition there was the £1000 paid out to Perronet Thompson for buying up the *Westminster*. In any case the loss was quite enough to alarm both his family and himself. Besides, his health had broken down under the strain of his unhappy love-affairs; he was sick of the disputes among the Radicals, and was turning ever more towards a more constructive project, his plan for Colonial development. It is not clear what, if anything, Mill paid him when he took over the *Review*, but he had evidently determined not to let it fail, and at the beginning of 1838 it was his and his alone.

Mill as Editor behaved as would be expected, with energy and kindness. He never failed to read a contribution and particularly enjoyed looking at the work of new writers, saying that he could detect intellectual honesty from the handwriting. He scarcely ever broke a connection once begun: when it became necessary to put off Blanco White, a worthy old professor who had given his life to exposing the evils of Catholicism in revenge for the sufferings of his two sisters in a Spanish nunnery, his letter of rejection was a masterpiece of affectionate tact, and was followed by the gift of a very rare book.[56] If he made a mistake, as in accepting an article from Dr. Bisset which he was subsequently disinclined to print, he refused to let it fall to the charge of the *Review*, and paid the necessary £25 to the author out of his own pocket.[57]

Financially, the *Review* was a constant drain upon Mill, and he was not at the time a wealthy man. He would, he told Nichol, willingly give up the India House if he "had £300 a year free from anxiety and literary labour, but I have at most £100".[58] Robertson, of course, was paid a salary, and they allowed a pound a page to such of their contributors as would accept it. The bookseller, in addition to his printing charges, was permitted to farm the advertising for his own profit. The Paris agent was paid Frs. 250 per issue with a further allowance of Frs. 125 for advertisement.* With these generous expenses it is hardly surprising that their hopes of self-sufficiency proved to have been too sanguine. Their first number lost them over £100. With economy and ingenuity this was eventually reduced to £33, the smallest debit figure ever achieved by the *Review* while under their control.[59]

At least, his personal losses enabled Mill to stand above his critics and indulge his inclinations. He resolved, despite his growing unpopularity with Roebuck and the Grotes, to press on even more strongly with his old intention to turn the Radicals into Liberals and the *Review* into a vehicle of culture. In the literary sphere his persistent efforts to collar new contributors had been meeting with success. Through Carlyle he had got an article from Leigh Hunt. Fox and Bulwer had at last written as they had for a long time promised. Charles Buller had reviewed *Pickwick* enthusiastically. Nichol was still writing, and Napier, and Harriet Martineau, whom Mill would as soon have been without. Robertson, too, was useful, but had to be closely watched. Once, contrary to Mill's express instructions, he published an article he had written defending female authors against "Crokerisms", or scurrilous onslaughts in the press.† His remarks about "blackguardising" and "lying" were taken as personal insults by Abraham Hayward, Mill's former tilting partner in the Debating Society, who vindictively tried to hold the proprietor responsible.[60] There was also Mill's own work. His glowing tribute to his friend Armand Carrel, the delicate-looking Republican editor, the Fonblanque of France, recently killed in a duel while defending his journalistic reputation. And his delightful appreciation of the writings of Alfred de Vigny. But it became increasingly hard

* Frs. 250 equalled about £10 at that time.

† So called after J. W. Croker, the author of the famous article against Keats in the *Quarterly*, and a man who boasted of his slashing anonymous attacks on women.

to keep the standard up, and the editors were forced at times to accept padding for lack of anything else to print.

In extremity, Mill turned once more to Sterling, now in Madeira. Carlyle, having achieved his main object of weaning his disciple away from religious orthodoxy, and now wishing to turn him from poetry to prose, felt that the *London and Westminster* would serve his purpose and added his support to Mill's appeal:

"Since I began writing, John Mill has been here; he is of purpose to write to you himself, and get your help in his Review, which has now become wholly his. What will you do? Mill himself means really well, and according as you mean, all the way he goes."[61] Sterling was still hesitant. "Mill", he replied in his best Carlylese, "might as well try to extract Twelfth Cake from Remainder Biscuit as to get vigorous interpretation from me. However he is an honest affectionate fellow whom I trust . . . and I should be right happy to help him if I could.

"At the best I should have some hesitation. I fear do what he will, if the [L and W] is to be a Radical Organ it must show a bad carping sneering partisan newspaper kind of spirit which I thoroughly hate."[62]

When Sterling returned to England, however, the secular mood overtook him altogether. In the summer of 1838 he founded a club which met to dine and talk on the first Tuesday of each month at the Piazza Coffee House in Covent Garden. To the scandal of the orthodox, a dozen or so of Sterling's closest friends, varying in religious conformity from church dignitaries such as Wilberforce and Thirlwall, to notorious infidels like Carlyle and Mill, were usually in attendance. Moreover, no grace was said when they sat down. Originally known as the "Anonymous Club", it soon changed its title at the desire of the members to the "Sterling Club".* It was still flourishing after Sterling's death; and when the appearance of Archdeacon Hare's limping biography surrendered his memory to the organs of doctrinal chauvinism as that of an apostate and recusant priest, the rumoured transactions of the Sterling Club provided them with the best scandal they had had since the Prince Consort had been caught playing chess in his apartments on a Sunday afternoon.

Having moved so far towards becoming "one who flung abroad the standard of open rebellion against the Lord Almighty", as

* See Mill on the Sterling Club in letter to Harriet, 31 March 1849 (Hayek, p. 149).

the evangelical *Record* afterwards denounced him,[63] there was no more room for moral scruples, and Sterling produced for the *Review* an allegoric article on Montaigne. Mill and Robertson were delighted, more delighted than he thought the thing was worth, and he refused to take their punctual payment:

> "I found here Robertson's note and draft and should have written to you about it even if I had not heard from you. I wish you to tell me in confidence whether the Review pays its expenses. If not I shall take the liberty of tearing up the draft. We may make other arrangements for the future—but if the Review puts you to any expense, I shall beg of you to accept the gift of my Scratchings about Montaigne in token of the sincere affection with which I am
>
> Yours ever
>
> John Sterling."[64]

His next contribution, about Simonides, elegist of Thermoplyae and Marathon, was submitted with a warm postscript indicative of his change of mind: "May your shadow, i.e. the Review, never be less!"[65] Its colourful improbability caused Mill grave embarrassment. "If it be necessary to stand up against the almost unanimous opinion both of the believing and unbelieving world (who would agree in considering it impossible that a miracle should have been wrought in the name of false gods), I should like it to be on some occasion which required it and on which my own convictions went with it",[66] he protested. Nevertheless, "Simonides" appeared in the number for December 1838.

Sterling had also proposed to review *Sartor*, now at last appearing, in the wake of the *French Revolution*, as a proper book, and was at first offended when Mill dissuaded him:

> "I shall be very glad to have my time to myself for other objects than reviewing Sartor so that from me you have no difficulty to look for. It is of course nothing to the purpose that I do not see the force of the objection . . . But if you want poignant novelettes no doubt you are right."[67]

Mill then explained the wider project he had had in mind, and Sterling swung to the opposite pole of intense enthusiasm. He agreed that *Sartor* had already been reviewed to death; instead, he would make a grand appraisal of Carlyle as a whole, his faults and virtues, his style and all his works. It was a year before it was finished, a year full of more intimate conference with Mill than he had yet experienced. Unlike the subject of his monograph, Sterling resolutely continued to refuse all payment, but in the end permitted Mill to ease his conscience with a gift of books.

First Carlyle, and now Sterling! For the Philosophical Radicals to have the lucid pages of their party chronicle defiled by the ragings of a wild emotionalist was bad enough, but a clerk in holy orders, even a suspect one, was overmuch. Mill's breach with the Grotes and Roebuck, already serious, widened to others and grew permanent: it led to his giving up the society of many of his former friends, and to recriminations on their part, blaming Harriet Taylor quite unjustly for the change in him. When Fonblanque supposed him an adherent to the "Grote conclave" he violently repudiated it:

> "What is the meaning of *your* insisting upon identifying me with Grote and Roebuck and the rest? . . . Have you forgotten what I am sure you once knew, that my Radicalism is of a school the most remote from theirs at all points which exist? *They* knew this as long ago as 1829, since which time the variance has been growing wider and wider. I never consented to have anything to do with the London Review but for the sake of getting together a body of writers who would represent radicalism more worthily than they did: you never could be induced to help me in this and until I could find such persons who would I could do little—but in proportion as I did find such persons I have been divesting the review of its sectarian character and have even gone this length, that when Molesworth ceased to feel that the review represented his opinions I took it off his hands, and am now myself the proprietor of it. In the face of this it is rather hard to be accused of ascribing all wisdom and infallibility to a set from whose opinions I differ more than from the Tories."[68]

In their eyes he was going to perdition and carrying his review along with him. The appearance in August 1838 of his criticism on the inviolable Bentham seemed to them, as it was meant to seem, a solemn final recantation. Five years before, in 1833, he had expressed his change of view on Bentham's philosophy at the request of Lytton Bulwer, who was then compiling a book called *England and the English*. Bulwer had thought his criticism excellent, and wished to publish it as it stood, but Mill at that time had refused outright for fear of his father. "It is not, and must not be, known to be mine",[69] he wrote to Nichol, and in the end Bulwer had to print it hugger-mugger as an appendix.

Now the article was taken out again and polished up. It appeared[70] as the first of two comparing Coleridge and Bentham, to the disadvantage of the latter, as the two great seminal minds of their generation.

The good old man had gone to his peculiar fathers in June 1832 a week or two after the passage of the Great Reform Bill he had done so much to frame. On his own instructions he was not buried; his body was carelessly draped in a sheet, and carried in a piano-dealer's van to the Webb Street School of Anatomy, where it was the first corpse voluntarily offered for dissection. Amidst angry peals of thunder, Dr. Southwood Smith made an impressive oration to the assembled friends and students before going to work with a knife. Bentham's skeleton was then dressed up in his usual clothes and given a waxwork head by Mme. Tussaud. He was seated in a chair, "Dapple" was thrust into his gloved hand, and for two successive years he presided over a dinner of his disciples, until the macabre effect so told upon the guests that the reunions had to be discontinued. In the library of University College he may still be seen, in a smart glass case, with his real head between his feet: every so often he is taken out and shaken and punched to keep the moths at bay.

His White-Knightly quality, his hopeful common sense, uncontradictable but yet not quite screwed down, was the basis of Mill's final estimate of his old friend. "He was a boy to the last" he wrote, and from that sprang both his virtues and his limits. He was completely kindly and optimistic, completely positive and practical in outlook. As a blaster of prejudice and catchwords he had no equal, and his practical achievements were immense. His political tenets, although they stopped short of protecting society from the tyranny of the proletariat implicit in complete democracy, secured more than could have been hoped for in his time. As for the law, "he found the philosophy of law a chaos, he left it a science: he found the practice of the law an Augean stable, he turned the river into it which is mining and sweeping away mound after mound of its rubbish". All this did not invalidate, however, the fact that he saw only half of any problem; indeed, it was because he saw one half so clearly that he was able to do so much. "For our own part, we have a large tolerance for one-eyed men, provided their one eye is a penetrating one: if they saw more, they probably would not see so keenly, nor so eagerly pursue one course of inquiry. Almost all rich veins of original and striking speculation have been opened by systematic half-thinkers."

On the other hand, continued Mill, half vision is no aid to a philosopher, for truth is a synthesis. "Every circumstance which gives a character to the life of a human being, carries with it its peculiar biases: its peculiar facilities for perceiving some things, and for missing or forgetting others. . . . No whole truth is possible but by combining the points of view of all the fractional truths." In this faculty Bentham was completely lacking. Of respect for other minds possibly finer than his own he was quite devoid. He wrote in a vacuum, as though his treatises on human affairs were the only ones that had been made; and any body of thought which disagreed with his, including that of Plato, he contemptuously dismissed as "vague generalities". He was thus driven back for information upon his own resources, which were quite unfitted for the task. He had no experience of many sides of the human state, nor was he able to imagine them. "He never knew prosperity and adversity, passion nor satiety: he never had even the experience which sickness gives. . . . His own lot was cast in a generation of the leanest and barrenest men whom England had yet produced, and he was an old man when a better race came in with the present century. . . . No one, probably, who, in a highly-instructed age, ever attempted to give a rule to all human conduct, set out with a more limited conception either of the agencies by which human conduct *is*, or of those by which it *should be* influenced."

The effect of precise reasoning, which was his real mastery, from such slender premises was disastrous. Human nature as revealed in his "Table of the Springs of Action" was hopelessly incomplete and confined entirely to self-interest, and it was on this view of human nature that his entire philosophy was built. His political system was a mere list of checks and balances, whereby the interests both of rulers and their subjects were weighted towards socially useful actions and away from those that were harmful. His social system took no account of any difference between one individual and another, one stage of civilization and another, or even of racial characteristics. Ethically, he regarded actions purely from the moral standpoint of general expediency: of their other aspects he had no idea at all. That what was morally admirable might not be beautiful, or that what was moral and beautiful might still not be lovable, never occurred to him. He had no knowledge of psychic nuances; poetry was for him misrepresentation.

V

The lasting achievement of the Radicals dated from these years of strife and failure, although to most of them it seemed at first a backwater. When Molesworth arrived in London just after the Reform Bill of 1832, one branch of radical thought was beginning to examine the possibility of systematic colonization. It might, they thought, provide a welcome alternative to the grim action of misery and vice in relieving the pressure of population. At the same time, the development of wealthy dominions overseas might be achieved more profitably by assisted emigration than by penal transportation, which they considered ineffective as a punishment and detrimental to the interests of the colonies.

Molesworth joined the National Colonization Society recently formed by Edward Gibbon Wakefield, and in 1834 the whole question of transportation came to a head. The Melbourne government were fearful of the effect on wages of the new workmen's movement towards combination, as expressed in the Grand National Consolidated Trades Union. By way of making an example, they picked upon six harmless and illiterate Dorchester labourers, who had been in the habit of holding oddfellow's meetings as a means of mutual assistance and society on the cheerless winter evenings. They were prosecuted under an obsolete statute, originally devised to punish mutiny in the Navy, and were savagely sentenced to seven years' transportation to Van Diemen's Land.

Shortly afterwards it came to light that a small aristocratic clique in Northern Ireland had formed a chain of secret societies called the Orange Lodges. Under the guise of freemasonry, their real object was to put the Duke of Cumberland on the throne of England at his brother's death instead of his niece Victoria, who was a female and a minor, and was likely to come under Whig influences. In January 1836 Molesworth shrewdly pointed out in the *London Review* the inequality of the law, demanding that the Duke and his treasonous associates should be prosecuted under the same statute as the Tolpuddle Martyrs, and should be packed off in their turn to the hulks. This was not done; but the Orange Lodges were disbanded. The next year Molesworth moved for and obtained a select committee on transportation under his own chairmanship. It was said "probably no volume was ever published in England of which the contents were so loathsome as the appendix to that Committee's Report".[71] As a result, though not for another thirty years, transportation was eventually abolished.

On the positive side, that of assisted emigration and organized development of the colonies, Molesworth could act only through his own pocket, since the enterprise was left to private companies. He joined the South Australia Association in 1834, and later became director of the New Zealand Association, but was hampered by obstruction from the Colonial Office, and by bitter opposition from the Church Missionary Society, who felt that the conditions "out there" were too corrupting for any white men other than missionaries to endure.

Although he was less immediately successful in this field, there began to grow up in his mind, and in the minds of those who assisted and succeeded him, a grand new design: a visionary dream of a free Commonwealth of associated democracies, industrially busy, decently taught and clad, bound together only by the intangible cords of common aims and interests. More and more it lured him away from the fruitless machinations of home politics, from the disappointed ideals of the *London and Westminster Review*. He lived to see the foundations of dominion self-government laid in Canada, Australia, and New Zealand: and he died in harness as Colonial Secretary in Palmerston's cabinet.

Associated with Molesworth in Wakefield's National Colonization Society were his two close friends John Mill and Charles Buller. These three linked the movement to the parliamentary Radicals, and to the dramatic issues woven round the enigmatic figure of the Earl of Durham. John George Lambton, "Radical Jack" as he was later known, was born of good old country stock. His father, who used to come to Westminster for the opening of the session honestly attired in a suit of homespun made from the wool of his own sheep, was stopped on one occasion by a supercilious usher who refused him entrance. The mistake was rectified, and as he was about to pass inside, the fellow held out a wheedling hand: "I hope your honour will give me something to remember you by another time." "Indeed I will", replied the squire, and caught him a staggering blow on the side of the head. Much of this spirit was transmitted to the son who at the age of five inherited the great estates.

His nature was an unstable mixture of impulse and formality. A saving grace of liberal principles, instilled by an early tutor, survived the patrician influences of Eton and the Tenth Hussars. At twenty, he spoiled his military chances by making a Gretna Green elopement with a girl who died soon afterwards. Instead of giving way to heartbreak, he took the family seat in Parliament, and made a profitable second marriage with the daughter of Lord Grey. Before long he had a peerage and was in his father-in-law's cabinet, where he played an important part in the Reform Bill drama.

He was no Whig. By instinct he was Tory; only his impatience and his burning sense of wrong set him apart, as it had done Cobbett and Burdett, in a lonely backwater of politics demanding a return to days he thought must be good because they were indubitably old. In the Reformed Parliament he resigned office, and remained a brilliant, arrogant element, dangerously independent, and a possible focus for the dissaffected members of any party. He drew upon himself the full wrath of the government, expressed with a savagery of which only Brougham, his one-time friend, then Lord Chancellor, was capable. From the bitter judgement of his colleagues, Durham appealed to the people. And the people, with their constant expectation of a champion from the ranks of the sun-born, so accepted him. When he spoke in Glasgow in October 1834, more than a hundred and twenty thousand persons assembled on the green to hear him.[72]

The significance of it was not lost on Mill. Always trying to establish his third party, always on the look-out for a leader, he would have soon despaired had he confined his vision to the pettiness of his associates. It was that hundred thousand strong that carried him on, the long, slow, patient line of the people gathered expectant round a single spruce figure. Expectant of what? That, Mill hoped, he would himself be able to decide. "We now see", he wrote to Nichol in November 1834, "the importance of the rallying point which Lord Durham has afforded. *Any* banner, placed so high that what is written upon it can be read by everybody, is all-important towards forming a party; but Lord Durham has really acted with consummate skill and in the best possible spirit. Whether he is ever minister or not, we have a great prize in him."[73] "His words", he told d'Eichthal, "have been taken up by the entire nation, the whole progressive party is solidly behind him. There are already several petitions to the king to make him minister. None the less, he will not be minister now nor perhaps ever: he is too vain, too imperious, and too much the slave of his own 'temperament'.—But I have no fear for us."[74]

Mill did not meet him face to face, knowing that in a contact where personal values were immediate and decisive, his scholarly standing and bookish approach would be unacceptable. Instead, he worked silently through Lytton Bulwer, adulatory, pseudo-Byronic, and well-connected. In January 1835, Bulwer wrote to Durham in terms of suitable homage, asking whether his lordship considered it a wise move for him, with his nebulous parliamentary following, to join the new party, the Philosophical Radicals. He admitted doubts about some of their policies, about the standing of some of their members, and the attitude of the aristocracy towards them. But he also hinted at their better propensities, and clearly pointed to their vacant chair of leadership.[75] Durham's reply, characteristically clear and haughty, carried no recognition of the offer:

> "As for the party to which you allude, I fairly confess that *I never before heard of its existence, or rather, of its being about to exist.* Until I know, therefore, of whom it is likely to be composed, and what are the avowed objects of its formation, I cannot advise my friend to join it."[76]

Bulwer wrote again, enclosing the party bulletin and a list of members, but by this time it was too late. Shrewd Melbourne, sensing danger, packed Durham off on a delicate mission as ambassador to St. Petersburg, where he would be out of the way for two years, and where, perhaps, he might by his impetuosity ruin himself.

No sooner had he gone than Melbourne, in the fashion of Richard II, abruptly sent Brougham too to "tread the strange paths of banishment". By it he earned the animosity of a dangerous man, but for the moment he obtained the peace and quiet he desired. The two years passed off all to quickly, and in the summer of 1837 Durham returned, not ruined in the least and as recalcitrant as ever. What would he do? That was the question that had the whole country by the ears.

"The eternal question in everybody's mouth", wrote Greville in his diary, "is what Lord Durham is to have, as if it was indispensable that he should have something. When Durham left England, he was the elected chief of the Radicals. Now that he is returned, the Radicals still regard him as their Chief, look anxiously to his introduction to the Cabinet. Charles Buller, whom I met the other day, said, in reply to my asking him if the Government would gain the election, 'I think they will gain anyhow, but *if they are wise* they will gain largely.' I said 'I wonder what you call being wise?' He said, 'Take in Lord Durham.'"[77] But to this, Melbourne would in no wise give consent. He played a waiting game, and, being a lucky fellow, there in due course came his way, as he thought, a far more admirable solution.

There was trouble in the Canadas. The arrangement dividing the country into two, Upper and Lower, West and East, had outworn its first purpose of pacification, and now tended to prevent all sense of national unity. In the eastern province of Quebec, discontent was endemic owing to the large French and Catholic majority. The west, Ontario, was colonized by loyalist emigrants from the United States; and people accustomed to a democratic climate were governed by an executive over whom they had no control apart from a limited vote in money matters. Overall, economic conditions were archaic, and the system for bringing forest and prairies into cultivation was lethargic and corrupt. Roebuck, regarding the question from the orthodox radical standpoint, had for the last ten years demanded the severance of the two provinces from the crown. Since the inception of the *London Review*, these and other shortcomings of Canadian Government had been tirelessly deplored. In 1837 small revolts broke out in each of the provinces. The Americans, still burning with dull anger at the humiliations of 1812, fingered their muskets and looked hungrily across the border. At home, in a generation vividly aware of the events of 1776, counsel was divided. "It has come to a fight", Mill wrote to Nichol, "and right or wrong originally, the question now is, will this country give men and money to prevent a colony by force from separating when it has a mind to it?"[78]

Here, thought Melbourne, was the ideal use for Durham. It was a task that would tax his undeniable capacities and power of command. If he succeeded, the Government could claim the credit: if he failed, it would be the end of him. In any case, it would get him out of the way. Besides, Durham was interested in the Colonies: like Molesworth, Mill, and Buller, he was a member of the Colonization Society, and was President of the New Zealand Association. What Melbourne did not know, and could not have understood if he had known it, was the great principle these few men shared between them, the principle of self-government within the Empire, worked out by Edward Gibbon Wakefield in Newgate gaol while serving a term for his unpopular habit of abducting heiresses. In Canada itself there had been frequent demands for responsible government; but, it transpired, they were really no more than a modest plea that responsible men be sent to govern them, instead of fools. In England it was commonly thought that Canada would inevitably go the way of the United States, and Durham was later told by a leading reformer of Upper Canada that he was "the first statesman to avow a belief in the possibility of a permanent connection between the colonies and the Mother Country".[79] Yet, those who believed in this principle found the Canadian problem straightforward and redeemable; although by no means easy.

The conditions demanded by Durham were very stiff. He insisted on dictatorial powers, and himself conducted the necessary Act of Parliament in the Lords, while Charles Buller acted for him in the Commons. Neither Whigs nor Tories were particularly enamoured of the idea, and when Buller was met with loud cries of "No!", Melbourne whispered to Russell that the mission was the greatest blunder they had yet committed.[80] The Bill was passed, reluctantly, at last.

The next thing was the question of Durham's retinue, about which he was more unmanageable than ever. He spurned the high-born pensionnaires, who were offered him in great profusion, insisting on picking for himself a small staff composed entirely of his confederates in the Colonization Society. As head secretary he chose Charles Buller. That was bad enough from the government's point of view, for Buller was not merely a Radical, he was a sort of Pantagruel; a burly fellow with an inexhaustible sense of humour, and an unfavourable name for playing practical jokes. They approved even less of Durham's next choice. Wakefield, who was probably the true father of the British Commonwealth, had acquired by his lady-snatching such a shocking reputation that any public function of which he was a part was doomed to irremediable distrust. "If you touch G.W. with a pair of tongs it is utter destruction, depend upon it",[81] wrote Lord Melbourne anxiously. But Durham was adamant, and the most they could get from him was an undertaking that the evil genius should go as his private adviser, without any official post.

Meanwhile Mill was busy working out the wider bearing of the negotiations. Great as were the prospects for Canada and the world if Lord Durham were successful, his success would also make it very probable that before long there would be no one to defy his popularity and he would be Prime Minister. A Radical Prime Minister was a stake to play for. "Give us access to him *early* and I will be d——d if we do not make a hard fight for it",[82] he told Robertson. So bright did the possibilities appear, he was even prepared to side with Grote and Roebuck in their attack upon the government. The hour for humouring the ministry was past. Melbourne was doomed. Unless the Radicals struck now in strength the Tories would come in, Canada and Durham would be lost. "A Durham ministry within a year" must be the slogan; or, at the very least, "a modification of the *personnel* of the ministry; not even a Durham ministry, but a *Whig* ministry unfettered on the finality of the reform bill". On that issue Mill would sink his differences, violent though they were, with the most bigoted of the Radicals, he warned Fonblanque. "I cannot, because I differ from them, join like you in crying them down for sacrificing their own popularity in maintaining *my* opinions about Canada, and while I myself seek the radical party where it *is*, not where it is *not*, and endeavour to rest upon the general body of radical opinion in the country, I will not throw overboard the most honest men in public life for standing nobly in the breach on a great occasion."[83] To make his purpose plain, he wrote an article in the *Review* defending Durham's claim for plenary powers, and giving him a hearty send off; while Molesworth to the last moment assiduously tutored Buller.

The deadly web of daily politics hung about Durham's mission, all unknown to him. After a leisurely embarkation of his family, of an enormous domestic train, and of plate chests weighty enough, or so Buller's mother feared, to sink the ship, the Earl's steamer paddled off. Melbourne, before they left, had given personal assurances—"As far as I am concerned, and I think I can answer for all my colleagues, you will receive the firmest and most unflinching support." The Queen, too, at his bidding sent a note of royal encouragement about "this important difficult duty": yet, while the smoke still hung dark on the horizon, Melbourne whispered treachery in his sleeve—"the final separation of those colonies might possibly not be of material detriment to the interests of the mother country".[84]

The first thing to settle on arrival at Quebec was the fate of the hundred and sixty rebels still languishing in prison there and at Montreal. Durham hit on a statesmanlike solution. On 28 June, the Queen's Coronation Day, he issued an Ordinance granting a general amnesty, excepting only the ringleader, Papineau, and a score of others, who were banished. An example was made without a drop of blood, and all Canada was amazed and jubilant. Here, they thought, at last was a true Governor: even the exiles drank his health on board the ship which carried them away. Next, with such military force as he could muster, he showed the flag at Niagara, and the Americans were suitably impressed. Then, leaving Lower Canada in the hands of a special council, he set out for the west. Adding local experts to his staff of advisers as he went along, he plunged into the detail of economic and administrative grievances, before investigating the wider questions of the Union of the provinces, representative government, and systematic emigration.

These measures, which seemed on the spot so reasonable, seemed quite otherwise at home. The Tories thought he had let treason go unpunished, and had sided with the rebels: the Whigs, that he was threatening the sovereignty of the English parliament by recommending a colonial one: the Roebuck Radicals, that he was riding roughshod over the legitimate claim of the French population for independence, by forcing upon them Union with Upper Canada. Should the factions unite upon the point, they could easily overset the government. Brougham, whose vindictive memory was long, now saw his chance to ruin Durham certainly, and Melbourne probably, and to be revenged on both his enemies at a single blow. Being a lawyer, he knew how to pick a quibble; Durham, he said, in sentencing the rebels by ordinance, had acted *ultra vires*: and by this thin precipitate all the opposing criticisms were released. Melbourne did not hesitate to sacrifice his envoy. Durham, returning with his family and Buller from a drive along the river, found letters from the Prime Minister and the Colonial Secretary full of congratulations and promises of support—and also a New York paper of a later date announcing that his ordinance was disallowed and his authority rescinded.

He resigned as a matter of course. All Canada, despairing of the future, entreated him not to desert them. Said Buller: "I do not think it would have been impossible for Lord Durham to have made himself King of Canada, if he had been fool enough to have wished it."[85] If he had only had a year, it is now maintained, he would have "removed all real grievances, satisfied every reasonable demand and established adequate systems of municipal government and education in both Upper and Lower Canada".[86] Instead, after less than half that time, he sailed for England on 1 November 1838. A second rebellion started as soon as the news of his departure spread.

To Mill it seemed that everything was turning out beyond his fondest hopes. The development of Canada within the Empire was assured. It was only necessary to proclaim the truth of what had happened, and the government would be discredited, Durham would return a strong and outraged hero. Both his objectives were almost within reach, and he exhorted Molesworth to snatch the opportunity. "The present turn in Canada affairs brings Lord Durham home, incensed to the utmost (as Buller writes to me) with both Whigs and Tories—Whigs especially, and in the best possible mood for setting up for himself: and if so, the formation of an efficient party of moderate Radicals, of which our Review will be the organ, is certain—the Whigs will be kicked out never more to rise, and Lord D will be head of the Liberal party, and ultimately Prime Minister. I am delighted with Buller . . . he is the man for us, and we shall have him and make a man of him yet. . . . There is a great game for you to play in the next session of Parliament."[87]

But the fight had gone out of Durham. He was tired, and mortally ill. Dispirited at his betrayal, on his way home he set about his final duty of making out the report he was to lay before Parliament. He drafted it himself, with the loyal help of Wakefield and of Buller, and a remarkable document it was.[88] Besides recommending the reunion of the provinces and dominion self-government, besides faithfully examining the administrative problems, it looked out beyond Canada to the permanent aspirations of mankind. It was the full expression of a great belief, the monumental justification of a stormy unfulfilled career.

At the time, it was more than likely that the report would be lost under the tumultuous flood of political recrimination. Durham's enemies were numerous and active. Brougham and his dogs were in full cry. Greville renounced him on behalf of the aristocracy. "He has done nothing in Canada, he took himself off just as the fighting was going to begin, his whole conduct has been visited with universal disapprobation . . . he who is brimful of pride and arrogance, and of an overweening sense of his greatness and his rank."[89] Roebuck, while the mission was at sea, unloosed in the *Spectator* a series of dangerous attacks, combining a deadly accuracy with a violent misrepresentation of which none but he was capable.[90] Immediately following came the news of Durham's farewell proclamation to the Canadians, in which he had set out his plan for the future of their country and the full story of his frustration. However necessary this was for the salvation of the empire, it was as regards home opinion more than tactless. To Melbourne the coincidence seemed a happy one: there was a growing colour in the country to the charges of high-handed action, and he frankly prepared to abandon his emissary, report and all.

Writing again to Molesworth a month after his first exultant letter, Mill was perplexed and worried. "What think you of all this rumpus in Canada? I find all the Whigs and moderates here blame Lord Durham for the Proclamation, and he has already the greater part of the real Radicals against him for the Ordinance. But I think the Liberal party in the country generally is with him. I mean to stand by him . . ."[91]

With that assurance, Durham's cause was in sure hands. Upon the ferment of repudiation and declaim there fell, of a sudden, the sedative drops of clear authentic wisdom. First in the *Spectator* and other journals, in fragments snatched hastily from the press; and then in full in the *London and Westminster Review* for December 1838, came "the word in season",[92] a compelling and authoritative voice:

> "He has been thwarted, but he has not failed. He has shown how Canada ought to be governed, and if anything can allay her dissensions, and again attach her to the Mother Country, this will. He has, at the critical moment, taken the initiative of a healing policy. He has disposed of the great immediate embarrassment—the political offenders. He has shown to the well-intentioned of both sides an honourable basis on which they may accommodate their differences. He has detached from the unreasonable of one party their chief support—the sympathy of the United States, and it is reserved for him to detach from the unreasonable of the other the sympathy of the people of England. He comes home master of the details of those abuses which he has recognized as the original cause of the disaffection, prepared to expose these as they have never before been exposed, and to submit to Parliament, after the most comprehensive enquiry that has ever taken place, the system on which the North American colonies may be preserved and well governed hereafter. . . . If this be failure, failure is but the second degree of success; the first and highest degree may be yet to come."

The result of these words was sudden silence. The main charge against Durham had been one of tyranny, and there was no one who imagined that if John Stuart Mill defended him there was a further inch to gain upon that score. Gradually other writers in other journals, hitherto intimidated by the uproar, began to see on what lines the defence could be taken up.[93] Mill's article was unpopular with his own readers, many of whom assented to Roebuck's dislike of Lords and arbitrary dealings, and it curtailed by one-third the sale of the *Review*. But, he said: "It is some satisfaction to me to know that, as far as such things can ever be said, I saved Lord Durham—as he himself, with much feeling, acknowledged to me."[94]

Molesworth went down to Devonport and organized a great reception. Durham waited for Buller to arrive, then they all set off for London. Their journey, partly owing to Molesworth's efforts and in part spontaneously, was roses all the way; it was, to the disgust of Greville, "a sort of triumph; and he has been saluted with addresses and noisy receptions at all the great towns through which he passed".[95] In the approaches to London, Molesworth handed over to Hume, and the vociferous welcome accompanied them right into the capital. Melbourne hastened to turn the occasion into a ministerial success. Within a few months Russell blandly introduced a bill on behalf of the government proposing the reunion of Upper and Lower Canada. Durham, his work safe, willingly left them masters of the field. A few days after the Royal Assent was given to the bill, he died, like Lawrence in another generation, the victim of the dream of commonwealth, the perfidy of government, and the monstrous inertia of the Colonial Office.

Mill, having struck his timely blow, was called to the Continent, and was not in England during the final stages of the drama. He cherished still, however, the brightest hopes of Durham's leadership, was still negotiating with Bulwer for his block of votes, and even hoped that Durham could be persuaded to take over the *Review*. He instructed Robertson to keep him fully informed of all developments, and was bitterly disappointed at the results:

> "He [Lord Durham] may be quite right, and there may be no better course to be taken than the one he means to take, but it cannot lead to the organization of a radical party, or the placing of radicals at the head of the movement,—it leaves them as they are already, a mere appendage of the Whigs: and if there is to be no radical party there need be no *Westminster Review*, for there is no position for it to take, distinguishing it from the *Edinburgh*.
>
> For my own part, I feel that if the time is come when a radical review should support the Whigs, the time is come when I should withdraw from politics . . . In short, it is one thing to support Lord Durham in *forming* a party; another to follow him when he is only joining one, and that one which I have so long been crying out against. . . . As for the *Review*, even if he would bear the whole expense, and leave me the entire control, I doubt *now* whether I should accept it. . . . I do not feel clear about publishing even another number."[96]

With the death of Durham, the Philosophical Radicals as a parliamentary party came to an end. Buller, much sobered by his experiences, became a Whig, and took small government appointments. Most of his time for the rest of his short life was devoted to colonial development and emigration. So was that of Molesworth, when he later returned to Parliament, for as a result of his part in the Durham affair he was forced by his constituents to resign. Grote also resigned, of his own free will, and retired into his History of Greece. Others, like the Austins, were leaning more and more towards the Tories, who, with Peel regenerate, and with Lord Ashley, offered some promise of social reforms. The equivocal Bulwer lost his seat in 1841, the year when Roebuck, lonely, obstinate, and fierce, was reinstated for Bath. Had all depended upon this handful of cantankerous theorists, Mill's long efforts would have been a prodigal waste, for they never were properly speaking a party at all. Yet in another sense they were the largest party in the land, for they sought to represent the mass of the underprivileged, of whom the hundred thousand gathered about Durham on Glasgow Green were but a small fraction. They, weary of the crotchets of their parliamentary leaders, now turned to other courses. The veteran Francis Place, seeing at last that his confidence had been misplaced, wrote to Mill saying that he would waste no more time "with men who are infirm of purpose". Mill showed the letter to Fonblanque and remarked: "I shall keep it as a memorial of the spiritless heartless imbecility of the English Radicals."[97]

Thus the people refused their mandate. As there was nothing to be had from inside Parliament, they decided to besiege it from without. They scrawled on a charter the same six points the Radicals had so long and vainly pressed, signed it with a million and a quarter names, and paraded it to Westminster. The demonstration failed. Bitterly, they recognized that in the end the only dependable poor man's friend was the poor man himself. The radical creed vanished for a time into the forging shops of the Trade Unions, to emerge as the Labour Party, secure in its six points and a great deal else beside.

VI

During the years of Mill's activity as an editor and politician, Harriet's share in his work was commonplace and feminine. It was she, for instance, who persuaded Mill, at John Taylor's request, that his two latest Italian refugees, Mazzini and Usiglio, should be taken on as writers for the *Review*. Although she played no open part in the business decisions, everything was submitted to her judgement—so much so that Cavaignac unkindly labelled her the "Armida of the *London and Westminster*", Armida being, in a popular opera by Rossini, a siren who lured sailors to their doom.[98]

No sooner had Robertson become sub-editor than there came a flood of contributions from his friend Harriet Martineau. Now Harriet Taylor had come to hate Miss Martineau for the relish she took in relating the details of the first meeting of the lovers at John Taylor's house. When Harriet Martineau sent in, at the time of Queen Victoria's accession, a prattling account of the young Queen's early life, the hand of Harriet Taylor is clearly traced in the violence of Mill's objections to Robertson: "It will give us an air of *attempting* and not *attaining*, the sort of ignorance of courts which most excites the ridicule of those who know them, especially when exhibited in sententious, goody, small moralizing. Altogether I cannot reconcile myself to its insertion in any shape . . ."[99] Robertson protested that he had invited the article, that his honour was committed, and so forth, but Mill would have none of it. "I detest that vile Queen thing more than ever for being the cause of the first real difference we have ever had about the Review. But I cannot see the force of what you say about our being committed. . . . As for H.M. you have only to say to her that it is necessary for the Review to ménager me, and that I have seen the article and decidedly object to it. . . . As for me, I am willing, as in this case I am bound, to take entirely upon myself the resentment of a very spiteful person rather than admit the article."[100] Robertson, attempting to mend matters, landed a big catch by getting Browning to promise an advance copy of *Sordello.* Mill coldly replied that if he did send it in, it must be reviewed, but that he himself would not be able to do it. The opportunity was lost, for no better reason than that Robertson had met Browning at Harriet Martineau's house.

Aside from these unseemly wrangles, Harriet Taylor's influence on Mill at this time was soft and womanly. She soothed him in anxiety; she worried about his health. She afforded him emotional release. In this respect she was completely adequate. When they were both in town they strolled out from Kent Terrace across Regent's Park and made their lover's alley in the Zoo, where they were safe from interruption even by her favourite brother:

"I think I had best not hope to see you today dearest *dearest* because Arthur is coming and will be here at the time you would come—but tomorrow *certainly* for I *could not* be longer without. I will get the stupid ticket and we will go for an hour to see our old friend Rhino—will you dear come here and take me tomorrow about five?"[101]

When she was in the country, she went eagerly to the Post Office for his letters—they always dealt, for privacy, through Poste Restante—and carried them off to read alone on Keston Heath:

"I went this morning there in the hopes of your word my delight and there it was—believe all I can say when I tell you how happy I am, that is, how happy you make me.

This sweet letter has been with me at every moment since I had it and it keeps me *so* well *so* happy *so* in spirits—but I cannot tell thee how happy it made me when first I read it on the highest point of the nice common with those glorious breezes blowing—It has been like an equinoctial tempest here ever since you left. Mama and C [Caroline] are here—I like it and it does me good—in the absence of the only good I ever wish for.

Thank God however the promised summer which was to be so much is come and will be all it was to be—has been already so much. I am to see you on Saturday; indeed I could not get on without.

I cannot write better today—tho' I never *felt* better or more.

Adieu my only and most precious—til Saturday.

Dear Saturday!"[102]

On 19 December 1838 John Taylor wrote to a business contact in Italy, Messrs. G. H. Gower.

"Dear Sirs,

I am on the point of leaving London with Mrs. Taylor who is very seriously unwell, and strongly recommended to try the effects of a milder climate. She intends to proceed to Pisa where she has relations and I hope and trust she will derive benefit from passing the winter in a warm and genial air.

Mrs. Taylor may probably find it most convenient to receive what money she requires in Leghorn, in which case may I beg the favour of your passing one hundred and fifty pounds sterling to her credit, and reimburse yourselves by valueing upon my firm for the amount.

John Taylor

Mr. David Taylor and Sons"[103]

What Harriet was suffering from was not exactly specified, but the arrangement was that she should go to her brother William and his Italian wife Emilia. At the same time, Mill, who had just returned from Axminster, where he had been enjoying his usual walking tour in the best of health, also proved to be indisposed, with pains in the chest and a disordered stomach. Although none of his family believed it to be anything very serious, and Wakefield was surprised that one so mortally ill could work with such vigour on the Durham case, it was sufficient to induce the family practitioner to order him to take sick leave and go abroad for six months. Wakefield and Buller, who needed more than all his friends to know his whereabouts at that time of crisis, were under the impression he was going to Malta. In fact, both Harriet and Mill were indefinite about their plans. Where they were really heading for was Naples, and they were both in the highest spirits, except that Mill, never a good sailor, was dreading the effect on his dyspepsia of the sea voyages in front of them. It seems that Harriet, having recommended him some nostrum against seasickness, felt that it would be better for him not to use it during the channel crossing when he would be alone, but to wait until they faced together the second journey from Marseilles to Leghorn, which they planned in preference to crossing the snow-bound Alps:

"*My Beauty*—

What a nice walk that was! I am quite thoroughly enjoying the thought of this journey. I write this word only to say, do not dear take that thing I told you of in Regent Street. Do not, for I would rather very much that you would not—when that day comes you shall do whatever you like if you happen to remember it you *darling*—

I shall hear this evening from thee all about our nice tomorrow—

Adieu—CARO" [104]

Harriet crossed to Boulogne just before Christmas, and reached Paris a few days later. There, John Taylor, her gallant escort, left her with Helen, or Lily as they called her, and returned to England. His duties were immediately taken up by Mill, who arrived as soon as he had gone. Mill was in very poor shape. The crossing had exceeded his worst anticipations. Owing to a confusion over the tides, he was at sea for eighteen hours, each of them more damaging than the last. Nevertheless, he pressed on to Paris, whence the lovers started at once for the warmer south, posting as far as Chalon despite the additional expense. The weather was bitterly cold—so cold that their breath froze on the windows of the carriage, and denied a view of the pale refrigerated landscape.

From Chalon they sailed down the Saone and the Rhone, through Lyons and Avignon to Marseilles, at that time still the quickest means of accomplishing the journey. From Marseilles, they took a French warship for Leghorn, Harriet spending the voyage prostrated by a headache. On 11 January 1839 she called on the worthy Mr. Gower, but instead of drawing money arranged that he should pass the credit on to Rome. Thither they proceeded, after a visit to Pisa had established that William Hardy and his wife were out of town; not, evidently, to Harriet's regret, since she had never told them she was coming. After a week or two in Rome they went on to Naples, Harriet once more transferring her credit; and, since Naples was the goal they had preordained, they made a leisurely stay of some three weeks. They had covered their traces well—so well that they could risk unusual intimacy. They stayed in the same hotel, the *casa Brizzi.* And, south of the Bay, in beautiful, discreet Sorrento, they took rooms on the same floor at an inn called *La Sirena.**

In March they were back again in Rome, Mill reporting to his family that his condition seemed to be on the mend since he started a regimen of macaroni instead of meat: but, he added resignedly, he would be thankful if he only avoided getting worse, since at his age of thirty-three, hardly anybody continued to have the same vigorous health they had in early youth. In Rome he ran across Carlyle's brother John, one of that curious class of Britons who reside more or less permanently on the Continent. He also found Sterling wintering there with Dr. Calvert, a friend with whom he had joined forces in Maderia. Sterling contrived to see a good deal of Mill, taking great pride in showing him the Sistine Chapel, and other artistic glories. It was the first time they had been thrown into each

* Sixteen years later, when revisiting Sorrento, Mill wrote to his wife: "Here I am, darling, and at the same inn, *La Sirena,* which looks as pretty as possible; only I think we were not on the ground floor which I am now. By the bye I only ascertained today, by finding the number of the house in Mrs. Starke, that my inn at Naples, the *Hotel des Etrangers,* is the very casa Brizzi which we were in, though not then *called* a hotel." (Hayek, p. 221.)

other's company with any continuity, and as a result, their friendship deepened from cordial admiration into intimate affection. Later on, when he lay dying, Sterling wistfully recalled the spring day they spent on top of the Baths of Caracalla:

> "They are huge walls and arches of brick rising perhaps 60 or 70 feet from the ground in the midst of lonely vineyards on the Eastern side of Rome. We sat there with the city behind us, and in front the Campagna, or open plains, with the ruins of the brown aqueducts, and high and bright beyond the whole range of Alban Hills, rising up to the Monte Cavo where stood of old the temple of the Latin Jupiter. Mr. Mill is a man to feel the nobleness of such a prospect, and we were very happy sitting there in the air as if we had been a thousand leagues from all the world but that of Antiquity."[105]

For all that, Sterling does not seem to have been made aware of Harriet's presence in the city. He was still a clergyman, if only nominally; and Mill was perhaps unwilling to risk another precious friendship foundering, as had Roebuck's, on the rocks of conscientious interference.

And so they went their ways: Sterling back to England, Mill and Harriet with her little daughter on to Venice. At the end of May they set off homewards, jaunting pleasantly through the Tyrolean Alps to Innsbruck, and from there to Munich, "altogether . . . a most cheerful place", said Harriet, "and if as dissipated as people say presents an argument for dissipation".[106] Thence through Germany and Brussels to Ostend. Mill reached his desk at the India House punctually on 1 July, after six months' absence, looking, according to his brother Henry, tolerably well but a good deal thinner. Harriet and Lily stayed a few days at the Ship Inn at Dover, and then went on to Brighton, where they were joined by the two boys Herbert and Haji, while John Taylor, who had evidently taken advantage of their absence to put in hand repairs at 17 Kent Terrace, found them a temporary abode. It thus happened that Harriet on her return to London lived for a time in apartments in Wilton Place; a circumstance sufficient to inspire Carlyle, who did not know her husband was there too, to indicate to Sterling that she was living clandestinely with Mill:

> "Mill . . . was looking but indifferently; he professed not to be sensibly better at all by his last-year's journeying. Mrs. Taylor, he further volunteered to tell me, is living not at the old abode in the Regent's Park, but in Wilton Place, a street where as I conjecture there are mainly wont to be *Lodgings*. Can it be possible? Or if so, what does

it betoken? I am truly sorry for Mill: he has been a most luckless man since I came hither, seeming to himself all the way to be a lucky one rather. He seems to fear that the Review will have to cease; a thing I regret but do not wonder at."[107]

Fortunately Sterling was unsordid; nor was his friendship once accorded easily undermined. He answered, "Yesterday's post brought me a pleasant letter from Mill along with yours. But he says no word of that miserable matter you hint at. I think it is a good sign of a man that he feels strongly that kind of temptation, but a far better one that he both feels it and conquers it, which I shall trust that Mill has done and will do."[108]

In October, Harriet went to Yorkshire to see her parents for the first time since their move to their country residence at Birksgate. She was enchanted with the house, the view, the furniture; above all with the warmth. "I should like you to come and see it", she wrote to Taylor; "it is so lovely—both Papa and Mama want you to come very much. . . . Papa busies himself in the garden and reading and Mama is as usual all warmth and kindness—Cary too is very well tho' she complains a little, but that is only owing to the ennui of Ley's absence."[109] A month later, back in London, she called on Lizzie Flower whom she had not seen for several years. Lizzie, sinking rapidly from consumption, and cut off almost entirely from society by her association with Fox, wrote excitedly to her sister, Sarah: "She was very sweet and tender, and looked at me with eyes full of real love."[110]

Whatever the effect of their holiday upon Mill's health, Harriet had plainly profited from it: she was in excellent spirits, on the best of terms with her family, and solicitous for her friends. A winter's idyll on the Bay of Naples; spring in Rome; an early summer spent amidst the Alpine flowers—it had been a happy, careless time; the happiest perhaps of her whole life with Mill. At about this period she left her little house at Keston, and moved to Walton-on-Thames, where her husband had leased another for her. For the next ten years she lived there mostly, making frequent journeys by the railway up to town. It was well placed for other excursions she continually made to Brighton, Ryde, and the whole of the south of England. She had an inveterate love of travelling and asserted, contrary to the general experience, that instead of exhausting, it refreshed and invigorated her.

VII

During Mill's absence, Robertson had been left in charge of the *Review*. He had managed the editorial duties faithfully enough; but by his brashness he had offended many people. He was, Carlyle wrote to Emerson, "a rude Aberdeen Lawyer, a great admirer of mine, too, with whom I conjecture I cannot act at all: so goodbye to that".[111] The change of opinion in the great man had been occasioned by a difference over an article on Cromwell which Mill, before he left, had arranged for Carlyle to write. During the winter, Robertson wrote to tell Carlyle he need not trouble as he intended to see to it himself. Carlyle was once more furious; he broke off all connection with the *Review*, and determined to devote his efforts to a full study of the Protector, which eventually became his *Cromwell's Letters and Speeches*.

The situation demanded all Mill's tact. Fortunately, Sterling's long-promised appreciation of Carlyle was ready in the summer, and Mill was glad to find it full of praise amounting nearly to worship. He showed it to Harriet, and she quite agreed that it was very timely. He wrote gratefully to Sterling:

> "Carlyle having called on me the day I received your letter, I gave him the copy destined for him. He expressed great interest about it—and seemed to expect something much less favourable than he will probably find it. Putting together my idea of the man and of the thing, I cannot think but that he must be on the whole greatly pleased with it.
>
> Taking the article altogether, . . . I yet think there has been nothing published for many years so likely to fix the attention of the best spirits and to be a source of light and warmth to them—and instead of thinking of it as you say you do with little pleasure, it will always be one of the most agreeable facts in my connection with the review that this article appeared in it. I am even now not alone in thinking that it will be received by many as the appearance of a not insignificant element in the present chaos of English opinion—and that many will look out eagerly for the future manifestation of the same."[112]

About Carlyle's feelings Mill was not mistaken. He was able to write again a few days later:

> "As I finish this letter, behold a note from Carlyle. He says: 'Sterling's is a splendid article; in spite of its enormous extravagance some

will like it; many are sure to talk of it, and, on the whole to be instructed by it. No man in England has been better reviewed than I—if also no one worse.' So far so good; and as for the 'extravagance', I doubt not his modesty applies that appellation mainly to the praise."[113]

Mill published it, with a graceful editorial comment, in October 1839, in the same number as the offending article on Cromwell, the effect of which was thereby so much mollified that Carlyle began to think of renewing his own contributions. In January 1838 he had mentioned to Mill a paper he had contemplated writing on the Chartists, but had postponed because of his course of lectures for that year. Now he had taken it up again; but Lockhart of the *Quarterly* declined it, feeling its strictures rather too strong against his aristocratic clientele. Hearing that Mill was to issue one final number of the *London and Westminster* he offered it to him, provided of course that the contributions on this occasion were not to be gratuitous. Mill was enthusiastic:

"It is a glorious piece of work, and will be a blessed gospel to many if they read it and lay it to heart. I took a great piece of paper to make notes upon, but found scarcely any to make. . . . It would delight me much to let this be the last dying speech of a Radical Review. I do not think a radical review *ought* to die without saying all this and no one else could say it half as well. Any number of copies of it might be printed in pamphlet form from the same types."[114]

But it came to nothing, and the farewell copy of the *Review* appeared without the additional adornment. Carlyle, feeling that his Chartism warranted a wider reading among the Tories than the *Westminster* could command, sold it to *Fraser's* to be published as a pamphlet. Where interest beckoned, friendship never hampered him. Besides, he felt no obligation to the *Review*. He continued to feel, as he had always felt, that the editors had treated him unfairly, and even that he should have been editor himself. Writing his *Reminiscences* long afterwards, he declared, "worse I could not have succeeded than poor Mill himself did as editor (sawdust to the masthead, and a croakery of crawling things, instead of a speaking by men)"[115]—a sad appraisal of a management who had gladly paid him £50 for anything he cared to offer them, and at a time when he was little known. Speaking of his rise to fame, it was Sterling's friendship, Sterling's devotion to him he acknowledged. To Mill, to Mill's *Review*, to Mill's intervention with Sterling even, he made no public tribute, although well aware of what he owed.

Having freed himself from his sense of obligation to Carlyle, Mill's only desire before parting with the *Review* was to complete his justificatory attack upon his father's school of thought. As he explained to Sterling, "If I carry on the review to another number it will be partly in order to publish in it an article on Coleridge which I have always thought desirable as a counter-pole to the one on Bentham. I shall write the article whether it appear in the review or elsewhere—and have begun a fresh study of Coleridge's writing for that purpose. . . . It would be of most essential service to me to receive any suggestions or warnings from you, . . . and especially such as would preserve me against overlooking any of the great thoughts . . . which he has contributed to the philosophy . . . of the age."[116] Sterling's advice was liberally provided, and the resultant essay[117] was the only thing of any value in the number for March 1840, except for a suitable companion piece on Emerson by Richard Monckton Milnes.

Coleridge and Bentham, Mill began, represented the ageless antithesis of order against progress. The two existed by denial of each other, and there was a relation between them. The problem went down to the roots of human knowledge, to the question how the mind grew conscious of the world outside itself. To Coleridge, as to all transcendental philosophers, it seemed that every object of experience, however apparently real, was no more than a symbol calling up the appropriate idea intuitively present in the mind. The Benthamites did not deny the possible existence of realities beyond the reach of human faculties. But the random peopling of the natural world with supernatural essences appeared to them unwarranted and disorderly. They held that the transcendentalists were too ready to proclaim as absolutes things capable of simpler explanation. Intuitions should be kept to an irreducible minimum, to the residue of undemonstrable truths remaining after the processes of reasoning had gone as far as they were able. Given only the human mind itself, they claimed, with its faculties of memory and association, of recording sensations and relating them together, the rest of the universe could be accounted for.

His own position in this much debated controversy was, Mill stated baldly, alongside Locke and Bentham. "We see no ground for believing that anything can be the object of our knowledge except our experience. . . . We are therefore at issue with Coleridge on the central idea of his philosophy." But he regarded it as a problem incapable of objective determination, the personal inclination of the individual being decided by his temperament. It was a question o fthe creative mind against the critical, of the imperative against the interrogative mood; and in daily life the common person tended to filch what he required from either side. When reason would not support an impulse, a conviction often did; just as when sentiment grew stale, experience began to count as wisdom. Practical truth was always a reconciliation.

The outcome as he saw it was more important in politics than in philosophy. Was a form of government the symbol of a hidden entity invested with the authority of the infinite, or was it a convention set up by men to be pulled down when it no longer served their purposes? Was the State a leviathan with a propulsion of its own, or was it no more than a free association of the individuals who composed it? Was the fact that a belief had been held by a majority of the human race over a long period, evidence of its intrinsic truth, or might it turn out to be a superstition? Such were the points at issue, and if the answers lay with the intuitionists, then authority was absolute and the individual was its slave.

Not that Coleridge maintained authority to be necessarily perfect. On the contrary, he held that it was frequently distorted, giving, like a twisted mirror, a false reflection of the truth it represented. He too was a reformer. And of the two methods of reform, his and Bentham's, Mill at this time generally favoured that of Coleridge. The Benthamites were unrealistic. They believed that the individual man was infinitely teachable, and an unerring follower of his own interest; that he would therefore speedily learn to identify his own good with that of the community. All government, they thought, was at the best a necessary evil, a temporary restraint pending increased enlightenment. Here, at the heart of their formula, there was a yawning gap. Between the self-interest of the individual and the greatest happiness of the greatest number there was no natural link, and all efforts to convert the one into the other by a system of legislative penalties and rewards must fail. Coleridge sought improvement through a surer means, the continuity of the human craving for tradition and propriety. History, to the Benthamites a dusty record of the crimes and follies of mankind, was to Coleridge an inspiring chronicle of the gradual unfolding of society. He wished to refashion and use what Bentham wanted to destroy. Instead of smashing the hard nut of convention and throwing away the pieces, he desired to discard the shell and to preserve the kernel.

Looking back upon the articles, Mill later felt that in censuring Bentham before full value had been gained from his iconoclasms, he had been inopportune. The more so, seeing that Bentham had made small pretence to philosophy, and was principally concerned with practical abuses. So in the version left to posterity in the *Dissertations and Discussions*, Mill softened the force of his criticism. As for his praise of Coleridge, he let it stand, being, as he said, an error on the favourable side. His object was to show that if Coleridge was blind to the truths excluded by established creeds, Bentham was equally ignorant of the truths which they contained. That though the two systems of thought were violently opposed, they were also complementary. To show, in fact, "that a Tory philosopher cannot be wholly a Tory, but must often be a better Liberal than Liberals themselves, while he is the natural means of rescuing from oblivion truths which Tories have forgotten, and which the prevailing school of Liberalism never knew."

The permanent value of the essays rests upon their exposition of Mill's concept of synthetic truth. For him, truth was no single element, but a gem of many faces, each capable of different, even contradictory appearance. It was impossible to grasp the whole from a single point of view; and, conversely, every honest point of view achieved an aspect of the truth. That any act of vision depends at least as much upon the situation and the circumstances of the seer as upon the object seen, was Mill's position in philosophy. It was the theme which ran consistently throughout his life and works, the constant factor in the shifting ground of his development. It throws light on his relation with Harriet, not as his flatterer but as his opposite; with Sterling, not as his disciple, but his friend. It explains his disastrous approaches, first to Carlyle and later on to Comte. It explains why his *Review* was a pantechnicon. It was the groundwork of his *Logic*, and the structure of his *Liberty*. It was the reason why he endured criticism and delighted in correction; the secret of his personal charm, and of his reputation. It was in these essays, in his reconciliation of gigantic adversaries, that he best displayed his power of drawing from opposites a truth greater than either of them could attain alone. It was tolerance, not as weakness, but as creative force.

VIII

All that he could do through the *Review*, Mill felt, had now been done. The political audience he had been addressing, the Parliamentary Radicals, had entirely disappeared. His future usefulness would lie in other fields. His duty, he was sure, was still the improvement of society: but he realized that he had been too sanguine and precipitate in attempting to secure direct conversion by means of pamphleteering. It was becoming more and more clearly evident to him that "the mental regeneration of Europe must precede its social regeneration, and, also, that none of the ways in which mental regeneration is sought will do."[118] As once before, in the days of the Debating Society, he had made the mistake of thinking the task was simpler than it was.

Besides the time and effort it involved, his editorship had cost him a substantial sum of money on each of the seven numbers he produced except the last, which by the deliberate slimness of its contents escaped with a deficit of £33. In all, he had spent some £1500. He therefore resolved to part with it. In order to keep it, so to speak, within the family, he made it over at a nominal price to William E. Hickson, a wealthy shoe manufacturer, his lifelong friend and one of his loyal contributors; who shared the liability with another, Henry Cole. Mill stipulated only that the radical tone should be preserved, and that the original name of *Westminster Review* should be resumed. His attempt to keep Robertson's salary intact was defeated by the strict economy applied by Hickson. Giving his own labour as editor and author free, and dividing any profit there might be between the contributors in place of regular payment, Hickson reduced the cost. And, despite the difficulty of obtaining writers on such meagre terms, he carried it on for ten more years before selling it for £300 to John Chapman. Mill continued to give occasional contributions, though he began to place his more important work in columns with a wider class of readers, like the *Edinburgh*. He did not regret his efforts in a hopeless cause, although he had offended several friends, especially Mrs. Grote, with whom for some time he was not on speaking terms, and had given others an opportunity to sneer at him. Carlyle lost no time in doing so, to Sterling: "The *Westminster Review* has come into the hands of Cole and Hickson; to be conducted on new principles! What words are adequate? No words."[119]

JOHN STERLING
from an engraving, after a painting by B. de la Cour in 1830.

BOOK FIVE

CAUSE AND EFFECT

1830–1849
aet. 24–43

Picture Post Library

JOHN STUART MILL and HELEN TAYLOR

I

MILL'S *System of Logic* took thirteen years to write. He began it in 1830, when he was only twenty-four. In his role as a reformer of the world, he knew that it was not enough to champion measures immediately necessary for social improvement. Something fundamental and comprehensive was required. He resolved to go to the heart of the matter, to the theory of thought itself. It would be an arduous business; but, as he told Gustave d'Eichthal, "Good seed is never wasted; it takes root, and springs up somewhere. It will assist the general reconstruction of the ideas of the civilized world for which ours is but a period of preparation. . . . That is why, 'cast your bread upon the waters, and it will return to you after many days'."[1]

He had learned at an early age that all reactionary values were based upon easy general assumptions, which were held to be universal truths, intuitively known, beyond the power of reason to explain. Logic, from time immemorial, had centred around man's faculty of creative thought, of putting together two propositions and from them drawing a third, believed to be entirely new and entirely inescapable. Generations of scholars had spent immemorable lives thrashing out the rules and pitfalls of this process, and it was taken for granted as the only legitimate method of adding to human knowledge. Its formal or scientific title was the Syllogism: its pet name was reasoning. In its pure form, it consisted of deduction from a general law to a particular case. Whoever had the power to discover and establish general laws, could control and fashion the whole texture of human thought. In days when erudition was confined to the authoritative element in society, it was an invaluable weapon for conservatives. The learned classes had been extremely nimble at reaching the conclusion best suited to their purpose from a portentous but conveniently undemonstrable affirmation. Whole treatises, prolonged and solemn, boiled down to something of this kind:

> The King can do no wrong.
> James I is King.
> Therefore James I can do no wrong.

There was, therefore, a natural affection between those interested in keeping things as they were, and the process of deductive reasoning.

Men of a scientific turn of mind had for centuries demanded a less fallible criterion for the general truth than the authority of the scriptures or the general opinion of mankind. Some, like Bacon, had looked towards induction, the experimental faculty. By the systematic study of particular cases, they claimed to build up a body of evidence with the universal validity of a general law. But, said the syllogist, it could not be done. However far they went in collecting evidence, they could never aspire to universality, because they could never be certain they had examined every possible case. The proper function of induction was to check by experience the findings of deduction. It was confirmatory, not creative.

Others, like Descartes, sought to escape from dogma by asserting that the individual conscience was the originator of general truths. This argument turned against itself. It led either to the utter scepticism of Hume, wherein logic became futile; or to the Protestant philosophy, which rejected one authority only to replace it by another equally mandatory and inscrutable. The syllogists received it gladly. Their general laws were still inviolable, safe from scientific probing. They were absolutes, born mysteriously with the mind, intuitively accepted, and unchallengeable. The moral sense was a far more vital sanction than the writings of the early fathers or the common consent of man.

Mill's attack upon the intuitionists was in part a legacy from his father, and in part an aesthetic pastime, for he loved keen reasoning. His sterner purpose was to show that general laws derive from the experience of the senses and the association of ideas; to discredit intuitions, in order to get at practical prejudices in morals, politics, and religion. Ultimately, as he later wrote to one of his few German admirers, Theodor Gomperz, he hoped to place "metaphysical and moral science on a basis of analysed experience, in opposition to the theory of innate principles so unfortunately patronized by the philosophers of your country and which through their influence has become the prevailing philosophy of Europe. I consider that school of philosophy as the greatest speculative hindrance to the regeneration so urgently required of man and society, which can never be effected under the influences of a philosophy which makes opinions their own proof and feelings their own justification."[2]

At the time when he began to write, he had to confront, from the stark outmoded ruins of eighteenth-century thought, the intuitionists, freshly entrenched with their rich and up-to-date philosophies. He had to meet them on the ground of their own choosing. He did it typically enough, by compromise. He did not attempt to dispute the legitimacy of deduction as the definition of reasoning. But he did dispute the absolute nature of the general truth, and declared that it was in fact the product of induction. His main object was to rehabilitate induction. To show that although reasoning went from the general to the particular, the general itself was but a summary of particulars. That the full process of thought was from particular evidence to general laws, and then from general laws again to particular cases, which were verified from experience of other cases.

He began by a definition of his field. Logic, he said, was the science of all operations of the mind which the mind itself was able to judge by evidence. That is to say, of all phenomena appreciable by the senses. From the first, he excluded much metaphysical speculation about things-in-themselves, and the nature of the mind, which the intuitionists would have wished to have drawn in. At the same time, he rejected their counter limitation that logic as he defined it was no more than "the science of the formal laws of thought". He claimed his right to explain as much as he could of the comprehensible universe without recourse to intuitive understanding, and denied the right of his opponents to limit him in advance.

To drive home his attack, Mill had to lay siege to the frowning citadel of the Syllogism. This he was quite disposed to do, for he considered its boast to be the method of creative knowledge utterly unfounded. To his mind, the conclusion of a valid syllogism, so far from being a new or original thought, was from the beginning implicit in the major premise. The syllogism was of value only as a means of classification, as a safety step for identifying a particular case with a general class to which it properly belonged. What was of interest was the general proposition, and how it was arrived at.

He went on to describe the growth of knowledge as he saw it in the light of his father's theory of psychology. The mind of man in its untutored infantile condition, he said, is in a state of horrifying and puzzling confusion. It lives in a world where sensations and impressions come tumbling in upon each other in a kaleidoscopic chaos which can be neither understood nor managed nor foretold. The function of the mind is to reduce them into an orderly sequence of events. It does so by means of its two faculties of memory and association, and the operation being dependent upon experience only, is wholly an inductive one.

Gradually the phenomena are classified in groups. Gradually, permanent relations are seen to exist between them, and these are the beginning of general laws. The advantage of a law is that the mind is able to deal with it as an entity, without considering in detail the multifarious phenomena of which it is a summary. As the laws of a given group become defined, there is the foundation of a science. In a science, the same process is repeated, and the laws still further reduced into more general laws, which are found to be applicable to all members of the group. So, in the end, a science reduces an enormous number of phenomena to a handful of general laws, and when it is impossible to reduce them any further, the science is said to be exact. Then, and then only, it is permissible to reason deductively from its general laws to any further particular phenomena that may occur.

Among themselves, the sciences are related in a hierarchy, the laws of the more exact commanding and embracing those of the less. King of all is mathematics, because its laws are fewest in number, and are valid for the whole range of known phenomena. At the time when he was writing, Mill maintained, the only physical sciences sufficiently reduced to proceed by process of deduction were mathematics and physics. The others, organic sciences, chemistry, biology, and physiology, remained inexact, and must continue to develop by induction. As for the social and moral sciences, they were still so disorderly and diffuse that they were scarcely sciences at all. It was, however, to be assumed that as human knowledge widened and inductive evidence increased, they too would reach the status of exact sciences. Also that other relations between phenomena would become apparent, and new sciences would be born; taking their place either as branches of existing sciences, as astronomy was a branch of physics, or else as separate sciences at the bottom of the scale.

Thus far Mill got by 1832. He had next to expound his theory of induction, but of induction at that time he could make "nothing satisfactory". For five years he left it fallow, during the more immediate excitements of his affair with Harriet, the undertaking of the *Review*, and the added responsibilities consequent upon his father's death. In 1837 Dr. Whewell's *History of the Inductive Sciences* provided him with the impetus he needed. He dissented from it violently, and it brought him into a lengthy bout of logical fisticuffs with its distinguished author. Dr. William Whewell, D.D., twelve years Mill's senior, was Professor of Moral Philosophy at Cambridge, and was shortly to become Master of Trinity in succession to Dr. Wordsworth, the brother of the poet. Sydney Smith remarked of him: "Science is his forte and omniscience his foible." When the fellows of Trinity, in their donnish way, told him he was at variance with the *Encyclopaedia Britannica* about Chinese music, he replied, "Ah yes, my views have changed considerably in the years since I wrote that article." He was a formidable example of Mill's philosophic adversaries. Their conflict terminated after fifteen years, with Mill pricking and goading the eminent divine all around the *Westminster Review*, describing his cherished *Elements of Morality* as "one of the thousand waves on the dead sea of commonplace".[3]

Whewell declared that universal truths carried with them a degree of certainty, a sensation of inevitable necessity, which no induction from experience could achieve, however far pursued. He lodged his case upon the apparent necessity existing in the theorems of Geometry, adding that as mathematics was by common consent the master science embracing all the others, whatever was true of its general laws must also be true of the rest.

All of this Mill strenuously denied. There was, he said, no such thing as a necessary truth. The geometric definitions were not universal truths at all, but were arbitrary assumptions accepted because it was supposed that "unless such a conception were possible, mathematics could not exist as a science". They were like the rules of a game. They existed because geometry existed, not the other way about. "When, therefore, it is affirmed that the conclusions of geometry are necessary truths, the necessity consists in reality only in this, that they correctly follow from the suppositions from which they are deduced. Those suppositions are so far from being necessary, that they are not even true. . . . There exist no points without magnitude; no lines without breadth, nor perfectly straight. . . . A line as defined by geometers is wholly inconceivable."[4] The rest of mathematics derived, in the last instance, from the laws of Arithmetic, the science of numbers, which were all experimental laws based on the evidence of the senses.

The apparent necessity of general truths, Mill said, was really a feeling that the reverse of a proposition was not only false but unimaginable. It was an illusion built up by repeated confirmatory experiences which had not at any time been contradicted. Whewell had cited the laws of the solar system and of gravitation as examples of truths intuitively recognized as soon as they were propounded, although contrary to all previous theory. He did not mention that they were determined inductively by Galileo and Newton in the teeth of bitter opposition from his own predecessors, the orthodox supporters of what were then held as infallible laws.

Making fun of Whewell, though a tempting occupation, was not of itself sufficient for Mill's thesis. He had to show that everything deduction was supposed to do induction could do better. That without completely exhaustive evidence it was still possible to induce a general law applicable to particular cases not hitherto considered. That induction was no mere cataloguing of experience, but the only fertile system of reasoning wherein the conclusion was greater than the premises. This section of the work was the most difficult as well as the most important. Yet he wrote it off in two months, in the summer of 1837, when he was still suffering from the effects of his serious breakdown of the previous year.

Proof by induction is only possible on one assumption which at first has the appearance of a giant intuition. It assumes that nature is uniform; that what has happened once will happen again in the same conditions. For if it were not so, there could be no relation between events and no grouping of evidence. In working on this assumption, Mill said, he was not being inconsistent. He had never claimed to get rid of intuitions altogether. He had claimed that the method of reasoning was the best which depended least upon them.

Granted that nature is uniform, Mill was able to show that the entire universe of man's experience could be reduced into general laws governed by cause and effect. Causation is the constant relation between a phenomenon and the sum of the positive conditions necessary to produce it. To explain something is to announce its cause, to bring a hitherto unrelated and therefore puzzling phenomenon under the bracket of a familiar law. The limit of explanation is reached when causation cannot be followed any further, and the remaining inexplicable phenomena are left in the air, apparently uncaused, and, as the opposing school would have it, necessary or intuitional. But although they are not yet explained, it does not follow that they never will be. As knowledge grows, the number of first principles outstanding will be progressively reduced. Theoretically, the process can continue until the whole body of phenomena is seen to depend upon one supreme all-motivating general principle, or First Cause.

It is only very seldom that a cause is plain and simple. Usually a cause is a combination of different causes, working together or against each other to produce a modified effect, as in the law of the parallelogram of forces. This circumstance has given rise to much loose phraseology. "Pure chance", for example, cannot exist, since every event must have a cause. "Chance" means only that we cannot gauge the causes at work, and so cannot predict the event. Similarly, there is no such thing as an exception to a law. The discovery of a true exception would immediately destroy the validity of the law. What is meant by an exception is that some other law has intervened between a cause and its effect and overruled it. Thus, a gas-filled balloon is no exception to the law of gravity: gravity is fully operative upon the balloon, but another cause predominates, compelling it to rise. Mill was specifically careful not to discredit miracles. He was likely to offend religious sentiment enough, without committing outright blasphemy. Miracles, he said, do not conflict with the law of causation. They do not dispense with cause; they claim the direct intervention of an overriding supernatural cause. And, since that is a legitimate contingency in causation, they are not incredible. He contented himself by saying that many fabulous entities, satyrs, centaurs, witches, fairies, giants, mermaids, ghosts, and even the occult works of darkness, fulfilled the same conditions and are no more inconceivable. The only question in such cases is the reliability of the evidence.

Mill went on to examine the various methods of induction appropriate to different sciences. In general, the only means available were observation and experiment. Experiment was the quicker and more certain, because it permitted a number of possible causes to be tried out with a view to seeing which of them produced a particular effect. On the other hand, experiment required laboratory conditions, the physical assembly of components and the exclusion of confusing influences. Frequently these conditions could not be obtained, as in the case of astronomy where, owing to the impossibility of having sun and moon and stars to play with, the only method of procedure was by observation of what happened in the heavens.

To assist in the collection of evidence by observation, there were various devices of which the chief was the Empirical law. It was a law of provisional validity, a means of stating that a relation of events had been observed but not accounted for. A typical example was the early attitude towards eclipses, which were known to be regular phenomena and could even be predicted, although they were not properly explained until they were brought under causation by the general law of the Solar System. An Empirical law did not have the same force as a fully established law of cause and effect, but nevertheless it had a definite status. It was stronger than Hypothesis. An Hypothesis was a generalization tentatively set up on slender evidence to see whether or not it could survive. It could give no better conclusion than that a proposition was very likely true; and it had to be abandoned at the first contradiction: whereas an Empirical law had the authority of a general law within the limits of the conditions of time, space and circumstance under which it had been experienced. Within these limits, it was supported by complete inductive evidence, while outside of them, there being no evidence, there was no means of knowing whether it applied or not.

From Mill's neat theorem of the whole of human knowledge there protruded only one untidy end, one problem to be solved before he could claim to have dispensed with necessary truths entirely. It related to the properties of things. How, for instance, does the mind know that soot is black? By experience, certainly. But there is no question in this case of causation; soot cannot be said to have caused the blackness nor can the blackness have caused the soot. Ultimate properties of matter exist universally without being caused. Here then is an invariable relation independent of causation. Like an obstinate piece left over from an elaborate construction set, it did not fit in anywhere: and yet a place had to be found for it. Eventually Mill confessed that the evidence was consistent with there being a general law of relation in coexistence, equivalent to the law of Causation in succession. His theory of Kinds, admitting a second law of nature distinct from his original assumption, was not achieved without reluctance, for he had a horror of natural laws. Apart from the handle they presented to the ever-watchful intuitionists, he felt it as a sort of intellectual disgrace to confess that anything was inexplicable. It offended the genuinely aesthetic pleasure he derived from a completely logical argument.

There was one gleam of consolation. Mill had always been troubled that the degree of credulity attached to beliefs based on equally sufficient evidence should vary. A man could believe that all crows were black, and be sure that if it were not universally so he would have heard of it; yet in meeting a traveller who said he had seen a white crow he would scarcely raise an eyebrow. But the same man would never believe soot could be white, even if he found his own chimney full of it several times in succession, at least until he had been forced to discard every other explanation short of admitting that the soot was white. Conversely, "why is a single instance, in some cases, sufficient for a complete induction, while in others myriads of concurring instances, without a single exception known or presumed, go such a very little way towards establishing an universal proposition? Whoever can answer this question knows more of the philosophy of logic than the wisest of the ancients, and has solved the problem of Induction."[5]

Here at last was the solution. The law of coexistence of properties was an Empirical law. It only held valid within the conditions of time, space, and circumstance wherein it had been experienced, and was not challenged by any contradication outside those limits. Evidence of a white crow was readily accepted because the limits of the law of blackness in crows were comparatively narrow, confined to a country or perhaps a continent; whereas soot was believed to be black the whole world over, and evidence to the contrary would discredit a general law. In such a conflict, as one or the other must be denied, the general law, having wider validity, must be believed and the contrary evidence rejected, at least until it had occurred so frequently that its limits were greater than those of the law. Belief in an Empirical law was apportioned to its universality. The only wholly inconceivable event was a contradiction of a universal law.

Into the category of Empirical laws, said Mill, fell all the laws of the abstract sciences, the so-called necessary truths, and the great law of Causation itself. It was a law so vast in scope that it commanded all phenomena the human mind was capable of experiencing, and within those limits was known to be invariably true. Since the limits were virtually universal, it was virtually a universal law. But not completely so. For what happened beyond the range of human faculties it could give no guarantee. It was entirely possible that in the deepest hidden recesses of the stellar regions, where the mind of man could not yet pry, the law of cause and effect might not be valid, and nature might not be uniform. His original assumption was shown to be built on experience by a process of induction. There was no "necessity" about it after all.

Quod Erat Demonstrandum! In great good humour Mill went on, in the autumn of 1838, to operations subsidiary to Induction, a collection of after-thoughts; and to Book V on Fallacies, where he had a glorious time enumerating the various snares surrounding the logician, and illustrating them with examples from the works of his opponents, including the favourite maxims of Dr. Whewell. On his return from Italy in 1839 he was all prepared for his final assault upon the Moral Sciences, but the next winter his deliberations were interrupted by a sad event.

II

Early in 1840 his second brother Henry, only nineteen years of age, sustained a dangerous spasm of consumption. He was the darling of the family, a "beautiful young creature, almost ethereal in the exquisite delicacy of his outline and colouring, and with a most musical voice".[6] "Dear Henry! So affectionate and sympathetic",[7] his sister Harriet sorrowfully recalled in her old age, while John Mill spoke of him as "a brother who, if he had lived, would probably have been one of the most remarkable men of our times, as he was already one of the most lovable".[8] He had been destined to follow his elder brother James Bentham into the Indian Civil Service, and only that December John had taken him to Haileybury where, after two years at University College, London, he was to have taken the usual training.

His mother decided he required a warmer climate, and in February they set out, accompanied by his sister Clara, for Falmouth whence they intended to take the mail packet to Madeira. On arrival they found that the boat had sailed, and were stranded with the invalid on their hands. Fortunately, John Sterling and Dr. Calvert, bound for Madeira on the same errand, had reached Falmouth a week or so before but were delayed by unfavourable winds and had resolved to winter there. Sterling appealed on their behalf to Barclay Fox, the son of a wealthy and cultivated family of Quakers, extremely numerous and influential in the district. Between them they reclaimed Mrs. Mill's passage money which was held in forfeit, and found lodgings for her on the Terrace, and very soon the kindly Foxes extended their friendship to all the exiles. The diarist of this family was the youngest daughter, Caroline, a pert girl of twenty-one with a nimble pen and a propensity for collecting autographs. She quickly formed a lifelong attachment to Clara Mill, and something more than an attachment to John Sterling, whose astonishing eloquence and faintly feminine charm immediately bewitched her. Sterling was still theoretically a curate, with a wife and family of six, while she was a pious Quaker girl, so neither was capable of the smallest impropriety. But as her private diary was filled with him all and every day, their mutual affection seems a more likely explanation of his sudden decision to spend the rest of the winter in Falmouth, than the official one that he found the locality interesting in a geological way, while it suited Calvert's hobby of stuffing birds.

So Caroline listened as Sterling lectured on every occasion and on every topic. They went to see the great beam of a steam engine cast, and while R. Cloke, the foreman, danced about the foundry in an agony of excitement, Caroline regretted that they had not brought some chestnuts to cook by the heat which was being wasted, and received a discourse on the theory of Utility. Particularly she liked to hear Sterling's debonair familiar tales of the lives of the literary great in London, of Wordsworth, and of Coleridge. Of his great friend Carlyle—how, when Count D'Orsay went to sketch him in his Chelsea atelier, the Scotch girl who opened the door was so amazed at the unaccustomed splendour of D'Orsay's clothing that she ran off in a fright.

Before long they fell to discussing the Mills, and Sterling began to tell Caroline about the phenomenal elder brother, another of his friends. "A man of extraordinary power and genius, the founder of a new school in metaphysics, and a most charming companion. . . .[9] Mill has singularly little sense of the concrete, and, though possessing deep feeling, has little poetry. He is the most scientific thinker extant—more than Coleridge was, more continuous and severe."[10] When it grew certain that Henry Mill would not recover, and it was announced that this stern and fabulous personage was coming down, she was consumed by eager agitation.

John Mill arrived in the middle of March, and was brought by his sister Clara to the Foxes. Caroline was reassured by his appearance. He was undoubtedly distinguished, but good-looking and quite young for a philosopher. "He is a very uncommon-looking person—such acuteness and sensibility marked in his exquisitely chiselled countenance, more resembling a portrait of Lavater than any other that I remember. His voice is refinement itself, and his mode of expressing himself tallies with voice and countenance."[11] She stood her ground, trying to draw him out, and was pleased to find him not unbending. "He talked enthusiastically of Sterling: I remarked on his writing being much more obscure and involved than his conversation even on deep subjects. 'Yes,' he said, 'in talking you address yourself to the particular state of mind of the person with whom you are conversing, but in writing you speak as it were to an ideal object.' 'And then,' said I, 'you can't ask a book questions'; which, I was proud to be informed, was what Plato had said before me."[12]

Gradually her awe gave way to more familiar admiration. During a walk, the process of unhooking a bramble from her dress made him "philosophize on the power of turning annoyances into pleasures by undertaking them for your friends—a genuine alchemy". He readily promised to get some famous autographs for her, including Guizot's. He confided that he felt his early lack of boyish amusements as a heavy disadvantage. "He told us that his hair came off 'when you were quite a little girl and I was two and twenty'. He has", Caroline added, "such a funny habit of nodding when he is interested in any subject." Very soon she was scolding him for taking too little care about his health.

Mill was indeed in very excellent spirits, so excellent that in the circumstances there appears to be something heartless in such entries as the following in Caroline's diary:

> "March 22. Henry Mill has been dividing all his things amongst his family, a deeply affecting employment to them all. They think him growing decidedly weaker, and take it by watches to sit up with him. . . . J. S. Mill gave a very interesting sketch of the political history of India, the advantages derived by its princes from our supremacy there."

But these people were not really heartless. They were all philosophers, for whom death was a spectacle for solemn regret, but not for despair or horror. Moreover, consumption was a common fatality about which nothing could be done: of their little group alone, Sterling and Calvert were already doomed, while Mill certainly believed himself to be so. Therefore in the intervals of vigil they all enjoyed the pale tentative whispers of the coming spring, and Mill and Sterling made the most of the calamity by which they had been brought together for the second time running at that expectant season of the year. They explored Pendennis Cavern; Mill proposed to leave burning as an offering to the gnomes the candles they had used to light the way. They had an alfresco luncheon at Penjerrick, and Mill interrupted the conversation to remark "on the elation of spirits he always experienced in the country, and illustrated it, with an apology, by jumping". The evenings were filled with student talk. "John Mill joined us at dinner, and Sterling came to tea. . . . The evening was then devoted to a glorious discourse on Reason, Self Government, and subjects collateral, of which I can give but the barest idea. Sterling was the chief speaker, and John Mill would occasionally throw in an idea to clarify an involved theory or shed light on a profound abysmal one."[13] He consented in his spare time to sit for Cunningham, the local portrait painter, the result being, according to Caroline, very beautiful; "quite an ideal head, so expanded with patient thought, and a face of such exquisite refinement".*

Henry's end was drawing near. His sister Harriet had joined the others several weeks before: on the second of April, the youngest brother George arrived: and on the fourth, surrounded by those who loved him, the boy died. Standing one on each side of the deathbed, and eyeing each other with solemnity, the good Calvert said to Mill: "This sort of scene puts an end to Reason, and Faith begins." The other emphatically answered, "Yes".[14]

* The portrait was probably not a good one. Calvert, who also sat to Cunningham, remarked of the result that it was a good piece of painting, "but not the Dr. Calvert that I shave every morning". (*Caroline Fox*, by Wilson Harris, p. 95.) It seems to have originated the medallion reproduced in Elliot's *Letters* and included in this book. Writing to Mill after the Falmouth visit, Sterling said: " . . . not having seen your head according to Cunningham of course I can give no opinion of it. Any sort of likeness of you would give me pleasure. I wish you would get Morrison to make a medallion then any of your friends could have copies to any extent." (MS. letter, 21 September 1840. Library of King's College, Cambridge.)

On 10 April Mill returned to London, and the party broke up. Sterling had rejoined his family at Clifton. Calvert settled permanently in Falmouth till his own death two years later. He was a kindly man, with a wry sense of humour: when his weakness reached the point where he could walk no longer, he bought himself a pony for £5, and called it "Z".

To the Foxes, Mill sent a large parcel containing all the *London and Westminster Reviews* from their beginning, with notes in his own hand, and the names of the writers attached to the articles. For Caroline he made a Calendar of Odours, containing the names of the flowers and shrubs that scent the air according to the months, beginning with the laurel and ending with the lime. He also entered into a long and helpful correspondence with her brother Barclay. To Sterling he wrote of their increasing friendship:

"I rejoice greatly that we met at Falmouth; independently of the good, of many kinds, which your presence did, it is very much now, and more than I thought it would be, that my last recollections of Henry are shared with you. If he had lived he would certainly have been an additional bond between us, and now that he is dead his memory will be so, and perhaps, as you say, he is conscious of it. I do feel, as you do, that we have been more to each other lately than ever before. . . . Even now I am very far from appearing to you as I am, for though there is nothing that I do not desire to show, there is much that I never do show, and much that I think you cannot even guess."[15] Did he consider admitting his friend to supreme intimacy, by telling him frankly of his love for Harriet? In any case he never did so: Falmouth was the last interlude of any length they spent together. While for his part Sterling was embarrassed by less vital matters: "I am very glad to learn", he wrote, "that the elder Foxes do not look askant on the intercourse that you and I have had with the younger ones. This is a luck I should hardly have expected from them considering what is the usual character of Quakerism in our day."[16]

In May 1840 Caroline Fox and her sister went to London, and joined the fashionable gathering at the hall in Portman Square to hear the later stages of Carlyle's course of lectures about Heroes and Hero Worship. They sat next to Mill's sister Harriet, who introduced them to her neighbour on the other side, Jane Carlyle. Close in front of them were Dr. Whewell and Samuel Wilberforce. Mill himself was absent. He and Harriet Taylor had attended the earlier performances, but at the second, the "Hero as Prophet", he had disgraced himself. For when the orator launched into his favourite denunciation of "Benthamee Utility, virtue by Profit and Loss", and had reached the rhetorical passage "if you ask me which gives, Mahomet or they, the beggarlier and the falser view of Man and his Destinies", Mill had risen to his feet, pale, but unable to contain himself, and called out a decided "No!"[17] After which Harriet Taylor seems to have given away their tickets.[18]

Caroline Fox was suitably impressed by the rugged simplicity, the indomitable strength and the glow of genius in the speaker's face, and was especially struck by the impatient, almost contemptuous way he waved aside applause. She emerged entranced, despite Jane Carlyle's demure undertone about her husband's sufferings as a lecturer: "It is so dreadful for him to try to unite the characters of the prophet and the mountebank: he has keenly felt it." Caroline and her sister returned with Harriet Mill* to Kensington Square, where, she records, "we were most lovingly received by all the family. John Mill was quite himself. He had in the middle of dinner to sit still for a little to try and take in that we are really here. . . . Walked in the little garden, and saw the Falmouth plants which Clara cherishes so lovingly, and Henry's cactus and other dear memories. Visited John Mill's charming library, and saw portions of his immense herbarium; the mother so anxious to show everything, and her son so terribly afraid of boring us. He read us that striking passage in *Sartor Resartus* on George Fox making to himself a suit of leather. How his voice trembled with excitement as he read, 'Stitch away, thou noble Fox: every prick of that little instrument is pricking into the heart of Slavery, and World-worship, and the Mammongod.' . . . Mrs. Mill gave us Bentham's favourite pudding at dinner!"[19]

Ten days later she went with the Mills to visit John in the India Office, where he entertained them nobly, talking copiously all the time. And on 3 June she attended a party at the Mills' where the Carlyles were present and the fun was furious. On leaving, she found her postillion in a drunken slumber on the coach-box and demanded a hackney carriage, "but J. S. Mill was delightfully ignorant as to where such things grew or where a likely hotel was to be found". Shortly afterwards when she was visiting at Clifton, Sterling told her that Mill "was never in so good a state as now".

* Mill's sister Harriet, not Harriet Taylor. The author regrets that so many female characters in the book are called either Harriet or Caroline. He can only assure the reader that he has done his best to distinguish between them.

III

All that Mill had so far written of his *Logic* was the groundwork, the technical argument. The most significant portion, the bearing of logic on the present and the future of humanity, he had saved for the concluding book. On his return from Falmouth he set about the task. He desired to show that the moral sciences, those involving human nature, although confused and inexact, were none the less the ultimate sciences, transcending all the physical sciences upon which they depended. Like the rest, they were subject to causation. In the end, human actions were predictable, and mankind could control its destiny.

He recast the theory of man's knowledge of causation into a persuasive, if very sweeping, sociological survey. In the beginning, the universe appeared a chaos of unrelated happenings where nothing was orderly and nothing was secure. To escape the misery of perpetual fear, men had come to attribute everything to arbitrary or capricious action by a superhuman agency which must be dreaded and placated. The state of superstition still existed among primitive communities, but was being progressively abandoned as more and more phenomena were scientifically explained and brought under the natural order of causation. The only major body of phenomena still supposed to be supernaturally directed were the volitions of human beings, and the inference was that they too would eventually be found to conform to general laws.

This brought him to the great question of the freedom of the human will, and here he found himself in a dilemma. If the will of man was subject to causation, how could a man be held responsible for his actions? Since every effect must have a cause, his volitions were determined by circumstances beyond his own control, by his upbringing and education, by his mental and physical condition. The Necessarian doctrine, as proclaimed by the followers of Robert Owen, was originally a plea in mitigation for the poor. But to Mill an unfree will seemed an atrocious concept. He wished, characteristically, that whether true or not, the doctrine of necessity could be believed by everybody regarding the actions of others, and yet be disbelieved about their own. Beyond that, he had no use for it. It was socially dangerous; individually, it was demoralizing and degrading. That it could be put to dangerous uses was soon to be stated in no measured terms by Frederick Engels: "It does not occur to any Communist . . . to believe that . . . in general, the single Bourgeois can act otherwise . . . than he does act. . . . The Revolution must come."*

If, on the other hand, the human will were free, then it could not be subject to the law of causation and Mill must at once admit the claim of the intuitionists that it was a supernatural entity produced by Providence; and also that there could be no such thing as a moral or a social science within his meaning of the word.

Now Mill was first of all a humanist, who carried the stern standard of utilitarianism into philosophy itself. If logic brought him to conclusions repugnant to the interests of mankind, he had no hesitation in using his great powers to bend the logic. In his dilemma, he as usual tried to reach a reconciliation. The will of man was free, he said, and yet at the same time it was not free. It was quite true that the will at any given moment was determined by the character, and that the character was caused by many circumstances, over some of which a man had no control. But over others he had control by means of his will, and he was able to select most of the circumstances which would decide his future character. Although Mill's argument does not stand up—although he represented character as the cause of will and will as the cause of character—it enabled him to say: "A person feels morally free, who feels that his habits or his temptations are not his masters, but he theirs: who even in yielding to them knows that he could resist; that were he, for any reason, desirous of altogether throwing them off, there would not be required for that purpose a stronger desire than he knows himself to be capable of feeling."[20]

Leaving the subject rather hastily, he proceeded to examine the interrelation of the moral sciences. Like the physical sciences, they had their hierarchy, being dependent one upon the other, the simpler commanding the more complex. The first of them was psychology, or the study of the individual mind, which derived from two fundamental general principles, memory and association of ideas. Next came the question how, given these laws of mind, various types of individual

* *Condition of the Working Class in England in 1844.*

character were produced by differences of environment. He admitted that, being based on rough observation only, the laws established would be very crude. But he maintained that it should be possible at least to indicate how varying sets of circumstances tend to modify the nature, and to mould the will; how, for example, poverty tends to breed bitterness, although other factors may frequently intervene to prevent it. This science of the individual character he called Ethology, regarding it as an indispensable step between the study of the mind and any study of mankind in the mass. He proposed to write a book about it, as a sequel to the *Logic*, and a necessary preliminary to Sociology.

Failure to observe the proper order of the sciences, he said, was the reason why previous attempts at reducing Sociology to general rules had all been unsuccessful. Some theorists, mistaking it for an experimental subject such as chemistry, had approached it by induction. They had taken examples from the historical past, and from them built experimental laws which they then verified, or attempted to verify, from human evidence in the present day. They had forgotten that the experimental method required laboratory precision not found in the confused morass of history, where all the facts could never be completely tabulated, and where it was impossible to find two cases that were exactly parallel. As a result, they had achieved a philosophy of history totally divorced from the characteristics of single human beings. Inevitably, by generalizing on the species without sufficient study of its members, they were led to set man in society above man as an individual creature. The organic theory of the state appeared to Mill a fallacy with hideous propensities. Society was a mixture, not a compound; a bag of bullets, not a molten ingot. "Men are not, when brought together, converted into another kind of substance, with different properties, as hydrogen and oxygen are different from water. . . . Human beings in society have no properties but those which are derived from, and may be resolved into, the laws of the nature of individual man."[21]

Another group of sociologists who were in error were those who, while rightly perceiving that the science ought to be deductive, had made the mistake of taking Geometry for their model. From very few, or even from a single principle of human nature, they set up rigid and purely abstract laws to apply at all times and in all places. In this class came the Benthamites, and especially his own father: they, basing all upon self-interest, had sought to make a permanent system out of a creed admirably suited to achieve the particular purpose of the Reform Bill.

In truth, said Mill, Geometry and Sociology were poles apart. The one was the most exact and unconditional of all the sciences: the other, the least reduced and the most prone to local variations. The springs of human action were not few but many, and no doctrine could be sound which failed to allow for their interweaving. In Sociology, as in Astronomy, experiment being impossible, the only method of procedure was by observing the behaviour of the material available, and by careful dissection of the counteracting influences at work. From the fractional study of living men, empirical laws of man could be built up, and could be applied within the same limits to whole societies. One such possible field was Political Economy, or man in pursuit of wealth. But economic laws applicable in England might not be true in India or France, where they were modified by different social conditions and national characteristics. The conclusions of economics were true only of one aspect of man, and must be balanced and corrected by man in all his other aspects. In this manner, it would eventually be possible to construct a theoretical man in society, an integrated figure with all his motives accurately assessed, and all his proclivities laid bare. A man of straw, who must then be verified by the study of real men in actual societies, and from the study of history, the archive of social observation. If ever the conduct of men singly and in groups ceased to appear capricious and became predictable, Sociology could be reduced to general rules. The final mysteries of the external world would be explained, and knowledge would be complete.

The individual was so significant, that he was the means and test of all society: so perfectly compact, that he was able, with his own native faculties, to compass the whole universe of his perception. Already, the individual was for Mill the sum of all philosophy, and most of the shortcomings of his logic can be traced to the obstinacy with which he laboured that belief. Curiously, the sharpest contradictions came from the very sciences he had most hoped to foster. His theory of induction failed because he claimed for reason more than it could achieve. His psychology was shortly shown to be painfully inadequate: the clear faculties of memory and association by which he set such store, soon proved to be no more than obvious wavelets dancing upon the dark and turbulent ocean of the subconscious mind. By attempting to draw the mentality of man direct from the physical sciences, he overlooked the great science of inheritance; the teeming world of intervening causes, furred, feathered, and four-footed, which are the real connection between man and his environment. It was to nature first, and not to human nature, that he should have directed observation.

It is true that at the time he wrote the *Logic*, the theory of Evolution had not been formally propounded. Also, that when he heard of it, he gave it greater credit than many of his contemporaries. For on reading the *Origin of Species* he called it "an interesting hypothesis," which at that time was what it was; whereas Whewell indulged in a bitter indictment of Darwin for setting the Creator on one side, and Carlyle exclaimed, "May the Lord confound all such dreary insolences of loquacious blockheadism, entitling itself Science!"

Nevertheless, Evolution was already in the air when Mill was writing.* And by failing to take account of it in the seven revised editions of the *Logic* which followed at intervals during the remainder of his life, he neglected much that could have been of service to him. In the first place, Darwin provided a beautiful example of the inductive method applied to the construction of a new and inexact science. For five years he voyaged patiently in the good ship "Beagle," before he would adopt the general opinion that inherited variations exist at least among the simpler forms of life. Then, reading Malthus, he grasped a second generalization; that as species multiply more rapidly than the food they need, there must always be a struggle for existence. Setting the two together in a simple syllogism, he at once deduced a law of cause and effect between them. If species were variable by inheritance, and if there was a struggle for existence, those variations would continue which were best suited to the struggle. This provisional general law he verified by exhaustive evidence, and it became the law of Natural Selection, from which depended the whole theory of Evolution.

Moreover, Evolution would have given Mill a valuable weapon against the Intuitionists. By admitting inherited mental characteristics, he could have taken the miraculous flavour from the word innate. He could have attributed to natural causes many mental

* Chiefly owing to Charles Lyell's *Principles of Geology*, 1830–1833, which damaged the theory of Creation by explaining that changes in the earth's surface had occurred naturally, over an immeasurable period of time, from causes which were still at work. Darwin's *Journal* was published in 1839. In 1845 Robert Chambers further adumbrated the theory of Evolution in his *Vestiges of Creation*. The *Origin of Species*, of course, did not appear until 1859.

phenomena, like the instincts or the moral sense, not easily described as personal acquirements. To assist the memory of man he could have adduced the primeval memory of the race: and where individual experience was not enough, he could have drawn on the inherited experience of the ages.

Taking it all in all, if Mill worked with insufficient tools, he still worked in the right direction. Much has been added to what he said, but little to deny it. He left nothing further to be gleaned from the ground which he had covered. His work was a comprehensive text-book, elegant in style and startlingly clear in content. While arguing his case, he admitted his difficulties honestly, and reconciled views so inimicable that they were not usually expressed in a single treatise. He defined the methods of investigation appropriate to the different sciences, and he cleared ancient misconceptions. The Science of Ethology is still unwritten. It is a sobering reflection that until it is, until it can be fully understood how people and races come to be as they are as a result of their circumstances, no great improvement can be hoped for in the field of human relations; and all our tremendous advances in material science must serve more to the constriction than to the enlargement of the human spirit.[22]

The first draft of the *System of Logic* was finished in November 1840, but "no bookseller is likely to hear anything about it from me for many months", Mill wrote to Barclay Fox.[23] In accordance with his invariable practice, he completely rewrote it during 1841; at Sterling's insistence, although much against his will, he combined the process with a reading of Hegel and other German logic. By Christmas it was ready, and was sent to John Murray's who, after hesitating for two months, eventually returned it. In April 1842 it was eagerly accepted by J. W. Parker with the enthusiastic approval of his reader, upon the terms then customary of half net profits: but it was too late to bring it out that season, and it had to wait another year. The otherwise aggravating delay proved in one respect a benefit. For Alexander Bain, then a young student at Aberdeen, and a fervent worshipper of Mill, went to London in the summer vacation, and gained an introduction to his hero through John Robertson, the former editor of the *Review*. He was much flattered at being asked to read the proofs, and provided valuable suggestions, including many examples of the various inductive methods. Thus improved, the book appeared in March 1843.

Except for the minor, though essential, services of Bain, and for the influence of Auguste Comte in the section on the moral sciences, the *Logic* was singularly the work of its author only. It is of particular interest from the biographical point of view, because of all Mill's major works it was the only one not seriously influenced, or even in part dictated, by Harriet Taylor. Mill was under no illusion about its probable popularity. He forbade Caroline Fox to read it all because, he said, "it would be like my reading a book on mining because you live in Cornwall—it would be making Friendship a burden."[24] "I don't suppose many people will read anything so scholastic", he told her brother Barclay: "it is probably worth your reading it, while I am certain it is not worth it to your sisters."[25]

He was therefore astonished when it became an immediate success. From the first, sales exceeded all anticipations, and "the book was asked for by unexpected persons, and appeared in shop-windows where he never thought to see it".[26] Oxford at once adopted it: and although Cambridge was rather slower in the uptake, probably owing to the ruffled feelings of Dr. Whewell, it was for the next half-century the groundwork of natural science in the Universities. His friends rallied round him. John Austin wrote for permission to review it in the *Edinburgh*, in order to forestall the enemy. Grote called it "the best book in my library". Caroline Fox dutifully read the chapter on Liberty and Necessity which Mill had appointed for her, but did not say what she made of it: she preferred to hear what Sterling had to say. "It will last as long as England", he wrote to his father enthusiastically; and, to another friend: "John Mill has completely finished and sent to the bookseller his great work on Logic, the labour of many years of a singularly subtle, patient, and comprehensive mind. It will be our chief speculative monument of this age."[27] Bain wrote a forty-page article for the *Westminster*, so laudatory that Mill sternly expurgated it. He was far more pleased at a hundred page attack in the *British Critic* by the Newman-Puseyites, in the course of which they said that if his "principles be adopted as a full statement of the truth, the whole fabric of Christian Theology must totter and fall".[28]

IV

The culminating chapters of Mill's *System of Logic*, wherein logic was applied to human problems, owed much to his association with another intellectual prodigy, eight years his senior. Auguste Comte's philosophy had been virtually complete since 1822, when he was twenty-four. Since parting from the Saint-Simonians, Comte had obtained a post at the École Polytechnique, the College of Military Engineering in Paris, and had devoted all his efforts to the completion of his monumental *Cours de Philosophie positive*. He presented his conclusions to the world during the thirteen years it took Mill to achieve his own.

Like Mill, his object was to achieve a systematic survey of the entire field of human knowledge. Like Mill, he severely limited his field to a scientific enquiry based upon the observed laws of causation, and excluded even more strictly any metaphysical speculation into the essence of "things in themselves". Like Mill, he inevitably gave offence to theological preconceptions. He was heretical enough to conclude from his study of Astronomy that the universe was not made for man, but that man grew up in the universe: that man inhabited the earth not because the conditions had been specially created to his requirements, but because, like any fungus, he would grow wherever the necessary conditions could be found.

Unlike Mill, he was not content to stop at the provision of a method for pursuing the various sciences. His philosophic treatise was specifically undertaken as a necessary prelude to political applications of a far more sinister purport. It hung upon his theory of society, which had advanced from the innocent transitions between critical and organic epochs of his Saint-Simonian days. Every brand of knowledge, he now said, passes successively through three stages, each of which culminates in a single explanation of all the facts of causation, first theological, then metaphysical, and eventually positive, or scientific. The three phases depended on the development of mind, and not only does every individual pass through them at different periods of his life, but civilizations as a whole must also pass through them. Periods of social calm are those when knowledge is attuned to the social order which enforces it: unrest occurs when the state of knowledge is moving to the subsequent phase, and the social framework is not yet moving with it.

The positive stage was the final phase of knowledge, beyond which the human mind was not equipped to go. It had begun at the Reformation, and was still in progress. The basic sciences, physics and mathematics, were already reduced to their ultimate laws; others were still inexact to some degree. The last to be finalized would be the most complex science, and the one most dependent upon all the others. This, which Comte called Social Physics, was Sociology. It would establish the laws and ordering of society appropriate to the positive state of knowledge. Since the positive was the final state of mind, the positive social order would be the final social order. When it was written, human knowledge would be complete. And when it was applied, progress would be at an end.[29]

The first volume containing the pith of the Positive Philosophy reached England in 1837, and Mill read it just at the time when he had completed his own theory of induction. He was at once struck by the almost unerring agreement they had reached, apparently by widely different paths of reasoning, on the entire question of logical method in science, and on the proper method of procedure. He read the succeeding volumes avidly, concluding that it was "one of the most profound books ever written on the philosophy of the sciences".[30] In November 1841 he wrote Comte a letter of warm congratulation, pointing out the extent of their agreement, and suggesting that they commence a correspondence intended to clear up one or two minor points of difference, before launching a great new philosophic system simultaneously in their two countries. In his exuberance, he quoted Voltaire. "When an Englishman and a Frenchman can agree, they must certainly be right."[31]

The discussions that began under such happy auguries were based on misunderstanding. To Comte, it seemed that Mill had come to him for elaboration of a few points in a work of genius which his mind was not yet good enough to grasp. From first to last, Comte's letters had a tone of parental guidance and correction: it never occurred to him that Mill could disagree with him. He simply thought that Mill was in the vanguard of the school of Positivism which was bound to spring up everywhere, and was only faintly astonished that England of all countries should be first to lead the way. He decided that, in following him, Mill showed an acumen uncommon in his countrymen.

Although Mill's first enthusiasm gave some grounds for the mistake, he regarded himself not as Comte's follower but as his colleague. He thought that where so much was agreed, the rest was capable of reconciliation. He was prepared to go half-way, and as usual a generous half; but he did not realize that he was travelling towards a fixed and immovable object. Nor could he yet know the final trend of Comte's philosophy. He must indeed have known that it would be dogmatic and restrictive, for that was apparent in every page Comte ever wrote. In speaking of Astronomy he had asserted that, since the faculties of men were not equipped for further exploration, knowledge began and ended with the solar system. What Mill did not see was that for Comte the existing social institutions were the facts of Sociology, just as the stars in their courses were the facts of Astronomy. The function of the Positivist was to examine them and establish a true theory of how they worked, but not to try to change their nature. And the revolutionary or progressive theorists who said that marriage, the family, the possession of private property, and the like, were not all they ought to be, must in Comte's eyes, seem just as wildly unscientific as if they had said that the sun ought to go round the earth, or that parallel straight lines ought to enclose a space.

Mill was therefore taken unawares when in 1842 the last volume of Comte's work appeared, containing an impassioned defence of the existing social relations, and complaining that "even the Family, which, amidst the fiercest revolutionary tumults, had been on the whole respected, has been assailed in our day in its very foundations, by attacks on the hereditary principle [in property] and on marriage." Nevertheless, while insisting on the value of the institutions, Comte admitted they were far from perfect, and under Positivism would be substantially reformed. This was what Coleridge had also said, and Mill accepted it. He gleaned besides several excellent notions for the revision of the last book of his *Logic,* and for a time the discussion continued smoothly.

Mill strongly approved of all that Comte had said about the necessity for moral and mental improvement to precede the regeneration of society, and even approved the idea of promulgating a set of sociological maxims, which should have the emotional force of a religion. He agreed that in social as in scientific matters, the general public must accept the guidance of experts who were more "positivized" than they themselves could hope to be; and that these experts should comprise a sort of philosophic priesthood, with advisory powers sharply distinguished from the powers of government, like the division between the temporal and spiritual powers in the Middle Ages. He even coined the name "Pedantocracy" for this body, which much delighted Comte. Comte, for his part, did Mill a great honour. When his complimentary copy of the *Logic* came, he was in the midst of a course of Cerebral Hygiene; a periodic treatment whereby, in order to preserve the purity and clarity of his own genius, he refrained from reading a single word that anyone else had ever written. He interrupted the process against his habitual rule especially to read Mill's book, and was greatly pleased by its praises of himself.

It was not until they came to discuss the supposedly secondary matters that stood between them that the rift appeared. Their difference hinged on the theory of psychology, which Mill maintained was a science in its own right, ranking in the hierarchy after physiology, and before the social sciences to which it was an essential prelude. But Comte was determined that all states of mind had physical causes, and that what we call the mind was no more than a physical mechanism. He even went so far as to compose a science of phrenology, allocating to each faculty and inclination a geographical situation in the head. He therefore regarded psychology as an elaborate form of physiology, and moved direct from physiology to the social sciences without any intervening studies of the individual mind. "Humanity", he said, "must explain man; not man humanity." And from that he reached the concept of society as a living entity more significant than the individuals who compose it.

This was to Mill's eyes bad enough. But the other result of Comte's psychological theory was even worse. For since the mind depended on the body, woman, whose brain was physiologically smaller than man's, was by nature inferior in intelligence just as she was inferior in physique. And that being so, all attempts to alter the natural subordination of women in the marriage tie or in society were doomed to failure, because "the economy of the human family could never be inverted without an entire change in our cerebral organism, and the only possible result of resistance to natural laws would be to deprive Woman of the enjoyment of her proper welfare by disturbing the family and society."

Mill tried all he could to soften this harsh and unconditional opinion. He admitted that women had smaller brains. He admitted that in the present, as well as in the historical past, women proved inferior to men in intellect, Queen Elizabeth and other remarkable individuals notwithstanding. He tried to get Comte for his part to concede that a fairer test would be to see what inferiority remained when all differences between the sexes traceable to education, environment, and circumstance had been removed. Comte would not concede it. Woman, he said, to compensate for her lack of brain, and partially as a result of it, had a superiority in feeling and emotion. Her function was to soothe and sympathize with men, to educate and care for children, and to keep both in close harmony with the kindly sentiments of private affection and general brotherly love, the foundation of the Positive society. She was to be loved and protected, pampered and even worshipped. But her mental condition was one of permanent childishness: she was quite incapable of abstract reasoning or unimpassioned judgement, and to allow her responsibility in society or in the affairs of state was biologically absurd. As for that notorious George Sand, he added, going about in trousers and masquerading as a man, she was a deplorable spectacle.

The battle raged all summer in 1843, until in November Comte, irritated beyond measure at the obstinate blindness of his rebellious follower, broke it off on the ground that it could do no good, since Mill's mind had not yet reached the stage where it could grasp the fundamental truths so long evident to himself. Mill agreed with him. He could give no further ground. Comte had, in effect, set up humanity as a kind of beehive with Woman for its queen, an idea which struck Mill as being as repulsive as it was false.* Still, he did not like to give up all hope of persuasion: besides, if this were to be the fruitless all, he would like to take back some of the concessions he had made. In doubt, he had recourse to his "almost infallible counsellor". He copied out the relevant part of the correspondence, and gave it to Harriet for her opinion.

Her reply was characteristic. It left no doubt of what she thought of Comte, and provided shrewd encouragement for Mill:

> "These have greatly surprised and disappointed me: and also they have pleased me. All this regarding only *your* part in them—Comte's is what I expected—the usual partial and prejudiced view of a subject which he had little considered, and about which it is probable that he is in the same state that Mr. Fox is about religion. If the truth is on the side ~~we~~ I defend I imagine C would rather not see it.

* A later generation of Positivists in England actually ran a journal called the *Beehive*.

Comte is essentially *French*, in the sense in which we think French mind less admirable than English—Anti-Catholic, Anti-Cosmopolite.

I am surprised in your letters to find your opinion undetermined where I had thought it made up—I am disappointed at a tone more than half apologetic with which you state your opinions— and I am charmed with the exceeding nicety elegance and finesse of your last letter.

Do not think I wish you had said *more* on the subject, I only wish that what was said was in the tone of conviction, not of suggestion.

This dry root of a man is not a worthy coadjutor scarcely a worthy opponent. With your gifts of intellect of conscience and of impartiality is it probable, or is there any ground for supposing, that there exists any man more competent to judge that question than you are?

You are in advance of your age in culture of the intellectual faculties; you would be the most remarkable man of your age if you had no other claim to be so than your perfect impartiality and your fixed love of justice. These are the two qualities of different orders which I believe to be the rarest and the most difficult to human nature."[32] *

Harriet's judgement was decisive. When, later on, Bain asked Mill to show copies of the correspondence to a friend of his, Mill agreed with great reluctance, saying he had made too many concessions and would never show them to anyone again. "Comte's taking to you is what I should have expected", wrote Mill to Sarah Austin, who had just met Comte in Paris on his introduction. "Reste à savoir whether his taking would hold unless kept up by homage and services to himself."[33]

The sequel proved that Mill's dissension was a timely one. In 1852–1854, Comte published his *Système de Politique positive*, being the promised application of his philosophy to the actual social order. It consisted of a highly elaborate religious system with the abstraction Humanity usurping the place of the Supreme Being, and with a priesthood of philosophers fortified by a Positive Catechism, hymns, vestments, sacraments, and all other necessary paraphernalia. As one enemy described it, it was "Catholicism minus Christianity". Regulation was carried into the minutest details of daily life. The good Positivist would cross himself, not in the conventional manner, but by tapping his head with his finger three times at the points where the impulses of love, orderliness, and progress were supposed by phrenology to reside. He would pray three times a day, for a total of two hours, once to each of his household goddesses, his mother, wife,

* It must not be supposed that this polished letter represents Harriet's first reaction to the correspondence. There also exists what appears to be a draft, filled with almost incoherent denunciation of some man provisionally identifiable as Comte (MT Coll. Box III/106).

and daughter, "representing severally the past, the present, and the future, and calling into active exercise the three social sentiments, veneration, attachment, and kindness".[34] He would use every artifice to render their images "as life-like, as close to the reality, as near an approach to actual hallucination, as is consistent with sanity".[35] If, while so doing, he found himself at a loss for words, he was permitted to fill up by quoting passages from the more invocative of the poets. He was to retire from work when he was sixty-three. When he died, if he was worthy, he would be canonized by his parish elders; his memory would be incorporated as a fragment of the Supreme Being, and his remains would be reverently laid in the *bois sacré* surrounding every temple of Humanity.

The middle class, which Comte considered parasitic, was to disappear. Society would be rigidly divided into rich and poor. Employers of labour, who would be regarded as salaried bailiffs of the state, would decide for themselves what proportion of their profits was sufficient to sustain them in their heavy responsibilities. The *prolétaires*, in addition to free lodging, education, and medical attendance, would receive a pound a week with extra rates for piece-work. The man was to bear rule within the family; a woman would not be allowed to defile herself by earning money or by owning property. Dowries would be abolished. Divorce was to be prohibited, and second marriages regarded as indelicate. Church weddings would entail a vow of eternal widowhood.

The world was to be broken up into small republics. Ireland, Scotland, Wales, were to be separated from England; Algeria was to go to the Algerians, Corsica to the Corsicans; France proper was to be made into seventeen states. In each, dictatorial powers for life were to be exercised by the three principal bankers, selected by their predecessors. Supreme over all reigned the spiritual power of the Grand Pontiff of Humanity, Paris succeeding Rome as the religious metropolis of the world.

Fortunately for his intended flock, in the years between the *Philosophy* and the *Politics*, the Grand Pontiff's devastating logic had melted into sentiment. Unhappily married himself, he fell in love with Clotilde de Vaux, the unfortunate wife of a convicted felon. For a year he adored her, sublimely, though without any hope of consummation: then she died, leaving him, much softened, to adore her memory. In consequence, his political system excluded all brutality. "Altruism", a word of his own coining, was to be its end and test.

In the new society there would be no force or violence: the moral feelings of mankind would be the only court of law.

Even so, Comte's powers as a dictator were to be spectacular. Although humane, they were extremely scientific. Since in the positive state progress would be at an end, there would be no further use for independent thought. It would be demoralizing and unsettling. He therefore provided for its extirpation. Anyone of ability would be absorbed into his sacerdotal body, and so pressed into his service. To allow for his own fallibility, he proposed to decree from time to time some one topic of pressing importance, upon which the entire intellectual resources of the globe would concentrate simultaneously. From their findings, he would get what little advice he needed. Thereby, mischievous speculation would be usefully distracted, and the sacred emotion of solidarity encouraged. To finish once and for all any remaining desire for change, any further "insurrections of the living against the dead", all books, except for a hundred of his own choosing, were to be burnt in a gigantic holocaust amidst tumultuous rejoicing.

"Others may laugh, but we could far rather weep at this melancholy decadence of a great intellect",[36] gasped Mill. Looking back upon it, he was horrified to think how he had courted a mind capable of conceiving such monstrosities; and he had every reason to praise Harriet for her prescience. "Comte", he said, "had lived to plan the completest system of spiritual and temporal despotism which ever yet emanated from a human brain, unless possibly that of Ignatius Loyola. . . . The book stands a monumental warning to thinkers on society and politics, of what happens when once men lose sight in their speculations, of the value of Liberty and of Individuality."[37]

To cap it all, Comte in his preface warmly congratulated Louis Napoleon on his coup d'état, "a fortunate crisis which has set aside the parliamentary system and instituted a dictatorial republic". Louis Napoleon was perhaps the only man Mill ever really hated, and just because he had done those very things. In subsequent editions of the *Logic*, Mill left out most of the laudatory passages that had so much gratified his colleague. In the *Autobiography* he cut his acknowledgement of his debt to Positivism to a very slender margin. And later on, as though still brooding over his undue admissions, he wrote two long articles for the *Westminster Review*, explaining his true opinion. They were reprinted as a book in 1865 under the title *Auguste Comte and Positivism.*

At the time, however, of Harriet's assault on Comte in the early forties, Mill could not disengage himself so easily as that. Like other men in other moonshine escapades, he found his rash advances had produced responsibilities unlooked for at the time. And, as he had already experienced with Carlyle, discipleship was all the weightier a burden for being involuntary. Comte, since 1837, had drawn a modest emolument of some £400 a year from his various positions at the École Polytechnique, chief among them being that of Examiner, which provided about half of this amount. It would normally have been adequate for his wants, had he not had to face unusual losses. First, he quarrelled with his father, and so lost a small but useful patrimony. Next, his wife left him. Although a woman gifted to a rare degree with moral and intellectual elevation, she had, he said, been brought up on vicious principles, and was unable to achieve a proper estimate of the position of her sex in the Positive economy.[38] As was natural to him, he told Mill, in pensioning her off he had gone far beyond what was generally considered necessary, giving her an annuity of £120, almost a third of his own income. Worse soon followed. His appointments at the Polytechnique depended, to his unspeakable, almost incredulous disgust, upon a yearly re-election by his colleagues. Though this was usually unanimous, a complete formality, his unorthodox religious and scientific views had created many enemies, and the whisper was going round that he was half deranged. When therefore in a preface to the last volume of his *Philosophy*, he gratuitously insulted the body of professors, the clique against him gained their way; in July 1844 his reappointment as Examiner was defeated by a narrow margin, depriving him of £240 a year.

A year before, when the first possibilities of the disaster had begun to loom, Comte had written to acquaint Mill of his fears. Mill was himself at that time in grave financial embarrassment owing to the American Repudiation of 1842, an inability to refund capital investments on demand, leading in England to the closure of many private banks and a general collapse of credit. In this crisis, a chronic situation in the forties as a result of exuberant speculation overseas, Mill lost a thousand pounds, besides several thousands of his father's trust money for the family, which he had to replace from his own resources. Nevertheless, he immediately offered to come to the assistance of a brother thinker, should his fears materialize. Happily, at that time the necessity did not arise; but now when the storm broke Comte turned at once to Mill in his distress. While fully cognizant of Mill's affection, he was, he said, unable to accept his generosity except as a last resort, because, under Positivism, it was forbidden for philosophers to depend upon each other. It was, however, specified that in the Positivist state, the community would be responsible for keeping them in an appropriate degree of comfort, and the wealthier adherents of the creed should have the privilege. Mill should therefore make it known to the richer Positivists among his English friends that an opportunity had come for them to recognize their duty.

Mill first of all tried Grote, who had on his introduction met Comte a few months earlier during a visit to Paris, and was a keen admirer of his writings. It was a lucky touch, for Grote immediately produced £120, half of the total sum to be made up. Comte was delighted. It would enable him, he said, to continue six months longer, by which time, he was certain, the plot against him would have been exposed, and he would be safely back again in office. But in December his exclusion was confirmed; and, despite the personal intervention of John Austin with Guizot, the Prime Minister, nothing could be done to reinstate him until the next election the following July. Accordingly, Comte wrote for the remainder of the subsidy, comprising two contributions of £70 and £50 collected from Molesworth and a wealthy banker called Raikes-Currie, neither of whom had ever met Comte personally any more than, for that matter, had Mill himself.

In July 1845 Comte again failed to be reinstated, and wrote to say that these sordid anxieties over money were becoming extremely bad for his Cerebral Hygiene, and he hoped his English friends would not leave their great munificence of the previous year half-uncompleted. This time Grote sent only £24. No doubt, Comte thought, since he had borne the heavier share before, Grote was leaving it to the others to make up the balance. But the others sent nothing. By September Comte's needs were pressing, and he wrote indignantly to Mill asking him to make a new appeal to Molesworth. Mill had to explain that it was useless: "I know how trifling for a man like you, is the salary of 5000 Frs [£200] that remains to you. But all the same, since you still have that sum, Sir W. Molesworth no doubt considers that your embarrassment, although deplorable, does not amount to a case of absolute necessity."[39]

This stung Comte to the quick. He replied that for eight years past he had enjoyed a modest comfort, as much his by habit as it was by right. As for economy, he said, he had practised it extensively in the past year. He had reduced his wife's annuity by a third. He had also cut his personal expenses. But these savings were less than half what he had lost. They did not lessen the responsibility resting on those who had withdrawn the protection they had at first justly, and, he would gladly say, nobly, conceded to him. They had added an unexpected defection to a notorious injustice, and all they had finally achieved was to delay by a year the measures he would be compelled to undertake for his own support. He could see now that he had been mistaken in expecting anything but churlish conduct from the vulgar English, and he would be forced in all honesty to put a preface to this effect in his next book.[40]

Mill saw at once that serious misapprehensions were at work. While all Comte said about the duty of disciples putting their goods at the disposal of their master was very true, he explained, the trouble was that neither Grote, Molesworth, nor Raikes-Currie had ever accepted Comte as their leader. On the contrary, while admiring both him and his speculative work, they all dissented violently from his sociological conclusions. They did not therefore feel under any obligation to support him permanently. What they had given, they had given out of sympathy and admiration, to help him over a difficult period until his reinstatement. They had never intended it as the first instalment of an annual tithe.

He had spoken plainly. So plainly that even Comte could catch his drift. At first he did not believe it. But gradually it dawned upon him that his school of Positivists in England was a castle in the air. It did not exist, and never had. The realization was more bitter to him even than the loss of money. Perhaps, he threatened, rich people would have occasion to regret that they had ill-treated the philosophers, who alone could protect them against the violence of popular uprising. Upon tones such as these, the voluminous, if unelevating, correspondence of two great thinkers drew to a rancorous close; and what had started as an *entente* of minds, ended in disaccord. Mill, who had been the first to slacken, made sure he was the last to end. When he received an appeal got up by Comte's own countrymen, he subscribed £10, intimating precisely that it was not an annual contribution. He also wrote a note to Grote advising him to do the same.[41]

Theoretically, the Positive state was supposed to embrace the globe in thirty-three years from its conception. All would be completed in the lifetime of the first Grand Pontiff. It was not to be. Comte quarrelled violently with his followers in France; and the forsaken genius had to scrape along as best he could, tutoring and writing articles, until he died from cancer at the age of sixty in 1857. In London, Frederic Harrison became the chief apostle. George Eliot, G. H. Lewes, Harriet Martineau, and the Richard Congreves were among the devotees. For a time, a Church of Humanity flourished in Lamb's Conduit Street. But whether by bomb blast or for lack of faith, it has long since disappeared, complete with its adornments, the busts of the ideal dead, the Pedantocracy dead and gone.

V

After his sojourn with the Foxes in the spring of 1840, Sterling spent a year at Clifton with his family, going to Torquay for warmth at the dead of winter. There, he took fond interest in Mill's young brother George, then aged sixteen, who was also showing the dreaded symptoms of consumption. But in April 1841 Falmouth once more drew Sterling back. In May he uprooted his family again, in order, he said, to be near Calvert, who had chosen it for his death place. "So you are really to have Sterling always with you", Mill wrote to Barclay Fox. "I congratulate you heartily—there is no place where I would rather wish him—except with me."[42]

Since ill-health drove him from his curacy in 1835, Sterling had taken more and more to a literary career, and Mill had gone to great pains to encourage him. Apart from the articles he had got Sterling to write for the *Review* under the guise of kindness to himself, Mill had successfully introduced him to Black of the *Morning Chronicle*. On being admitted to the closely guarded secret of Sterling's anonymous poem "The Election", Mill put a notice of it in that paper, and at the same time arranged a welcome for it in the *Westminster*—to no avail, for it sold very poorly. Sterling turned to dramatic poems, "Strafford" and "Richard Cœur de Lion", but his progress was slow, and even when they did appear they made no great sensation. What was worse, Emerson, who was trying to bring out an American edition of Sterling's works at Boston, somehow fell among thieves, and they were pirated. Sterling had an article or two in *Blackwood's*, and in the *Quarterly*, once more through Mill's influence, this time with Lockhart. But though he loved the trade of writing, it brought him no money sufficient for the needs of his expansive family. "It seems the price of wisdom is still so much above that of rubies that it finds no purchaser in the market",[43] he told Mill. He recalled regretfully that in 1839 illness had compelled him to decline the chair of Moral Philosophy at Glasgow, worth £700 for six months' lecturing in the year, which Mill, who had been asked for a nomination by Professor Nichol, had offered unsuccessfully both to him and to Carlyle.

Truly, as Mill had foretold, Sterling had come to fill the place of his favourite brother Henry, and was all the better loved for being habitually unfortunate. Early in 1843 he burst a blood vessel in moving a heavy table. While still very weak in bed, he sustained a crippling blow. Both his wife and his mother died suddenly, on the same day and within an hour of each other. Mill hastened to offer any help that he or his family could give to his friend or the six children. He received an affectionate answer:

> "You and Carlyle, Hare and Francis Newman—the feeling how deeply I can rely on you for the love that is worth all the benefits in the world does me good at every moment, and did so even in the dreadful moments (they were so unexpected) that I can still not think of without closing my eyes and shuddering. The kindness of the Foxes has been beyond all my previous notions of what human beings could do for each other."[44]

In June 1843, Sterling, his own health now quite broken, went with his children to Ventnor, Isle of Wight, where Mrs. F. D. Maurice, the wife of his old friend and brother-in-law, kept house for him. In spite of a visit to London where he saw Carlyle for the last time, and another to see Caroline Fox at Falmouth, life was dull without his friends around him. "Let me know as soon as you can when you will come. You know how glad I shall be of your visit",[45] he asked Mill.

Mill came at the beginning of October, and of this, their last meeting, Sterling wrote in glowing terms to Emerson:

> "On Sunday last I had indeed a visit from an old Friend who delighted me by his cordial candour,—John Mill, son of the historian of India, and in many ways notable among us now. His big book on Logic

is, I suppose, the highest piece of Aristotelianism that England has brought forth, at all events in our time. How the sweet, ingenuous nature of the man has lived and thriven out of his father's cold and stringent atheism is wonderful to think, and most so to me, who during fifteen years have seen his gradual growth and ripening. There are very few men in the world on whose generous affection I should more rely than on his, whose system seems at first (but only *seems*) a Code of Denial."[46]

In January 1844, Sterling appears to have proposed to Caroline Fox. After a great struggle with herself, she refused him out of family duty, because of his heterodox religious views, although she loved him and well knew that he was dying. For him, the gloom thickened. "There is nothing new here. Life plods on dimly enough through the mild winter, but leaves small trace behind it",[47] he told Mill. In April and May he had two ghastly chest attacks, and Mill wrote a letter saying all a man could ever say to call back his friend on the very threshold of the grave:

"And there is one thing which cannot be said to you too often, because I have seen before that there was real need of saying it. If there should be but little chance of your recovering anything like solid or perfect health . . . I am afraid that you will think . . . that it is better to be dead. I enter most perfectly into such a feeling, and should very likely feel the very same if I were, as I have several times thought I would be, in your circumstances, but I cannot conceive anything more completely mistaken than in your case such a feeling would be.

"If you were never able to go through any active exertion, or to write a single line, except an occasional letter, or to exercise any influence over mankind except the influence of your thoughts and feelings upon your children and upon those by whom you are loved and valued, you would still be, I sincerely think, the most useful man I know. It is very little that any of us can do, except doing good to those nearest to us. . . . There are certainly few persons living who are capable of doing so much good by their indirect and unconscious influence as you are, and I do not believe you have ever had an adequate conception of the extent of influence you possess, and the quantity of good which you produce by it. Even by your mere existence you do more good than many by their laborious exertions. I do not speak of what the loss of you would be . . . none of us could hope in our lives to meet with your like again, and if we did it would be no compensation; and when I think how many of the best people living are at this moment feeling this, I am sure that you have much to live for."[48]

Mill kept him plied with articles, and letters provocative of argument: and then, in August, he sent his extreme blessing:

"I have never so much wished for another life as I do for the sake of meeting you in it. . . . I shall never think of you but as one of the noblest, and quite the most lovable of all men I have known or ever look to know."[49]

Sterling lingered for another sultry month, neither dead not yet quite living, godspeeded but not embarked, hovering over the void of the unknown. At last, on 8 September 1844, ten days before the end, he made his reply, and also his farewell:

"My dear Mill,

We neither of us can need assurances of what we are to each other, but your letters have a tone in them that I would fain reply to fittingly if I could. But I am so weak that I dare not in the least give way to any strong feeling or it leaves me completely broken and helpless. I have been looking at old letters of my own (yours you shall have again) and how much I find, if that were wanted, to put me in mind of you. How many many scores of times have I been thinking how we sat together on the Baths of Caligula. Let us hope to meet upon some other height with a still nobler prospect. Heaven keep you. Always and entirely yours.

John Sterling."[50]

Of the joint executors responsible for editing Sterling's literary remains, Carlyle thought himself an indifferent man of business, and so the lot fell on Archdeacon Julius Hare, "a nervous, dragged looking man".[51] It was an unhappy plight for an Anglican dignitary, who could do no other than deplore the lapse of his convert and former curate from the faith. The result served only, as he had wretchedly foreseen, to anger all friends of Sterling and to raise the wind of orthodox intolerance. The scandal of the Sterling Club blew to a frenzy. It became necessary for someone to still the tumult. There was no lack of brave impulsive spirits ready for the task. Emerson talked a good deal of doing it. Sterling's brother Anthony collected together all the letters. Mill was about to start, but was deterred by the earnest entreaties of Caroline Fox, who feared that the participation of so celebrated a free-thinker could only make things worse. At last, in 1851, when all that remained of Sterling's name had been ground up, scattered and forgotten, and all was calm again, Carlyle came out with his famous *Life*. He depicted Sterling as a saintly, affectionate but effete young man, successively misguided first by Coleridge and then by Hare, until eventually rescued by himself. Caroline was so upset that she never called at Cheyne Row again.

VI

During the forties, the affairs of Mill and Harriet fell into a ragged and uneven strain. For this their personal fortunes were in part responsible. Harriet, on returning from Brighton in the summer of 1840, was perhaps as well and happy as ever in her life; "we have had the most lovely season and have enjoyed the sea thoroughly",[52] she told Miss Fox, the daughter of W. J. Fox. But her good state did not continue. Her second visit to her family at Birksgate in September was not the amiable affair that it had been the year before. She fell foul of her sister Caroline, whom she suspected of monopolizing their mother, and of making a league with her brother Edward to rule everybody and everything. Caroline had by this time married her drunken lawyer Arthur Ley, who had been since the death of the eldest brother Thomas a trustee of Harriet's marriage settlement. Harriet's profound dislike and distrust of him led to a quarrel lasting till her death, becoming more or less violent as Caroline was alternately an object of pity for being bullied by him, or of anger for defending him.

Even the good-natured John Taylor was drawn into it. On suggesting, "merely to gratify Cary", that they should invite the Leys to dinner when they came to London, he was promptly told by Harriet to ask them when she would not be there; an idea unthinkable enough to extort one of his rare rebukes—"one really is so vexed about this that I don't know I shall propose anything again",[53] he remarked. By May 1842 Caroline seems to have wished to patch their difference, for, she wrote to her "dearest sister", "It would be such a relief to me if you would write and say that it is all past and that you will think nothing more of it, for I can't bear there to be any anger between us . . . do write to me."[54] But it all broke out again two months later when Taylor's brother-in-law Joseph Travers, the other trustee to the settlement, went abroad, leaving the future interests of Harriet's children in the sole hands of Arthur Ley. Harriet earnestly begged Carlyle to fill the vacant place, and Taylor called on him to the same purpose: but although he was persuaded to go with Mill to spend a week-end at Walton and discuss the matter with her, he declined. He was not a good enough business man, he said. Eventually John Ingram Travers, the brother of Joseph Travers, was appointed.

In addition to family troubles, Harriet's health gave way. Quite suddenly, in June 1841, she, who had always hitherto seemed quite strong, "with hardly any warning lost the use of her legs almost entirely",[55] and by winter had grown still worse. Although she recovered slowly from the attack, it marked the beginning of a general breakdown; paralysis and rheumatic pains recurred at intervals, later accompanied by neuralgia and indigestion. From this time on she mostly lived at Walton as an invalid. She was now thirty-four. Her beauty had begun to fade, and, as a result of her nervous disorder, the early vivacity of her quick emphatic temperament became more and more tempestuous. Moreover, she began to apply the great liberal principles she had learnt from Mill, not only to her own problems but to those of others, in a hectoring and righteous manner. When, for instance, John Taylor's mother died in August 1842, it was in direct defiance of well-meaning orders issued by Harriet, through her husband, that she was "necessary to himself, to her grand-children and to all her family, and that she *ought as a duty* to *exert* herself" to keep alive.[56]

Mill's own condition underwent a similar decline. In the summer of 1840 he had been in a splendid state when he entertained the Quaker Foxes, and dined out with Guizot and Bishop Thirlwall, and the interesting young Tory William Gladstone. He had some trouble with his chest in December 1841, but had completely recovered by the time Caroline Fox saw him again when dining at the Mills the following May:

> "John Mill in glorious spirits; too happy to enter much into deep things. He alluded to the indescribable change and growth he experienced when he made the discovery that what was right for others might not be right for him. Talked of life not being all fun, though there is a great deal of fun in it. . . . He is greatly relieved at having finished his 'Logic', and is going to mark the best passages for me with notes of admiration. He said 'My family have no idea how great a man I am!' He is now saving up his holidays for a third journey to Italy; he had serious hopes of an illness in the winter, but was conscientious enough not to encourage it."[57]

At this same season Bain went along by the side of Robertson to the India House. He was full of excitement, an excitement rare in so prosaic a man. He was going to meet his hero. As they passed the commissionaire, resplendent in a cocked hat, and entered the dingy capacious building, his expectation mounted. They walked down a long passage, up two flights of stairs, through the waiting-room where some of the messengers were brewing tea; through the long gallery in which the Examiner's clerks sat nosing their quills in their cubicles by the windows, or chatting in front of an enormous fire, for like most clerks they kept a hot and fetid atmosphere. And when at last they knocked on the door of a private room, guarded by an outer door of confidential green baize latched back to the wall, Bain became quite breathless.

It was a large room, with three tall windows looking into a small brick courtyard. At one end was the fireplace; on one side of it stood a desk deep in loose papers; on the other, a table buried under piles of India despatches all done up with tape. Opposite the fireplace was a bookcase. The space between the two, a distance perhaps of thirty feet, was bare. Bain heard a clock strike the hour, but noticed that he could not see it from the windows. As for the Assistant Examiner, Mill, he stood by his desk, with his face turned to the door as they entered. He was tidily dressed in a black suit with a silk necktie to match; for although when his years became the change, he abandoned his dress-coat for a surtout, black was his invariable colour. "His tall slim figure, his youthful face and bald head, fair hair and ruddy complexion, and the twitching of his eyebrow when he spoke, first arrested the attention: then the vivacity of his manner, his thin voice approaching to sharpness, but with nothing shrill or painful about it, his comely features and sweet expression—would have remained in my memory though I had never seen him again."[58]

Mill used to reach his office at ten o'clock. While studying his despatches, he would eat the breakfast prepared for him by the messengers—a boiled egg, tea, and bread and butter; he ate or drank nothing further until his simple dinner at six when he got home. For reading, he was generally on foot, pacing the length of his room with his papers in his hand. He wrote at a high reading desk, either standing or sitting on a tall stool. Only half his time of attendance was given to the service of the Company. His work, careful and copious as it was, he completed comfortably in three or four hours, the remaining two or three being spent talking to the constant visitors, or to other officials in their rooms, or else in his own pursuits; for the greater part both of the *Logic* and the *Political Economy* was written in this way, as well as nearly all his private letters. As David Masson, another of his visitors, wrote:

> "His reception of me had always been kind, one especial act of kindness having been his offer, on my first call, or my second, to read anything of mine in manuscript. This was a form of kindess of which large use was made, and of which he really liked use to be made by the men of letters —and especially the young men of letters—within the circle of his acquaintance. I remember the studious politeness with which he framed the offer in my case. I was not to think it would be a trouble to him; on the contrary, it would be a favour; he had plenty of time, and nothing he liked so much as reading manuscripts!"[59]

Every summer for the next five years, and after that, having no academic duties to take him out of London, all year round, Bain called twice a week at the India House punctually at four o'clock, to walk back with Mill to his mother's house in Kensington Square. Sometimes, on arriving at the Mills' he was invited in, often meeting another privileged young admirer, G. H. Lewes, whose dearest wish Mill was able to satisfy with an introduction to Comte. Frequently, too, he would find Masson there, chatting with Mill's sisters and their mother. Masson thus describes them:

> "They were a remarkable family. When they were all together, you saw, at the time I speak of, besides Mill himself, then thirty-eight years of age, his mother, a widow since 1836, still a comely lady for her years, and a kindly and most competent hostess; four daughters yet unmarried; and one younger son,—all these five looking up to John now as their head, and their link of honour with the rest of the world; but all of them, even to the youngest, remembering also their dead father, by whom to the very last days of his life, they had been carefully and even rigourously educated. Not one of the five but bore the stamp of their upbringing in a certain superiority both of character and intellect."[60]

In the summer of 1842 came Mill's losses in the American Repudiation, and a great deal of consequent worry. At the same time, Harriet grew much worse. All this, coupled with the phenomenal labours of preparing the *Logic* for the press, reduced him that winter to a low, persistent and morose depression. For two whole years he had no proper holiday; both because he could not afford it, and because his desire to be near Harriet, or, as he expressed it to Comte, "most pressing personal relations",[61] restricted him to London. But with the spring in 1844 came the dawn of better things.

Harriet was better. It was, as thirteen-year-old Helen wrote in her diary, "a sort of spring year—all spring".[62] On 23 May, accompanied by Haji, they arrived at Brighton in dazzling sunshine, and at Whitsun they "walked by the sea singing Gloria in Excelsis while the moon shone".[63] In June Harriet and Helen set out on a two months' tour of Normandy, sailing about by river steamer between Rouen and Havre. Mill was certainly with them, for he was absent from London at that period, and had told Sarah Austin in February that he was saving up his leave for "a real holiday in summer"[64] which would set him up for some time. From Caen, on 24 June, Harriet wrote to her husband that she both felt and looked quite splendid. Helen also was very well indeed:

> "She enjoys the Churches, Dinners, and Diligences immensely, but grumbles excessively whenever we come in contact with people, as in the crowded steamboat. She has all the intolerance of a young person for anything strange, and could not find words strong enough to express her dislike of the French on the steamboat because they talk so much and so fast—indeed their tongues seem never to weary, and the great heat, which makes the little girl cross, seems only to make them more lively."[60]

"I think I have enjoyed my birthday this year as much as I ever have", Helen entered in her diary on 27 July. On 3 August they reached Havre by diligence, and were intending to go on to Dinan, but the news contained in the letters they then received decided their immediate return to England. For Mill was apprised that Comte's letter describing his dismissal from the École Polytechnique had been waiting for him for ten critical days, and hurried off to London to attend to it. The others made a more leisurely journey, stopping for several days in Southampton on the way, then went to London by the railway for a day or two. On 16 August Helen was able to write exultantly: "Here we are at our own beautiful Walton. It is as beautiful as Avranches, and the moonlight nights among the tall trees are as solemn and still as the Cathedral."[66]

VII

Mill's incidental writings at this period were not numerous, but they were masterly summaries on a variety of subjects ranging from the history of Athens and Sparta to contemporary political crises. In style and presentation they were smooth and crystal clear, a marked advance on anything that he had done before, and their range of easily commanded knowledge was stupendous. Moreover, they were for the most part uncontentious, and come down to the present day as elegant essays unmarred by disputation.

The only exception was an article which appeared in the *Westminster Review* for October 1842, and was an excellent example of Mill's devastating system of controversial attack. Samuel Bailey, the Scottish philosopher, while calling in question the generally accepted dictum of Bishop Berkeley on the nature of sight, had rashly and unintentionally given a dangerous opening to the Intuitionists which Mill decided could not pass unchallenged. Instead of overwhelming his victim with superior eloquence and authority, Mill indulgently proceeded to set out the best argument that could be made for the case that Bailey meant to state; and then he summarily demolished it. Bailey was furious, and replied accusing Mill of deliberate misrepresentation. His tone, Mill said to Bain, was peevish. Mill therefore wrote again in the *Westminster* in May 1843. He apologized for his lack of understanding: he had assumed that of two possible arguments open to him, Bailey had meant to take the better, whereas he had now made it clear that he preferred the worse. Whereupon Mill demolished that as well, and rather more severely than the first.

Although history never was Mill's special field of knowledge, it had now become his hobby. His historical outlook was contained in two articles written in the autumn of 1843 and the summer of 1845, about the works of two eminent Frenchmen, Michelet and Guizot.*

The concepts of any age, as he had learnt from Comte, were the concepts most suitable to its requirements, and those best calculated

* (1) "Michelet's History of France", *Edinburgh Review*, January 1844. (2) "Guizot's Essays and Lectures on History", *Edinburgh Review*, October 1845. Both reprinted in Mill's *Dissertations and Discussions*, Vol. 2.

both to preserve order and to ensure development. The object of history was not to make the past ludicrous in comparison with the present: it was to review the past as a chain of causes and effects from which it should be possible to predict the future. Both Guizot and Michelet, he felt, contributed to the philosophic view of history. While resting upon sound research, they gave a glimpse of the ideas that dominated epochs. Michelet's work in particular, Mill observed, "is a history of the middle ages, quite as much as of France; and he has aimed at giving us, not the dry husk, but the spirit of those ages."

Within their sweeping survey of European civilization, Mill found much that was compatible with Comte's doctrines of the complementary historical stages, theological, metaphysical, and positive, and of the continuity of history. The Roman Empire disintegrated; but it did not disappear. It left towns, island systems of municipal organization. It left the idea of a cohesive imperial order. It left a valuable body of law. And it left the seamless robe of the Christian Church, a fabric of moral authority, learning and instruction, spread over and enfolding all the rest. By distinguishing between the spiritual and temporal powers, the mediaeval Church, Mill thought, for the first time liberated conscience from the civil law, and so did more to promote freedom of thought than all the fires it kindled ever did to extinguish it.

Into this half-ruined structure of imperial institutions stormed the barbarians, bringing with them their fresh raw principles of the sturdy independence of the individual and voluntary association for a common purpose. The result was Feudalism, a loose hierarchy of highly organized societies each huddled round its castle, and held together by the reciprocal needs of protection and agricultural services, defined not by legal codes but by local custom. When by the inevitable monopoly of power the smaller were merged in the larger, and Feudalism in its turn gave place to the modern epoch of the national monarchy, it did not decay, but rather expanded itself into the Positive phase of human progress. For, "At no period of history was human intellect more active or society more unmistakably in a state of rapid advance, than during a great part of the so much vilified feudal period."

Though Mill's roseate opinion of the middle ages was shared by most of his generation, his reasons for it were peculiarly his own. He saw a world where each man had to make his own decisions, and was not only a more important but a more responsible creature than he had since become. He saw an era when men rose up in hosts for the militant pursuit of an ideal. An era of widening knowledge, and increasing tolerance even of the Moslem enemy. In particular, the only era in history when women were treated with equality; when the Châtelaine was as good as her Lord in everything save actual ferocity. When the Virgin Immaculate was installed in heaven while Jeanne d'Arc ranged the earth. "But the poor middle age, its Papacy, its chivalry, its feudality, under what hands did they perish? Under those of the attorney, the fraudulent bankrupt, the false coiner."

In his enthusiasm for a philosophy of history, Mill even swallowed Guizot's ingenious vindication of his own increased conservatism. A constitutional monarchy on the English pattern, such as he was now supposed to serve in France, could not succeed, said Guizot. It worked in England, for the exceptional reason that England had never been properly feudal. The Norman conquest was undertaken by a brotherhood of barons who arrived with insufficient force; and the King had to bargain, first with them, and then with the natives, in parliamentary conclave. In France, and other countries where feudal authority had been fully effective, parliamentary government could never be more than a temporary balance between the alternatives of despotism and republicanism.

Fuller reflection upon the menacing implications of arguments like this revealed to Mill the gins and snares of casuistry lurking in the fair field of historical generalization. He gave up his search for an overall theory of history, and, at the same time, his attempt to found the new science of Ethology. Both branches of enquiry were, he felt, insufficiently developed to provide general laws in any way exact. He decided instead upon a more limited scrutiny of man in society. Political Economy, or the study of man in pursuit of wealth, was a branch of knowledge in which he had been steeped since early youth, and was well qualified to tackle.

In 1844 he published his five *Essays upon Some Unsettled Questions of Political Economy*, the bulk of them written fifteen years before. With this preparation he began his second major work, the *Principles of Political Economy*. He did not aspire to anything more than a blending and a thorough exposition of already existing treatises. He began in the autumn of 1845. By the end of the winter he was half-way through. Considering the extent and detail of the work, it is clear that it came easily to him. At the same time he was revising the *Logic*, and rewriting important sections of it, for the second edition which appeared in April 1846. In the summer, he took a two months' holiday, and was further distracted by two long articles for the *Edinburgh.**

In the winter of 1846 more pressing matters intervened. The bad potato harvests in Ireland produced a desperate condition of famine and starvation, and Mill hastened to put forward remedies. For five years he had had facilities for writing leaders in the *Morning Chronicle* whenever the fancy took him, and now for four months he practically monopolized the editorial page. Not until the end of January 1847, when the staff of the *Chronicle* had sufficiently mastered the theme of his articles to carry them on unaided, was he able to return to his *Political Economy*. Even so, the first draft was completed during March. Of the eighteen months which had passed since its commencement, only ten had been used for composition, and even those were full of interruption.

Mill differed from his predecessors, from Adam Smith, Ricardo, James Mill, and M'Culloch, because he regarded Political Economy as a continuation of his *Logic*, a natural descent from the theory of knowledge as a whole to a detailed enquiry into one field of human activity. His basic assumption was that the concept Economic Man was no more than a conventional symbol for the fact that whatever else he may or may not do, man invariably pursues wealth, and that to do so is a part of his nature and one condition of his existence.

So regarded, Political Economy was but a small compartment of Sociology, the least complete of all the sciences, and the most liable to continual modification by the laws of all the others. Its conclusions had no higher status than that of empirical truths, its effects following upon their causes only within certain conditions of time and place and circumstance. Mill's theory of historical progression led him to believe that economic ideas should be judged for stability in their particular era, and for assisting the transition to the next. Not as absolute in themselves, but as contributory to eventual absolutes.

In consequence, his work retained great breadth and flexibility. He saw that what was sound economic doctrine in one state of civilization might not be at all appropriate in another. That an economic

* (1) "Duveyrier's Political Pamphlets", *Edinburgh Review*, April 1846. (2) A review of the first two volumes of Grote's *History of Greece*, *ibid.*, October 1846.

gambit such as the paper currency, a benefit in an advanced society, might have had disastrous repercussions among the Druids, or their modern equivalent in the dusky jungle. Economics depended on society, not society on economics. Since he believed that human knowledge was marching towards completion, he also believed the social order would finally achieve perfection, and bring with it a kind of economic paradise.

In his review of Political Economy as a static science, Mill did little more than gracefully repeat the fundamental principles laid down by his predecessors. The laws relating to production and exchange, such hard facts as the dependence of wealth upon production, of profit upon the cost of labour, or of prices upon the cost of production: the purely token nature of money: the effects of a debasement of the currency: the necessity of balancing imports with exports; the mutual benefit to be derived by all nations from a lively flow of trade: and the ultimate identification of all economic terms with labour: all these were established truths, and have come to be received in the present day as commonplaces.

It was when he turned from the static to the dynamic side of the science, to economics as related to social progress, that Mill entered regions far distant from those normally occupied by Political Economists. Although production and exchange were bound by positive laws, the same was not true of the manner in which the fruits of production were distributed. The rights of property rested on no absolute sanction, but upon social conventions, made by men, and variable from one age or one community to another. The most that could be done was to show, not which institutions of property must exist in a given community, but which were the most just and convenient in that state of civilization, and the most conducive to its advance. And so the various forms of Socialism, Fourierism, Saint-Simonianism, even the Communism of Louis Blanc and the Owenites, appeared to him not as dangerous heresies, but as interesting experiments to be examined in the single light of their expediency as compared with private enterprise.

Even so viewed, however, they could not stand up. If all property were held in common, and everyone were guaranteed an equal or even a graduated share in the fruits of production, everyone would be incessantly occupied in evading his fair share of the work. For mankind was still immeasurably removed from the standards of moral excellence any such system would require. He quoted from the report of a Swiss industrialist to illustrate the shortcomings of the British workman in his present state:

> "Whilst in respect to the work to which they have been specially trained they are the most skillful, they are in conduct the most disorderly, debauched, and unruly, and least respectable and trustworthy of any nation whatsoever whom we have employed. . . . When the uneducated English workmen are released from the bonds of iron discipline in which they have been restrained by their employers in England, and are treated with the urbanity and friendly feeling which the more educated workmen on the continent expect and receive from their employers, they completely lose their balance."

To which Mill added, "This result of observation is borne out by experience in England itself. As soon as any idea of equality enters the mind of an uneducated English working man, his head is turned by it. When he ceases to be servile, he becomes insolent."

All systems of communal ownership, then, were "almost too chimerical to be reasoned against". Even in ideal circumstances, private enterprise would be superior. "There has never been imagined any mode of distributing the produce of industry, so well adapted to the requirements of human nature on the whole, as that of letting the share of each individual . . . depend in the main on that individual's own energies and exertions. . . . It is not the subversion of the system of individual property that should be aimed at, but the improvement of it."

His definition of private property, however, soon took the smiles away from the faces of conservatives. "Nothing is implied in property but the right of each to his (or her) own faculties, to what he can produce by them, and to whatever he can get for them in a free market." There was no such thing as a right of inheritance. A man had a right to bequeath his property once and once only: he had no right to fix entails and perpetuities. If he died intestate, and failed to exercise his right, the state had a claim on his whole property. Similarly, there was no right of property in land. No man made the land. It was a natural commodity and a limited one, the original inheritance of the whole species. Mill shared Ricardo's theory of rent, that landlords were a parasitic class maintaining a monopoly protected by law. No matter what happened to prices, wages, or the fair profit of capital, the one class who always gained were the one class who contributed nothing to production, the *rentiers*.

In societies based predominantly on agriculture, the ownership of land by private inheritance was not only inexpedient but iniquitous. The large estates should be redeemed, the waste lands reclaimed, and all should be divided out into small peasant properties. He quoted Arthur Young's conclusion:

> "Give a man the secure possession of a bleak rock, and he will turn it into a garden: give him a nine year's lease of a garden, and he will convert it into a desert. The magic of property turns sand to gold."

Besides encouraging efficiency, peasant ownership was a source of self-respect, an education in free cooperation between equals for a common purpose, and a restraint upon over-breeding, since all mouths had to be fed directly from a limited area.

Everywhere peasant ownership had been tried, it had been successful. In America, with its endless expanses of land, it had been adopted as a matter of course. In France, it was one of the few satisfactory achievements of the Revolution. Particularly in Ireland, Mill conceived, the system of land tenure was at the bottom of the trouble. Ownership was confined to a small number of landlords who mostly lived in England, and thought only of how to increase their rents. As a result, the tenant farmers had to pay a crippling price for land, were mercilessly evicted if they could not pay it, and had neither money nor incentive for the improvements necessary to make the insufficient acres feed the people. He suggested that the government should divert to the establishment of peasant properties on waste areas, the same sum they would otherwise have to outlay in public assistance. But the government were too much scared of innovation. Instead of making the peasantry into respectable landowners, they degraded them into paupers, a course saved from complete disaster only by the sudden disappearance of two-and-a-half million Irishmen, who joined the massive human tide flowing across the Atlantic.*

Like monopoly in land, monopoly in industry created a scarcity value, and destroyed the incentive of competition which was the mainspring of private enterprise. Since large businesses produced goods more cheaply than small, there was always a tendency for monopoly to grow up of its own accord, and so far as the loss in incentive was compensated by greater efficiency, the tendency must be endured. Public expediency was the only test. So viewed, the legal protection of

* These views on Irish land tenure, the continual burden of Mill's leading articles in the *Morning Chronicle*, were developed at the time of the Fenian risings in a pamphlet called "England and Ireland" published by Longmans in February 1868.

monopoly by means of tariffs and other devices was undesirable, save in a few special cases. The inventor of a new process should be rewarded by a temporary patent in the fruits of his discovery. New colonies or other young communities should be protected until they were established. And, more significantly, all ventures properly classed as public utilities should be held as state monopolies, so that society gained both by greater efficiency and by a share in the profits.

> "In the case of railways, for example, no one can desire to see the enormous waste of capital and land (not to speak of increased nuisance) involved in the construction of a second railway to connect the same places already united by an existing one; while the two would not do the work better than it could be done by one, and after a short time would probably be amalgamated. Only one such line ought to be permitted, but the control over that line never ought to be parted with by the state, unless on a temporary concession, as in France; and the vested right which Parliament has allowed to be acquired by the existing companies, like all other proprietory rights which are opposed to public utility, is morally valid only as a claim to compensation."

This instruction, made within twenty-five years of the opening of the first railway, and almost exactly a century before it was carried into effect, was possibly due less to prophetic insight than to the violent irritation expressed by both Mills, father and son, at the continual spoiling of their favourite rambles by the random tracks of the juggernaut.

The most insidious form of competition was for wages. Like Ricardo, Mill believed that there was in the price paid for any article a fixed sum available for the payment of labour, the amount left over after deduction of the other costs of production, such as the materials consumed and the minimum rate of profit necessary to induce the capitalist to outlay his money. Thus, in the whole field of industry, there was a total wage fund, and no action of the workers by strikes and combination, of the government by legislation, or of the capitalists themselves could alter it. The amount received by each worker as wages was entirely dependent upon the number of workers between whom it must be divided.

That, as Mill had accepted from Malthus, was always the maximum number who could scrape a living. Despite temporary fluctuations, wages tended irresistibly towards the bare subsistence level. For if, by some event such as plague, the number of workers was reduced and wages increased, the balance would soon be restored by an immediate increase in breeding. And if, on the other hand, the wage fund were temporarily reduced by a calamity like the collapse of credit, the toll of misery and starvation would cut the population to the point where it could be maintained exactly on the total sum remaining for wages. There was no artificial means of breaking through the cycle. Emigration *en masse* was a valuable temporary remedy, but the relief so gained would soon be swallowed up by the improvident breeding of those who remained. Technological improvements enabling more to be produced at lower cost would for a time provide low prices and relatively higher wages: but production could not for ever speed faster than the increase in population. Food could be imported cheaply from abroad, and certainly there was every reason why the government should refrain from measures which kept food prices high and resulted in counter tariffs; but there again the food must be paid for in other goods, and was limited by the rate of home production. In the end, the resources of the whole world would be stretched to the full, and world population would be checked only at the point where all could live, and do no more than live.

The only permanent remedy was to change the tendency of the population to increase, and in the absence of artificial means, it could only be done by the development of self control in the individual. Education by itself was not enough, said Mill, since it was impossible to teach the very poor.

> "For the purpose therefore of altering the habit of the labouring people, there is a need of a twofold action, directed simultaneously upon their intelligence and their poverty. An effective national education of the children of the labouring class is the first thing needful: and, coincidentally with this, a system of measures which shall (as the Revolution did in France) extinguish extreme poverty for one whole generation."

Here again, the creation of a class of peasant proprietors was his solution for agricultural areas. In the meantime, much could be done by means of a censorious public opinion. The Church, it was true, had long discountenanced promiscuous intercourse and the birth of illegitimate children, but it went too far in praising marriage as an alternative. Wedlock certainly ensured that every child was the responsibility of some family, but it did not follow that the responsibility was properly recognized. Married improvidence was directly encouraged by a large body of sentimental persons, who refused to face Malthusian facts because they thought them brutal. Instead, they proclaimed that God sends food enough for every mouth, enjoined a prudish silence about sex, insisted by indiscriminate charity on enabling the poor to continue their deadly indulgence, and set up the large family as a model, pointing proudly to the achievements of royalty, squire, and parson in that respect.

> "While a man who is intemperate in drink is discountenanced and despised by all who profess to be moral people, it is one of the chief grounds made use of in appeals to the benevolent, that the applicant has a large family, and is unable to maintain them." *

In so far as he held that the law of population determined the wages of labour, Mill was, as he later admitted, mistaken.† There was no such thing as the wage fund. Wages did not inevitably tend to the minimum subsistence level, nor was it impossible to raise them by legislation or combination. Profits did not, as Ricardo had supposed, entirely evaporate into the pocket of the landlord as rent, or else go back to production in the form of capital. There was a considerable margin annually consumed by the capitalists themselves in luxury expenditure or unproductive speculation. There was, as Mill perceived in another part of his treatise, a direct relation between low wages and high profits. Not only the great landlords but the financier and man of business plundered their finery from the earnings of the poor, and they could all have been stripped of most of it without losing their inclination to invest capital in production for the hope of further gain.

Malthus' main contention, on the other hand, the invariable tendency of population to overrun the means of subsistence, remained as it had always been, the foundation of the entire social philosophy of Mill. For this, if excuse were needed, good contemporary reasons could be given. The population figures for the British Isles, already doubled in the first half of the century, still curved dangerously upward at the rate of a thousand a day. To anyone who daily walked as Mill did, through the foul crush of London in the time of Mayhew, to an office whence he administered unwanted millions of Indian Ryots, it was obvious that the toll of misery and vice was no inhuman theory but a hideous fact. And now, in the present day, the spectre of world famine has once again begun to

* Mill elaborated this line of thought in the *Edinburgh Review* for April 1845 while reviewing a book called *The Claims of Labour* by his acquaintance Arthur Helps, who had extolled the increasing disposition of the well-to-do to show Christian charity to the poor.

† See page 488 below.

loom. In Mill's opinion, an uncontrolled birth-rate was all that stood between men and ultimate Utopia. Although he would regret that physical devices should take the place of moral discipline, he would probably have regarded the general introduction of effective contraceptives as the greatest social benefit since the discovery of America.

Given family planning, Mill foresaw a happy prospect for humanity under his revised form of private enterprise. Prosperity demanded an increasing production and increasing thrift. Both of those conditions seemed, in the middle of the nineteenth century, to be indefinitely assured. The better security provided by orderly government against crime, plague, riot, and natural calamities such as fire and flood, were a great encouragement to brisk business and to public confidence. Even war, in those halcyon days, seemed about to become an antiquated barbarism:

> "Wars, and the destruction they cause, are now usually confined, in almost every country, to those distant and outlying possessions at which it comes into contact with savages."

England, and eventually the world at large, seemed to be reaching the first dawn of boundless and perpetual wealth. The rapid march of man's scientific conquest of the material world promised an endless improvement in industrial processes. As machines developed, people would be able to get more and better goods for less and less labour. Better communications would remove the last fluctuations of price and value due to local shortages or temporary vagaries of climate, and with them all necessity for hoarding. More and more capital would become available to industry, and, with the disappearance of the *rentier* and his capacious pocket, it would all flow into productive channels. If it ever came about that production had all the capital it required and did not need to put out tenders for any extra, there would be a perfect economic equilibrium. The public, having no further incentive to invest, and feeling perfectly secure, would cease to accumulate further capital, and would live comfortably on their salaries and income, spending the surplus they would formerly have saved upon better conditions of life, and the greater enjoyment of leisure. Moreover, as the inheritance tax drained off the great unearned fortunes, there would be a constant tendency towards equality. In the end, there would be extremes neither of wealth nor poverty, the difference in income being determined wholly by personal capacity and effort.

The advent of the Stationary State presumed that the limit of improvement in production had been reached. Also that there were no longer any external attractions, backward colonies, ravaged or undeveloped regions, to drain off surplus capital with the promise of gain. Also that population had been fixed at the overall figure which could be adequately supported. It was not therefore an immediate prospect. Nevertheless, that these conditions should one day pertain throughout the world was, said Mill, as sure as death.

It had been the fashion with other economists to deplore "this irresistible necessity that the stream of human industry should finally spread itself out into an apparently stagnant sea. . . . That, to however distant a time incessant struggling may put off our doom, the progress of society must end in shallows and in miseries." Not so Mill. Man meant more to him than economics. Everlasting competition held no lure:

> "I confess I am not charmed with the ideal of life held out by those who think that the normal state of human beings is that of struggling to get on; that the trampling, crushing, elbowing, and treading on each other's heels, which form the existing type of social life, are the most desirable lot of human kind, or anything but the disagreeable symptoms of one of the phases of industrial progress. . . . While minds are coarse, they require coarse stimuli, and let them have them. In the meantime, those who do not accept the present very early stage of human improvement as its ultimate type may be excused for being comparatively indifferent to the kind of economical progress which excites the congratulations of ordinary politicians; the mere increase of production and accumulation. For the safety of national independence it is essential that a country should not fall much behind its neighbours in these things. But in themselves they are of little importance. . . . It is only in the backward countries of the world that increased production is still an important object."

And nature meant as much to him as man:

> "There is room in the world, no doubt, and even in old countries, for a great increase of population, supposing the arts of life to go on improving, and capital to increase. But even if innocuous, I confess I see very little reason for desiring it. . . . A population may be too crowded, though all be amply supplied with food and raiment. It is not good for man to be kept perforce at all times in the presence of his species. A world from which solitude is extirpated, is a very poor ideal. Solitude, in the sense of being often alone, is essential to any depth of meditation or of character; and solitude in the presence of natural beauty and grandeur, is the cradle of thoughts and aspirations which are not only good for the individual, but which society could ill do without.

Nor is there much satisfaction in contemplating the world with nothing left to the spontaneous activity of nature; with every rood of land brought into cultivation which is capable of growing food for human beings; every flowery waste or natural pasture ploughed up, all quadrupeds or birds which are not domesticated for man's use exterminated as his rivals for food, every hedgerow or superfluous tree rooted out, and scarcely a place left where a wild shrub or flower could grow without being eradicated as a weed in the name of improved agriculture. . . .

It is scarcely necessary to remark that a stationary condition of capital and population implies no stationary state of human improvement. There would be as much scope as ever for all kinds of mental culture, and moral and social progress; as much room for improving the Art of living and much more likelihood of its being improved, when minds cease to be engrossed by the art of getting on. . . . Hitherto it is questionable if all the mechanical inventions yet made have lightened the day's toil of any human being. They have enabled a greater population to live the same life of drudgery and imprisonment, and an increased number of manufacturers and others to make fortunes. They have increased the comforts of the middle classes. But they have not yet begun to effect those great changes in human destiny, which it is in their nature and in their futurity to accomplish."

The achievement of the ideal state by private enterprise left little room for the consumption of capital by the government. Expenditure for military purposes would be negligible: police, and the ordinary executive and administrative functions, would cost the minimum. In examining the sphere and duties of government, Mill, in the liberal tradition, entirely denied the organic conception of the state, and confined it to the position of referee of a spontaneous progress to a predetermined end. He grudgingly allowed its right to levy taxes either direct or indirect to ensure its own continuance; although, he observed, "the burden of taxation in our own country is very great" (income tax had just gone down from 7*d.* to 6*d.* in the pound).

In its authoritarian aspect, Government interference should be kept to the minimum necessary to protect its subjects from the infringement of their rights by force and fraud. Compulsory legislation beyond that point would be unnecessary, since no one knows better how the shoe pinches than he who wears it, and each man is normally the best judge of his own interest. In many cases it was actually injurious. The great majority of company law and trading regulations, in addition to being an enormous waste of time and money, had a confusing and depressing effect on enterprise. Exceptions to this rule, however, would be children who, as persons not yet capable of deciding and defending their own welfare, had a claim to special protection from the state, not only against industrial exploitation, but especially against the parental tyranny of their own families. Above all, the state had an absolute obligation to provide compulsory education "either gratuitously or at a trifling expense", since "the uncultivated cannot be competent judges of cultivation". But in this connection it was to be remembered that the government must not in any way direct the course of actual teaching: "to possess such a control, and actually exert it, is to be despotic. A government which can mould the opinions and sentiments of the people from their youth upwards, can do with them whatever it pleases."

In its advisory or constructive capacity, the government had greater latitude. It could take over the land, coal, iron, and other natural properties of the community, and all industries fairly designated as public utilities, either working them itself, if its management of them was efficient, or hiring them out on temporary contracts. It could set up a national bank in open competition with private banks; it could build fire-stations and hospitals. But it must bear in mind that over-centralization of executive offices tends to make government too unwieldy for its real function of wise legislation. In all these matters it should make full use of local government and voluntary bodies, both on that account, and also because of the excellent lessons in citizenship acquired by the public from participating in such affairs.

VIII

With the first draft of the *Political Economy* completed, Mill spent the remaining nine months of 1847, from March to December, in rewriting it. Harriet, in her enforced retirement at Walton, was taking a keen interest in his progress. The *Logic* had slipped into print without her intervention, but that was never to be the case again. Every line received her scrutiny. For the dry principles of economics she cared little: but of human nature she felt herself at least as much a judge as Mill himself. As a Friend of the Species, she favoured the socialist form of society as an ideal. But at the same time her gentility perceived such coarseness in the common people, that she thought it unattainable until much had been done to render them less vulgar. She therefore agreed with Mill's assessment of socialism as being chimerical, at any rate for the immediate future. She did, however, observe that his description of the ultimate Utopia had a somewhat bourgeois tone: that while for business men and bankers many mansions were allowed in the financial Arcady, there was little hope the poor would ever reach it. And she insisted on his appending a further chapter, taken almost from her own lips, outlining the means for the reformation of the working classes.

Throughout this chapter, she laid emphasis upon the development of character by rugged and personal self-help. The paternal relation between rich and poor; the friendly watchfulness on one hand and the dog-like loyalty on the other, so wistfully conjured up by the Merry-Englanders "whose dissatisfaction with the Present assumes the form of affection and regret towards the Past" (Carlyle had sent Harriet an inscribed copy of his *Past and Present* in 1843), was not only an historical myth, but not even an adequate ideal, Mill wrote, at Harriet's bidding:

> "The poor have come out of leading-strings, and cannot any longer be governed or treated like children. To their own qualities must now be commended the care of their destiny.... Whatever advice, exhortation or guidance is held out to the labouring classes, must henceforth be tendered to them as equals, and accepted by them with their eyes open. The prospect of the future depends on the degree in which they can be made rational beings."

Besides the indispensable public education, and the voluntary restriction of population, the proper means towards this end was the cooperative industrial undertaking. Peasant proprietorship, though admirable in backward agricultural communities, was not enough in the heavily industrialized conditions of the present day. "The aim of government should be not solely to place human beings in a condition in which they will be able to do without one another, but to enable them to work with or for one another in relations not involving dependence." For this reason also, the various schemes developed by enlightened capitalists for making their workers shareholders and partners in their factories, mines or fisheries, although praiseworthy, were insufficient.

What Mill and Harriet wished to see were associations like the Rochdale Pioneers, the original title of the Cooperative Wholesale Society, which, starting in 1844 with 28 members and a capital of £28, achieved in sixteen years a capital of over £37,000, a membership of 3450 and an annual profit of nearly £16,000. The members of such societies would learn, through experience, the most sensible form of organization, not trying to divide up all proceeds equally on a communistic pattern, but paying out a minimum wage supplemented by a bonus according to deserts. A substantial proportion of the annual profit would be put back into general capital, and considerable funds be set aside for social and welfare benefits, covering almost every want defined a century later in the Beveridge Report excepting one. All provision for maternity was rigorously forbidden as a dangerous incentive to reckless breeding. Industrial or commerical undertakings of this sort would have such tremendous advantages in cutting costs and getting rid of middlemen that they would finally drive out privately managed firms entirely. And when the Stationary State eventually arrived, it would be a State made up of these cooperative businesses, each composed of members adequately paid, responsible, and well enough educated to get full advantage from the greater leisure that would then be possible. But any tendency between the societies to merge and swallow one another voluntarily must be discountenanced. Competition was the only means to improved production, the only safeguard against the natural laziness of mankind. The Socialists were wrong in thinking it an evil to be overcome. "They forget that wherever competition is not, monopoly is; and that monopoly, in all its forms, is the taxation of the industrious for the support of indolence, if not for plunder."

With Harriet's considerable additions, the book was sent to press in December 1847. By this time, in addition to her part share in the authorship, she had begun to take Mill's business affairs in hand. The contract struck with Parker was, like that for the *Logic*, based on half net profits, but in this case, at her insistence, the publisher's rights were confined to a single edition. Mill warmly praised her. "The bargain with Parker is a good one and that it is so is entirely your doing—all the difference between it and the last being wholly your work, as well as the best of the book itself so that you have a redoubled title to your joint ownership of it."[67] She was soon able to turn the reservation to good use. Before the third edition was agreed, Mill, who was normally undemanding in such matters, wrote sternly to Parker, telling him that he was far from satisfied with his share of the profits from the last, and that with a book so successful as this had been, he expected to get at least £300 from the next printing.[68]

Early in 1848 the proofs were coming through. Harriet, who already felt "more like a ghost than a living person" from her exertions, found herself so enmeshed in the details of publication that she had for the second time to defer a holiday at Brighton with her husband. "I am so taken up with the Book which is near the last and has constantly something to be seen to about binding, etc., that I could not leave town before the beginning of April if even then", she told him.[69] Indeed, her intense preoccupation in her literary partnership made her a little easy with John Taylor's interests. When Mill was offered the joint management of the *Morning Chronicle*, she suggested enthusiastically (although unsuccessfully) that her husband should buy it up for him, in order, as she said, to save it from the Tories.[70]

The work at last complete, the climax came when the author, swept away by gratitude, proposed to preface it with a tribute to his Muse.

"To
Mrs. John Taylor
This attempt to explain and diffuse ideas
Many of which were first learned from herself
is
with the highest respect and regard
dedicated" *

was what he wished to print on the thousand fly-leaves of his textbook on economics.

Harriet was immensely flattered at the prospect. To tell the truth, it left her rather breathless. But perceiving it to be a matter in which her husband ought to be consulted, she wrote him a candid, cordial letter:

"I am somewhat undecided whether to accept its being dedicated to me or not—dedications are not unusual even of grave books, to women, and I think it calculated to do good if short and judicious . . . yet I cannot quite make up my mind—what do you advise—on the whole I am inclined to think it desirable."[71]

* The full inscription may be seen in Professor Hayek's *J. S. Mill and Harriet Taylor*. The above, which is an extract, gives a fair idea of the whole.

She was apparently surprised and not a little vexed to receive John Taylor's strong reply:

> "Consideration made me decidedly think, as I did at the first moment of reading your letter, that all dedications are in bad taste, and that under our circumstances the proposed one would evince on both author's part, as well as the lady to whom the book is to be dedicated, a want of taste and tact which I could not have believed possible. . . .
>
> It is not only 'a few common people' who will make vulgar remarks, but all who know any of us—The dedication will revive recollections now forgotten and will create observations and talk that cannot but be extremely unpleasant to me. . . .
>
> I much regret, as I always do, differing in opinion with you. But as you asked me what I advised, I have not hesitated to give my opinion."[72]

In the end, they reached a compromise unsatisfactory to all. The dedication was restricted to a few gift copies, and Harriet had to find an ingenious cover for her husband's unexpected touchiness. "I should have said that the Dedication was confined to copies given to friends at my especial request", she explained to Fox, "and to the great disappointment and regret and contrary to the wish and opinion of the Author. My reason being that opinions carry more weight with the authority of his name only." The practice was repeated in the second edition, but in the third edition in 1852 the inscription was omitted altogether. By that time John Taylor was dead and Harriet had married Mill, so, she informed her brother Arthur, "it would have been no longer appropriate".[73]

The Principles of Political Economy was published in April 1848. As a text-book it enjoyed an immediate and lasting reputation. In England it ran into thirty-two editions in fifty years, and almost as many again in the present century. Within six months Mill received a complimentary copy of the American edition, and it was soon translated into many foreign languages. In the field of pure economics, its extensive influence was somewhat mischievous. Mill had made no special study of his subject before beginning to write. In fact, since composing his *Essays upon Some Unsettled Questions of Political Economy* in 1829, he had read virtually no economics at all. His utter failure to take any account of the advances that had been made in the intervening twenty years, had the effect of retarding the development of the science for an entire generation. As a work on social philosophy, it was received with outcries by "numerous sentimental enemies, and still more numerous interested enemies in sentimental guise".[74] It goaded Ruskin to indulge in economic controversy in *Unto this Last*, and was more effectively manhandled by "that creature Dickens" in *Hard Times.** On the other hand, it found unexpected favour with the Christian Socialists, "the Kingsley set", who asked for and obtained permission to reprint Harriet's chapter on the future of the working classes.

It was widely and energetically misunderstood. George Jacob Holyoake, who, as founder of the Rochdale Pioneers was a sturdy personification of the virtues of self-help among the workers, published it as a serial in his weekly republican periodical *The Reasoner*, so that it might be made available to his public, who could not afford to pay the thirty shillings that it cost. Unfortunately, he could not refrain from adding a hearty introduction loudly welcoming Mill as an adherent to militant atheism. For this, he earned a sharp rebuke from Harriet. "I am disgusted with the mixture of impudence and imbecility of this *foolish* creature Holyoake", she wrote to Mill:

> "I suppose he too must be answered. What do you think of the ci-joint notion of an answer? I should like to see your answer before it goes, if quite convenient.
>
> "I fancy I should say that the morality of the Reasoner appears to me . . . to be as intolerant slavish and selfish as that of the religion which it attacks. . . . The fool ought to be sharply set down by reasons, but he is such an *excessive* fool and so lost in self-sufficiency that he will cavil and prate say what you will. . . . I am glad of the quarrel with him as I am glad not to have your name and influence degraded by such a connection. . . . *The fact is* his irreligion like Fox's liberalism is a trade."[75]

A little later Mill also had to take to task, though for quite opposite reasons, an admirer in New York who had sent him a clipping from the *North American Review*:

> "The article is laudatory enough to satisfy an appetite for praise much stronger than mine. But the writer is one whose tone of thinking and feeling is extremely repugnant to me. He gives a totally false idea of the book and of its author when he makes me a participant in the derision with which he speaks of Socialists of all kinds and degrees. . . .
>
> On the population question my difference with the reviewer is fundamental, and in the incidental reference which he makes to my

* "That creature Dickens, whose last story, *Bleak House*, I found accidentally at the London Library the other day and took home and read—much the worst of his things, and the only one of them I altogether dislike—has the vulgar impudence in this thing to ridicule rights of women. It is done in the very vulgarest way—just the style in which vulgar men used to ridicule 'learned ladies' as neglecting their children and household etc." (Mill to Harriet, 20 March 1854, MS. letter in the library of King's College, Cambridge.)

assertion of equality of rights . . . of women, the tone assumed by him is really below contempt. But I fear that a country where institutions profess to be founded on equality, and which yet maintains the slavery of black men and of all women, will be one of the last to relinquish that other servitude."[76]

Mill himself was convinced that his views on property were outspoken to the point of daring, but the uproar he expected on this count was the one effect that never followed. The revolutionary events all over Europe which coincided with the appearance of his book—the barricades in Paris, the rising of the United Irishmen, the massed parading of the Chartists—introduced people to more savage doctrines; and those who grew accustomed to the sanguinary threats of the Communist Manifesto were not to be alarmed by a mild and reasoned argument in favour of heavy death duties, national education, and cooperative societies.

On the contrary, he was continually taken for the champion of conservatism. He decided that, for the second edition which followed almost at once, a stronger statement of his case, so far from being intemperate, was necessary in order to make it understood at all. He was, therefore, disposed to soften the severity of his judgements against Socialism. But the violent change in Harriet's mind produced by the events of 1848 was a complete surprise to him. Her passionate and downright sympathy with the oppressed, her robust and practical common sense, two qualities more commonly found together in women than in men, made her feel that the condition of the poor was far more miserable than she had at first supposed. That their degraded tendencies were the result of evil circumstances. That the desired improvement of their minds might after all be accomplished very rapidly, since they had shown themselves possessed of courage enough to stand up and demand their rights. Especially, she felt, a lot of the objections to the communal ownership of property were nothing more than humbug:

"Among other trash did you observe Hume said—'To interfere with the labour of others and to attempt to establish community of property is a direct violation of the fundamental laws of society'. What a text this would be for an article which however no paper would publish. Is not the Ten Hour's Bill an 'interference' etc etc? Is not the 'interference' with their personal freedom by this Suspension Bill * a 'violation' etc, what is the meaning of 'fundamental laws of society'—

* The suspension of Habeas Corpus during the Irish rebellion, July 1848.

the very point in debate on the subject, communism, on which he professed to be speaking.

Oh English men!
English intellect!"[77]

She told Mill to abolish, in the second edition, all his objections against Socialism and Communism.* She demanded a complete reversal of his economic treatise in its most essential feature. And she obtained it, though the process cost him infinite pain and worry. The work which had set out to expose all schemes of communal ownership as wild fancies, came within a year to regard them as "the most valuable elements of human improvement now existing".

She objected "strongly and totally" to a passage in the first edition indicating that security in the necessaries of life was in itself a largely overrated source of happiness. And, although Mill pointed out that she had suggested it herself in the first place, that it had always seemed to him the strongest part of the argument, and that its omission would imply a direct change of front, he was forced to give way. His disavowal of the aims of Socialism so confidently expressed in 1848 was replaced in 1849 by the brief contradiction:

> "On the Communistic scheme, supposing it to be successful, there would be an end to all anxiety concerning the means of subsistence: and this would be much gained for human happiness."[78]

Again, Mill's jealously held opinion that the natural indolence of men would render industries unworkable in a socialist community where the incentive of competition was removed, she now held to be untenable. And the offending passage disappeared, although he vigorously protested it would mean that "all the two or three pages of argument which precede, and of which this is but a summary, are false and there is nothing to be said against Communism at all—one would only have to turn round and advocate it."[79] Fourierism, which had originally been dismissed with the other brands of Socialism as contrary to the laws of human nature, and "almost too chimerical to be reasoned against", now received a long examination and full praise as an ultimate objective. She even insisted that Socialism, instead of awaiting the regeneration of humanity by a long and distant process of education, should be immediately introduced, seeing that the children of the community could be made perfect in ten years, "if there were a desire on the part of the cleverer people to make them perfect".[80] But at this point Mill refused to go her pace, observing

* In 1848 there seems to have been little or no distinction between the two.

merely: "With every advance in education and improvement, their system tends to become less impracticable, and the very attempt to make it succeed would cultivate, in those making the attempt, many of the virtues which it requires."

By the time the third edition was ready in 1852, Harriet had finally won the day. "Whatever may be the merits or defects of these various schemes", Mill then admitted, "they cannot be truly said to be impracticable." Instead of the welfare state encouraging over-population by removing all motive for prudential restraint, "the communistic scheme has the recommendation of tending in an especial degree to the prevention of that evil." Free enterprise, instead of being the best possible mode of distributing the produce of industry both in the present and in any imaginable condition of human nature, could now hold its own only if improved almost beyond recognition:

> "If therefore the choice were to be made between Communism with all its chances and the present state of society with all its sufferings and injustices: if the institution of private property necessarily carried with it as a consequence, that the produce of labour should be apportioned as we now see it, almost in an inverse ratio to the labour: . . . if this or Communism were the alternative, all the difficulties, great or small, of Communism would be but as dust in the balance. But to make the comparison applicable, we must compare Communism at its best, with the regime of individual property, not as it is, but as it might be made. The principle of private property has never yet had a fair trial in any country, and less so, perhaps in this country than in some others... We are too ignorant either of what individual agency in its best form, or Socialism in its best form, can accomplish, to be qualified to decide which of the two will be the ultimate form of human society."

The decision between Communism and Capitalism, which were now regarded as systems with equal possibilities for satisfying the economic wants of man, was to rest in future upon the next need of human beings, personal liberty. The doubt, and a doubt shown to have been shrewdly keen by the experience of the twentieth century, was whether with Communism or its various modifications "there would be any asylum left for individuality of character; whether public opinion would not be a tyrannical yoke; whether the absolute dependence of each on all, and surveillance of each by all, would not grind all down into a tame uniformity of thoughts, feelings, and actions. . . . No society in which eccentricity is a matter of reproach can be in a wholesome state."

Harriet's astounding, almost hypnotic control of Mill's mind was not confined to reversing the direction of his economic theory. She extended it to other branches of his thought. At the time when the third edition of the *Political Economy* was preparing, Harriet was working on a treatise about the disabilities of women. Her increasing absorption in that one particular injustice was sharply reflected in Mill's work as well. He incorporated it as a vital part of the population problem, and it became the fundamental issue of his entire social philosophy, a theme repeated and developed in one way or another in practically everything he subsequently wrote. In the third edition of his *Political Economy* he inserted a new paragraph at the point where he was discussing means of checking thriftless breeding:

> "There would be no need, however, of legal sanctions, if women were admitted as on all other grounds they have the clearest title to be, to the same rights of citizenship with men. Let them cease to be confined by custom to one physical function as their means of living and their source of influence, and they would have for the first time an equal voice with men in what concerns that function: and of all improvements in reserve for mankind which it is now possible to forsee, none might be expected to be so fertile as this in almost every kind of moral and social benefit."

Passages like these, almost certainly Harriet's, occurred throughout the work, outlining the conceptions later contained in the *Liberty* and *Subjection of Women*—the same conceptions she had faintly defined in her incompleted essays twenty years before. They now became the most evangelical of Mill's convictions, and the basis of his claim to be considered a progressive, original sociologist.

Those who were jealous of Harriet's success with Mill or else incredulous of her powers, and there were many of each in her immediate circle, cynically attributed his high opinion of her to her skill in remembering his ideas and giving them back to him as though she had thought them out herself. Carlyle did much in his sly way to perpetuate this view after Mill was safely dead, by telling Charles Eliot Norton, whose faithful notebook never forgot such pieces, that "those great dark eyes, that were flashing unutterable things while he was discoursin' the utterable concernin' all sorts o' high topics"[81] were at the bottom of the problem. To make certain of his point, he also told John Morley, "She was full of unwise intellect, asking and re-asking stupid questions."[82] And of the many who have felt moved to make a special study of the prophet, like David Wilson and Professor Emery Neff, none has bothered to question his inference that flattery was the key of Harriet's power over Mill.

A man like Mill, to whom unearned praise was so distasteful and deliberate contradiction so welcome, would never have been deceived by stratagems of that kind, and generally the charge of flattery has met with little credence. But practically all of his assessors, including Leslie Stephen, Leonard Courtney, and the editors of the *Encyclopaedia Britannica* (edition of 1940), have been reluctant to believe that Harriet had the share in his work which he expressly stated. They have been driven to elaborate circumlocutions, in order to explain his many unmistakable assertions of her intellectual influence as sentimental misconceptions or as chivalrous extravagances, without giving him the lie direct. They look to the violence of his emotional craving, and conclude that in satisfying it she charmed and bewitched his mind. Bain came closest to the mark. He recalled Mill's love for Sterling, a man of quick sensibility and provocative enthusiasm, and decided that Harriet's nature must have been the same. He also remembered that when he once remarked on the power of stimulation as a source of mental energy, Mill eagerly replied, "There! stimulation is what people never sufficiently allow for."[83]

It is difficult on the face of it to see why Mill, who was so soberly and carefully exact in every other matter, should be discredited in this. He claimed that the partnership was one of mutual benefit, he providing intellectual fuel for Harriet's rapidly expanding mind, and testing in return his judgements against a brain abnormally receptive both of ideal aims and of the hard facts of the present. So that, he said, they went forward in complete companionship both intellectual and emotional. Recent evidence confirms that his was no overstatement. From 1846 onwards, Mill's entries in his chronological list of published works are marked with increasing frequency as "a joint production with my wife", and the *Political Economy* is so styled.[84] The influence she had gradually extended over him now ended in complete ascendancy, and his further writings were "not the work of one mind, but of the fusion of two".[85] When Harriet required him to deny his main political belief, he meekly answered: "This is probably only the progress we have always been making, and by thinking sufficiently I shall probably come to think the same—as is almost always the case, I believe always, when we think long enough."[86] This, and other similar statements in their correspondence, make it plain that her predominance was even more complete than he himself pronounced. Except for the *Logic*, the principles underlying the more important works of John Stuart Mill were defined, although not actually composed, by Harriet Taylor. And whatever in them cannot be ascribed to his lucid reasoning must be attributed to the sheer force of her personality.

IX

How far during these twenty years did their unmarried intimacy extend? Reading the passionate terms of their letters, it is difficult not to think that they were lovers in every meaning of the word. "Far from being unhappy or even *low* this morning, I feel as tho' you had never loved me half so well as last night—and I am in the happiest spirits and *quite quite* well part of which is owing to that nice sight this morning",[87] wrote Harriet, after one of their week-ends in the country. And again, when Mill went away for a fortnight on a walking tour: "I should be low rather to think of the enormous length of time that has to be passed before I am again to see the light of my life, my most admired my most beloved—the only inclination I have, not being able to see you, is to write such words as these—*darling sweetest dearest.*"[88] Add, that they defined chastity as "sexual intercourse *with* affection"[89]: that for a time at least they debated an elopement: that only a very few of Harriet's letters escaped her general injunction to Mill to make sure that he destroyed them: that, while at home they were hypersensitive and secretive, at sunny Sorrento they gaily took rooms on the same floor of *La Sirena*—and the world would rush to its conclusion.

The world, however, would be quite mistaken. It is quite certain that they never went to bed together, "at that time", as Mill said in the *Autobiography*. Harriet herself requested him to say so:

"Should there not be a summary of our relationship from its commencement in 1830—I mean given in a dozen lines—so as to preclude

> other and different versions of our lives at Kesn [Keston] and Waln [Walton]—our summer excursions etc. This ought to be done in its genuine truth and simplicity—strong affection—intimacy of friendship and no impropriety. It seems to me an edifying picture for those poor wretches who cannot conceive friendship but in sex—nor believe that expediency and the consideration for the feelings of others can conquer sensuality. But of course this is not my reason for wishing it done. It is that every ground should be occupied by ourselves on our own subject."[90]

If the truth were not as she described it, to write thus to her lover would have been indelicate and pointless.

There was certainly a need for such a statement. At the time, there was lively speculation on the matter; not unnaturally, for they were both ardent, handsome, and, in the early stages of their affair, young and sound of body. Later, when the charge of immorality could not hold in the face of Mill's integrity and the placidity of John Taylor, it became the fashion to assume that he was undersexed, a more disgraceful shortcoming in the eyes of his manly and athletic critics. "In the so-called sensual feelings, he was below average", said Bain; "he made light of the difficulty of controlling the sexual appetite."[91] "The sea may be ignored, but not sex, which is everywhere", howled Wilson, "they who ignore it suffer . . . Doctors might agree he should marry or take a mistress and quit Mrs. Taylor; but who was to tell him that, after his father died?"[92] Leslie Stephen was at once more daring and more smug: "His feelings, however, were, I take it, as tender as a woman's. They were wanting, not in keenness, but in the massiveness which implies more masculine fibre. . . . The most eminent women, hitherto at least, are remarkable rather for docility than originality. Mill was especially remarkable, as I have said, for his powers of assimilation. No more receptive pupil could ever be desired by a teacher. Like a woman, he took things—even philosophers—with excessive seriousness: and shows the complete want of humour often—unjustly perhaps—attributed to women. . . . When Carlyle, in his hasty wrath, denounces 'shams' with a huge guffaw, Mill patiently unravels the sophistry, and tries to discover the secret of their plausibility."[93]

Within these bellows of the dominant male is contained the imputation that Mill's alleged lack of sexuality accounted for his unpalatable doctrines about women. For though he could not be argued down by reason even after he was dead, it could be asserted he was more a woman than a man, and, as a woman, need not be listened to.

The facts are otherwise. The most noisy man is not often the most potent, nor is the profligate necessarily the most truly amorous. There is every reason to suppose that Mill endured the sensual torments in all their normal urgency, despised them not in ignorance but in conquest, and fought them just as fiercely as any mediaeval saint. But for a different, and special reason. He was not ascetic. He approved of any form of genuine enjoyment; but he believed the physical pleasures to be less acute and far more transitory than the spiritual, and that the coarse texture of the one could soon dull the appreciation of the other. Neither Mill nor Harriet was austere. Sex of itself was not for them a thing of shame, but a question of personal inclination limited by the expediency of the circumstances. "What any persons may freely do", Mill wrote, "with respect to sexual relations should be deemed to be an unimportant and purely private matter, which concerns no one but themselves. If children are the result, then indeed commences a set of important duties towards the children, which society should enforce upon the parents much more strictly than it now does. But to have held any human being responsible to other people and to the world for the fact itself, apart from this consequence, will one day be thought one of the superstitions and babarisms of the infancy of the human race."[94]

In their own case, inclination was sapped by intellectual prejudices. It seemed to them that half of humanity, because it was not strong enough to resist, was more or less politely set aside for the satisfaction of the animal requirements of the other half, and women were denied all free share in the arrangements and decisions concerning even that one function. So viewed, the sexual relation became for them revolting and unjust. It encouraged in the one sex pompous selfishness, and in the other, petulant servility: and it debased society to the level of a farmyard. It also seemed to them that all the economic evils in the world grew from the inability of mankind to control its lust. So long as an extra coin in the wage packet served only to produce a wanton rush to oblivious embraces, all hopes of ease and plenty were in vain. And being full of poetic longing for the destiny of man, the spectacle was enough to cause a carnal disgust in both of them. Therefore, although Mill wanted the completest union possible with Harriet; and though Harriet loved him well, respected, and even perhaps a little feared him, each was personally disposed to stop short of physical passion, and they were sure that for example's sake they were bound to do so.*

To these restraints was added their regard for the feelings and reputation of John Taylor, and here they showed a lack of understanding. Believing as they did, and as they expected him also to believe, that the sexual question was a small and unimportant aspect of the matter, it is difficult to see why they thought their abstinence should be any great consolation to him. Yet they gave him that assurance as though it were all that he could ask, and seem never to have considered that they did him greater injury in other ways. His domestic comforts were curtailed: his habits of life upset: in professional circles, in the chapel, and in his club, he became a figure of ribald fun. Nor did their bearing do much to lessen his embarrassment: for by varying from careless defiance to excessive prudence, it gave every appearance of guilt. To know that his wife and her lover did not sleep together can have little contented him, since everyone who did not believe that they did so apparently considered that they should.

While they required John Taylor to share the responsibility for their grand passion, the lovers were more jealous of Harriet's reputation than of his. During the forties, they retired from social life completely. For this there were many reasons. It is no doubt true, as Mill told Caroline Fox, he got no good from society and did more by staying away. Once he had parted with the *Review*, he was glad to withdraw to more contemplative pursuits. Harriet's illness, too, restricted her engagements; while the death of many of their closest friends, Lizzie and Sarah Flower, John Sterling, and Charles Buller, removed much of the pleasure of going out. Besides, they had each other, and that traditionally is company enough. "When I was happy, I never went after any one; those that wanted me might come to me",[95] Mill remembered sadly.

But incontestably the main cause of their retirement was the fear of gossip. Bain says that when he arrived in London in 1842, the affair was the familiar talk of all the circle. Despite their statutory innocence, and although they "did not consider the ordinances of

* Betty Miller, in her *Portrait of Robert Browning* (1952), has drawn an interesting comparison between Harriet and Elizabeth Barrett, as women of similar brilliance and identical ailments, exerting an equally absolute power over their admirers. She suggests that, had Elizabeth Barrett wished it, the poet too was ready to undergo a long sentence of platonic adoration.

society binding on a subject so entirely personal",[96] they had a more than normal dread of being talked about. Bain goes on to recall that now and then, when Mill was due with Harriet at Kent Terrace, his cherished walk back from the India House would go no further than the Bank, where his hero ceremoniously and in silence boarded an omnibus for Regent's Park. Harriet was even more discreet. Her daughter Helen, whose diary recorded all other visitors at this period, made no mention of Mill either at Walton or elsewhere, though he was continually in attendance both at home and abroad. When Mill was with them at Caen in 1844, Harriet did not wish her son Herbert to visit her family at Birksgate, "because there would be no end to questionings and wonderments at everything I do".[97] Another time when she was expecting Mill, she cautioned her long-suffering husband not to breathe a word; "he does not tell even his own family *where* he goes for his holiday as I do hate all tittle-tattle. Therefore I do not mention it either except to you."[98] And to Mill himself, on a critical occasion after Taylor's death, she wrote: "I must see you soon—it occurs to me that it might be well to go down to Walton to spend next Sunday. As there is no one there but old Mrs. Delarne it wd not do for anyone to sleep there but me and Lily as she is too old to do anything—but even a day would be much after such an interval."[99]

All this is not to say, however, that at this period Mill broke with all his friends because of their incautious references to Harriet. The legend is so invariably repeated that it is time to examine the foundations on which it rests. The first example given is Harriet Martineau. Now that Harriet Martineau gossiped is undeniable: but there is no evidence that she was dismissed on that account. From Mill's letters to Robertson at the time of the *Review*, it is clear he already thought her a cantankerous and opinionated creature, the hard and narrow core of the sectarian radicalism he was trying to puncture. He never liked her: she was not his friend. And from the first she disapproved of Harriet for being frivolous. "Such women as Mrs. Opie and Mrs. John Taylor", she pronounced cathedrally, "ought to have been superior to the nonsense and vanity in which they participated."[100]

Harriet Grote was also a shrewd incorrigible gossip. When Bain first came to London, she had quarrelled with Mill: but there again, her remarks about "baiting hooks with carrion", and other objections to his conduct of the *Review*, were quite sufficient explanation. After

Grote left politics things soon mended, Mill being able to turn confidently to him for help in refloating Comte. Bain records that in the summer of 1845, whenever Grote came up from the country he hastened to arrange walks and talks with Mill, and that Mill's attitude was one of filial respect, while Grote expressed doubts about Mill's dangerous trifling with the Coleridgeans. In 1846 the first two volumes of Grote's history appeared, and were welcomed by Mill in the *Edinburgh*, a labour of love in every sense; and during that year he corresponded both with Grote and with his wife. In the summer Bain was asked to stay with them at Burnham Beeches on Mill's recommendation. Early in 1849 when subsequent volumes of the history came out, Mill wrote effusively, and put an advertisement in the *Spectator*. There is no sign of any breach during the later forties, and it is impossible to suppose that the timid Grote could have preserved such close relations with a friend who was barred by his vigorous wife. There are, however, indications of a temporary estrangement later on, and it appears that Mrs. Grote was neither quick enough nor warm enough in her felicitations to the happy pair on their eventual marriage.

Sarah Austin was another gossip. In November 1839 she wrote a more than usually affectionate letter beginning "dearest John", and begging him to visit her sick and gloomy husband, as he alone could cheer him up.[101] Shortly afterwards the Austins went abroad, and throughout the forties Mill had a constant exchange of friendly letters with them both. But in March 1848 they had a decided difference of opinion over the uprising in Paris. The Austins, who were living on the spot, were filled with horror at the spectacle of Red Revolution. Passports were suspended, and they had some fears as to whether they would ever get out alive. John Austin wrote a letter to the *Times* expressing sentiments of conservative foreboding.

To Mill, the revolution seemed not bloody rebellion but a necessary blow for freedom; and the measures of the Provisional Government, not craven compromise but wise and liberal statesmanship. On seeing John Austin's letter, he was quite incredulous, and wrote indignantly to Sarah. "Who can it be that takes Mr. Austin's name in the *Times* and attempts to imitate his style? . . . There were several things in it which it is very disagreeable that Mr. Austin should be supposed to have written, especially the flattery of the *Times*—the meanest, most malicious, and most hypocritical among our very low newspaper press."[102]

Sarah's answer disillusioned him. The truth was that since he had last seen them, both the Austins had become more scared and unprogressive than the Tories. Inevitably, when they were privileged with one of the special copies of the *Political Economy*, they did not like it, and alienated their old friends the authors.

From then on the breach widened. As soon as they reached England, the Austins busied themselves about the welfare of Guizot, who had arrived in exile penniless and dramatically disguised as a footman. Mill had also been a warm admirer of Guizot when he was ambassador in London in 1840, and he remained enthusiastic about his *History*. But the duplicity and petty tyranny of Louis Philippe's régime had undermined his respect for the man who had been throughout the guiding hand. Accordingly, the news that the Austins and a whole family of Guizots were all to settle at Weybridge was one of Harriet's reasons for wishing to give up her house at Walton. She did so only just in time, for in January 1849 Mill received a call from Austin:

> "He said he had after much difficulty and search taken a house at Weybridge, and that he liked the place, but he did not (I have no doubt purposely) say anything about wishing that I should visit him there or anywhere. . . . Nothing was said about her or about the copy of the Pol. Ec. but it is necessary to *prendre un parti*. What should it be?"[103]

Things went from bad to worse. In April 1849 Mill published a glowing defence of the Revolution and the Provisional Government in the *Westminster*, a scathing reply to an attack by Brougham. The Austins retorted by becoming close friends with Louis Napoleon, who had been serving with their son-in-law as a special constable during the Chartist riots. Whereupon Mill added a paragraph to the *Political Economy*, specially in order to call Louis Napoleon an "unprincipled adventurer". There was ample dissension between Mill and Sarah Austin without reference to Harriet.

It is true that Roebuck was specifically put away by Mill, but that was for frankly advising him to abandon his affair, not for spreading scandal. It had happened years before, at the very beginning of the romance, when all was still hot-blooded and excitable. It happened, also, on the morning after a public humiliation, and it may be that Roebuck, who was impetuous in speech, was not so tactful as he later thought he had been. The only other person who directly tackled Mill concerning Harriet was Bain. Receipt of an inscribed copy of the *Political Economy* gave him an excuse to question Mill about the fabulous creature. He says he was considered to have done a very rash thing, and that he did not feel disposed to reopen the subject very often. But to his surprise he was not frozen to silence or roundly accused of being impertinent. Mill seemed quite pleased that he had asked, and treated him to a vehement speech about the "apostle of progress".

It appears, then, that although Mill put off several people who had gossiped, until he finally married Harriet gossip was only a contributory cause. All had offended him in other ways. Remarkably, the one who escaped just punishment for his sins was the very one who shouted most about it, the arch gossip of them all, Carlyle. Like many other things to Mill's disadvantage, Carlyle's accusation of wintry unfriendliness formed part of the statement he deliberately made to Norton as soon as he heard that Mill was dead. "What! John Mill dead! Dear me, Dear me! John Mill! how did he die and where?" The old man was deeply shocked, and nostalgic memories welled into his mind so mournfully that their discreditable flavour was concealed. At last he came to the question of their parting:

> "Well, John Mill and I were very near friends for many years, and I know not what parted us, but I remember the last time we ever met. It was when your country woman, Margaret Fuller, was here. She brought me a letter from Emerson, to which I wanted to do honour, and I determined to ask some o' the people she would like to meet her at dinner, and John Mill among them. And I went one day to the India House to invite him, and before I got there I met him coming along the street, and he received me like the very incarnation o' the East Wind, and refused my invitation peremptorily. And from that day to this I've never set my eyes upon him, and no word has passed between us. Dear me! And many a night have I laid awake thinkin' what it might be that had come between us, and never could I think o' the least thing, for I'd never said nor harboured a thought about that man but of affection and kindliness. And many's the time I've thought o' writin' to him and sayin' 'John Mill, what is it that parts you and me?' But that's all over now. Never could I think o' the least thing unless maybe it was this. One year the brother o' that man Cavaignac who was ruler for a time in France,—Godefroi Cavaignac, a man o' more capacity than his brother,—was over here from Paris, an' he told me o' meeting Mill and Mrs. Taylor somewhere in France not long before, eatin' grapes together off o' one bunch, like two love-birds. And his description amused me, and I repeated it, without thinkin' any harm, to a man who was not always to be trusted [Charles Buller], a man who made trouble with his tongue, and I've thought that he might perhaps have told it to Mill, and that Mill might have fancied that I was making a

jest o' what was most sacred to him; but I don't know if that was it, but it was the only thing I could ever think of that could ha' hurt him."[104]

The year of Carlyle's dinner party for Margaret Fuller was 1846. The year Godefroy Cavaignac was in London and met Carlyle was 1835. The year that Mill knew him in Paris was 1833. It seems improbable that Mill would cut Carlyle for tattle he had made eleven years before about events which were thirteen years old. Nor was he likely to have picked on that, when Carlyle had been engaged ever since in spreading tales of far more infamous bearing, like his remark to Sterling about Harriet going into lodgings in 1839.

Their correspondence did not end in 1846, but continued at a leisurely pace until Mill's death: the manuscripts are now preserved in the National Library of Scotland. Mill sent him an inscribed copy of the *Political Economy* in 1848 and the *Liberty* in 1859. Nor was it the last time they ever met. In 1851 the Irish patriot Gavan Duffy wished to persuade Mill to stand for Parliament in the Irish cause, and called on Carlyle for an introduction. Duffy states that Carlyle then went with him to see Mill.[105] Carlyle's descriptions of his alleged ill-treatment are full of inconsistencies. It is not even certain that the encounter in the street took place at all, for he told another enquirer that he had invited Mill by letter, and the letter was never answered.[106] Also, in the same breath, that Mill was offended because he disliked the *Liberty*. But the *Liberty* was not published until thirteen years after the incident in question.

Wilson has tried to explain that "it is the pillow that sunders families as the Muslims say",[107] and that the philosophers were separated by a pique between their women. It is true that Jane, despite her first marked fancy, did not care for Harriet later on. She told Duffy, "When one was first told that the strong woman of the *Westminster Review* had gone off with a man whom we all knew, it was as startling an announcement as if one heard that a woman of your acquaintance had gone off with the strong man at Astley's; but that the partners in this adventure had set up as moralists was a graver surprise."[108] She added that Harriet was "a peculiarly affected body. She was not easy unless she startled you with unexpected sayings. . . 'come down and see us', she said one day (mimicking her tone), 'you will be charmed with our house, it is so full of rats.' 'Rats!' cried Carlyle, 'Do you regard *them* as an attraction?' 'Yes' (piano), 'they are such dear innocent creatures.' "[109] Harriet probably had equally little time for Jane, for when Jane made use of her invitation in April 1845, and went one afternoon to call, young Helen recorded in her diary "she appears to me to be somewhat of a humbug".[110]

Whatever the relations between the ladies, there is no doubt that Carlyle grew to hate Mill, and contrived a long, ingenious, eminently successful disparagement of his reputation. The real reason for their parting was, as he told Duffy, "that Mill and he had ceased to see much of each other in later times, as, in fact, they had nothing at all in common".[111] Mill had been trying to make him realize that for fourteen years, and now when he did realize it, it made him bitter. They had nothing in common at all. Their philosophies, if Carlyle can be said to have had a consistent philosophy, were as strongly contrasted as their temperaments. Besides, Mill no longer had the *Review*, or friends more consequential than his, while he for his own part no longer needed money or literary contacts. Above all, Mill had refused to be his disciple. Clearly, Mill had done him many wrongs. And so when Carlyle heard the rumour that Mill had been harsh and icy to his friends, he found it convenient to substantiate the charge by including himself among the martyrs. When he told Norton "I never knew a finer, tenderer, more sensitive or modest soul among the sons of men. There never was a more generous creature than he, nor a more modest",[112] that was not the general burden of his statement. His tears were crocodile. And the worthy scholar had scarcely snapped his vade-mecum shut, and left to catch the steamer back to Harvard, before Carlyle sat down and wrote his real feelings:

> "Goose N. came down to me today—very dirty—very enthusiastic—very stupid and confused, with a daily newspaper 'containing two articles ineffably sublime and heart-interesting upon Mill'. Two more blusterous bags of empty wind I have seldom read. 'Immortal fame!' 'First spirit of his age!' 'Thinker of thinkers!' What a piece of work is man with a penny-a-liner pen in his hand." *

* This jotting, quoted by the much abused Froude in *Carlyle's Life in London*, has been studiously ignored by Alexander Carlyle, Wilson, and other members of the personal bodyguard: presumably, under their own convention that much of what Carlyle wrote about people on the spur of the moment did not do justice to the great man's generosity, and must therefore be suppressed. See Wilson's own account, in his preface, of how he burned one or two Carlyle manuscripts, in the possession of Carlyle's youngest sister, in Canada in 1895.

"Goose N." is provisionally identified as Norton by a previous reference, viz.: "I made Miss Bromley take me up to Norton's (poor N. has had an attack of pneumonia)." (Carlyle to Dr. Carlyle, 22 March 1873, quoted in *New Letters of Thomas Carlyle*, ed. Alexander Carlyle, 1904.) Certainly, Norton called on Carlyle on 9 May 1873, and first told him of Mill's death.

That, of course, had not yet been written when in 1864 Moncure D. Conway, another peripatetic American, noticed sharply that "Mill always seemed to me to grow suddenly aged when Carlyle was spoken of". If it had been, he would have been less shocked by Mill's painfully murmured charge: "Carlyle turned against all his friends."[113]

X

All revolved round Harriet, and Harriet was very spoilt. Two men were devoted to her; both were distinguished, and one was rich. She managed the household of the one and the philosophy of the other. Both were perfectly content that the extraordinary equipoise should last indefinitely. Mill, congratulating d'Eichthal on his marriage in 1841, wrote: "That certainly will not happen in my case, for marriage in this country, nine times out of ten, changes a superior man into quite the opposite, without making him happy."[114] He was well indoctrinated.

She had her country villa and her London mansion. She had every freedom to indulge her restless passion for travelling; and while John Taylor paid her bills, one or other of the men was ready to be her escort whenever necessary. Helen was her constant handmaiden both at home and abroad.

Those whom she permitted to be intimate friends were always and for ever ecstatic. In April 1847 Sarah Flower Adams wrote to her, when clearing up the personal belongings after the death of her sister Lizzie:

> "In the blank leaf of one of her books, is this pencilled memorandum in her handwriting: 'The Divine Government to Mrs. Taylor; and the diamond ring she gave me, for Helen.'
>
> The ring will be sent to you in a day or two—The book as soon as I return to town—which will be when the warmer weather comes—I have been ill since seeing you, with a cough—it is gone since coming here.

> I have always let the hair take its own form. This tress to you, is the first that has laid itself round like a willing living thing, in its accustomed curl. It is the love of the Beautiful lingering in it yet—
>
> For me—why should I not say what I feel—The recollection of you brings tears in my eyes often, tears of tender reverence for what was and is and ever will be one of the *choicest* remembrances of my life."[115]

"I had Mrs. Adams on Tuesday", wrote Harriet to her husband pettishly, in her own version of Sarah's visit during March.

> "She looks *most* wretchedly—but this seems chiefly because she gives herself up to passionate fits of crying—ten minutes, five minutes, after she will laugh quite merrily. She is no way altered in character during the eight or ten years I have lost sight of her—she is even more what she calls 'impulsive'—what I call horribly sentimental. It is a way of taking life most disagreeable and 'antipathique' to me. Her account of all that old set is mad and disagreeable—as far as you can call it *an account*, which consists of scattered words and expressions very hard to form any intelligible notion of facts from. . . .
>
> One cannot get on with such people. She describes that Mr. Adams '*was ruined*' (her favourite expression) in Dec*r*. but that now they are very grand. She is a great boaster, and very curious, and a bit of a gossip. But she means well."[116]

Within a few months Sarah too was dead.

Wilson makes out that Harriet "played the invalid and neglected her duties".[117] That is quite untrue, and completely foreign to her masterful character. The children adored her. On the first day of 1847 Helen wrote, "Yesterday we sat up until twelve and heard the clock strike. A Happy happy happy happy New Year I wished dearest one, and wish her always every day."[118] Harriet was proud of her children, and yet quite detached. She wrote affectionately about them to her husband:

"Thanks for your long amusing letter. I had a letter from each of the 'gars' this morning. . . . Lilkin has been writing to you, but she likes scrambling over the commons and the rocks much better than sitting down to anything. . . . She is so well and rosy it is delightful to see."[119] Her correction of them was firm, and remorselessly liberal. "I cannot love you if you are not good", was all she ever said to Helen.[120] "I am much concerned to hear that Haji has not lost the cough", she instructed Taylor. "He systematically refuses to pay any attention to my advice on that subject or on any other. . . . He needs to be told most decidedly that in his case a long continued cough will prove mortal—of this I feel sure—and *if* having been told this by you as well as by me, he still persists in neglecting to use the means pointed out to him of curing it—I can only feel that I have done my utmost for him and that he has a 'right' to do as he pleases with himself."[121]

From 1838 to 1845 the two boys boarded at Mr. Underwood's school in Manchester Square, where they learnt languages by starting to read without any attempt at grammar—the same system by which Mill had learned. Mill himself took private lessons in German from Underwood. He also lent the boys books suitable for their growing minds from his library at Kensington—Reid, Brown, Locke, Hume, Hobbes, James Mill, and Berkeley.[122] They kept up their friendship with Mill's younger brother George, and were welcomed by the family at Kensington. George visited them in return both at Kent Terrace and at Walton. He was the best source of information about Harriet for the cautious but inquisitive Bain.

On the whole, Harriet got on least well with Herbert. She certainly saw least of him. In 1845, when he was seventeen, he joined his father in the business, and that kept him mostly at Kent Terrace. In April 1846 he went to America and returned a year later, Harriet anxiously enquiring of her husband whether he should not come home by the steamer. "That is as safe as anything can be, while about sailing there is always some risk. What do you think?"[123] Herbert's independent journeyings in the New World seem to have turned his head a little, and he preferred the company of his worldly father, taking his side in any dispute that might arise. Early in 1849 he planned another trip, and did not even write to tell his mother he was going, an omission which caused Mill to agree with her that he was "a very great fool (at present)".[124]

Algernon, or Haji as he was always known, missed most of the excursions to the Continent. But his mother saw plenty of him in the holidays and took him for jaunts to the seaside. In February 1849 when he became nineteen, Mill was asked to speak about him to the Chairman of the East India Company. He promised to do so, but nothing apparently came of it. Haji, though intelligent, lacked fibre, and was generally a disappointment to his family.

Helen was kept always at her mother's side. She seems to have received little in the way of formal education, and was left much to herself to go sightseeing during their tours abroad and to pick up what she could: this she was well able to do, but she would willingly have given up the continual wanderings for the studious serenity of Walton. Her reading was wide and voracious. During 1846, when she was fifteen, it included works by Shakespeare, Carlyle, Coleridge, Emerson, Bulwer, de Stael, Schiller, Lady Blessington, Jeremy Taylor, Jane Austen, Maria Edgeworth, and Schelling. The books, apart from a few provided by her mother, she ordered to Walton from the London Library which had opened in 1840. She commented fully and decisively on all of them in her diary. Her favourite was *Macbeth*: Lady Blessington she described as "trash". From an early age she had a fiery concern for feminine rights. She was a quick, high-spirited and imaginative little girl, with more than a touch of poetry in her. "I went on Thursday to town and saw Papa and Haji", she wrote. "I had to wait some time at the Coach office in the Regent's Circus and was amused by people coming in wishing to go or send things to every part of the world. It is the office for Waghons express to India and apparently for every important affair connected with travelling."[125] At Rome, at Brussels, and Rouen, she was in and out of cathedrals all the time. As a child, her favourite game was playing at Mass with Haji. As she grew older she acquired a vivid interest in the stage, learning by heart the roles of Portia and Lady Macbeth.

Harriet was determined that her children should not suffer the same lack of emotional development as Mill had done. She took them to the theatre and the opera. She encouraged their religious fervour, and carefully instilled a love of music. Herbert sang for several months in the choir of St. George's Cathedral, Southwark. Haji and Helen went to churches of all denominations, but preferred the Catholic because of the greater blaze of ceremonial beauty. They often went to Westminster Abbey and thought it the finest of Anglican cathedrals, but Helen regretted that it had so few stained glass windows. "Protestantism does not suit churches", she remarked. "To make it effective, to make one feel it, their services should be celebrated in a sunny forest, or on a mountain, then its simplicity would be fine."[126] Harriet, herself a great lover of sacred music, occasionally went with them, and when they got home, played beautifully on the piano. Once, as they were coming out of the Church of Our Lady in St. John's Wood after the celebration of High Mass, she said, "It was like taking Heaven by Storm."[127] Sometimes, Mill went too.

In 1846, Harriet was very gay. In the summer, accompanied in all probability by Mill, who again admitted to having been "out of London and even out of England"[128] at about this time, she took a two months' holiday down the Rhine, travelling in part once more by steamboat, to the disgust of Helen who found the incessant eating of the Germans just as tiresome as the talking of the French had been two years before. Back at Walton in July, Harriet received a visit from her handsome brother Alfred, just returned from Adelaide. A week later she was in the Isle of Wight. At Sandown, haunted ever for Mill by her love of its beauty, she and Helen shared a single machine and joyously bathed. Wherefore it became a place of hallowed memory for Helen too. In the spring of 1847 Harriet had some of her relatives to stay. In the summer, Mill was expecting another holiday in Paris, but whether or not they went is not quite clear. In the autumn, she paid a return visit to Birksgate, although to everybody's disappointment John Taylor was detained in London by the crisis in the City.

Her husband, Mill, her children, and her friends—Harriet had little trouble with them. It was her own family, her parents, her brothers and sister that caused the difficulty. Early in 1848, due no doubt to her winter's labours with the *Political Economy*, her health deteriorated: besides a return of her paralysis and rheumatic pains, she suffered from what she called "faceache". For that condition, which was probably a form of chronic toothache and at the root of all her trouble, she took laudanum, which, she complained, gave her colds. Altogether she was in no state to face the annual visit of her mother and her sister Caroline, who brought her own family with her. So she left her husband to take the main part of the burden:

> "I suppose the Birksgates will come for their usual long stay. I fully enter into your feeling on the occasion. Had I better come to town when they do, do you think? I only wish to do what will make the infliction least to you. What do you think of my coming to K.T. for a week or ten days (God knows I do not think I can stand it longer) and then going to Brighton when you could come down on a Sunday or two, it being your month of freedom, and I might invite them once? I really can think of nothing else except running away altogether, and that is not fair to you."[129]

With the *Political Economy* safely published, she spent the summer of 1848 in an energetic but unsuccessful search for a new house. In addition to the impending menace of the Austins and the Guizots, the nice little house at Walton had been spoiled since all the trees had been cut down and a nest of "poor people's poor little places" erected opposite. Her health was still bad, and once she felt most unwell in the train. "Lily got out and got a captain biscuit and a sandwich, part of which set me to right, and at the Pier Hotel they gave us some very good oxtail soup which was a great comfort."[130] Her cures were always most improbable.

In November she settled at Worthing, where she was joined by Mill, who wrote his essay on the revolution of 1848 there under her guidance. He too was in a very bad state. During the summer, while entering Hyde Park, he fell over a loose brick by a pump at the Kensington Grove Gate and injured his hip. His doctor applied a belladonna plaster, and, although Mill very soon ripped it off, his eyes were affected by it, and he became temporarily blind as well as lame. Harriet went from bad to worse: she took Tinch of Bark for her indigestion, and iodine for her legs, the latter in the form of pills combined with mercury. They definitely improved her legs, but, being too concentrated, produced horrific symptoms of their own, "much pain at the back of the head, palpitations, and general excitement, besides loosening the teeth . . ."[131]

At Worthing, Helen had a derangement of the stomach; and then on top of all, the usually sturdy John Taylor developed obstinate internal pains, and when prescribed a diet refused to stick to it. "He is very particular in eating stale bread and taking little wine etc. at home", Herbert reported, "but he cannot always resist temptations at the Club which I think do not do him much good."[132] Harriet tried to coax him back, and firmly overruled his quibbling: "I do not fancy *ale*, even tho' the pale bottled kind, would suit you for long. I suppose when you take it you take no wine—the mixture of beer and wine is always so unwholesome."[133] Her excellent advice was disregarded. Her brother Arthur turned up from Australia, and her husband, throwing caution to the winds, wrote with gusto, "Herbert sends his love—we are to dine at the Club today and to have a *crack* dinner at Arthur's expense. . . . I fear it is not very prudent on my part to go."[134]

Harriet began to think of the south of France: there were too many invalids about, she felt, for her to deal with all at once in her weak state. She was quite unable to face further visits from her family in the spring. Besides, the English winter was drawing on. She sounded Herbert, who said that it was a good idea, and that he thought his father could be induced to accompany her, at any rate part of the way. She wrote suggesting it, but Taylor's answer was discouraging: he recalled their experiences of bitter cold at Boulogne in 1838, and said it would be folly for her to go in her condition. He added that he was not up to it himself, and could not in any case leave his business. If she insisted upon going, she must take Haji or Herbert instead.

Then her father fell ill as well, at Birksgate: it was rumoured that he might be dying. Arthur, who was staying with her, had to go and see about the Will, and there was some prospect that she ought to follow him. That settled it. She would leave immediately after Christmas. She asked her husband to get her £100 in traveller's cheques, from Coutts'. He still demurred. Apart from the danger to herself, how could she leave when her father was so ill? And would it not look strange, after pleading her inability to travel as a reason for not going to Yorkshire, if she immediately dashed away to Pau?

She simply had to get away. She was driven to desperate tones:

> "I am very sorry to find you say *you are sorry* I am going to Pau. I can assure you I do not do it for my pleasure, but exceedingly to the contrary, and only after the most *anxious thought*—indeed I am half killed by *intense anxiety*. The near relationship to persons of the most opposite principles to my own produces excessive embarrassments, and this spring it must be *far* worse than usual owing to the constant presence in London of A[rthur], whom I must either neglect (which is very disagreeable to me) or admit into a degree of intimacy which must inevitably lead to an interference on the part of Birksgate. . . . I therefore think that my going away for the next four months would *cut* the difficulties I feel about this spring, while I should return at a season (May) and in health to exert myself during the summer months. . . . I think . . . you will see how completely my going is a matter of expediency. . . . It is always so undesirable to make family quarrels if it is possible to avoid them. . . . Your saying that you are sorry I am going has given me ever since I read your note so *intense* a headache, that I can scarcely see to write. However it is only one of the vexations I have to bear and perhaps everybody has—just as I got so far, a letter from A has come in, which I think exonerates me from staying in England on my father's account",

she ended up triumphantly.[135]

The family spent Christmas of 1848 together at Kent Terrace, and on Boxing Day Harriet and Helen set off. As Paris was still in a state of smouldering insurrection it was necessary, despite her protestations, that someone should go with them; and so Mill hobbled and groped his way along beside them. Fortunately the sea was calm, and Paris quiet. After a tiring three hours in the station waiting-room, they managed to get a carriage empty except for an elderly priest, so Harriet was able to put her feet up on the seat. They had an easy journey down. Mill felt sad as he returned alone to England.

He got back in a shocking state. His mother wrote to George and Clara in Madeira, anxiously describing how, as he was not to use his eyes, she was going to arrange for a man to take down his dictation so that he could get on with the new edition of the *Political Economy*. He was terribly restless. "We played at cards till 12 o'clock last night and between while he played upon the Piano without music some of his own compositions."[136] He could not walk as usual to and from the India House, and he had to approach his office by a labyrinth of corridors in order to avoid climbing the long staircase. Bain tried to help by introducing him to a specialist, who wanted him to take the new water-treatment. But Mill was too impatient. "His view of the medical art", complained his follower, "was that it should restore a shattered frame by something like magic."[137]

Somehow or other he got through the *Political Economy* and carried on his normal work. He also managed to write at length to Harriet. Luckily, it was an exceptionally mild winter. At Walton, where he paid periodical visits of inspection, many of the spring flowers were out by the third week in February, and daffodils were in bud. As he began to mend, his one interest was how to get special leave from the India House in order to fetch Harriet from Pau, and he wrote discussing longingly every detail of their circuitous journey home. He drove himself unmercifully, and by the middle of March was able to take the train to Watford, and walk the twenty miles back to town via Harrow without any subsequent ill effects, which he considered a very satisfactory test.

Harriet meanwhile, as she had predicted, felt better as soon as she reached the sunny territory of the Basques. She and Helen got very pleasant lodgings with a magnificient view of the distant Pyrenees. They were in the most fashionable situation, overlooking the *Place Royale*, where the band played on Sundays and everybody promenaded up and down, and where sometimes in the evening there was a great display of fireworks. She felt sorry for the English people wintering there, for they looked bored: they destroyed the native gaiety by stalking puritanically with their prayer books in their hands. It was as warm as summer in England, and so still that a candle would burn all night in the middle of the *Place* as steadily as in a room. They got good dinners in their rooms for two francs each: their *Patron*, in convulsions of politeness, expressed horror at their paying a franc a bottle for wine, obtained outside, and asked to be permitted to supply them with a better vintage at only fifteen sous. The only drawback was that at Pau, unlike all other French towns Harriet had ever been in, there was no proper bookshop: and owing to the inefficiency of the postal service, she did not at once receive the *Times* which John Taylor was sending regularly. "But it would be quite useless and impossible to complain; the very suggestion of complaining about anything done by *l'Autorité* makes the French look aghast at one's boldness. . . . They certainly need revolutions for they have no political freedom of any kind apparently, and they do not know what freedom is for they have never tried it."[138]

The mail arrived at last, bringing with it news that her husband's health was not much better. She immediately resumed her attack against his artful dodges. Port was his trouble. "You must remember that the number of *glasses* he allows", she warned, "means of the *ordinary* size." She advised him to try French wine instead. "I find the change to it from the stronger Spanish wines has so *alternative* an effect. . . . I think the ordinaire quite as wholesome or more so than the higher priced kinds . . . it is to be got, as you know, very good at Hedges and Butler's. All French wines contain an astringent quality, which acts more on the stomach than the bowels." That done, she turned to other matters. She was adept at managing a household from a distance. Taylor was to give the landlord at Walton notice that they would be leaving in September. The Californian Gold Rush offered fine opportunites of placing drugs in the *placiemento*: was he going to send out quinine? She reassured him he was right about the servants: "I knew Cook took spirits occasionally as they almost all do—but . . . I thought it only in a permissible quantity. Now that she is aware that she is observed, I hope she will not exceed."[139]

At the end of March she had most disquieting news, and at a very inconvenient time. She had to make her choice between her men, and she did not hesitate.

Harriet to John Taylor, Pau, 30 March 1849:

"I have just received your letter of the 26th and am more concerned than I can express to hear so poor an account of your progress. . . . I entirely agree in the wisdom of going to Brighton for change of air. . . . If I only consulted my own inclination I should come back to England immediately on the receipt of your letter in hopes of being able to be of use to you.—The reason I cannot do this is that I have arranged with Mr. Mill to meet me on the 20th of April when he is to have three weeks holiday on account of his health which has been the whole winter in a very precarious state, . . . and both Clark and Alexander the oculist say that a complete change and cessation from all work is absolutely necessary to save his sight. . . . I shall therefore return with him as far as Paris and I shall get back the earliest that I possibly can in hopes of being of use to you. . . . I feel it a duty to do all in my power for his health . . ."[140]

She left for Bagnères in the Pyrenees on 17 April, and Mill joined her there. But as the rain was incessant, and there was snow as well, they soon left for Toulouse; whence they made a leisurely return to Paris, waiting to get inside places in the diligence. They lingered several days in Paris before going on, as usual, separately to England.

Harriet reached Kent Terrace late at night on 14 May, and sustained a staggering shock. John Taylor's pains were caused by cancer, not by port. They told her he was dying.

She was frantic. Her father had died at Birksgate on 3 May, but she scarcely noticed it in her anxiety for her husband. As the disease advanced steadily to its inevitable end, she flung herself into nursing him with impetuous abandon, and for more than two months she and Helen were continually at his bedside. She felt so impotent.

"The being in the midst of such a solemn and terrible fact surrounded entirely by people destitute of all ideas . . . makes me feel like a caged lion sometimes when I feel that I cannot do more for him—They are all however perfectly kind and considerate only they take it as a matter of course that what the doctors say is and must be all and *look so coolly to the result.*"[141]

Fortunately her health withstood the strain much better than could have been expected, and Mill was always close at hand. Having no proper status, he hung around her rather helplessly, but was ready with whatever comfort he could give. Sometimes she permitted him to do some little service:

"Will you send any Mags. or Revs. you have, for him—if you have any that is.
He has got, for July, the New Monthly and the Quarterly.
Especially I want the Edinburgh *at the earliest* possible.
Don't call again."[142]

Sometimes she was able to confide in him, and so relieve her feelings:

28 *May* 1849 "He is most patient and firm and endures with the utmost strength and courage—but *why* should he have these torments to endure! What good to anybody is all this—he never hurt or harmed a creature on earth. If they want the life why can't they take it—what useless torture is all this! and he is so sorry and hurt to give so much

labour to me—he feels that I am the greatest good to him and feeling that no servant could do what I do for him enables me to keep up. He said 2 days since 'well if I *do* recover it will be entirely owing to you!' How cruel to feel that his chance is so slight—alas I feel as if he besides you is the only life I value in this wretched world. He is so thoroughly true direct honest strong and with all the realities of *nice* feelings, as I constantly see now."[143]

Early June "You talk of my writing to you 'at some odd time when a change of subject of thought may be rather a relief than otherwise'! *Odd time*! indeed you must be ignorant profoundly of all that *friendship* or *anxiety* means when you can use such pitiful narrow-hearted expressions. The sentence appears to have come from one of the Miss Taylors. It is the puerility of thought and feeling of any utterly headless and heartless pattern of propriety old maid. . . . Good God shd you think it a relief to think of somebody else some acquaintance or what not while *I* was dying? If so—but I will say no more about this— . . . my heart is wrung with indignation and grief."[144]

9 *July* "You have no notion what a mistake you make in saying it could be no more contagious than a fractured skull. Anyone who saw and watched this and thought so must already have got a fractured skull. I have very little doubt that it is as often contagious as Typhus or plague. It seems very like the latter—probably all are contagious . . ."[145]

All this Mill bore with love and understanding. He even managed to divert her interest, despite herself, to other things. John Sterling's brother, Captain Anthony Sterling, had written for permission to print certain passages referring to Mill in Sterling's letters to Carlyle.* Although Harriet had already given decided views against it, Mill now deliberately brought the matter up again on the ground that having given a half promise he found difficulty in refusing. As he must have expected, he drew out upon himself her whole pent-up excitability:

"I know that you place great vanity in not being vain but with me a love of truth as well as vanity would make repugnant to me the myself giving the world an appreciation of me made by an evident inferior who makes it with all the air of judging from a height which is conceivable. A second thing which hurts me intensely tho' it does not surprise me is your perfect madness to put your own hand and seal to the mention of your name and character soi-disant appreciatingly by a man who you perceive was weak and foolish enough to be in agreement with his correspondent in judging your relation with some unknown woman in unknown circumstances. Of course the old bugbear words 'married

* MT Coll. 49/21 is a document in Mill's handwriting, marked "Extracts from letters of Sterling to Carlyle respecting me". The extracts are for the most part extremely flattering, and contain no mention of any gossip about Harriet.

woman' were at the bottom of this unanimity of fear and sorrow which these men honoured (or disgraced selon moi) you with. Nowadays I would have thought that with our opinion we must thoroughly despise men who have not got out of that baby morality and intellect. That you cd. be willing to have these things printed hurts me more deeply than anything else I think could do. It has disturbed my mind and feelings even amidst these trying days and nights. But if you have engaged yourself about them some of them must stand."[146]

It led her on to scorn almost every man whom Mill had ever liked: "Tocqueville is a notable specimen of the class which includes such people as the Sterlings Romillys Carlyles Austins—the gentility class—weak in moral, narrow in intellect, timid, infinitely conceited, and gossiping. There are very few men in this country who can seem other than more or less respectable puppets to us."[147] It put an end to all hopes of poor Captain Anthony Sterling publishing his book. But Mill had distracted her mind in the only possible way, and with that he was quite satisfied.

John Taylor died on 18 July 1849. Harriet scribbled a note to her sister-in-law Eliza Taylor who had been considerate and kind throughout:

"To the last he had the same affectionate manner and cheerful tone of voice and what I had so much feared—pain at the end—he was altogether without. He spoke half an hour before the last moment in his usual gentle affectionate way and at the last there was not the slightest suffering of any kind. He was sleeping when for half an hour I perceived that the breathing was rather quicker than usual . . ."[148]

She was utterly exhausted, but she could not yet give way. "Feeling has to remain in abeyance", she told Mill, "while the many absolutely necessary mechanical details are ordered and attended to by me who never saw anything of the kind before and having no person *whatever* but the three children to advise with—it is the most trying time.*

"I do not know *where* he should be laid—having no connection with any place—I have thought of either Kensal Green or Hampstead as not too far? Tell me what you think! Write to me enclosed to Herbert at Cross Street."[149]

She relied upon him much in the emergency. She had decided on Kensal Green. Did he know if there were any choice of site? Was it true she had to find her own clergyman? And if so, did he know of one

* Herbert reached Liverpool from New York on 4 June.

who would be suitable? Herbert had insisted on putting a notice in the papers to stop the flood of enquiries which he had to answer. She thought it was too soon. "Tell me if it *struck* you as indecent haste?"

At last she reached the delicate and all-important question whether Mill should or should not attend the funeral. She could not make up her mind. Her first reaction was to say *of course*. But then, she wanted all to be exactly as her husband would have wished, and as in his case that was more or less synonymous with what the world approved, it was necessary to have an eye to etiquette. In that regard she had a "feeling of 'better not', grounded on the sort of distance which of late existed".

But then again, would not Mill's absence be taken for a lack of respect? Everyone had either heard or was sure to hear "(through Arthur if no other way), of the Dedication—of our intimacy—and on the side of his relations, nor that I know of on mine, there does not appear to be any médisance. (Indeed the kindness and attention to me of all his relations is as marked as the neglect of these by mine.) . . . Does not therefore absence seem much more noticeable than coming? On the other hand nothing is more true of common world than 'out of sight out of mind'. . . ."[150]

It was all very difficult. Herbert on the whole inclined against Mill going, but then Herbert like his father had "a sort of ostrich instinct, like morally timid people, always *not to do*—while my instinct is always to *do*".

What did Mill think?

His reply is not to hand, but it seems probable that Mill did not attend the funeral.

BOOK SIX

THE HOPED-FOR HEAVEN

1849–1858
aet. 43–52

JOHN STUART MILL

from the portrait by G. F. Watts, in 1873, in the National Portrait Gallery.

I

THE death of her husband was no help to Harriet's difficulties. Perhaps it might have been if she had loved him more, or even if she had loved him less; for certainly she had loved him, in some complicated manner of her own. It never occurred to her that she had used him badly. Her power of rationalization was so immense, everything she did appeared to her so necessary and correct, that she never wondered whether he was satisfied. And any qualm she may have felt was banished during her final weeks of ferocious guardianship. He was a fixed familiar feature in her daily life, an acquiescent factor constantly available for deployment in her scheme for family arrangements. Her feeling for him was the feeling of the primitive female for everything pertaining to her home. She was not therefore capable of the cynical shrug which would have dismissed his memory with his body, enabling her to turn at once to her other more close attachment. Nor, since she had refused his bed and scorned his comradeship, could she feel at his death that the completeness of their understanding entitled her to grasp her freedom joyfully. In consequence his ghost remained within her.

It was John Taylor who had kept the balance steady. For nearly twenty years he had ignored humiliation. While watching with indulgent admiration his wife's mercurial efforts to persuade herself that she was loyal to him, he had held himself ready to be convinced by her, and had acceded to the many unexpected projects she found necessary for the purpose. For Mill, it is probable he had no special fondness, and that his stiffness was reciprocated. But if he thought his rival something of a humbug, or if Mill looked on him as a barbarian, both men, out of regard for the delicacy of Harriet's feelings kept these natural prejudices well in check, and treated each other with rigid although distant courtesy. Except when he was asked to subscribe, as in the matter of the dedication of the *Political Economy*, to antics passing beyond all bounds of worldly decorum, John Taylor made no protest. And so long as he himself could see no reason for complaint, nobody else had any right to do so.

Now that he was gone, however, it was quite another matter. Harriet and Mill had lost the barrier protecting them from the criticisms of the world. What were they to do? It was certain that, at all costs, they must live together. Should they then get married? They shared a sharp distrust and disapproval of that institution in theory and in practice, and both at various times had given public utterance to their feelings. But they had seen enough of the hounded atmosphere presiding in the illicit establishment of Eliza Flower and Fox to know that the alternative meant unnecessary misery. The more so since in the intervening years the Victorian fashion of conjugal propriety had begun to spread its stifling shroud over the whole field of personal morality. Harriet was no George Sand: her contempt for the conventions was confined to intellectual rebellion, and the circumstances of her actual life were ruled by a violent concern for the decency of appearances. Nor could Mill afford to take the risk. There were many among the clerical and conservative schools of thinking who, alarmed at the social heresies he propounded, and smarting at their inability to refute him in debate, would willingly have ruined him if he had provided them with so sensational an opportunity.

Marriage seemed to be the only way. Even that course was attended to a disagreeable extent by embarrassment and awkwardness. During the long years of their intimate relationship, they had been able to take refuge in the principle that the friendship of two adult individuals was an affair concerning no one but themselves, since it involved no answerable consequences to any other party. They had thus been able to protect their privacy by imposing upon their friends and families a chilly and unnatural silence, in the pretence that a subject of absorbing if affectionate interest was so ordinary as to be not worth mentioning.

The principle would be overset by marriage. However quiet and secular the ceremony; however severe the exclusion of all festivity, of all well-wishing, the plain fact of registration implied a request to society to take formal notice of a personal connection; implied, in return for legal recognition, a public declaration of a definite responsibility, the one towards the other and together towards the world. As husband and wife, everyone, even the most vulgar, would be free to indulge his fancy on them. Comparisons would be drawn between their present and their past demeanour: old discussion would be revived, speculations of the most offensive nature would be bandied, the pure flower of their devotion trampled underfoot. Whichever way they turned, it seemed, the hideous shape of ridicule lay crouched to pounce upon them.

This situation they debated long and anxiously. They examined it inside and out, from back and front, searching for the best, or at any rate the least objectionable solution. To make things worse, when John Taylor's will was read, they found that he had loyally left her in unconditional enjoyment of his fortune, thereby opening a further possible line of calumny against Mill should be marry her. A long delay was deemed essential, and in the meantime they must continue as before, only with even greater caution.

The next two years for Mill were stagnant and disconsolate. His desire, it is true, was on the spiritual plane, but his suffering was not for that reason any less severe. His loneliness was just as void, his longing just as sharp as that of more lusty amorists, nor did he have the occasional assuagement they usually enjoyed. In addition, his health, though mending slowly, was not by any means robust, and his whole nervous temperament remained in a low debilitated state. Outwardly, he maintained mechanical normality, carrying on his routine at the India House, and pursuing with furious energy his botanical rarities across the length and breadth of the Home Counties. His inward feeling of unending restlessness is expressed in a personal scrap which somehow escaped the strict censorship imposed by Harriet and himself upon their relation at this time:

> "The days seem always short to me as they pass. The time that seems long, the time that I am often impatient of the length of, is the time till spring—the time till we have a home, till we are together in our life instead of this unsatisfactory this depressing coming and going, in which all disagreeables have so much more power than belongs to them, and the atmosphere of happiness has not time to penetrate and pervade in the way I know so well even by the most imperfect experience and which then it will always . . ."[1]

For his own real work he had no heart. With Bain's assistance he made some serious revisions for the third edition of his *Logic*, in order to rebuff the ponderous forays of Dr. Whewell. He also wrote the most forceful dissertation of his life against Carlyle, who had outraged every liberal feeling dear to him in an article, "The Nigger Question", of which the disastrous consequences were to mature after fifteen years, despite Mill's immediate attempt to neutralize them.* But apart from these unwelcomed and obligatory duties, he produced, and apparently engendered, nothing of significance during this period. The day's march of his intellect was halted; and for the first time since his early mental revolution, the royal progress of his principles ran slow and turbid.

He became acutely conscious of his own shortcomings. More and more strongly it appeared to him that his capacity was exhausted, and, compared with the obvious genius of Harriet, inadequate even to outline the diaphanous ideals they were determined to render solid on the earth. He now believed, as he repeated constantly in different ways, "I am but fit to be one wheel in an engine not to be the self moving engine itself—a real majestic intellect, not to say moral nature, like yours, I can only look up to and admire."[2] Henceforward he conceived it as his task, not to release fresh forces in himself by feeding upon her inspiration, nor yet to be the spokesman of a full and fruitful partnership, but to carve out and polish the faultless jewels latent in the rich mine of her personality.

The first result of his new attitude was a range of newspaper articles and letters about specific injustices inflicted by society upon its weaker members. "Corporal Punishment"; "The case of atrocity near Bideford"; "The Law of Assault"; "Punishment of Children"; "Wife Murder"—all these topics, physical brutalities in daily life, were far removed from Mill's usual animadversions on political or economic theory. In his manuscript record of his printed works he scrupulously marked them down as "very little mine", until eventually after marriage he described them as "a joint production with my wife, like all my newspaper articles on similar subjects, and most of my articles on all subjects".[3] In tone they were aggressive, and the argument was biting rather than philosophic. When, for example, to satisfy a public clamour resulting from a sudden incidence of husband-poisoning—a crime inspiring an especial dread in the male imagination—the Liberal Government introduced a bill restricting the sale

* See page 464 below.

of arsenic in small quantities to men, the Home Secretary received a violent protest signed by Mill against "the gross insult to every woman in the country". "Does the criminal calendar, or the proceedings of the police, show a preponderance of women among the most atrocious criminals? Everybody knows that the direct contrary is the truth, and that men out-number women in the records of crime in the ratio of four to one. On what supposition are men to be trusted with poisons and women not, unless that of their peculiar wickedness? . . . If the last two or three murderers had been men with red hair, as well might Parliament have rushed to pass an Act restricting all red-haired men from buying or possessing deadly weapons."[4]

Soon a more ambitious project came in view. For some time Mill had been most anxious to get Harriet's essay on the disabilities of women into print. "I do not think that anything that could be written would do nearly so much good on that subject, the most important of all, as the finishing of your pamphlet,—or little book rather, for it should be that", he had told her in February 1849. "I do hope you are going on with it—gone on with and finished and published it *must be*, and next season too."[5] During her period of mourning, naturally, it had been put aside, but in October 1850 the meeting of a Women's Rights Convention at Worcester, Massachusetts, gave Mill an opportunity to coax her back to work. By the following spring he was able to offer it as an article to W. E. Hickson, to whom he had sold the *Westminster Review* ten years before, and it appeared in the issue for July 1851.

Contributions were still not publicly attributed to their authors, and since Mill had deliberately given the editor the impression he had written it himself, either to ensure its publication or else for fear that Harriet should be dubbed a bluestocking, it was generally taken to be his. Both of them were well aware that it was not a very striking paper. They refused permission to reprint it to John Chapman, after he took over the *Westminster Review* with George Eliot as his assistant, lest it "should be supposed to be the best we could do, or the real expression of our mind on the subject".[6] And the brash Holyoake was soundly reprimanded for selling it in thousands to the working classes, badly printed and without leave asked. But it was remarkable in the breath of its claim for equal rights in property, in occupation, and especially in family status, at a time when women were only just making the first tentative petitions for a vote. It was intended as the groundwork of a fuller treatise they designed to write together, which Mill ultimately had to undertake alone. It was Harriet's only publication after her youthful contributions to the *Monthly Repository*, her authorship not being avowed until her death, when Mill included it in his *Dissertations and Discussions.*

In these pursuits they occupied themselves as best they could, until at last in the spring of 1851 the time arrived when they could take their next eagerly awaited steps. Mill was careful to protect them both against a charge of inconsistency, and any possible rumour that he was marrying Harriet in order to get control of John Taylor's money. On 6 March he wrote out a formal protest against the existing law of marriage in respect of the powers it conferred upon the husband:

> ". . . I, having no means of legally divesting myself of these odious powers (as I most assuredly would do if an engagement to that effect could be made legally binding on me) . . . declare it to be my will and intention, and the condition of the engagement between us, that she retains in all respects whatever the same absolute freedom of action, and freedom of disposal of herself and of all that does or may at any time belong to her, as if no such marriage had taken place; and I absolutely disclaim and repudiate all pretension to have acquired any *rights* whatever by virtue of such marriage."[7]

The next thing was to break the news to their respective families. This delicate mission, Harriet seems to have taken in her stride. Her father had died six weeks before her former husband: almost his last action had been to throw the family into turmoil by beginning a financial quarrel with his son Arthur, the only member of the family for whom Harriet had real sisterly feeling. Arthur was now back in Australia, and all her other brothers were resident abroad. Her sister Caroline was more than taken up with her own reprobate of a husband, and from her mother she never put up with any nonsense. She had a letter of good wishes from John Taylor's sister Eliza, regretting only that "so very many painful memories of the past arise",[8] but her wistful sorrow was quickly dissipated, and they remained on the best of terms.

Mill, on the other hand, being less socially accomplished, made more heavy weather. He had been living all this time at home in Kensington. His brother James was still in India: George, the youngest, was gradually dying of consumption in Madeira. Willie, his eldest sister, and Jane and Mary, the two youngest, had now married and left home. The household therefore consisted, apart from his ageing mother, of his middle sisters Harriet and Clara, who incidentally were the two who knew him best. It is not conceivable that this exclusively feminine circle, by no means unintelligent, was deluded by his morose reticence from grasping the significance of John Taylor's death, and its logical effect upon their favourite brother. What should they do, how were they supposed to act, when he at last announced his marriage to the extraordinary creature whom they were not allowed to mention, let alone to meet; and whom good taste almost forbade them to discuss among themselves? What about her was so vastly different from other women? If only he would speak, would give them some chance of bringing to the open his taut personal obsession. But although forthcoming upon all indifferent topics, upon this of singular importance he remained quite blank.

As month followed month and season turned to season, the tension in Kensington Square gathered force. The knitting needles clicked, the silken dresses rustled restlessly, and the silent anxiety verged upon hysteria. At last, after nearly two years of it, he declared abruptly that he was about to marry Mrs. Taylor. Willie and Jane, from abroad, hastened to send congratulations, and received brief acknowledgements giving some account of his immediate plans. Those in the vortex did not escape so easily. They had decided to wish him well and feel their way, and his mother was probably stating their considered policy when she told his old friend Horace Grant: "She believed and trusted it would be for [his] happiness, though it would cause the removal of a good son, who had always saved her much trouble and annoyance in her affairs."[9] Indeed, it was a sensible and prudent attitude, seeing that they were too petrified to be capable of any further action. But as luck would have it, it was entirely insufficient. Mill had evidently decided that on hearing the news they should hurry off to call on Harriet, who was still living at Kent Terrace. Their failure to do so seemed to him a deliberate insult to the woman of his choice. He was mortally offended.

And so the tragic paradox came about, that when twenty years of dangerous liaison had passed harmlessly away, the marriage which should have mended everything and made strangers friends, marked the beginning of irreparable discord. The preparations for the wedding went ahead in a seclusion that was practically stealthy. Harriet, accompanied by Algernon and Helen, slipped out of town to take up at Melcombe Regis, near Weymouth, the temporary residence required by law; they were joined for the Easter holidays by Mill, who had already made a preliminary visit. Here, in the depth of country where they were unknown, they were married on Easter Monday 1851 by the local Registrar, Mr. Richards, in the office of the Superintendent Registrar, Mr. Dadson: Harriet's two children were the witnesses, and nobody else was present. Mill without thinking signed the register in his customary manner, without writing his christian names in full, and when the error was pointed out to him, got into such a state of nerves that he tried to squeeze in the missing letters, giving the whole a botched and unauthentic character. They shook hands with the Registrar, and with the Superintendent Registrar. The bridegroom fumbled for the fee. They then returned to their lodgings and to the work they had in hand, the preparation of Harriet's article for the press. After a week they went back to London, and the cheerless nuptials were completed by a bald notice in the *Times*. The mistake about his signature so preyed upon Mill's mind that over a year later he wrote a letter to his wife, making a formal record of the occurrence, and begging her that they should be married all over again, and this time in a church.

For all their precautions, they did not succeed in averting the attention of old friends. John Chapman, worldly and experienced where women were concerned, found it worth while noting in his diary, "had a long conversation with Miss Martineau who gave me the history of J. S. Mill's relations with Mrs. Taylor, now his wife".[10] And Carlyle, accepting two invitations to "at homes" from Lady Harriet Baring, now Lady Ashburton, took the opportunity of remarking: "John Mill, did you see in the *Times*, is wedded to his widow Taylor; a fact in biography: poor good Mill! He has not announced it to anybody."[11] As a result, Lord Ashburton, with the effortless civility of an aristocrat, wrote genially to Mill, asking permission to call upon his wife with a view to winning them back into society.

His appeal was doomed to failure. The happy couple planned to find themselves a suitable small house sufficiently far from London to discourage visitors, but not so far as to prevent Mill getting to his work, and then to go as soon as possible for a Continental holiday, giving the dust a chance to settle. In the meantime they were at home to nobody except to W. J. Fox, the trusted witness of their early meetings.

In such a constrained, resentful atmosphere, Mill's family had little chance of putting right their unintended solecism. Nevertheless, mother and sisters, they were all resolved to try. They ignored the unkindness of not being invited to the wedding, and as soon as a discreet interval had passed, one of them went to the India House to make the first overtures. The result was most discouraging, Mill bluntly refusing to admit her. It seems, however, that his wife responded by urging him to make a formal call, and in due course they appeared, as smart and stiff as tailor's dummies, in the little Kensington drawing-room. For Mill, this meeting with his unforgiven family was an unbearable embarrassment. They had, he thought, gratuitously insulted him and the woman he adored, unmindful of all he had done for them. And then, how was he to confess to his beloved, that paragon of beauty, miracle of intellect and arbiter of taste, that "superior being": how could he explain to her that these dowdy, commonplace females, as they now appeared to him, were his flesh and blood? What would she think of them or of him? He was suffused with shame; and, like a schoolboy escorting his people to a prize-giving, dared hope only that they would somehow manage to behave less foolishly than usual. He was as chilly as a block of marble, unapproachable and unresponsive. For the women who had suffered and shared with him, for whom his leadership, his joy or melancholy had been as elemental as the sun and rain, it was too much to bear. They did not blame Harriet for the change in him: they did not even blame John. They only knew that since their love displeased him, they felt the goodwill ebbing from their faces, and the springs of affection drying out obediently but for ever.

Harriet did the best she could. She asked after Willie's daughter, little Clara King, who had heard so much of Helen and Haji from her Uncle George; and on the strength of Harriet's effort to be cordial, the elder Clara, who had wisely kept her room during the disastrous interview, decided to make a last approach through her. Taking the child with her as an innocent intermediary she called on Harriet some days later, only to be turned from the doorstep by her brother, who popped out on them like the Long-Legged Scissor Man. That was the end. The youngest of the sisters, Mary Colman, a courageous woman of thirty-one, on escaping to the calmer climate of her own home down at Bristol, to her children, her pious husband and her Ragged Schools, felt impelled to write a long remonstrance to her brother in which all his inexplicable cruelties were chronicled:

"I finish a painful task with one last request, urging you by the only feeling that now seems remaining to you, 'your love for your wife' not to throw this from you as coming from one of a family now evidently hateful to you, but to read it through without irritation, judge from what motives it has sprung, and ask yourself if your present course is likely to conduce to her happiness.

P.S. If this should close all intercourse between us as I think possible it will be to me very painful, but at least the sting will be wanting of thinking that I have shrunk from the duty of honesty towards you."[12]

The gathering tempest broke upon the unsuspecting shoulders of the unfortunate George Mill. He alone of Mill's relations had some intimate knowledge of Harriet, and the Taylors were very fond of him. In November 1848 he had been driven by tuberculosis to leave the India House, where for four years he had been working under the guidance of his brother, and go abroad. John Taylor had written in great anxiety to his wife at Pau, and she in her turn wrote to Haji:

"The account I hear of George and my knowledge of that insidious disease make me very much fear for him, and I most earnestly and anxiously wish that he may live. It is very important in writing to him to say very little about his health, and not to seem to think of it as anything more than a common cough, because if a person thinks themselves consumptive the effect on the spirits has the utmost possible tendency to produce or to accelerate that fatal disease. I think he would much like to hear from you and perhaps you have already written."[13]

As his great friend David Masson wrote of him, George was a very engaging youth:

"Less tall than his brother, but of compact and agile figure, with finely cut features, bright eyes, and a most winning sweetness of expression, . . . he had inherited no small share of the keen family ability. . . . He carried within himself an almost Shelley-like intensity of belief, quiet and undemonstrative in the main, but that might break out suddenly in some Shelley-like action. But this you had to discover gradually, so gentle was his demeanour, so sweetly reasonable his talk, so ready was he for anything gay and humoursome. . . . All in all, I have known no more lovable a nature than young George Mill."[14]

For some reason, Mill had recently been feeling more and more unkindly to his brother, perhaps because he thought he knew too much, and suspected him of giving too many scraps of information to the eager ears of Bain and of his sisters. In any case, in the spring of 1850 Mill wrote to George, harshly accusing him of gross impertinence. George, in defending himself, begged that the faultless Harriet ("the best umpire I could find") should be called upon to judge between them. His plea went unheeded. Mill wrote again a fortnight before his marriage, giving his full opinion upon the political shortcomings of Lord John Russell and on other topics, but entirely omitting any mention of the great step he and Harriet were about to take. George therefore knew nothing about the marriage until a month after it was over, when he received a cryptic statement of the fact, presumably from one of his terrified sisters. Since he had a passionate admiration for his famous brother, nearly twenty years older than himself, he was naturally shocked and hurt at Mill's distressing lack of confidence. In sending Harriet his congratulations, inevitably belated, he made reference, though not at all in powerful terms, to the pained state of his feelings. But sorrow was not his principal emotion. The solace of his suffering had been to follow enthusiastically every utterance and action of the figure who seemed to him so noble and tremendous. He had long been convinced of the evils of matrimony, and regarded the relation between Harriet Taylor and his brother as an heroic challenge to the conscience of society. In their capitulation, it appeared to him that they had struck their colours, and inexplicably, because, as he understood their case, they had nothing to gain by marriage and scorned the ultimate licence it conferred. There must, he concluded, be some other explanation. This "great and good" man, this "clever and remarkable" woman, could surely never have betrayed their principles. In great concern, he wrote to his old friend Haji, expressing his bewilderment. The letter arrived just as Mill's battle with his sisters was reaching its crescendo. Haji had no more sense than to show it to his mother.

She sat down impulsively and tore off a stinging answer:

"I do not answer your letter because you deserve it—that you certainly do not—but because tho' quite inexperienced in the best way of receiving or replying to an affront I think that in this as in all things, frankness and plain speaking are the best rule, as to me they are the most natural—also it is best that every one should speak for themselves. Your letters to me and Haji must be regarded as one, being on the same subject and sent together to us. In my opinion they show want of truth modesty and justice to say little of good breeding or good nature which you appear to regard as very unnecessary qualities.

Want of justice is shown in suggesting that a person has probably acted without regard to their principles which principles you say you never [understood?]. Want of modesty in passing judgement on a person thus far unknown to you—want of everything like truth in professing as you do a liking [?] for a person who in the same note you avoid calling by their name using an unfriendly designation after having for years addressed them in to say the least a more friendly way.* In fact want of truth is apparent in the whole, as your letters overflow with anger and animosity about a circumstance which in no way concerns you so far as anything you say shows and which if there was any truth in your profession of regard shd be a subject of satisfaction to you. As to want of the good breeding which is the result of good feeling that appears to be a family failing.

The only small satisfaction your letter can give is the observation that when people desert good feeling they are also deserted by good sense—your wish to make a quarrel [?] with your brother and myself because we have used a right which the whole world, of whatever shade of opinion, accords to us, is as absurd as unjust and wrong.

Harriet Mill"[15]

As though this were not clear enough, Mill claimed for himself the privilege of carving up his brother, and after making a draft or so, sent him a further letter expressing the same sentiments only rather more judicially. Haji also wrote, adding his little meteor to the thunderbolt. The unhappy invalid defended himself with considerable spirit, but his exile was made harder by the knowledge that he had lost all contact with those whom he held dear at home. Two years later he took it on himself to hasten the miserable end of his existence.

From now on, Harriet added her ebullient temper to her husband's overwhelming arrogance, and although the running fight with the remainder of the family continued for another year, the final breach was not in doubt. Mill charged them with petty gossip, and demanded "only common civility".

Clara answered:

"I do not pretend to judge you, I only cannot understand you, but under such circumstances to have any personal intercourse with you, could only be painful, and tho' I by no means admit that I deserve your contempt, I do not conceive that my acquaintance can be of any importance to your wife. We did not seek each other's acquaintance before her marriage nor ever should have done so—on what ground then begin it now?"[16]

* George Mill had ended his letter:

"Believe me dear Mrs. Taylor (I can't forget the old name)
Yours affect*ly*
Geo. G. Mill"

The letter begins "Dear Madam".

Mill retorted:

"You are entirely mistaken if you suppose that I said you had been uncivil to my wife, I said you had been wanting in all good feeling and even common civility to *us*. My wife and I are one.

You flatter yourself very undeservedly if you think that either my wife, or I for her, seek your acquaintance. You had an opportunity of seeking hers if you chose and you showed in every negative way in which it is possible to show a thing that you did not choose. My wife is accustomed not to seek but to be sought, and neither she nor I desire the acquaintance of anybody who does not wish for ours."[17]

One by one the links of kinship were deliberately broken, until at last nothing remained but the pitiful figure of Mill's mother, scurrying helplessly to the India House to plead for reconciliation. Having been scorned for thirty years by an icy and ungenerous husband, she now found herself despised by her equally icy eldest son.

In this instance, time was no great healer. Two years later, in April 1854, when their mother lay in mortal pain, dying from a tumour in the liver, Mill's youngest sister Mary wrote again, with cold distaste:

"My mother is very unhappy because she thinks that she has not behaved well to your wife. She is constantly urging me to go to Blackheath and call on her, saying that it would please you very much and nothing will divert her mind from this one point. She is still very weak, unable to stand, and thinks evidently that you are very angry with her and do not come to see her on that account.

. . . Will you therefore either let me know what you think we had better do, or, for my mother's sake, write *her* a few lines to prevent her from wishing us to go, or in some way set her mind at ease."[18]

By way of doing so, Mill wrote to his mother two days later:

"My dear Mother,

I received on Saturday another of Mary's vulgar and insolent letters. The impertinence appears the only motive for writing them and I cannot waste my time in answering any more of them. In this she affects to think that I wish to see her. Will you tell her, that neither I nor my wife will keep up any acquaintance with her whatever.*

I hope you are gaining strength and will soon be quite well again. When you are able to write will you let me know how you are. I need not say that we shall be always glad to see you.

Yrs. affy.
J.S.M."[19]

* A very violent sentence here deleted in the draft.

His mother rallied her strength in order to reply herself:

"My dear John

I will try and write a few lines to you, I have been able to get down stairs with assistance for these two or three last days, and I hope I shall get stronger now I am able to sit up.

I was very much surprised at the message you sent to Mary the last time you wrote, but I did not deliver it, as I was sure it would make her very unhappy, she has gone to the country.

I did not know what she wrote to you, that could have given you cause to be so much displeased with her.

We always hoped to be upon good terms with Mrs. Mill and her family—your Marriage gave us all pleasure as you had chosen a Wife who was capable of entering into all your pursuits and appreciate your good qualities.

I trust that I shall soon get strong and that Mrs. Mill will do me the favour to come and take a family dinner with me. In the meantime present my kind regards to her.

Your ever aff*te* Mother
H. Mill."[20]

Two months later, Mill was warned by his sisters that his mother's end was near. He went once to visit her, but he had been urgently ordered abroad by his own doctors, and was not able to put off his departure. Before he left, he asked her in a hurried note, which she was too ill to understand, to appoint somebody to succeed him as executor to her will. She died a week afterwards, and when the news reached him he was far away in Brittany. He showed no particular emotion, even on reading the letter the old lady left for him:

"I did not mention the furniture in my will which you were so kind as to leave for my use, but as some of it is a great deal worn, I hope you will take the best of it, and do as I should have done if I had considered it my own, give the rest to your two unmarried sisters, Clara and Harriet. Your plate is taken care of and will be restored to you by your sisters.

God bless you my dear son, I sincerely hope that you and Mrs. Mill will enjoy many many years of uninterrupted happiness."[21]

He stiffly instructed Charles Colman, Mary's husband, upon whom the executorship had fallen, that the furniture was to be divided equally among all his sisters; also the plate, since, as he explained to Harriet, "to us it would only be worth its weight as old silver".[22] His sisters, however, haughtily refused to take it. For his own part, Mill was strongly inclined to deal the same about a share of his mother's money—some four or five hundred pounds—which came to him by entail. But as Harriet dissented violently from his opinion, he hastily decided to accept it. "About the matter of my mother's inheritance, of course as your feeling is so directly contrary, mine is wrong, and I give it up entirely."[23]

II

The house selected by Mill and Harriet as their retreat was the last but one on the left in Blackheath Park. Seven or eight miles out of London, and half a mile from the nearest station, it was described by a later visitor as "a square, plain, brick mansion in a little plot of ground . . . but with a characteristically English air and look in its seclusion behind a wall, and trim thick shrubbery, and the ivy covering one side and affording a shelter for innumerable twittering sparrows. Over the way is a wide open space of rolling meadow bounded far off by a blue outline of distant hills."[24] They took it on a twenty-year lease for £150 a year, quite a high figure in those days. Evidently, their eye was keener for amenity and situation than for structural soundness, for the foundations were intrinsically defective, and the incessant cracking of the walls owing to their unequal settling involved heavy bills for carpenters, plasterers, painters, paperhangers, plumbers, and glaziers. Mill was later twice driven to the expense of underpinning the building, the whole cost of necessary repairs amounting on average to half the annual rent, to say nothing of the further £300 dilapidations he was held liable for at the expiry of the lease. But these practical troubles, along with all their greater ones, were still ahead of them when they first moved in, in the autumn of 1851. They had each other and a home, and they could feel that they had really earned their happiness. They drew their curtains on the misty humours of the park, shutting out the distant lamps and musky odour of the smouldering leaves. By their own fireside they sank into matrimonial intimacy.

Seclusion they had certainly obtained. They never went out, except when Mill occasionally attended a meeting of the Political Economy Club. Bain, who had recently returned to London, was no longer allowed to wait on him for his daily walk from the India House, and, since he was never invited to Blackheath, lost all opportunity for conversation except briefly during office hours, or when he and Grote were now and again permitted to accompany Mill to Charing Cross, the station for Blackheath. During the seven years they lived there, Fox and his daughter, Theodor Gomperz and Pasquale Villari, two visiting scholars, and the great Mazzini, were about all they reckoned, as Mill courteously put it to the latter, "among the few persons to whom we can sincerely say that they may feel sure of being welcome".[25]

In fact, the Mills were so absorbed in the exploration of each other's personality, that they regarded any outside encounter as an unwelcome interruption to be avoided whenever possible. They were not lonely in the least degree. Helen lived with them, and, for the first five years of marriage, so did Haji, who had grown into a sickly, rather feckless youth. Herbert, with whom they did not get on so well, lived, when he was not travelling in America, in the City; before long, he got married. They had a cook named Kate, and hired a jobbing gardener to trim their tiny orchard: in spring he raised peas and early strawberries under Harriet's watchful eye, and gloomily carried out her orders about the use of lime. They kept tame song birds, and put up a green and white pet stand for them in the garden. And, to complete the household, Harriet had a beautiful white Persian cat.

Every morning they chatted pleasantly, until Mill left for the office sometime after nine. At six he came in again, bearing the family mail, and performed the rite of making tea, his sole domestic duty. When it was light enough, they always strolled out on the common and admired their view. Then, after supper, while Harriet sat in her own chair by the fire, he would play chess with Haji, or they would read, or, now and again, she would ask him to play the piano. When that happened, he sat down at once and after a few introductory chords began to play music out of his head exactly as it came to him. When he had finished, Harriet, who played beautifully herself, would ask what theme had been running in his mind, and he would tell her it had been clouds driven before a storm, or a dirge; a battle, or a procession. For her, he would play for hours, or when he was by himself. But he never would play when they were not alone. On Sundays he strode off into the country, his tin box for botanical specimens under his arm, and by combining rail and foot travel he went far afield. He would eat a healthy lunch at an hotel, and return at nightfall fresher than he had started, after walking sometimes more than twenty miles. Haji records that in all the time he spent with them, including half a dozen continental journeys—the severest test of temper—and innumerable English ones, he "never knew him to utter a cross word or show impatience in her regard, nor to demur to any expressed wish on her part; and, it must be added, she no less considered his wishes in all things".[26]

The first year of marriage, 1852, slipped by happily enough. Mill wrote his last most caustic estimate of Whewell, and yielding to Chapman's importunity, allowed him to produce it in the *Westminster* for October. Chapman was delighted to the point of indiscretion, and George Eliot had to remind him sternly that his policy of including philosophical and temperamental enemies in the same number was going to cause them some embarrassment, since the Editors were still nominally in agreement with every view expressed :

> "As to James Martineau, there is no doubt that he will write; 'self-interest well understood' will secure that. Pray, how came you to tell him that J. S. Mill was going to write? I have told you all along that he would flatly contradict Martineau and that there was nothing for it but to announce contradiction on our title page."[27]

Mill contributed a public letter in support of Chapman in his case against the Bookseller's Association, a clique of publishers who fixed a high retail price for books and refused supplies to any bookseller who undersold them. Chapman, backed by an indignant congregation of authors under the chairmanship of Dickens, won his case, and the Bookseller's Association was abolished.

In March, the third edition of the *Political Economy* came out. Otherwise, Mill did little in this year. Perhaps, for the first time in his life, he browsed idly upon the lotus of domesticity, for a remarkably large proportion of his less enlivening letters were prefaced by euphemisms such as "Want of time has prevented me", or "The pressure of my occupations has left me no leisure until now". If it was so, it did not last. The following year they awoke from their day-dream to find the grim figure of death hovering about them.

Pulmonary consumption, or phthisis, as tuberculosis was then known, was the scourge of the nineteenth century. Being a disease which thrives best in conditions of overcrowding and under-nourishment, it flourished as never before or since in the great wen of London, where these conditions were aggravated by the soot-laden smoke from myriad factory and residential chimneys mingling with the icy fog rising like a miasma off the Thames.

The general attitude towards the disease was curious. Not only was it regarded as incurable, but it was thought to be purely hereditary, and not at all infectious. In consequence, whole families, as they huddled fatalistically in their stuffy homes each one waiting for the blow to fall, unwittingly condemned themselves, and were swept away piecemeal. The only treatment was, for those who could afford it, to go to Madeira or some other place with a soft warm climate, where the sufferings of the patient were allayed and the end prolonged, although it was also made more certain since the germs equally benefited from the change of air. The rate of death from this cause was five times as heavy in 1850 as in the present day; and of the small circle of people in Mill's life—all people, after all, coming from the politest kind of homes—his own father and two of his brothers; Harriet's brother Thomas Hardy, John Sterling, and Dr. Calvert, Eliza and Sarah Flower, eight in all, had already been carried off.

It has since become known that although everyone is exposed to the disease at one time or another, and most become to some extent immune, anyone may be grossly infected by close contact with another sufferer. It is also known that "those suffering from the chronic type of pulmonary disease with cavities are, perhaps, the most dangerous of all, such cases producing, as a rule, copious expectoration of a sputum heavily charged with bacilli while, being relatively resistant, they often survive for years and are well enough to remain at home."[28]

Now Mill was typical of these chronic cases. His letters describe in detail his racking cough, the thick uncontrollable expectoration tinged with blood, and his feverish sweating in the night. Suddenly, Harriet too fell ill with the familiar symptoms. She had no particular record of lung trouble, and her many previous ailments had been apparently of a nervous kind. So it seems almost as certain that Mill gave her consumption, as that his father had originally given it to him long years before, when they worked at logic and political economy across a narrow table.

For the moment at least they declined to recognize the sentence of death either for themselves or for each other, and of the two, Mill's own condition caused the greater alarm. At the end of August 1853 he took his wife to Sidmouth, where it was hoped the sea air would help her to recuperate. Then, in the autumn, as soon as he could get leave from the India House, they set out on their doctor's advice for the south of France, accompanied as always on these voyages by Helen. At Nice, Harriet was taken desperately ill with a haemorrhage of the lung, and her life was saved only by the prompt action of a resident Englishman, Dr. Cecil Gurney. They still regarded it as an isolated attack, and as soon as she was fit to move went on to Hyères, where Mill left the ladies immediately after Christmas. From the comparative warmth of the *Place des Palmiers*, he went into a world of bitter cold where everything sparkled with frost which burnt the fingers. At Avignon, it chanced that he had to wait the inside of a day for a coach connection. And, as the *mistral* was howling down the Rhone, he went into the *Hôtel de l'Europe* to write to Harriet. "This inn", he said, "seems good. It has plenty of rooms on premier and an easy staircase. Of the eating I only know a very good sweet omelette and excellent tea (as at Marseilles) besides good coffee and excellent butter which was the only thing bad at Marseilles."[29] He noted appreciatively that it was a place where they might stay another time. He could not know the tragedy that other time would bring.

Owing to the deep snow and the icy roads, his journey home took the best part of ten days. He arrived in Lyons, chilled to the bone, and heartily weary of the bleak, snow-clad fields. Because the Saône was frozen over he could not go on as usual by the steamer; he had to take the omnibus, which broke down on the way and reached Chalon twenty-four hours overdue. Finally, in the train from Paris to Boulogne he was snowed up, for a further twenty-four hours. Once in Boulogne, he raced to the Post Office, where the expected letter from Harriet was waiting for him and put him back in spirits. His crossing was mercifully smooth and swift, and before long he was splashing through the drenching black slush of London in a thaw.

During the unavoidable separation from his wife, Mill grappled valiantly with the unaccountable caprices of his household Gods. On first returning to Blackheath he noticed how cold and desolate the old place looked. His fond gaze turned irresistibly towards Harriet's empty chair, and his thought ranged gloomily on the unending desert of isolation which divided them. But, like any man of spirit in his situation, he thrust aside these maudlin influences. It was, after all, their home; a pleasant home even in her absence, and indeed her presence seemed to hover over it. Unacquainted as he was with the technique of daily living, he resolved to keep it going exactly as she would wish. Methodically, almost superstitiously, he ensured that her last enjoinders were carried out to the very letter. The two chairs which ought to be at the ends of the sideboard were, he observed, still there; and the things she had tied round them for some unobvious purpose of her own were still in place. He moved the table nearer to the window as she had directed, making sure the side where he would sit at meals was opposite the middle of the fire. He was of course to write to her in the greatest possible detail several times a week; but in case she should still be insufficiently informed of his state of mind, it had been decided that he should record some *pensée* of a general nature every day which she could read on her return, and for this purpose a diary was procured. Then, after making some promised medical researches in a fat text-book, he went virtuously to bed, not wholly dissatisfied with his performance.

He should not have been so cocksure.

> "It rained torrents in the night and in the morning Kate knocked at the door and said that the water had come in again—it had indeed, in at least a dozen places, reaching as far as the beau milieu of the room so there is another plastering job inevitable—and it was every way unlucky as there was no way of getting at the place to bale out the water, which lay apparently so deep that no doubt the pipe was stopt up. There was nothing to be done but to go again to Smith's, and say that the place he had mended was worse than before. Again unluckily the old fellow was out and not expected for a day or two but his son promised to go immediately, and take a ladder."[30]

After this he gradually lapsed into the slothful parsimony of the solitary male. By having meat for tea, he saved himself the trouble of going out at night for dinner. He read a book at meals, a thing he never did when Harriet was there. As for the leaks, he discovered it was folly to be wise: "The men came yesterday but, Kate says, only stayed about 10 minutes during which they cleared the pipe and 'hammered down something'—the water has not come in since—adieu with a thousand loves", he hopefully reported.[31]

His first contact with the cost of living horrified him, and he grew morbidly convinced he was being cheated:

> "This morning Kate announced that she had no kitchen candles or soap; the last owing to her having washed things for Haji. I said you expected her stores of all sorts would last till March. I said I would write to you about it and in the meantime to order 1 lb of each from

Dalton. She also said that there were only potatoes for two or three days. The last had were a bushel on the 3rd November: have they not gone very fast, considering Haji's three weeks absence and that when he was here (until the last week) they were only wanted one day in the week? What does the tax gatherer mean by charging us 12/– for 'armorial bearings'? Can he mean the crest on your dear little seal? Webster's bill is 'examining correcting and cleaning foreign marble clock 15/–, new winder 2/6. Cleaning and repairing carriage clock, (which he spoiled) 12/6'. . . ."[32]

He sternly determined on retrenchment, and on putting the Staff in its proper place at any price:

"I paid Kate's wages. She is exactly all you said—very pleasant to speak to and be served by—but her *excuses* are like a person with no sense or head at all and she requires *much* looking after. She says Parson's bill is wrong because it charges, during all Haji's absence, about twice the quantity of meat she professes to have had, and she has twice taken the bill to make him alter it, but of course she *has* had the meat, and last Sunday the fact that a large piece of the roast beef had been cut off was as palpable as in the worst case I remember with the former cook. I showed it to her of course not charging *her* with anything but that she might know I had noticed it."[33]

As he rapidly found out, he was entirely wrong in much of this, and soon had to divert his effort to his own defence. A chance remark by his physician about his underclothes led to a sharp enquiry from Harriet as to the condition of his wardrobe. His reply was glib enough:

"As to care about my appointments in going to Clark—I have been attentive to them. I always use one of my best shirts, those with the invisible buttons, not the linen because they were so much older. The braces I will attend to—hitherto those I bought at Nice have seemed good enough. The criticisability of the flannels was not as to their quality, for they were very good, and quite new—but he thought them not thick enough and recommended wearing another set [?] (with short sleeves) over them which I have done ever since. I got a new hat the other day in honour of him (and Mrs. Winter), and on the whole have behaved very well in the matter, though I say it that shouldn't."[34]

Now Mrs. Winter was a tradeswoman whose bill he had recently been to pay, and his flippancy seems to have been regarded as ill-timed, for he soon had to write again in a more humble tone:

"I was annoyed with myself for what I wrote about the appointments when I read your comment. When I go next to C which will probably

> be on Tuesday I will put on an old linen shirt. The flannels were from Brier's, but I will get some from Capper's today or tomorrow and will discard the second flannel though I am sure C meant it quite seriously."[35]

Towards the end of his vigil, Mill's eagerness for his wife's return was sharpened by another quite unanticipated excitement. The neighbour, Powell, sent a note to say that he had found a boisterous colony of rats along the wall dividing the two properties, and since the local ratcatcher had drawn a blank on his side, he feared they must be coming across from Mill's. Responsibility being thus disputed, Mill applied confidently to Harriet for instructions; and, as an interim measure, he sent Haji round with an answer to Powell's note.

> "Mr. J. S. Mill is obliged to Mr. Powell for his information and will have his side of the garden wall examined."

This, he proudly told her, he felt to be "safe and *un*committing". But a day or two later, Kate showed him in great alarm how the rats had broken out from their bridgehead during the night, gnawed a hole under the door between the coal hole and the scullery, and had now gained a lodgement in the outhouse where, she said, they made a tremendous uproar. The outhouse, he found, was locked. And he had not got the key. "I do not know what it is best or indeed possible to do", he confessed to Harriet in despair, "but to leave things as they are till we meet." From her answers he discovered to his joy that she had taken the new complication in her stride, and he was only too glad to accept her criticism of his own mishandling. "I am so sorry", he replied, "the few words I wrote to Powell vexed her. . . . I shall now do at once what my dearest one recommends, that is, her last recommendation." Accordingly, he sent for the blacksmith to pick the door of the outhouse; and he wrote Powell a resounding reprimand, settling upon him the full responsibility for all the rats. He then sent for the ratcatcher, and charged him to explore both houses thoroughly. The ratcatcher spent a day on Powell's premises and caught one rat. Next day he went to Mill's, searched everywhere, but saw no sign of a rat. "So that it is plain", Mill jubilantly ended, "there were none, but the one he drove from Powell's and which afterwards returned there and was caught."[36] He had no further trouble from the audacious Powell, who presumably was left to pay the piper.

III

Behind the little trials of family life there loomed the darkening shadow of declining health. When Mill returned to the India House after leaving Harriet at Hyères, all his colleagues flocked to his room, pressing their anxious questions and wringing him by the hand, while his old friends Grote and Prescott hurried round from their banking house as soon as they heard that he was back; between them all, they made it quite apparent they had doubted whether they could hope ever to see him again. Only his superior, Thomas Love Peacock, head of the Examiner's Office, had the good sense to avoid the topic of illness altogether: after mentioning a visit he had had from Mill's only remaining brother James, who had just come back from India, he plunged gruffly into official matters as though nothing at all had happened.

In truth Mill's condition was very serious. While attending to his wife in Nice, Dr. Gurney had felt bound to tell him some disquieting things about himself, and the rigours of his journey home, the cruel exposure and immense fatigue, had aggravated all his symptoms. His cough was worse, his pulse was high, he lay awake and sweated in the night, and he was alarmed to find traces of blood in the mucous which he spat up every morning. Soon after his return, he went again to take the advice of Sir James Clark, Physician in Ordinary to Queen Victoria. Sir James, like many of his breed, was enigmatic. After a thorough examination, in which he puzzled his patient by directing all his attention to the left lung whereas Mill knew the right had always been the one to give him trouble, he looked grave but at the same time reassuring. He could find, he said, no trace of organic disease; but when Mill asked him point-blank "then you find nothing the matter with my lungs beyond catarrh?" he answered ominously, "not at present".[37] He prescribed hemlock pills and mustard poultices, which Mill wondered whether Kate could make or he himself apply. He recommended stouter clothes. He promised to consult his dossier on the case. Then, warmly patting the stony shoulder of his patient, he told him to come again in two or three weeks, if not completely cured by then.

In spite of several other visits, the symptoms grew worse and worse, and Mill began to cast uneasily about for other information:

"I. have been reading a little book which I remember seeing advertised years ago but did not get it supposing it to be some merely quackish thing, but an edition having been readvertised just now I got it—called the Curability of Consumption, by Dr. Ramadge—and it is not a quackish thing at all—the writer is evidently well entitled to an opinion having been Senior Physician to the Infirmary for Diseases of the Chest.* I wish I had seen the book long ago—I certainly think any person would be very foolish to let themselves die of consumption without having tried him and his treatment. . . . The number and quality of the cases of success which he cites, even in an advanced stage of consumption, are such as quite entitle him to a trial."[38]

About the middle of March 1854 the dreaded blow descended. Clark confessed that it was consumption after all, and he had known it all along. He added that there was nothing he could do beyond advising cod-liver oil as a palliative. At first Mill tried to keep the news from Harriet. Although he had taken every opportunity of reassuring her by saying she could not possibly have consumption herself, and that his own condition was far worse than hers, he remained extremely worried about her. She was mending slowly in the warm air of the Mediterranean, but was still very easily tired, and the least fatigue brought on her pains in the chest. He had made her stay where she was until the unusually frigid weather in the north had given way to spring, and she and Helen were just now slowly making their way to Paris, posting in the little carriage he had procured for her in Hyères, which she had determined to bring home since she could not sell it for a reasonable price. She was very much exhausted by the journey—at Dijon they had to take to the railway, carriage and all—and since it had been arranged that he was to join her in Paris for fear the channel crossing should lead to another haemorrhage, he decided not to hasten her or add to her anxiety, but to keep the diagnosis to himself until they were together. Accordingly he wrote about indifferent things, and confided only in his diary:

"March 31st. Apart from bodily pain, and the grief for the grief of those who love us, the most disagreeable thing about dying is the intolerable ennui of it. There ought to be no slow deaths."[39]

For his own part, he refused to give up his case as hopeless, as Sir James Clark had done, but went instead to Ramadge. Ramadge

* *Consumption Curable*, by Francis Hopkins Ramadge, M.D. (1793–1867) First published London, 1834.

had original and consoling views about consumption. He thought it was far more common than was generally supposed, and very seldom fatal. He had not, like other specialists, confined his researches to cases known to have died of the disease. He had deliberately examined the lungs of non-consumptive corpses, and had found in most of them traces of tuberculosis which had somehow been arrested. He concluded that many of those then going about in the best of health must unknowingly have suffered from it at some previous time. In consequence he offered hope where others only shrugged their shoulders. He had a very prim and quiet manner; but every time Mill went to see him, his eyes glinted as he showed him a new bundle of letters from the patients he had healed. He spoke with great confidence of a cure, and said he had never had so favourable a case. He refused to admit that his treatment could possibly fail if properly tried. Mill, while sceptical enough, was sufficiently impressed to acquire the necessary apparatus. Three times a day for periods of half an hour he dutifully breathed through a sort of metal trumpet which delayed his respiration, with the object of keeping his lungs expanded and preventing the growth of further tubercles. After a fortnight, being no longer able to conceal the truth from Harriet, he told her the whole story, but could add that for whatever reason he was beginning to feel a definite improvement.

In the middle of April, since he was not well enough to go to her in Paris, she risked the crossing and joined him at Blackheath. The new circumstances in which they found themselves could now come under closer discussion, and they proceeded to recast their whole scheme of life. In the first place, the possibility of an early death for either of them (and whichever it might be, Mill was certain it would be equally fatal to his career), filled him with a desire to get through as much as possible of the work they had planned for the remainder of their lives in the shortest possible time. He had long been convinced of the need for haste, for even before her illness he had written:

> "We must finish the best we have got to say, and not only that, but publish it while we are alive. I do not see what living depository there is likely to be of our thoughts, or who in this weak generation that is growing up will even be capable of thoroughly mastering and assimilating your ideas, much less of re-originating them—so we must write them and print them, and then they can wait until there are again thinkers."[40]

He now gave up the idea of publication, and devoted his efforts to getting everything down in draft. In fact, after his final article on the later volumes of Grote's *History of Greece* in the *Edinburgh Review* for October 1853, which gave great pleasure to the author and led to some sort of a *rapprochement* with Mrs. Grote, he published nothing during the rest of his married life except some botanical notes in the *Phytologist*. Nor, except for the vicarious support he gave, at Harriet's wish, to G. O. Trevelyan's plan for the introduction of a competitive Civil Service, did he concern himself in the various measures of the passing day.

That did not however signify, as Bain suggests, that he was worn out or incapacitated by his illness. On the contrary, he was constantly at work, and the worse his health became the more vigorously he wrote. His two great works, the *Logic* and the *Political Economy*, he now regarded simply as a prologue, as an establishment of first principles. The more essential part of his task still lay before him, the application of those principles to a variety of topics of a practical and widespread daily interest. His object was that they should "get most of it into a fit state for printing—if not in the best form for popular effect, yet in the state of concentrated thought—a sort of mental pemican, which thinkers, when there are any after us, may nourish themselves with and then dilute for other people".[41] He planned with Harriet a list of the subjects to make up a book of essays, which became, with very little material alteration, the foundation of most of his later publications, of the *Liberty*, *Utilitarianism*, *Representative Government*, the unfinished *Chapters on Socialism*, and the posthumous *Three Essays on Religion*.

On 7 February 1854 Mill wrote to Harriet:

> "I finished the 'Nature' on Sunday as I expected. I am quite puzzled what to attempt next—I will just copy the list of subjects we made out in the confused order in which we put them down. Differences of character (nation, race, age, sex, temperament). Love. Education of tastes. Réligion de l'Avenir. Plato. Slander. Foundation of Morals. Utility of Religion. Socialism. Liberty. Doctrine that Causation is Will. To these I have now added from your letter, Family, and Conventional. It will be a tolerable two years work to finish all that. Perhaps the first of them is the one I could do most to by myself, at least of those equally important."[42]*

* Mill's views on the subjects mentioned were later elaborated in his works as follows:

Nature, and Utility of Religion: *Three Essays on Religion*, 1874
Liberty and Conventional: *On Liberty*, 1859

Harriet replied:

"About the Essays dear, would not religion, the Utility of Religion, be one of the subjects you would have most to say on—there is to account for the existence nearly universal of some religion (superstition) by the instincts of fear, hope and mystery etc, and throwing over all doctrines and theories, called religion, and devices for power, to show how religion and poetry fill the same want, the craving after higher objects, the consolation of suffering, the hope of heaven for the selfish, love of God for the tender and grateful—how all this must be superseded by morality deriving its power from sympathies and benevolence and its reward from the approbation of those we respect.

There, what a long winded sentence, which you could say ten times as well in words half the length."[43]

The "Utility of Religion", when it eventually appeared, dealt faithfully with all these points. Said Mill, "Your program of an essay on religion is beautiful, but it requires you to fill it up—I can try but a few paragraphs will bring me to the end of all I have got to say on the subject. What would be the use of my outliving you! I could write nothing worth keeping alive for except with your prompting."[44]

Furthermore, the first draft of the *Autobiography*, which they felt to be their most important, almost sacred duty, and intended as a summary of their whole spiritual and intellectual life, was put in hand. "I shall never be satisfied unless you allow our best book the book which is to come, to have our *two* names on the title page. It ought to be so with everything I publish, for the better half of it all is yours, but the book which will contain our best thoughts, if it has only one name to it, that should be yours",[45] Mill told her. He pressed on with it, and shortly afterwards reported: "The fact is that there is about as much written as I *can* write without your help and we must go through this together. . . . But of what particularly concerns *our* life there is nothing yet written, except the descriptions of you and . . . of what I owe to you *intellectually*."[46] "I feel sure dear", she responded mildly, "that the Life is not half-written and that half that is written will not do."[47] The draft was complete by 1856; it differed

Socialism: *Chapters on Socialism*, Unfinished
Doctrine that Causation is Will: *Examination of Sir Wm. Hamilton's Philosophy*, 1865
Réligion de l'Avenir: *Auguste Comte and Positivism*, 1865, and *Utilitarianism*, 1861
Foundation of Morals, Education of Tastes: *Utilitarianism*, 1861
National Differences of Character: *Representative Government*, 1861
Plato: Article "Plato", *Edinburgh Review*, April 1866
Family: *Subjection of Women*, 1869; *On Liberty*, 1859

little in essentials from the version posthumously published, and covered the first and most important two-thirds of its length.[48]

The *Subjection of Women* clearly grew, and was intended to grow, out of Harriet's article "The Enfranchisement of Women". "I only wish the better thing we have promised to write were already written instead of being in prospect", said Mill in 1854. "In any case the article will of course be in any collection or rather *se*lection of articles which we may either publish in our life, or leave for publication afterwards, and whichever we do it shall be preceded by a preface which will show that much of all my later articles, and all the best of that one, were, as they were, my darling's."[49] The *Dissertations and Discussions*, an anthology of Mill's articles published in the *Edinburgh* and *Westminster Reviews*, was debated and the contents settled. *Auguste Comte and Positivism* was suggested by Chapman's incessant demands that Mill should do something on the subject for the *Westminster*. The plan was for the moment dropped because Harriet feared it must include flattering references to the hated Harriet Martineau, whose translation of Comte's *Système de Philosophie positive* had recently appeared. Even the *Examination of Sir William Hamilton's Philosophy* seems to have been projected in shadowy outline, under the title "Doctrine that Causation is will".

Mill ceased to make distinction between Harriet's mind and his. In little things as well as great, he followed where she led. As in the choice between communism and free enterprise, he did not hesitate to change his views. He who, as a loyal Radical, had been a protagonist of the secret Ballot, became in the *Representative Government* its chief opponent. He who had told Caroline Fox that he was opposed to capital punishment, was able afterwards to speak in Parliament against a bill for its abolition. Even his humour took its colouring from Harriet. Helen records in her diary how she went with her mother to see the American dwarf, Tom Thumb, and that "we were 'greatly pleased' and 'much amused' ". Bain walking with Mill in Trafalgar Square, and talking seriously as usual, was amazed to find, as they passed a poster featuring GENERAL TOM THUMB AS ROMULUS, stark naked save for spear and helmet, that Mill was suddenly convulsed with laughter.

It is certain that every major work Mill published after the *Political Economy*, was drafted or at any rate planned during his first few years of married life. And Harriet, though she did not write them, suggested, approved, and interpolated every one, dictating parts verbatim. In so far as Mill's influence, theoretic or applied, has been of advantage to the progress of the western world, or indeed of humanity at large, the credit should rest upon his wife at least as much as on himself. For, as he observed in the *Autobiography*, "when two persons have their thoughts and speculations completely in common . . . it is of little consequence in respect to the question of originality, which of them holds the pen."[50] His continual assertions to that effect were neither, as it has been the fashion to make out, exaggerated chivalries, nor the fulsome aberrations of a man who had fallen under the witchery of the other sex. They were, over a long period of time and in a wide variety of circumstances, his most ardent conviction. A conviction now seen to have been based upon an abundant body of evidence.

He worked with fearful urgency. The whole question seemed to him to be how much they could get done before the hand of death divided and thereby silenced them:

> "I hope we shall live to write together 'all we wish to have written' to most of which your living is quite as essential [as] mine, for even if the wreck I should be could work on with undiminished faculties, my faculties at the best are not adequate to the highest subjects and have already done almost the best they are adequate to. Do not think darling that I should ever make this an excuse to myself for not doing my very best—if I survived you, and anything we much cared about was not already fixed in writing you might depend on my attempting all of it and doing my very best to make it such as you would wish, for my only rule of life *then* would be what I thought you would wish. But I *am not fit* to write on anything but the outskirts of the great questions of feeling and life without you to prompt me as well as to keep me right. So we must do what we can while we are alive—the Life being the first thing—which independent of the personal matters which it will set right when we have made it what we intend, is even now an unreserved proclamation of our opinions on religion, nature, and much else."[51]

Another effect of the prospect of continual illness was to make them wonder whether they should not go and live somewhere out of England. Apart from its unhealthiness they had no great love for London, nor did they feel any sentimental bondage to their native land. They both loved France, and Harriet was fond of Italy; they would have taken up a Continental life at once, had it not been for Mill's work at the India House. The question of his retirement thus arose, and the problem became one of money. Why they should have felt themselves to be hard up is not at all apparent, since his salary was at this time £1200, and Harriet had been willed full use of all John Taylor's assets. It seems that Mill, true to his scruples, refused to include her portion in their family reckonings, and it was no doubt swallowed up in allowances for her children, of whom only Herbert was working, and he was extravagant by nature. Mill did not count upon any regular income from his books, although both the *Logic* and *Political Economy* were still selling steadily, and his receipts from publishers for 1853 amounted to £375, a large return, as he contentedly remarked, "to have come in one year from writings of which money was not at all the object".[52] So they decided to leave the question of retirement until they had at least £500 a year safely deriving from gilt-edged investments. Although they worked towards this figure by means of stiff economy (Mill, for example, saved two-pence on each of his letters to Harriet by sending them unstamped and allowing her to pay the postage in French currency), they had, in January 1854, reached only £420 and could not achieve their aim for at least another year.

A more important point was that of pension. If Mill retired voluntarily, the Directors were not bound to any figure, whereas if he were compelled to leave for reason of his health, they were almost certain to grant him two-thirds of his salary, or eight hundred pounds a year. That would, as he observed, "make a very great difference in the aspect of matters".[53] Unless therefore it grew obvious they were to be parted by death in the very near future, in which case they both would wish to take their pleasure and their leisure at once rather than miss it altogether, it would pay him to keep on at the India House for another year or so. Especially so since Mill had grounds for hoping that his doctors would order him abroad for the winter, giving them a six month's holiday at the Company's expense. Sick and already over-occupied though he was, he tore into his official duties so that the Directors should have no reason to refuse him leave, and accomplished in two months the work of five-and-a-half. He almost resented any suggestion by the doctors that he was getting better quickly.

He need not have worried, for in June 1854 his general condition, and particularly the speed at which he was losing weight, caused them to pack him off immediately. Since it again seemed likely he would have to retire at once, he took the opportunity of scouring Brittany for a place where they could live. At the same time the Directors, alarmed at his talk of leaving, made a special addition to his salary of

£200 a year, gave him reason to suppose that his pension prospects would be the highest they were allowed to give by law, and removed all doubts about the winter leave. This enabled him to relax the stringent saving, and to insist that Harriet should have the medical comforts she had denied herself:

> "Then about the things required by bad health which you say we are unable to have—let us have them, that is *you* have them darling, at least up to our income—we are now living much within it—and we are not likely to lose more than £300 a year. . . . So we can judge well enough what we can afford, and have everything desirable which is consistent with it."[54]

As Harriet was suffering from an abscess in her side, which eventually had to be surgically treated, he left her at Blackheath and set out for the Continent alone. He hated sea voyages at the best of times, and as his course took him down the tumultuous Race between Alderney and the Cherbourg Peninsula, he arrived in Jersey in a depressed and sour state. To make matters worse it rained incessantly, and he was delayed a day because the steamer which was to have taken him to St. Malo had gone on an excursion to Alderney, and was prevented by a gale from getting back in time. But once ashore in France his spirits bounded up. The genial air, the rocky territory, were admirably suited to his taste; he walked prodigious distances, regardless of his illness. Living was cheap: at Lannion he got his room, an omelette for supper with the tea he always insisted on making for himself, and eggs for breakfast in the morning, all for four francs; while the country butter about which of all things he was most particular, he found delicious. He got to know a fellow Englishman named Pope, who, until Mill wearied of him, served for a time to while away the long days of travelling by diligence:

> "He turned out a pleasant person to meet, as, though he does not seem to me to have any talent, he is better informed than common Englishmen—knows a good deal of French history for example, especially that of the Revolution—and seems either to have already got to or to be quite ready to receive, all our opinions. I tried him on religion, where I found him quite what we thing right—on politics, on which he was somewhat more than a radical—on the equality of women which he seemed not to have quite dared to think of himself but seemed to adopt it at once—and to be ready for all reasonable socialism—he boggled a little at limiting the power of bequest which I was glad of as it showed that the other agreements were not merely following a lead taken. He was therefore worth talking to and I think he will have taken away a good many ideas from me."[55]

Mill began to put on weight. In the first three weeks he gained four pounds, and another two in the next ten days. His feverishness abated and his chest expanded. As he felt his strength returning he walked ever more vigorously and with increased enjoyment. When he returned to England at the end of July, his inexpensive holiday—the whole seven weeks cost only £31—had achieved a miracle. For whether owing to Ramadge's advice, or to his own extraordinary energy when on the brink of death, his consumption was arrested. There was talk, at the time, that his right lung had collapsed. It seems possible that he had by his exertions anticipated a modern treatment. Although he suffered periodically from other ailments, chiefly indigestion, his lungs gave no further dangerous trouble for the remainder of his life.

When the nights drew in and the time drew near for the promised winter excursion, which was meant to take them to the Isles of Greece, the glorious Acropolis, the sapphire Adriatic and the silver bays of the Aegean, it turned out that Harriet was not well enough to go. Mill, perhaps prompted by the success of his summer tour, the first he had undertaken singly since his visit to Sir Samuel Bentham over thirty years before, decided to carry on alone. So he took her to Torquay, where she rented a house and asked her mother and her sister Caroline to stay with her. Leaving her to winter in this safe though disputatious female company he returned to Blackheath, gathered up his bags, and set out the following day, 8 December 1854.

He was miserable at first. At Boulogne he was sick on the quay, and scarcely able to totter up the steps. On claiming his luggage in the customs shed, he found that his portmanteau had burst open, breaking one of his bottles of cod liver oil and spilling the invaluable fluid all over his neatly packed linen. Paris looked its very worst, dark, soaked, and uncomfortable, so he left at once for Bordeaux. He stared out gloomily from the windows of his first-class carriage, a rare luxury taken because of the new system of heating, so much better than anything he had experienced on English trains. He watched the French peasants scratching stolidly at their flat and soggy acres with square-headed hoes, and wondered they could ever make a living. He felt as though he were being whirled away from a safe haven into a void of uncertainty. He almost determined to take the next train back to Harriet.

It was not until he reached Montpellier, where he caught up with his earlier life, that he achieved a more cheerful frame of mind. "I walked out twelve kilometres on the road I best knew, being that which leads to the château formerly of the Benthams, but which has ceased to be theirs these twenty years or more—I found my recollections in no particular way inaccurate."[56] The inn was very good. The *table d'hôte* was the best he had ever tasted and the service quite exceptional. He was particularly pleased to find the library took the *Post* and not the *Times*.

From Montpellier he went on to Avignon, where he stayed over Christmas, no doubt again in the comfortable *Hôtel de l'Europe*. For what reason he could not properly tell, the old city of the schismatic Popes held a peculiar, an insidious fascination for him. He made the formal excursions to the *Pont du Gard*, where he scrambled about the galleries of the Roman aqueduct, and to the fountains in Petrarch's valley of Vaucluse, where the waters rumbling in the heart of a precipitous pine-clad mountain roar out in a torrent of indescribable commotion. Full of pleasure, he continued to Marseilles, from whence he crossed to Genoa.

At Rome in the middle of January, he found an old friend Frederic Lucas. A few years previously, Lucas with Gavan Duffy had formed the deputation inviting Mill to stand for Parliament in the Irish interest. He had recently become a Catholic, and was inseparable from his confessor, a Father Kyne; but as Mill found the latter "not disagreeable nor much in the way" they toured together through most of the appropriate collections and museums. Mill was duly impressed with the paintings and the sculptures. He visited the graves of Keats and Shelley. He went to Rossini's opera *La Cenerentola*. He even attended high mass in St. Peter's:

> "The music, which as usual was all vocal, gave me no pleasure—it was either the Gregorian chant or some of that very old church music which is much the same. When it was over I saw the procession pass out —the cardinals and bishops followed by the Pope * carried above the heads of the crowd in his chair, then the guardia nobile and the soldiers. I did not expect to find the Pope's features so entirely insignificant—he is not like an Italian. The Cardinals had all sorts of physiognomies, austere, sensual or bland, but almost all of them marked features of some sort."[57]

Gradually, his colourful occupations, coupled with the increasing strength which he attributed to the excellent local brewing of tea, his

* The reactionary Pius IX, who a few weeks earlier had pronounced the dogma of the Immaculate Conception.

sovereign anodyne, aroused creative turbulence in Mill. One day as he was climbing the steps of the Capitol, pondering upon the grand tyrants of the past and the more petty persecutions of the present, he suddenly saw how a short essay he had written the year before, on Liberty, could, and should, grow into a whole volume:

> "So many things might be brought into it and nothing seems more to be needed—it is a growing need too, for opinion tends to encroach more and more on liberty, and almost all the projects of social reformers of these days are really liberticide . . ."[58]

To his delight his counsellor agreed, and from that day forward the idea began to grow and to be fashioned in his mind:

> "We have got a power of which we must try to make a good use during the few years of life we have left. The more I think of the plan of a volume on Liberty, the more likely it seems to me that it will be read and will make a sensation. The title itself with any known name to it would sell an edition. We must cram into it as much as possible of what we wish not to leave unsaid."[59]

In Naples, the light-hearted gaiety of the streets infected him, and he was once again made drunk and drowsy by the natural beauty of the place. Deliberately, and as a pilgrimage, he repeated the excursions he had made with Harriet sixteen years before. He was horrified to find that an outbreak of official prudery had banished from the galleries many of their favourite works of art:

> "The precious King of Naples has shut up the Venus Callipyge and the other Venuses on pretext of public decency—the Pope too has done the same to the Venus of the Capitol. If these things are done in Italy what shall we come to next? I take it as a matter of course that the Venus de Medici will be under lock and key by the time we go to Florence."[60]

When he reached Palermo, he was aggravated by the intrusion of English residents. "O these English! The gossiping gossip hunting of English living idly at a place like this."[61] He resolved to make a tour of southern Sicily, a very rugged undertaking. He hired a muleteer and his two animals. They made a curious group as they set out. The soberly clad philosopher of nearly fifty, a copy of Theocritus and of Dante in his pocket, dangling his long legs against the flanks of his bony beast: the swarthy Sicilian following, driving the second mule piled high with books and baggage. Mill was not an experienced rider, and before they had gone far his enthusiasm began to wane. The roads were unspeakable; the rain drenching and continuous. The peculiar amble of his steed was worse than anything he had ever dreamed. A few miles, and he was in agony. A few more, and he was compelled to get down and stumble painfully on foot through all the puddles and the mud. After the midday halt he changed places with the guide, perching himself on top of the baggage as a cushion. He got little sleep at the inn where they stopped the night, on the hard boards covering a rickety trestle bed. He arose in the morning scarcely able to move, with the prospect of almost three weeks more of this excruciating form of travel still before him. But he consoled himself with the consideration that for a man apparently dying of consumption only six months previously, his performance was surely a good promise for the future. "It will", he asserted gamely to his wife, "be an incomparable excursion if only I am able to go on with it."[62]

Happily, his squire was capable of everything. He did all the foraging, and although the bread was yellow, hard and tasteless, the country milk was excellent. When they halted, he prepared the meals, while Mill busied himself with the enormous teapot produced like Benjamin's cup from the bottom of the saddle-bags. When Mill had to go to a local doctor about his thumb, infected by thorns acquired while botanizing, the fellow made up as a matter of course the prescribed poultice of lettuces and rice, and applied it with miraculous results.

Eventually the rains abated and Mill's fortitude increased. He began to make light of his discomforts. "Another flea hunt night and morning", he laconically recorded on 10 March: "this time there were rather fewer, and of these fewer escaped. I believe I brought them all from the last two places. I should not believe there were any here if it did not seem impossible that they should not be continually brought here. (N.B. in the middle of this sentence I stopt and caught one)." Indeed, he became so expert in his routine massacres that when the warmer weather brought out another kind of pest he was quite contemptuous of their lack of fight. "The mosquitoes here are remarkably stupid, for they let themselves be killed with scarcely an effort to save themselves. Perhaps however it is I who have become more dexterous, by practice in hunting a more nimble insect."[63]

All the same he was not sorry to reach Syracuse and civilization. With great good-will on both sides, and not a little relief on his, he paid off his equerry and patted the ironic looking mounts. In the boat which took him from Messina to Corfu, he lay flat on his back in the cabin and ruminated happily. "The pictures I have carried away from

Sicily are a perfect treasure of recollections for as much longer as I live . . . I *should* like to see them again with her. . . . *Living* in Sicily however I do not think would suit us. Perhaps Corfu would do better. We shall see."[64]

See he did. From the first he was enchanted with the island, a gem set in blue seas under a dazzling sun. The Colonial Secretary for the Ionian Islands, Bowen, quickly learned of his arrival and invited him to breakfast. Bowen was a Fellow of Brasenose, an erudite author and a great admirer of Mill's *Logic*. Upon Mill revealing the idea he had in mind, he became enthusiastic. He said it had often surprised him that so few English people settled in Corfu. Living was cheaper by half than it was in England; his predecessor, who had a sizeable family, had kept a carriage and several horses on his salary of £500 a year. He added that the Residency either of Zante or of Cephalonia would fall vacant within a year, and was sure that Mill could have the appointment for the asking. He would get a house in town and country: and, between themselves, the work would not take more than two hours a day.

Bowen insisted on introducing Mill to the High Commissioner at once, and haled him off to the garrison library, where they found his Excellency reading the English papers. It happened that his tour of duty ended the next day, and as his successor, who duly arrived to a salute of guns, proved to be a man whose father Mill had known at the India House, Mill was invited to dinner that same evening at the Palace. One way and another, he was out to dinner almost every evening for the next few days, and they all put heavy pressure on him to accept the post. He very strongly inclined towards the golden offer, but the climate was too variable. As Harriet explained to her brother Arthur Hardy in Australia, "tho' much tempted I do not think we shall accept it, we both dread the heat which is said to be excessive in the summer."[65]

The Greece of the ancients had always been Mill's intellectual heaven. From reading he was familiar with the country; in imagination he had experienced every incident in its long history. So now when he at last approached Greek territory he came in genuine reverence, though fully aware that the glory had long since departed. He first gazed in admiration at the Parthenon and the Acropolis. Then, with a young Irishman he had picked up in Corfu, a fellow botanist, he climbed Pentelicus. As always when he was on mountain tops, everything else was driven from his mind by "the more than earthly beauty". On the way down they collected plants by the armful, so many that they were hard put to it to carry them, and Mill was busy drying, examining and sorting them far into the night.

The hills were honeycombed with brigands' lairs, and he had to reassure Harriet he would not repeat his Sicilian odyssey without the advice of the British ambassador, Sir Thomas Wyse, to whom he had an introduction. "You might well say", he teased her, "that some other person's savoir faire was wanted 'in addition' to mine—I could not help laughing when I read those words, as if I had any savoir faire at all."[66] However, Wyse informed him, with the assent of the French minister who was with him at the time, that the brigands designed to be a political rather than a criminal embarrassment, and therefore did not usually molest travellers, though they thought nothing of burning and plundering whole villages.

So he set out to explore the northern hinterland with a guide, and yet another young man, this time from Cumberland. "We form quite a caravan, having four horses and two mules, three for ourselves and the guide, three for luggage and utensils, beds, provisions etc. also three muleteers and a cook: all this being provided for the 25 francs a day we each pay, which also includes the remuneration of the guide. . . . My travelling companion Dawson is pleasant mannered and seems desirous of information but very little educated and even leaves out many an *h*—which one would not have expected from his appearance or the tones of his voice, or his general manner of expressing himself."[67] In the fierce and desolate mountains round Thermopylae they came into bandit country, and on presenting the letters they had from Sir Thomas Wyse were given the armed escort a dozen strong to which they were by law entitled. These, deploying anxiously but without incident, brought them safely through the famous pass, past Delphi and Parnassus, all of which Mill found below his expectations, until they came in easy range once more of Athens, where they arrived on 15 May.

Three days later he was off again, this time towards the south, and alone save for the guide, which was the mode he really best preferred. In Sparta he found he was expected to call upon a native judge, who made a practice of entertaining every traveller who came within his jurisdiction:

> "I went and found a house externally very like the barns I am usually lodged in, but internally with an approach to civilization: it is true that the floor of the principal room was boarded very like a hay loft, but there

were chairs or something like them, and two sofas which bore marks of having been slept on. Few Greeks sleep in a bed; a carpet or rug on the floor is their only couch, and even in the well-to-do houses in the villages and country towns not more than a couple of wooden stools to sit on, with boards round part of the room in the Turkish fashion, spread with some sort of cloths or carpets. The judge was at his court, but came at once on being sent for—casas de Grecia! I was entertained by his young ugly wife, his old strong looking careworn looking mother, and his seven or eight years old daughter by name Calliope, to hear which name cried about the house was very odd: I could exchange very little discourse with them, but they handed me, first, a long wooden tobacco pipe as tall as myself—I contrived to inform them that I did not smoke—then a tray with a glass of very nice sweetmeat, a glass of water, and a stand with about twenty spoons that I might take as many spoonfuls successively as I liked—twenty apparently silver spoons being I suppose thought a better arrangement than one plate. After this came the usual little china cup of café noir which is the common Greek civility and is what a Greek gives to anybody at a café: as an American gives a 'sherry cobbler', so a Greek gives a coffee, which being never strained and being served boiling hot, is always thick and the lower half undrinkable: this however being at a private house was better. The judge, Mr. Phangara, presently appeared—he spoke French pretty well, better indeed than he understood it when spoken. He is a pleasant mannered man, and seems to delight in the excitement of having foreigners in his house."[68]

The Spartan life was obviously good for Mill. His spirits were terrific, and he was eating, for him, enormously:

"I have been very well today, and have found out how to manage myself. I now have cutlets or chicken and potatoes for breakfast, without any bread—replacing bread and butter by rice either slighly au gras which they here call pillafe, or boiled into a solid mass with milk. With this I drink tea, often without sugar or milk. . . . Instead of being barely ready for dinner when I arrive at night, I am now hungry early, and when we stop about midday for the horses and men to eat, I eat a hard egg, and with a lemon which the guide takes with him and the fine mountain water of these regions he makes me some lemonade which, by means of a bottle of carbonate of potass. I convert into a delicious effervescing draught—the gas penetrates one's whole body, and the effect is like a slight intoxication by champagne and lasts several hours. The dinner lately is soup, chicken, and stewed prunes, and agrees with me perfectly. I get always stronger, and shall be an excellent traveller by the time I leave off travelling."[69]

For all his boasting, he soon decided he had had enough. With scarcely more than a passing nod for Zeus and the athletes of Olympia he hastened to the coast. Once back in Italy, he set out hot foot for Paris where, he had just learnt, Harriet was proposing to go and meet him. But being diverted from Bologna by reports of insurrection on the way, he found himself in Florence, and his homeward steps became less rapid. Since he was there, he reasoned it would be a pity not to see it, as he might never have another chance. And anxious though he was to be reunited to his "darling beauty", his months of independence seemed to have been somehow strangely sweet. His cough grew bad again; bad enough to hold him up, yet not so bad as to hinder him from seeing briefly all there was to see in Florence. He was utterly beguiled, not by the place itself, which he thought ugly and tasteless, but by its immense riches in paintings and in statues, sufficient to bring back the feeling Rome had given him of being bathed in art. The Venus de Medici had not, as he had feared, been locked up for indecency; as soon as he saw her he knew why:

> ". . . decidedly I do not like her. . . . Of course she is a beautifully formed woman, but the head is too *too* ridiculously small, as if to give the *idea* of having no room for brains—and they may well say she does not look immodest, for the expression of the face is complete old maidism."[70]

The woman of the place not coming up to expectations, Mill turned to other sources of amusement. He sought out his correspondent, Pasquale Villari, the historical philosopher. He found him a small dark vital Neapolitan nearly twenty years his junior, quick and highly stimulating: they walked and talked all afternoon till the fireflies came out, and then took tea together. One way and another, Mill tarried longer than he should at Florence. He began to have morbid doubts of Harriet's reception. Fearing her impatience, he hurried northward by Verona and Milan. In his haste he lost his indispensable tin box for collecting plants. He hated losing things, perhaps because of the fatal watch he once lost years ago: he bolstered himself by giving an account of his possessions:

> "I have lost nothing else of consequence in this journey—nothing beyond a pocket handkerchief which I lost on Pentelicus and an old shirt which must have been kept by some blanchisseuse—though I hardly ever failed to count the things and compare them with the note."[71]

To save time he decided to press straight on over the St. Gothard, although he knew the summit was still deep in snow, and would have to be traversed by sleigh. When he reached it, he found to his concern that the sledges were little things, entirely open, taking only two persons at a time. As the rain was soaking and perpetual he dared not risk the effect upon his cough, and choosing the lesser of two evils, he wasted another day. He therefore felt a little sheepish when he greeted Harriet in Paris on 22 June 1855.

IV

In his absence, Harriet's little house at Torquay had been anything but the intended nest of snug repose and family affection; on the contrary, it had been a minor bedlam of conflicting temperaments. Caroline and her mother, who had for some time past been living together, had bred between them a private understanding to the exclusion of the more independent sister. Within a fortnight, the Christmas harmony was shattered. Mill, from the safe distance of Montpellier, sided with his wife:

> "When you are for any time with the grand' mère your feelings and conscience are always revolted and nerves set on edge. You have said the truest of words—always dupe de votre cœur—you thought she felt *declining* and had the natural wish to give what she would feel agreeable, but you are not physically fit for that now—and why should you throw yourself away on one for whom Caroline is not only good enough but pleasanter to her than you?"[72]

Before long the old dispute over Caroline's husband and Harriet's marriage settlement came up again. All earlier efforts to dislodge Arthur Ley from his position as trustee had failed; and now the other trustee, William Thornton, Mill's staunch, reliable colleague at the India House, fell seriously ill. If he were to die, the whole of Harriet's money and the interests of her children would pass into Ley's hands. Hearing that Ley's brutality to Caroline had reached the physical plane, Harriet appealed to her to help get rid of him. Unaccountably, Caroline refused, and even intimated that her husband was a better guardian of the children's interests than was Harriet herself. Ley declared he would not resign without written instructions from Herbert who, since Mill, true to his promise, would have nothing to do with Harriet's property, managed all his mother's business. Herbert declined, according to Harriet, at Caroline's instigation, because although he had "showed throughout that he cared nothing about the matter itself, he would not lose the opportunity offered by Caroline of opposing me and his brother and sister".[73]

Mill arrived back in the middle of this painful and intricate situation. While thinking it most unfit that Ley should continue as trustee, he found that there was nothing he could do, except to have a distringas laid upon the stock so that it could not be transferred without due notice. This was done, but the rift continued. Although the Hardys, being a less sensitive if more tempestuous family than the Mills, did not carry out an absolute break, Harriet does not appear ever to have seen her mother or Caroline again. The only relieving feature was the respect and fondness accorded to Mill by all of them. That was most evident in Harriet's last letter from her mother, written just after Mill's retirement from the India House, when he had refused a place on the reconstituted board on grounds of health:

> "I was glad to see that Mr. Mill had received such a flattering testimonial to his talents and zeal. I regretted to see the reason given for his refusing the seat offered him. I hope his health is not seriously impaired. If change of air were needful to him, I hope I need not say how glad I should be to see him as my guest. Pray give my love to him and tell him so. I know it would be in vain to ask you—you have not enough interest in me to visit me."[74]

In the summer of 1855, Helen in her turn began to show symptoms of consumption. Harriet took her to see Ramadge, who was far from satisfied; but after Christmas she recovered, gradually and permanently. By the summer of 1856 Mill was at last able to tear himself away from the India House, and as they were all for once in a reasonable state of health, they set out for Geneva. There they were joined by Haji who, after a short-lived effort to become a farmer, had given it up and was now a temporary inmate of a monastery in Rome. After a pleasant six weeks Harriet and the rest went back to Paris, but Mill, who was still at the top of his form, could not resist a week's climbing in the French Jura. He met the others at Boulogne for the journey home.

With her own health more or less restored, and with her parents in an unusually prosperous way, Helen Taylor felt that the time had come when she might reasonably hope to achieve some degree of independence for herself. She was now twenty-five, and in all her life had scarcely left her mother's side for more than a day. From childhood she had exercised her emotions privately in elaborate games of make-believe. When she was fifteen, and wandering about in churches and cathedrals, little snatches of Shakespeare were always running in her head. " 'Is this a chapel which I see' . . . I am incessantly quoting Shakespeare",[75] she said to herself. Early in 1856 she wrote to the actress Fanny Stirling, asking whether she might take lessons from her. She was asked to call, and from that moment began one of the warmest friendships of her life. Fanny was a hard-working, affectionate and modest creature; she was touched by the depth of Helen's enthusiasm, and being also impressed by her quite untutored talent, decided to do her best to help her. Helen for her part was entirely swept away; she confessed to Haji that she had even thought of going with Fanny to tour America, though because of her mother's illness "that plan will not come to anything yet awhile if indeed it ever does, for I should not like to leave my precious darling for so long and be so far away from her."[76]

Soon after they got back from Switzerland, Helen broached the subject to her mother. Quite understandably, Harriet strenuously demurred. For all that she had written about the professional equality of women, she had a prudish horror of the repertory stage; and since families are always last to recognize a talent, she had a dread that Helen would make a fool of them in public. Besides, at Blackheath, Helen supervised the housekeeping. Harriet could not do without her. And Helen's practical services apart, they were so emotionally interlocked that they might well have been twins.

Helen managed to get permission for Fanny to come and call. From the first, Fanny was charmed and enslaved by Harriet, while Harriet liked her for her unassuming gratitude and for her warmth of feeling towards Helen. A bond of union was struck. Once, while Mill was away on a walking tour, Fanny went to stay at Blackheath, and Harriet gave her the ultimate privilege of reading a letter she had had from Mr. Mill. Fanny worshipped Mr. Mill. At the time of his retirement from the India House, she wrote to Harriet: "It has been a pleasure to see Mr. Mill so spoken of lately. I have felt how your eyes would brighten—the sight of his name carries me to a certain home at Blackheath that seems to me to combine oh! so much! strength—elegance—poetry—comfort (not too poetical to stuff your ducks!!!)—can God understand that I look at what seems such happiness with envy."[77]

Indeed, Fanny and Harriet got on so well it began to seem that Helen might be free. "Helen—who should be the object of interest between us, and whom I believe we both love tho' differently—is I fancy rather a stumbling block", observed Fanny, "for I am always fancying you may feel that but for me this passion of hers might die a natural death."[78] It showed no sign of doing so, and eventually it was agreed that she should have her way. To avoid notoriety, she would always be known as "Miss Trevor": no one should ever know where she was or what she was doing. In order to conceal her whereabouts, Helen was to send her letters to Mill at the India House, and Harriet was to reply in envelopes preaddressed by Helen. The secrecy was intense. On one occasion Harriet dissuaded Fanny from visiting her at Blackheath because she supposed that Fanny could not speak French, and therefore that the servants would overhear every word they said. As for Helen's physical and moral safety, a "decent middle aged person" would be found by Fanny to look after her without knowing who she was.

And so, on 21 November 1856, "Miss Trevor" set out for Newcastle escorted by her brother Haji. The pangs of parting were severe. Even before her cab reached Euston, Helen had written once, and a second time before her train rumbled into Peterborough. At first she was all for coming home again, or else for having Harriet with her on her travels. But Harriet soon became resigned to the *fait accompli*:

> "I shall calm down by degrees—I feel clearly this dearest girl that deeply as I feel and thank you for the offer of sacrifice you make your happiness only must be considered and if you are happy I shall I hope become so in time. I must be with you sometimes, I hope often, but generally or always as you propose that I could not do—I could not leave alone my one generous firm unchanging friend and that when his health is not strong, for any other motive than your health."[79]

Helen quickly settled down, changed her lodgings at 15*s.* a week for the more professional 5*s.* quarters, and learnt that she could not after all play Lady Macbeth for a year or two. Harriet plied her with advice. She sent voluminous costumes by the boxful: about money she was generous—"I did not answer what you said in one letter about money dear—I always feel that all we have is in common and you are to have and use whatever you like—we have always been perfectly one about that darling."[80]

At last the great day came, when Helen was Jane Shore ("it is a very theatrical part—I have got to scream, to faint, and to die on the stage"). She was a queen. "I wore the velvet gown low at the neck and with short sleeves. The jet coronet with the large black veil, my hair as I wear it best at home; the jet girdle, the little ruby cross you gave me at Boulogne, the Genoa gold bracelet on one arm and the garnet bracelet on the other."[81]—"What a beautiful bracelet,—those are real garnets", cooed all the other girls. How Harriet's face shone as she read to Mill the plain and diffident account, exactly confirmed by Haji in a separate letter, of how the audience warmly clapped "Miss Trevor" on her first appearance, and still applauded at the final curtain, despite her almost inaudible voice, her cold declamatory tone and manner. Of how the whole troupe gathered in the wings around the flushing débutante and asked her how she felt:

> "That notion they all have that you must of course be frightened shows what a low class they generally are connected with theatres, as no well bred young lady would show any, or feel much trepidation on such an occasion and I was sure you would not."[82]

How angry she was, after this, when there were for a time no parts for Helen. How she raged, when they asked her daughter to be a singing fairy in the pantomime. And how she tried to soothe the outraged feelings. "Do not feel disappointed dear one—you are tired and overdone, it will take a turn and go better before long no doubt. . . . All day I have kept repeating Oh my dearest girl you must not you shall not be disappointed. Keep up your spirits my darling for my sake, you cannot yourself be more interested in succeeding than I am for you. There is *nothing* I would not do to help you . . ."[83]

For the first month or two it was not possible for Harriet to go north. Mill, at the India House, she found, was especially busy with the Indian Mutiny; and as he had terrible pains in the head, she would not leave him. They all spent Christmas down in Brighton, and afterwards Helen took a part offered to her in Glasgow. Early in February Mill's headaches got so bad that the Chairman ordered him to take a few days off, and he was able to accompany Harriet as far as Edinburgh, returning to Blackheath while she went on to Glasgow. Her visit was not much of a success: she waited endlessly in her rooms for Helen, whose rehearsals very often kept her late. After a week she was ill again, and so was Helen; but Harriet was so afraid of being discovered in the city where her daughter had been acting, that she refused Mill's earnest entreaties to be allowed to come and join her.

Instead, at risk of her life, she got up and moved to Edinburgh. That settled it. Mill went and brought her home, and packed her off again to Brighton.

She made a good recovery. In September 1857 they took a belated summer holiday. Mill spent it striding about the Lake District; while Harriet and Helen, once more with a gap in her engagements, wandered disconsolately between Blackpool and Leamington Spa. Next year, Harriet remained at Blackheath, and sent her husband to spend his July week in the Derbyshire Peaks, with her maternal blessing:

> "Tuesday morning—I have just got your dear letter and shall send this and my last night's scrap to Bakewell. I hope you will get among wilder country—Matlock seems fitter for an excursion together at some future time. I was very poorly yesterday partly [because] the sudden heat was very exhausting. . . . I am so glad to hear you have got some plants—Oh, I do so hope you will have pleasant scrambles and stay out as *long as possible* and then come home perceptibly better for the change and the fresh air.
>
> Your note to Mr. Bumpus went yesterday and the good little book came this morning. Adieu my dearest love and just as I say so comes out the bright sun as if to say yes to it all."[84]

V

During these years, the mismanagement of the Crimean war and the alliance with the hated Emperor of France disgusted Mill so much that he took no part in public affairs. He could not have done so had he wished, for his office duties kept him fully occupied. In March 1856 his two superiors, Hill and Peacock, both retired, and he became Chief Examiner. It was the post his father had held before him, carrying with it the responsibility of a Secretary of State. At the same time his friend Thornton, whose appointment as his assistant he had made the condition of his own promotion, was seriously ill. In order to avoid his compulsory resignation, Mill undertook all his work for a whole year in addition to his own. Then, early in 1857, came the first rumblings of the Indian Mutiny. His jump in salary from £1400 to £2000 was more than offset by the increase in his labours, and he had less time to spare for his casual visitors, for Bain, or for the ever-welcome rat-tat of Grote's walking-stick upon his door.

The Mutiny tolled the bell upon the old East India Company. There had long been a bitterness among the commercial interests at the back of the Whig party against the exclusive privileges it enjoyed. Piece by piece they had been worn away, and when the Company's charter came up for renewal in 1833, an assault was launched against the last of them, the monopoly in the China Tea Trade. On that occasion it had fallen on James Mill to make a stout defence under many searching inquisitions before a Select Committee of the House of Commons. Largely owing to his fire and masterly knowledge, the charter was renewed. The Company retained the government but lost the China Tea, and was left in proud if pyrrhic possession of responsibility without any special advantages, except what it was able to derive by virtue of prestige.

There had also been a feeling, steadily growing, that the rule over so vast a territory, with its unnumbered millions of human lives, was too great a matter to be left in the hands of a private organization. That the machinery, the weightiest of its kind in history, including a complete colonial service and a sizeable naval and military establishment, was cumbersome, fortuitous and obsolete. The Mutiny brought the feeling to a head. Palmerston bowed to the pressure put upon him. At the end of 1857 an Act for the Better Government of India was introduced. The Company was to be swept away. A Secretary of State was to be appointed, with an advisory board of fifteen experts in Indian administration. And the Queen was eventually to adopt the imperial title. In short, India was to be nationalized.

It was fitting at this final crisis that John Mill was sitting at his father's desk. That is not to say that in defending the East India Company they either of them acted simply out of loyalty to a concern whose fee they pocketed although its aims and objects were alien to their own. On the contrary, they were convinced that in India, as in primitive communities of the ancient world, despotism was the only possible system for the time, and in this sense they believed the Company to be unrivalled. They had faith in its record of systematic expansion, of slow and steady enlightenment, and in its long tradition of loyal service. Dangerous radicals as they were as far as Europe was concerned, for India they were more tory than the Tories. If they had lived in India all their lives, they could not have had a greater dread of doctrinaire and headlong policies.

In John Mill's case, his objection to the new proposals had a deeper philosophic root. He had a strong aversion to the Whig passion for making dominion governments directly dependent on the English Parliament, as he had shown in the case of Canada. As he later wrote in his *Representative Government*:

> "The government of a people by itself has a meaning and a reality; but such a thing as government of one people by another does not and cannot exist. . . . It is not by attempting to rule directly a country like India, but by giving it good rulers, that the English people can do their duty to that country; and they can scarcely give it a worse one than an English Cabinet Minister, who is thinking of English, not Indian politics. . . . The only mode which has any chance of tolerable success is to govern through a delegated body of a comparatively permanent character. . . . Such a body did exist in the case of India; and I fear that both India and England will pay a severe penalty for the short-sighted policy by which this intermediate instrument of government was done away with."[85]

He therefore willingly set to work to draw up the petition against the bill which was to be presented in Parliament on behalf of the Company. He traced the achievements of the Company in the past; how they had consolidated a magnificent empire in the east at the very time when the government were losing one in the west, and had ruled it in the intervening hundred years without costing a penny to the English taxpayer. He challenged a full enquiry into the causes of the mutiny, emphasizing that the control already held by the government over the actions of the Company entitled them to any blame there was. He sketched the ominous effects to be produced upon the Indian mind by the arrival, at a time of turbulence, of a new administration backed by an overwhelming military force. He remarked that the new advisory council must be wholly independent of the minister. And he pointed out that the former double government by means of a home department provided a valuable deliberative check on the executive, similar to the part played by the House of Lords. Lord Grey, when he first saw it, said it was the ablest state-paper he had ever read.*

* 3rd Earl (1802–1894). Son of Lord Grey of the Reform Bill, and the great Colonial Secretary in Lord John Russell's cabinet 1846–1852. In his youth he was a member of Mill's Debating Society, and as an elder statesman an occasional correspondent.

The Directors, too, were very pleased with it. Being themselves of a pragmatic rather than a philosophic turn of mind, they were surprised to find how much theoretic eloquence could be brought to the support of what they secretly knew to be a rather hopeless case. When the stockholders of the Company met to dot the i's and cross the t's of Mill's fortunate appoggiatura, William Thornton could scarcely believe his ears when one of them blandly spoke of it as having been written by a certain other official who was sitting by his side, "adding after a moment's pause, 'with the assistance, as he understood, of Mr. Mill'."

> "As soon as the Court broke up, I burst into Mill's room, boiling over with indignation, and exclaiming 'What an infamous shame!' and no doubt adding a good deal more . . .
>
> 'What's the matter?' replied Mill, as soon as he could get a word in, 'M— (the Director) was quite right. The petition was the joint work of Hobson and myself.'*
>
> 'How can you be so perverse?' I retorted. 'You know that you wrote every word of it.'
>
> 'No', rejoined Mill, 'you are mistaken: one whole line on the second page was put in by Hobson.' "[86]

As it happened, Palmerston's government was turned out over the Conspiracy to Murder Bill before the India Bill was passed, and Lord Derby's more accommodating cabinet, while carrying it through, adopted many of Mill's suggestions.† He was the first to be invited by the new Secretary of State to take a seat on the advisory council, but he declined. Although from conviction he had done his best to save the Company, for his own sake he would have been less glad than sorry if he had succeeded. As it was, he took the opportunity of retiring with full honours and a handsome pension of £1500, which unless his health had given way again, he could not otherwise have done until he became sixty in another eight years time. His earlier decision to carry on had proved well worth while, and all seemed to be happening for the best.

No sooner was his resolution made known, than Thornton made a suggestion leading to a curious episode in their friendship:

* Hobson—name fictitious.

† Conspiracy to Murder Bill—a Bill permitting the arrest and punishment of those who conspired in England against the life of foreign princes. It was introduced at the demand of the French Government following the failure of Orsini's plot against Napoleon III. Mill, writing to Pasquale Villari, described it as "the miserable attempt of Palmerston to drag the British nation in the mud by making it the annex of the French police".

"Talking over that one day with two or three of my colleagues, I said it would not do to let Mill go without receiving some permanently visible token of our regard. The motion was no sooner made than it was carried by acclamation. Every member of the Examiner's office—for we jealously insisted on confining the affair to ourselves—came tendering his subscription, scarcely waiting to be asked; in half-an-hour's time some £50 or £60—I forget the exact sum—was collected, which in due course was invested in a superb silver inkstand, designed by our friend Digby Wyatt, and manufactured by Messrs. Elkington.

Before it was ready, however, an unexpected trouble arose. In some way or other Mill had got wind of our proceeding, and, coming to me in consequence, began almost to upbraid me as its originator. I had never before seen him so angry. He hated all such demonstrations, he said, and was quite resolved not to be made the subject of them. He was sure they were never altogether genuine or spontaneous. There were always several persons who took part in them, merely because they did not like to refuse—and in short, whatever we might do, he would have none of it.

In vain I represented how eagerly everybody, without exception, had come forward; that we had gone too far to recede; that if he would not take the inkstand we should be utterly at a loss what to do with it, and that I myself should be in a specially embarrassing position. Mill was not to be moved. This was a question of principle, and on principle he could not give way.

There was nothing left, therefore, but resort to a species of force. I arranged with Messrs. Elkington that our little testimonial should be taken down to Mrs. Mill's house at Blackheath by one of their men, who, after leaving it with the servant, should hurry away without waiting for an answer."[87]

This plan succeeded, and on later visits Thornton found the inkstand unobtrusively established in the drawing-room; but whether it was by feminine intervention he could not tell, for it was never spoken of again.

VI

Towards the end of 1858, Mill and Harriet were free at last. Financially, they were assured for life. Their health, apparently, was better than it had been for years, better than they had so recently expected it could ever be. They had no family ties. The young were fairly launched—not, certainly, exactly as they would have chosen, since one was on the stage, another in a monastery, and the third in business—but none the less they were self-determined and, comparatively speaking, settled. At last, after twenty-eight years, they were free to write their books, free to visit openly together all the places Mill in his loneliness had carefully marked down.

They resolved to take their time. They would go to Montpellier, then on to Hyères for a leisurely winter in memory of bad times past. After that, who knew? Italy, Greece? One year, two years, or for ever? The Ionian sea was beckoning them with its blazing terraces and sapphire waves. Impatiently, without waiting for Mill's notice to expire at Christmas, they shook away the damp October mists of England.

Helen came down from Aberdeen to see them off. When their train drew out of London, she went to watch Fanny Stirling in the *première* of Wilkie Collins' drama, *The Red Vial*. The play was a wretched failure. Afterwards, she went to stay at Fanny's house in Brook Street. They drank a glass of wine as Mill and Harriet crossed the Channel, and wished them safe return.

Travelling always did Harriet good, and at Paris all was well. They drove about in a carriage all one day. In the Bois de Boulogne, under the bronze leaves of the chestnuts, Harriet showed Mill the new alterations, to his pleasure. In the town, the ladies in their brown and yellow *modes* looked very gay. They dined at the *Frères Provençaux*, where Harriet learned a new dish, oysters steamed with Parmesan—"very good if you had been there to share it",[88] she told Helen. Over everything there was a soft autumnal glow.

They went on to Dijon, Mill making the arrangements still with his customary lack of *savoir faire*. "The fact is", Harriet told her daughter, "we always get the last seats in the railway carriage, as I cannot run on quick, and if he goes on he never succeeds, I always find him running up and down and looking lost in astonishment, so I have given up trying to get any seats but those that are left."[89] Everything was normal. Helen sighed with relief, and returned to Aberdeen.

At Lyons, Harriet had a cough, with fever, the usual kind of thing. They delayed a week and then pressed on, for they had to get to the south. They took precautions. A chair was fetched, and porters, to carry her into the station. At Valence they took a private *coupé*. But it had been too much—the hissing of steam, the clanging bells, the chilly glare of the gas lamps, the interminable waiting-rooms and the slippery platforms—she arrived at Avignon in a state of collapse. And so at last they came together to Avignon. They went to the inn, the comfortable inn, and one of the best in France. They had the best rooms. Yet the floors of red tiles with their thin carpets over could not keep out the draught, not all the coming and going of chambermaids with footstools could keep the cold away. She could not sleep, if she lay down she could not breathe, so she spent the time propped in a chair, her low voice stilled, her great dark eyes staring out between the pillows. The first day she wrote to Helen that she was better, that the worst was over. The local doctors came, but their drugs were too mild; she concocted some she was accustomed to, from the store she carried with her. The second day Mill was alarmed, and wrote, but only wrote, to the doctor in Nice who had saved her life before:

"Avignon Oct. 28 1858

Dear Dr. Gurney,

My wife is lying at the Hotel de l'Europe here so very ill that neither she nor I have any hope but in you to save her. It is a quite sudden attack which came on at Lyons, of incessant coughing which prevents sleeping, and by the exhaustion it produces has brought her to death's door. I implore you to come immediately. I need hardly say that any expense whatever will not count for a feather in the balance.

I am dear Dr. Gurney
very truly yours
J. S. Mill."[90]

Next day she rallied, and Mill at her direction wrote to Helen to say again the worst was over and she was not to think of coming, because "it wd be a very great pity to break your good arrangements which are a great pleasure to her to hear of". Another day passed, and another, and then on 1 November "Miss Trevor" received a telegram which read:

> "She is not better or perhaps worse have written to beg Dr. G to come."[91]

The next day she seemed better, she had to be better, they had to get on to Montpellier, they had so much to do. But still the doctor did not come and did not come, and day and night now made no difference, but her coughing was quieter and her spirit still, and then suddenly another paroxysm, a little gasp, and the beautiful dominant genius lay dead in the face of her uncomprehending lover.

BOOK SEVEN

THE SAINT OF RATIONALISM

1858–1873
aet. *52–66*

I

OUTSIDE the old walls of the city of Avignon, about a mile to the south-east, lies the town cemetery of St. Véran, in a flat unprofitable region of the dead. It is a crowded acre surrounded by a high wall, full of exorbitant monuments to grief and family pride. But in Provence the soil and sun are fruitful. High rows of cypresses along the wall give privacy. Flowering trees and shrubs break up the ranks of the dear departed. And in the dusk of summer evenings, nightingales abound.

Here Harriet was buried. As the earth went thundering down upon her coffin, it seemed to Mill as if he were being crushed. For a whole long day he had been alone with the body of his wife, a day of procession in garish clarity of stark unthinkable events. Greyly, he had recalled that she had left instructions what to do in an emergency. He had groped vaguely for her note:

> "Will you dear remember this memorandum—If I sh*d*. be some night taken so ill as to be unable to speak, or even to die suddenly you know I cannot bear that the servants sh*d*. get to my papers and I shall therefore from to-night always leave all places locked and put away my keys on the hook behind the window curtain thus they wd. not be found until you came."[1]

Somehow, he had managed to write a formal note to the Mayor of Avignon, enclosing a thousand francs for the community poor, reminding himself savagely in writing it, that his beloved wife, Harriet Mill, née Hardy, had died at Avignon on 3 November 1858. "It is doubtful if I shall ever be fit for anything public or private again", he wrote to Thornton when sending the miserable notice for the *Times*. "The spring of my life is broken."[2]

Then Helen had arrived. She had left Aberdeen the moment she got the wire. As soon as she reached Avignon, she had written to her brother:

> "Dear Haji—it is all over—but I too was too late too late too late. He cannot write he suffers so dreadfully—he was twenty-four hours all alone—I must try to take care of him now. He tells me to say there was a change for the better when he wrote to you and afterwards it was so sudden writing was out of the question. *All* will be over when you get this—there is no possibility of delaying things more. He means to go to England almost immediately and quickly but we shall certainly return here for a time at all events before very long—I shall at least for I must go with him. He says there is no necessity of a business kind for you to come to England but if you do you will probably find us at home. Direct to us at home. I cannot write dear—I am utterly stupefied by the blow.
>
> Your wretched sister."[3]

Mill was still a man to dominate his circumstances. Any emotion he could not express was always capable of rational conversion. In the face of utter desolation, action began where inclination failed. For him, as for Helen, there could be no possibility of giving in. It was a question of continuing in a dedicated key.

His first care was the laying out of his little fortune, so arduously gained and now so valueless. As if extravagance were in itself a comfort, he sent money upon money to the Mayor, and to the pastor of the Protestant Church. Although the number admitted to any degree of intimacy with him in Avignon was to be negligible: although to the peasantry he was to appear a solemn and mysterious recluse known variously as "M. Émile", "Maister Lord", or simply as "l'Anglais", he was determined to make up as best he could the treasure the community had lost in Harriet. Dr. Gurney, who had taken a week to come the hundred and fifty miles from Nice, and had arrived too late for everything except the funeral, was persuaded to accept a fee of £1000, the sum a leading specialist had received for going from London to Nice to save a patient.

Soon another prospect dawned, causing him to delay his immediate desire to return to Blackheath. Near the cemetery, separated only by one or two green fields, there was a small white house, the *Hermitage de Monloisier*. During the revolution, it had been seized from the nuns of Sainte-Praxède and sold by the Convention, since when it had been used by a member of the *Académie de Vaucluse* as a week-end villa. It was a small square building with a tiled roof and green Venetian shutters. It had only five small rooms. It was approached from an almost unused road by an avenue of tall sycamores and mulberry trees, ending in a kind of road-screen made of hornbeams. Behind this lay some flower beds, then the house, with a trellis hidden by wisteria. At the back there was a garden, and beyond, a thick dark spinney full of nightingales. From the upstairs windows, looking towards the north, it was possible to see into the graveyard. Within three weeks Mill had bought it, and, according to Maurice Barrès, had installed in it the furniture from the room in the *Hôtel de l'Europe* where Harriet had died. He then went home with Helen to an atmosphere of less harrowing memories.

II

On 30 November 1858 he wrote on heavy mourning paper to his publisher, J. W. Parker:

> "You can have my little book 'On Liberty' for publication this season. The manuscript is ready; but you will probably desire to look through it, or to have it looked through, by someone in whom you confide, as there are some things in it which may give offence to prejudices.
>
> Should you decide to publish it, I propose that we should make the same arrangement as we made for the *Political Economy*, viz: to publish one edition at half profit, and if another is called for, make a fresh agreement respecting it."[4]

It had, as a matter of fact, been ready eighteen months. It had been written and rewritten, every word had been discussed and weighed. It had been kept on hand, luxuriously awaiting any amendment that some day might seem desirable. Now Harriet was dead, that was no longer a possibility; both Mill and Helen affirm that in this book especially the ideas were mostly hers; and since her voice was silent, no one else would be allowed to alter it.

Although Mill called *On Liberty* "a kind of philosophic textbook of a single truth", it was really more of a hymn or incantation. It was intended rather to excite than to persuade. There were a dozen other names he might have given it, but he deliberately chose the one among all others which in every age has most surely caused men to perform intellectual somersaults. The essay was, in genesis, Harriet's early paper on "Toleration", elaborated in her lifetime, dressed in Mill's most graceful prose, and authorized from the depths of his sage majestic knowledge. But of course that was not all. It was intended as the consummation of their life together, a joint statement of the values to be borne in mind while urging the onward progress of mankind towards perfection. Mill added to it his entire personality. It knitted up the nebulous aspirations running through his works, and proclaimed the unity underlying all his thought. Its roots ran back through the solid ground of Anglo-Saxon Puritanism, to draw their nourishment from the distinctive feature of Christian civilization, the power and importance of personal identity. The pulse of the book invoked Mill's constant ideal of human intercourse, an Athenian society tempered by the Socratic frame of mind.

Liberty, seen through the medium of one so purposely eclectic, necessarily became the confluent of many streams of thought. Specifically, the sturdy eighteenth-century view of society as a lubricant to completely fashioned entities continually in friction, was the undercurrent of the work. "That so few now dare to be eccentric, marks the chief danger of the time"[5]—the challenging assertion was Mill's final tribute to the Bentham brothers. His father's psychology, giving a sealed validity to individual experience, led to a sweeping limitation of the sphere of government. "The only purpose for which power can be rightfully exercised over any member of a civilized community, against his will, is to prevent harm to others. His own good, either physical or moral, is not a sufficient warrant."

Superimposed on downright individualism came the more complex, mystical theories of the nineteenth century. The revolt from the completeness of limited men, from the stultifying effort to resolve in puny terms the transcendental motives of the universe, brought, in the social field, the emphasis from the single human being to the corporate purpose of the race. Comte, and the philosophic view of history, had let in the principle that only at a certain stage in their development did either societies or individuals become capable of bettering themselves by their own free agency. The Saint-Simonians had made a practical attempt to prove a widely held belief, that individuals could be perfect only when society anticipated and enforced its own perfection.

Straddled between the rival generations was the paramount issue of western political theory. If each individual were acknowledged as a sovereign fragment of society, how could there be imposed the discipline necessary to pursue a common object for the good of all? No one, certainly, contested Wilhelm von Humboldt's statement, "The true end of man . . . is the highest and most harmonious development of his powers to a complete and consistent whole. Freedom is the grand and indispensable condition which the possibility of such a development presupposes."[6] That splendid edict, which had not appeared in English until 1854, sixty years after it was written, was in no way new. In origin it was at least as old as Plato. It did not, however, follow automatically that individualism in von Humbolt's sense was the best means to the appointed end. There had always been a powerful opinion that the highest human possibilities could be reached only by obedience to and in the service of either an authoritative religion or the state. Mill was very far from wishing to discredit or suppress the social instinct. On the contrary, he eagerly looked forward to the time when it would be invested with the solemn force of ritual. In his *Utilitarianism* he deliberately used it as the link between the Benthamite self-interest and the ultimate selflessness required by ethics. The danger was, he said, "not that it should be insufficient, but that it should be so excessive as to interfere unduly with human freedom and individuality".

Two concepts, each of immense significance for the future of mankind, perpetually flouted and denied each other. As in the conflict between Coleridge and Bentham, Mill was convinced that they could, and must, be reconciled. He started from the ancient redoubt, the inherent right of the individual to freedom. He carried the fight to the higher ground where the enemies of freedom were encamped, to the security and interest of society. Freedom, he maintained, was precious to the commonwealth: the real traitor was intolerance.

Comte's conclusions had warned him that the general adoption in human affairs of any single system, however sound theoretically, led straight to social strangulation. Nor was there any safeguard in political democracy. The old Utilitarians, fighting the tyranny of a few, had taken refuge in the rough justice of the many. De Tocqueville had revealed that this was no more than a change of masters:

that under majority rule, not only might the servitude of forty-nine per cent be greater than that of ninety-nine under enlightened despotism, but, which was worse, the mental vitality of the whole society would be less.

Such were the lines of speculation which flowed together in the *Liberty*. The problem, as Mill debated it, went far beyond the forms of government. They, in the ideal systems which he was discussing, were assumed to depend upon the opinion of the governed. "Deeper than opinion lies the sentiment which predetermines opinion."[7] It was the underlying sentiment at which he struck. To Mill, the groping of the human spirit for its best way of life appeared so tentative and delicate, that safety lay in the greatest possible variety of experiments and the most equal balance possible between them all. The prospect of the race depended upon the power of original thought, upon the individual rediscovery of old truths, and upon the invention of new. Great minds had only this in common, that they were always part of the minority. It followed that society, in its own best interest, should encourage minority opinions. For one thing, the minority opinion might be true; or, if false, it might contain a part of the truth so far unrecognized. While if the general opinion was correct, contradiction was still a necessary tonic. Truth unchallenged withered into commonplace. Thought was vital only when it was created, not received. More deadly even than violent persecution was "the deep sleep of a decided opinion".

It was not sufficient for society to refrain from unnecessary interference with individual peculiarities of conduct. The public at large must actively stimulate diversity, must carry a revolt against the prevailing despotism of custom. "The demand that all other people shall resemble ourselves grows by what it feeds on. . . . Its ideal of character is to be without any marked character; to maim by compression, like a Chinese lady's foot, every part of human nature which stands out prominently."

The *Liberty* came out in February 1859, at a very unpropitious time. At one end of the intellectual scale, the Oxford movement was expounding a mysticism more and more dogmatic. At the other, parliamentary reform was in the air: for better or worse, democracy was coming and the people knew it: the people, not the individual, were to be the sovereign. In the intervening span, the *Origin of Species*, also published in 1859, led to the theory of inherited racial characteristics, and provided a new, scientific footing for inveterate prejudices. Everyone was tired of do-nothing government. Dickens, Ruskin, Carlyle, Kingsley, all were whipping up the social conscience. The advance of science promised boundless rewards for corporate action and increased interdependence. Tory, trade unionist, Comtist, Christian Socialist, all preached greater solidarity. The tide was setting for Collectivism, and although there was profound disharmony about the form it was to take, all were agreed that man had no significance apart from the group or society of which he happened to be part. Before long, it would be stated academically with general approval, "There can be no claim on society such as constitutes a right, except in respect of a capacity freely to contribute to its good."[8] The era of the beehive state was dawning, and the freedom of the individual was going out of fashion.

The main objections to Mill's views on liberty were, first, that "discussions about liberty are in truth discussions about a negation".[9] Second, that they made constructive government impossible. Neither argument is sound. Liberty is no more a negative because it means the absence of constraint, than health is negative because it means the absence of disease: both are positive conditions of well-being. It was not freedom from, but freedom to, that interested Mill. His principles left room for a good deal of social legislation, especially in the fields of education and of local government. As for the question of practicality, human affairs are fluid and the issue is comparative. If the liberal ideal expects man to be virtuous, the collective ideal requires perfection in society. Both are unlikely, but while there is a strong belief that a flawless individual once existed, no one ever said the same about a state. Where neither system tallies with the facts, it is wise to adopt the one least likely to do harm. Mill's doctrine of liberty may be incomplete, but it is more coherent than collectivism, which must either baldly assert that might is right, or else seek refuge in the sophistry of the general will. Society is not an organism. When the finger is cut, the whole body bleeds; but when a man dies, unless he is heroic or ignoble, society at large is unaware. It is the individual, not the race, who sins or soars. It is the individual who is responsible.

At the time, however, the abstract merits of the case were left in the background. The point was that the whole intellectual climate was opposed to Mill. It is true, the *Liberty* was widely read. Charles Kingsley, finding it in Parker's bookshop, read it then and there, remarking that it made him a clearer-headed, braver-minded man on the spot. In only two years, a Russian edition gave it access to the main citadel of European reaction. But although it was studied, it was not applied. Lady Amberley, an ardent liberal, wondered why it did not make more stir in people's way of thinking. The reason was, that it ran contrary to the terms of the pervading outlook, and the common reader found it too unsettling. Caroline Fox, supposing its purpose was to drag her most sacred thoughts before the devil's advocate, called it "that terrible book, so clear, and calm, and cold"—"Mill makes me shiver, his blade is so keen and so unhesitating",[10] she wrote. It bemused Mill's allies as much as it annoyed his adversaries. Bain, for example, said "it takes a little reflection to see what he is driving at".[11]

Sir James Fitzjames Stephen, Leslie Stephen's elder brother, was Mill's junior by more than twenty years. He was very up-to-date. He believed, like the old Radicals, that men must be driven into a dictated form of virtue by exploitation of their natural vices, the hope of gain and fear of penalties. He followed the precept to its logical conclusion, and emerged a cut-and-dried authoritarian. In a series of papers later published as a book called *Liberty, Equality, Fraternity*, he roundly attacked Mill both in principle and detail. The essential distinction between self-regarding acts and acts affecting other people was, he said, entirely fictitious. There was no such thing as an action without consequence to others. He felt that Mill went much too far in praise of eccentricity: "originality consists", he said, "in thinking for yourself, not in thinking differently from other people." The quiet enquiring manner in which Mill pursued his thesis offended his propriety. Mill had observed, "Fornication must be tolerated and so must gambling; but should a person be free to be a pimp or keep a gambling house?" Thundered Stephen, "I do not think that the State ought to stand bandying compliments with pimps. . . . My feeling is that if society gets its grip on the collar of such a fellow it should say to him, 'you dirty rascal . . .'." A little persecution, he maintained, was an invaluable thing for keeping people's minds alert and uncomplacent. "To attack opinions on which the framework of society rests is a proceeding which both is and ought to be dangerous. I do not say that it ought not to be done in many cases, but it should be done sword in hand."

"He does not know", said Mill to Bain, "what he is arguing against; and is more likely to repel than to attract people."[12] Still less did the distinguished lawyer realize what he was arguing for. When he turned from criticizing liberty to present an alternative system of society, he expressed ideas which in the present day have a familiar and disagreeable ring. They serve to point and emphasize the warning Mill wished to impress upon his generation:

> "The essence of life is force."
>
> "The way in which the man of genius rules is by persuading an efficient minority to coerce an indifferent and self-indulgent majority."
>
> "Progress has its drawbacks, and they are great and serious."
>
> "I do not envy the Englishman whose heart does not beat high as he looks at the scarred and shattered walls of Delhi or at the Union Jack flying from the fort at Lahore."[13]

Indignant as were the protests of the new authoritarians, the recriminations of the old guard were even more emphatic. Henry Larkin, a good little clergyman who had volunteered to compile the indexes for Carlyle's books, and had drawn the maps for *Frederick the Great*, describes how:

> ". . . one morning when I entered his study, I found him as usual sitting at his table, but evidently in a condition of great suppressed irritability, with Mill's *Liberty* lying before him, which someone, perhaps Mill himself, had sent him. I believe the book had recently been published, but I cannot say positively. Certainly I had until then never seen it, or heard of it.
>
> After I had discharged my trifling business, he rose angrily from the table with the book in his hand, and gave vent to such a torrent of anathema, glancing at Christianity itself, as filled me with pain and amazement. He addressed himself directly to me, almost as if *I* had written the book, or was in some way mixed up with it in his mind. I felt terribly hurt; but what could I say against such a wide-rushing torrent of invective? . . .
>
> I know the book well enough now, . . . and I will only say that, putting myself honestly in Carlyle's place, I do not wonder that his indignation was beyond endurance. It must have been to him, in the incisiveness of its attack and the taking popularity of its style, like a vision of the great red dragon standing triumphant before him, ready to devour the fruit of his soul's travail as soon as it was born. Since that day, I have never heard him express more utter abhorrence of anything than I have, more than once in late years, heard him express of the crowing, God-denying, death-stricken spirit, now making such 'great signs' with our fashionable sciences and life-philosophies,—and all the world wondering after it!"[14]

"As if", Carlyle groaned to his brother, "it were a sin to control, or coerce into better methods, human swine in any way; . . . Ach Gott im Himmel!"[15]

There was, then, little to be done for liberty in 1859. The rationale of European thought had settled for a season in another groove. Mill knew it when he wrote. "If the claims of Individuality are ever to be asserted, the time is now, while much is still wanting to complete the enforced assimilation. . . . If resistance waits till life is reduced *nearly* to one uniform type, all deviations from that type will come to be considered impious, immoral, even monstrous and contrary to nature."

He did his best to rescue his own age. He failed, and an age of darkness followed. But the stuff he handled was imperishable. Liberty could not for ever be outmoded.

> "The worth of a State, in the long run, is the worth of the individuals composing it; and a State which . . . dwarfs its men, in order that they may be more docile instruments in its hands even for beneficial purposes, will find that with small men no great thing can really be accomplished; and that the perfection of machinery to which it has sacrificed everything, will in the end avail it nothing, for want of the vital power which, in order that the machine might work more smoothly, it has preferred to banish."

When authority, in whatever form, had done its worst. When men were tired of being led obediently to ruin; it was then, Mill thought, that the teachings of the *Liberty* would have their greatest value. "And", he added, "it is to be feared that they will retain that value a long time."[16]

III

At Blackheath, through the murky winter of 1858, Mill struggled to express his gross despair. That it was useless he well knew. "The little you saw of her", he wrote to Theodor Gomperz, "may have been enough to make you surmise that there was much more to see, but nothing I could say would give you the smallest idea of what she was or of what her loss is to me."[17] All his patient answers to condolences, to Grote, Pasquale Villari, to his sisters, and to Arthur Hardy in Australia, repeated this same burden, the impossibility that anyone could understand what Harriet had been. Grief, he realized, was a highly private form of pain. He who had been singularly unmoved at the death of his own parents, now welcomed its full intensity. When some years later, Holyoake, as editor of the *English Leader*, voiced a popular opinion that Queen Victoria was making too aristocratic a fuss over her bereavement, Mill deplored his "monstrous assertion that a woman who says . . . that she is 'heartbroken' must be out of her mind."[18]

The more difficult it seemed to communicate his loss to others, the more determined he became to try. The *Liberty* was prefaced by a glowing dedication. Another, equally glowing, introduced her essay "The Enfranchisement of Women" in his *Dissertations and Discussions*, handed over to the publisher at the same date. A year later he was at work on yet a third, even more elaborate tribute. It was to be inscribed upon the chaste and costly tomb of white Carrara marble he was raising over her grave at Avignon.

promotion
"As zealous and active in the cause of human improvement." "As earnest and active in promoting the great interests of mankind." Whichever way he wrote it, the deep poetry he sought eluded him;

and every word of praise he added made the testimony less credible and more vague.

AS EARNEST FOR THE PUBLIC GOOD
AS SHE WAS GENEROUS AND DEVOTED
TO ALL WHO SURROUNDED HER
HER INFLUENCE HAS BEEN FELT
IN MANY OF THE GREATEST
IMPROVEMENTS OF THE AGE
AND WILL BE IN THOSE STILL TO COME
WERE THERE BUT A FEW HEARTS AND INTELLECTS
LIKE HERS
THIS EARTH WOULD ALREADY BECOME
THE HOPED-FOR HEAVEN

There, at last, he had to leave it, not because he was satisfied, but because he could do no more. That it was effusive did not bother him. Many years earlier, while working up a tablet to the memory of his father, he had told Sarah Austin:

> "I do not however think that it is a fault in an epitaph to be pretensious (if I may coin such a word), provided it does not pretend to more than is thought just by friends and admirers. People expect that an epitaph shall contain what a man's admirers think of him—not what is thought by all the world." *

He fell short of this humane standard by failing to be plain. In consequence, he was thought to be obsessed. Bain spoke of his "extraordinary encomiums"; Grote said, "only John Mill's reputation could survive such displays"; Goldwin Smith observed that "Mill's hallucination as to his wife's genius deprived him of all authority wherever that came in".[19] The common concern of his friends, all in their different ways distinguished, that he would injure his philosophic credit, is understandable enough, since none of them ever once met Harriet. But recently it has become evident that Mill's description of Harriet's share in his work was no more than the truth,† while as for her personal qualities, there can be no doubt of her extraordinary power and charm. In speaking of her, extravagance came naturally. "It seems to me", Helen wrote to Haji, "I can never sign Lily any more—I was *her* Lily—now I am no longer anybody or

* John Stuart Mill to Sarah Austin, 20 April 1837, in the King's College Collection. The Shorter Oxford Dictionary attributes the word "pretentious" to 1845.

† From the block of private letters published by Professor Hayek in his *John Stuart Mill and Harriet Taylor*, 1951.

anything but a miserable wretch."[20] And Fanny Stirling, who in her trouping had certainly encountered both the artificial and the genuine in feminine personality, told Helen: "The knowing you and yours was an event in my uneventful life and the more I read or see or hear of anything or anyone of beauty or mind the more strongly I am reminded of her who to my poor narrow way of seeing things had more of strength, and beauty and poetry generosity and goodness than I've ever yet met with in woman."[21] Harriet herself, in one of her moments of rare insight, told her lover, "the desire to give and to receive feeling is almost the whole of my character."[22] That was perhaps the final word on the temperamental aspect of her influence.

From time to time during the remainder of his life, Mill took out the text of his *Autobiography* and tried again to set out dispassionately what above all he wished posterity to know. The result was always the same. Superlatives clogged his meaning, and he whose whole training had been to give exact form to his convictions, whose supreme talent was that "what he aimed to make you see you saw as plainly as a conspicuous object set in sunshine",[23] devised only a shadowy memorial to a huge but purely personal experience. Contemplation of her nature ended invariably in worship and never in revelation. Some years after her death, round a comfortable fire in the house of trusted friends, Helen, who was trying to give them a glimpse of the treasured memory, stopped suddenly. "She said, 'I am such a bad interpreter of my mother, I hardly like speaking of her'; whereupon Mill stood up and said with tears in his eyes, 'no one could interpret her, she was above everyone and inspired everyone.' "[24]

In his first keen misery, his only wish was to publish the hoard of work they had accumulated during their marriage, and then die. "To us who have known what it is to be with her and to belong to her", he wrote to Arthur Hardy, "this silly phantasmagoria of human life devoid of her, would be utterly meaningless and unendurably wearisome, were there not still some things to do in it which she wished done, and some public and other objects which she cared for, and in which therefore it is still possible to keep up some degree of interest. I have been publishing some of her opinions, and I hope to employ what remains to me of life (if I am able to retain my health) in continuing to work for them and to spread them, though with sadly diminished powers now that I no longer have her to prompt and guide me."[25]

Perversely, it was Helen, and not he, who was taken ill. His own health, so long precarious when he had most wanted it, was more robust than it had been for several years. As he worked, he made a good recovery. And although his own world seemed dead, the world of others rumbled on, impinging on him now and then with claims he felt he had to honour. A coming philosopher of high originality and promise, Herbert Spencer, who had first attracted his attention by an amiable attack upon the *Logic*, being penniless, asked for his help in getting a place in the reconstituted India Office. Mill gave him a strong testimonial, and regretted being no longer in a position to do more. Soon, a friend of longer standing was in need of his assistance. Bain, the first volume of whose treatise on analytical psychology, *The Senses and the Intellect*, had been printed at Mill's recommendation by his own publisher J. W. Parker, was having difficulty in getting the second volume, *The Emotions and the Will*, accepted, since the first had been a loss. Mill immediately wrote to Parker:

> "Both Mr. Grote and myself are very desirous that the remaining volume should be published, as it is more popular than the first both in subject and execution and we think it likely not only to sell better but to add to the sale of its predecessor. We are therefore willing if you will publish the second volume this season, to guarantee you against loss by it, to the extent of £100 (that is each of us to the extent of £50)."[26]

The offer was accepted, and when the book appeared Mill furthered its success with a full and enthusiastic review in the *Edinburgh* for October 1859.

Whether owing to this renewal of an old alliance in well-doing (since helping Comte, in 1856 Mill and Grote had lent Holyoake £70 to assist him over the financial consequences of a rash act of friendship), or whether, as Mrs. Grote claimed, he was touched by their warm sympathy, he went to see the Grotes for the first time in sixteen years and gradually allowed himself to be coaxed into coming more often. Little by little he began to emerge from his retirement. Early in May 1859 he recommenced his regular attendance at the meetings of the Political Economy Club. There, he incidentally acquired the lifelong devotion of John Elliot Cairnes, later his trusted authority and adviser on economic matters. Cairnes was the first of the ever widening group of talented young men which surrounded Mill henceforth, as unfailingly as though he were Socrates himself:

> "There was a discussion after dinner led off by J. S. Mill in which most of the persons, your humble servant amongst the number (don't damn my impudence) took part—It was carried on in conversational fashion no one leaving his chair and with the exception of the first speaker no one speaking for more than five minutes—I never knew a question better discussed. Mill spoke like a leaf from 'the Principles'....
>
> But my greatest triumph has to be recorded yet. On leaving, J. S. Mill happened to be going the same way, and actually took my arm and walked along Pall Mall with me! You would suppose from his manner that *I* was conferring the compliment upon *him*."[27]

Mill and Helen, she mended in body and he to some extent in mind, returned to Avignon at the end of May and moved into their cottage at St. Véran, a proceeding which kept Helen busy most of the next two years improving on the building and rescuing the garden. For the first awkward days she managed to persuade Mill, who expressed a hunger and thirst for mountains, to go climbing in the Cevennes, but he soon returned and set about the matter of the tomb with extreme impatience. When the order was first placed in February, Pascal, the Avignon architect, had promised to complete it in three and a half months, from the time the marble arrived from Italy. But since Mill insisted that to ensure a matching grain all the pieces must be cut from a single block, pure white, veinless and unstained, it was not until July that it reached Marseilles, and he was recalled by telegram from Bagnères in the Pyrenees.

It then turned out that the enormous block was only large enough to provide the main slab for the top. While it was being cut and shipped up the Rhone towards Avignon, an order for the sides was placed in Paris. Mill and Helen spent the restless interval gardening in the cemetery. At the head of the grave they planted a single white camelia. They littered the earth around it with violets and pansies, jasmine and honeysuckle. They set a square hedge of spindle trees and laurels for seclusion, and surrounding all, a light railing of wrought iron mounted in marble, with a little gate. The two gravel paths leading to the shrine, though not within Mill's plot, were tended lavishly. "Last week", wrote Helen, "we planted laurels, roses, and myettes, and willow, ash, and laburnum trees. We planted more than a hundred rose bushes last week and we intend to put in some more still when the standard roses come. . . ."[28]

But it was now late autumn, and still the marble had not come. Mill was frantic. "Time appears to have an extraordinary importance with

Mr. Mill", grumbled Derville et Çie, the Parisian contractors. When it did arrive, one piece was defective: as they would not take it back, he was compelled to buy another from them for an extra 3000 francs. This he was still waiting for at Christmas, and, as he would not go away until the tomb was finished, he had to put off the trip they had proposed to make to Greece or Egypt.

At last, at the end of March 1860, it was ready. Helen warned Haji to attend the opening, brooking no excuses:

> "I—and I think I may say *we*—shall be extremely disappointed if you are not here at the time of its erection. We have looked forward to it as quite an epoch, and we feel strongly that we ought to be all present on the occasion. . . . As to expense I hope you will not consider that. . . . When you consider the immense expense that the whole thing has been and will be, only for the sake of showing a sentiment and a feeling, what is this comparatively small addition, to show that you share the feeling with us?"[29] *

The grave became a sort of holy place. Whenever he was at Avignon, Mill invariably spent an hour each day at the cemetery, gardening or talking with his guests: and when returning from his frequent absences, he always stopped there before going home. It grew into a part of the Victorian world. George Eliot and G. H. Lewes, passing through Avignon on their way to Florence in 1861, paused to look and wonder, as did everybody else.

The monument completed, Helen and Mill slipped off to the Pyrenees again for a month or two. The scenery was beautiful in spring, and Mill had an extremely successful expedition, collecting enough rare plants to make the subject of some special articles in the *Phytologist*. But Helen had a wearying time, trundling along doggedly in her awkward clothes, travelling sometimes four hours on foot and eight on horseback in a day, in scorching sun, on rocky mountain trails; sinking knee deep in snow over the passes, splashing through the thaw, stopping at desolate little inns where no lady traveller had ever been seen before. It was by no wish of Mill's that she underwent these hardships. Quite the reverse.

"It is a great happiness to me to be a support to you under depression", he wrote during one of their brief separations, "but it would be very painful to me to think that I should always continue

* It must have cost about £1500. In 1905, after Helen had gone to live with her niece Mary Taylor in Torquay, the house and fields were sold. The town of Avignon, in return for a payment of 3000 francs, agreed to undertake the upkeep of the grave for ever.

to be the only one, as I must necessarily fail you some day and I can never be at ease, unless either by means of persons or pursuits, you have some other resource besides me, and I am sure my own darling would feel as I do."[30]

It must have been some curious penance of her own, some sacrifice to her mother's memory, that made her see it as her duty to become to Mill all he proclaimed that Harriet had been. Her two years on the provincial stage had been a busy time of promise. Now she at once gave up the pleasures of the green-room. Twenty-five years attendant on her mother, for the next fourteen she scarcely left Mill's side. Mill gave her grateful credit in his *Autobiography:*

> "Surely no one ever before was so fortunate, as, after such a loss as mine, to draw another prize in the lottery of life—another companion, stimulator, adviser, and instructor of the rarest quality. Whoever, either now or hereafter, may think of me and of the work I have done, must never forget that it is the product not of one intellect and conscience but of three, the least considerable of whom, and above all the least original, is the one whose name is attached to it."[31]

She lived her part so well that she destroyed herself. "Miss Trevor" and Lily, the sprightly child of curious fancy, disappeared: Helen Taylor only continued to exist. After Mill's death, she became the jealous guardian of all his thoughts and relics. She grew priggish and overpowering; eventually, mean, suspicious, truculent and sometimes half beside herself with passion. She became a great light in her various causes, Women's Suffrage and the London School Board. For the rest, she clung on grimly at Avignon. Thirty years later her niece Mary Taylor found her there, the house dilapidated and the garden overgrown. "At Avignon", said Mary, "her one occupation consisted of picking up leaves and twigs in the garden. . . . It is true to say that her existence at Avignon was almost a death in life, a living death."[32] But when at last she was prevailed upon to give it up, and went to live with Mary in Torquay, she became a plump and rosy old lady; an old lady who loved to go for rides in motor buses, who climbed spryly to the coach-box; an old lady who chuckled at the conjuring at Maskelyne and Devant's.

IV

Mill's mind was further distracted from his sorrow by his absorption in a problem of political organization which erupted fortunately in 1859. The Tory fears of democracy had been so generally belied by the results of the Reform Bill of 1832 that it seemed to Disraeli advantageous for the party, in their new role as protectors of the poor against the monsters of laissez-faire, to embark upon a further limited extension of the right to vote. In these circumstances Mill felt that the time had come to publish the animadversions he and Harriet had long since outlined on the subject, and they duly appeared as a pamphlet entitled *Thoughts on Parliamentary Reform.*

It was really a political corollary to the *Liberty*. Both Mill and Harriet had readily admitted that universal suffrage was not only just and inevitable, but of paramount importance as a means of social education. The question was how best to welcome it, and at the same time alleviate the intermediate risks involved in handing over sovereign decision to a working class majority in their existing credulous and unenlightened state.

On re-examining the problem now, when Harriet was dead, Mill struck a solution so convincing that he inserted it on his own authority. Although it was equitable that everyone should have a voice in government, it was quite another thing to say that everyone should have an equal voice. Such a proposition sprang from the old radical slogan "each to count for one, and only one"; this part of his early faith Mill cast incontinently overboard. "It is the fact", he stated baldly, "that one person is *not* as good as another." There should be a plurality of votes, based strictly upon education and ability, not upon wealth or social station; so that while a factory owner or a country gentleman should have, say, four votes and his workmen only one or two, a professor should outdo them all by having five or six. In this way, while everyone enjoyed the basic right to vote, real power would be vested in those who, in Mill's opinion, were most able to use it well and wisely. At the same time he proposed that everyone applying for electoral registration should be required "to copy a sentence of English in the presence of the registering officer and to perform a common sum in the rule of three." "If ever there was a political principle at once liberal and conservative", he remarked, "it is that of an educational qualification. None are so illiberal, none so bigoted in their hostility to improvement, none so surreptitiously attached to the stupidest and worst of old forms and usages, as the uneducated. None are so unscrupulous, none so eager to clutch at whatever they have not and others have, as the uneducated in possession of power. An uneducated mind is almost incapable of clearly conceiving the rights of others. . . . Recent example has shown that, if it subverts a constitution, it is as likely to do so in favour of despotism as of democracy."*

He then dealt with the proposal that votes should be cast confidentially in ballot boxes, another radical dogma given up at Harriet's behest. Mill was never slow to change his mind: consistency he rated as a very minor virtue, often indistinguishable from obstinacy, a rigid clinging on to outworn prejudices long after they had ceased to have any value. In this case, he maintained, the danger of bribery and intimidation of the electorate had passed away. The voting list was now too large, the polling machinery too secure, for corruption in that form to be effective. The more pressing problem was to prevent the elector voting in his own personal interest at the expense of the great body of people, and especially women, whom he was supposed to represent. This could only be achieved by making him vote in public, so that the exposure of his selfishness might shame him. Even when all should have a vote, the ballot would still be undesirable. Anyone responsible enough to vote, must not flinch from stating his preference openly.

No sooner was the pamphlet printed, than Mill received from an unknown barrister named Thomas Hare his recently published treatise on Proportional Representation, advocating, Mill thought, a far better system than his own. Hare was all in favour of redefining the franchises and boroughs on an equal basis, but he also suggested there should be a single roll of candidates and a single electoral

* In the civilized West of the present day, where the universal vote and the ability of the voter to read and write are commonplaces, a body of argument so heavily in favour of the "pedantocracy" sounds unattractive. But in Africa and India, where the momentous apparatus of democracy is being applied wholesale and for the first time, the educational qualification may still prove a valuable intermediate measure. And as for the despotism of a majority, it must be remembered that obtaining the support of the masses by deliberate misinformation has become the essential factor in the technique of modern tyranny.

register for the whole country. By dividing the number of voters by the number of seats available it would then be possible to find the minimum number of votes any candidate must get to be elected. Each voter was to nominate any candidates he wished, and in whatever order he preferred. When the count was made, if his first choice had already acquired the requisite number of votes, or if it transpired that he could not eventually do so, that name was to be disregarded, and the elector's vote was to be reckoned for the first candidate on his list who had not yet reached the quota. When every vote had been recorded, every seat would have been exactly filled. Since none of those cast for an overpopular or an unsuccessful candidate had been wasted, every elector would have had one effective vote, while every body of opinion in the country of sufficient strength to command one quota of votes would be sure of representation.

The scheme encountered every conceivable criticism short of a fair trial. It was, some said, too complicated, too mathematically nice, and put a faith in the mentality of the electorate quite beyond their capabilities. Others felt that it would destroy the supposedly close relationship between the member of parliament and his constituents. It was commonly thought that it would kill the party system, and make cabinet government a babble of conflicting policies, a perpetual deadlock. Alternatively, that the power of the main parties would soon contrive to turn its provisions to their own advantage, and so defeat its object. A Tammany caucus was gloomily foreboded. However, in small, well-educated, closely-knit societies where Proportional Representation, in various forms, has since been tried, it has, on the whole, worked well. It is even yet possible that England may resort to something of the kind to solve her electoral anomalies.

Mill, at any rate, took instantly to the idea. It had never been his wish to deprive the poorer classes of the majority representation due to their preponderance of numbers. He had only feared that in winning district after district even by a narrow margin, they might gain seats in the House out of all proportion to their real majority. The adoption of Hare's scheme would ensure that six hundred of the best heads in the country were elected, instead of party hacks and local worthies. The effect on the electorate would be especially beneficial; the wide choice of candidates and the certainty of personal representation would bring keener interest and more careful thought. New ideas would be brought continually before the nation; new sections of opinion, now disheartened and deserted, would revive in unexpected strength.

By a single reorganization of the existing system, Mill saw that all his political difficulties could be swept away. There would be no further objection to universal suffrage. The safeguards of plural voting, even his cherished educational qualification, could be discarded. Moreover, Hare agreed with him on many parenthetic points: the undesirability of payment for members of parliament, the restriction of election expenses to a fifty pound deposit; in particular, that women should have votes on exactly the same terms as men. Mill was overjoyed. He also found that the author had not only worked the matter out in thorough detail, but, with lawyer's aplomb, had thoughtfully drafted the statute necessary to make it law.

"Dear Sir", Mill wrote excitedly. "Having been absent from home, it is only within the last few days that I have had an opportunity of reading and studying your book—which I have done with no ordinary feelings. You appear to me to have exactly, and for the first time, solved the difficulty of popular representation—and by doing so, to have raised up the cloud of gloom and uncertainty which hung over the futurity of representative government and therefore of civilization. . . ."[33]

The two men met, and became good friends. "I like Hare more and more. I like very much the expression of his face",[34] said Mill to Helen. He acclaimed Hare's book in an article in *Fraser's* for April 1859. In 1861 he again defended it with heat in his *Representative Government*, a didactic recapitulation of his whole political theory. He lost no opportunity in urging the adoption of the scheme to his influential correspondents in Australia, the United States, and among the cotton operatives of Manchester. It became, after women's suffrage, the greatest practical interest of his life. When he was himself in Parliament, he brought it forward as an amendment to the Reform Bill of 1867. But, to the disgust of Hare's two daughters sitting in the gallery, the House was both jocular and inattentive until called to order by Lord Cranbourne, who protested gamely, "*any* plan proposed and entertained by such a great thinker as Mr. Mill deserved respect".[35] In his *Autobiography* Mill gave his final verdict:

> "I saw in this great practical and philosophical idea, the greatest improvement of which the system of representative government is susceptible; . . . I can understand that persons, otherwise intelligent, should, for want of sufficient examination, be repelled from Mr. Hare's plan by what they think the complex nature of its machinery. But

anyone who does not feel the want which the scheme is intended to supply; anyone who throws it over as a mere theoretical subtlety or crotchet, tending to no valuable purpose, and unworthy of the attention of practical men, may be pronounced an incompetent statesman unequal to the politics of the future."[36]

From the first, his only doubt was that Hare's somewhat statistical style of presentation might scare his readers into thinking the scheme complex and unworkable. He was therefore highly delighted when in February 1860 another of his new friends, Henry Fawcett, produced a pamphlet to explain and simplify it. Fawcett was a rapt admirer of Mill. According to Leslie Stephen, his Cambridge colleague, he knew the *Political Economy* as a Puritan knew the Bible, and at his lectures his answer to all questions was the same—"Read Mill." His enemies said he knew no other book. He was a large and genial fellow, with a thunderous voice and a reverberating laugh. At the age of twenty-seven, young and full of promise, he had recently been blinded by his father, who had shot him in both eyes while aiming at a partridge. There never was a man who overcame a handicap so quickly and completely. He learned to catalogue his clothes so that he could order what he wanted from his gyp by numbers. In the street he never failed to hear the tapping stick of a blind beggar, and to give him alms. He even rowed stroke in a Dons' boat club called "The Ancient Mariners". Mill greatly respected his courage in dictating such a pamphlet less than two years after the accident, and gave him full encouragement.

"You have selected well the object of your present efforts. We can never do enough in pressing forward Mr. Hare's plan. . . . It is an uphill race, and a race against time, for if the American form of democracy overtakes us first, the majority will no more relax their despotism than a single despot would. But our only chance is to come forward as Liberals, carrying out the democratic idea, not as Conservatives, resisting it."[37]

He went on to assure Fawcett that his blindness, so far from disqualifying him from a political career, would "be very much in your favour, not only by exciting interest and neutralizing envy and jealousy, but because it will cause you to be much more and sooner talked about."[38]

And so it turned out. Fawcett was elected to Parliament along with Mill in 1865, and soon became a favourite of the house. For a time they worked together, the blind disciple and his master. "If this fellow had eyes", remarked Disraeli, "how one should damn them."[39] After Mill's defeat Fawcett continued as his unofficial representative in Parliament, accepting his instructions gladly, whether for the women's movement, national education, or the preservation of the common lands. His gallant wife, Millicent Garrett, and their daughter, became active suffragettes. He formed a Radical Club in London, which Mill joined, and a Republican Club in Cambridge. Gladstone eventually made him Postmaster General, and he introduced parcel post, postal orders, post office savings stamps, and cheap telegrams before he died in office in 1884.

V

In August 1860, Helen and Mill returned to Blackheath. Although a London house was no longer strictly necessary; and despite the expense of its rickety foundations—a disease which seems to have infected the whole locality, since the objectionable neighbour, Powell, was also underpinning frantically—they resolved to keep it on. For the next few years they divided their time fairly equally between their two establishments, which resembled each other so closely that Mill, who had visited Blackheath during the past winter, evidently found it quite confusing:

> "I found Haji looking pale but, I thought, with a more animated (or rather less dead) expression of countenance than usual. He seems disposed to be amiable. Puss (who seems to have entirely forgotten me) quite startled me by her size—rather bulk than stature. It may be an illusion, from having been used to a little puss and little doggy (to whom remember me) especially as the teapot also looked as if it had grown."[40]

He added that, as directed, he had bought a revolver and fifty cartridges for the use of the amazon Helen at Avignon, and would bring them with him. "I hope they won't stop it at the Customs House. I believe importation of arms is prohibited, not to mention that they may think I intend to fire at the Emperor."

Haji, in the interval, had occupied the empty house. He was cared for in their absence by the usual domestic, at this time Elizabeth, whom Helen kept in deepest mourning in order to maintain the London end of the bereavement. He spent his time writing up his experiences in Italian monasteries, and courting Ellen Gurney, a sister of Doctor Gurney of Nice. Although, to the amazement of his uncle Arthur Hardy, he had pulled himself together sufficiently to join the Rifle Volunteers being raised against an expected French invasion, he remained a bilious, sulky, rather pompous youth.

In October 1860 Haji's wedding took place near Norwich, Mill signing the register, to the gratification of the verger. He also visited the happy couple in their new abode at Limpsfield. It was not to be a fortunate alliance. The wife died four years later. Of the three children, the eldest daughter became a religious fanatic, and went to live with pious friends in Canada. The son, Cyprian, joined the Navy, but soon afterwards went mad and had to be confined. While Mary, after nursing Haji for the last thirty years of his life, in the course of which time he almost starved them both to death by an excessive addiction to vegetarianism, performed the same function for her Aunt Helen, retrieving her from her querulous senility.

Back in Avignon in 1861, Mill was as near as he ever became to complete recovery, or rather resignation. "Life here is uneventful", he wrote to Thornton, "and feels like a perpetual holiday. It is one of the privileges of advanced civilization, that while keeping out of the turmoil and depressing wear of life, one can have brought to one's door all that is agreeable or stimulating in the activities of the outward world, by newspapers, new books, periodicals, etc. It is, in truth, too self-indulgent a life for anyone to allow himself whose duties lie among his fellow-beings, unless, as is fortunately the case with me, they are mostly such as can be better fulfilled at a distance from their society, than in the midst of it."[41]

He was beginning to enjoy a life of leisure and detachment as a commentator on earthly affairs and a writer of books. In the same year, 1861, he wrote the *Subjection of Women,* his supreme contribution to practical philosophy, although he did not yet publish it. He also brought out in *Fraser's* a series of articles later gathered into the volume called *Utilitarianism*, which he had written in 1854, finished in 1859, and refurbished in 1860.

In these he attempted to reaffirm the authority of Bentham's formula by filling in the gap between the pleasure seeking of the individual and the greatest happiness of the greatest number. For if man is moved only by the pursuit of personal pleasure or the fear of personal pain: and if, as Bentham emphatically claimed, "quantity of pleasure being equal, push-pin is as good as poetry", how could the existence of the higher virtues be accounted for, let alone encouraged? Above all, what of the extraordinary fact of altruism, the fact that men, even rough unsaintly men, were capable of self-sacrifice for the sake of others, without hope of reward or thought of praise? To deny the virtue of such actions, and the glow they bring to the heart—to say either that they were foolhardy, or performed with expectation of ulterior gain, would be to deny morality altogether. On the other hand, to admit that they sprang from intuitive benevolence would go far towards confirming the divinity of the moral sense, and upsetting the rationalistic theory of psychology. The only way out was for Mill to say there was, after all, a difference in quality of pleasures; that the happiness derived from goodness outweighed all others, even life itself, and that the really virtuous man was also the most discriminating in his selfishness.

To the obvious objection that virtue is usually not its own reward, he returned a specious answer: "It is indisputable that the being whose capacities of enjoyment are low, has the greatest chance of having them fully satisfied. . . . It is better to be a human being dissatisfied than a pig satisfied, better to be Socrates dissatisfied than a fool satisfied. And if the fool, or the pig, is of a different opinion, it is because they only know their own side of the question." But the pig and Socrates are of entirely different constitution, and if happiness is all, the pig in his piggery is, to all common experience, happier than Socrates in his misery. Morover, once a spiritual qualification is admitted to pain and pleasure, the whole closely woven fabric of Bentham's sanctions falls to pieces. Necessarily so, since it was never intended to be a code of ethics, but a yardstick of sociological or legalistic measures. It did not attempt to cover crimes for which prison, and death, are no dishonour; or virtues for which medals are an insult.

Nevertheless, Mill overcame the incoherence by which scholars are generally afflicted when they approach the fulness of human nature, and gave an eloquent description not of what is, but of what ought to be. He foresaw:

". . . the possibility of giving to the service of humanity, even without the aid of belief in a Providence, both the psychical power and the social efficacy of a religion; making it take hold of human life, and colour all thought, feeling, and action, in a manner of which the greatest ascendancy ever exercised by any religion may be but a type and foretaste. . . . The deeply-rooted conception which every individual even now has of himself as a social being, tends to make him feel it one of his natural wants that there should be harmony between his feelings and aims and those of his fellow creatures. . . . This feeling in most individuals is much inferior in strength to their selfish feelings, and is often wanting altogether. But to those who have it, it possesses all the characters of a natural feeling. It does not present itself to their minds as a superstition of education, or a law despotically imposed by the power of society, but as an attribute which it would not be well for them to be without. This conviction is the ultimate sanction of the greatest happiness morality."

In the same year he proposed to write an article for the *Westminster* on the philosophy of Sir William Hamilton, who seemed to him to be making a praiseworthy attempt to reconcile the rival systems of the Transcendentalists and the Scottish school of Common Sense. But a preliminary survey of the works of that great pedant revealed, behind the bulwark of his erudition, a sea of error so expansive and so menacing, that Mill determined grimly on a full examination. He resolved to make of it a metaphysical sequel to his *Logic*.

He was in fact reverting steadily towards his original and natural function as a protagonist in lofty dialectics, linked only remotely to the concerns of daily life. But now the mean world kept breaking through. The scandals of public life, the work of friends, above all the fight with tyranny, continually upset his thoughts; for Harriet had made of him a watchful guardian of freedom.

He had, for instance, to notice Palmerston's pigheaded opposition to the Suez Canal. He thought Palmerston a fool, and a dangerous fool. The objection made, the wretched excuse that British interests would suffer, besides being untrue, was the very type of thing responsible for the widespread belief abroad that British foreign policy was always sinister. A belief inevitable enough, in view of the national habit of pretending cynical motives even for generous policies. To help correct it, Mill gave a stirring dilatation on the virtues of his native land, an account unusual and refreshing from one who was so frequently its critic:

"There is a country in Europe, equal to the greatest in extent of dominion, far exceeding any other in wealth, and in the power that wealth bestows, the declared principle of whose foreign policy is, to let other nations alone. . . . Any attempt it makes to exert influence over them, even by persuasion, is rather in the service of others, than of itself: to mediate in the quarrels which break out between foreign States, to arrest obstinate civil wars, to reconcile belligerents, to intercede for mild treatment of the vanquished, or finally, to procure the abandonment of some national crime and scandal to humanity, such as the slave-trade. . . . If the aggression of barbarians force it to a successful war, and its victorious arms put it in a position to command liberty of trade, whatever it demands for itself it demands for all mankind. The cost of the war is its own; the fruits it shares in fraternal equality with the whole human race. Its own ports and commerce are free as the air and the sky: all its neighbours have full liberty to resort to it, . . . nor does it concern itself though they on their part, keep all to themselves, and persist in the most jealous and narrow-minded exclusion of its merchants and goods.

A nation adopting this policy is a novelty in the world; so much so, it would appear, that many are unable to believe it when they see it."[42]

This mild honeymooning between Mill and his country did not for long continue. The American civil war broke out. For Mill, who had studied its approach for years, it was a clear-cut issue. The North's was "the good cause". John Brown was a "true hero". The South had launched "an aggressive enterprise of the slave-owners to extend the territory of slavery"; their success would be "a victory of the powers of evil". As for their famous right to secede, it was no more than the right Dick Turpin might have claimed to secede "because the law of the country would not suffer him to rob and murder on the highway". Here, then, in this struggle, which he felt from the beginning "was destined to be a turning point, for good or evil, of the course of human affairs for an indefinite duration", was a case where his own people should, as he believed to be their wont, exert their influence in the service of others, arrest an obstinate civil war, and put an end to a national crime and scandal to humanity. "It may be imagined with what feelings", he exclaimed,

"I contemplated the rush of nearly the whole upper and middle classes of my own country, even those who passed for Liberals, into a pro-Southern partisanship: the working classes, and some of the literary and scientific men, being almost the sole exceptions to the general frenzy. I never before felt so keenly how little permanent improvement had reached the minds of our influential classes, and of what small value were the liberal opinions they had got into the habit of professing. None of the Continental Liberals committed the same frightful mistake. . . . It was not generally believed in England, for the first year or two of the war, that the quarrel was one of slavery. There were men of high principle and unquestionable liberality of opinion, who thought it a dispute about tariffs . . ."[43]

Worse followed. There was the Trent Affair. When a naval officer of the United States boarded the British steamer "Trent", and arrested two Confederate envoys who were passengers between neutral ports, war loomed imminent. The memory of Yorktown and Saratoga rankled on, and there was a general feeling that the Yankees were too saucy. Flags were waved. Bayonets were sharpened. Louisa Stanley, a cultivated English lady, shared the common indignation. "I can*not*", she wrote, "believe N. America can be such a Fool as to engage in *such* a strife. It is much comfort to feel quite sure we shd. knock all her pride & insolence out of her—& she wd get properly humbled—The *expense* of doing this wd be too great to bear thinking of."[44]

Mill put forth every power he possessed. In *Fraser's Magazine* he praised the patience and restraint his countrymen had shown in face of undoubted wrongs and provocation. He asserted that the amends the American government had made—an apology, and the release of the two envoys—were sufficient, even handsome. He went on to advocate war, should it be necessary, but for the other side, for the North against the South, who, he said, had every intention of carrying slavery into the British colonies and dominions. "For these reasons I cannot join with those who cry Peace, peace. . . . War is an ugly thing, but not the ugliest of things: the decayed and degraded state of moral and patriotic feeling which thinks nothing *worth* a war, is worse. . . . A man who has nothing which he cares more about than he does about his personal safety, is a miserable creature who has no chance of being free, unless made and kept so by the exertions of better men than himself." He ended shrewdly by reminding his incalculable public that Jefferson Davis, the Southern leader, was the very man who had insisted on the odious "repudiation" which had touched so many English pockets.[45]

He fortified the Lancashire cotton operatives in their voluntary economic martyrdom. He deplored the Southern bias of the English press reporters, particularly "that poor gobemouche Mackay in the *Times*, who simply retails the stuff he hears from a disreputable clique at New York, almost all of them personally interested in slavery either through commerce or politics. . . . Their following consists chiefly of the mob of Irish emigrants."[46] He besought John Lothrop Motley, author of the *Rise of the Dutch Republic* and American ambassador to Austria, not to mistake what he read in the papers for the real voice of England:

"You will find that, whenever any name is attached to these wretched effusions, it is always that of some deeply-dyed Tory—generally the kind of Tory to whom slavery is rather agreeable than not, or who so hate your democratic institutions that they would be sure to inveigh against you whatever you did. . . . As long as there is a Tory party in England it will rejoice at everything which injures or discredits American institutions, but the Liberal party, who are now, and are likely to remain much the strongest, are naturally your friends and allies."[47]

In the original version of the *Political Economy*, he had made some very unflattering references to America. "They have the six points of Chartism, and they have no poverty: and all that these advantages seem to have done for them is that the life of the whole of one sex is devoted to dollar hunting, and of the other to breeding dollar hunters." In the sixth edition now preparing, the offensive passage was struck out root and branch. He wrote whole folios of letters confirming Cairnes in his adherence to the cause, and when Cairnes wrote a book entitled *The Slave Power* and dedicated it to Mill, he was delighted:

"I do not think there is an opinion or a sentiment in the book with which I substantially disagree; and this is so very generally the case when I read anything you write, that I feel growing up in me, what I seldom have, the agreeable feeling of a brotherhood in arms. This feeling being one of the pleasantest which life has to give, I owe you thanks privately as well as publicly for adding as much to it as you have done by your present volume."[48]

The Slave Power gave him an opportunity of saying some more on the subject, this time in the *Westminster Review*. He was determined that "a few, if only a few, known writers and speakers, standing firmly by the Americans in the time of their greatest difficulty, should effect a partial diversion of their bitter feelings, and make Great Britain not altogether odious to the Americans."[49]

On this account he was for a time displeased with Thornton. He told Fawcett he was "not at all surprised that Thornton is not with us on the American question. Though a superior person on many points, on others he feels with the herd, and one never knows which these last may be."[50] On the other hand, he saluted his old adversary Dr. Whewell, who was so strongly for the North that he would not suffer the *Times* to be in his house. "No question of our time has been such a touchstone of men", he cordially wrote, "has so tested their sterling qualities of mind and heart as this one, and I shall all my life feel united by a sort of special tie with those, whether personally known to me or not, who have been faithful when so many were faithless."[51]

Next came the matter of the Alabama Claims. A vessel named, significantly, "Alabama" was, as the United States Consul very well knew, a man-of-war then building at Birkenhead in the yards of Messrs. Laird. Despite his representations on the subject, and in defiance of all neutrality laws, she was able to elude the Port Authorities and put to sea. She lay off Anglesey for two days without any effort at pursuit, then made her way to the Azores, where she received her armament brought from Liverpool in two British ships. She was then taken over by a Confederate crew, and had two racy years as a raider on the high seas before she was sunk off Cherbourg in 1864. The government of the United States was, not unnaturally, very much offended, particularly since it was suspected that two other ships, the "Florida" and "Shenandoah", had come into being in a similar manner. A long controversy ensued, in which Mill took the part of the Americans and addressed a letter to Mr. Gladstone, then Chancellor of the Exchequer and at the height of his popularity in the prosperous sixties. The great man answered courteously, inviting him to breakfast. In the end, the government stopped their sinuous protestations and finally agreed to arbitration.*

Of Lincoln, whom he greatly admired, and with whom he would certainly have had a great deal in common, Mill wrote to Cairnes:

> "What I now principally feel is that the death of Lincoln, like that of Socrates, is a worthy end to a noble life, and puts the seal of universal remembrance upon his worth. He has now a place among the great names of history, and one could have wished nothing better for him personally than to die almost or quite unconsciously, in perhaps the happiest moment of his life. How one rejoices that he lived to know of Lee's surrender."[52]

Mill's main concerns were summed up in a letter to Parke Godwin, the New York *litterateur*:

> "I have never believed that there was any real danger of a quarrel between the two countries, but it is of immense importance that we should be firm friends. And this is our natural state. . . . Most of the dislike and suspicion which have existed towards the United States were the effect of pure ignorance; ignorance of your history, and ignorance of your feelings and disposition as a people. It is difficult for you to believe that this ignorance could be as dense as it really was. . . .

* The British were eventually ordered to pay $15,500,000 in gold.

Everyone is vaguely inculcating gentleness, and only gentleness, as if you had shown any signs of disposition to take a savage revenge. I have always been afraid of one thing only, that you would be too gentle. I should be sorry to see any life taken after the war is over (except those of the assassins), or any evil inflicted in mere vengeance; but one thing I hope will be considered absolutely necessary, to break altogether the power of the slaveholding caste. Unless this is done, the abolition of slavery will be merely nominal. If an aristocracy of ex-slaveholders remain masters of the State legislatures they will be able effectually to nullify a great part of the result which has been so dearly bought by the blood of the Free States."[53]

VI

In the middle of all this, Mill and Helen took their promised holiday in Greece; for her, a single visit to a land of legend; for him, a second homecoming to the ruins of a civilization which was the earliest source and constant nourishment of his philosophy.

Leaving Avignon at the end of dark January 1862, they made their way through Italy to Ancona, then crossed by steamer to brilliant Corfu, now in its last years of British mandate. In March they were in Athens, where they set to work to equip themselves for two expeditions, one to Arcadia and the Peloponnese, one to the northern mainland and Euboea. Athens was once more full of tales of brigandage. Mill was disturbed to learn that one of his curious hermit-like acquaintances had recently been molested, and forced to deliver up his hidden funds, some two or three hundred pounds, under the threat of boiling oil. However, he persuaded Helen that the brigands seldom attacked the English, on the rather optimistic grounds that they knew that if they did so the government would find the compensation too expensive, and would come and rout them out.

Apart from themselves there were seventeen in the party, servants, guides, and soldiers. They travelled on horseback over craggy roads, through mountains and by feverous swamps. They pitched their tents in solitary places, in plains or valleys, in the ruins of old cities, or on the grass beside the mountain springs. "Sometimes in forests", Helen told Fanny Stirling, "where our men lit huge fires, throwing on the trunks of two or three whole trees, to keep the wolves from our horses. Sometimes we were in wild and desolate regions deserted even by the shepherds and their flocks, and where we heard the cry of jackals, the owls and the night hawks all night."[54]

By mid-June they were back in Athens. In the Parthenon, they discussed where the statue of Athene must have stood, a much debated point. Helen distinguished herself by going directly to a certain place and saying "I believe that it was here", an opinion afterwards accepted by Cortius the German archaeologist and his team. When asked her reason, she said that in a Catholic church the image of the Virgin would have stood there.[55] They went on by sea to Smyrna and Constantinople, then in July started slowly homewards by way of the Danube, Vienna, and Switzerland, reaching Avignon in September 1862.

In October, Thornton went to stay with them, and wrote an encouraging account to Henry Fawcett and Mill's other anxious friends in England:

> "At eight o'clock we breakfast; then, if there is no special plan for the day, Mill reads or writes till twelve or one, when we set out for a walk which lasts till dinner-time. In the evening Mill commonly reads some light book aloud for part of the time. This, I fancy, is his ordinary mode of life while here, but he is now laying himself out to entertain me, and almost every other day we make a long carriage excursion, starting directly after breakfast, and driving twenty or thirty miles on end and not returning till sunset or later. We have already visited in this way Petrarch's valley of Vaucluse, the Roman monuments at St. Remy, and the curious feudal remains of Les Baux, and tomorrow we are to go to the famous Pont du Gard. Mill tells me that they seldom let a week pass without making some such excursion, but that this year they have postponed all until my arrival. You may imagine how much I am enjoying myself, and no small part of my pleasure consists in seeing how cheerfully and contentedly, if I may not say how happily, Mill is living. I feel convinced that he will never be persuaded permanently to abandon this retreat, for here, besides the seclusion, in which he takes an almost morbid delight, and a neighbourhood both very interesting and in its own peculiar way very beautiful, he has also close at hand the resting-place of his wife, which he visits daily, while in his stepdaughter he has a companion in all respects worthy of him."[56]

Not all Mill's friends were as fortunate as Thornton. There was, for instance, the sad case of young Theodor Gomperz, Mill's German translator and intense admirer. Gomperz had been one of the very few privileged to stay at Blackheath during Harriet's lifetime; passing through Austria on their way back from Greece, Mill and Helen paused, and eagerly renewed the old association. Quite unknown to both of them, Gomperz, in the heady Viennese summer, completely lost his heart to Helen. Mistaking Mill's friendly letters for an encouragement, he followed them to London, intending to press his suit. Before he could bring himself to do so, they had left for Avignon, where, in the spring of 1863, the distraught lover proposed that he should visit them. By this time, it had dawned on Mill that more than scholarly friendship was betokened by the constant presence of Gomperz. After anxious discussion with an incredulous Helen, he sent a reply that even a far less sensitive man would have taken as a sharp refusal.*

> "Come by all means if you like, though I should not for an instant have thought of proposing it to you. . . . If, knowing this, you still like to come, I can only say that I shall be glad to see what I can of you; and I should not have said so much if you had not expressed yourself as if your motive for coming to Avignon was chiefly to see us; and I should very much regret that you should either be disappointed or think us unfriendly in case you should see less of us than you expect."[57]

Gomperz was so upset by grief and worry that he went clean off his head. Mill was deeply shocked. He had not intended his letter to be rude, he said, although, "Knowing as I now do the state of your feelings, I can well understand your being pained by it. . . . I thought I was using a freedom which I could not have taken with a mere acquaintance, but which I was even bound to use with a friend."[58] The visit took place as soon as Gomperz was well enough to travel, but the unfortunate man never fully recovered from the blow.

Deliberately, Mill was beginning to widen his acquaintance. He reopened a correspondence with his old friend Gustave d'Eichthal which had been closed for more than twenty years, and occasionally went to see him on his way through Paris. By contrast with the impenetrable privacy at Avignon, life at Blackheath, when they were there, was practically convivial. Among his new associates was a young journalist, John Morley, whose article in an obscure radical review on the importance of encouraging a wide variety of ideas caught

* See *Theodor Gomperz, Briefe und Aufzeichnungen,* by his son, Heinrich Gomperz, Vienna, 1936, Vol. I. I am indebted to Professor Hayek for this information. Gomperz later published the only collected edition of Mill's works.

Mill's watchful eye and led him to issue a summons, since he "felt a strong wish to know who was its author, as it shows an unusual amount of qualities which go towards making the most valuable kind of writer for the general public".[59]

Helen was a practised housewife and a conscientious hostess. Soon, five o'clock Saturday dinners at Blackheath became almost weekly functions. They took place in a room surrounded by tall bookcases with classic plaster busts on top, and an engraving of Raphael's Madonna over a warm fireplace. The guests included the Grotes, the Bains, the Amberleys, the Fawcetts, the Cairnes, with their American neighbour Moncure D. Conway, who was an Emersonian and the successor of Fox at South Place Chapel. Thornton, Morley, Herbert Spencer, Cliffe Leslie, Louis Blanc the French socialist and exile, Lyell the geologist, Schuyler, later American chargé d'affaires in Moscow, and his wife, a descendant of Alexander Hamilton. By far the majority were of the younger generation. They would go down by train from Charing Cross. They would find the familiar lonely figure waiting on the platform to walk up with them to the house, while Helen drove with the ladies in the carriage.

Mill was a splendid host. Charles Eliot Norton, after making the pilgrimage with his wife, recorded: "His manner is entirely that of a gentleman and man of the world, with a tender grace and sweetness about it rarely met with. . . . He is entirely simple, and modest, . . . there is nothing epigrammatic, or strained, in Mill's talk. . . . It was interesting because the man himself was interesting. . . . It showed indeed in its range the variety and liveliness of his sympathies, and the quickness of his perceptions,—but had you been listening to it, without knowing who the man was that was talking, you would not have learned from it that he was Mill, though you would have been sure that he was a man of powerful intellect, and of a well-trained mind."[60] Mill quickly put people at their ease. Strolling with Conway, for example, he turned the conversation on to Emerson, and Conway broke into an animated tale of how, as a youth in Virginia, a sentence from Emerson had awakened in him a new thought and aim which ultimately revolutionized his life. At that, Mill paused on the road, and said, "That is something which should be engraved on a man's tomb." "Although", Conway went on, "in his countenance there was a tinge of melancholy, it was serene; and there was some twinkle in his eyes when he uttered an epigrammatic criticism on one or another politician who had acquired popularity or power. He was a man of delicate sentiment, eloquent manners, and affectionate nature."[61] He also liked to make others talk. Morley recalled that once, after dinner, he challenged Herbert Spencer to expound shortly the fundamental ideas of his philosophy. Spencer did so, in a discourse of twenty minutes, and Mill was very much pleased, drawing Morley's attention to Spencer's power of expression. Morley agreed. But Fawcett, an intensely practical person, was horribly bored.

Mill's relationship with Spencer was very odd. In temperament they were plain opposites. Where Mill was painstaking, Spencer was reckless. Where Mill was open-minded, Spencer was opinionated; so that, although Mill was fourteen years the senior, they were very much on even terms. Where Mill was reflective, Spencer was a spontaneous genius. When going to work on a subject, Mill read enormously and thoughtfully first; then sat down and wrote, and re-wrote, until all that pleased him out of several conflicting treatises had become fused into an harmonious whole. Spencer, on the other hand, scarcely ever read a book of any sort, and when he did it was usually a novel. As a boy, he was so idle he was unable to go to a university because he could not pass the entrance examinations. Yet he produced complete systems of Psychology, Biology, Sociology, and Ethics, of undoubted brilliance and marvellous lucidity. Although, "of history he knew nothing, of English literature very little, of German literature not a word", he was endowed with "a natural facility for attracting from every quarter facts which bore upon any theory he was promulgating, though without any effort to himself".[62] He was tall, and ruddy; healthy and vigorous, but extremely susceptible to nervous excitement and excruciating headaches. So much so that he always carried earplugs, in order, if a conversation threatened to become too stimulating, to prevent himself from listening. Finding in violent exercise the best relief for his congested mind, he used to dictate his philosophy to his secretary while playing racquets or rowing on the Serpentine, stopping to reel it off in uninterrupted periods of perhaps twenty minutes at a time.

When confronted with a problem, Mill was as pertinacious as a bulldog. He never let go, but worried and worried at it until it came completely clear. Not so Spencer. Once, when George Eliot, who for a time it seemed likely he would marry, asked him why his brow was unwrinkled, seeing how much he must have thought, he answered, "I suppose it is because I am never puzzled." "O!" she cried, "that's the most arrogant thing I ever heard uttered!" He then explained that when he encountered something he could not comprehend, he never bothered with it, but put it away in the back of his mind where it would remain perhaps for years. Until one day, usually while thinking of something else, he would suddenly have a little mental flash, and there it would be again, completely solved and perfectly phrased, ready to go down in his book. With a little of Mill's dogged application, he might have been an even greater thinker. Certainly, Mill thought so. "He is so good", he told Bain, "that he ought to be better."[63]

Philosophically, they were akin, but far from being identical. As an individualist, Spencer went even further than Mill, maintaining that a man was justified in refusing to pay taxes, provided he gave up all claims to be protected by the state. He also claimed to be a Utilitarian, to the extent that he believed that individual happiness was the end of life, that self-love and social would eventually prove to be the same, and that the only valid test for the morality of an action was, how far its motives accorded with those ends. On the other hand, having explored the theory of natural selection, or, as he called it, the survival of the fittest, four years before Darwin, his views were naturally coloured by evolution and heredity. He confirmed the innate, intuitive character of the moral sense, and denied that it could, as Mill maintained, be wholly accounted for by the experience of the individual.

Being, before all else, a scientist, Spencer held the law of Causation to be absolute and invariable, inferring a necessity between cause and effect. This was contrary to Mill's philosophy. Spencer also supposed a supreme Cause, a Creator of causation, and he called it the Unknowable. He proposed to test the absolute nature of any truth by what he called the Universal Postulate, the inconceivability of the opposite. He carried absolute causation into the field of morality and social science. The Utilitarian morality, the set of rules conducive to general happiness, was not enough. He "conceived it to be the business of moral science to deduce, from the laws of life and the conditions of existence, what kinds of action *necessarily* tend to produce happiness, and what kinds to produce unhappiness. Having done this, its deductions are to be recognized as laws of conduct; and are to be conformed to irrespective of a direct estimation of happiness or misery."[64]

All this, inferring as it did, a rigid authoritative moral code with a divine sanction, was very uncongenial to Mill. It seemed like a moulding of his own philosophy into the requirements of the intuitionists, a kind of trading with the enemy; and he could see no fundamental difference between the new Unknowable and the old Jehovah. Yet, though a confused philosophy, it was without doubt plausible. "He is a considerable thinker, though anything but a safe one", he told Bain; "and is on the whole an ally, in spite of his Universal Postulate. . . . But this is Spencer all over; he throws himself with a certain deliberate impetuosity into the last new theory that chimes with his general way of thinking, and treats it as proved as soon as he is able to found a connected exposition of phenomena upon it. This is the way with his doctrine of Heredity, which, however", Mill ended in perplexity, "will very likely prove true."[65]

There was, therefore, a certain amount of muddle in their dealings. In his *Utilitarianism* Mill listed Spencer with the goats, and Spencer wrote protesting at great length, only to find himself still worse misrepresented in the *Hamilton*. On this occasion G. H. Lewes, then editor of the *Fortnightly Review*, urged him to denounce Mill in its columns. Mill was quite unruffled at the prospect: "Nothing can be more agreeable to me than to hear that you are going to answer me in the *Fortnightly Review*. I hope you will not spare me." If, he said, Spencer made out a strong enough case, he might reply, perhaps through the same review. But not unless it was essential. "I have had enough for the present, of writing against a friend and ally." On the very day when Spencer was correcting the proofs of his attack, he dined with Mill. When it came out, Mill patiently corrected the new edition of his *Hamilton* twice, and the sixth edition of his *Logic*, until Spencer was entirely satisfied.[66]

Spencer, who was quite incapable of earning his living, was by this time very hard up, and in 1866 his publishers, who were producing his treatises by subscription, closed down on him for lack of funds. Sooner than let the series end, Mill, who had already acted at some cost as an Honorary Proprietor to Spencer's unsuccessful paper called the *Reader*, at once wrote offering to guarantee the publisher from loss, as he had done in the case of Bain, up to whatever figure they should lay down as sufficient. He was careful to salve his rival's vanity, which was notorious:

> "I beg that you will not consider this proposal in the light of a personal favour, though even if it were I should still hope to be permitted to offer it. But it is nothing of the kind,—it is a simple proposal of cooperation for an important public purpose, for which you give your labour and have given your health."[67]

Nevertheless, Spencer refused, and Mill, after trying to persuade Grote to get a place for him on the Senate of London University, went round to see Spencer's publisher, Chapman, and came to a secret agreement with him. He gathered enough friends to buy up two hundred and fifty copies of the next issue, and sent out a circular bearing names as distinguished as John Tyndall, T. H. Huxley, and John Lubbock, besides his own. The death of Spencer's father at that moment relieved the situation and the circular was withdrawn; but not before American admirers had collected $7000 in bonds and a gold watch for him.[68] Spencer, perhaps not having grasped Mill's rare and liberal view on scholarly disagreement, never got over what he called "a generosity that might almost be called romantic". At Mill's death he wrote a full account of the affair for the *Examiner*.

Of all Mill's new found friends, the best were Lord and Lady Amberley.[69] Amberley was the eldest son of Lord John Russell: Kate, the fourth daughter of Lord Stanley of Alderley. At the time Mill came to know them, they were both about twenty-two and newly wed. They were really a kind of fairy-tale couple. They were handsome, young, and gifted: liberal, nobly born, reasonably rich, "a mixture of fun and earnestness", and very much in love. In accordance with the adage, both died young. But while they lived they shone through the heavy atmosphere of mid-Victorian pretension and convention like two fireflies in the night.

Amberley first met Mill dining at the Grotes in March 1864, when he was just down from Cambridge. He was not particularly impressed. "He speaks in a very gentle voice, and is not in appearance like a great man", was all he recorded in his journal. Three months later, during half-a-year of exile imposed by his mother in the hopes of preventing him from marrying Kate, Amberley found himself staying at the *Hôtel de l'Europe* in Avignon. While he was there, he thought, he ought to call on Mill. First he paid a visit to the cemetery, and admired the grave. Then he went on to the philosopher's house, and found him working in the garden. Mill took him into his study and they had a talk. "Interesting, but not satisfactory", noted Amberley, "as I felt as if I were detaining him from more agreeable pursuits." Next morning Amberley went back to the cemetery, and copied out the epitaph.

The next encounter happened when, in February 1865, Mrs. Grote decided to give a house party at her new residence near Shere in Surrey. Her mind was in a desperate confusion, owing to the strange behaviour of her husband. On emerging from his thirty-two years' labour on the *History of Greece*, carefree and rather lost, the "Historian" had unaccountably stepped out with a young lady by the name of Miss Durant. Miss Durant was a sculptress. Mrs. Grote was very much upset. She knew that it was not her husband's fault. It was, she admitted, "common for old men to have deep passions late in life, she had known several cases of it; two old men had had passions for her and in one case it had hastened the old man's death." All the same, she could not but feel her husband's folly in throwing away, after forty years of "affectionate confiding intercourse", "the only real balm for the ills and infirmities inherent to the decline of age".[70] Nor could she hope that his reputation, which was dearer to her than anything else, would not be damaged. In short, he "had made an old fool of himself".

At this moment, the crisis and climax of the whole affair, she was determined that no mark should be apparent on the sheer surface of their usual relationship. So she began to think of sending invitations. She was now on the best of terms with Mill and Helen. Kate she had known for several years, and had brought very much under her influence, styling herself an honorary aunt. Although she did not know Amberley so well, she had taken pains to win him over too, and had offered her redoubtable assistance in the agitation and intrigues before the wedding. These four guests, then, met each other at the station.

It was the first time Kate had seen Mill. Of course she had heard a good deal of him, and had read the *Liberty* twice before she was eighteen; but she was not disposed to venerate him more than the other grave distinguished personages she had been accustomed to see stalking through the family mansions during her gay and cultivated maidenhood. Amberley, though he often spoke of Mill, used no exaggerated terms. Under the guidance of Mrs. Grote, they even tended a little to make fun of him. Between themselves, they were in the habit of calling him, irreverently, "the Lama".

All this was altered during that memorable week-end. On the way up from the station, Kate and Helen rode, while Mill walked with Amberley, and praised him for his speech as candidate in an unsuccessful by-election, which had attracted unfavourable comment from the *Times* and *Punch*. On the Sunday, after breakfast, while Grote worked sulkily on the proofs of his *Plato*, the others talked, and Mill said Amberley ought to stand again for Parliament, this time for Westminster. In the afternoon, Mill, Amberley, Grote, and Helen went for a long walk in the rain. Mill told Amberley all about Hare's scheme (and later sent him books on it). Mrs. Grote drove out with Kate to meet them in the carriage, and took the opportunity of regaling her with stories about Harriet. "After dinner", Kate records, "Grote and Mill talked metaphysics, beyond me quite, and complimented one another on their new books. . . . Mill told us Comte said that the reason a room gets better for speaking in is that the wood gets a sympathy with the sound and learns to give it back better."

Monday was a repetition of the Sunday. Again they sat talking all the morning. Again they walked or drove all afternoon. Kate had a long chat with Mill, and was very deeply moved:

> "He was talking about everyone being wished to be alike and do alike, and I told him that we met with opposition for going to the country and not going out as everyone did and people were always wanting A to shoot to be like everyone else so he advised me to answer 'I did not wish him and he did not intend to be like everyone else but something more and of use in his time and for that solitude and study were necessary and not to be always in the world'.
>
> The whole conversation was deeply interesting and made a great impression on me—I felt he was so congenial and sympathetic to me, and that all he said was fr. such a true and elevated point of view. It did one great good to hear him and raised one into a hopeful state of mind. He said the wish and intention to do good was good in itself—and he said the great thing was to consider one's opponents as one's allies; as people climbing the hill on the other side. This view he said was becoming more held every day—He altogether gave one hope . . ."

Next day, it all came to an end:

> "Tuesday 21 Feb.
>
> Mill and Miss Taylor left at 11 and walked to the station—Mill said he had been very glad to meet Amberley . . . I am so happy at A knowing him and Mill's appreciating him. It is of course more pleasure to hear him praised or rather commended by Mill than all the praise or blame of the world—I do trust never to mind more what the world says, than I do now; for now it is quite indifferent to me, I know all his motives are noble and great and unselfish, only to be admired."

They were both full of Mill. When they got back to London, Lord John Russell teased his son by asking if he had got nearer his Millennium by his visit. They did not care. As Mrs. Grote told Helen in a P.S. to a letter:

"Lord and Ly A were *enchanted* wi *their* visit & Lady A quite 'cottoned' wi *you.* I am glad you both were pleased wi your stay here. *I* enjoyed it very completely in spite of the bad *weather*. 'Historian' gone to London . . ."[71]

Kate opened a correspondence with Helen which continued regularly till her death. Dinners and visits became frequent. When Kate's white Pom had pups, Mill was given one: he called him "Kalos", Greek for beautiful, although Kate thought him very ugly. Because Kate said their kinsman Dean Stanley would like to see the day when Mill could preach in Westminster Abbey, she had a serious quarrel with her mother, ending in her stamping out without saying goodbye, and not making it up for a whole week. In 1869 the Amberleys stayed at St. Véran on their way through Avignon to Rome. A few months later, Helen offered them the use of Blackheath while they were searching for a house. When they found one, Mill and she were Kate's first guests at Ravenscroft.

The intimacy was very great, and for the worldly interests of the Amberleys, a disastrous one. Not that they followed Mill blindly, to the exclusion of their own judgement, or that he would have permitted them to do so. They frequently disagreed with him. In the case of Governor Eyre, for instance, they thought he pressed too far with his prosecution; and like all other landed families, they thought his attack on the Irish landlords was unjust. Amberley approved of the Contagious Diseases Acts,* despite Mill's personal persuasion to oppose them: and, at dinner at Blackheath, Helen and Mill defended Cairnes' proposal for a national conscript army, while the Fawcetts and the Amberleys disliked it.

But the whole texture of their thought was steeped in Mill's opinions, dangerously advanced; and their contempt for society together with their determination to act up to their beliefs made them rash. In vain, Mrs. Grote warned them that one so young as Amberley should not follow "the example of Mill, whose creed all recognize as the extreme democratic" and should guard himself "from going beyond the limits of a conscientious liberal in public speaking". Amberley not only continued to refuse to go out shooting, but became a keen Malthusian. He consented to become Vice-President of "The Dialectical Society", which included in its membership such questionable names as Mr. Bradlaugh, Dr. John Chapman, and Dr. Drysdale.

* See page 465 for Governor Eyre; page 451 for Irish Landlords; and page 501 for Contagious Diseases Acts.

At his very first meeting he stated, from the chair, that "if ever we are to escape, as a nation, from poverty, it must be by the limitation of the size of our families . . . and after all it turned out to be a medical question how this could best be accomplished without injury to the health. . . . In America ladies were in the habit of keeping back their families, but the methods they employed seemed to him to be dangerous to health. Hence he should much like to hear a discussion as to whether some innocuous measure might not be discovered."

Although the proceedings were supposedly private, the ghastly sentences leaked out. They were eagerly pounced on, puffed up, tossed about and used to defeat him at his parliamentary election. The *British Medical Journal* repudiated them "with indignation and disgust". The *Medical Times* spoke of "unnatural crimes", and whispered ladies had been present. The local paper scarcely could believe that the scion of a noble house should advocate "infernal practices", and demanded that he should be "scouted by every decent man and woman. Is he fit for a legislator who would introduce into virtuous England not only the political licence of America, but what we cannot err in calling one of the most horrible of its vices?" The Roman Catholic Bishop of Liverpool preached against Amberley for wishing to stifle children in their birth.

The uproar was immense, already quite sufficient to spell ruin and disgrace in families less toughly constituted than the Russells and the Stanleys. Yet before it had properly subsided, Kate emerged in her turn, quite unapologetic, not merely a feminist, but a shockingly prominent feminist. The Amberleys were social outcasts. They were ridiculed as cranks where they were not reviled as firebrands.*

They never regretted it. When Mill was elected for Westminster, Kate told Helen, "You should have seen how delighted Amberley was much more pleased than if *he* had been elected for this he said was of national importance".[72] When Mill was defeated, Amberley wrote, "I wish I had a seat for a liberal borough and constituents willing to accept you as a member, as I should have been proud to resign in your favour".[73] When Mill died, Kate told her mother, "We can think of nothing but poor Helen Taylor." There were plans for Helen to come and stay with them, to live near them, to have the children to take care of.

* Amberley also became the author of a scheme for abolishing war by means of a League of Nations. It was printed by John Morley, in deference to Mill's urgent intervention, in the *Fortnightly Review* for May 1871.

It was not to be. In June 1874 Kate died suddenly of diptheria, caught while nursing her small daughter who had picked it up while they were on the Continent. "Infinitely as I have suffered myself", wrote Amberley to Helen, "I have not forgotten to feel for you in the loss of a friend who was so truly anxious to do all in her power to make your life a little less unhappy."[74] Robbed of his wife and daughter at a single blow, Amberley lost all interest in life. Eighteen months afterwards, he died too.

The friendship had one lasting memorial. When Kate's third child was born in 1872, she wrote to Helen:

> "Do you mind god-mothering my little *boy*. I had always somehow counted on a girl to be called 'Cordelia Helen' but as it has turned out a 'Bertrand William' and a girl may never come will you give him your blessing and guidance? We hesitated to ask such a favour of Mr. Mill otherwise I wish he too cd. have been god-father—for there is no one in whose steps I wd. rather see a boy of mine following in ever such a humble way, than in Mr. Mill's."[75]

Helen replied, from Austria.

> "Dearest Kate
>
> I should like to be godmother to your little boy and should take as much interest in him as in a little girl, for one of the sweet and attractive things about children is that one finds just as much earnestness and sweetness and purity about the boys as energy and courage about the girls, till, alas! they fall under the influence of the vulgar world. . . . Mr. Mill says if you wish it he does not think that it would conflict with his opinions to enter into that relation . . ."

And so, in due course, a cup arrived for Bertrand Russell, with a suitable inscription on it. The child grew and thrived. He was fed on asses' milk. He was "a fine bright boy full of activity and observation". Before he was two, "he insisted on lifting all alone an *enormous* book out of the shelf to a little stool where he sat down with it open before him—in a fit of laughter at his own wisdom". "Bertrand is so lovely and teachable quite ready to be worked on and moulded", reported Kate a fortnight before her death. He can only have met his godfather while he was too young to remember; but afterwards Helen seems to have looked after him for a short time.

VII

From 1863 to 1865 Mill was happy with his *Examination of Sir William Hamilton*. It appeared in April of the latter year, and bore so striking a resemblance in many ways to his father's *Fragment on Mackintosh* that one is forced to wonder whether effusions of this kind were not a family failing. They both amounted, under the guise of a sharp sarcastic criticism of the work of a Scottish dignitary, in each case already dead, to a violent onslaught on the whole psychology and philosophy of the Intuitionists. The "Examination", however, was considerably longer than the "Fragment". It was deliberately polemical, and each edition was carefully revised and embellished with footnotes dealing with the objections bestowed upon the last. Moreover, since many of the points at issue have since been abandoned as either insoluble or irrelevant, it is for a modern reader astonishingly dry.

For some time past, philosophers who agreed in nothing else had been equally chary about the character of the external world. On the one hand, Hume, by carrying free speculation to its logical extremes, had shown that the existence of anything outside the mind was, so far as reason went, conjectural and insusceptible of proof. On the other, the Intuitionists, eschewing reason, had taken refuge from Hume's scepticism in essences, in things-in-themselves, in shadowy noumena. To the hard-headed Scottish school of Common Sense, it seemed that it was time to stop disputing the agenda and get down to business. They felt it was obvious that the daily world of matter did exist; and, furthermore, that they themselves existed, along with the scruples and intuitions of which they were acutely conscious. If reason could not prove these things, then there was something wrong with reason. They wished to rescue intuitionism from German mysticism, and set it back on a less metaphysical footing. It was along these lines that Reid, and Brown, and Dugald Stewart had been working.

Mill was hard put to it. In his *Logic*, following faithfully from Hume, he had attempted to build up a convincing account of the whole apparent universe on the single postulate of the mind and its ability to receive sensations. He had taken the professional position, that the objective existence of the external world was an open question, and one of which the importance had been magnified. Now, confronted with men who asked bluntly if he believed in the external world or not, he had to be more precise, and in being so, made valuable admissions. Matter, he said, was the permanent possibility of sensation. Consciousness was the expectation of sensation, based on the assumption of the uniformity of nature. What then was memory, upon which depended the association of ideas? Memory was the present consciousness of a past sensation. But since he could not further explain it, he was forced very grudgingly to admit it as another unaccountable faculty of mind, an extra intuition. Much to the disgust of Bain. "For myself", said Bain, "I never could see where his difficulty lay." Mill was also closely questioned on the Freedom of the Will, which in the *Logic* he had left in a most unsatisfactory compromise. Further admissions in that direction appeared more than likely.

At this point he was mercifully delivered by Sir William Hamilton, who enabled him to go over to the attack. Hamilton, the heir and successor to Reid and Brown, was a very learned man with a tremendous reputation. The minuteness of his scholarship was famous. He thought nothing of giving up two years to proving his family title to a baronetcy. In support of the contention that reason was unequal to the tasks imposed upon it, Hamilton unearthed an old logical puzzle known as the antinomy, a device whereby the mind was faced with two alternatives, both equally inconceivable, but one of which must be true. Space, for example, must either be limited or unlimited. When compelled to choose between alternatives beyond the power of reason, the mind depended upon Faith, he said. "The last and highest consecration of all true religion must be an altar to the unknown God."

His follower, Mansel, an Oxford Professor and later Dean of St. Paul's, took the opportunity afforded by this view of solving the religious problem of the existence of evil. It had been asserted that if God were good, he could not countenance evil, much less perform it: whereas if he were all-powerful, he must be able to prevent it if he wished: and therefore he could not be both. In his Bampton lectures, published as *The Limits of Religious Thought*, Mansel laid it down that this was an antinomy, and the goodness and omnipotence of God must be accepted as an act of Faith. From which it followed that evil did not really exist, and that in the Bible what appeared by human standards frankly immoral deeds were, in the case of Jehovah, converted by a moral miracle into good.

This doctrine stirred Mill to the deepest indignation. Not on religious grounds, for he regarded religious opinions as a very private matter. He allowed great latitude to all doctrinal utterances; and carefully refrained from publishing any religious statement during his own lifetime. As a matter of fact, when his *Three Essays on Religion* were published at his death, it transpired that his views were far less rigidly determined than his adherents had supposed. In the first, written under Harriet's guidance in 1854, he decided there was no evidence in the behaviour of the natural world, in its murderous greed, its calamitous convulsions, to indicate the work of a benign Creator, although there was some evidence of design. In the second, of about the same date, he found that religion was capable of being morally and socially valuable to mankind, but that a Religion of Humanity could fulfil this function as well or perhaps better than Christianity. But the third, written in the winter of 1869 long after Harriet's influence was withdrawn, was much more sympathetic to the Christian faith. In it, he concluded that the evidence from design in nature was, after all, enough to justify a belief in a benevolent God who took pleasure in his creatures' welfare. Not indeed an omnipotent God, for he never overcame the idea that if God could prevent evil and did not do so, he could not be good. But a God limited in power, either by forces of evil, or, more probably, by obstacles to the process of creation not evident to human consciousness. He also said of immortality that, since the physical part of the mind was only a condition, not the cause of mental life, there was a faint chance for the survival of the spirit. And to the specific claims of Christianity he paid this tribute:

> ". . . Whatever else may be taken away from us by rational criticism, Christ is still left. . . . About the life and sayings of Jesus there is a stamp of personal originality combined with profundity of insight, which . . . must place the Prophet of Nazareth, even in the estimation of those who have no belief in his inspiration, in the very first rank of the men of sublime genius of whom our species can boast. When this pre-eminent genius is combined with the qualities of probably the greatest moral reformer, and martyr to that mission, who ever existed upon earth, religion cannot be said to have made a bad choice in pitching on this man as the ideal representative and guide of humanity. . . . It remains a possibility that Christ actually was what he supposed himself to be—not God, for he never made the smallest pretension to that character and would probably have thought such a pretension as blasphemous as it seemed to the men who condemned him—but a man charged with a special, express, and unique commission from God to lead mankind to truth and virtue."

Mill's shadowy approach to what he had pronounced unknowable, his yearning to be in the twilit land of half-belief, caused grave consternation to his followers, many of them respected pillars in the strict community of agnostics. John Morley sorrowfully disclaimed it in the *Fortnightly*. Fitzjames Stephen in the *Pall Mall Gazette* called it "a diet of anaesthetic". Professor Bain, while praising Mill's courage in admitting his change of mind, was especially perturbed about his reputation. If Helen is to be believed, Bain went to the lengths of "pirating" the *Three Essays*, presumably in order to soften their impact in some way. He had once heard Mill remark, "To my mind the only permanent value of religion is in lightening the feeling of total separation which is so dreadful in real grief", and took this to mean that Mill was seeking an anodyne, whether consciously or not, for the loss of Harriet. Whatever the reason, there can be no doubt that Mill's final outlook on religion was a state of what he elsewhere called "Imaginative hope", and that he had been in that state for at any rate ten years.*

It was not therefore because he disbelieved in God that he hated Mansel's doctrine. Rather the reverse. To put God above morality, to say that what man knows to be evil is really good, seemed to him to be degrading God. Apart from invalidating human ethics, apart from disastrous social consequences, it could not fail to take all trust and dignity from worship, reducing it to the primitive level of fear, superstitious flattery, and appeasement. It would set God up as an arbitrary capricious tyrant, and pull man down to servile brutishness. It was a notion utterly, almost physically, repugnant to him. He called the *Limits of Religious Thought* "a detestable to me absolutely loathsome book".[76]

"When I am told that I must believe this", he thundered in his *Examination*, "and at the same time call this being by the names which express and affirm the highest human morality, I say in plain

* Early in 1862, Mill wrote to a correspondent, Arthur Weguelin Creene:

"I am desirious to explain, that neither in the *Logic* nor in any other of my publications had I any purpose of undermining Theism; nor, I believe, have most readers of the *Logic* perceived any such tendency in it. I am far from thinking that it would be a benefit to mankind in general, if without any other change in them, they could be made disbelievers in all religion; nor would I willingly weaken in any person the reverence for Christ, in which I myself very strongly participate. . . . That the world was made, in whole or in part, by a powerful Being who cared for man, appears to me, though not proved, yet a very probable hypothesis." (MT Coll. I/72.)

terms that I will not. Whatever power such a being may have over me, there is one thing which he shall not do: he shall not compel me to worship him. I will call no being good, who is not what I mean when I apply that epithet to my fellow-creatures; and if such a being can sentence me to hell for not so calling him, to hell I will go."

VIII

For once Mill was on the popular side. The Christian Socialists were not enamoured with Mansel's idea of a God whose morality was inscrutable. Once that was admitted, it would soon be possible to claim that the depths of poverty, the worst exploitation of the factory system and the horrors of the workhouse, were all part of the divinely ordered plan against which nothing either could or should be done. Maurice, who had been wrangling with Mansel, sent his copy of Mill's book to Kingsley, calling it "a grand and affecting theological statement".[77] Kingsley, for his part, had been attempting to explain away the apparent cruelty and injustice of many actions attributed to God by the incontrovertible authority of the Bible. He was strenuously contesting the assertion that the destruction of the Canaanites was opposed to human standards of morality. He had made deep researches showing that the Canaanites richly deserved their fate. They were, he said, a vicious lot. But finding this line of argument laborious, and, for some indefinable reason, of questionable benefit to his case, he welcomed Mill's eloquent vindication of the human conscience, giving it high praise from the pulpit of the Chapel Royal.

Backed by such an unexpected weight of clerical approval, Mill could afford to ignore the fulminations of the sabbatarian press, the *Record*, which called him "chief of the Satanic School in England", and the editor of the *Morning Advertiser* who accused him of the most revolting atheism. Moreover, his normal secular following was increased by further fortunate chances. Taine, the rising French historian and philosopher, reviewed him with boundless admiration. Augustus de Morgan, the brilliant mathematician and logician (as a boy, he is said to have read algebra like a novel), with whom Mill was carrying on an engaging academic correspondence, was greatly pleased. de Morgan was no lover of Hamilton, who had pirated his principle "the Quantification of the Predicate". Even Dr. Whewell warmly thanked Mill for the copy he had sent him, he too having been offended by the attacks Hamilton had made on his theory of mathematics.

On the other hand, the Scots were seriously put out. Mill had not only outraged their common sense by questioning the existence of the external world; he had flouted the memory of their national philosopher. In vain, Grote sought to restore peace by a reconciliatory article in the *Westminster*. Carlyle joined in the general resentment up in Edinburgh. He was fresh from his inauguration as Rector of the University, that notable occasion when, it is said, "there was an audible motion, as of breath long held, by all present: then a cry from the students, an exultation; they rose up, all arose, waving their arms excitedly; some pressed forward, as if wishing to embrace him, or to clasp his knees; others were weeping . . ."[78] His triumph was completed by the belief that his adversary had overreached himself.

At one of the banquets held in Carlyle's honour, Lord Neaves was among the guests. Lord Neaves was a judge, given to composing facetious ballads in his spare time, and was in great demand at Edinburgh celebrations. After dinner, he enlivened the proceedings with a song, specially written for the purpose. Verse 8 is sufficient to indicate the general tone: *

"We banish hence Reid's Common Sense;
We laugh at Dugald Stewart's blather;
Sir William, too, and Mansel's crew,
We've done for you and Mind and Matter.
Speak no more of Mind and Matter:
Mill with mud may else bespatter
All your schools of silly fools,
That dare believe in Mind and Matter.

Stuart Mill on Mind and Matter,
Stuart Mill on Mind and Matter,
Stuart Mill exerts his skill
To make an end of Mind and Matter!"

* The full text of this ballad may be found in Lord Neaves' *Songs and Verses, Social and Scientific, by an old contributor to 'Maga'*, 1868.

The whole table was in a roar, and nobody more so than Carlyle, who quite lost his appearance of exhausted philosophical detachment. Indeed, he amazed his host by his vivacity and capers. He shouted out the choruses. He waved his knife as if it were a baton. " 'Stuart Mill on Mind and Matter, Stuart Mill on Mind and Matter' he chanted laughingly along with Lord Neaves every time the chorus came round, beating time in the air emphatically with his fist."[79]

Mill felt that a quiet retort would not be out of place. His contribution to Carlyle's flood of congratulations was a short note, which, Jane said, made her start and give a little scream. "Please thank Mrs. Carlyle for her rememberance of me", he wrote crisply. "I have been sorry to hear a rather poor account of her health, and to see by your Edinb. address that your own is not quite satisfactory."[80]

In one way and another, Mill found himself coming very much before the public eye. And if most of the reasons for it were not those he would have predicted, in one respect at least he was master of his fate. In March 1865, about a month before the *Hamilton* came out, he received a letter asking whether he would be willing to stand as Parliamentary candidate for Westminster at the forthcoming General Election, if a circular letter should reveal a general desire among the electors for his nomination.

Mill was in two minds what to answer. In 1851, he had refused to stand, but times had changed since then. Then, he had held an important post at the India House and, like his father before him, was disqualified from public office by the will of the Court of Directors. Then, he had been just about to marry Harriet, and wanted privacy and peace; now, alas, he had no such happiness. Besides, that had been only an offer of an Irish seat; this was a free invitation to stand for Westminster; and Westminster to a Liberal was like Mecca to the Moslems, the heart of a tradition. He had a great desire for practical achievement. The struggles of the Reform Bill era, his part with the Philosophical Radicals and the *Westminister Review*, were still fresh in his mind, though other things had intervened. He was immensely flattered at the spontaneous determination of the Westminster electors, and fully conscious of his duty to respond to the call of his fellow citizens.

On the other hand, he was more than doubtful whether he could be of more service to the community in Parliament than out of it. As he wrote to Theodor Gomperz:

"I am, indeed, reduced to wondering whether I shall ever be able to resume those quiet studies which are so prodigiously better for the mind itself than the tiresome labour of chipping off little bits of one's thoughts of a size to be swallowed by a set of diminutive practical politicians incapable of digesting them. One ought to be very sure of being able to do something in politics that cannot be as well done by others, to justify one for the sacrifice of time and energies that might be employed on higher work. Time will show whether it was worth while to make this sacrifice for the sake of anything I am capable of doing towards forming a really advanced liberal party; which, I have long been convinced, cannot be done except in the House of Commons."[81]

Eventually he temporized, waiting to see what the committee would say when they heard his terms, which he made extraordinarily stiff. He wrote thanking them for the honour they had done him, and consenting to be nominated if so desired, on four very strict understandings. First, that if elected he would not undertake the charge of any local interest. Second, that since his only object in Parliament would be to promote the opinions expressed in his writings, he would elaborate them as might be required, telling his constituents the votes he intended to give and his reasons for them. Beyond that he would give no pledge of party loyalty. Third, that he would not advertise or offer himself to the constituents in any manner. Fourth, he would not pay a pennyworth towards the cost of his election, because it was a scandal that only rich men could afford a seat in Parliament, and because the enormous expense deterred many of the best candidates from running. There was something to be said for this opinion. The virtuous Amberley, shocked to find that his victory at the Nottingham by-election of 1866 was gained by indirect corruption, resolved at his next election to limit his personal expenditure to £500. When the total accounts came in they were found to amount to £5143 which had to be paid by his unfortunate relations, and even then he had not won the seat. His father, accustomed as he was to the grand bribery of the bad old days, was horrified. He thought that £1500 should have been enough. Mill concluded by congratulating the Westminster committee on their excellent notion of a circular letter to the electorate, inviting their views about his nomination. He suggested that, in order to give the electors the best possible choice, the names of several other candidates should be added to the list besides his own, particularly Sir J. Romilly, and his old friend Edwin Chadwick, the sanitary reformer.

When this unique communication was published in the *Daily News* for 23 March 1865, the result was that Mill's name leapt into national prominence. A well-known public figure was heard to say that God Almighty would have no chance of being elected on such a programme. The demand for his books soared. The first edition of *Hamilton* sold out in two months. and Bain had to help him go to work on a sixth revision of the *Logic*. More satisfactory still was the effect upon his cheap editions. For a year past he had been negotiating with Longmans (Parker having died about 1860, the two firms had merged) to bring out those of his works most likely to attract the working classes at a price within their reach; when Longman could not bring them low enough, he had arranged to forego entirely his usual half profits. The prices finally agreed were the *Political Economy* at 7*s.*, falling to 5*s.* after the first 4000: the *Representative Government* at 2*s.*, and the *Liberty* at 1*s.* 4*d.*, although Mill still thought that it should have been 1*s.* *

These were now appearing, and they sold like wildfire. A thousand copies of the *Liberty* went in the first week, and within five years the *Political Economy* had topped ten thousand. Nor, to Longman's surprise, did the People's Editions interfere with the sale of the library copies. There was talk of a complete edition of his works.†

The students of St. Andrews University elected him, without consulting him, to be their Lord Rector, and were not at all dismayed at hearing they would have to wait a year for his inaugural address. Mill was slyly pleased at his own craftiness about the parliamentary nomination. "I have gained this by it," he wrote to Edwin Chadwick, "that what are thought the most out-of-the-way of all my opinions, have been and are discussed and canvassed from one end of the country to the other, and some of them (especially women's voting)

* In August 1870 Mill was asked by William Trant, a working man, to add the *Logic* to his list of cheap editions. Mill declined, thinking there would not be enough demand. Instead, he ordered Longmans to send Trant at his expense several copies of all his works except those available in the cheap editions. One copy of each was for Trant himself: the rest he was to distribute among working men's clubs and libraries as he thought best. Two years later, Trant wrote to say that all the books had been very widely read, except in a few cases where club members were unable to read at all. (Correspondence in MT Coll., Vols. I and II.)

† This was never published. Mill wrote to Longman, "I have sometimes thought of such a thing myself, but am inclined to think that the most suitable time would be after my death, as I am likely, so long as I live, to make material improvements in every new edition of my larger works." (MT Coll. I/93.)

are obtaining many unexpected adhesions. I reckon this a good stroke of practicality, whether I am elected for Parliament or not."[82]

Needless to say, the Westminster electors at a general meeting adopted him, conditions and all, and opened a subscription to pay for his campaign. Mill quickly replied to their questions on specific policies. He was all for Reform, but dead against the Ballot. He advocated a firm hand with France: economy but no disarmament: a mixture of direct and indirect taxation: no religious disabilities. Landed estates should be subject to death duties: the purchase of commissions must be stopped: flogging must be abolished both in the army and outside, except for crimes of violence: as for strikes, the less the government interfered the better—but the same must also apply to lockouts.

As time wore on, the chances of success looked slim. Mill was not the official Government candidate. His committee were working hard, yet what could they achieve? James Beal, Thomas Beggs, William Brewer, W. T. Malleson, Hon. Sec.—honest English names enough, but not a single peer or prelate in their number. What match were they for Captain Grosvenor, the Liberal Party's choice, or (since two members had to be elected) for the Tory power invested in the comfortable figure of W. H. Smith?* Mill did not help at all. He would have nothing to do with the traditional tokens and encouragements. Kate Amberley, for instance, always got an orange bonnet from her mother to wear at her husband's hustings. But Mill would have no favours. For a long time, he refused to have his photograph taken for display. He declined to come home to show himself to his committee: even Helen gave up hope. Instead, he brooded like a stern Olympian deity at Avignon until the end of May; then, as the day grew nearer, removed himself yet further from the scene of action. On 18 June, Waterloo Day, and barely three weeks from polling day, he was still sunning himself rather ostentatiously at Mont Doré les Bains.

Yet somehow all was getting done. W. D. Christie, the friend of Mill's younger brother James, was electioneering valiantly in *Macmillan's Magazine*. G. H. Lewes wrote in the *Fortnightly* in his support. Chadwick and Holyoake were working at the back of the committee. Amberley, forsaking the party line although himself a candidate for Leeds, gave up Grosvenor's faction and joined Mill's.

* The "Son" in "W. H. Smith and Son".

Four ladies, friends of George Eliot, drove round Westminster with placards on their carriage.[83] Subscriptions were mounting up, from unexpected quarters. Fortnum and Mason's gave £50, Debenham's £100, a leading wine merchant in Bond Street (probably Hedges & Butler with whom John Taylor and Harriet had dealt) a further £100. "Look at the list", Mill gleefully exclaimed; "next to none of them are representative men. They are people from here, there, and everywhere who have happened to like my books."[84] Longman the publisher ventured to say that he was going to vote for Mill, because he felt very strongly that he ought to be in Parliament, "although I must frankly say I think you go a little too far on some points".[85] On 9 June 1865, Lord John Russell, assessing the state of affairs with his usual acumen, observed, "I expect Mill to come in for Westminster, and tho' I am far from agreeing with him, I think he is too distinguished a man to be rejected."[86]

At the beginning of July, with just ten days to go, Mill at last consented to come home. Not, as he said, on account of election business, but because he had promised to attend a meeting of the Political Economy Club. His committee pounced on him. He was finally induced to make two speeches, on the grounds that it was only fair for the public to be told, before they voted for him, exactly what his aims and objects were. The first meeting, for the electors proper, was decorous enough. The second, being for voteless working people, who, Mill insisted, had as much right to hear their representative as had anybody else, was a much tougher business. The Victorian working men were just as burly and forbidding as the rest of their uncompromising generation.

Mill was laboriously explaining his political faith, when suddenly there came an interruption. A bill-board was brought in, bearing the deadly words from his *Thoughts on Parliamentary Reform.*

"THE LOWER CLASSES,
THOUGH MOSTLY HABITUAL LIARS,
ARE ASHAMED OF LYING."

They asked him, had he written that? For a second he paused, but he never wavered. He answered clearly, "I did." There was another pause. Then, instead of the stony silence, the discontented mutterings he expected, the whole of the stolid audience rose to greet him. They clapped, they whistled; cheered, and stamped their feet. Their leader, George Odger, stood up beaming and announced that "the working classes had no desire not to be told of their faults; they wanted friends, not flatterers."[87] It was a riot. Over the hoardings of Westminster another quotation was placarded in enormous letters.

"IF SUCH A BEING CAN SENTENCE ME TO HELL, TO HELL I WILL GO."

At the polls on 12 July 1865, Grosvenor and Mill carried the election, Mill having a majority of 700 over W. H. Smith.

IX

The new session opened in February 1866 under auspices favourable to Mill. During the recess Palmerston had died, and with him the last obstruction to further electoral reform. The veteran Lord John Russell was once again Prime Minister, but he placed the real authority in the vigorous and capable hands of Gladstone, Chancellor of the Exchequer and Leader of the House. Moreover, since the majority was not a large one, an unusual amount of influence was attached to the actions of independent-minded members such as Mill, and true to his word he at once began to make the most of it.

He soon put an end to rumours that he was to be offered a place in the Cabinet, either the Duchy of Lancaster or the India Board. His first action was to vote against his own party in favour of an Irish amendment, supported by only four other non-Irish members. A week later, he made his maiden speech, attacking a proposal by Mr. Robert Lowe, a senior Liberal, to compensate landholders for their losses in the recent cattle plague. Mill said they had already been indemnified enough by the consequent rise in the price of meat. "The hon-member for Westminster is a great deal too clever for us in this House,"[88] growled Mr. Lowe. Two days afterwards Mill was vehemently opposing the government plan to forestall the expected rebellion in Ireland by suspending the Habeas Corpus Act. He had a great respect for Bright, and a strong sympathy with the Irish peasants. He was convinced that the whole trouble sprang from the attempt to impose the English system of agricultural tenure upon Ireland, where it was completely out of place, to the advantage of the already oppressive landlords. His ill-disciplined deeds were impelled no doubt by these opinions. But they certainly did not increase his favour with his colleagues. "Mill's speaking", Kate Amberley wrote sorrowfully, "seems to bore the house, they say he has spoken too often—much, and cannot be heard. I am very sorry his first speech was not a good one and well prepared."[89]

He became so unpopular he decided to lie quiet for a time. He had done himself no good in any quarter by being more liberal than the Liberals. At the opening of the session the Tories had been rather frightened of him. Most of them had never to their knowledge seen a philosopher before, and did not quite know what he would do to them. They expected a forensic giant, an embodiment of pure passionless reason. Instead they saw "a slight frail figure, trembling with nervous irritability. He poured out a series of perfectly formed sentences with an extraordinary rapidity suggestive of learning by heart; and when he lost the thread of his discourse closed his eyes for two or three minutes till, after regaining his composure, he could again take up his parable. Although his oratory was defective, he was clearly speaking with intense feeling and was exceedingly sensitive to the reception by his audience."[90]

"Ah, I see", Disraeli sneered when he first saw him in the House; "the finishing governess."[91]

J. A. Roebuck, Mill's one time friend and still his warm admirer, was also in the House. He was so anxious for Mill to succeed in Parliament that he could not refrain from giving sound advice from his own long experience. But as he was still under the banishment imposed by Mill over thirty years before for his well-intended interference about Harriet, he could only do so through an intermediary:

"19 Ashley Place
S.W.
March 9 1866

My dear Chadwick

There will be directly a great opportunity for Mill—I do not presume to address him directly, but possibly he may listen to you and through you I would speak.

Gladstone's coming reform bill is the occasion—That bill will be received on Monday, by all the really important men in silence, the fools who love talking, and to hear their own voices will jabber on the occasion—But the second reading, will afford the opportunity of which

I speak. Mill if he pleases, may make what ought to have been his début. If he will speak as a philosopher putting Bright and all paltry influences on one side, coming forth in his own great strength aye majesty depend upon it, the House would listen and be delighted. Let him be himself, clear bold and *understandable* (there is a new word) and he will put his mark upon the debate . . .

Having determined what to say, he ought to plant himself steadily on his feet, give the right pitch and tone of voice, then earnestly and with perfect simplicity, make his opening statement—The House will be anxious to hear him—Let him show, that he is no mere puppet, that he is no man's follower—but one possessed by strong opinions—well thought opinions—and really anxious to have those opinions fairly and honestly laid before his country he with his great powers, will be able to captivate his country and to lead them in the course he desires— . . . —If he follows these badly expressed counsels he will succeed.

Yrs very truly
J. A. Roebuck."[92]

Mill did listen to the counsels, and Roebuck proved to be quite right. At the second reading of the Bill, he duly rose on Friday 13 April, to deliver a carefully prepared and measured speech. It was steeped in philosophic wisdom, yet at the same time it faithfully upheld his party leader. It was accepted as his maiden speech, and the House was pleased. Kate, who was present in the gallery, said in her journal, "J. S. Mill spoke directly after, very well, so clearly and distinctly I heard every word he said without any trouble. It was a most comprehensive speech going over all the good things Reform had done and wd do. He was very much cheered while he spoke and when he sat down also and every time his name was mentioned later in the evg. After he had done, every one got up to go away . . ."[93]

Roebuck wrote glowingly to Chadwick, telling of Mr. Speaker's high admiration—Mill assuredly deserved it—it laid open to him the highest offices in the administration of the country—an epoch in Parliamentary oratory, the outpouring of a great, honest, yet modest mind—and so forth. He ended with one further suggestion for improvement. "He has a habit of joining his hands behind him, and rolling from side to side, looking like a schoolboy saying his lesson. Now I would suggest to him, to stand for some minutes every day before a cheval glass, with a card in his hand; to make a little speech, and watch carefully his own demeanour."[94] *

* After Mill's death, Roebuck and Helen entered into correspondence over the account given in the *Autobiography* of the original estrangement. When Helen assured him how often in the last twenty years Mill had spoken of him

Mill had learnt his lesson about the content as well as about the style of his speeches. Henceforth he was faithful to the party line. Shortly afterwards, a small clique of deserters led by Lowe, mostly like Mill's own colleague Grosvenor, the elder sons of peers distrustful of reform, bound themselves into the "Cave of Adullam" and pulled down the government. Mill stood firm. His addresses to his electorate during the crisis were models of propriety, demanding a General Election so that the traitors could be justly punished by their constituents. After the government resigned, on St. Swithin's Day, he proposed Gladstone's health at the Cobden Club dinner, and was almost overcome with tears. When Lord Derby's Tory government came in, and the rapier-like Disraeli, as his Chancellor, cynically carried the "leap in the dark" Reform Bill, Mill remained defiant and unsubdued. He had already won his spurs against the Tories. He irritated them intensely by his unwearying reflections on the landed gentry, until they learnt to retaliate by reading up and quoting at him fragments from his own works. Once, when the fatal Liberal Reform Bill was in committee, Sir John Pakington taunted him in this way, recalling the passage in the *Representative Government* where he said the Conservatives were the stupidest party in the state. Mill replied:

> "I never meant to say that the Conservatives are generally stupid. I meant to say that stupid people are generally Conservative. I believe that is so obviously and universally admitted a principle that I hardly think any gentleman will deny it. Suppose any party, in addition to whatever share it may possess of the ability of the community, has nearly the whole of its stupidity, that party must, by the law of its constitution, be the stupidest party; and I do not see why honourable gentlemen should see that position as at all offensive to them, for it ensures their being always an extremely powerful party. . . . There is so much dense, solid force in sheer stupidity, that any body of able men with that force pressing behind them may ensure victory in many a struggle, and many a victory the Conservative party has gained through that power."[95]

with gratitude and affection, Roebuck was pathetically affected. "I am sure that Mill's mind changed with regard to myself during the later years of his life", he answered. "The last letter I received from him, was in a tone of tenderness, that spoke of old times and old feelings. . . . Indeed the contents moved me so much that I tried to find his apartments in Victoria Street but was unsuccessful, and desisted from further enquiry thinking that I perhaps had overrated the meaning of the passage. I am indeed glad to hear that he felt respecting me as in his youth he was accustomed to feel." (MT Coll. VIII/28–30.)

This repartee was generally considered excellent parliamentary fun. Indeed, we are told, "the House fairly burst into a roar of laughter, men on all sides thoroughly appreciating the humour of the thing".[96] Gladstone was still talking about it a month later. He said it was the most pungent and clever thing that Mill had ever said.*

Mill's relation with the party leader was, Bain thinks, more intimate than anybody realized. Gladstone had long been in the habit of consulting him. In 1861, Gladstone and Lowe had put him through a sharp examination in the committee-room of the House of Commons, about his unheard of proposition that income tax ought to be graded according to earned and unearned income. It ended, as in the matter of the Alabama Claims, with Mill being invited to breakfast to discuss it further. In 1866, upon being told of Mill's distress at the Government's defeat, and how he had said he had never hoped to be under a leader for whom he could feel so much sympathy and respect, Gladstone answered, "Poor fellow, he has all through been most kind and indulgent to me."[97] It was probably no accident that, as soon as he became Prime Minister with a commanding majority behind him, Gladstone hastened to pass legislation on almost every one of the questions nearest to Mill's heart. The disestablishment of the Protestant Church in Ireland, and the first of the famous Irish land reforms: the Married Women's Property Act, the National Education Act, the abolition of religious tests in the Universities, and the end of bought commissions in the army—all were carried in Gladstone's first great ministry which followed, as it happened, immediately after Mill's defeat.

When Leonard Courtney asked Gladstone for a contribution to his *Life of J. S. Mill*, Gladstone sent a memoir kindly meant though killingly sententious:

> "We well knew Mr. Mill's intellectual eminence before he entered Parliament. What his conduct there principally disclosed, at least to me, was his singular moral elevation. I remember now that at the time, more than twenty years back, I used familiarly to call him the Saint of Rationalism, a phrase roughly and partially expressing what I now

* Compare this with the fate of another of Mill's jokes in Parliament. In March 1868 Disraeli's Government, sooner than disestablish the Irish Protestant Church, proposed instead to endow the Roman Catholic clergy as well. According to Courtney, Mill, who had been called Utopian for his pamphlet in favour of peasant-proprietors in Ireland, retorted that this was "Kakotopian"—"too bad to be put into practice—a rigidly academic phrase, which did not amuse the House".

mean. Of all the motives, stings, and stimulants that reach men through their egoism in Parliament, no part could move or even touch him. His conduct and his language were, in this respect, a sermon. Again, though he was a philosopher, he was not, I think a man of crotchets. He had, I think, the good sense and practical tact of politics, together with the high independent thought of a recluse.

I need not tell you that, for the sake of the House of Commons at large, I rejoiced in his advent, and deplored his disappearance. He did us all good. In whatever party, whatever form of opinion, I sorrowfully confess that such men are rare."[98]

Mill was a very conscientious member. Like his venerable colleague Lord Henley, he would sit for hours listening to dull debates, while others occupied themselves by reading or writing, or by going to sleep. He took his full share of committee work. And he expressed himself freely if no political issue were at stake, sometimes even against the opinion of advanced Liberals; as in his defence of capital punishment, or when his determination to thwart the Emperor of the French led him to criticize his party's pacificism in agreeing to the Declaration of Paris. On that occasion, in a speech not unworthy of another well-known figure in a later age, he deplored the weakening of British naval strength. "We have put away the natural weapon of a maritime nation", he declared, "it is a national blunder."[99] His hatred of Napoleon also led him to attack the extradition laws with the utmost vehemence, and he found himself on a Select Committee, with the result that England for a time retained its character as a political sanctuary. His judgement was not always right. In urging the Government, with a moving reference to the interests of posterity, to pay off the national debt before the country's coal seams were exhausted, he was off the track of possible events. And his sense of proportion failed him when, from personal irritation, he described the practice of smoking in non-smoking railway carriages as a flagrant case of oppression by a majority.

Generally, he avoided the main controversial issues of the day. His object in going to Parliament was to promote and draw attention to ideas either so advanced or so unpopular that no one else would handle them. So long as the great party battles were competently led by others, he saw no cause to interfere. In consequence, both enemies and allies thought him ineffectual; they listened respectfully, they enjoyed deriving uplift, but their attention drifted easily away. When Disraeli entered the House for the first time as Prime Minister, Mill was speaking, and he had to pause for several minutes until the uproar had subsided. Often by the time he got his hearing it was late in the day and most members had slipped off home. Or it was near the end of the session, and the government would claim that while what he said was doubtless very true, they really must hurry up and pass the Bill. But he intended to start new lines of thought, not to carry through new laws, and in this he was successful.

He gradually drew about himself a small, politically insignificant coterie. Fawcett, McLaren, Buxton, Amberley, Torrens, W. E. Forster, Thomas Hughes, and P. A. Taylor—with their help, and with expert advice from outside Parliament, he was able to raise projects which he well knew were too far before their time to interest either side. He made use of the debate on Disraeli's Reform Bill, a perplexing and uncomfortable interlude for other members of his party, to ventilate his dearest aims, Hare's scheme for Proportional Representation, and Votes for Women. Prompted by Chadwick and other municipal reformers, and in his capacity as a city member, he had the honour of introducing the first proposal for a London County Council. It met complete indifference: but the movement thus begun continued, and eventually in 1888 the project was accepted. He tried to persuade the Tory government, as the price of his followers' votes for their Corruption Bill, to include in it various improvements in the conduct of elections. But Disraeli, after luring them with fair promises, and gaining Mill's voice for his own purposes in the main debate, deserted them in committee. Nevertheless, most of the improvements have since been adopted as a matter of course. As has, for example, Fawcett's proposal that the fair cost of an election, the polling booth and the returning officer's fee, should be a charge on the local rates, with nothing demanded from the candidate beyond a small deposit as an earnest of good faith.

Occasionally Mill was forced, by the urgency of some threat to freedom, some gross though transitory injustice, to appear in the turbulent arena of day to day affairs. Then, he invariably took a leading, sometimes a spectacular part, though usually an unpopular one. Curiously enough, the first case of this sort was in response to an appeal from the Tory government, to intervene in the national interest and stop a revolution they seemed to be bringing on themselves.

In July 1866, the defeat of Gladstone's Reform Bill, and his replacement by the Tory administration of Lord Derby and Disraeli, aroused great impatience in the London populace for the further extension of the electoral franchise, an impatience fanned and exploited by the activities of the Reform League. Formed in 1864 with the express intention of hurrying things up, the Reform League was a peculiar hybrid. Its enormous membership recalled the unwieldy tactics of the Chartists, but its leadership was that of a keen political instrument. Edmond Beales, its President, was a scholar of Trinity College, Cambridge, a lawyer, and eventually became a judge.* His lieutenant was a Colonel Dickson. There was a feeling in Tory circles that Gladstone, later so famous for his handling of mass-meetings, was in some way involved behind the scenes.

Beales began to organize vast concourses of people as an agitation for Reform. The government retaliated by threatening to close the parks, the only places in the city suitable for meetings of that size, on the grounds that the parks were royal gifts intended for national recreation, and that mass demonstrations were a form of public nuisance. Feelings ran high. Ugly groups began to hang about, glaring at the carriages of the gentry as they bowled along serenely. Handbills appeared, which read, "Wanted, 10,000 costermongers on their donkeys to parade Rotton Row, to test the question as to whether this or any other portion of Hyde Park belongs to a class or to the entire people."

The League announced a meeting in Hyde Park for seven o'clock on Monday 23 July. On the orders of the Home Secretary, the Chief Commissioner of Police posted a notice on the park gates, saying they would be closed at five. Questions were asked in Parliament, and Mill roundly abused the government. But Disraeli was able to assure the Queen, who was also asking questions, that "all was over, and over well".

On the day appointed, workers from all over the country streamed in orderly contingents down Oxford Street and the Edgware Road, 69,000 strong, converging at the Marble Arch, where they found the police drawn up in force. They stopped. The leaders, Beales, Holyoake, Bradlaugh, Dickson, went forward and demanded entry. This being refused, the parade proceeded as arranged to Trafalgar Square, where, after a good deal of shouting, they dispersed. But while the parley was going on, some of Bradlaugh's men, less orderly than the rest, started pulling up railings to force a way into the park. This greatly amused the crowd of sightseers. Joyfully they surged forward

* Edmond Beales of the Reform League not be be confused with James Beal of Mill's election committee.

and joined in. In no time they had torn down a mile of railings, careered across the precious flowerbeds, raced over the forbidden turf, and started throwing stones at wealthy houses in Belgravia. Soldiers were summoned. But before they got there, late at night, everyone had finished rioting and had gone to bed. They could only march strictly through the empty park, and then return to barracks.

Next morning Beales, with the other leaders, called on the Home Secretary. They stressed their restraint and discipline under great provocation, laid all the disturbances of the previous night to his account, and demanded permission to hold one further meeting in the park to establish the right of free assembly there. Now Spencer Walpole, though described by Holyoake as "a sensitive and cultured gentleman", was not a man of great resource and daring. Being (like Lord Lundy) very easily moved to tears, he broke down and wept piteously. The stern reformers, unnerved by a display of feeling so uncustomary in Tory cabinet ministers, left sheepishly under the impression they had gained their point, and Beales went straight to Hyde Park with a notice saying no further meetings would be held there, "except only on next Monday afternoon at six o'clock, by arrangement with the Government".

The news was quickly spread among his followers, and preparations for the meeting went forward in full swing. But Walpole's colleagues, when they heard of it, were furious. In vain did the unhappy man protest he had given no such undertaking. "This fiasco of Walpole's", Lord Derby muttered. The War Office was alerted. Leave was cancelled. Walpole sent for the deputation to return. Holyoake alone came, and made himself most unpopular for doing so, an unpopularity increased when Walpole thanked him publicly in the press for his cooperation. At this stage, only a man of commanding influence with the working classes could have any chance of dissuading them from their purpose; and if they were not dissuaded, there would be bloodshed, perhaps another Peterloo. There were only three men in the country who could do it. One was Bright, but he was out of town. Another was Gladstone, who was watching the turn of events with grim satisfaction. Desperately, Walpole turned to Mill. And Mill went down, with a few of his friends, to attend a conference with the Council of the League.

It was not easy going. He explained why he was there, the evils they would bring upon themselves if they persisted in the meeting.

The leaders, for the most part, saw his point, and had in fact already said the same. But the working men were in an ugly mood. They were in a majority on the Council. They were angry, stubborn and defiant. And there were 70,000 more of them outside. Mill tried a different line. He asked them to look at the principles of the thing. Their course of action could be justified only "if the position of affairs had become such that a revolution was desirable, and if they thought themselves able to accomplish one". To this argument, rather surprisingly, they yielded: but as part of the trouble was that none of them were ready to accept the blame for giving way with the main body of the League, they made it a condition that Mill himself should come and speak at a general meeting to be held in the Agricultural Hall at Islington, instead of in the park, at the original time and date. Now Mill had never had much to do with the Reform League: they wanted the ballot, they did not want votes for women, and in particular he disliked their readiness to proceed at once to a trial of physical force if any opposition was made to their demands. However, since they were obdurate, and since it was clear that the unfortunate Holyoake would probably be torn in pieces if he did not go, he finally agreed. He was able to tell Walpole his success. And, he adds, "I shall never forget the depth of his relief or the warmth of his expression of gratitude."

Cold comfort. On the Monday afternoon, Mill walked with Holyoake from Westminster to Islington. Whatever their forebodings on the way, the reality on arrival far surpassed them. This is how the *Daily News* described the scene:

> "Last night probably the most numerous and imposing demonstration of popular feeling that was ever exhibited under a single roof took place in the Agricultural Hall." After saying that the place was already packed before the main procession arrived, so that it seemed as if they never could get in, the report continues. "But, like the affluents of some spacious lake, the successive streams of human beings moved forwards through the mass inside till at length they blended, and became one solid, compact and homogeneous substance. At this moment the prospect from the platform was truly wonderful. Tens of thousands of stalwart men, evidently belonging to the working class, packed in front of the platform, the galleries all round the building so filled as to leave no spaces vacant, the bands playing popular and patriotic music, and the banners arranged in the distance presented a spectacle such as could scarcely be equalled in any other part of the world. The open doors on the Liverpool-road side added to the demonstration, for through them could be seen the thousands who were unable to find admission inside."

Mill and Holyoake elbowed their way forward to the place of crucifixion. Two blinding lights were shining on the platform; the rest of the great building was in deep shadow. There were more than twenty thousand people within earshot; some of them clung to the tops of the pillars like Lincoln Imps, others sat in the girders of the roof. The noise was indescribable. After a hurried conversation among the sponsors of the meeting, it was decided that G. J. Mantle, who had a massive voice, should introduce the speaker. "His sentences", says Holyoake, "seemed shot from a culverin. His throat opened like the mouth of a tunnel." He announced that Mill would speak, and at that there was a reasonable silence. The *Daily News* continues:

"Mr. J. S. Mill M.P., who supported the resolution, on rising was received with loud cheers from all who could hear the announcement of his name. The hon. Member, who seemed deeply impressed by the spectacle of the teeming and swaying multitude before him, said: 'Ladies and gentlemen, this building is a sufficient guarantee that the cause of reform will suffer nothing by your having determined to hold your meeting here instead of repeating the attempt to hold it in the park. But I do not want to talk to you about reform, you do not need to be stimulated by me on that subject. . . . One of the objects of such meetings is demonstration. You want to make a display of your strength, and I tell you that the countries where the people are allowed to show their strength are those in which they are not obliged to use it. As regards the Parks, your chairman, who is a lawyer, does not doubt your right to meet in them. . . . Your protest has been made, and you have—I think wisely—determined not to renew it. . . . The government, without abandoning what they thought were their legal rights, might have permitted the park for one meeting when permission was asked, and I think it would have been a wise policy and a gracious act to have granted it—(tremendous cheers)—but it was refused.' At this point the crowd in front of the platform became, from the inevitable effect of pressure, so tumultuous and noisy that it was impossible for the hon. gentleman to proceed so as to make himself audible even to those who were nearest to him, and accordingly he made no attempt to complete his remarks."

He was, however, able to extricate Holyoake safely, and walk back with him to Westminster. "I really believe", he said modestly in his *Autobiography*, "that I was the means of preventing much mischief."[100]

Under the circumstances, Disraeli's attitude was, at the best, ungrateful. "The constant demonstrations in the streets of London", say his biographers, "and the countenance afforded to the agitators by many of the Radical leaders, such as J. S. Mill and Bright, made

Disraeli anxious. He wrote to his wife on 26 July: 'I hope with energy and prudence we may overcome the difficulties, but it is very obvious to me that the affair is encouraged by our opponents underhand, with the view of upsetting the Government. I think they will fail.'" Walpole was replaced by the more redoubtable Gathorne Hardy; and in May 1867, nearly a year later, the government, having found they had no legal right whatever to prevent meetings in Hyde Park, introduced a bill especially to obtain it. In August, when it was well on its way to becoming law, the leaders of the Reform League lobbied Mill, and he injudiciously agreed to meet them with a few other radical members in the tea-room of the House of Commons. The government made the most of this: they accused him of "presiding at a meeting within the precincts of the Palace at which measures of physical force were proposed"[101]—a totally false accusation; none the less, the meeting was against the rules, and Mill had to apologize to the Speaker. But the government had miscalculated. It was near the end of the session, and for once Mill was able to turn this to advantage. By speaking in unbroken succession, he and his little troop contrived to play out time. They had plenty to say, and went on saying it. No division could be taken. The bill could not be passed that session. It was dropped, never to be brought in again; and it remains a cherished right for anyone to say whatever he likes in Hyde Park, and for anyone else to listen to him.

When contrasted with his bearing at the Agricultural Hall, Mill's conduct in a different mood at another critical juncture bears evidence to his versatility as a demagogic orator.

At the end of the American Civil War, a great number of disaffected Irishmen, who had been whiling away their exile bearing arms for one side or the other, returned to Ireland. During their stay in the United States they had bound themselves into a Fenian Brotherhood, an international organization with the avowed intention of attacking England wherever and whenever possible. When therefore they got home, the Government expected trouble. Their revolutionary paper, the *Irish People*, was suppressed, Habeas Corpus was suspended, and a great number of them were locked up, although "Head Centre" Stephens managed, with the connivance of a prison warder, to escape to France. The rebellion broke out in 1867, but was easily put down by the police. They had been tipped off by an informer, and the cause found little support among the peasantry, because the Catholic priests denounced it as being Jacobin. The leaders were tried in Dublin. Two of them, Colonel Burke, who had fairly earned his rank while fighting for the South, and M'Cafferty, were condemned to death. Appeal had failed, reprieve had been refused; the scaffold was building, the coffins had been measured.

At this point Mill stepped in. He had already made himself very unpopular by his continual assertion that the trouble in Ireland was due not to the Irish but the English. He now felt that the execution of these men would be not only an injustice but a dangerous blunder. He organized a deputation of fifty M.P.'s of both parties, and all nationalities, English, Irish, Scotch. With these he called, on 25 May, at the house of Lord Derby, the Prime Minister. Mill spoke adroitly, alluding to the occasion of the Queen's birthday as an appropriate one for royal clemency. "My Lord," he ended, "we must sincerely apprehend that the fact of executing these men will make them heroes and martyrs. You must remember that the cause of Irish nationality has not yet had its martyrs." But in vain. Lord Derby, says the *Daily News*, "in his reply maintained an unruffled firmness that, under the circumstances, was remarkable".[102]

That very evening, Mill was to address a meeting in St. James' Hall, on the subject of Disraeli's Reform Bill. The hall, though not so large as the Agricultural Hall, was packed. The doom of the Fenians was in every mind. By now the hangman must be on his way. This time, Mill did not wish to still the popular excitement. The hall was within easy range of Lord Derby's residence; he wished to make Lord Derby's windows rattle. He rose to speak. Here is an extract from the *Daily Telegraph's* account:

> "A pause, and then came a shout—a roar—a tumult, that noise which, coming from a stirred and excited multitude, sounds nearly as terrible when it is sympathizing as when it is hostile or threatening. No need to mention Mr. Mill's name; every one present seem to know him personally."

He soon forgot about reform. And, while he had been jocular about the Compound Householder, keeping his audience in high good humour, he now became intensely grave. He was deliberately provocative.

> "I should like to know whether you think that we have any right to hold Ireland in subjection unless we can make Ireland contented with our government? (Cries of No, No.) That expression of your sentiment will resound through Ireland, and win the hearts of her people to you. Let me ask you now: Do you think the Irish people are contented with our government? (Cries of No, No.) Is that your fault? (No. No.)

Do you think that those men who have been driven desperate by the continuance of what they think mis-government . . . do you think, I say, that those men are not fit to live for that reason?"[103]

Having put them in a frenzy, Mill left and hurried back to the House of Commons. From there, on 27 May, he was able to announce to Helen the government's capitulation:

"dear—all is as it should be. Disraeli, in answer to the O'Donaghue, has announced the Queen's consent to the remission of the capital sentence: and if he had not, the O'Donaghue, Sir John Gray and two others were prepared and determined to go to Balmoral tonight—my regards to pussy—you ever affectionate JSM."[104]

Mill's most sensational incursion into practical politics had started in the previous year, in 1866. Instead of defending an old established privilege, he was prosecuting an abuse of power. Instead of pleading for the lives of two misguided Irish rebels, he was trying to bring to justice, and if he could do it, to the gallows, the Governor of a Crown Colony. He was fighting for the principle he loved above all others against the iniquities performed under the cloak of government by a dunderheaded martinet.

The great liberal achievements of the middle of the century had brought nothing but disaster to the island of Jamaica. The slaves had been freed, but freed only to starve. The planters, having to find wages, could not compete with the price of slave-grown American sugar: one by one they left their estates, or watched them falling into decadence about them. The end of protective tariffs in England, which brought bread to so many hungry mouths, brought to Jamaica only the loss of a safe market, and further ruin.

News of this state of things, on reaching England, aroused great sympathy in anti-slavery and missionary circles. Carlyle was thereupon inspired to dilate upon the subject in the first and most savage of his *Latter Day Pamphlets*, printed in *Fraser's* for December 1849 under the title "Occasional Discourse on the Nigger Question". He deplored the "rosepink sentimentality" of those who pitied the distant blacks while surrounded by misery at home. He went on to say that the whole trouble in Jamaica was due to the natural indolence of the natives, to "beautiful blacks sitting there up to the ears in Pumpkin", filching land to grow their special delicacies instead of toiling faithfully for their white superiors. "What say you", he enquired "to idle Black gentleman, with his rum-bottle in his hand . . . no breeches on his body, pumpkin at discretion, and the fruitfulest region of the earth going back to jungle round him?" He spoke of the "beneficent whip", and hinted at the reintroduction of slavery.

Mill was appalled, so appalled that he emerged from convalescence to attack Carlyle publicly. In the next number of the same magazine, he eloquently assailed the famous doctrine Might is Right:

> "The author issues his opinions, or rather ordinances, under imposing auspices; no less than those of the 'immortal gods'. . . . This so-called 'eternal act of Parliament' is no new law, but the old law of the strongest,—a law against which the great teachers of mankind have in all ages protested: it is the law of force and cunning; the law that whoever is more powerful than another is 'born Lord' of that other, the other being born his 'servant'. . . . I see nothing divine in this injunction. If 'the gods' will this, it is the first duty of human beings to resist such gods. . . . The history of human improvement is the record of a struggle by which inch after inch of ground has been wrung from the maleficent powers, and more and more of human life rescued from the iniquitous dominion of the law of might."

He ridiculed the "everlasting duty" of work for work's sake—"This pet theory of your contributor about work, we all know well enough." He corrected Carlyle's colourful but most erratic economics, and suggested that the thews and sinews of the countless slaves worn out in hacking back the jungle really had more to do with the creation of the plantations than "brave Colonel Fortescue". He went on to deal with "the great ethical doctrine of the Discourse, than which a doctrine more damnable, I should think, never was propounded by a professed moral reformer, that one kind of human beings are born servants to another kind". It was "a true work of the devil"

Carlyle called this resounding confutation "shrill, thin, poor, and insignificant". "No use", he said, "in writing that kind of criticism." And there at least he was unfortunately right. The mischief had been done: his own article was reprinted as a pamphlet and circulated widely. It matched exactly the opinion of the Colonial Office. Such too was the opinion of Governor Edward John Eyre when he arrived at Kingston in 1862 to take up temporary command while Sir Charles Darling went on leave. Eyre was a sturdy man in his prime fifties, a former explorer in Australia, a keen churchman in a forthright formal way. He had had considerable experience of the Colonial Service in New Zealand, Trinidad, and the Leeward Isles. He was not very brainy, in fact he mistrusted brains; but he knew what he liked and what he didn't. As his approved biographer claimed, "from infancy he never saw anything but the object he had in view, and took no heed of any obstacles in the way of his attaining it". He was a strong man, the very embodiment of all Carlyle felt his Man of Action ought to be.

He especially prided himself on his swift intuitive judgement. There was, he decided, no distress to speak of in Jamaica. Most of the talk about distress was really sedition, which was extremely rife, and was deliberately fanned by the Baptist missionaries, who went about educating the natives and spreading dissatisfaction with the loca magistracies. Only a firm hand, and a cool nerve, could prevent a general rebellion and the massacre of the whites whom the blacks outnumbered thirty to one. Having stored his gloomy preconceptions in the back of his mind, he set to work on his administration.

What had at first been passable he made bad, and what had been bad before he made worse by clumsy arrogance. During his first years of office, he antagonized the whole of Kingston by permitting speculators to build a tramway through the main thoroughfare of the city, a tramway later described by British engineers as "rubbish" when they uprooted it, at a total cost to the taxpayers of £13,500. He grew very unpopular. It was with hasty steps that he went down to meet the ship bringing Darling back and ending his lieutenancy; and it was with grim pale lips he turned away when he learned that Darling had not come, that his own appointment was confirmed. He was afraid.

In February 1865 a Baptist missionary, Dr. Underhill, wrote to the Colonial Secretary, Cardwell, describing the true state of affairs in Jamaica. His account ran directly contrary to the report supplied by Eyre, but Eyre was able to persuade Cardwell that Underhill, activated by jealousy of the Church of England, was spreading deliberate falsehood. The result was that the natives, who had trustfully petitioned the Queen to alleviate their misery by a concession of crown lands, received a curt answer to the effect that the only cure for their plight was for them to work harder and so earn more wages—a reply which Eyre triumphantly plastered all about the island. Nobody for a moment believed that the Queen herself would have written such a letter, and indignation against Eyre became extreme. In the capital, one of the leading papers said: "Among the indifferent Rulers that the Colonial Ministers, patronage or interest have thrust upon us, we hesitate not to say that none has equalled his Excellency." The web of his own psychology was closing in on Eyre. If this were the attitude of his more coherent subjects, what, oh what, must the black anonymous hordes be planning? His world became a narrow nightmarish dread, peopled by vague and murky shadows, where only his overbold image of himself strutted aggressively between his white charges and frightful violence. His terror and hatred became concentrated on the figure of one man, George William Gordon, who had caused him several small annoyances, and represented all the things he hated most, being Baptist, half-caste, fairly literate, and politically active.

In October 1865 a rebellion broke out at the small town of Morant Bay, occasioned chiefly by more than usually untactful handling of the alleged Queen's Letter. A band of about four hundred native malcontents approached the court house, and clashed with the local Volunteers. The Riot Act was read. The insurgents continued to advance. The Volunteers fired in volley, killing seven. While they were reloading, the rebels attacked, butchering a similar number with crude weapons. They then disappeared into the hinterland, and during the next few days sporadic outbreaks occurred in one or two other settlements. In all, twenty-two men were killed by the rebels, of whom about half were white, and thirty-five were wounded. In no case were women or children molested in any way.

In this extremity the Governor, or some say Colonel Nelson, his chief of staff, acted with admirable promptitude. Troops and gunboats were ordered to the troubled area, martial law was proclaimed. Eyre himself went down and set the tone for the subsequent reprisals by waiting to see the first batch of twenty-seven rebels brought before the drumhead courts martial he established, and then hanged without ceremony. Back in Kingston five days after the original outbreak, he was able to give assurances that there was no question of a general rebellion; that the savage local rioting in the east end of the island was sealed off, and had in fact already been suppressed.

But now another spirit in him got to work. It happened that the Baptist Gordon, now in Kingston, had formerly been a magistrate at Morant Bay, and it all seemed plain to Eyre that his bitterest enemy had been the master-mind behind the whole conspiracy. Since Kingston was not under martial law, he issued a warrant for the arrest of Gordon, and, upon his surrendering to it, clapped him on board a gunboat and ran him down to Morant Bay. Ramsay, the Provost Marshal, was instructed to find the evidence to hang him, and manfully set about his task by flogging everyone he thought might be a witness. Gordon was swiftly brought to trial before a court which was quite improperly constituted. The President was Lieut. Brand, a young naval officer who was thoroughly enjoying his unusual powers, and had insisted on hanging the first rebel with his own hands before

Eyre's very eyes. Gordon was allowed no counsel and no witnesses. He had not even got his glasses, which had been taken by the sailors as a souvenir, to read the depositions. He was condemned to death. The sentence was personally confirmed by Eyre, and Gordon was hanged two days later. He was not hanged next day because it was a Sunday.

Eyre was very satisfied with the smooth working of his device for getting rid of inconvenient persons. Accordingly martial law was not repealed, but kept in force for a whole month, the maximum period allowed by law. During this interval the process was repeated seventy times. The executions continued with the hideous orderliness common to all judicial massacres. Flogging was wholesale, and indiscriminate of age or sex. One man was put to death for sedition because he bared his teeth at Ramsay while being flogged.

By now there had not been the least sign of resistance from the broken rebels for some weeks, and to justify such measures, it was necessary to keep the excitement going artificially. The Colonel who was sent to clean up the interior was especially warned to be utterly ruthless. But as he was a humane and conscientious soldier, Eyre arranged for a friend of his, Major-Gèneral Forbes-Jackson, who lived along the route to Stony Gut, to keep an eye on him. The General, a retired Indian Army officer who later introduced himself to the Royal Commission as "a little bit of an eccentric person", joined the expedition, waving his revolver enthusiastically, to "fight the enemy of the Queen in the bush". At first he tried to take command of the regiment as senior officer. That being refused, he capered off ahead of the troops, plunging about like a harrier in the scrub, a macabre Don Quixote who saw movement in every thicket and a menace in each ravine. At last the soldiers, fearful he might do some harm to them or to himself, took his revolver and removed the chamber. But his tales of bloody savagery so worked upon the Colonel that when they met a drove of terrified natives coming unarmed to plead for his protection, he shot about a hundred out of hand. When he afterwards learnt what he had done, he went mad, and, on his way back to England, threw himself overboard and was drowned.

The martial law expired at last and violence ended. It transpired that in payment for the twenty-two original victims of the rioters, 586 lives had in all been taken, by far the greater part of them by sentence of court martial, and over a thousand houses gutted: no count could be given of the numbers flogged. Eyre easily induced the Legislative Assembly to pass an act indemnifying him by name, and all others who worked under him, for whatever had been done, and then to vote for their own abolition. In his report to Cardwell, he wrote elaborately and with pride:

> "So widespread a rebellion and one so effectually put down is not, I believe, to be met with in history, and speaks volumes for the zeal, courage, and energy of those engaged in suppressing it. . . . One moment's hesitation, one single reverse, might have lit the torch which would have blazed in rebellion from one end of the Island to the other; and who can say how many of us would have lived to see it extinguished."

At home, the news made an uncomfortable stir in Victorian drawing-rooms. Eyre was suspended, and a Royal Commission was sent out. In April 1866 they reported faithfully enough that, while Eyre had shown praiseworthy vigour in stamping out a planned resistance to authority which might otherwise have had disastrous consequences, he was nevertheless to blame for continuing martial law long after it had become unnecessary, and for sanctioning punishments so excessive as to be horrifying. Particularly, they condemned the trial and execution of Gordon as wholly illegal and unjust.

Faced with facts no longer in dispute, public opinion divided sharply along the line of preconceived ideas about the colour problem, households frequently being split in two. Without question the great mass of average thought defended Eyre. The horrors of Cawnpore were still quite fresh in memory, and the bumptious imperialism which was to lead to the interminable conquests of Zulus and Ashantees was just about to dawn. There were women, as well as men, who had no time for "sentimentalizing over a pack of black brutes".[105] And inevitably there was a good deal of talk of "saving the women of England from a fate which is left unexpressed by the term dishonour".[106] Some agreed with Kingsley, that the blacks deserved all they got for being heathen. Others felt like Tennyson, that Britons must hold their own. Taken all in all, the great majority concurred with Carlyle's euphemism: "Poor Eyre! . . . Such his reward for saving the West Indies, and hanging one incendiary mulatto, well worth the gallows, if I can judge."[107]

On the other hand, the intellectual flower of the country was determined that the atrocities must not be allowed to pass without a protest, or be condoned in the name of the people of Great Britain.

Philanthropists of Exeter Hall, Buxton, Thomas Hughes: scientists like Huxley and Spencer, who could see no major biological difference between black and white; Liberals like Bright and P. A. Taylor; Radicals of the old stamp like Fitzjames Stephen; Morley, Frederic Harrison, and Goldwin Smith—these all formed themselves into a Jamaica Committee, where they came under a hand steadier and more implacable than any of them. For Mill not only hated Caesarism; he had a nice legalistic sense as well. His youthful poring over Bentham's *Evidence*, and his long friendship with John Austin, had been sure to leave their mark. The principle involved was whether the protection of the law of England was to stop short at her shores, or whether it was to reach out over her dependent colonies. Whether actions which in England would be unpardonable and revolting crimes were, because they occurred in far away Jamaica, to be taken lightly as unfortunate mistakes.

Mill sent out legal representatives with the Royal Commission, to make sure they did not fudge the evidence. He issued a pamphlet laying out the whole case, with the aims and objects of the Jamaica Committee plainly stated. Membership soared; soon there were over three hundred influential names behind him, including seventeen M.P.s. He made a terrific denunciation of Eyre in Parliament, and asked question after question. But the Government proposed nothing beyond dismissing Eyre without a pension, leaving the army and navy to make their own enquiries into the behaviour of his subordinates. This would, of course, result only in a few amendments to Queen's Regulations on the conduct of courts martial. Mill resolved on sterner measures. He had taken counsel's opinion, and found that a charge of murder could be brought. He announced his intention of hunting Eyre to death through every channel of the English law.

He was commonly thought to be going much too far. Most people agreed with W. E. Forster, at that time Cardwell's junior at the Colonial Office, that "we can recall Eyre as unfit, we can censure him as a fool; but we have no right to punish him as a criminal."[108] Buxton resigned from the committee, leaving Mill its titular as well as its actual leadership. Mill became extraordinarily unpopular with all classes. Every week, in addition to protests from his constituents, he received anonymous letters, some abusing "the Mill atheist of Westminster, lately M.P., but now a dog", others threatening to shoot him next time he entered Parliament. He was accused of being vindictive. He did not deny it. It would, he said, be a good thing if everyone were a little more vindictive where the rights of others were concerned. "I have never in the whole course of my life felt myself called upon to take practical action on any matter on which I felt more clear."[109]

The opposition saw their opportunity. An Eyre Defence Committee was formed, and a fund opened to pay for his expenses. Carlyle took, for him, an active part. He wrote a public letter on its inauguration, and sent £100. He also took the chair at the first meeting, to prove that "my old coat is not afraid of a little mud on the sleeve of it, as superfiner ones might be".[110] He tnen won Ruskin to the cause, leaving him to bear the brunt.

In August 1866 Eyre reached Southampton and was enthusiastically received by his supporters. He acted with great craft. He displayed amazement at the excitement that was going on. He professed complete ignorance of most of the atrocities, but nevertheless boldly claimed entire responsibility for himself. He then went to earth in Shropshire, where any criminal indictment must be brought against him, and would have, he knew, no countenance from the kindly Tory magistrates. He knew as well that time was on his side: that the jungle would grow over the distant pits in which the bodies of his victims had been thrown; that people would remember only the poor old country gentleman, broken, ruined, with a family to support, now so mercilessly hounded to his last penny and even to death. He maintained an invincible silence, hailed by his admirers as a dignified soldierly bearing. It enabled him to avoid being forced into admissions which might disclose that he, the stern repressor of the rebellion, had also been its panic-stricken cause.

Cheated for the moment of his main quarry, Mill turned upon the underlings, and here he was more successful. Eyre's chief of staff, Colonel Nelson (now Brigadier), and Lieut. Brand (now Lieut.-Comdr.) were charged at Bow Street Police Station with murder, and the magistrates passed the case for trial. In April 1867 the prisoners appeared at the Central Criminal Court of the Old Bailey before Lord Chief Justice Cockburn. He, in summing up, made it very clear that the deliberate extension of martial law, or rather absence of law, beyond what was strictly necessary was illegal: that the whole circumstances of Gordon's arrest and trial were illegal: and therefore that the charge should stand. But the defendants were never in any real danger. Throughout the instruction of the jury, the odious Brand, in the dock, whiled away the time drawing callous sketches of

Gordon being hanged. The Grand Jury disregarded the Lord Chief Justice and threw out the bill, and with it ended every hope of getting Eyre for murder.

Mill next tried prosecuting Eyre for misdemeanour under the Colonial Governor's Act. The Attorney General returned the papers with a chilling note, saying no action was intended by the Government. Mill then brought it as a private case. When it came up in Queen's Bench, Mr. Justice Blackburn, dissenting from the Lord Chief Justice, ordered the jury to throw it out. A civil action which a negro, Phillips, was persuaded to bring for damages for false imprisonment met with no better fate. The prosecution was at an end. Eyre, feeling himself safe at last, ventured to write to the papers in his own behalf. Carlyle drafted a petition for his reinstatement, but Lord Carnarvon in replying for the Government said "it is a most terrible case and one that is indefensible", and that he did not wish to speak of it.

With that the Jamaica Committee had to be content. In July 1868, two years after its inception, Mill issued a leaflet announcing its disbandment. Of its three main objects, he said, two had been obtained. For although they had failed to bring Eyre to justice, they had got a legal decision about martial law, and had roused public indignation against oppression in the dependencies. "Colonial Governors and other persons in authority", he added grimly in the *Autobiography*, "will have a considerable motive to stop short of such extremities in the future."

All the same, Eyre eventually came out on top. In 1872 the Liberal government voted him compensation for his costs in litigation. "After this", Mill wrote disgustedly, "I shall henceforth wish for a Tory Government." Three years later, Disraeli granted Eyre the pension of a retired Governor, and he lived on in respectable seclusion till his death in 1901. "Carlyle's conclusion", says the Dictionary of National Biography, "that Eyre was a just, humane, and valiant man, faithful to his trusts everywhere and with no ordinary faculty for executing them, was finally accepted. It is, however, impossible to understand the quiescent attitude of Eyre throughout the tragic crisis."[111]

X

On 30 April 1868 Gladstone defeated Disraeli on the Disestablishment of the Irish Church, and shortly afterwards there was an appeal to the country. Mill stood for Westminster again in November, but this time W. H. Smith, his opponent, was carried home, although the overall result of the elections was a convincing victory for the Liberals. Mill himself attributed his failure to the great superiority of the Tory party mechanism, and to the huge sums of money they laid out, while he again refused to pay a penny towards his own expenses. There was probably some truth in this, for certainly the Tories were keen enough to see him go.

But there were other reasons: the Eyre business had not done him any good, and his wilful interference in other elections was resented by many of his own party. Bouverie, for instance, who had been Liberal member for Kilmarnock for a quarter of a century, was not pleased when Mill suggested how very public spirited it would be if he retired in favour of Edwin Chadwick, for whom Mill had subscribed £100.

Mill's main interest in the election was not his own success, but the return of working-class candidates to Parliament. He sent money and letters of support to George Odger, among several others, some of them utter strangers. By doing so, he risked splitting the party vote for no good reason, since none of them had a chance of getting in. The worst case of this kind, and, despite his subsequent bland denials, one most damaging to his own cause, was his contributing ten pounds to Charles Bradlaugh who was standing for Northampton.

Bradlaugh was a militant atheist, the central figure in several prosecutions for publishing blasphemous papers. He was said to have been seen standing watch in hand in the market place, challenging God to strike him dead within ten minutes. He was so detested that a special fund had to be started for the working men who lost their jobs for supporting him. In siding with him, Mill not only endangered the election of his old friend Henley, the party contestant of the seat, but brought suspicion on his own respectability. *The Times*, the *Saturday Review*, and the Lord's Day Observance Society all attacked him. Even the devoted Kate Amberley said he was much too meddlesome and was behaving very badly.

To the tide of indignant demands for explanation rushing in upon him, Mill made a series of evasive answers. To some, he said that as Bradlaugh had no hope of being elected, he could not be said to be damaging Lord Henley's chances. To others, that whatever Bradlaugh's religious views might be, he wished to see him in Parliament because he was a man of obstinate and forthright character. To his Committee, who wrote that all was in confusion and that under the charge of atheism they had lost ground heavily, he replied defiantly:

> "If anyone again tells you that I am an atheist, I would advise you to ask him how he knows, and in what page of my numerous writings he finds anything to bear out the assertion. You will find he has nothing at all to say. If he talks about my subscription for Mr. Bradlaugh, he should be asked whether he thinks that the working men of Northampton, who have adopted Mr. Bradlaugh as their candidate . . . are all atheists."[112]

Helen, in Avignon, was furious at the variety of his excuses, and on seeing this letter in the *Daily News* was moved to chide him with an emphasis reminiscent of her mother:

> "It seems to me utterly unworthy of you, to speak mildly of it; and not to speak of its imprudence. That you could write such a letter shows how this electioneering hurry and excitement unfits you for writing and it seems to me the height of folly to go on varying your replies on such a topic instead of keeping as nearly as possible to one set form for everyone. I do not know which I dislike most—the assertion that to be called an Atheist is calumny, that you are as much one as Gladstone is a Catholic, or that dignitaries of the Ch. of England have spoken for you! ! ! Surely to use such arguments is to sacrifice all that it is worth while to be elected for. Then you go on to say you are no more an Atheist than all the working men of Northampton who support Bradlaugh; and you defy him to find anything in your writings to justify the assertion. I cannot tell you how ashamed I feel. And you actually invite the publication of this letter which makes me literally blush for you and must lower the opinion entertained of you by everyone who knows you and sees it. I beg and entreat of you, refuse utterly to say one word on this topic except what you have already said. Copy as literally as you can the letter I dictated (which I enclose) about Bradlaugh; and what you yourself said at the former election, about yourself. Do not disgrace yourself as an open truthful man; do not shut the door to all future power of usefulness on religious liberty by such mean and wretched subterfuges as this letter. Do not be drawn into saying one *fresh* thing great or small. That is what your opponents want you to do. . . ."[113]

Helen herself conducted all future correspondence about Bradlaugh.

Mill's defeat was probably viewed with a certain equanimity by the main body of the Liberal party, but to his little band of followers it was complete disaster. At the same time, Amberley was turned out, Chadwick failed to be elected, and Roebuck lost the seat he had held at Sheffield for nearly twenty years. To John Morley in particular, who at the age of thirty also failed at this his first election, it seemed that the end of the world had come. Mill's rejection was, he rather largely wrote, "as significant as the fall and disgrace of the great Turgot".[114] Mill himself, however, was undisguisedly elated, as he wrote to Cairnes:

> "I really have much difficulty in feeling as I ought to do about what is a real defeat to advanced Liberal opinions, so great and fresh is the pleasure of the feeling of freedom, and the return to the only occupations which agree with my tastes and habits. I hope to be quite as active for my opinions out of the House as I was in it, and more usefully so than I probably should have been during the next Session (if not Sessions) during which the Irish Church will engross nearly all the activity of Parliamentary men."[115]

As for Helen, she greeted him as though he were her warrior returning from the fray:

> "Dear Mr. Mill—
>
> How I wish you were not obliged to stay all these tedious days at Blackheath! I want you to be here that we may enjoy together the strange feeling of liberty and repose; instead of which you are surrounded by circumstances which bring forward all the disagreeable side of the Westminster failure—all the excitements and interests of party politics. . . . If I thought you would feel the result as a disappointment on the whole, I should so wish to be with you—indeed I think I should start off to meet you; only then I think you would laugh at me, not for sympathizing with you but for supposing you could dislike the result. . . . How I wish you were here! I shall be so impatient till you arrive! and now today it is divinest Avignon weather; the Ventoux streaked with sparkling snow; the air warm and balmy the sky intensely blue, the after-glow its most glorious. And then the two pussies seem to mew for you to come and admire them."[116]

So, leaving Broadwood's to pack and send his piano,* and dutifully bearing his homely trophies—a packet of curry powder from London, and a pot of "Jus de Limons et Glycerine" from the

* Now the property of Madame Jeanne de Flandrésey of Avignon.

Boulevard des Italiens for Helen's hair, Mill set out once more for the beauties of Provence. For the mysterious and purpling hills, the brown terraces of the wine crop, olive orchards, the heavy flowing Rhone, the yellow walls and spires. For the broken bridge with its chapel standing out into the flood, once joining the massive palace of the Popes to the Gothic village on the other bank, Villeneuve, the convenient annex for the mistresses of the Viceregent's court.

He went back to the chill of the Mistral whining down the river, to the marble tomb, to the villa hidden in the trees. Helen had made many improvements for him. Beneath the balcony running round two sides of the house where he strolled and mused in sunny weather, she had built in a bathroom, and a special place where he could sort and file away his plants. She had also built a long covered passage for him to walk in when it was cold or wet, as he had done years before with Jeremy Bentham in the cloisters at Ford Abbey. "Thus, you see", he wrote to Thornton, "I am in clover, and you may imagine with what scorn I think of the House of Commons, which, comfortable club as it is said to be, could offer me none of these comforts, or, more properly speaking, these necessaries of life. . . . I am lost in wonder and admiration of the ingenuity with which Helen has contrived to manage it all."[117] He declined invitations to stand again for other constituencies on whatever terms he liked to make, and he continued to indulge his whim of subscribing to the election expenses of working men.

During his time in Parliament, he had only the winters free for writing. In consequence his literary output was not large. During the recess of 1865, he wrote a stylish review of Grote's *Plato* for the *Edinburgh*, taking the opportunity to cover the whole field himself, with only occasional flattering references to the author. Early in February 1867 he delivered his Rectorial oration at St. Andrews. It was more of an essay on higher education than a speech, and not entirely successful, since he had no notion there were any limits to the amount of ground a university course could profitably cover. He was, however, gratified at the cheers he drew from the Divinity students when he touched upon free thought. Also in 1867 he began, with the help of Bain and Grote, a revised edition of his father's *Analysis of the Human Mind*, which he felt would now be likely to receive the popular attention denied it on its first publication because of the ascendancy of the mystic theories of the romantic age. His notes and introduction were a filial vindication of the associationist psychology he had protected stoutly through so many tortuous wrangles, and had, along with Bain and Spencer, done so much to bring back into favour.

It appeared in 1869, and marked the end of his purely philosophic work. Not that his intellect was tiring; on the contrary, he was as vigorous as ever. "There certainly is no blessing in human life comparable to liberty", he wrote to Amberley in congratulating him on their mutually regained freedom:

> "I envy you the pleasure of having got to a Latin Classic. I hope to be able to give myself the same satisfaction by-and-by. I have not read a Greek or Latin book for at least half-a-dozen years with the exception of Plato, whom I read right through preparatory to reviewing Mr. Grote's account of him. Cicero's philosophical writings are very pleasant reading, . . . but I like his orations and letters better. It is true I am much interested in everything that relates to that great turning-point of history . . . which is called the Augustan age—so solemn in its literary monuments, so deformed by the presence of Augustus in it. No historian has treated that cunning, base, and cruel adventurer as he deserved except Arnold in the 'Encyclopaedia Metropolitana' and Ampère in 'L'Empire Romain à Rome', merely because Virgil and Horace flattered him.
>
> But this kind of reading after all is but recreation. . . ."[118]

He was in his sixties now, and time was getting short for all he wished to do. In the winter of 1869–1870 he methodically finished his essay on Theism, the last of the *Three Essays on Religion*, and brought the *Autobiography* up-to-date. The next year he produced a seventh library edition of the *Political Economy*, and in 1872, carefully prepared the definitive eighth edition of the *Logic*. The *Dissertations and Discussions* had already been brought up to their final form in three volumes in 1867. As regards his major writings, therefore, he was ready for any eventuality.

The work of others continued to make claims upon him. Henry Thomas Buckle, a fervent admirer of Mill, who had set out to write a History of Civilization, had died in 1862 with only the introductory volume of his giant undertaking published, leaving an unsorted mass of relevant material and scribbled fragments. These Helen, at Mill's suggestion, began in 1865 to edit with a biographical introduction. The composition and the labour were her own. But Mill had to lend assistance in writing for information to friends and relatives of Buckle with results not always suitable for a sympathetic study, and he also had to find a publisher for her. Longmans eventually undertook it, and the *Miscellaneous and Posthumous Works of H. T. Buckle* appeared in three volumes in 1872.

Another personal commitment was John Morley, who in December 1866 had taken over the editorship of the *Fortnightly Review*. Morley was even more under Mill's influence than G. H. Lewes had been before him. The *Liberty* had come out during his final year at Oxford, and, according to one of his contemporaries, he knew it practically by heart. During the last year or two he had enjoyed closer familiarity with Mill than Lewes had ever done. From Mill's point of view, the *Fortnightly*, since its inception in 1865, had been all that he had once wished that the *Westminster* might be, a modern magazine wherein all opinions were admitted freely with a minimum of editorial dogma. All his favourite views were championed, Hare's scheme, his own election, Governor Eyre, votes for women, the House of Lords, land reform, peasant proprietorship in Ireland, trades unions, the conscription of a national army, and later, the Franco-Prussian war. It has been said that Mill was, to the *Fortnightly*, "the incarnation of its philosophy".[119]

Although Morley had inherited a galaxy of contributors—Walter Bagehot, George Eliot, Herbert Spencer, Frederic Harrison, Trollope, and Meredith—and added to them Huxley, Sidgwick, and Leslie Stephen, he had not yet rescued the review from its unpopular reputation as a Comtist and sectarian organ, or worked it up into the trumpet of enlightened Liberalism he later made of it. During these years Mills gave him articles, always freely, whenever asked or whenever he had anything to say. Indeed, regarding Morley as his natural successor, and recalling his own troubles with the *Westminster*, he gave him a complete monopoly. There were several articles on the nationalization of the land; one on the French philosopher Taine; one in December 1870 to stop the headlong dash into a war with Russia on behalf of France; a review of Sir Henry Sumner Maine on Village Communities; an appreciation of Berkeley's life and writings, Mill's favourite among the old philosophers; and finally, a few months before his death, a salute to Grote's valedictory *Aristotle*.

In November 1870 when Morley was ill, Mill wrote proposing that he should temporarily undertake the management of the *Fortnightly*. And in his will he left his copyrights to Morley "to be applied in aid of some periodical publication which shall be open to the expression of all opinions, and which shall have all its articles signed with the name of the writer".[120] Mill never ceased from helping periodicals of liberal inclinations in the financial difficulties he knew so well to be inescapable. One of the last letters ever written to him was from H. R. Fox Bourne, editor of the *Examiner*, declining £500 Mill had offered to save it from liquidation, and proposing instead that Helen should take it over.[121]

The worst of his distractions was his enormous correspondence. Since he first stood for Parliament he had become a national figure, or, more properly speaking, a sort of international oracle. From every corner of the civilized world, on every topic under the sun, letters flowed in upon him. There were books to acknowledge, meetings to address, individual hardships to assist, scholastic quibbles to be settled. An Australian wished to hear his views on the nationalization of the railways there. His friend Sir Charles Dilke asked how he thought prehistoric monuments could best be protected against vandalism. d'Eichthal tried to enlist him in the cause of making Greek a universal language. From the banks of the River Ohio came a book, with an almost illegible covering letter, to show that "the rudest members of society on the farthest limits of social intercourse with mankind have the same profound interest (for the future of the race) as those at the great centres of Thought".[122] Out of the blue, Henry George, the land reformer and exponent of the Single Tax, wrote to him from California about the problem of the Chinese coolie labour:

> "For myself, I have no doubt of your views, nor do I see how any one who has attentively read your works can doubt them; but your name is lugged into this controversy as frequently upon one side as upon the other, and a direct expression of opinion from you would be of great use. . . . You must be aware of the fact, but I think can hardly appreciate the reality, that in all parts of this country (and wherever our tongue is spoken) there are thousands of earnest men and women to whom your name is as familiar as a household word, and who do not merely admire your ability and appreciate your work, but regard you with all the feeling due to that highest of all characters,—the 'great, good man'."[123]

A doctor in Wimpole Street tried to get Mill's help against compulsory vaccination. A certain Wm. Riddle thought he had found a way to universal plenty by the centralization of steam power under international control. Two Russian professors from Yaroslavl desired an interview. An agency called Redpath and Fall wanted to arrange a lecture tour in the United States which "could be made equally pleasant and lucrative"

Everything worth an answer always got one, exhaustive, plain, and carefully thought out. Helen helped him faithfully. She learned to express his own ideas exactly in his serviceable, ocean-going style, and so was able to prepare his letters for his copying and signature. Gradually she took over whole blocks of correspondence, mostly to do with education, or the rights of women, or specific cases of abuse. So well did she succeed that it became impossible to tell the difference, except occasionally from the length, and Mill was once forced to shame and discomfort an over-eager friend who, in his anxiety to have the authority of the great name behind his cause, had taken the unpardonable step of publishing a letter without asking if he might. "I am particularly pleased at your approbation of the last sentence of my letter", observed Mill mildly, "because I can share in it myself, for it was dictated to me, as I wrote it word for word, by my dear daughter. We always agree in sentiments, but she sometimes can find better words to put them in than I can myself."[124]

It was a neat and thorough secretariat. Every letter of importance after they went to Avignon was filed away with the draft of the answer fastened to it. At Mill's death, Helen was able to write decidedly, "I have all my dear stepfather's letters, preserved, looked through from time to time by himself, arranged in order by myself, and left by him in my hands with directions, verbal and written, to deal with them according to my judgement. When the more pressing task of the publication of his MSS. is completed, I shall, if I live, occupy myself with his correspondence; if I do not live it will be for my literary Executors to decide what to do with it."[125]

A letter of advice she sent to Kate Amberley in September 1869 reveals how this most intimate confidence with Mill was reached, and throws a valuable light on their mutual method of work:

> "Don't be discouraged from writing because Lord Amberley criticizes you severely. It is an excellent thing to have a severe critic at home; I am a *very* severe critic on Mr. Mill; and I am continually reproaching him that he will praise everything I do, which I tell him shows indifference to whether I do it well or not. My dearest mother was a severe critic of everything I did and constantly stimulated me to go on trying to do well without in the least hiding from me the defects

of what I had already done. From this I have gained the advantage that I do not grudge any quantity of trouble, and am not discouraged at having to throw away what I have written and begin all over again two or three times if necessary. The faintest kind of disapprobation from Mr. Mill (when I am lucky enough to get it) suffices to make me cancel a whole article, or page after page in it, and often I am too dissatisfied with what I wrote to care to show it even to him. But believe me it is far pleasanter to have some one on whose sternness one can rely for anticipating what hostile critics might say, than to be thrown entirely on one's own judgement.

. . . You must remember that every woman who has been well educated begins at a disadvantage with men and with uneducated women; she has to *un*learn the letter writing style—the style of saying so little in as many words as possible and passing lightly from one subject to another. Will you let me see the article you have written and shall I suggest improvements in it? Mr. Mill tells me I alter other people's writings particularly well and should make a good editor from my power of seeing what they mean to say and bringing out their meaning with as few modifications of their own words as possible. I have a great deal of practice in doing this, beginning with Mr. Mill's writings which I go over five or six times, putting in words here, stops there; scratching through whole paragraphs; asking him to write whole new pages in particular places where I think the meaning is not clear; condensing, enlarging, polishing, etc. In short I take very much greater liberties with his things than with anyone else's, because there is no *amour propre* to be hurt in his case or mine, and I have confidence in him to reject my alterations if he does not really think them improvements."[126]

Clearly, as an author, Mill was very patient, and a lesson to all that cantankerous and embittered breed. Yet he too had his arrogance. It was fortunate, for instance, that he had no wish for honours or rewards. In December 1869 the Princess Royal of Prussia and Queen Victoria's daughter Princess Alice earnestly sought an interview at Avignon. Mill excused himself on grounds of health, although he had just returned from a holiday in the Alps, at the end of which he walked fifty miles in three days, and had even more lately entertained the Amberleys. To Chadwick, enquiring about the creation of Life Peerages, he replied that the House of Lords was obsolete, and that any such scheme would become a "refuge for the mediocrities of past administrations".[127] He thought Kings and Queens were also obsolete, except for the historical evidence the Queens provided of the excellence of women rulers. He took to task the Rev. Stephen Hawtrey because, in his otherwise admirable treatise on education, he seemed "to regard Eton as a favourable specimen of what a school can do in the way of moral and religious training; an opinion from which all that I know of the kind of article turned out annually from Eton into the higher walks of life in this country, leads me strongly to dissent."[128] And, with the Eton master who objected to this letter he was even more acerbic. "When you say that so many of your best boys go into the Guards, you say what amounts to an acknowledgement of utter failure in educating them morally either for the special responsibilities of a governing class or for the universal duties of a man."[129]

On the other hand, he was fully alive to the danger of intellectual standardization, and the necessity of bringing up a cultured aristocracy. "It is a great mistake to think that children are not benefited by living and growing up among models of beauty", he told James M. Barnard of Boston:

> "They are, on the contrary, more benefited than anyone else, though not, at the time, conscious of the benefit. I can trace a great influence in my own development to the accident of having passed several years of my boyhood in one of the few old abbeys which are still inhabited, instead of a mean and graceless modern house, and having at the same time and place been familiar with tapestries from Raphael's cartoons, which peopled my imagination with graceful and dignified forms of human beings. . . . The great desideratum in America—and though not quite in an equal degree, I may say in England too—is the improvement of the higher education. America surpasses all countries in the amount of mental cultivation which she has been able to make universal; but a high average level is not everything. There are wanted, I do not say a class, but a great number of persons of the highest degree of cultivation which the accumulated acquisitions of the human race make it possible to give them. From such persons, in a community that knows no distinction of ranks, civilization would rain down its influence on the remainder of society. . . ."[130]

His personal sympathy was large, and he gave as much time to individual problems as to social principles. Yet he did not lend himself to special pleading. To a schoolboy of fourteen who hopefully wrote to ask if corporal punishment ought not to be abolished, he made a sternly rational reply:

> "Sir,—To give a proper answer to your question would be to write the essay which you are intending to write. But if you wish for a mere opinion, expressed in few words, I would say;
>
> 1. Severe punishments of some kind are often necessary for boys, but only when they have been negligently or ill brought up and allowed to acquire bad habits.

2. Assuming severe punishments to be necessary, any other method of punishment that would be effectual is preferable to flogging. In the case, however, of certain grave moral delinquencies, chiefly those which are either of a cowardly or brutal character, corporal punishment in that or some equivalent form may be admissable."[131]

Mill's letters, naturally enough, reveal a great deal of the man. He was well aware of the horrors of war, but he had no use for Peace Societies. "I regard war", he said, "as an infinitely less evil than systematic submission to injustice."[132] He looked eventually to international arbitration backed by force. "If war between nations is ever to be put an end to, it can only be as war between individuals has been checked in civilized societies—by the creation of a police and an impartial umpire to settle quarrels."[133] In the meantime, he wished to see the regular army swept away and replaced, in the interest of both justice and efficiency, by a citizen army in which every able-bodied man should serve without exception:

"I do not think it safe to trust entirely to voluntary enlistment for the large defensive force which this and every other country now requires. The perfection of a military system seems to me to be, to have no standing army whatever (except the amount required for foreign possessions) but to train the whole of the able-bodied male population to military service. I believe that with previous school drill, six month's training at first and a few days every succeeding year would be amply sufficient for the infantry. This would not take away the young men from civil occupations to any material extent: the six months would be taken at the very beginning of active life; and there would be at once the greatest amount of force possible, and the strongest security against its being called out unnecessarily; for a service from which no one would be exempt would inevitably be unpopular unless the cause were one for which the nation at large felt a real enthusiasm."[134]

Innumerable societies thought that Mill would like to be on their committees. Occasionally they were right, and very often he sent money even when he disagreed with them. But sometimes they were startlingly wrong. The Secretary of the Neophyte Writers' Society was told:

"So far as I am able to collect the objects of the society from the somewhat vague description given of them in the prospectus, I am led to believe that it is not established to promote any opinions in particular; that its members are bound together only by the fact of being writers, not by the purposes for which they write. . . . Now, I set no value whatever on writing for its own sake, and have much less respect for the literary craftsman than for the manual labourer, except so far as he uses his powers in promoting what I consider true and just. I have, on most of the subjects interesting to mankind, opinions to which I attach importance, and which I earnestly desire to diffuse, but I am not desirous of aiding the diffusion of opinions contrary to my own; and with respect to the mere faculty of expression, independently of what is to be expressed, it does not appear to me to require any encouragement. There is already an abundance, not to say superabundance of writers who are able to express in an effective manner the mischievous commonplaces which they have got to say."[135]

He also refused to become a Vice-President of the Society for the Prevention of Cruelty to Animals, because, being supported largely by the upper classes, it concentrated on the brutalities of the poor and ignored the more luxurious cruelties of the rich. In this case, however, he continued to subscribe as he had done for many years, and at his death he willed the Society the princely sum of £500.

Counting himself averagely wealthy—between 1866 and 1870 his income ranged roughly speaking from £2500 to £2000, of which some £1800 represented his pension and income from investments, and the remainder royalties from his books—he gave money freely. Over the course of three years, he paid out nearly £1000 in 80 distinct subscriptions and donations, his gifts being notable for their variety rather than their size. The Women's Suffrage Society was, of course, the principal recipient. But the Protestant Charitable Fund, the Blackheath Volunteer Band, the Drinking Fountain Association, the Freedmen's Aid Society, the Railway Guards' Friendly Society, the Life Boat Fund, the Blind, a Working Men's Library in Ireland, a Wiltshire poacher under prosecution, and the Parsee Girls' School, all gained more or less from his generosity. He even seems, on occasion, to have turned out his pockets in the street, for there are in his account book entries like "Gave an English workman £1-7-10."[136] When he died, half of his total estate of £14,000 was given to charity.[137]

His accounts were precise even in imprecision. In the middle of a long list of casual payments—meals at the House of Commons, stamps, taxes, piano tuning, umbrella covering, coach mending, medicine, dog licence, plasterers, gardener, books, excursions and the like—he put down "Lost by mistake 16/10". Fortunately, Helen was a frugal housewife. They were therefore able to live comfortably within their income, despite their two establishments complete with servants, and still enjoy their favourite pursuits.

They continued to take holidays in the Alps. In the summer of 1871 at Lucerne they hired a rowing boat and spent six days plashing happily round the Lake. At Avignon, two or three times a year, they would climb up Mont Ventoux. Sometimes they were caught in sudden thunderstorms, and took shelter in solitary mountain farms where they were always welcomed, as Helen gratefully acknowledged:

> "Coffee, wine, milk, or the best of whatever the house afforded was always pressed upon us. Blazing fires lit, in spite of our protests, on bare mountain sides where wood is scarce; and guides offered for miles if we would accept them: and on the few occasions when we ventured to offer any gift in return, it was always refused, although with perfect courtesy, even by little children. Having wandered about for years on foot among the mountains of Provence, and knowing every valley and peak of the department of Vaucluse better than the streets of London . . . I may be permitted to testify to the kindly character of the Provençaux. . . ."[138]

They had many of their English friends to stay at Avignon. Among the French, they permitted only a few to share their intimacy, and those few were utterly devoted to them. There was M. Chauffard, the local doctor who had attended Harriet, formerly *Maire* of Avignon and a member of the *Légion d'Honneur*, whose books Mill took some pains in getting published. And there was the young Protestant Pastor, Louis Rey, on whose keen and liberal Gallic mind the contradictory features of Mill's character continued to exert a consuming fascination, to the end of his long life of ninety-nine years. After Mill's death he helped Helen with her legal affairs, and when she left Avignon, he undertook a Power of Attorney for the sale of her house and property. Later, he made two splendid public addresses, just before and just after the first world war, in favour of Mill's statue being erected in the *Place Crillon* facing the *Hôtel de l'Europe*. Jules Véran recalls that in the nineteen-thirties he found the old man musing in dim lamplight on a late October afternoon, and how, at the name of Mill, the whole of his aged face lit up.[139] His wife and daughters, too, were friends of Helen, and helped her in many ways. Three of the daughters are still very much alive.* Among the greatest treasures of the family are Mill's inkstand, a portrait of him, two vases which he brought from Athens, and his copy of Montesquieu's *Esprit des Lois*.

* In 1948.

The only activity in which Helen did not attempt to accompany her stepfather, was one he pursued the more energetically as he grew older, that of botany. When he died, he left behind him enormous albums full of pressed plants. Helen sent four packing cases of them as a gift to the Curator of the Royal Gardens at Kew, who in turn sent some of them to Harvard University. Others seem to have ended up in the Botanical Museum at Melbourne, Australia, where the lady in charge was much stirred to hear of their illustrious origin. Those containing specimens from Vaucluse were given to the Musée Calvet in Avignon, where they may still be seen. Mill was essentially an amateur collector. For him botany was not a science, but in a true sense, his sport. To Spencer, who had invited him on a fishing trip in Scotland, he replied "my murderous propensities are confined to the vegetable world".[140] So, it was fitting for his womenfolk to keep away, and leave him to choose his own companions. He never had the slightest difficulty in making friends. On his latest excursions he had tramped round England and Scotland with a young Scot called Irvine, who had spent some years collecting proverbs of all nations. As he was looking for a publisher for them, Mill sent him to call on the long suffering Longman.

At Avignon, while browsing in the Requien Collection of natural history in the Abbaye St. Martial,* Mill fell in with the supervisor, J. H. Fabre. Fabre at that time was just beginning to be known. He had raised himself from a peasant birth entirely by his own efforts; and having acquired an immense knowledge of entomology by minute and patient observation, rather than from books, he provided a fine example of the inductive method of achieving truth. Mill was immediately interested in him, and they found they had a community of tastes. Though Fabre was not primarily concerned with botany, his keen eye had not failed to pick up in the course of his rambles a great deal of information about plants as well as insects. They took to going out together, and Fabre became a frequent caller at Mill's sorting room at St. Véran. Soon Mill conceived the project of compiling a survey of the Flora of Vaucluse, and Fabre emphatically agreed to help him. They were well equipped for such an undertaking. Mill methodically gathered one of each species of plant and carefully catalogued it; while Fabre, who was always attracted by the tiny and bizarre, dealt with the exotic race of mushrooms. They trailed across the country of romance, over the hills and through the valleys;

* Now the Post Office.

Fabre, with his short brisk tread in front, Mill following with his long and pensive stride. In a whole day's outing they would hardly speak. Nor was that surprising; for Fabre would spend hours peering through his lens into a strange world peopled by grasshoppers and spiders, and Mill would lose himself in an equally private region of pure cones and tangents. "As one of these mathematical exercises", he confided to de Morgan, "it occurred to me to ask myself what is the curve of which the equation is $xy=a^2$? I soon came to the conclusion that it is a pair of opposite equilateral hyperbolas referred to the asymptotes. This being the case, what is there to say about the *other* pair of hyperbolas considered as referred to the same axes? The coordinates being in this case of opposite signs, the equation must be $xy = -a^2$ . . ."[141] Nevertheless, they understood each other well, the entomologist and the botanist.

It was part of Fabre's duty at the abbey to lecture to a convent school. Feeling that the subject matter of his discourse, like his audience, was too closely supervised and guarded, he determined to extend his usefulness. He began giving free public lectures to townspeople of both sexes, and Mill strenuously encouraged him in his decision. The results were disastrous. Fabre was never popular in Catholic circles: he was a naturalist, and since Darwin launched his bombshell, nature had become a dangerous business. Besides, he was far too brusque and *irregulier*. On finding him teaching the pure virgins of Avignon in plain and simple language about the sex habits of arachnids, his superiors' worst suspicions were confirmed. They instantly dismissed him from his post. Since he had never bothered with a formal contract, he had to leave at once. Since he had never saved a penny, he was facing ruin, with a wife and a large family of daughters to support. He had been too busy to make friends, and his Parisian patron had been broken in the same attack. Fabre was enraged, bewildered, and despairing. At last he wrote to Mill, who was away in Parliament. Mill at once sent Frs. 3000, without conditions and without receipt. He overcame Fabre's fierce peasant pride by telling him it was not intended as a personal favour, but to enable him to continue with his service to humanity—a formula which had often served its turn before, in similar circumstances. Fabre was free to seek his livelihood from scientific writings. Two years later, as soon as he was able to command advances large enough, he rushed off to St. Véran and poured the cash out into Mill's protesting hand, insisting upon adding another thirty francs as interest on a debt which, Mill assured him, existed nowhere outside his own imagination. That done, he hastened to shake off the dust of Avignon, and found himself a small retreat, as nearly as possible like Mill's, on the outskirts of Orange. Fabre never forgot the incident, and forty years afterwards, in his triumphant dotage, asked his biographer time and time again, if he was sure that he had got it down in full.[142]

Meanwhile, the two men continued to walk together in silence as of old. The *Flora of Vaucluse* took shape and swelled. When Mill died, Fabre wished to continue it alone, but was unable to get funds from the *Maire* of Avignon. The best he could do on his own account, he did. He worked devotedly, and eventually brought out his hefty treatise on the little mushrooms.

XI

Mill's wider interest in his later years was taken up with two great political issues of the future. One of these was the question of Socialism. The Reform Bill had come and gone without the consequence he so much feared, the stampeding of Parliament by a host of ignorant working men. In fact, not one of them so far had succeeded in passing its majestic portals, and from Mill's point of view there were too few rather than too many. Then his friend Thornton had produced a book discrediting the Wage Fund theory. That theory taught that it was useless for the workers to try to raise their wages by means of strikes and combinations, because they already shared between them all the money available for that purpose. In making a public recantation of his adherence to it, in two articles in the *Fortnightly*, Mill was widely thought to have signed the capitulation of classical Political Economy. He had given up his one remaining speculative objection to the labour movement, and by reason of his tremendous reputation gave great impetus to Trade Unionism all over Europe. When in 1872 five gas-stokers were sentenced to a year's imprisonment for conspiring to coerce their masters by plunging London into darkness, Mill said it was "a permanent disgrace".[143]

With both his political and his economic bogeys gone, he had to reconsider his position. He began to wonder whether after all Harriet, who had really been the Socialist of the family, had not been right as usual.

It has often been claimed that had he lived a little longer, Mill would have become the first and foremost of the Fabians. Certainly, when he died he was working at a book on Socialism, which he intended to be as exhaustive as the *Representative Government* and to outrank it in importance. When Helen published his somewhat inconclusive beginning for this book, he was found to have predicted the rise of Socialism as an inevitable consequence of universal suffrage.* Certainly, too, he was in favour of democracy, both as an ideal and, so far as was consistent with the public interest, as an immediate proposition. He was aware that the working classes endured many injustices, and was anxious to remove them. Not only because they were injustices, but because they stood in the way of that general elevation of the race towards happiness and dignity which was his constant preoccupation. National expediency was his sole measure of the rights of ownership. He favoured a strict limitation of inheritance. If he had been persuaded that it was necessary for the state to requisition any property whatever, and take over the direction of large slices of the national economy, he would have advocated it.

But this must not be pushed too far. He was very far from being a *sansculotte*. "What advantage is there in designating the doctrines of the Association by such a title as 'the principles of the political and social Revolution'?" he scolded the Nottingham Branch of the International Working Men's Association. "'The Revolution' as a name for any sort of principles or opinions, is not English. . . . The meaning intended . . . can only be guessed at from a knowledge of French, in which language it seems to mean the political ideal of any person of democratic opinions who happens to be using it."[144] Measures of nationalization would have seemed to him necessary

* *Fortnightly Review*, February, March, April 1879. See also *John Stuart Mill on Socialism*, edited by W. D. P. Bliss, Linden, Mass., 1891. *J. S. Mill*, by Julius West, Fabian Tract No. 168, 1913; *The English Utilitarians*, by Leslie Stephen, 1900, Vol. III, pp. 203–237, and Elliot's *Letters*, Vol. II, p. 334.

temporary evils, as in fact all government appeared to him to be. He would never have welcomed them as milestones on the way to a corporate existence. He was dyed liberal to the bone. He believed in individuality and self-development as ends in themselves and as the only means to the end of human welfare. Particularly he would have deplored the general modern rationale of state organics, whereby governments of every shade are allowed and even expected to act as though the community were something greater than the sum total of its parts.

Moreover, he never was convinced that such measures were necessary or even possible, as he pointed out quite clearly elsewhere in the book on Socialism. "Apart from all considerations of injustice to the present possessors, the very idea of conducting the whole industry of a country by direction from a single centre is so obviously chimerical that nobody ventures to propose any mode in which it should be done." Of industrial politics in the twentieth century style he had not the faintest concept. He thought strikes had a beneficial tendency towards promoting partnership between management and labour. He thought payment by the day would be immoral, and that piecework, coupled with fixed working hours and an increased rate for overtime, was the perfect system. The intricacies of mass-production never occurred to him. Friendly cooperation in a creative undertaking was the limit of his industrial imagination. He had a great respect for capital, and thought any tax upon it undesirable. He was a free-trader. And he was convinced that competition was the healthiest and most vital of the principles of economics.

It is true he wished to nationalize the land. He believed that a man was entitled to possess only what he could earn or make himself. As no man made the land, and since the landowner drew all the profit from its use while contributing nothing to its fruitfulness, Mill saw no reason why this ancient monopoly, originally obtained through favour and preserved for centuries by force of law, should not be abrogated.

Following on from his speech in Parliament about the Irish system of land tenure, he lent his active support to the Land Tenure Reform Association. He frequently addressed the meetings which they sponsored. He drafted a manifesto of their aims and objects, and arranged for Longmans to put it out at *6d.* The last two articles he published were written on behalf of the Association,* and in his Will

* In the *Examiner*, 4 and 11 January 1873.

he left them £500.* While allowing them to claim the right of the state to requisition on payment of fair compensation, he was determined that they should be cautious, because of the powerful opposition they were certain to excite. He wished them for the present to demand only the special taxation of augmented income from the land, due to new discoveries of natural wealth or to a sudden desirability of situation, and a capital gains tax in the event of sale. He consistently opposed a rival society formed by working men who thought the programme ought to be much bolder. "The furious and declamatory violence of their resolutions", he told Fawcett, "seems to show that they would have been a very intractable element in the other association, and that it is well rid of them."[145]

Their agitation for the immediate expropriation of the land clashed with another interest far dearer to him. "One thing I see clearly, that there will be more difficulty than ever in preserving the commons. The working-class speakers are filled with exaggerated ideas of the value of waste lands for cultivation, and apparently do not care at all for the preservation of natural beauty."[146] A few years previously on the foundation of the Commons Preservation Society he had written promising his fullest help. "The desire to engross the whole surface of the earth in the mere production of the greatest possible quantity of food and the materials of manufacture, I consider to be founded on a mischievously narrow conception of the requirements of human nature."[147] He enthusiastically backed successful movements in favour of protecting Epping Forest as a free resort within easy range of London, and of keeping open footpaths through the leafy glades of the New Forest. He was prepared to force the landlords to throw open their estates as public parks, sooner than let them be sequestered, and ploughed up to grow corn.

There is therefore little in Mill's activities over land reform to indicate that he was veering towards state socialism. "I am sorry to say", he told Pasquale Villari when sending him the pamphlet of the Association, "that the little tract has been reviewed in the *Deux Mondes* by a person so ignorant of my opinions as to call me a partisan of extreme centralization. It is about the last reproach I

* In 1891, Sir George Grey told a meeting of the Single Tax League at Sydney that Mill was not only President of the Association from 1868, but left them £3000 in his will. (*Pall Mall Gazette*, 25 April 1891.) Both these statements seem to be incorrect. In a letter to Fawcett on 24 October 1869 Mill said he had declined to become President. And Mill's Will in Somerset House states clearly that the sum was £500.

should have expected. But a large class of French writers make assertions of facts with a levity almost incredible."[148]

Mill's other great political concern was the birth and growth of the Suffragette movement. When on 20 May 1867, during the debate on the Reform Bill, he rose to move that the word "man" should be replaced by the word "person", the question of a woman's right to vote was heard for the first time in modern history in the legislative assembly of a civilized country. The boisterous humour of the House of Commons at first saw only what they took to be the absurdity of the subject, but as he proceeded they found themselves compelled to listen. It was a wise and reasoned discourse, appealing to expediency more often than to justice. He demolished all the obvious objections, that politics were not a woman's business, that women did not want to vote, that they preferred to wield the immense indirect power they had always had, or that they were already represented by the votes of their natural protectors. And he sketched the happy effects on family life of making men and women frank and confident companions. When he finished, after a short debate, a division was taken. There was a certain amount of buffoonery in the lobbies, and many who had promised to support Mill did not dare to face the ridicule. Even so, when the figures were announced, it was found he had got as many as 73 votes, or almost a third of the thin attendance.

Mill was very pleased. He had never expected that his motion would be carried: he had only meant to advertise it. His speech had been intended not as a climax but as an overture: not as a defiant Parthian shot, but as the first action in a carefully planned campaign. So far the opposition had been slight, and even crumbly. As he himself expressed it:

"The unexpectedly large minority which the proposal obtained, and the thought and discussion which it excited in quarters where the subject had never been thought of before, have given an immense impulse to the question. Numbers of men and women in all ranks have since given their adhesion to the movement; and agreement with it is rapidly becoming a badge of advanced liberalism."[149]

The next step followed swiftly. A month later he wrote to Cairnes:

> "The Women's question has been a most decided and important success, and it is truly astonishing how the right opinion is spreading both among women and men since the debate. We are now forming a society in London for the Representation of Women, and hope to get others formed in Edinburgh and Dublin, and elsewhere (there is

already a most efficient one in Manchester, which obtained the majority of the 13,500 signatures to this year's petitions). The proposed Society will probably be composed of an executive committee of ladies, a General Committee of both sexes subscribing one guinea a year, which will be the ultimate governing body, and ordinary members who will only subscribe a small sum per annum, will receive the reports and circulars, but have no part in the management. The chief members of the Executive Committee will be Mrs. P. A. Taylor, Miss Cobbe, Mrs. Stansfield, and Mrs. Fawcett. My daughter and I will be on the General Committee. Will you and Mrs. Cairnes give us leave to put your names upon it? And can you give any help for the formation of a society in Dublin?"[150]

The Cairnes were duly enrolled. So were Lord Houghton (Richard Monckton Milnes) and Lord Romilly. Mill counted his conversions singly, with a loving care, agreeing with Robert Browning,

"That low man goes on adding one to one,
His hundred's soon hit:
This high man, aiming at a million,
Misses an unit."

His hundred, so far as the Committee went, was in fact hit before the beginning of September and included thirty Members of Parliament. In the next few years he added, among many others, Francis Newman, brother of the Cardinal, and Charles Kingsley, despite the decided opposition of his wife. Fanny Kingsley was a strong antagonist of women's votes. So Mill invited them to spend a night at Blackheath, where it took him less than an hour to win her over too.[151]

But he was a high man as well, aiming not at one million but at many. To the editor of the American *Anti-Slavery Standard*, he observed, "the disabilities of women are now the only remaining national violation of the principles of your immortal Declaration of Independence".[152] At home, meetings were being held, and agitation was being fostered by every possible means. It even seems that during the preliminaries for the autumn election of 1868, a few women, taking advantage of a quibble raised in the *Fortnightly Review* by Dr. R. M. Pankhurst,* about the meaning of the word "man", contrived to slip past the revising barrister and got their names on to the electoral register—a case involving some engaging possibilities, as de Morgan jubilantly pointed out:

"The R.B. was right; he is not bound to know that Jane Smith is a woman, nor could he raise the question. I have a cousin whose wife is

* In 1879 Richard Marsden Pankhurst, Doctor at Law, married Emmeline Goulden, subsequently famous as Emily Pankhurst.

David. When the poll clerk sees a female claimant, I suppose he will be bound to say, 'Madam, you cannot be the Jane Smith on the list, for the law says that voters are all men. I must wait until some man comes forward and declares he is the person described.' Then the poll clerk may perhaps be subjected to an action."[153]

In one way and another the movement gathered force, and in March 1869, Mill wrote to Pasquale Villari in all sober judgement, "This cause is making very rapid progress here, and so great a number of women, and of the most distinguished women, have responded to the appeal which has been made to them, that success, though still distant, no longer seems to me as much as three years' distant."[154]

He hastened to throw more faggots on the fire. In the spring of 1869 he published *The Subjection of Women* which he had kept lying by him for eight years awaiting the decisive kindling moment. It was, like all his works, exhaustive, tracing the dominance of man from the rough dawn of history to the smoother methods of the present day. Carefully and clearly it exposed the disadvantages of women in each of the three great circus rings of life where every human being must perform, education, work, and home. It attacked the matter philosophically, examining the corrosive force of power both on the subject and still more upon her master. And, typically, it attacked the opposition on its strongest as well as on its weakest ground. It mentioned, but it did not linger on, the brutal and the base: it challenged the texture of even the most perfect union under the conventions then prevailing:

"The most favourable case which a man can generally have for studying the character of a woman, is that of his own wife: for the opportunities are greater, and the cases of complete sympathy not so unspeakably rare. And in fact, this is the source from which any knowledge worth having on the subject has, I believe, generally come. But most men have not had the opportunity of studying in this way more than a single case: accordingly one can, to an almost laughable degree, infer what a man's wife is like, from his opinions about women in general. To make even this one case yield any result, the woman must be worth knowing, and the man not only a competent judge, but of a character so sympathetic in itself, and so well adapted to hers, that he can either read her mind by sympathetic intuition, or has nothing in himself which makes her shy of disclosing it. Hardly anything, I believe, can be more rare than this conjunction. It often happens that there is the most complete unity of feeling and community of interests as to all external things, yet the one has as little admission into the internal life of the other as if they were common acquaintances. Even with true affection, authority on the one side and subordination on the other prevent perfect confidence. Though nothing may be intentionally withheld, much is not shown."

Of anything Mill ever wrote, *The Subjection of Women* aroused the most antagonism. Those who were always hostile became more hostile still. Fitzjames Stephen said it was "the strongest distinct illustration known to me of what is perhaps one of the strangest, and what appears to me to be by far the most ignoble and mischievous of all the popular feelings of the age". He obligingly went on to say that there was something practically indecent "in prolonged and minute discussions about the relations between men and women, and the characteristics of women as such. I will therefore pass over what Mr. Mill says on this subject with a mere general expression of dissent from nearly every word he says."[155]

"His intense arrogance", said *Blackwood's*, "his incapacity to do justice to the feelings or motives of all from whom he differs, his intolerance of all but his own disciples, and lastly, in natural consequence of these qualities, his want of playfulness in himself and repugnance to it in others, all combine to create something like antipathy."[156]

This time not only his enemies but his friends were horrified. "He leads us to suppose", said Bain incredulously, "that the relations of men and women between themselves may work on a purely voluntary principle."[157] "Rank moral and social anarchy",[158] said Frederic Harrison thirty years later. Herbert Spencer took the line that women should not vote because they could not fight—a view shared by de Morgan in a half-serious remonstrance. Charles Kingsley, though convinced, was cautious: he had, he said in a mysterious way, "arrived at certain conclusions thereon, which (in the face of British narrowness) I have found it wisest to keep to myself".[159] Kate Amberley alone was faithful. "I wish it cd be done without talk," she wrote, "but no reform was ever made without talk and without boring people out at last, and so I suppose we must be discussed and turned inside out for the next 20 years and then lawmakers will begin to see they had better give in and let us manage our own affairs and keep our own property and be guardian to our own children."[160]

Mill had not set out either to please his friends or to enrage his enemies. He had set out to stimulate discussion, and in that he was abundantly successful. Nearly everyone had strong opinions in the matter. Two editions of the book were rapidly exhausted, and arrangements were soon being made for its translation into German, French, and Polish. In that same summer of 1869, Moncure Conway visited an imperial mansion twenty miles from Moscow with his friend Schuyler, the American chargé d'affaires in Russia. To his astonishment, upon its being learned that he was a personal friend of John Stuart Mill, four dazzling princesses, the young daughters of the house, came and bowed before him, "declaring (in perfect English) that Mill's book demanding freedom for women was their Bible. 'Yes', said the eldest, 'I sleep with that book under my pillow'."[161] Mill sent a copy of the French edition to the poet Mistral, and it had the desirable effect of stiffening his ideal of womanhood: henceforth the heroines of the Félibre, though still romantic, were noticeably less limpid. From over the Atlantic, from Hartford, Conn., rang like a clarion the voice of Mrs. Isabella Beecher Hooker, sounding her thanks to God, her praise of Mill:

> ". . . For many years, I have contended (privately I mean and in my own heart) that men were by nature capable of as high moral excellence as women. . . . But of late I have been impressed more and more with the closer likeness to the divine nature which woman seems to bear, in that she is, more sensibly, if not more truly a *creator* than man is. . . . What father can say, 'Thou art my child' as a mother can?"[162]

This, Mill thought, showed a tendency to paint the lily, and in replying he felt bound to say:

> "I do not perceive . . . any ground for attributing a natural superiority in capacity of moral excellence to women over men. . . . The position of irresponsible power in which men have hitherto lived is, I need hardly say, most unfavourable to almost every kind of moral excellence. So far as women have been in possession of irresponsible power, they too have by no means escaped its baneful consequences."[163]

Mill well knew the strength of prejudice against him. At one end of the scale was James S. Blackie, a Professor at Edinburgh University, who maintained that men were trees and women flowers. At the other was the crofter's wife who said, when Helen consoled her on the death of her small son, "what troubles me is, they be all men folk up there, and won't know how to do for him".[164] At the root of all was the placid acceptance of the customary, the inveterate fear of novelty. Mill knew that what was wanted was to make the seemingly outrageous appear commonplace; in short, to advertise. With this in mind, he got Trübner to reprint his speech in Parliament, as well as Harriet's *Enfranchisement of Women*, and an article by Helen called *The Claims of Englishwomen*. It was the only occasion he ever lost money on his publications.

He knew that, in the end, however many just and chivalrous men spoke up for them, the only dependable friends of women as a class, as of all other classes, were themselves. The cardinal reason why women could not vote was that men did not want them to. From the start, Mill's chief discouragement was the extraordinary reluctance of women to come forward. A certain amount could be attributed to fear: a certain amount more to the servile station which had for so many generations been their lot. But by no means all: there was still a preponderance of women who genuinely and freely thought they were better off as they were.

What was needed was the force of example, and here Helen was first and foremost. "The existence of the Society", Mill said in his *Autobiography*, "is due to my daughter's initiative; its constitution was planned entirely by her, and she was the soul of the movement during its first years, though delicate health and superabundant occupation made her decline to be a member of the Executive Committee." It was she unaided who reproved first Mary Carpenter and then Miss Nightingale for pusillanimity, and later on enrolled them both. She was so prominent, in fact, that Charles Eliot Norton, writing to his friend Chauncey Wright, quite unjustly blamed her for Mill's whole interest in the cause. "Her words have an oracular value to him", he declared, "something more than their just weight: and her unconscious flattery, joined with the very direct flattery of many other prominent leaders of the great female army, have a not unnatural effect on his tender, susceptible and sympathetic nature."[165]

In October 1869, Helen and Mill decided that the time had come for their female supporters to take an active part. On the immediate question of finding a speaker for a meeting at Stoke-on-Trent, he wrote to the wife of his friend, P. A. Taylor:

> "I have written to propose to Mrs. Fawcett to take up the project; if she does not, would it be impossible for you to do so? . . . The cause has now reached a point at which it has become extremely desirable that the ladies who lead the movement should make themselves visible to the public, their very appearance being a refutation of the vulgar nonsense talked about 'women's rights women', and their manner of looking, moving, and speaking being sure to make a favourable impression from the purely feminine as well as from the human point of view."[166]

He wrote later to Croom Robertson:

> "You seem to us to underrate the value of a 'pretty face' in a lecturer on women's rights. As my daughter says, it is not for the sake of effect on men that it is important, but for the influence it has on the younger women."[167]

Kate Amberley filled the bill superlatively for one. She had listened enthralled in the Ladies' Gallery to Mill's historic speech in Parliament. Shortly afterwards she left for a six months' visit to America with Amberley, but on her return she was remorselessly enrolled by Helen. In a letter to a friend, she made her declaration of her faith. It was a neat summary of the salient points in the *Subjection of Women*:

> "As force no longer rules the world I see nothing in woman's nature and mental capacities to doom her eternally to the inferior position of a squaw or for the better sort a harem princess—I do not like that position as a lot of half the human race, and wd have woman in reality a help mate to man, an improving and equal companion . . .
>
> Opening every possible occupation and profession to women, giving them the same wages for the same work as to a man—letting women have their own earnings unmolested by a husband or father; opening the places of education and the prizes of it, to those who wish to make use of them; and lastly giving them the franchise, not as an end, but as a means of getting themselves heard and attended to—
>
> These are the things I wish for, and it is to make the life of a woman of the higher and lower classes more complete, less dependent, less animal and selfish and more noble and spiritual; in fact to make her a citizen and give her the chance of leading an honest and happy life—I could write for ever on this subject but the post is going."[168]

She raced round getting up petitions for the Married Women's Property Act. She gave £50 towards the opening of Girton, but was told by the Principal, Miss Davies, that her name was too dangerous for her to be on the Committee. Undaunted, she gave a scholarship of £50 for three years for women medical students recently admitted to the lectures at Edinburgh University. Then, in March 1869, she attended a full meeting of the Women's Suffrage Society in Hanover Square and sat on the platform between Helen and Amberley. She did not speak, although almost everybody else of importance in the movement did, including Mill himself, and Helen; Cairnes, Mrs. Fawcett, Mrs. Grote, and Mrs. P. A. Taylor.

In May a year later she took her baptism of fire. Supported by her husband on the dais, she read the paper she had been anxiously preparing for many months—the paper which had had the benefit of Helen's scrutiny—to a pompous looking lot of people in a dingy little hall at Stroud. There was hardly any clapping, and it seemed to fall very flat. To make matters worse, the petition they were all supposed to sign was left in a small room behind the stage, and scarcely anybody saw it. Even so, she earned several columns of condescending criticism in the *Times*. Her aunt Louisa Stanley wrote to say that she was terribly ashamed of her Goddaughter, and wondered she did not go to settle in America where their ways would suit her better. A few months later Kate was publicly laughed out of a party at the Gladstones. But she carried on. In February 1872 she rose triumphantly to speak at Bristol as President of the West of England Branch of the Society. She had Charles Kingsley and Lady Bowring among her many distinguished Vice-Presidents, and was received with great applause.

Neither Kate nor Helen nor the others minded that they made themselves notorious in gaining publicity for women's rights. At the same time, it was essential to be circumspect. Any hint of fanaticism would be fatal. The campaign was managed in a strictly rational key, and nobody could tell from Mill's unimpassioned utterances that the whole race of women for whom he spoke were an embodiment of his ideal Harriet. It was particularly necessary to avoid embroilment with sensational or scandalous proposals. The Bradlaugh affair had taught him prudence; he kept the women's movement quite distinct from universal suffrage. He was still more discreet about the question of divorce. His real views were suspected to be most advanced, as indeed they were:

> "My opinion on Divorce is that, though any relaxation of the irrevocability of marriage would be an improvement, nothing ought to be ultimately rested in short of entire freedom on both sides to dissolve this like any other partnership. The only thing requiring regulation would be the maintenance of the children when the parents could not arrange it amicably—and in that I do not see any considerable difficulty."[169]

But in the *Subjection* he was very guarded. His opponents, feeling themselves cheated, taunted him angrily: his friends were disappointed and surprised. He refused to be drawn by either, and for the rest of his life stuck to an official formula: "I do not think that the conditions of the dissolubility of marriage can be properly determined until women have an equal voice in determining them, nor until there has been experience of the marriage relation as it would exist between equals."[170]

Many people could not understand why he pursued what seemed to them the unimportant token right of voting, at the expense of other more immediate practical matters—the reluctant passage of the Married Women's Property Act, or the slow acceptance of the principle that women should be educated. This again was part of a deliberate policy. He did not ignore the other issues, he gave them every assistance in his power. "Much must also be attributed to the influence of one man", Professor Dicey says of him in relation to the Property Act.[171] When Girton was founded, he drew up the first examination paper on Political Economy—and an extremely stiff one it was too. He also took an interest in the expansion of the women's college in Bedford Square. At his death he left the enormous sum of £6000, nearly half his total estate, to the cause of women's education.*

No one was more aware than Mill of the extent of women's disability. He saw it as a hydra with a hundred heads. But he knew his time was short, and if he was to achieve anything, it could only be by piercing the monster through the heart. It seemed to him that once women were properly represented in Parliament, all their grievances would be swept away, as surely as the working-class vote would end in Socialism. "When that has been gained", he said, "everything else will follow."[172] Meanwhile the particular agitations gained an incalculable impetus from the general battle. A bill admitting women to the local government elections, for example, passed through Parliament practically unnoticed.

Nor is it commonly realized how close he came to success in his main purpose. His friends in the House of Commons formed the plan of moving his resolution that women should have votes as a formal protest every year on May Day, much in the way that Grote had done for years on the question of the ballot. The Liberal Government took little interest since it was not a party issue, and in 1870 the Women's Suffrage Act carried its first reading by a majority of thirty. To the general consternation of the House, it had to come up a second time. It was then found to have no fewer than 184 adherents;

* £3000 was to be set apart for the first university to open its degrees to women. A further £3000 was left to endow scholarships for female students only. In 1881 Professor Knight of St. Andrews wrote to Helen asking whether the bequest was still available, as they were thinking of carrying out that reform.

many waverers, encouraged by the victory, having overcome their fear of ridicule. In 1871 and 1872 it got 151 and 143 votes respectively. Had Mill lived a few years longer, he would very probably have got it through. It is an indication of his personal influence that, once he was dead, it took nearly fifty years and a world convulsion to bring enough opinion round, and that even then it was only achieved at the expense of riot, brutality, and martyrdom.

Although Mill's policy in furthering the rights of women was one of masterly discretion, there were times, as in his parliamentary life, when rank injustice forced him to be outspoken. The laws relating to venereal disease were such a case; and here, on a topic unsavoury enough to endanger the entire cause, he revealed quite clearly the giant indignation underlying his methodical campaign.

Prostitution, and its attendant evils, were very rife. In 1868, forty-three per cent of the out-patients at Guy's Hospital were venereal cases. In the great naval ports, so many sailors were being lured from their faithful watch and ward by scarlet women of one sort or another, that a number of Her Majesty's Ships were quite unfit for service. Now the dignitaries of the realm were men of the world, who knew prostitution as the oldest of professions, and generally preferred not to soil their hands with anything so distasteful. But when the disreputable trade broke out of its permitted province in the ill-lit streets and surreptitious lodging houses, and imperilled the Fleet, morality reinforced by patriotism demanded action. So, the so-called Contagious Diseases Acts were passed, empowering the police in certain places to take up any woman whose virtue they had reason to suppose was professionally easy, and subject her to a medical examination.

A number of enlightened people, like Florence Nightingale, felt these acts to be not only unjust but ineffective. They were, they felt, of a piece with the Puritan pillory and whipping-post. They were less considerate than the law in force until the reign of George III, by which women were to be burnt alive for treason because it was indelicate to expose their bodies on a gibbet. Mill shared these views, but knew the issue was a dangerous one—as dangerous as that of birth control, for which he had been prosecuted many years before. As he counselled one enthusiast, "though it is often a merit, it is only in peculiar cases a duty, in anyone to be a martyr for his opinions".[173] He therefore exercised the virtue of restraint, and in due course a body of women led by Mrs. Josephine Butler started such a general clamour that a Royal Commission was appointed. Mill then intimated that he would like to be called in evidence; and, as he was known to have knowledgeable if peculiar views on women, he was called.

How did he comport himself before this grave tribunal? Did he appeal to them, out of their manly strength to deal leniently with feminine frailty, to pity even though they must condemn? Or did he, like another figure long ago, stoop, and draw with his finger in the dust, as though he heard them not? He did neither of these things, although no doubt they were both implied in his burning cheek, his quivering voice, and in the nervous twitching of his temple. What he did was far more unexpected. He actually said it was the men who were to blame:

> "The object of the Act is not to protect those who voluntarily seek indulgence, but to protect the innocent from having these diseases communicated to them; that I understand to be the object. Now a woman cannot communicate the disease but to a person who seeks it, and who knowingly places himself in the way of it. A woman can only communicate it through a man; it must be the man who communicates it to innocent women and children afterwards. It seems to me, therefore, if the object is to protect those who are not unchaste, the way to do this is to bring motives to bear on the man and not on the woman, who cannot have anything to do directly with the communication of it to persons entirely innocent, whereas the man can and does."[174]

Gradually the main drift of this disastrous logic began to dawn on his astonished audience. He was cross-examined by Sir John Pakington, an old antagonist who had been the butt of his joke about the "stupid party".

"Am I right in inferring from the evidence you have been so good as to give us", began Sir John belligerently, "that you would not consider the fact of a very large proportion of the crews of our men-of-war and the soldiers of our army, being incapacitated for rendering service to the State by this terrible disease, an adequate reason for legislation of this kind?"

"Not for legislation of this kind", answered Mill; "but it might be for legislation of other kinds. I cannot say that I have considered the subject much, but I do not see why the State should not subject its own soldiers and sailors to medical examination, and impose penalties on them in case they are found diseased. I would not undertake to say that it might not, by means directly acting on soldiers and sailors, in a very considerable degree discourage that kind of indulgence. It is certain, at least I have understood so, that the impression on the minds of soldiers and sailors, is that it is not discouraged."

Sir John Pakington became shocked and pained. "Am I to understand you seriously to propose that in this country we should adopt a system of espionage over every man seen going into a brothel, and that men seen to go into a brothel should be subject all alike to personal examination?"

"I am not suggesting espionage, because I do not recommend the Acts at all: but if it is already in practice on women who go to brothels, I think the women should not be singled out to be subject to examination, but the men should be subjected to it also."

In despair, Sir John Pakington tried to make him mitigate his severity against the guilty man. Was not Mill aware, he asked, "that for a man to give his wife a disease of that description would be adjudged cruelty, and would be a ground for divorce, at all events *a mensa*?"

"Yes, but not complete dissolution of the matrimonial tie."

"You would make it so?"

"Yes."

"You would make it *a vinculo*?"

"Yes, *a vinculo*," replied the merciless philosopher, "accompanied with very heavy pecuniary damages for the benefit of the sufferers, the wife or children."

Fifteen years afterwards, the Contagious Diseases Acts were repealed.

XII

"One who knew Mill only through his writings knew but half of him, and that not the best half", said Fitzjames Stephen, his most decided critic.[175] As the shadows of his life began to lengthen, the mists of fame began to swirl up and obscure the man. Gone is the slender figure reclining in an armchair by the fire, with the cat Placidia purring at his feet, who rose and cordially received the reporter from the *Chicago Tribune*. The broad high forehead and the hatchet face; the grey and steadfast eyes; the thin, straight nose; the clean complexion and emphatic chin; the growth of curly light-brown hair running round the thinning cranium; the soft, incisive voice—all this is gone. In its place remains the legend left by Victorian misunderstanding, sedulously tinted by Carlyle, impressed by decades of schoolteachers and divines. A name, a black and shiny case left over from the days of horse-drawn cabs and gaiters. A name, indeed, to conjure with; a name at which, as one of Mill's modern adversaries has pointed out, we still instinctively take off our hats.[176] But a name erudite and respectable; sober, censorious, and sad; prodigious, and at the same time somehow awful, a kind of moral Great Agrippa. Above all, as dry as dust.

Still, while he lived, his friends could see him as he was, and for us too the foggy wreaths occasionally divide. News of the outbreak of the Franco-Prussian war reached him sitting in his garden at Blackheath. He struck his chair with vehemence, and cursed Napoleon, crying out, "What a pity the bombs of Orsini missed their mark, and left the crime-stained usurper alive."[177] Like everybody else, he was entirely taken in by Bismarck's stratagem.

> "The English public should know, and show that it knows, that this war has been brought on wholly by Napoleon, that the Prussians are fighting for their own liberty and for that of Europe; that England is bound to protect Belgium. . . . The volunteers ought to be armed with the newest and best rifles by public subscription. It is not a time for talking about peace and the horrors of war when our national existence may be soon at stake. At the same time it is wrong to attribute this war to France. . . . The Germans are right in saying that it is Napoleon and not France they are fighting. . . ." [178]

A few months later Mill and Helen were staying with the Amberleys at their new home, Ravenscroft, and were taking picnic lunches out to Tintern Abbey and the Forest of Dean, then goldening for autumn. He was in his highest spirits, walking everywhere, and always noticing the flowers and hedgerows. One evening after dinner he read them Shelley's *Ode to Liberty*. "He got quite excited and moved over it rocking backwards and forwards and nearly choking with emotion; he said himself: 'it is almost too much for one!'"[179] Then suddenly came catastrophic news that public order had collapsed in France, and Helen remembered she had left her precious Buckle manuscript in Avignon. After a sleepless night she decided they must go and fetch it. They dared not go through France for fear that Mill might be taken for a Prussian spy. So they went to Switzerland, and Mill waited there while she and her maid went on to Avignon. They came back more impressed than ever at the industry and discipline of the German troops.

In 1871 the lease ran out on the tumble-down Blackheath house, and he took a flat in Victoria Street, 10 Albert Mansions, where he was nearer to the centre of his quiet, illustrious circle. In June George Grote died, and to Mill's disgust an Abbey funeral was arranged. He walked reluctantly as pall-bearer, and, as they left the marble-cluttered aisles, remarked to Bain, "In no very long time, I shall be laid in the ground with a very different ceremonial from that."[180]

He had made peace with his family. His sister Mary Colman, who had caused the worst offence, was a good woman although inclined to dominance.* She had fallen on hard times. Her husband had separated from her; her favourite son, a sailor, was swept overboard during a gale in the Channel. Her circumstances were most depressed, and Mill to some extent retrieved his old and bitter wrong by coming to her rescue. He made her an annuity. He arranged for her daughter Minnie to go to Bedford College. And when her second son disgraced himself by robbing an office till, it was Mill who found the money for giving him another chance.

In March 1873 Sir Charles Dilke persuaded Mill to sit for his portrait to the famous artist, G. F. Watts.† A better likeness of him,

* Information kindly supplied in a letter from Mrs. Edna Gemmell, of South Africa, her grand-daughter.

† George Frederick Watts, R.A., O.M., 1817–1904: the first husband of Ellen Terry. Helen did not particularly like the painting, the only known one of Mill. It was offered to her by Lady Dilke, but at her suggestion the Dilkes kept it, and commissioned Watts to make a copy of it for the National Portrait

on a glittering April day, is preserved in the luminous writing of John Morley:

"He came down by the morning train to Guildford station, where I was waiting for him. He was in his most even and mellow humour. We walked in a leisurely way and through roundabout tracks for some four hours along the ancient green road which you know, over the high grassy downs, into old chalkpits picturesque with juniper and yew, across heaths and commons, and so up to our windy promontory, where the majestic prospect stirred him with lively delight. You know he is a fervid botanist, and every ten minutes he stopped to look at this or that on the path. Unluckily I am ignorant of the very rudiments of the matter, so his parenthetic enthusiasms were lost upon me. Of course he talked, and talked well. . . .

Rose was in some trepidation, but his simplicity and soft amiable way put her soon at ease, and all through lunch they chatted most sociably and gaily about the wildflowers, and birds, and weasels, in which he takes as keen an interest as she does. He was impatient for the song of the nightingale. Then I drove him to our little roadside station, and one of the most delightful days of my life came to its end, like all other days delightful and sorrowful."[181]

For Mill, as for Helen, Avignon was a perfect paradise in May. He was impatient to be gone. From there, on 26 April, he wrote eagerly to Fabre announcing his return and asking him to fix a day when they could make an expedition from Orange. Fabre replied enthusiastically:

"I am at your service any day you like. You decide, and let me know a day or two beforehand, so as to be sure to find me in on your arrival. It would be as well, I think, to wait until the present spell of bad weather has passed; the plants are still very backward. I will expect you in the first fortnight of May.

Our house is some distance from the town, about as far as yours is from Avignon. In order to avoid loss of time to both of us in coming and going, allow me to offer you our humble hospitality. There is a room at your disposal. Pray accept it; stay with me; you will be received with joy by all the family and you will do the greatest honour to honest folk who all revere you. While wishing as I do to have you stay with me during the short time you spend in Orange, I do not want to interfere with your usual arrangements. But do not refuse out of excessive courtesy; we shall all be more than happy to receive you."[182]

Mill would not wait. He replied next day:

"Dear Sir,

Thank you for you kind letter. If it were a question of coming only once to Orange it would certainly be better to put it off till later.

Gallery, where it may now be seen. An etching made from the portrait by the French engraver, P. A. Rajon, was bequeathed by Dilke to Westminster City Hall.

But there are, thanks to your discoveries, so many different varieties for me to gather in that region, which do not bloom at the same time, that I hope to make more than one expedition there this spring, of which the pleasure, like the fruits, will be all the greater for me if I am able to make them in your company.

I therefore propose to come to Orange next Saturday by the train which arrives at 11.46 (railway time) and to return here by the train leaving Orange at 5.40. As I shall not be staying the night, I should like, if I may, to take advantage of your generous hospitality by taking lunch with you."[183]

This letter was to be his last. On Saturday the third of May he duly made his expedition. After walking fifteen miles the hot day through, he went home tired and happy. But the evening air was chill. On the Monday he produced a fever. Towards evening, Helen called in Dr. Chauffard. He pursed his lips, and shook his head, and immediately wired for Dr. Gurney to come from Nice. Gurney arrived next day, and this is what he later said:

"The disease of erysipelas is endemic in the lowly-lying clay ground about Avignon. Mr. Mill knew the situation was not healthy, but purchased the house and grounds only because they were close to the cemetery where his wife was buried fifteen years ago, and in order that he might spend as much of his time as possible near her tomb. The house, moreover, was densely surrounded by trees, which he would not allow to be touched lest the nightingales abounding in that neighbourhood should quit the spot. The avenue under the shade of which he composed and studied was filled with these birds, and so tame were they, that when I paced up and down between my visits to his bedside, they followed me from tree to tree.

"Mr. Mill suffered but little, except in swallowing and from the heat and weight of the enormous swelling which by the time I arrived from Nice had already spread over his face and neck; and yet he learnt from me on my arrival the fatal nature of the attack with calmness and resignation. His expressed desire that he might not outlive his mental faculties, or suffer from long, wasting disease, was gratified, for his great intellect remained clear to the last moment."[184]

Mill died at seven o'clock on the morning of Wednesday 7 May 1873. Shortly before the end, he murmured, half delirious, to the wide-eyed Helen, "You know that I have done my work".[185]

His death was very sudden. So sudden that Fabre, coming over to lunch with him one sunny morning, was shocked to find him already in the tomb. He was dead before his sisters Harriet and Mary read of his illness in the papers, and asked to be allowed to come and nurse him. He was buried before Charles Eliot Norton leapt from his hansom on seeing the momentous newsbills in the London streets; before Bain on holiday in Venice received a telegram, and hastened to Avignon on the trail of his biography. Pastor Rey and his wife, who hurried round at once, arrived too late. Helen took them upstairs; and, as they stood by the plain iron bedstead, the Pastor offered up a prayer.

Mill was carried down next day along the short road to the familiar grave. A light, warm rain was falling. No notice had been given, and only five—Gurney and Chauffard the two doctors, the Pastor and his wife, and Helen—followed him. But when they reached the cemetery gates, a large spontaneous crowd stood dumb and damp. And, although there was a rushed and tasteless effort to get his remains for Westminster Abbey; although a bronze statue later rose up on the Thames embankment, these were his real memorial. All his life he had fought for them, and for the millions they represented; fiercely, though never with unfair weapons. All his life they had looked to him, half-comprehending, full of trust.

The Pastor made a short address, and read another prayer. Then Mill was laid beside Harriet in their marble sanctuary.

NOTES

These notes contain sufficient information to indicate the sources of quotations. For further details of publication, see the author's name in the appropriate section of the Bibliography.

Book One—TABULA RASA

Pages **8–31**

1. Bain, *James Mill*, p. 42.
2. Ibid., pp. 59, 60.
3. Ibid., p. 63.
4. Ibid., p. 52.
5. Ibid., p. 49.
6. Ibid., p. 112.
7. Graham Wallas, *The Life of Francis Place*, p. 91.
8. Sir John Bowring, *Memoirs of Bentham*, vol. X of *The Works of Jeremy Bentham*, ed. Bowring, p. 558.
9. Bowring, *Memoirs of Bentham*, p. 118.
10. Wilson Harris, *Caroline Fox*, p. 202.
11. Bowring, *Memoirs of Bentham*, p. 8.
12. Bain, *James Mill*, p. 100.
13. Bowring, *Memoirs of Bentham*, p. 567.
14. Elliot, *Letters*, vol. I, intro. p. xv.
15. Bain, *James Mill*, p. 119.
16. Ibid., pp. 88–90. General Miranda's death, no doubt the circumstance to which Bain alludes, occurred in 1816.
17. Bain, *JSM*, p. 5.
18. Bain, *James Mill*, p. 135.
19. Bowring, *Memoirs of Bentham*, pp. 479, 480.
20. Ibid., p. 480.
21. Graham Wallas, *Life of Francis Place*, pp. 49–53, 69.
    M. W. Patterson, *Sir Francis Burdett and his Times*, vol. I, pp. 240–294, 321.

22. Graham Wallas, *Life of Francis Place*, pp. 75, 76.
23. Bain, *James Mill*, p. 156.
24. A. W. Levi, "The Mental Crisis of John Stuart Mill". *The Psychoanalytic Review*, vol. XXXII, Jan. 1945.
25. MT Coll. 47/1.
26. Bain, *JSM*, p. 9.
27. J. S. Mill, *Autobiography*, p. 22.
28. Bain, *JSM*, p. 11.
29. Lady Bentham, *Memoir of Brigadier General Sir Samuel Bentham, by his Widow*.
    Lady Bentham, *The Life of Sir Samuel Bentham*.
30. Bain, *JSM*, p. 21.
31. King's. MS. Mill to Sarah Austin. Montpellier, 17 Jan. 1821.
32. J. S. Mill, *Autobiography*, p. 40.
33. King's. MS. Harriet Mill to the Rev. J. Crompton. London, 26 Oct. 1873.
34. J. S. Mill, *Autobiography*, p. 44.
35. Ibid., p. 47.
36. Janet Ross, *Three Generations of Englishwomen*, vol. I, p. 65.
37. Gordon Waterfield, *Lucie Duff Gordon*, p. 37. The cat, Sir John Langborn, lurks hidden in the unindexed forest of Bowring's *Memoirs of Bentham*.
38. Gordon Waterfield, *Lucie Duff Gordon*, p. 21.
39. Ibid., p. 32.
40. Bain, *JSM*, p. 28.
41. Bain, *James Mill*, p. 203.
42. Levi, "The Mental Crisis of John Stuart Mill". Extract from unpublished early draft of Mill's *Autobiography*.
43. Bain, *JSM*, p. 43.
44. Elliot, *Letters*, vol. II, p. 14.
45. *The Westminster Review*, no. 3, July 1824.
46. Bain, *James Mill*, p. 207.
47. Ibid., p. 285.
48. MT Coll. 48.
49. R. E. Leader (ed.), *Autobiography and Letters of John Arthur Roebuck*, p. 51.
50. Ibid., p. 27.
51. Bain, *JSM*, p. 39.
52. Bain, *James Mill*, p. 292.
53. Edward Dowden (ed.), *Correspondence of Henry Taylor*, p. 6.
54. J. S. Mill, *Autobiography*, p. 80.
55. Yale. This and the subsequent quotations are taken from a MS. correspondence between Bentham and J. S. Mill.
56. J. S. Mill, *Autobiography*, p. 71.
57. Bain, *James Mill*, p. 334.
58. Henry Solly, *These Eighty Years*, vol. I, p. 147.
59. Levi, "The Mental Crisis of John Stuart Mill". Extract from unpublished early draft of Mill's *Autobiography*.

60. J. S. Mill, *Autobiography*, p. 94.
61. Ibid., p. 97.
62. Ibid., p. 99.
63. Mrs. S. E. Henshaw, "John Stuart Mill and Mrs. Taylor". *The Overland Monthly*, Dec. 1874.
64. Levi, "The Mental Crisis of John Stuart Mill".
65. Voltaire, *Lettres Choisies*, vol. I, p. 115.
66. J. S. Mill, *Autobiography*, p. 100.
67. Algernon Taylor, *Memories of a Student*, p. 237.
68. J. S. Mill, *Autobiography*, p. 105.
69. G. L. Nesbitt, *Benthamite Reviewing—The Westminster Review 1824–1836*, p. 121.
70. Wilson Harris, *Caroline Fox*, pp. 72, 167.
71. William Knight, "Letters of J. S. Mill to Professor John Nichol". *The Fortnightly Review*, vol. LXI, May 1897.
72. Frederick Maurice (ed.), *The Life of Frederick Denison Maurice*, vol. II, p. 178.
73. Ibid., vol. II, p. 252.
74. J. S. Mill, *Autobiography*, p. 107.
75. Anne Kimball Tuell, *John Sterling*, p. 69.
76. J. S. Mill, *Autobiography*, p. 113.
77. Lord Macaulay, *Miscellaneous Writings and Speeches*, pp. 160 *et seq.*
78. Hayek, p. 133.
79. d'Eichthal, p. 82.
80. Ibid., intro. p. vi.
81. Ibid., pp. 15–17. Translated and paraphrased.
82. J. S. Mill, *Autobiography*, p. 116.
83. d'Eichthal, p. 27.
84. Ibid., p. 40.
85. Ibid., pp. 93, 101
86. Ibid., p. 111.
87. Ibid., pp. 125–127.
88. J. A. Froude, *Thomas Carlyle, a History of the First Forty Years*, vol. II, p. 224.
89. *National Library of Scotland*, MS. vol. 618. Mill to Carlyle, 17 Sept. 1832.
90. Elliot, *Letters*, vol. I, p. 75.
91. F. A. Hayek (intro.), *The Spirit of the Age—J. S. Mill*, p. 33.
92. T. Wemyss Reid, *The Life of Richard Monckton Milnes*, vol. I, p. 50.
93. Thomas Carlyle, *Life of John Sterling*, ch. XIII (1871 edn., p. 78). See also A. K. Tuell, *John Sterling*, pp. 98–110.
94. Leader, *John Arthur Roebuck*, p. 30.
95. Bain, *JSM*, p. 41.
96. J. L. and Barbara Hammond, *The Village Labourer*, 1760–1832, pp. 240–324 (esp. p. 308).
97. Bain, *James Mill*, p. 364.
98. Bowring, *Memoirs of Bentham*, p. 450.

Pages

103–111

99. Gerald Bullett, *Sydney Smith*, p. 310.
100. Elliot, *Letters*, vol. I, pp. 7–15.
101. Solly, *These Eighty Years*, vol. I, pp. 147–148.
102. Ibid., p. 204.
103. Lytton Strachey and Roger Fulford (eds.), *The Greville Memoirs, 1814–1860*, vol. II, p. 58.
104. Anna J. Mill, "John Stuart Mill's visit to Wordsworth, 1831". *The Modern Language Review*, vol. XLIV, no. 3, July 1949.
105. Bain, *James Mill*, p. 357.
106. Dowden (ed.), *Correspondence of Henry Taylor*, p. 40.
107. Edith J. Morley (ed.), *Henry Crabb Robinson on Books and their Writers*, vol. I, p. 404.
108. Anna J. Mill, "J. S. Mill's visit to Wordsworth, 1831".
109. MT Coll. 37. MS. Mill's diary of a walking tour in Cornwall, Sept. 1832.
110. Elliot, *Letters*, vol. I, p. 2.
111. Henry Taylor, *Autobiography*, vol. I, p. 78.
112. Hayek, p. 59.
113. Strachey and Fulford, *The Greville Memoirs*, vol. II, p. 52.
114. Ibid., vol. VII, pp. 285–287.
115. Dowden (ed.), *Correspondence of Henry Taylor*, pp. 326–327.
116. Hayek, p. 25.
117. Ibid., p. 80.

Book Two—FRIENDS OF THE SPECIES

115–125

1. The particulars of Harriet Taylor's background are taken from Mary Taylor's statement in Elliot, *Letters*, vol. I, p. xl; from some observations by Algernon Taylor in his *Memories of a Student*, p. 145; from information kindly supplied by Mrs. Helen Sutherland of Adelaide, a descendant of Arthur Hardy, and by the present owner of Birksgate, F. W. Rycroft, Esq.; from H. J. Morehouse, *History of Kirkburton and the Graveship of Holme*; from a letter referring to the portrait of Charles I, written by Harriet to her mother on Christmas Day, 1856 (MT Coll. 27/80); and a further reference in Helen Taylor's diary, 27 Feb. 1845 (MT Coll. 44). Harriet's birth certificate is quoted in Hayek, p. 23. Information about Thomas Hardy's medical career was kindly given by W. R. Le Fanu, M.A., Librarian to the Royal College of Surgeons.
2. MT Coll. 27/49. MS. Harriet to Arthur Hardy, 30 Oct. 1855.
3. Hayek, p. 24.
4. MT Coll. 28/143.
5. W. H. Griffin and H. C. Minchin, *The Life of Robert Browning*, p. 50.
6. W. J. Linton, *Memories*, p. 25.
7. MT Coll. 27/23, 30. Quoted by Betty Miller, *Robert Browning, A Portrait*, p. 35.
8. Ibid., Box III/77.

9. Hayek, pp. 76, 77.
10. MT Coll. Box III/87.
11. Ibid., 27/144.
12. Froude, *Carlyle, The First Forty Years*, vol. II, p. 190.
13. Elliot, *Letters*, vol. I, p. 70.
14. Ibid., p. 26.
15. MT Coll. 27/38.
16. Hayek, p. 36.
17. This, and the next quotation, are taken from the holograph MS. diary of Mill's walking tour with Henry Cole through Hampshire, West Sussex and the Isle of Wight, 19 July–6 August 1832, pp. 24, 26. In the Library of Mount Holyoke College, South Hadley, Mass.
18. Hayek, p. 41.
19. *Monthly Repository*, n.s. vol. VI, 1832, pp. 649–659.
20. Elliot, *Letters*, vol. I, p. 15.
21. Hayek, p. 275.
22. King's. MS. Mill to Fox, 7 Sept. 1833.
23. Griffin and Minchin, *Life of Robert Browning*, p. 58.
24. Hayek, p. 43.
25. Griffin and Minchin, *Life of Robert Browning*, pp. 58, 60.
26. Ruth Borchardt (ed.), *Four Dialogues of Plato*. Introduction.
27. MT Coll. 27/27.
28. Richard Garnett, *The Life of W. J. Fox*, p. 154.
29. Hayek, pp. 58 *et seq.*
30. Ibid., p. 38.
31. *National Library of Scotland*, MS. vol. 618. Mill to Carlyle, 17 Sept. 1832.
32. King's. MS.
33. Ibid., MS.
34. MT Coll. 2/317.
35. Elliot, *Letters*, vol. I, p. 62.
36. Hayek, p. 46.
37. Ibid., p. 49.
38. Ibid., pp. 51–53.
39. Elliot, *Letters*, vol. I, p. 79.
40. Hayek, p. 55.
41. Ibid., p. 92.
42. MT Coll. 27/27. Quoted by Betty Miller, *Robert Browning. A Portrait*, p. 35.
43. King's. MS. Mill to Fox, 14 July 1834.
44. Hayek, p. 93.
45. Ibid., pp. 95, 96.
46. Ibid., p. 45.
47. Leader (ed.), *John Arthur Roebuck*, p. 38.
48. Hayek, p. 99.
49. Ibid., pp. 99, 100.

Book Three—"A VERRA FOOLISH PIECE O' FRIENDLINESS"

Pages
157–186

1. Froude, *Carlyle, the First Forty Years*, vol. II, p. 161.
2. Thomas Carlyle, *Sartor Resartus*, ch. VII.
3. Froude, *Carlyle, the First Forty Years*, vol. I, p. 359.
4. Ibid., vol. II, p. 23.
5. Ibid., vol. I, p. 382.
6. Carlyle, *Sartor Resartus*, ch. X.
7. Froude, *Carlyle, the First Forty Years*, vol. II, pp. 189–190.
8. Elliot, *Letters*, vol. I, p. 16.
9. Froude, *Carlyle, the First Forty Years*, vol. II, p. 200.
10. Ibid., vol. II, pp. 209–210.
11. King's. MS. Carlyle to Mill. 4 Ampton Street, London, n.d.
12. Elliot, *Letters*, vol. I, p. 35.
13. Ibid., pp. 87–89.
14. A.C., p. 94.
15. *National Library of Scotland*, MS. vol. 618. Mill to Carlyle, 2 Feb. 1833.
16. Froude, *Carlyle, the First Forty Years*, vol. II, p. 18.
17. A.C., p. 71.
18. Elliot, *Letters*, vol. I, p. 68.
19. A.C., p. 80.
20. Elliot, *Letters*, vol. I, pp. 84, 85.
21. A.C., pp. 92, 93.
22. Froude, *Carlyle, the First Forty Years*, vol. II, p. 404.
23. Waterfield, *Lucie Duff Gordon*, pp. 51–56.
24. Hayek, p. 81.
25. Ibid., p. 81.
26. Ibid., p. 82.
27. Froude, *Carlyle, the First Forty Years*, vol. I, p. 346.
28. Hayek, p. 82.
29. Tuell, *John Sterling*, p. 243.
30. A.C. intro., p. viii.
31. Elliot, *Letters*, vol. I, p. 100.
32. J. A. Froude, *Thomas Carlyle, a History of his Life in London*, vol. I, p. 53.
33. Froude, *Carlyle's Life in London*, vol. I, p. 25.
34. Froude's account of this incident is still the best. See also Hayek, pp. 83, 84, and the authorities he lists on p. 292. In a letter to Carlyle, partly quoted in A.C., p. 107, Mill's sister Harriet goes on to say, "I can, perfectly well, remember our search, and my dear brother's extreme distress, and I fancy, tho' of this I do not feel so sure, that some pages were found." Carlyle in reply bade her

dismiss the whole painful incident from her mind. The originals of both letters are in the *National Library of Scotland*, MS. vol. 666, no. 109, and MS. 1778.

35. A.C., pp. 107, 108.
36. Elliot, *Letters*, vol. I, p. 102.

Book Four—THE LONDON AND WESTMINSTER REVIEW

1. King's. MS.
2. C. B. Roylance Kent, *The English Radicals.* A good account of the dissensions of the Radicals. See also, Mrs. Harriet Grote, *The Philosophical Radicals of 1832.*
3. Knight, *Fortnightly Review*, vol. LXI. Mill to Nichol, 10 July 1833.
4. W. J. Linton, *Memories*, p. 158.
5. Mrs. M. G. Fawcett, *Life of the Rt. Hon. Sir William Molesworth, Bt.*, p. 71.
6. King's. MS. Mill to Sarah Austin, 28 Jan. 1837.
7. Fawcett, *Life of Sir William Molesworth*, p. 63.
8. Ibid., p. 63.
9. MT Coll. 49. MS.
10. Fawcett, *Life of Sir William Molesworth*, p. 63.
11. Bain, *James Mill*, p. 349.
12. Ibid., p. 391.
13. King's. MS. Mill to Guilbert, 8 May 1835.
14. Alexis de Tocqueville, *Democracy in America*, ed. Philip Bradley, vol. I, intro. de Tocqueville to Mill, 3 Dec. 1835.
15. E. Rigby (Lady Eastlake), *Mrs. Grote*, pp. 114–115.
16. J. S. Mill, "Civilization". *London and Westminster Review*, April 1836. Reprinted in *Dissertations and Discussions*, vol. I.
17. Bain, *JSM*, p. 43.
18. Thomas Carlyle, *Letters and Memorials of Jane Welsh Carlyle*, ed. J. A. Froude, vol. I, p. 57.
19. Bain, *James Mill*, p. 409.
20. Alexander Carlyle (ed.), *New Letters of Thomas Carlyle*, vol. I, p. 16.
21. Froude, *Carlyle's Life in London*, vol. I, p. 74.
22. Hayek, p. 85.
23. Bain, *JSM*, p. 44.
24. A.C., p. 197.
25. King's. MS. Mill to Sarah Austin, 28 Jan. 1837.
26. Elliot, *Letters*, vol. I, p. 102.
27. MT Coll. 2/295. MS.
28. A.C., p. 110.
29. King's. MS.
30. A.C., p. 106.

31. A.C., p. 197.
32. King's. MS. Mill to Sarah Austin, 26 April 1837.
33. Ibid., MS. Mill to Aristide Guilbert, 19 June 1837.
34. David Masson, *Memories of London in the Forties*, p. 4. Bain, *JSM*, p. 59, note.
35. King's. MS. Mill to Robertson, Sept. 1837 [?].
36. F. Espinasse, *Literary Recollections*, p. 125.
37. Bain, *JSM*, p. 56, note.
38. King's. MS. Mill to Robertson, Sept. 1837 [?].
39. Elliot, *Letters*, vol. I, p. 108.
40. Fawcett, *Life of Sir William Molesworth*, p. 73.
41. Ibid., p. 71.
42. MT Coll. 2/337. MS. Sarah Austin to Mill, Malta, 3 March 1837.
43. King's. MS. Mill's reply to Sarah Austin, 26 April 1837.
44. *Edinburgh Review*, Jan. 1844.
45. Elliot, *Letters*, vol. I, pp. 103–106.
46. Bain, *JSM*, p. 57, note.
47. MT. Coll. 2/337 (see note 42).
48. King's. MS. (see note 43).
49. Mrs. H. Grote, *The Philosophical Radicals of 1832*, p. 28.
50. *Athenaeum*, 20 May, 1837.
51. Froude, *Carlyle's Life in London*, vol. I, p. 93.
52. A.C., p. 154.
53. C. E. Norton (ed.), *The Correspondence of Thomas Carlyle and Ralph Waldo Emerson*, vol. I, p. 107.
54. A.C., pp. 160–162.
55. Alexander Carlyle (ed.), *New Letters of Thomas Carlyle*, vol. I, p. 101.
56. Joseph Blanco White, *Life and Correspondence*, vol. II, pp. 341–342, 354.
57. C. Marion D. Towers, "John Stuart Mill and the London and Westminster Review". *Atlantic Monthly*, vol. LXIX, Jan. 1892. Mill to Robertson, 12 July, 1837.
58. Knight, *Fortnightly Review*, vol. LXI. Mill to Nichol, 29 Jan. 1837.
59. Towers, *Atlantic Monthly*, vol. LXIX.
60. Ibid. Also King's. MS. Mill to Robertson, watermarked 1837. Robertson's article appeared in the *London and Westminster Review*, April 1839.
61. A.C., p. 212.
62. A. K. Tuell, *John Sterling*, p. 76.
63. Ibid., p. 368.
64. King's. MS. Sterling to Mill, Aug. 1838.
65. Ibid., 4 Sept. 1838.
66. MT Coll. 48. MS. Mill to Robertson [?] 12 Sept. 1838.
67. King's. MS. Sterling to Mill, Aug. 1838.
68. MT Coll. 49. MS. Mill to Fonblanque, 30 Jan. 1838.
69. Knight, *Fortnightly Review*, vol. LXI. Mill to Nichol, 14 Oct. 1834.
70. *London and Westminster Review*. Aug. 1838. Reprinted in Mill's *Dissertations and Discussions*, vol. I.

71. Fawcett, *Life of Sir William Molesworth*, p. 142.
72. Chester New, *Lord Durham*, p. 262.
73. Knight, *Fortnightly Review*, vol. LXI. Mill to Nichol, 26 Nov. 1834.
74. d'Eichthal, p. 165.
75. Earl of Lytton, *The Life of Edward Bulwer, First Lord Lytton*, vol. I, pp. 496–497.
76. Ibid., vol. I, p. 498.
77. Strachey and Fulford, *The Greville Memoirs*, vol. III, p. 400.
78. Knight, *Fortnightly Review*, vol. LXI. Mill to Nichol, 21 Dec. 1837.
79. Lord Elton, *Imperial Commonwealth*, p. 289.
80. E. M. Wrong, *Charles Buller and Responsible Government*, p. 24.
81. Elton, *Imperial Commonwealth*, p. 288.
82. Towers, *Atlantic Monthly*, vol. LXIX. Mill to Robertson, 1837.
83. MT Coll. 49. MS. Mill to Fonblanque, 30 Jan., 3 Feb. and 6 Feb. 1838.
84. J. S. Morison, "The Mission of the Earl of Durham". *Cambridge History of the British Empire*, vol. VI, pp. 288, 289.
85. Morison, *Cambridge History of the British Empire*, vol. VI, p. 299.
86. New, *Lord Durham*, p. 387.
87. Fawcett, *Life of Sir William Molesworth*, p. 203.
88. Sir Reginald Coupland (ed.), *The Durham Report*, intro.
89. Strachey and Fulford, *The Greville Memoirs*, vol. IV, pp. 104, 105.
90. F. Bradshaw, *Self-Government in Canada*, p. 228.
91. Fawcett, *Life of Sir William Molesworth*, p. 204.
92. J. S. Mill, *Autobiography*, p. 151.
93. Stuart J. Reid, *Life and Letters of Lord Durham*, vol. II, p. 307.
94. Wilson Harris, *Caroline Fox*, p. 159.
95. Strachey and Fulford, *The Greville Memoirs*, vol. IV, p. 104.
96. Towers, *Atlantic Monthly*, vol. LXIX. Mill to Robertson, 6 April 1839.
97. Kent, *The English Radicals*, p. 346.
98. Hayek, p. 103.
99. Towers, *Atlantic Monthly*, vol. LXIX. Mill to Robertson, 28 Sept. 1837.
100. Ibid., 6 Oct. 1837.
101. Hayek, p. 116.
102. Ibid., p. 104.
103. MT Coll. 29/271. MS.
104. Ibid., 28/239. MS.
105. A. K. Tuell, *John Sterling*, pp. 52, 53.
106. Hayek, p. 110.
107. A.C., p. 225.
108. A. K. Tuell, *John Sterling*, pp. 70, 71.
109. MT Coll. 28/151. MS.
110. Garnett, *Life of W. J. Fox*, p. 186.
111. Norton (ed.), *Correspondence of Carlyle and Emerson*, vol. I, p. 215.

Pages

242–247 112. King's. MS. Mill to Sterling, 28 Sept. 1839. An earlier portion of this letter is quoted in Elliot, *Letters*, vol. I, p. 113.
113. Elliot, *Letters*, vol. I, p. 115.
114. A.C., p. 171, note.
115. T. Carlyle, *Reminiscences* (ed. J. A. Froude), vol. II, p. 186.
116. King's. MS. Mill to Sterling, 28 Sept. 1839.
117. *London and Westminster Review*, March 1840. Reprinted in Mill's *Dissertations and Discussions*, vol. I.
118. Caroline Fox, *Memories of Old Friends*. Ed. Horace N. Pym, 2nd edn. Mill to Barclay Fox, 1 Dec. 1842.
119. A.C., p. 233.

Book Five—CAUSE AND EFFECT

251–272 1. d'Eichthal, p. 173.
2. MT Coll. 1/29. MS. Mill to Theodor Gomperz, July 1854.
3. *Westminster and Foreign Quarterly Review*, Oct. 1852. Reprinted in Mill's *Dissertations and Discussions*, vol. II.
4. J. S. Mill, *A System of Logic*, bk. II, ch. v.
5. J. S. Mill, *Logic*, bk. III, ch. v.
6. Caroline Fox, *Memories of Old Friends*. Journal, Feb. 1840.
7. King's. MS. Harriet Mill to Rev. J. Crompton, 26 Oct. 1873.
8. d'Eichthal, p. 183.
9. Caroline Fox, *Memories of Old Friends*. Journal, 17 Feb. 1840.
10. Ibid., 25 March 1840.
11. Ibid., 16 March 1840.
12. Ibid., 16 March 1840.
13. Ibid., 21 March 1840.
14. Ibid., 6 April 1840.
15. Elliot, *Letters*, vol. I, p. 117.
16. King's. MS. Sterling to Mill, 10 June 1840
17. David Alec Wilson, *The Life of Carlyle*, vol. III, "Carlyle on Cromwell and Others", p. 85.
18. Hayek, p. 111.
19. Caroline Fox, *Memories of Old Friends*. Journal, 19 May 1840.
20. J. S. Mill, *Logic*, bk. VI, ch. II, para. 3.
21. Ibid., ch. VII, para. 1.
22. F. A. Hayek, *The Counter Revolution of Science*. Contains a warning of the dangers involved in approaching the Moral Sciences in a "scientistic" spirit.
23. Caroline Fox, *Memories of Old Friends*. Mill to Barclay Fox, 23 Dec. 1840.
24. Ibid., Journal, 16 June 1842.
25. Ibid., Mill to Barclay Fox, 6 May 1841, 14 Feb. 1843.
26. Bain, *JSM*, p. 68.
27. A. K. Tuell, *John Sterling*, pp. 74, 75.

28. Bain, *JSM*, p. 69.
29. Auguste Comte, *The Positive Philosophy*. Tr. Harriet Martineau.
30. Knight, *Fortnightly Review*, vol. LXI, Mill to Nichol, 21 Dec. 1837.
31. Lévy-Bruhl, p. 41.
32. Hayek, p. 114.
33. King's. MS. 26 Feb. 1844.
34. J. S. Mill, *Auguste Comte and Positivism*, p. 150.
35. Ibid., p. 151.
36. Ibid., p. 199.
37. J. S. Mill, *Autobiography*, p. 149.
38. Lévy-Bruhl, p. 102.
39. Ibid., p. 481.
40. Ibid., pp. 482–498.
41. Elliot, *Letters*, vol. I, p. 139.
42. Caroline Fox, *Memories of Old Friends*. Mill to Barclay Fox, 6 May 1841.
43. King's. MS. 17 July 1842.
44. Ibid., 29 April 1843.
45. Ibid., 11 Aug. 1843.
46. *A Correspondence between John Sterling and Ralph Waldo Emerson*. Ed. E. W. Emerson. Sterling to Emerson, 7 Oct. 1843.
47. King's. MS. 1 Feb. 1844.
48. Elliot, *Letters*, vol. I, p. 125.
49. Ibid., p. 127.
50. Yale. MS. Sterling to Mill, 8 Sept. 1844.
51. Caroline Fox, *Memories of Old Friends*. Journal, 17 May 1847.
52. Hayek, p. 112.
53. MT Coll. 28/155. MS. 23 Sept. 1840.
54. Ibid., 27/93. MS. 26 May 1842.
55. King's. MS. Mill to Sarah Austin, 4 Oct. 1841.
56. MT Coll. 28/158. Harriet to John Taylor, July 1842.
57. Caroline Fox, *Memories of Old Friends*. Journal, 31 May 1842.
58. Bain, *JSM*, pp. 64–65.
59. David Masson, *Memories of London in the Forties*, p. 99.
60. Ibid., p. 102.
61. Lévy-Bruhl, p. 154.
62. MT Coll. 44. MS. Helen Taylor's diary, 9 Sept. 1846.
63. Ibid., 30 May 1846.
64. King's. MS. 26 Feb. 1844.
65. MT Coll. 28/140. MS.
66. Ibid., 44. MS. diary, 16 Aug. 1844.
67. Hayek, p. 143.
68. King's. MS. 15 March 1852.
69. Hayek, p. 120.
70. Ibid., p. 119.
71. Ibid., p. 120.

72. Hayek, p. 121.
73. Ibid., pp. 124, 297.
74. J. S. Mill, *Autobiography*, p. 166.
75. Hayek, p. 125.
76. Elliot, *Letters*, vol. I, p. 138.
77. Hayek, p. 126.
78. For detail of variations in the editions of Mill's *Principles of Political Economy*, see the introduction and commentary by Sir W. J. Ashley to his definitive edition, first published London, 1909. Also Hayek, pp. 134–139, and notes, pp. 299, 300.
79. Hayek, p. 135.
80. Ibid., p. 145.
81. Sarah Norton (ed.), *The Letters of Charles Eliot Norton*, vol. I, pp. 496–497.
82. Wilson, *The Life of Carlyle*, vol. II, "Carlyle to the French Revolution", p. 380.
83. Bain, *JSM*, pp. 173, 149.
84. MT Coll, 36.
85. J. S. Mill, *Autobiography*, p. 133.
86. Hayek, p. 135.
87. Ibid., p. 45.
88. MT Coll. 2/320. MS. fragment.
89. Hayek, p. 291, note.
90. Ibid., p. 196.
91. Bain, *JSM*, p. 149.
92. Wilson, *The Life of Carlyle*, vol. II, "Carlyle to the French Revolution", p. 400.
93. Leslie Stephen, *The English Utilitarians*, vol. III, pp. 72, 73.
94. Elliot, *Letters*, vol. II, p. 382.
95. Bain, *JSM*, p. 169.
96. J. S. Mill, *Autobiography*, p. 161.
97. MT Coll. 28/140. MS. Harriet to John Taylor, 24 June 1844.
98. Hayek, p. 151.
99. Ibid., p. 164.
100. Harriet Martineau, *Autobiography*, London, 1877, vol. I, p. 299.
101. MT Coll. 2/280. MS. Sarah Austin to Mill, 7 Nov. 1839.
102. Elliot, *Letters*, vol. I, p. 135.
103. Hayek, p. 132.
104. *The Letters of Charles Eliot Norton*, vol. I, pp. 499, 500.
105. Sir Charles Gavan Duffy, *Conversations with Carlyle*, pp. 166–171.
106. John Beattie Crozier, *My Inner Life*, vol. II, p. 385.
107. Wilson, *Life of Carlyle*, vol. IV. "Carlyle at his Zenith", p. 349.
108. Duffy, *Conversations with Carlyle*, p. 222.
109. Ibid., pp. 166–171.
110. MT Coll. 44. MS. diary, Friday, 27 [?] April 1845.
111. Duffy, *Conversations with Carlyle*, p. 166.
112. *The Letters of Charles Eliot Norton*, vol. I, pp. 496–500.

113. Moncure D. Conway, *Thomas Carlyle*, p. 90.
114. d'Eichthal, p. 190.
115. Yale. MS. 18 April 1847.
116. MT. Coll. 28/163. MS. 19 March 1847.
117. Wilson, *Life of Carlyle*, vol. II, "Carlyle to the French Revolution", p. 400.
118. MT Coll. 44. MS. diary, 1 Jan. 1847.
119. Ibid., 28/142. MS. dated 27 May. No year.
120. *Amberley Papers*, vol. I, p. 372.
121. MT Coll. 28/176. MS. 24 March 1848.
122. Algernon Taylor, *Memories of a Student*, p. 213.
123. MT Coll. 28/164. MS. 6 April 1847.
124. Hayek, p. 136.
125. MT Coll. 44. MS. diary, 12 Dec. 1846.
126. Ibid., 2 Jan. 1845.
127. Algernon Taylor, *Memories of a Student*, p. 25.
128. Lévy-Bruhl, pp. 536, 538.
129. MT Coll. 28/176. MS. Harriet to John Taylor, 24 March 1848.
130. Ibid., 28/191. MS. Harriet to John Taylor, Aug. 1848 [?].
131. Ibid., 28/210. MS. Harriet to John Taylor, Nov. 1848.
132. Ibid., 28/131. MS. Herbert Taylor to Harriet, Nov. 1848.
133. Ibid., 28/210. MS. Nov. 1848.
134. Ibid., 28/206. MS. John Taylor to Harriet, Nov. 1848.
135. Hayek, p. 130.
136. Ibid., p. 133.
137. Bain, *JSM*, p. 91.
138. MT Coll. 28/221–223. MS. Harriet to John Taylor, Pau, Jan. 12, 23, 30, 1849.
139. Ibid., 28/225. MS. 27 Feb. 1849.
140. Hayek, p. 150.
141. MT Coll. 50/19. MS. Harriet to Mill, 4 June 1849.
142. Hayek, p. 155.
143. Ibid., p. 153.
144. Ibid., p. 153.
145. Ibid., p. 155.
146. Ibid., p. 158.
147. Ibid., p. 156.
148. MT Coll., 28/126. MS. fragment. No name, no date.
149. Hayek, p. 162.
150. Ibid., p. 163.

Book Six—THE HOPED-FOR HEAVEN

Pages
345–366

1. Hayek, p. 167.
2. Ibid., p. 165.
3. MT Coll. 36.
4. Elliot, *Letters*, vol. I, p. 160.
5. Hayek, p. 138.
6. King's. MS. Mill to Harriet, 20 March 1854.
7. Full text in Hayek, p. 168.
8. MT Coll. 28/128. 4 March 1851.
9. Yale. MS. Horace Grant to Mill, 27 July 1851.
10. Gordon S. Haight, *George Eliot and John Chapman*, p. 213.
11. Wilson, *Life of Carlyle*, vol. V, "Carlyle to Threescore and Ten", p. 21.
12. Hayek, p. 175.
13. Ibid., p. 139.
14. David Masson, *Memories of London in the Forties*, p. 105.
15. Hayek, p. 176. MT Coll. 47/17. MS. endorsed on back in Harriet's hand "copied July 16th 1851—sent to Madeira".
16. Hayek, p. 180.
17. MT Coll. 47/23a. MS. transcript by Mary Taylor of a pencilled note in Mill's hand, on the back of a draft of a letter to his mother dated 5 March 1852. The latter is quoted in Hayek, p. 181.
18. MT Coll. 47/26. MS. 3 April [1854].
19. Ibid., 47/27. MS. 5 April 1854.
20. Ibid., 47/30. MS. Sunday 11 April 1854.
21. Ibid., 47/37a. 27 March 1854. Enclosed in a letter from Charles Colman to Mill, dated 12 July 1854. Mill's mother died on 15 June.
22. Yale. MS. 24 July 1854.
23. Hayek, p. 210.
24. *The Letters of Charles Eliot Norton*, vol. I, p. 330.
25. Elliot, *Letters*, vol. I, p. 202.
26. Algernon Taylor, *Memories of a Student*, p. 11, note.
27. Gordon S. Haight, *George Eliot and John Chapman*, p. 58.
28. "Tuberculosis", *Encyclopaedia Britannica*, 1940.
29. Yale. MS. 30 Dec. 1853.
30. Yale. MS. Mill to Harriet, 26 August 1853.
31. MT Coll. 2/305. Mill to Harriet, 27 August 1853.
32. Yale. MS. Mill to Harriet, 14 Jan. 1854.
33. Ibid., 16/17 Jan. 1854.
34. Ibid., 12/13 Feb. 1854.
35. Ibid., 24 Feb. 1854.
36. Ibid., March and early April 1854.
37. Ibid., 12 Jan. 1854.
38. Ibid., 28 Feb. 1854.

39. Elliot, *Letters*, vol. II, p. 383.
40. Hayek, p. 185.
41. Ibid., p. 191.
42. Ibid., p. 192.
43. Ibid., p. 195.
44. Ibid., p. 197.
45. Ibid., p. 185.
46. Ibid., pp. 190, 194.
47. Ibid., p. 196.
48. A. W. Levi, "The Writing of Mill's Autobiography". *International Journal of Ethics*, July 1951.
49. King's. MS. Mill to Harriet, 20 March 1854.
50. J. S. Mill, *Autobiography*, p. 171.
51. Hayek, p. 199.
52. Ibid., p. 199.
53. Yale. MS. Mill to Harriet, 7 Feb. 1854.
54. Ibid., 4 July 1854.
55. Hayek, p. 208.
56. Yale. MS. Mill to Harriet, 20 Dec. 1854.
57. Ibid., 18 Jan. 1855.
58, Hayek, p. 216.
59. Ibid., p. 222.
60. Yale. MS. Mill to Harriet, 3 Feb. 1855.
61. Ibid., 24 Feb. 1855.
62. Ibid., 2 March 1855.
63. Ibid., 30 March 1855.
64. Ibid., 6 April 1855.
65. Hayek, p. 235.
66. Ibid., p. 234.
67. Ibid., p. 238.
68. Yale. MS. Mill to Harriet, 23 May 1855.
69. Ibid., 26 May 1855.
70. Hayek, p. 248.
71. Ibid., p. 250.
72. Yale. MS. Mill to Harriet, 22 Dec. 1854.
73. MT Coll. 27/51. MS. Harriet to Arthur Hardy, 8 June 1857.
74. Ibid., 27/87. MS. Harriet from her mother, 31 Aug. 1858.
75. Ibid., 44. MS. diary, 16 May 1846.
76. Ibid., 24/705. MS. Helen to Algernon Taylor, 4 May 1856.
77. Ibid., 54/27. MS. Fanny Stirling to Harriet, 23 Aug. 1858.
78. Ibid., 54/23. MS. Fanny Stirling to Harriet, 14 May 1858.
79. Ibid., 51. MS. Harriet to Helen, 25 Nov. 1856.
80. Ibid., 27 Nov. 1856.
81. Ibid., Helen to Harriet, 9 Dec. 1856.
82. Ibid., Harriet to Helen, 10 Dec. 1856.
83. Ibid., 52. MS. Harriet to Helen, 10 Feb. 1857.
84. Ibid., 28/237. MS. Harriet to Mill, 13 July 1858.

389–394

85. J. S. Mill, *Considerations on Representative Goverment*, ch. XLVII.
86. H. R. Fox Bourne (ed.), *John Stuart Mill—Notices of his Life and Works*, no. 2. "His Career in the India House", by W. T. Thornton.
87. Ibid.
88. MT Coll. 53. MS. Harriet to Helen, 14 October 1858.
89. Hayek, p. 261.
90. Ibid., p. 261.
91. Yale.

Book Seven—THE SAINT OF RATIONALISM

397–411

1. MT Coll. 53/30. MS. fragment.
2. Bain, *JSM*, p. 102.
3. MT Coll. 24/708. MS.
4. King's. MS.
5. All quotations in this section, unless otherwise specified, are from Mill's essay *On Liberty*.
6. Baron Wilhelm von Humboldt, *The Sphere and Duties of Government*, 1791. Tr. Coulthard, 1854.
7. Pattison, *Essays*, vol. II, p. 264. Quoted by A. V. Dicey, *Law and Opinion in England*, 2nd edn., p. 465.
8. T. H. Green, *Lectures on the Principles of Political Organization*, 1931 edn., p. 157.
9. Sir James Fitzjames Stephen, Q.C., *Liberty, Equality, Fraternity*, 2nd edn. 1874, p. 197.
10. Caroline Fox, *Memories of Old Friends*. Caroline Fox to E. T. Carne, 25 Nov. and 23 Dec. 1859.
11. Bain, *JSM*, p. 107.
12. Ibid., p. 111.
13. Fitjames Stephen, *Liberty, Equality, Fraternity*, pp. 51, 68, 99.
14. Henry Larkin, "Carlyle and Mrs. Carlyle: a Ten Years' Reminiscence". *British Quarterly Review*, July 1881.
15. Alexander Carlyle (ed.), *New Letters of Thomas Carlyle*, vol. II, p. 196.
16. J. S. Mill, *Autobiography*, p. 178.
17. Lord Stamp, "New Letters of J. S. Mill". *Times*, 29 Dec. 1938.
18. MT Coll. 1/77. MS. Mill to Holyoake, August 1864.
19. Bain, *JSM*, pp. 167, 171.
20. MT Coll. 26/1053. MS. fragment. Helen to Algernon Taylor [?].
21. Ibid., 54/32. MS. Fanny Stirling to Helen [early 1859].
22. Hayek, p. 98.
23. Gavan Duffy, *Conversations with Carlyle*, p. 167.
24. *Amberley Papers*, vol. I, p. 372.
25. MT Coll. 1/44. MS. Mill to Arthur Hardy, 14 May 1859.
26. King's. MS. Mill to Parker, 6 Dec. 1858.
27. MT Coll. 49. MS. J. E. Cairnes to Wm. Nesbitt [?] 9 May 1859 [?].
28. Ibid., 24/713. MS. Helen to Algernon Taylor, 23 October 1859.

29. MT Coll. 24/713. MS. Helen to Algernon Taylor, 23 Oct. 1859.
30. MT. Coll. 53. Mill to Helen, 14 Feb. 1860.
31. J. S. Mill, *Autobiography*, p. 185.
32. MT Coll. 58/3. MS. Mary Taylor's diary, 1904–1906.
33. Elliot, *Letters*, vol. I, p. 215.
34. MT Coll. 53. MS. Mill to Helen, 17 Feb. 1860.
35. *Amberley Papers*, vol. II, p. 39.
36. J. S. Mill, *Autobiography*, pp. 181, 182.
37. MT Coll. 57. MS. Mill to Henry Fawcett, 5 Feb. 1860.
38. Ibid., 26 Feb. 1860.
39. Monypenny and Buckle, *Life of Benjamin Disraeli*, vol. V, p. 501.
40. MT Coll. 53. MS. Mill to Helen, 26 Jan. 1860.
41. W. L. Courtney, *Life of John Stuart Mill*, p. 139.
42. J. S. Mill, "A Few Words on Non-Intervention". *Fraser's Magazine*, Dec. 1859. Reprinted in *Dissertations and Discussions*, vol. III.
43. J. S. Mill, *Autobiography*, p. 188.
44. *Amberley Papers*, vol. I, p. 139.
45. J. S. Mill, "The Contest in America" *Fraser's Magazine*, Feb. 1862. Reprinted in *Dissertations and Discussions*, vol. III.
46. Elliot, *Letters*, vol. I, p. 304.
47. Ibid., p. 264.
48. MT Coll. 55/9. MS. Mill to Cairnes, 24 June 1862.
49. J. S. Mill, *Autobiography*, p. 190.
50. MT Coll. 57. MS. Mill to Fawcett, 6 March 1862.
51. Elliot, *Letters*, vol. II, p. 37.
52. MT Coll. 55/40. MS. Mill to Cairnes, 28 May 1865.
53. Elliot, *Letters*, vol. II, p. 32.
54. MT Coll. 23/660. MS. 6 July 1862.
55. Moncure D. Conway, *Autobiography*, vol. II, p. 14.
56. Elliot, *Letters*, vol. I, p. 262.
57. Ibid., p. 293.
58. Lord Stamp, "New Letters of J. S. Mill". *Times*, 29 Dec. 1938.
59. F. W. Hirst, *The Early Life and Letters of John Morley*, vol. I, p. 52.
60. *The Letters of C. E. Norton*, vol. I, p. 330.
61. Moncure D. Conway, *Autobiography*, vol. II, p. 14.
62. Elliot, *Letters*, vol. I, p. xxvii, intro.
63. Ibid., vol. II, p. 4.
64. Herbert Spencer, *Autobiography*, vol. II, p. 121.
65. Elliot, *Letters*, vol. I, p. 310.
66. Herbert Spencer, *Autobiography*, vol. II, p. 121.
67. Ibid., p. 134.
68. Hugh Elliot, *Herbert Spencer*, p. 31.
69. Except where otherwise stated, the whole account of Mill's friendship with the Amberleys is taken from *The Amberley Papers*, eds. Bertrand and Patricia Russell, 2 vols., London, 1937.
70. MT Coll. 21/298, 299. MS. Harriet Grote to Helen Taylor, 11 Nov. 1867 and 29 Nov. 1868.

71. MT Coll. 21/291. MS. Harriet Grote to Helen, 22 Feb. 1865.
72. Ibid., 19/12. MS. Kate Amberley to Helen, 12 July 1865.
73. Yale. MS. Amberley to Mill, 18 Nov. 1868.
74. MT Coll. 19/6. MS. Amberley to Helen, 7 Sept. 1874.
75. Ibid., 19/45. MS. Kate Amberley to Helen Taylor, 16 June 1872.
76. Elliot, *Letters*, vol. I, p. 272.
77. Frederick Maurice (ed.), *The Life of F. D. Maurice*, vol. II, p. 498.
78. Moncure D. Conway, *Autobiography*, vol. II, p. 87.
79. Wilson, *Life of Carlyle*, vol. VI, "Carlyle in Old Age", pp. 59, 60.
80. *National Library of Scotland.* MS. vol. 618, Mill to Carlyle, April 1866.
81. Lord Stamp, "New Letters of J. S. Mill". *Times*, 29 Dec. 1938.
82. Elliot, *Letters*, vol. II, p. 33.
83. L. and E. Hanson, *Marian Evans and George Eliot*, p. 252.
84. Elliot, *Letters*, vol. II, p. 39.
85. MT Coll. 1/84. MS. Longman to Mill, April 1865.
86. *Amberley Papers*, vol. I, p. 394.
87. J. S. Mill, *Autobiography*, p. 199.
88. Edward R. Russell, *The Autobiography of J. S. Mill.*
89. *Amberley Papers*, vol. I, p. 470.
90. Leslie Stephen, "Some Early Impressions". Cutting from *The National Review* in MT Coll. 45/52.
91. Monypenny and Buckle, *Life of Benjamin Disraeli*, vol. V, p. 501.
92. Yale. MS.
93. *Amberley Papers*, vol. I, p. 483.
94. Elliot, *Letters*, vol. II, p. 59.
95. W. L. Courtney, *Life of J. S. Mill*, p. 147.
96. Algernon Taylor, *Memories of a Student*, p. 122.
97. *Amberley Papers*, vol. I, p. 516.
98. W. L. Courtney, *Life of J. S. Mill*, pp. 141, 142.
99. Hansard, *Parliamentary Debates*, vol. 189, 5 Aug. 1867.
100. Authorities for the Hyde Park episode are: J. S. Mill, *Autobiography*, pp. 203–205. G. J. Holyoake, *Sixty Years of an Agitator's Life*, vol. I, p. 105. Monypenny and Buckle, *Life of Benjamin Disraeli*, vol. IV, pp. 450–452. W. L. Courtney, *Life of J. S. Mill*, pp. 151–153. J. MacCabe, *Life and Letters of G. J. Holyoake*, vol. I. *Charles Bradlaugh*, by his daughter Hypatia Bradlaugh. Elliot, *Letters*, vol. II. p. 77. *Daily News*, Tues. 31 July, 1866. *Dictionary of National Biography*, Edmond Beales, 1803–1881.
101. Hansard, *Parliamentary Debates*, vol. 189, 13 Aug. 1867.
102. *Daily News*, Mon. 27 May 1867.
103. Ibid.
104. MT. Coll. 1/99. MS. 27 May 1867.
105. Wilson, *Life of Carlyle*, vol VI. "Carlyle in Old Age", pp. 62, 63.
106. Hamilton Hume, *The Life of Edward John Eyre.* App. Speech by Professor Tyndall.
107. Froude, *Carlyle's Life in London*, vol. II, p. 329.

108. T. Wemyss Reid, *The Life of W. E. Forster*, vol. I, p. 389.
109. Elliot, *Letters*, vol. II, p. 112.
110. Froude, *Carlyle's Life in London*, vol. II, p. 329.
111. The main authorities used in describing the Eyre case are: T. Carlyle, "Occasional Discourse on the Nigger Question", *Fraser's Magazine*, Dec. 1849. J. S. Mill, "The Negro Question", *Fraser's Magazine*, Jan. 1850. J. S. Mill, *Autobiography*, pp. 207–210. Sydney Olivier, *The Myth of Governor Eyre*. Hamilton Hume, *The Life of Edward John Eyre*. W. F. Finlason, *The History of the Jamaica Case. Jamaica Papers No. 1*, issued by the Jamaica Committee, 1866. MT Coll. Box I/41, *Statement of the Jamaica Committee*, 15 July 1868. *Dictionary of National Biography*, Edward John Eyre.
112. MT Coll. Box V/1. Cutting from the *Daily News*, Nov. 1868.
113. Ibid., 53. MS. Helen to Mill, 12 Nov. 1868.
114. F. W. Hirst, *The Early Life and Letters of John Morley*, vol. I, p. 147.
115. MT Coll. 55/67. MS. 4 Dec. 1868.
116. Ibid., 53. MS. 19 Nov. 1868.
117. Elliot, *Letters*, vol. II, p. 177.
118. Ibid., p. 196.
119. E. M. Everett, *The Party of Humanity—The Fortnightly Review*, 1865–1874, p. 292.
120. Somerset House. The Will of John Stuart Mill.
121. MT Coll. 2/275. MS. 5 May 1873.
122. Ibid., 1/139. MS. Geo. W. Thompson, West Virginia, to Mill. Aug. [?] 1869.
123. Ibid., 1/138. MS. 22 Aug. 1869.
124. Elliot, *Letters*, vol. II, p. 174.
125. MT Coll. 53. MS. postscript.
126. *Amberley Papers*, vol. II, p. 311.
127. Elliot, *Letters*, vol. II, p. 199.
128. Ibid., p. 86.
129. Ibid., p. 91.
130. Ibid., pp. 226–227.
131. Ibid., p. 48.
132. Ibid., vol. I, p. 133.
133. MT Coll. 1/152. MS. Mill to Patrick Henessy, Aug. 1870.
134. Elliot, *Letters*, vol. II, p. 291.
135. Ibid., vol. I, p. 180.
136. MT Coll. Box IX/2. Mill's account book, Jan. 1866–Dec. 1870.
137. Somerset House. The Will of John Stuart Mill.
138. MT Coll. 8/122. MS. draft.
139. Jules Véran, "Le Souvenir de Stuart Mill à Avignon", *Revue des Deux Mondes*, Sept. 1937.
140. Herbert Spencer, *Autobiography*, vol. II, p. 213.
141. Yale. MS. Mill to Augustus De Morgan, 28 Oct. 1864.
142. G. V. Legros, *La vie de J. H. Fabre, Naturaliste*.
143. E. M. Everett, *The Party of Humanity*, p. 284.

489–504

144. Elliot, *Letters*, vol. II, p. 347.
145. Ibid., p. 223.
146. Ibid.
147. Ibid., p. 56.
148. Ibid., p. 341.
149. MT Coll. 45/13. MS. Mill to the Editor of *The Anti-Slavery Standard*, U.S.A., 4 July 1867.
150. Ibid., 55/57. MS. 30 June 1867.
151. Charles Kingsley, *His Letters and Memories of His Life*, ed. Mrs. Fanny Kingsley, vol. II, pp. 294–295. Also MT Coll. 19/21. MS. Kate Amberley to Helen Taylor, Oct. 1869.
152. MT Coll. 45/13. MS. 4 July 1867.
153. Sophia De Morgan, *Memoir of Augustus De Morgan*, pp. 382, 383.
154. Elliot, *Letters*, vol. II, p. 192.
155. Fitzjames Stephen, *Liberty, Equality, Fraternity*, pp. 220, 222.
156. "Mr. Mill on the Subjection of Women". *Blackwood's Magazine*, no. 647, Sept. 1869.
157. Bain, *JSM*, p. 130.
158. Frederic Harrison, *Tennyson, Ruskin, Mill*, p. 310.
159. Charles Kingsley, *Letters and Memories*, ed. Fanny Kingsley, vol. II, p. 295.
160. *Amberley Papers*, vol. II, p. 282.
161. Moncure D. Conway, *Autobiography*, vol. II, p. 165.
162. Yale. MS. 10 Aug. 1869.
163. Elliot, *Letters*, vol. II, p. 214.
164. Moncure D. Conway, *Autobiography*, vol. II, p. 14.
165. *The Letters of Charles Eliot Norton*, vol. I. Norton to Chauncey Wright, Siena, 13 Sept. 1870.
166. Elliot, *Letters*, vol II, p. 219.
167. Ibid., p. 349.
168. *Amberley Papers*, vol. II, p. 299.
169. Elliot, *Letters*, vol. I, p. 187.
170. Ibid., vol. II, p. 212.
171. A. V. Dicey, *Law and Opinion in England*, 2nd edn., p. 386.
172. MT Coll. Box V/10. Article by Dr. Georg Brandes in the *Pall Mall Budget*, 10 March 1882.
173. Elliot, *Letters*, vol. II, p. 265.
174. The quotations in this episode are from *The Evidence of John Stuart Mill taken before the Royal Commission of 1870 on the Administration and Operation of the Contagious Diseases Acts of 1866 and 1869. Reprinted verbatim from the Blue Book.* The pamphlet was printed under the auspices of the National Association for the Repeal of the Contagious Diseases Acts.
175. *The Letters of Charles Eliot Norton*, vol. I, p. 331.
176. R. J. White, "John Stuart Mill", *The Cambridge Journal*, vol. V, Nov. 1951.
177. Wilson, *Life of Carlyle*, vol. VI, "Carlyle in Old Age", p. 213.

178. Elliot, *Letters*, vol. II, p. 267.
179. *Amberley Papers*, vol. II, p. 375.
180. Bain, *JSM*, p. 133.
181. This extract is compounded from two of Morley's letters. One to his great friend Frederic Harrison, which was subsequently used for Mill's obituary in the *Fortnightly Review*, vol. XIII, N.S. 1873. The other to his favourite sister Grace, printed in *The Early Life and Letters of John Morley*, by F. W. Hirst, vol. I, pp. 236–237.
182. MT Coll. 2/272. MS. Fabre to Mill, 29 April 1873. (Translated.)
183. Ibid., 2/328. MS. Mill to Fabre, 30 April 1873. (Translated.)
184. Mansfield Marston. *The Life of John Stuart Mill*. Obituary Pamphlet. 1873.
185. Pastor Louis Rey, *John Stuart Mill en Avignon*, p. 13. For further accounts of Mill's death and funeral, see *The Literary Guide and Rationalist Review*, 1 July 1907.

BIBLIOGRAPHY

A. THE WORKS OF JOHN STUART MILL

The following list is confined to works which have appeared in book form, together with the more important pamphlets. A full account of Mill's subsidiary writings may be found in his own manuscript record (MT Coll. 36). This has been published under the title *Bibliography of the published writings of John Stuart Mill.* Ed. Ney MacMinn, J. R. Hainds, and James McNab McCrimmon. Northwestern University Studies in the Humanities, no. 12. 1945.

The Rationale of Judicial Evidence. From the MSS. of Jeremy Bentham. Edited, with a Preface, by J. Stuart Mill. 5 vols. London, 1827.

The Spirit of the Age. A series of articles in *The Examiner,* Jan–May 1831. Reprinted as a volume, with an Introduction by F. A. Hayek. Chicago, 1942.

Notes on Some of the more Popular Dialogues of Plato. A series of articles in *The Monthly Repository,* Feb. 1834–March 1835. Reprinted as a volume, under the title *Four Dialogues of Plato—J. S. Mill,* with an Introduction by Ruth Borchardt, 1946.

A System of Logic. 2 vols. London, 1843. The definitive edition is the 8th, published in 1872.

Essays on some Unsettled Questions of Political Economy. Written 1830-1831. London, 1844.

Principles of Political Economy. Described by Mill as "A joint production with my wife". 2 vols. London, 1848. The definitive edition is the 7th, published in 1871. Reissued with an Introduction, notes, and commentary on editorial variations, by Sir W. J. Ashley, London, 1909.

On Liberty. London, 1859.

Thoughts on Parliamentary Reform. London, 1859.

Dissertations and Discussions. Mill's anthology of his occasional writings. 2 vols. London, 1859. 3 vols. 1867. 4 vols. 1875.

Considerations on Representative Government. London, 1861.
Utilitarianism. Reprinted from *Fraser's Magazine*, Oct.–Dec. 1861. London, 1863.
An Examination of Sir William Hamilton's Philosophy. London, 1865.
Auguste Comte and Positivism. Reprinted from the *Westminster Review*, April and July, 1865. London, 1865.
Analysis of the Phenomena of the Human Mind, by James Mill. Edited, with additional notes, by John Stuart Mill. London, 1869.
The Subjection of Women. Written in 1861. London, 1869.

PUBLISHED POSTHUMOUSLY

Autobiography. Ed. Helen Taylor. London, 1873. The definitive version is the John Jacob Coss edition, Columbia University Press, New York, 1924. Reissued 1944.
Three Essays on Religion: Nature, the Utility of Religion and Theism. London, 1874.
Chapters on Socialism. Reprinted from the *Fortnightly Review*, 1879, under the title *Socialism—John Stuart Mill.* Ed. W. D. P. Bliss. Social Science Library Series. Linden, Mass., 1891.
On Social Freedom. Reprinted from the *Oxford and Cambridge Review*, June 1907. Introduction by Dorothy Fosdick. New York, 1944.

PAMPHLETS

Inaugural Address to the University of St. Andrews, 1 Feb. 1867. London, 1867.
Speech on the Admission of Women to the Electoral Franchise, 20 May 1867. London, 1867.
England and Ireland. London, 1868.
The Evidence of John Stuart Mill, taken before the Royal Commission of 1870 on the Administration and Operation of the Contagious Diseases Acts of 1866 and 1869. Reprinted verbatim from the Blue Book. Issued by The National Association for the Repeal of the Contagious Diseases Acts, London.
Programme of the Land Tenure Reform Association, with an explanatory statement by J. S. Mill. London, 1871.
Speech in favour of Women's Suffrage. 12 Jan. 1871. Edinburgh, 1873.

B. MANUSCRIPT SOURCES

The Mill-Taylor Collection, British Library of Political and Economic Science. 58 bound volumes of letters, and 9 boxes of miscellanea.
The John Stuart Mill Collection. Yale University Library. About 450 letters, drafts and fragments.
The Keynes Library, King's College, Cambridge. Includes 114 letters and 6 miscellaneous items.

The National Library of Scotland, MS. vol. 618. 116 letters between Mill and Carlyle.

The Library of Mount Holyoke College, South Hadley, Mass. A holograph manuscript diary of Mill's walking tour with Henry Cole through Hampshire, West Sussex, and the Isle of Wight, 19 July–6 Aug. 1832. It is understood that this document is now being prepared for publication.

Somerset House. The Will of John Stuart Mill.

C. BIOGRAPHICAL SOURCES

BAIN, Alexander. *James Mill, a Biography*. London, 1882.

—— *John Stuart Mill, a Criticism*. London, 1882.

BARRÈS, Maurice. Article in the Avignon weekly *L'Accent*, 26 Jan. 1947.

BRANDES, Dr. Georg. *Eminent Authors of the Nineteenth Century*. Tr. R. B. Anderson. New York, 1886.

CARLYLE, Alexander (ed.). *Letters of Thomas Carlyle to John Stuart Mill, John Sterling and Robert Browning*. London, 1923.

—— *New Letters of Thomas Carlyle*. 2 vols. London, 1904.

CARLYLE, Thomas. "Occasional Discourse on the Nigger Question." *Fraser's Magazine*, Dec. 1849.

—— *Reminiscences*. Ed. J. A. Froude. 2 vols. London, 1881.

—— *Letters and Memorials of Jane Welsh Carlyle*. Ed. J. A. Froude. 3 vols. London, 1883.

—— *The Correspondence of Thomas Carlyle and Ralph Waldc Emerson*. Ed. C. E. Norton. 2 vols. Revised edn. Boston, 1886.

CHARLES-ROUX, J. *J. H. Fabre en Avignon*. Paris, 1913.

CHRISTIE, W. D. *J. S. Mill and Mr. Abraham Hayward, Q.C.* London, 1873.

—— "Mr. John Stuart Mill for Westminster." *Macmillan's Magazine*. May, 1865.

COLE, Sir Henry. *Fify Years of Public Work*. London, 1884.

CONWAY, Moncure D. *Autobiography*. 2 vols. Boston and New York, 1904.

—— *A Memorial Discourse in Honour of John Stuart Mill*. London, 1873.

—— *Thomas Carlyle*. New York, 1881.

COURTNEY, W. L. *Life of John Stuart Mill*. London, 1889.

COX, C. M. *The Early Mental Traits of 300 Geniuses*. Genetic Studies of Genius, II. Stanford, Cal., 1926.

CROZIER, John Beattie. *My Inner Life*. 2 vols. London, 1908.

D'EICHTHAL, Eugène (ed.). *John Stuart Mill, Correspondance Inédite avec Gustave d'Eichthal*. Paris, 1898.

Démocratie du Midi. Avignon newspaper, 8th May–4th June 1873.

DE MORGAN, Sophia Elizabeth. *Memoir of Augustus De Morgan*. London, 1882.

DOWDEN, Edward (ed.). *Correspondence of Henry Taylor*. London, 1888.

DUFFY, Sir Charles Gavan. *Conversations with Carlyle.* London, 1892.

—— *My Life in Two Hemispheres.* London, 1898.

DUMAS, Alfred. "Stuart Mill et Mistral." *Mémoires de l'Académie de Vaucluse.* 1927.

ELLIOT, Hugh, S. R. (ed.). *The Letters of John Stuart Mill.* 2 vols. London, 1910.

ESPINASSE, F. *Literary Recollections.* London, 1893.

EVERETT, E. M. *The Party of Humanity. The Fortnightly Review,* 1865–1874. Chapel Hill, North Carolina, 1939.

FAWCETT, Mrs. M. G. *Life of the Rt. Hon. Sir William Molesworth, Bt.* London, 1901.

FONBLANQUE, E. B. *Life and Labours of Albany Fonblanque.* London, 1874.

FOX BOURNE, H. R. (ed.). *John Stuart Mill—Notices of his Life and Works.* London, 1873.

FOX, Caroline. *Memories of Old Friends.* Ed. Horace N. Pym. 2nd edition. London, 1882.

FROUDE, J. A. *Thomas Carlyle, a History of the First Forty Years.* 2 vols. London, 1882.

—— *Thomas Carlyle, a History of his Life in London.* 2 vols. London, 1884.

GARNETT, Richard. *The Life of W. J. Fox.* London, 1910.

—— *Thomas Carlyle.* London, 1887.

GIBBS, J. W. M. (ed.). *Early Essays by John Stuart Mill.* London, 1897.

GILCHRIST, H. H. (ed.). *Anne Gilchrist, her Life and Writings.* London, 1887.

GOMPERZ, Heinrich. *Theodor Gomperz, Briefe und Aufzeichnungen.* 2 vols. Vienna, 1936.

GREVILLE, Charles. *The Greville Memoirs 1814–1860.* Ed. Lytton Strachey and Roger Fulford. London, 1938.

GRIFFIN, W. H., and MINCHIN, H. C. *The Life of Robert Browning.* London, 1910.

GROTE, Mrs. Harriet. *The Personal Life of George Grote.* London, 1873.

—— *The Philosophical Radicals of 1832.* London, 1866.

HAGBERG, Knut. *Personalities and Powers.* Tr. Elizabeth Sprigge and Claude Napier. London, 1930.

HAMILTON, Mary Agnes. *John Stuart Mill.* Makers of the New World Series. London, 1933.

HANSARD. *Parliamentary Debates.* 1865–1868. London.

HARRIS, Wilson. *Caroline Fox.* London, 1944.

HAYEK, F. A. *John Stuart Mill and Harriet Taylor.* London, 1951.

—— "J. S. Mill's Correspondence." *Times Literary Supplement.* 13 Feb. 1943.

HENSHAW, Mrs. S. E. "John Stuart Mill and Mrs. Taylor." *The Overland Monthly.* San Francisco, Dec. 1874.

HIMES, Norman E. "John Stuart Mill's attitude towards neo-Malthusianism." *The Economic Journal,* Jan. 1929. Economic History Series no. 4—Supplement.

HIRST, F. W. *The Early Life and Letters of John Morley.* 2 vols. London, 1927.

HOLT, Winifred. *A Beacon for the Blind—Henry Fawcett.* London, 1915.

HOLYOAKE, G. J. *John Stuart Mill, as some of the Working Classes knew him.* London, 1873.

—— *Sixty Years of an Agitator's Life.* 2 vols. London, 1892.

HYDE, Francis E. "Utility and Radicalism, 1825–1837." *Economic History Review,* vol. XVI. 1946.

KINGSLEY, Charles. *Letters and Memories of his Life,* ed. Mrs. Fanny C. Kingsley. 2 vols. 2nd edn. London, 1877.

KITCHEL, A. T. *George Lewes and George Eliot.* New York, 1933.

KNIGHT, William. "Letters of J. S. Mill to Professor John Nichol." *Fortnightly Review,* vol. LXI, May 1897.

LARKIN, Henry. "Carlyle and Mrs. Carlyle: a Ten Years' Reminiscence." *British Quarterly Review,* July 1881.

LASKI, Harold (ed.). Introduction to *The Autobiography of John Stuart Mill.* The World's Classics Edition. Oxford, 1924.

LEADER, R. E. (ed.). *Autobiography and Letters of John Arthur Roebuck.* London, 1897.

LECHALIER, M. (ed.). *Les Annales Municipales de la Ville d'Avignon,* 1929.

LEGROS, G. V. *La vie de J. H. Fabre, Naturaliste.* Paris, 1924.

LEROUX, Ernest (ed.). *Lettres d'Auguste Comte à John Stuart Mill, 1841–1846.* Paris, 1877.

LEVI, A. W. "The Mental Crisis of John Stuart Mill." *Psychoanalytic Review,* vol. XXXII. Albany, N.Y., Jan. 1945.

—— "The Writing of Mill's Autobiography." *International Journal of Ethics,* July 1951.

LÉVY-BRUHL, L. (ed.). *Lettres Inédites de John Stuart Mill à Auguste Comte.* Alcan, Paris, 1899.

LINTON, W. J. *Memories.* London, 1895.

London Review, 2 vols. 1835–1836.

London and Westminster Review, vols. III and XXV, Jan. 1836—vol. XXXIII, March 1840.

LYTTON, Earl of. *The Life of Edward Bulwer, First Lord Lytton.* 2 vols. London, 1913.

MACCABE, Joseph. *The Life and Letters of George Jacob Holyoake.* 2 vols. London, 1908.

MARMONTEL, Jean François. *Mémoires d'un Père.* 4 vols. Paris, 1804.

MASSON, David. *Carlyle Personally—Two Edinburgh Lectures.* Edinburgh, 1885.

—— *Memories of London in the Forties.* Ed. Flora Masson. London, 1908.

MAURICE, Frederick (ed.). *The Life of Frederick Denison Maurice.* 2 vols. 3rd edn. London, 1884.

MILL, Anna J. "John Stuart Mill's visit to Wordsworth, 1831." *The Modern Language Review,* vol. XLIV, no. 3, July 1949.

MILL, John Stuart. "The Negro Question." *Fraser's Magazine.* Jan. 1850.

MINEKA, F. E. *The Dissidence of Dissent. The Monthly Repository, 1806–1838.* Chapel Hill, North Carolina, 1944.

Monthly Repository. New Series. 1827–1835.

MONYPENNY, W. F., and BUCKLE, G. E. *The Life of Benjamin Disraeli, Earl of Beaconsfield*. 6 vols. London, 1916.

MOREHOUSE, H. J. *History of Kirkburton*. Huddersfield, 1861.

MORLEY, Edith (ed.). *Henry Crabb Robinson on Books and their Writers*. 3 vols. London, 1938.

MORLEY, John. *Critical Miscellanies*. 2nd series. London, 1877.

NESBITT, G. L. *Benthamite Reviewing. The Westminster Review, 1824–1836*. New York, 1934.

NEW, Chester. *Lord Durham*. Oxford, 1929.

NORTON, Sarah (ed.). *The Letters of Charles Eliot Norton*. 2 vols. London, 1913.

OKEY, Thomas. *The Story of Avignon*. London and New York, 1911.

OLIVIER, Sydney H., Baron. *The Myth of Governor Eyre*. London, 1933.

Quotidien du Midi. Avignon newspaper. Sat., 12 April 1913.

RAMADGE, Francis Hopkins, M.D. *Consumption Curable*. London, 1834.

REID, T. Wemyss. *The Life of Richard Monckton Milnes, First Lord Houghton*. 2 vols. London, 1890.

REY, Louis, Pasteur, *Le Roman de John Stuart Mill*. Paris, 1913.

—— *John Stuart Mill en Avignon*. Vaison, 1921.

RUSSELL, Bertrand, and Patricia (eds.). *The Amberley Papers*. 2 vols. London, 1937.

RUSSELL, Edward R. *The Autobiography of J. S. Mill*. Liverpool, 1874.

SOLLY, HENRY. *These Eighty Years*. 2 vols. London, 1893.

SPENCER, Herbert. *Autobiography*. 2 vols. London, 1904.

STEPHEN, Leslie. "Some Early Impressions." *The National Review*. Cutting in MT Coll. 45/52.

STEPHENSON, H. W. *Sarah Flower Adams*. London, 1922.

STERLING, John. *A Correspondence between John Sterling and Ralph Waldo Emerson*. Ed. E. W. Emerson. Boston, 1897.

TAYLOR, Algernon. *Memories of a Student*. 2nd edn. London, 1895.

TAYLOR, Harriet. "The Enfranchisement of Women." *The Westminster and Foreign Quarterly Review*, vol. LV, July 1851.

TAYLOR, Henry. *Autobiography*. 2 vols. London, 1885.

Times. "John Stuart Mill." Obituary article. 10 May 1873.

TOWERS, C. Marion D. "John Stuart Mill and the London and Westminster Review." *The Atlantic Monthly*, vol. LXIX, Jan. 1892.

TUELL, Anne Kimball. *John Sterling*. New York, 1941.

TYNDALL, John, Professor. *New Fragments*. London, 1892.

Union de Vaucluse. Avignon Newspaper. May 1873.

VÉRAN, Jules. "Le Souvenir de Stuart Mill à Avignon." *Revue des Deux Mondes*. Sept. 1937.

VISSAC, Marc de. "John Stuart Mill." *Mémoires de l'Académie de Vaucluse*, vol. XXIV., 1905.

WALLAS, Graham. *The Life of Francis Place*. London, 1898.

WATERFIELD, Gordon. *Lucie Duff Gordon*. London, 1937.

WELLINGTON, Samuel. "John Stuart Mill—the Saint of Rationalism." *The Westminster Review*, Jan. 1905.

WEST, Julius. *John Stuart Mill.* Fabian Society Tract no. 168. London, 1913.

Westminster Review. vols. I–XXIV. 1824–1836.

WHITE, Joseph Blanco. *Life and Correspondence.* 3 vols. London, 1845.

WILSON, David Alec. *The Life of Carlyle.* 6 vols. London, 1923–1934.

WRONG, E. M. *Charles Buller and Responsible Government.* Oxford, 1926.

D. PHILOSOPHICAL AND CRITICAL

ALBEE, Ernest. *History of English Utilitarianism.* London and New York, 1902.

ALEXANDER, F. P. *Mill and Carlyle.* Edinburgh, 1866.

"ANTICHRIST". *The Jesus Christ of John Stuart Mill.* London, 1875.

BENTHAM, Jeremy. "Introduction to the Principles of Morals and Legislation." *The Works of Jeremy Bentham,* ed. J. Bowring, vol. I. London, 1838.

Blackwood's Magazine. "Mr. Mill on the Subjection of Women", no. 647, Sept. 1869.

BONAR, James. *The Tables Turned.* London, 1931.

British Quarterly Review, "John Stuart Mill's Autobiography", vol. LIX. Jan. 1874.

BROWNE, W. R. *The Autobiography of J. S. Mill.* London, 1874.

CATLIN, G. E. G. Introduction to *The Rights of Woman by Mary Wollstonecraft and The Subjection of Women by John Stuart Mill.* Everyman's Library, no. 825. London, 1929.

CAVANAGH, F. A. *James and John Stuart Mill on Education.* Landmarks in the History of Education series. London, 1931.

COLERIDGE, S. T. *On the Constitution of Church and State.* London, 1828.

COMTE, Auguste. *The Positive Philosophy of Auguste Comte.* Tr. Harriet Martineau. Intro. Frederic Harrison. 3 vols. London, 1896.

COURTNEY, W. L. *The Metaphysics of J. S. Mill.* London, 1879.

DAVIDSON, W. L. *Political Thought in England: The Utilitarians, from Bentham to J. S. Mill.* Home University Library, no. 106. London, 1915.

DE TOCQUEVILLE, Alexis. *Democracy in America.* 12th edn. Intro. Philip Bradley. 2 vols. New York, 1945.

DICEY, A. V. *Law and Opinion in England.* 2nd edn. London, 1914.

Dublin Review. "Evolution and Faith." "The Rule and Motive of Certitude." July 1871.

ELLIOT, Hugh S. R. Preface to *J. S. Mill and the Protection of Infant Industries.* Cobden Club Pamphlet. London, 1911.

ENGELS, Frederick. *The Condition of the Working-class in England in 1844.* Tr. Florence K. Wischnewetsky. London, 1892.

GREEN, T. H. *Lectures on the Principles of Political Obligation.* London and New York, 1931.

GRIFFITH, G. Talbot. *Population Problems of the Age of Malthus*. Cambridge, 1926.

HALÉVY, Élie. *La Formation du Radicalisme Philosophique*. 3 vols. Paris, 1904.

HARRISON, Frederic. *Tennyson, Ruskin, Mill*. London, 1899.

HAYEK, F. A. *The Counter Revolution of Science*. Chicago, 1952.

HULL, Alban. *The Political Ideas of J. S. Mill*. Huddersfield, 1935.

HUMBOLDT, Baron Wilhelm von. *The Sphere and Duties of Government*. Tr. Joseph Coulthard. London, 1854.

HUXLEY, Julian. *The Living Thoughts of Darwin*. Living Thoughts Library. London, 1939.

JENKS, Edward. *Carlyle and Mill*. Cambridge, 1888.

JOAD, C. E. M. *Guide to the Philosophy of Morals and Politics*. London, 1938.

KENT, C. B. ROYLANCE. *The English Radicals*. London and New York, 1899.

LASKI, Harold J. *Political Thought in England: from Locke to Bentham*. Home University Library, no. 121. London, 1920.

—— *The State in Theory and Practice*. London, 1935.

LAUGEL, Auguste. "Les Confessions de John Stuart Mill." *Grandes Figures Historiques*. Bibliothèque Contemporaine. Paris, 1875.

MACAULAY, Lord. "Mill's Essay on Government." *Miscellaneous Writings and Speeches of Lord Macaulay*. Popular edn. London, 1889.

MACCUNN, John. *Six Radical Thinkers*. London, 1907.

MALTHUS, Thomas Robert. *An Essay on the Principle of Population*. London, 1798.

MANSEL, Henry Longueville. *The Limits of Religious Thought*. London, 1858.

MARITAIN, Jacques. *An Introduction to Logic*. London, 1937.

MILL, James. *Essays on Government, etc. Reprinted from the Supplement to the Encyclopaedia Britannica* (*5th edn.*). 2nd edn. London, 1828.

—— *A Fragment on Mackintosh*. London, 1835.

MORLAN, George. *America's Heritage from John Stuart Mill*. New York, 1936.

NEFF, Emery. *Carlyle and Mill*. 2nd edn. New York, 1926.

—— Introduction to *On Liberty and Other Essays*. Modern Reader series. New York, 1926.

—— *Carlyle*. London, 1932.

OLIVIER, Sydney H., Baron. "J. S. Mill on Socialism." *Today*, vol. II, n.s., 1884.

RADCLIFFE of Werneth, Lord. *The Problem of Power*. Reith Memorial Lectures 1951. London, 1952.

ROBERTSON, John M. *Modern Humanists*. London, 1908.

—— *Modern Humanists Reconsidered*. London, 1927.

ROUSSEAU, Jean Jacques. *Du Contrat Social*. Ed. C. E. Vaughan. Modern Language Texts. 2nd edn. Manchester, 1926.

RUSSELL, Bertrand. *Freedom and Organization*. London, 1934.

—— *A History of Western Philosophy*. New York, 1945.

—— *Authority and the Individual*. Reith Memorial Lectures, 1948. New York, 1949.

SIDGWICK, Henry. *Method of Ethics*. London, 1874.
STEPHEN, Sir James Fitzjames, Q.C. *Liberty, Equality, Fraternity*. 2nd edn. London, 1874.
STEPHEN, Leslie. *The English Utilitarians*. 3 vols. London, 1900.
TAINE, Hippolyte A. *English Positivism. A Study on J. S. Mill*. Tr. T. D. Haye. London, 1870.
WHEWELL, William, D.D. *Of Induction, with especial reference to Mr. J. Stuart Mill's "System of Logic"*. London, 1849.
WHITE, R. J. "John Stuart Mill." *The Cambridge Journal*, vol. V. Nov. 1951.
WHITTAKER, Thomas. "Comte and Mill." *Reason: A Philosophical Essay with Historical Illustrations*. Cambridge, 1934.

E. GENERAL

ANON. *Anonymous Journalism*. London, 1855.
ATKINSON, C. M. *Jeremy Bentham*. London, 1905.
BAIN, Alexander. *Autobiography*. Ed. W. L. Davidson. London, 1904.
—— (ed). *The Minor Works of George Grote*. London, 1873.
BENTHAM, Jeremy. *A Plan for Universal and Perpetual Peace*. Grotius Society Pamphlet. London, 1927.
—— ("Gamaliel Smith, Esq."). *Not Paul, but Jesus*. London, 1823.
BENTHAM, Lady. *Memoir of Brigadier General Sir Samuel Bentham, by his Widow*. Papers and Practical Illustrations of Public Works. London, 1856.
—— *The Life of Sir Samuel Bentham*. London, 1862.
BEVERIDGE, Sir William H. *The Pillars of Security*. London, 1943.
BLISS, Trudy. *Jane Welsh Carlyle*. London, 1949.
BOSANQUET, Theodora. *Harriet Martineau*. London, 1927.
BOWRING, Sir John. *Memoirs of Bentham. The Works of Jeremy Bentham*, ed. J. Bowring, vol. X. London, 1843.
BRADLAUGH, Hypatia. *Charles Bradlaugh, by his Daughter*. London, 1894.
BRADSHAW, F. *Self-Government in Canada*. Studies in Economic and Political Science series. London, 1903.
BULLETT, Gerald. *Sydney Smith*. London, 1951.
BULWER, Edward, Lord Lytton. *England and the English*. London, 1833.
CARLILE, Richard. "What is Love?" *The Republican*, 6 May 1825.
CARLYLE, Thomas. *Sartor Resartus*. First published, Boston, 1835.
—— "The Diamond Necklace." *Critical and Miscellaneous Essays*, vol. V. London, 1871.
—— *The French Revolution*. First published, 3 vols., London, 1837.
—— *Chartism*. First published, London, Dec. 1839.
—— *On Heroes, Hero-Worship*, etc. First published, London, 1841.
—— *Past and Present*. First published, London, 1843.
—— *Life of John Sterling*. First published, London, 1851.
—— "Letters from Thomas Carlyle to the Socialists of 1830." *New Quarterly Review*, vol. II, 1909.

COLLS, Rev. J. F. *Utilitarianism Unmasked*. London, 1844.
COOK, Hartley Kemball. *Over the Hills and Far Away*. London, 1947.
COUPLAND, Sir Reginald. Introduction to *The Durham Report*. Oxford, 1945.
CRAWFORD, Alexander H. *Recollections of James Martineau*. London, 1903.
CUNNINGHAM, W. *The Growth of English Industry and Commerce in Modern Times*. 2 vols. Cambridge, 1917.
DE TOCQUEVILLE, Alexis. *Recollections*. Ed. J. P. Mayer. New York, 1949.
DODDS, John W. *The Age of Paradox. England 1841–1851*. New York, 1952.
DUNN, Waldo H. *Froude and Carlyle*. London, 1930.
ELLIOT, Hugh S. R. *Herbert Spencer*. Makers of the Nineteenth Century series. London, 1917.
ELTON, LORD. *Imperial Commonwealth*. London, 1945.
FINLASON, W. F. *The History of the Jamaica Case*. London, 1869.
FOOT, Isaac. *Michael Verran and Thomas Carlyle*. London, 1946.
GALT, J. *Annals of the Parish*. Edinburgh, 1821.
HAIGHT, Gordon S. *George Eliot and John Chapman*. Yale, 1940.
HALÉVY, Élie. *A History of the English People in the Nineteenth Century*. 6 vols. London, 1951.
HAMMOND, J. L., and Barbara. *The Village Labourer, 1760–1832*. London, 1911.
HANSON, L., and E. *Marian Evans and George Eliot*. London, 1952.
HAYEK, F. A. *The Road to Serfdom*. London, 1944.
HOUGHTON, Lord (Richard Monckton Milnes). *Monographs, Personal and Social*. London, 1873.
HUME, Hamilton. *The Life of Edward John Eyre*. London, 1867.
JAMAICA. *Observations on the Royal Commission*. Anon. London, 1866.
—— "Jamaica—Who is to blame?" Reprinted from *The Eclectic Review*. London, n.d.
JAMAICA COMMITTEE. *Jamaica Papers*, no. 1. London, 1866.
JAMES, Henry, Sr. "Some Personal Recollections of Carlyle." *The Atlantic Monthly*, vol. XLVII, May, 1881.
LARKIN, Henry. *Carlyle and the Open Secret of his Life*. London, 1886.
LEA, F. A. *Carlyle, Prophet of Today*. London, 1943.
LUCAS-DUBRETON, J. *La Restauration et la Monarchie de Juillet*. Paris, 1926.
MAINE, Sir Henry Sumner. *Ancient Law*. 14th edn. London, 1891.
MARSTON, Mansfield. *The Life of J. S. Mill*. London, 1873.
MARTINEAU, Harriet. *Autobiography*. 3 vols. London, 1877.
—— *Five years of Youth*. London, 1831.
—— *History of the Thirty Years Peace*. London, 1877.
MILL, James. *The History of British India*. 4th edn. Ed. H. H. Wilson. 9 vols. London, 1848.
MILLER, Betty. *Robert Browning. A Portrait*. London, 1952.
MORISON, J. S. "The Mission of the Earl of Durham." *Cambridge History of the British Empire*, vol. VI. Cambridge, 1930.
MORLEY, Edith J. *The Life and Times of Henry Crabb Robinson*. London, 1935.
NEVILL, John C. *Harriet Martineau*. London, 1943.

OGDEN. C. K. *Jeremy Bentham.* Centenary Lecture. London, 1932.
PATTERSON, M. W. *Sir Francis Burdett and his Times.* 2 vols. London, 1931.
PLANTA, Edward. *A New Picture of Paris.* London, 1818.
QUENNELL, Peter (ed.). *Mayhew's London.* London, 1949.
REID, Stuart J. *Life and Letters of Lord Durham.* 2 vols. London and New York, 1906.
REID, T. Wemyss. *The Life of W. E. Forster.* 2 vols. 2nd edn. London, 1888.
RIGBY, E. (Lady Eastlake). *Mrs. Grote.* London, 1880.
ROSS, Janet. *Three Generations of Englishwomen,* 2 vols. London, 1888.
ROSS, W. G., Colonel, R.E. *Oliver Cromwell and His Ironsides . . . as they are represented by Thomas Carlyle.* London, 1889.
SMITH, Rev. Sydney. *Works.* 3 vols. 3rd. edn. London, 1845.
STEPHEN, Leslie. *Studies of a Biographer.* 4 vols. London, 1902.
STRACHEY, Lytton. *Queen Victoria.* New York, 1921.
TAYLOR, Helen (ed.). *Miscellaneous and Posthumous Works of Henry Thomas Buckle.* 3 vols. London, 1872.
THOMPSON, Thomas Perronet, Colonel. *Exercises, Political and Others.* 6 vols. London, 1842.
TREVELYAN, G. M. *Illustrated English Social History.* 4 vols. New York, 1952.
URE, Dr. Andrew. *The Philosophy of Manufactures.* London, 1835.
VOLTAIRE. *Lettres Choisies.* Collection des Classiques Garnier. 2 vols. Paris, n.d.
WADE, John. *The Black Book, or Corruption Unmasked.* London, 1820.
WALKER, Hugh. *The Literature of the Victorian Era.* Cambridge, 1921.
WALLAS, Graham. *Human Nature in Politics.* 3rd edn. London, 1920.
—— *The Great Society.* London, 1914.
—— *William Johnson Fox, 1786–1864.* London, 1924.
—— *Jeremy Bentham.* London University Foundation Oration, 1922.
WESTERMARCK, Edward. *The Origin and Development of the Moral Ideas.* London, 1906.
WOODHAM-SMITH, Mrs. Cecil. *Florence Nightingale.* London, 1949.
YOUNG, Norwood. *Carlyle, His Rise and Fall.* London, 1927.

INDEX

"A" ("ANTIQUUS"), press sign of John Mill, 133
ABBAYE ST. MARTIAL (Avignon), 486; now Avignon Post Office, 486 n.
ABERDEEN, 211, 242, 271; "Miss Trevor" acts in, 392; news of Harriet's illness, 393; 398
ACADÉMIE DE VAUCLUSE, 399
ACCIDIE, John Mill suffers from, 75, 80; Carlyle's similar complaint, 160
ACROPOLIS, 374, 378
"A CRISIS IN MY MENTAL HISTORY", 79
ADAMS, MRS. WILLIAM BRIDGES. *See* Flower, Sarah
ADAMS, WILLIAM BRIDGES ("Junius Redivivus"), articles on Divorce, 124; marries Sarah Flower, 148; 328
ADELAIDE, Alfred and Arthur Hardy in, 116; 331
AGRICULTURAL HALL (Islington), Mill addresses mass meeting at, 460-1; 462, 463
ALABAMA CLAIMS, 426, 455
ALDERNEY, 373
ALEXANDER, CZAR, 28
ALICE, PRINCESS (Daughter of Queen Victoria), Mill avoids meeting in Avignon, 481
ALISON, SIR ARCHIBALD, John Mill's review of, 175
ALLEN, WILLIAM, 29
ALPS, 238; Harriet and Mill in Tyrol, 240; 481; 485
AMBERLEY, LADY (KATE), 33 n., 404, 430; Mill's young friends, 434; meets Mill and Helen, 437–9; sudden death, 439; 449; 452; Mill's Reform Speech, 453; 474; Helen's letter on criticism, 480–1; supports Mill on Suffrage, 495, 498; works for Women's cause, 498–9; speeches for Society, 499; at Ravenscroft, 505
AMBERLEY, LORD, 430; calls on Mill, visits tomb, 434; develops friendship with Mill, **435–7**; Mill's influence on, **437–9**; speech on birth control, 438; on League to abolish war, 438 n., death, 439; supports Mill's election, 449; 457; loses seat, 475; 477, 480, 498; 504
Amberley Papers, 59 n., 81 n.
AMBLESIDE, 131
AMERICA. *See* UNITED STATES
AMPÈRE, JEAN JACQUES, 477
AMPTON STREET, Carlyle's lodgings, 170
Analysis of the Human Mind, 14; James Mill starts in 1822, 53; young reformers, led by John, study, 69; 106; Mill revises, 476
ANATOMY, SCHOOL OF (Webb Street), Jeremy Bentham's corpse dissected, 222
Annals of the Parish, 53
Annual Review, The, 12
ANONYMOUS CLUB. *See* STERLING CLUB
"ANTIQUUS", 133
Anti-Slavery Standard, 493
APOSTLES (Cambridge Society), proposed expedition to free Spain, 99; 106, 109
ARCADIA, 427
ARISTOTLE, 478
ARMY, BRITISH, Volunteers, 10, 11; flogging in, 13; 31, 420, 487; Mill's election platform, 449; 455, 470, 478; Mill on conscription, 483; 502, 504
ARNOLD, DR. THOMAS, 96, 477
Arthur Coningsby, 183
ARTICLES, MISCELLANEOUS, Mill's articles and letters on specific injustices, 346, 347
ASHBURTON, LORD AND LADY. *See* BARING, BINGHAM, AND LADY HARRIET
ASHLEY, LORD, 192, 235
ASSOCIATION, THEORY OF, **14–16**, 48, 53, 69, 106, 158, 254, 267, 269, 276, 410, 431, 441, 476, 477

ASTRONOMICAL OBSERVER (Edinburgh), 178, 180
ATHENAEUM (Club), John Mill elected to, 107
Athenaeum, The, 215
ATHENE, Helen finds correct position for statue, 428
ATHENS, Mill's article on, 293; Mill's first visit to, 378–9; return to, 427, 428; 485
ATTWOOD, THOMAS, 101, 192, 193
Auguste Comte and Positivism, Mill reprints his *Westminster* articles as book, 280; 369 n., 370
AUGUSTUS, Mill's opinion of, 477
AUSTIN, CHARLES, 51, 52; impressed by John Mill's ability, invites him to Cambridge, 52; 69; joins London Debating Society, 70; 87, 109
AUSTIN, JOHN, **50–1**, 52, 62, 104; course in Jurisprudence at University of London, 127; Carlyle's description of, 169; ill-health, 178; 179, 196; dislikes Carlyle in *London Review*, 214; 235; review of Mill's *Logic*, 272; 282; letters to *Times* on Paris Revolution, 322; political break with Mill, 323; 331, Harriet dislikes, 338; 470
AUSTIN, LUCIE (DUFF GORDON), 50, 179
AUSTIN, SARAH (*née* TAYLOR), neighbour of Mills in Queen Square, tutors John Mill's sisters, 4, 6; 50–1; teaches John Mill German, 74, 87, 106, 119, 121; translates German literature, 163; 174; passion for Prince Puckler Muskau, 178–9; 197; Mill's complaint of overwork, 208; helps with *London Review*, 209; 213, 214, 235, 278, 292; differences with Mill, 322, 323; Harriet objects to, 331; Mill on epitaphs, 408
AUSTRALIA, Hardy brothers in, 116; South Australia Association, 225; 332, 348, 378, 407, 417, 465, 479; Mill's botanical specimens in Melbourne, 486
AUSTRIA, 424, Mill and Helen visit on return from Greece, 429
Autobiography, cheerless childhood, 24; women's education, 25; early draft on mother; 33; 34, 35, 71 n.; mental crisis, 79; 80, 80 n.; on Maurice, 95; 151 n., 280; on relations with Harriet, 317; first draft of, 369; Harriet's share in work, 371; Mill's continued attempts to describe Harriet, 409; tribute to Helen, 413; verdict on Proportional Representation, 417, 418; 453 n., 461; final opinion on Eyre prosecution, 472; brought up to 1870, 477; existence of Suffrage Society due to Helen, 497
AVIGNON, 239; Mill's pleasure over Hôtel de L'Europe, 361; 375; Harriet's illness and death at, 393–4; 397; Mill known as "M. Émile Maister Lord", "l' Anglais", 398; Mill and Helen return, 411; Harriet's tomb, 412, 412 n.; 413, 419, 420, 427, 429; Thornton's description of, 428; 429; Amberley visits, 434; 437, 449, 474, 475, 475 n., 480, 481; English friends visit, 485; French friends, 485; 486, 487, 488, 504, 506, 507, 508

BACON, FRANCIS, 88; Robertson's article on, 211; 252
BAGEHOT, WALTER, 478
BAGNÈRES, Mill joins Harriet at, 336; 411
BAILEY, SAMUEL, Mill's article attacking, 293
BAILEY, SAMUEL (of Sheffield), 196
BAIN, ALEXANDER, 9 n., visits Ford Abbey, 28; 33 n., 39 n., considers John Mill's achievement not exceptional, 40; 54 n., 59 n., describes James Mill at home, 76; John Mill's breakdown due to overwork, 79; 107 n., 154 n., 206 n., 211; assists Mill with *Logic*, 271; reviews *Logic* in *Westminster*, 272; 278; visit to India House, description of Mill, **289–90**; on Harriet, 316; Mill undersexed, 318; on relation of Mill and Harriet, 320; 321, 322, 323, 324; 329, 334; assists with revisions for third edition of *Logic*, 346; 352; sees little of Mill after Mill's marriage, 358; 368; Mill's humour, 370; 388; uncertainty over *Liberty*, 404; 408; Mill's help in publishing his books, 410; 430; Mill on Herbert Spencer, 432, 433; 441; belief that Harriet's death responsible for Mill's change in religion, 443; 448; Mill's influence with Gladstone, 455; 476, 477; horror over *Subjection of Women*, 495; Mill's comment on Grote's Abbey funeral, 505; 507
BALARD, ANTOINE JEROME, John's first friend, 47 n., 66
BALLOT, SECRET, Grote moves once a year, 193; 215; under Harriet's influence, Mill opposes, 370; 415; against in election proposals, 449; Reform League want, 460; 500
BARCLAY (tenant farmer), 3, 4, 5
BARCLAY, DAVID, 8, 9 n.
BARING, BINGHAM (LORD ASHBURTON), effort to call on Mill's wife, 350
BARING, LADY HARRIET (LADY ASHBURTON), 110; Greville's report of John Mill's attachment to, 110 n.; 350
BARNARD, JAMES M., Mill on education, 482
BARRÈS, MAURICE, 399
BARRETT, ELIZABETH, 320 n.
BARROW GREEN, Jeremy Bentham invites Mill family to visit, 18, 19; 21, 26
BARTON, MISS. *See* STERLING, MRS. JOHN
BATH, Roebuck reinstated for, 235
BATHS OF CALIGULA. *See* BATHS OF CARACALLA
BATHS OF CARACALLA, J. S. Mill and Sterling visit, 240; Sterling recalls, 287

BAYSWATER, Fox and Eliza Flower move to, 149; Austins move to, 178; Sterling moves his family to, 183
BAZARD, ARMAND, supplanted as leader of St. Simonians, 96; John Mill meets in Paris, 100
BEAL, JAMES, Member of Mill's Westminster election committee, 449; 458 n.
BEALES, EDMOND, President of Reform League, 458, 458 n., 459
BEDFORD SQUARE, COLLEGE OF, Mill's interest in, 500; sends Mary Mill's daughter to, 505
Beehive, The, Saint-Simonian journal, 277 n.
BEGGS, THOMAS, 449
BELGIUM, 504
BENTHAM, GEORGE (son of Brigadier Sir Samuel), 43; introduces John Mill to botany and teaches him to swim, 44; John Mill's criticism of his book on Logic, 65
BENTHAM, JEREMY, 11; meets James Mill, **12–19**; pamphlets, 13, 14; theory of pleasure and pain, 15; early history, 16–19; need for amanuensis, 17–18; reverence for Milton, 21; offers to be guardian to John Mill, 22; 24; rents Ford Abbey, 26; 27, 28; attacks Church, 29–30; his life at Ford Abbey, 32; 37, 38, 41, 42, 43, 44, 48; *Traité de Legislation*, 49; description of, 50; 52, 53 n., 54, 59; starts new Radical review, 62; 63, 64 67, 68; *Rationale of Judicial Evidence*, insists John Mill take credit for editing, 72–3; 74, 80 n., 85, 98, 101, 102, 104, 106, 192, 198, 213; Mill's criticism of, 221; death, dissection, 222; Mill's estimate of, 222–3; Mill's articles comparing Bentham and Coleridge, 244–6; 265, 400, 401, 420, 421, 470, 476
BENTHAM, LADY (Wife of Sir Samuel), 43; efforts to teach social accomplishments to John Mill, 44–6
BENTHAM, BRIGADIER SIR SAMUEL (Jeremy Bentham's brother), 16; 30, 35; home in France, 40; **42–3**, 44, 48, 51, 97, 375, 400
BENTHAMITE (-ISM). *See* UTILITARIANS
Benthamite Reviewing, 63 n.
BERKELEY, BISHOP, 293, 329; Mill's appreciation of, 478
BERTHOLLET, MME., 41
BIRKSGATE (YORKSHIRE). Hardy family home, 115, 116; Harriet's first visit, 241; Harriet's second visit, 288; 321
BIRMINGHAM, 101, 192
BIRTH CONTROL, John Mill's distribution of pamphlets, 56–9; Mill's remedies for over-population, 301–3; Harriet's view, 307, 314, 315, 437; Amberley on, 438
BISMARCK, 504
BISSET, DR., 8, 217
BLACK, JOHN, editor of *Morning Chronicle*, 53; James Mill's influence with, 54; John Mill's letters, 54; 101 n., 102; fights duel with Roebuck, 193; 284
BLACKBURN, JUSTICE, 472
BLACKHEATH PARK (Mill's home in), 355; description of, **357**; secluded life of Mills, 358; Mill and household problems, 361–4; 367, 373, 374, Helen the housekeeper, 384; 386, 391, 398; Mill and Helen return to, 407; 419, 429; Saturday dinners, 430; 437, 475; Voluntary Band, 493; Mill leaves, 505
BLACKIE, JAMES S., 496
Blackwood's Magazine, 285; attacks *Subjection of Women*, 495;
Black Book, or Corruption Unmasked, 61
Black Dwarf, The, 58
BLANC, LOUIS, Mill considers his communism as experiment, 297; 430
Bleak House, Mill objects to ridicule of women's rights, 311 n.
BLESSINGTON, LADY, 330
BLISS, W. D. P., 489 n.
BOGHURST CHURCH, 18
BOIS DE BOULOGNE, 392
BONAPARTE (BUONAPARTE). *See* NAPOLEON BUONAPARTE
BOOKSELLERS' ASSOCIATION, Mill's public letter against, 359
Book of the Church, 63
BORDEAUX, 207, 374
BOSANQUET, THEODORA, 110 n.
BOTANY, George Bentham starts John Mill's interest in, 44; Mill walks with Graham and Roebuck, 67; 107, 139; herbarium, 265; 345; Mill's Sunday walks, 359; notes in *Phytologist*, 368; Mill in Sicily, 377, 378; Mill on Pentelicua, 379; Mill loses collecting box, 381; articles in *Phytologist*, 412; herbarium in Avignon, 476; Mill's sport, 486; Mill's collections dispersed, 486; Mill and Fabre, 486–7; 506, 507
BOULET, MLLE., 44
BOULOGNE, 178, 207, 212, 238, 332, 361, 374, 383, 386
BOUVERIE (Liberal Member for Kilmarnock), 473
BOWEN, (Colonial Secretary for Ionian Islands), 378
BOWOOD, 16, 26
BOWRING, SIR JOHN, Jeremy Bentham's biographer, 18; editor of *Westminster Review*, 64; 101, 127; in Parliament, 192; 193, 194; Mill defends father's memory, 213
BOWRING, LADY (Sir John's second wife), 499
BOW STREET, John Mill at, 57; Eyre's assistants charged at, 471
BOYD, LIEUTENANT ROBERT, cousin of Sterling, 99
BRADLAUGH, CHARLES, 437, 458; Mill supports for Parliament, 473, 474; 475, 499
BRAND, LIEUT. (later Lieut.-Comdr.), 467, 471

BRASENOSE COLLEGE, 378
BREWER, WILLIAM, 449
BRIGHT, JOHN, Mill's respect for, 451; 459, 461, 470
BRIGHTON, Mill ordered to, 205; 207; Harriet in, 240; Harriet's frequent visits to, 241; 288, 292, 309, 331, 335; Harriet, Helen and Mill spend Christmas at, 386; 387
BRISTOL, Colman home in, 351; Kate Amberley's speech at, 499
British Critic, Newman-Puseyites attack *Logic*, 272
BRITISH AND FOREIGN SCHOOL SOCIETY, 29
BRITISH AND FOREIGN UNITARIAN ASSOCIATION, 118
British Medical Journal, 438
BRITISH MUSEUM, John Mill and Roebuck visit, 67; 187
BRITTANY, 356; Mill searches for home in, 372; Mill's tour, 373–4
BROOKE, REV. STOPFORD, Defends Mill against Hayward's attacks, 72 n.
BROUGHAM, LORD HENRY, association with James Mill, 6; 12, 13, 61, 101, 102, 195, 216, 226, 227; enmity for Durham and Melbourne, 231; attacks Durham, 232; 323
BROWN, THOMAS, 6, 329; Mill's attacks on Scottish school of Common Sense, 440, 441
BROWNING, ROBERT, 120; youthful love for Eliza Flower, 122, 123; John Mill's criticisms of "Pauline", 135–6; 136 n., 199, 236, 237, 320 n., 493
BUCKENHAM CASTLE, James Mill and John visit Lady Harriet Baring at, 109
BUCKLE, HENRY THOMAS, Helen edits his works, 477, 478; 505
Bull Dog, The, 56
BULLER, CHARLES, in London Debating Society, 72; 106, 110 n.; John Mill visits in Cornwall, 131, 141; tutored by Carlyle, 162; 168, 170, 179, 183; in Parliament, 192; 193, 194, 195, 196, 213; on radical defeat, 215; 218; in Colonization Society, 225; on Durham, 227, 228; secretary for Durham's Canadian mission, 229; 230; on Durham's success in Canada, 231; Mill's opinion of, 232; assists Durham with Report, 232; 234; becomes a Whig, 235; 238; death of, 320; 324
BULLER FAMILY, 106, 152, 162, 165, 174, 197, 230
BULWER, EDWARD LYTTON, in London Debating Society, 70; in Parliament, 192, 193; 197; Mill on *Sir Thomas Browne*, 209; Mill on changes in *Review* after James Mill's death, 214; 218; Mill on Bentham's philosophy for *England and the English*, 221; letters to Durham on Radicals, 227; 235, 330
BULWER, HENRY LYTTON, 70
BUMPUS (Bookseller), 387
BURDETT, SIR FRANCES, 13, 29; arrest of, 31; 102; becomes a Tory, 193; 226
BURKE, COLONEL, 463
BURROW, HARRIET. *See* MILL, MRS. JAMES
BURROW, MRS. (Mother of Mrs. James Mill), 9, 25 n.; John Mill's letter to, 35
BUTLER, MRS. JOSEPHINE, 501
BUXTON, CHARLES, 457, 470; resigns from Jamaica Committee, 470;
BYNG, Radical candidate, 193
BYRON, LORD, 19, 25, 78; John Mill and Roebuck debate on, 82; 131; 152

CAEN, 292, Mill and Harriet at, 321
CAIRNES, JOHN ELLIOT, first meets Mill, 410; 411; dedicates the *Slave Power* to Mill, 425; Mill's letter on Lincoln, 426; 430; 437; Mill's relief over election defeat, 475; Mill asks to assist Women's Suffrage Society, 492, 493; 498
CAIRNES, MRS. JOHN ELLIOT, 493
CALENDAR OF ODOURS, Mill sends to Caroline Fox, 267
CALVERT, DR., Sterling's friend, 239; in Falmouth, 261; 263, 263 n., 264, 284, 360
CALVINISTS. *See* NON-CONFORMISTS
CAMBERWELL GROVE CHAPEL, 120, 122
CAMBRIDGE UNIVERSITY, 19, 47; James Mill refuses to send John to, 49; Union debates, 52; 70, 72; Sterling at, 99; 162, 194, 198, 255; success o. *Logic* at, 272; Fawcett's use of *Political Economy*, 418; 419, 434, 458
CANADA, 225, 228, 229, 230; popularity of Durham, 231; rebellion on Durham's departure, 231; Durham's Report on, 232, 233; union of Upper and Lower, 234; 389, 420
CANNING, GEORGE, 36
CAPITAL PUNISHMENT, Harriet changes Mill's views on, 370; Mill defends in Parliament, 456
CARDWELL, EDWARD, 466, 469, 470
CARLILE, RICHARD, 54, 55, 58
CARLYLE, ALEXANDER, 151 n., 326 n.
CARLYLE, DR. JOHN (Brother of Thomas), 143, 239, 326 n.
CARLYLE, MRS. (Mother of Thomas), 160–1, 164, 166
CARLYLE, JANE WELSH, on d'Eichthal, 96; 157; committed to marry Carlyle, 162; 165–6; 169, 170; 171, 178; meets Harriet, 179–83; 184, 185, 186; on Mill's health, 205; 206, 264, 265; dislike of Harriet, 325; 326, 446
CARLYLE, THOMAS, 84, 86, 96, 96 n., 104, 107, 111, 126; description of John Mill, 128; 129, 136, 140, 142, 147, 151 n., **157–87**; origin, 158; comparison with James Mill, 159; mental crisis, 160; marries Jane Welsh, 162; German metaphysics, 163; Craigenputtock, 165;

Sartor Resartus, 167; first impressions of John Mill, 169; friendship with John Mill, 170–3; meets Harriet, 179; meets Sterling, 183; criticisms of his style, 184; *French Revolution*, 185–7; 194; 205; visits Mills at Dorking, 206; description of Mill's condition, 206; gossip about Mill and Harriet, 207; 209; articles for *London and Westminster*, 210; Radicals object to Carlyle articles, 214; Mill's praise of *French Revolution*, 215; lectures, 216; Carlyle on *Review* finances, 217; 218, 219, 221; further gossip about Mill, 240; 241; *Cromwell* 242; pleasure over Sterling article, 243; indignation against Mill and *Review*, 243; 244, 246, 247, 261; "Hero as Prophet" lecture, 264; 265, 270, 281, 285; *Life of Sterling*, 287; refuses trusteeship of Harriet's children, 288; 307; on Harriet's influence with Mill, 315; 318; to Norton on relations with Mill, 324; 325; hatred of Mill, 326; Mill on, 327; 337, 337 n., 338, 346, 350, 403; abhors *Liberty*, 405; at Edinburgh, 445; 446; on "Niggers", 464; 465, 466, 469, on Eyre Defence Committee, 471; drafts petition for Eyre, 472; 504

Carlyle's Life in London, 326 n.

Carnarvon, Lord, 472

Caroline. *See* Ley, Caroline

Carpenter, Mary, 497

Carrel, Armand, 147, Mill's tribute in *Review*, 218

Casa Brizzi (Naples) (Hotel des Étrangers), Harriet and Mill stay in, 239; Mill returns to, 239 n.

Catherine, Empress, 42

Cato Street Conspiracy, 91

Cavaignac, Godefroy, John Mill meets in Paris, 147; 236, 324, 325

"Cave of Adullam", 454

Cenerentola, La (Opera), 375

Cephalonia, 378

Cévennes Mountains, Mill climbs in, 411

Chadwick, Edwin, 127, Mill suggests his Committee canvas for, 447; 448, 449; intermediary between Roebuck and Mill, 452, 453; arranges Mill's proposal for London County Council, 457; 473, 475, 481

Chambers, Robert, 270 n.

Chancery Lane, Owenites debating hall in, 69; London Debating Society meetings at Freemason's Tavern, 70

Chapman, John, buys *London and Westminster*, 247; Harriet's article on "Enfranchisement of Women" published by, 347; 350; induces Mill to write again on Whewell, 359; 370, Mill's agreement on publishing Spencer, 434; 437

Chapters on Socialism, 369 n.

Charles X (France), 100

Chartists, Carlyle's article on, 243; 312, 323, 458

Chauffard, Dr., Avignon friend of Mill, 485; 507, 508

Cheyne Row, Chelsea, 182, 185, 287

Chicago Tribune, reporter's description of Mill, 507

Chief Examiner, *See* East India Company, Examiner's Office

China Tea Trade, James Mill defends East India Company, 388

Chrestomathia, Jeremy Bentham's plans for universal education, 29; 59

Christian Socialists, 84; reprint Harriet's working-class chapter from *Political Economy*, 311; 403; enthusiasm for Mill's *Hamilton*, 444

Christie, W. D., defends Mill against Hayward, 72 n.; electioneers for Mill, 449

Christopher Street, 4 (Finsbury), John and Harriet Taylor's first home, 117; 118; John Mill's visits to, 128; Taylors move to Kent Terrace, 141

Church of England, Bentham's *Church-of-Englandism*, 29; 38, 53, 63, 84, 119, 183, 184; James Mill's attack, 197; 301; disestablishment in Ireland, 455, 455 n., 466, 473, 474

Church-of-Englandism, 29

Church of Our Lady (St. John's Wood), 330

Church Missionary Society, 225

Cicero, Mill's opinion, 477

Circus, Franconi's, 44–5

Citizen King. *See* Louis Philippe

City of London, India House, 55; 67; Grote's home, 68; John Taylor's business, 110, 116; 331; Herbert lives in, 358

Civilization, 207

Civil Service (Competitive), Harriet's interest in, 368

Claims of Englishwomen, The, Helen's article, 497

Claims of Labour, The, 302 n.

Clark, Sir James, 335, 363, 365, admits Mill consumptive, 366

Clapton, W. J. Fox's home in, 144, 149

Clay, Sir William, 193

Clifton, Sterling's family live at, 264; 265, 284

Cobbe, Miss, 493

Cobbett, William, 13, 102; in Parliament, 192; 193, 226

Cobden Club, Mill proposes Gladstone's health, 454

Cochrane, John George, Publisher of *Foreign Quarterly Review*, 174

Cockburn, Lord Chief Justice, 72, 471, 472

Coleridge, Samuel Taylor, 25, 29, 61, 79; influence of, **83–4**; 85, Mill calls on with friends, 86; 93, 107, 163, 184; Mill's article comparing Bentham and

Coleridge, 221; Mill's final article in his *Review* on Bentham and Coleridge, 244–6; 261; Sterling's comparison of Mill and Coleridge, 262; 275, 287, 401
COLE, SIR HENRY, 71 n., 107, 107 n.; walking tour with Mill in south of England, 139; takes over *London and Westminster* with Hickson, 247
COLLECTIVISM, Growth of, 400–1, 402–3
COLLS, JOHN, 18, 32
COLMAN, CHARLES (married Mary Mill), 356, 505
COLMAN, MARY. *See* MILL, MARY
COLMAN, MINNIE (Daughter of Mary Mill), Mill sends to Bedford College, 505
COLONIAL DEVELOPMENT, 217, 224, 225, 228, 235
COLONIAL OFFICE, 225, 234, 465, 470
COLONIAL SECRETARY, 225, 231, 466
COMMON SENSE, SCOTTISH SCHOOL OF, 6, 422; Mill's attacks on, 440; reactions to Mill, 445
COMMONS, HOUSE OF, 229, 388; Mill in, **451–7**; 462, 464, 476, 484, 492, 500
COMMONS PRESERVATION SOCIETY, Mill promises aid, 491
COMMONWEALTH, BRITISH, First conceptions of, 225; 229
COMMUNISM, 69; Saint-Simonian, **92–3**, 97, **103–4**, 400; Engels quoted, 267; 312; confused with Socialism, 313 n. *See* SOCIALISM
COMTE, AUGUSTE, 47 n., 92, 93, 94, 138, 246, influence on *Logic*, 272; *Cours de Philosophie positive*, 273; correspondence with Mill, 274–8; acute differences with Mill, 277; Harriet's judgement, 278; *Système de Politique positive*, 278–80; personal misfortunes, 281; loses post at Polytechnique, 282; Mill collects money for, 282; anger over defection of English "disciples", 283; correspondence with Mill ends, 283; 291, 292, 293, 322, 370; 400; 401, 410, 436
COMTISTS. *See* POSITIVISM
CONDILLAC, ÉTIENNE BONNOT DE, 48
Condition of the Working Class in England in 1844, 267 n.
CONGREVES, RICHARD, 284
CONSPIRACY TO MURDER BILL, 390, 390 n., 456
CONSTANTINOPLE, 97; Helen and Mill visit, 428
CONSUMPTION, James Mill's mother dies, 7; Harriet's brother dies, 116; Flower girls' symptoms, 122; James Mill's attacks, 197; Henry Mill ill, 207; Mill's lungs damaged, 208; Eliza Flower dying, 241; 260; Henry Mill's death, 263; Calvert's death, 264; George Mill ill, 284; Sterling dying, 286; Sarah Flower's death, 328; 348, George Mill dying, 352; **359–60**; Harriet seriously ill, 361; Mill ill, 366; Ramadge offers Mill hope, 367; Mill's alarming condition, 372; Mill's consumption arrested, 374; 377, 381, Helen's symptoms, 383; Harriet's death, 393–4.
Consumption Curable, 366
CONTAGIOUS DISEASES ACTS, 437, 501; Royal Commission on, 502; Mill called in evidence, **502–3**
"CONVERSATION SHARP", 106
CONWAY, MONCURE D., 327, description of Mill, 430; on *Subjection of Women* in Russia, 496
CO-OPERATIVES, 307–8, 312
CORFU, 377; Mill considers settling at, 378; Helen and Mill visit, 427
CORN LAWS, 39, 61, 194
CORPORATION AND CHURCH PROPERTY, John Mill's article on, 106
CORRESPONDING SOCIETY, THE, 31
CORRUPTION BILL, 457
COULSON, WALTER, 53 n.
"COUNT CAGLIOSTO", 176
Cours de Philosophie positive, 273–6
COURTNEY, LEONARD, 316, 455, 455 n.
COURTS MARTIAL (in Jamaica), 467; Gordon condemned, 468; 470, 471
COVENT GARDEN, 109, 219
COX, MISS C. M., 40
CRAIGENPUTTOCK, John Mill fails to visit, 143; Jane's inheritance, 165; Carlyles retire to, **166**; 170, Emerson visits, 171; 173, 174, 176, Carlyles leave, 178
CRANBOURNE, LORD, 417
CRIMEAN WAR, 387
CRISPE, SIR NICHOLAS, Harriet's ancestor, 115
CROKER, J. W., 218 n.
"CROKERISMS", 218
CROMPTON, REV. S., 25 n., 33 n.
Cromwell's Letters and Speeches, 242, 243
CROYDON, Mill summer place at, 68
CUMBERLAND, DUKE OF, 224
CUNNINGHAM, Mill's portrait, 263; 263 n.
CURRENCY JUGGLE, John Mill's article on, 106

Daily News, 448; mass meeting at Agricultural Hall, addressed by Mill, **460–1**; 463, 474
Daily Telegraph, Mill's address at St. James's Hall on Irish rebels, 463
DANTE, 376
"DAPPLE", Bentham's stick, 50, 222
DARLING, SIR CHARLES, 465, 466
DARWIN, CHARLES, 270, 270 n., 432, 487
DAUBISSON, M., 45
DAVIES, MISS, Principal of Girton, 498
DAVIS, JEFFERSON, 424
DAWSON, MR., Mill's travelling companion in Greece, 379
DEBATING SOCIETY. *See* LONDON DEBATING SOCIETY
DEBENHAM'S, 450
DECEMBRISTS, 91

DECLARATION OF INDEPENDENCE, 493
DECLARATION OF PARIS, 456
DEDICATION OF *Principles of Political Economy*, John Taylor objects to Mill's dedication to Harriet, 309–10; 339
"DEFINITION OF POLITICAL ECONOMY", 207
DELPHI, Mill's trip to, 379
Democracy in America, John Mill's review of in the *London* and *Edinburgh Reviews*, 199–203
DERBY, LORD, adopts Mill's suggestions for government of India, 390; 454, 457, 459; Mill's M.P. deputation calls on, 463
DESCARTES, RENÉ, 252
Deux Mondes, Revue de, 491
DIALECTICAL SOCIETY, THE, Amberley a vice-president, 437; Amberley speaks on birth control, 438
Dialogues of Plato (Translation by J. S. Mill), 136
Diamond Necklace, The, 176, 182, 210
DICEY, PROFESSOR A. V., Mill's part in Married Women's Property Act, 500
DICKENS, CHARLES, 215; attacks *Political Economy* in *Hard Times*, 311; 311 n., 359, 403
DICKSON, COLONEL, 458
Dictionary of National Biography, 472
DIDEROT, DENIS, Carlyle's article on, 174, 176
DILKE, LADY, offers Mill's portrait to Helen, 505 n.
DILKE, SIR CHARLES, 479; Mill's portrait by Watts, 505, 505 n.
DISRAELI, BENJAMIN, 414, 419; on Mill, 452; 454, 455 n., 456, 457, 458; blames Mill and Bright for people's demonstrations, 461; 462, 463, 464; pension for Eyre, 472; 473
DISSENTERS. *See* NON-CONFORMISTS
Dissertations and Discussions, 246, 378; contents settled with Harriet, 370; given to publisher, 407; final form, 477
Dissidence of Dissent, The, 121 n.
DIVORCE, 124; Harriet on, 125; Harriet and John Mill on, **137–8**; Carlyle on, 182; Comte's attitude to, 279; Mill's discretion on and true opinion, 499
DORKING (Surrey), 53; James Mill buys cottage at Mickleham, near Dorking, 104; 105; 106; 145, 175; 197; 205; Carlyle's description of cottage, 206
D'ORSAY, COUNT, 261
DOVER, John Mill's first trip, 41; Harriet and Helen stay at, 240
DRYSDALE, DR., on Mill's night in prison, 59 n.; 437
DUFF GORDON, LUCIE. *See* AUSTIN, LUCIE
DUFFY, GAVAN, requests Mill to stand as Irish member, 325; Carlyle tells reason for break with Mill, 326; 375
DUMONT (Jeremy Bentham's French translator), 12 n., 16 n.; John Mill first reads, 49; 53 n.; John Mill's work on Dumont's translation of *Rationale*, 72
DUNCOMBE, SLINGSBY, 192
DURANT, MISS, Grote's friend, 435
DURHAM, EARL OF, **225–6**; reply to Bulwer's letter on Philosophical Radical party, 227; 228; demands for Canadian mission, 229; amnesty ordinance, 230; reactions to ordinance, 231; forced resignation and departure, 231; 232; Mill defends, 233; triumph on return, 234; death of, 234; 235, 238
"DUVEYRIER'S POLITICAL PAMPHLETS", Mill's article on, 296; 206 n.

EAST INDIA COMPANY, 36, **55**, 89; end of **388–90**; James and later John Mill defend Company, 388, 389, 390
—EXAMINER'S OFFICE, James Mill's appointment to, 36; James Mill's promotion and John Mill's appointment, 55; 66; John Mill's first salary, 80; James Mill the Chief Examiner, 104; 105; John Mill's promotion, 204; Mill third Examiner, 208; Bain describes Mill in his office, 290; Mill receives friends, 291; Peacock the Chief Examiner, 365; Peacock retires, 387; Mill as Chief, 387–90; Mill retires, 390; Mill's tribute from office, 391
—INDIA BOARD, 36; Mill's pension, 372; Mill's petition, 290; 446
—INDIAN CIVIL SERVICE, James Bentham Mill in, 204; 260
—INDIA HOUSE, 36, 47, 53, **55**, 57, 62, 66, 67, 74, 107, 141, 147, 153, 159, 183; John Mill debarred post as editor, 191; both Mills debarred from politics, 193; 206, 207, 218, 240, 289; Bain's description, 290; 291, 321, 324, 334, 345, 351, 352, 355, 358, 361, 365, 371, 372, 373, 378, 382, 383, 384, 386, 446, 451
Ebenezer Elliot, 176, 177
ÉCOLE POLYTECHNIQUE, 273; Comte loses post as Examiner, 281; 292
EDINBURGH, 3, 4, 5; James Mill at university, 6; Carlyle in, 160; Carlyle and Jane in, 165; 174, 178, 194, 386, 387; anger over Mill's *Hamilton*, 445; 492
Edinburgh Review, The, 6; James Mill contributes to, 12; 13, 29; founding of, 61; James Mill's attack on, **62–3**; Carlyle's articles in, 86; Macaulay's reply to James Mill, **87–88**; 102, 131, 165, 166, 169; reject Carlyle's articles, 176; Mill's review of de Tocqueville, 199, 209; 214 n., 234; Mill's articles in, 247; 272; Mill on Guizot and Michelet, 293; Mill's reviews of Grote and Duveyrier, 296; 302 n., 322, 336; later review of

Grote, 368; 370; Mill's review of Bain, 410; Mill's review of Grote's Plato, 476
EDINBURGH UNIVERSITY, James Mill attends, 6; Carlyle at, 159, 160; Carlyle elected Rector of, 445, 446; 496; scholarship for women medical students, 498
EDUCATION, GENERAL, James Mill's article on, 14; theories of, 14–16; of the time, 19, 20; John Mill on, 133; Reformed Parliament annuities, 191, 192; 206 n.; London School Board, 413; 482
EDUCATION, HIGHER, Religious tests abolished in Universities, 455, 455 n.; Mill's address on, 476; Mill's opinion of American needs, 482
EDUCATION OF JOHN STUART MILL. *See* MILL, JOHN STUART
EDUCATION, NATIONAL, Roebuck's proposal, 153; 191; Mill in *Political Economy*, 301; and again, 306; Harriet's ideas on, 307; 312; Act for, 455
EDUCATION, NON-SECTARIAN, 29, 31, 102, 127
EDUCATION, UNIVERSAL, Jeremy Bentham's scheme for, 29
EDUCATION, WOMEN'S, 25; Harriet's views on, 125; in the United States, 202; Comte on, 277; Helen on, 481; 484; Fabre's lectures, 487, 494; Kate Amberley's contributions, 498; Mill's activities and contributions, 500; 505
"*Education of Women*", 125
D'EICHTHAL, GUSTAVE, 91; on John Mill, 93; effort to convert Eyton Tooke and John Mill, 95–6; 97, 99, 129, 171; Mill's letter on Durham, 226; 251; Mill's letter on marriage, 327; Mill renews friendship with, 429; on Greek as international language, 479
ELDON, LORD, 101
Election, The, Sterling's anonymous poem, 284
Elements in the Art of Packing, The, 13
Elements of Morality, 255
Elements of Political Economy, 39, 69, 87
ELIOT, GEORGE, 154 n., 284, 347, 359; in Avignon to see Harriet's tomb, 412; 431, 450, 478
ELKINGTON, MESSRS., 391
ELLIOTT, HUGH S. R., 263 n., 489 n.
ELLIS, WILLIAM, 52, 69
EMERSON, RALPH WALDO, 20; meets Carlyle, 171, 172; 210, 216, 217, 242; article on, 244; Sterling's letter on Mill, 285; 287, 324, 330, 430
EMIGRATION, growing interest in, 224–5; 231, 235, 299, 301
Emotions and the Will, The, 410
Encyclopaedia Britannica, James Mill's "Education" in fifth edition, 14; 30; James Mill's "Government", 62; 87, 255; 1940 edition on Mill, 316
Encyclopaedia Metropolitana, 477
ENFANTIN, BARTHELÉMY PROSPER, leader of Saint-Simonians, 96; 97, 100
Enfranchisement of Women, The, Harriet's article published, 347; groundwork for Mill's *Subjection*, 370; Mill's tribute to Harriet, 407: reprinted by Mill, 497
ENGELS, FREDERICK, 267
England and the English, 221
England and Ireland, 299 n.
English Leader, The, 407
English Utilitarians, The, 489 n.
ENSOR, MR., accompanies John on his first trip, 41
ENTOMOLOGY. *See* FABRE, J. H.
Esprit des Lois, 485
Essay on Government, 62, 87
Essays on some Unsettled Questions of Political Economy, 105 n.; published 1844, 295; 310
ETHOLOGY, 268, 271, 295
ETON COLLEGE, 19, 23, 226; Mill's views on, 481, 482
EVOLUTION, THEORY OF, Mill's reactions to, 270; 432
Examination of Sir William Hamilton's Philosophy, 369 n., 370, 422, 433; written 1863–1865, 440; resemblance to James Mill on Mackintosh, 440; 443, 446, 448
Examiner, The, 13, 62; Fonblanque takes over from Hunts, 97; 98, 102; John Mill's articles in, 105, 133; 135; John Mill reviews "Songs of the Month", 136; "The Spirit of the Age", 168, 169; 173; John Mill's help for, 176; 193, 196, 209; Spencer's account of Mill's generosity, 434; Mill's offer of financial aid, 479; Mill's last two articles, 490 n.
EXAMINER'S OFFICE. *See* EAST INDIA COMPANY
EXETER HALL, 470
EYRE DEFENCE COMMITTEE, Carlyle takes chair, 471; Ruskin follows, 471;
EYRE, GOVERNOR EDWARD JOHN, 437, 465; mis-management and unpopularity, 466; rebellion, 467–9; Mill's denunciation of, 470; Eyre's return to England, 471; legal compensation and full pension, 472; 473, 478

FABIANS, 489, 489 n.
FABRE, J. H., Mill meets, 486; Mill and Fabre make excursions together, **486–7**; loses post, 487; Mill's assistance, **487–8**; 506; last expedition with Mill, 507
FALCONER, THOMAS, John Mill's assistant on *Review*, 196; 204; 207; inefficient, 210; replaced by Robertson, 211
FALMOUTH, Home of Quaker family, the Foxes, 119; Mill and Sterling meet Foxes, Henry Mill's death, **260–3**; 264; 265, 266; Sterling returns to, 284; 285
FAWCETT, HENRY, disciple of Mill, 418; worked with Mill in Parliament, 418–9;

Postmaster General, 419; 425, 428, 430; 431, 437, 457, 491, 491 n.
FAWCETT, MRS. HENRY (*née* Garrett), active suffragette, 419; 430, 437, 493, 497, 498
Feast of Pikes (*French Revolution*), 185, 187
FÉLIBRES, 496
FEMALE SUFFRAGE. *See* WOMEN'S SUFFRAGE
FENIANS, 299, 462; Mill's speech for, **463–4**
FERDINAND VII, King of Spain, 99
"FINALITY JOHN" (Lord John Russell), 192
FINSBURY, South Place Chapel, 116; Taylors' first home, 117; 120, 121; Taylors leave, 141
FLANDRÉSEY, MME. JEANNE DE, 475 n.
Flora of Vaucluse, Mill's project with Fabre, 486–8
FLORENCE, 376; Mill's visit to, 381; 412
FLOWER, BENJAMIN, 123
FLOWER, ELIZA (Lizzie), 109, **121–3**; Harriet's intimacy with, 123; 124, 126, 130, 131, 136, 139; relation with W. J. Fox, **144–5**; continued intimacy with Harriet and John Mill, 146; 148; leaves South Place community with Fox, 149; 151 n., 152, 181; dying of consumption, 241; 320; bequest to Harriet, 327; 344, 360
FLOWER, SARAH (SY-Sallie—Mrs. W. B. Adams), **121–3**, 127, 136; marriage 148; 151 n., 152, 241, 320; visits Harriet, 327–8; 360
FONBLANQUE, ALBANY, 62, 70; takes over the *Examiner*, 97, 98, 102, 107, 135, 169; in financial difficulties, assisted by John Mill, 176; John Mill requests articles for new Review, 196; 209; Mill on Parliamentary Radicals, 212; Mill's definition of his radicalism as opposed to "Grote conclave", 221; Mill on Radicals' position on Canada, 230; 235
FORBES-JACKSON, MAJOR-GENERAL, 468
FORD ABBEY, life of Jeremy Bentham and Mill family in, **26–36**; 43, 476, 482
FORDYCE, DR., father of Lady Bentham, 43
FOREIGN POLICY, BRITISH, Conspiracy to Murder Bill and Mill's opinion of, 309, 390 n.; Mill's praise of, 422–3; Mill's efforts over American Civil War, 423–7; Mill's influence with Gladstone on Alabama Claims, 426; 449, 456, 478, 504
Foreign Quarterly Review, 169, 174
FORSTER, W. E., 457, 470
Fortnightly Review, 194 n.; Spencer attacks Mill, 433; Amberley's article on a League of Nations, 438 n.; 443, 449; edited by John Morley, champions all Mill's favourite causes, 478; Mill recants opinions on Wage-Fund, 488; 489 n.; Pankhurst on "man", 493;
FORTNUM AND MASON, MESSRS., subscribe to Mill's election fund, 450
FOURIER, CHARLES, 97, 297; Mill's change over Fourierism, 313
FOX, BARCLAY, 261; correspondence with Mill, 264; 271, 272; Mill on Sterling's move to Falmouth, 284
FOX, CAROLINE, 261–5; friendship with Sterling, 261; description of Mill, 262; on Mill's portrait, 263; in London, 264; dines with Mills, 265; visits Mill at India House, 265; 272, 285; Sterling proposes marriage, 286; requests Mill not to write Sterling's life, 287; breaks with Carlyle, 287; 289, 320, 370; opinion of *Liberty*, 404
FOX, CHARLES JAMES, 8, 60
FOX FAMILY (Falmouth), 119, 261, 264, 284; 285, 289
FOX, GEORGE, 265
FOX, MISS (Daughter of W. J. Fox), 288, 358
FOX, W. J., 62, 96; **120–4**; 126; introduces John Mill to Harriet Taylor, 127–8; 132, 132 n., 134, 135, 136, 137; John Mill's confidant, 141; 144–5, marital crisis, **148–9**; 152, 175, 177, 179; Carlyle's description of, 180; 181, 191, 193, 194, 196, 199, 209, 218, 241, 277, 288, 310, 311, 344, 350; visits Blackheath, 358; 430
FOX, MRS. W. J., 123, 144, **148–9**
FOX BOURNE, H. R., 479
Fragment on Mackintosh, 197, 440
FRANCE, 40; John Mill's first trip to, 41–6; 92, 95; John Mill's knowledge of, 97, 98; the Revolution of 1830, 100; 128, 132, 147, 163, 174, 175, 201, 202; Harriet and John Mill in, 207; 210, 218; Harriet and Mill in, 238, 239; Harriet and Helen tour Normandy, 292; 293 n. 294, 295; peasant ownership, 299; ownership of railways, 300; 301, 324, 332; Harriet and Helen in south of, 334–6; Mill joins Harriet for return trip, 336; Mill and Harriet in south, 361; Mills consider retiring to, 371; Mill's walking tour in Brittany, 373; Harriet's last excursion, 392–4; Harriet's death at Avignon, 394; 462, 478; Mill's opinions on Franco-Prussian war, 504; for life of Mill and Helen in Provence, see AVIGNON.
FRANCO-PRUSSIAN WAR, 478, 504
Fraser's Magazine, 168, 176, 177, 182, 210; Mill's article on Proportional Representation, 417; Mill's articles on Utilitarianism, 420; Mill on American Civil War, 424; Carlyle on "Nigger Question", 464; Mill's reply to Carlyle, 465
FREEMASON'S TAVERN, 70
FREDERICK THE GREAT, 405
French Revolution, *The*, 171; Carlyle's decision to write, 174–6; the burning of,

185–7; 206, 210; Mill's eulogy in *Review*, 215; 220
Frères Provençaux (Paris), 392
Froude, James Anthony, 326 n.
Fuller, Margaret, 324; 325

Galileo, 88, 256
Galt, John, 53
Garrett, Millicent. *See* Fawcett, Mrs. Henry
Gemmell, Mrs. Edna (Grand-daughter of Mary Mill), 505 n.
Geneva, Harriet, her children, Mill, George Mill in, 207; Harriet, Helen, Haji and Mill revisit, 383
Genius, John Mill's plea for original thought, 133; 136, 203
George, Henry, Mill's name as "great, good, man", 479
George III, 11, 59, 501
German Literature, Sarah Austin translates, 163; Carlyle studies, 163–5; 169; Sterling studies in Germany, 183; Carlyle lectures on, 216; Mill reads, 271
Germany, 163; Sterling in, 183; Harriet and Mill visit, 240; Harriet and Helen travel in, 330
Gibbon, Edward, 19
Gillies, Mary, 122
Gillies, Margaret, 122
Girton, College of, 498, 500
Gisborne, Thomas (the Younger), 193
Gladstone, William, 72 n., 289, 419, Mill meets over Alabama Claims, 426; 451, 452, 454, Mill's influence with, **455–6**; 457, 458, 459, 473, 474, 499
Glasgow, 29, Durham's speech, 226; 235, Helen on stage, Harriet's visit, 386
Glasgow, University of, 136, 194 n.; chair of Moral Philosophy declined by Carlyle and Sterling, 285
Glen (Carlyle's friend), 174
Globe, Le (Saint-Simonian Journal), 96
Globe, The, 204
Godwin, Parke, 426
Goethe, 165, 176, 184
Gomperz, Heinrich, 429 n.
Gomperz, Theodor, Mill's German translator, 253; 358, 407; falls in love with Helen, 429; only complete edition Mill's works, 429 n., 446
"Goose N". *See* Norton, Charles Eliot
Gordon, George William, Eyre's antipathy to, 467; condemned and hanged, 468; 471
Goulden, Emmeline. *See* Pankhurst, Emily
Government, James Mill's article on, 62
Graham, George John, John Mill's friend, 52; 62, walks with John Mill, 67; visits Mill home, 68; 74, 76; in Paris with John Mill, 100; 105, 105 n., 108, 110; dines with Harriet Taylor, 128; 205
Grant, Horace, visits Mills at Dorking, 206; in Examiner's office, 206 n., 349
Gravel Pit (Hackney), Chapel of, 116, 120, 123
Gray, Sir John, 464
Great Exhibition, 107 n.
Great Reform Bill. *See* Reform Bill (of 1832)
Greece, 91; Athenian democracy, 133; 374, Mill's first visit to, **378–80**; 392, 411; Helen and Mill visit, **427–8**; 429
Greene, Arthur Weguelin, 443 n.
Greville, Charles, 106, 110, 110 n.; on Durham, 227; on Durham's reported failure, 232; 234
Grey, Lord (2nd Earl), 226, 389 n.
Grey, Lord (3rd Earl), on Mill's petition for the East India Company, 389; 389 n.
Grey, Sir George, 491 n.
Grosvenor, Captain, 449, 451, 454
Grote, George, 62, **68**; John Mill's group meet at house of, 69; 74, 99, 101, 174; in Parliament, a yearly resolution for secret ballot, 193; 196; dislikes Carlyle in *Review*, 214; re-elected, 215; 218; Mill repudiates "Grote conclave", 221; 230; resigns from Parliament, 235; praise of *Logic*, 272; money for Comte, 282; 283; Mill's review of *History of Greece*, 296; 322, 358, 365; Mill's review of later volumes of *History*, 368; 388, 407, 408; assistance for Bain, 410; 430, 434; his friendship with Miss Durant, 435; 436, 437, 445; Mill's review of *Plato*, 476; assists with revision of James Mill's *Analysis*, 476; 477; Mill reviews *Aristotle*, 478; 500; funeral, 505
Grote, Mrs. Harriet, 33 n.; marries George Grote, 68; 81, 106, 195, 202; on Mill's conduct of the *Review*, 214; 218, 221, 247, 321, 322, 368; Mill calls on Grote again, 410; 430; introduces Amberleys to Helen and Mill, **434–7**; 498
Guards, The, 482
Guilbert, Aristide, 201, 211, 218
Guizot, François, 261, 282, 289, 293, 293 n.; J. S. Mill on, **294–5**; 323, 331
Gurney, Dr. Cecil, saves Harriet's life, 361; 365; Mill sends for, 393; arrives in Avignon after Harriet's death, 394; Mill's generosity to, 398; Haji marries his sister, 420; attends Mill in Avignon, 507; 508
Gurney, Ellen. *See* Taylor, Mrs. Algernon

Habeas Corpus, suspension of, in Ireland, 312 n., 451, 462
Hallam, Arthur Henry, 99, 216
Hamilton, Sir William, 422; Mill's *Examination of*, **440–1**; 443, 444, 445
Hard Times, attack on Political Economy, 311

HARDY, ALFRED (Brother of Harriet Taylor), 116, 331
HARDY, ARTHUR (Brother of Harriet Taylor), Harriet's favourite, 116; 237, 310, 332, 333, 339, 348, 378, 407; Mill's despair over Harriet's death, 409; 420
HARDY, CAROLINE. *See* LEY, CAROLINE
HARDY, EDWARD (Brother of Harriet Taylor), 116, 117, 147
HARDY, EMILIA (Wife of William Hardy), 238, 239
HARDY, GATHORNE, Home Secretary, 462
HARDY, HARRIET. *See* TAYLOR, HARRIET
HARDY, REV. JOHN, 115
HARDY, THOMAS (Eldest brother of Harriet Taylor), 116, 288, 360
HARDY, THOMAS (Father of Harriet Taylor), early obstetrician, 115; 117, 126, 149; at Birksgate, 241; 333, 348
HARDY, THOMAS (Novelist and Poet), 115
HARDY, THOMAS (founder of Corresponding Society), 31
HARDY, MRS. THOMAS (*née* HURST—Mother of Harriet Taylor), 115, 151, 237, 241, 331, 348, 374; quarrels with Harriet, 382; respect for Mill, 383
HARDY, WILLIAM (Brother of Harriet Taylor), 116, 238, 239
HARE, ARCHDEACON JULIUS, 183; biography of John Sterling, 219; 285; joint executor with Carlyle, 287
HARE, THOMAS, Mill's enthusiasm over his Proportional Representation, 415–7; 418, 436, 457, 478
HARRISON, FREDERIC, chief apostle of Positivists, 284; 470, 478; attacks *Subjection of Women*, 495
HARTLEY, DAVID, 14; John Mill's group study his psychology, 69; 160
HARVARD UNIVERSITY, Mill's botanical specimens, 486
HASLAM, Irishman, 58
HAWTREY, REV. STEPHEN, 481
HAYEK, F. A., 132 n., 151 n., 219 n., 239 n., 309 n., 408 n., 429 n.
HAYWARD, ABRAHAM, John Mill's opponent in Debating Society, 72; attacks Mill after his death, 72 n., 218
HEGEL, 271
HELPS, ARTHUR, 302 n.
HENLEY, LORD, 456, 473, 474
HENSHAW, MRS. S. E., 79
HERBARIUM (OF J. S. MILL). *See* BOTANY
HERMITAGE DE MONLOISIER (Avignon), Mill buys, **398–9**
HERO, THE, Carlyle's conception of, 164; 165; Carlyle's lectures on, 264, 265
HEUSCHRECKE, COUNSELLOR, 168
HICKSON, WILLIAM E., 205; takes over *London and Westminster Review*, 247; prints Harriet's article on disabilities of women, 347
HIGH COMMISSIONER (OF IONIAN ISLANDS), 378
HIMES, NORMAN E., 59 n.
Histoire Parlémentaire, 210
HISTORY, PHILOSOPHY OF, 92, 94, 98, 103, 268, 273, 294, 295, 400
History of England (Macaulay's), 89
History of Greece (Grote's), 68, 235; Mill's review of first two volumes, 296; 296 n.; Mill's review, later volumes, 368; 435
History of India (James Mill's), 10, 12, 20, 30; completed, 36; 285
History of the Inductive Sciences, 255
History of the Revolution (Thiers), 177
HOBBES, THOMAS, 69, 329
HODGKINS (Sub-Editor, *Morning Chronicle*), 101, 101 n.
HOLYOAKE, GEORGE JACOB, publishes *Political Economy* for workers, 311; reprints Harriet's article on women's disabilities, 347; 407; Grote and Mill assist, 410; 449, 458; Mill's help over Reform League, **459–61**
HOME SECRETARY, and meeting in Hyde Park, 458, 459, 462
HOOKER, ISABELLA BEECHER, 496
HOOPER (Bookseller), 211, 218
HORACE, 477
HÔTEL DE L'EUROPE (Avignon), 361, 375; Harriet's death, **393–4**; 399, 434, 485
HOUGHTON, LORD. *See* MILNES, RICHARD MONCKTON
HUGHES, THOMAS, 457, 470
HUMBOLDT, WILHELM VON, 401
HUME, DAVID, 7, 160, 252, 329, 440
HUME, JOSEPH, 6, 30, 193, 215, 234, 312
HUNT, JOHN, 13, 97
HUNT, LEIGH, 13, 97, 218
HUXLEY, T. H., 434, 470, 478
HYDE PARK, 40, 332, 458, 459, 460, 461; Government Bill to prevent meetings defeated by Mill, 462
HYÈRES, 361, 365, 366, 392

Illustrated English Social History, 56 n.
Illustrations and Proofs of Population, 56
Incondita, 123
INDIA, 36, 55, 77, 108, 262, 269, 302, 330, 348, 365; Act for better government of, 388; Mill's belief in eventual self-government of, 389; Act passes, 390
INDIA HOUSE. *See* EAST INDIA COMPANY
INDIA OFFICE, Mill refuses post on new council, 383; Secretary of State and 15 experts to be appointed, 388; Mill first expert invited, 390; 410, 451
INDIAN CIVIL SERVICE. *See* EAST INDIA COMPANY
INDIAN MUTINY, 386, 388, 389
INHERITANCE. *See* PROPERTY, RIGHTS OF
INNS OF COURT, 66, 70
INTERNATIONAL WORKING MEN'S ASSOCIATION, 489
INTUITIONISTS, 83; Mill on Coleridge, 244; Mill's attack on, 252–3; 258, 267, 270, 293, 433; Mill's final attack on, 440

IONIAN ISLANDS, Mill's first visit to, 378; Helen and Mill visit, 427
INTELLIGENCE QUOTIENT, 40
IRELAND, 103, Orange Lodges, 224; Mill's articles in *Morning Chronicle*, 296; land tenure in, 299; 325, 375, 451, 452, 455 n.; disaffected Irish return to, 462; Mill on government of, 463, 464; Disestablishment of Church, 473; 475, 478, 484, 490
IRISH, 101, in Reformed Parliament, 192; 299, United Irishmen, 312; 325, 375, 378; emigrants in New York, 424; 437, 446, 451; Fenians, 462; Mill's efforts to save rebels, 463–7
Irish People, The, 462
IRONS, REV. JOSEPH, 120
IRVINE, Mill's walking companion, 486
IRVING, EDWARD, 160, 162, 164
ISLE OF WIGHT, Harriet on holiday, 117; John Mill's interest in, 132; 285; Harriet and Helen in, 331
ISLINGTON, 116; Agricultural Hall meeting, **460–1**
ITALY, 91, 97, 207; Harriet and Mill in, 208; long excursion of Harriet and Mill, 237, 238, **239–40**; 260, 289, 371; Mill's third trip to, **375–7**; and return through, 381; 392, 411; Helen and Mill in, 427

JACOBIN, Mill as, 103; 462
JAMAICA, 464, 466; rebellion, **467–9**; 470
JAMAICA COMMITTEE, 470; Mill's unpopularity over Eyre case, 470; fail to bring Eyre to trial, 471; bring trial against underlings, 471; disbanded, 472; Mill's conclusions, 472
JEFFREY, LORD FRANCIS, 6; takes James Mill's articles in *Edinburgh*, 12; 61; befriends Carlyles, 165, 166, 167; 176, 178, 215
JEVONS, WILLIAM STANLEY, on Mill, 81
Johannes Agricola, 123
John Stuart Mill and Harriet Taylor, 132 n., 309 n., 408 n.
JONES, GALE, 69
JOURNALS (of J. S. Mill), 107, 132
"JUGGERNAUT OR JUG", 29
"JUNIUS REDIVIVUS". *See* ADAMS, WILLIAM BRIDGES
JURISPRUDENCE, 127, 178

"KALOS", Mill's dog, 437
KATE (Cook at Blackheath), 358, 362, 363, 364, 365
KEATS, JOHN, 61, 199, 218 n.; Mill visits tomb of, 375
KEMBLE, FANNY, John Mill calls on, 109
KEMBLE, JOHN MITCHELL, 99, 109
KENSINGTON SQUARE, new Mill home, 208; Caroline Fox visits, 265; Mill's friends call at, 291; 329, 348; Mill and Harriet call at, 351
KENSINGTON, James Mill moves family to Vicarage Place, Church Street, 104; 185; James Mill buried in Kensington Church, 205
KENT TERRACE, No. 17 (REGENT'S PARK), Taylors move to, 141; 147; Mill calls at K. T., 141; 151, 182, 185, 204, 205, 237, 240, 331, 333, 336, 349
KESTON HEATH, Harriet's country cottage in, 151, 151 n., 204, 237; Harriet leaves, 241; 318
KEW, ROYAL GARDENS AT, Helen sends Mill's botanical specimens to Curator of, 486
KING, CLARA (Daughter of Wilhelmina Mill), 351
KING, DR. (Husband of Wilhelmina Mill), 205 n.
KINGSLEY, CHARLES, 311, 403; opinion of *On Liberty*, 403, 444, 469, 493; caution on Women's suffrage, 495; 499
KINGSLEY, FANNY (Wife of Charles), won to Women's Suffrage by Mill, 493
KINGSTON (Jamaica), 465, 466, 467
KINTORE, EARL OF, 3
KNIGHT, PROFESSOR, 500

LABOUR PARTY, 235
Lady of Shalott, Mill's review of, 199
LA FAYETTE, MARIE JOSEPH, 91, 100
LAMB, CHARLES, 170
LAMBTON, JOHN GEORGE. *See* DURHAM, EARL OF
LANCASTER, JOSEPH, 29
LANCASTER SCHOOL, 29, 31, 127
Lancet, The, 192
LAND, OWNERSHIP OF, 38; Mill contends no rights of, 298; peasant proprietorship, 299; 301, 302, 307, 437, 449; in Ireland, 452; 454, 455, 455 n., 478; Mill's articles on nationalization of, 478; 479, 489, 490, 491
LAND TENURE REFORM ASSOCIATION, Mill's interest in, 490; Mill wills £500 to, 491; sends pamphlet to Villari, 491
LANGBORN, SIR JOHN (cat), 50
LANSDOWNE, LORD, 16
LARKIN, HENRY, On Carlyle's violent reaction to *On Liberty*, 405
Latter Day Pamphlets, 464
LAUSANNE, Mill and Harriet visit, 207, 208
LEADER, JOHN TEMPLE, 213
"LEAGUE OF NATIONS", Amberley's scheme for abolishing war, 438 n.; Mill on international arbitration enforced by international police, 483
LECTURES (CARLYLE'S), on German Literature, 216; on Heroes and Hero Worship, 264, 265
LEE, ROBERT E., 426
LEGENDRE, ADRIEN MARIE, John Mill dissatisfied with his "Ratio", 44
LE HARDY, CLEMENT, 115
LEITH WALK, 160, 163, 167

L'Empire Romain à Rome, 477
LESLIE, CLIFFE, 430
Letters of John Stuart Mill, 263 n., 489 n.
Letters and Journals of Lord Byron, 131
LEWES, G. H., 153 n., 284 ; visits Mill home, 291; in Avignon to see Harriet's tomb, 412; 433, 449, 478
LEWIS, SIR GEORGE CORNEWALL, 196, 214, 214 n.
LEY, ARTHUR, Caroline Hardy marries, 116; 241, 288, 348; refuses to resign trusteeship of Harriet's children, 383
LEY, CAROLINE (Sister of Harriet Taylor), 116, 151 n., 237, 241; quarrels with sister, 288; 331, 348, 374; further quarrels with Harriet, 382–3
LIBEL, LAW OF, Jeremy Bentham exposes abuses of, 13; John Mill on, 63
LIBERALS, 70; Mill's efforts to turn Radicals into, 218; Mill's hopes for Party of, 232; 233, 246, 346, 404, 418, 423, 425, 449, 451; Mill too Liberal, 452; 454, 456, 470; Liberals vote Eyre compensation, 472; Liberal victory, 473; reactions to Mill's defeat, 475; 490, 492; 500
Liberty. See *On Liberty*
Liberty, Equality, Fraternity, 404
Life of J. S. Mill (Courtney), 455
Life of Napoleon (Scott), 63
LIFE PEERAGES, 481
LILY. *See* TAYLOR, HELEN
Limits of Religious Thought, The, 441, 443
LINCOLN, ABRAHAM, Mill's admiration for, 426
LOCKE, JOHN, 14, 198, 244, 329
LOCKHART, JOHN GIBSON, 61, 243, 285
Logic (of J. S. Mill). See *System of Logic*
LONDON, James Mill's impressions of, 8; 56; London streets, 302; 360;
LONDON COUNTY COUNCIL, 457
LONDON DEBATING SOCIETY, Formation and first meetings, **70–2**; 74, 77, 82, 83, 84; John Mill leaves, 85; 87, 90, 93, 107 n., 183, 218, 247, 389
LONDON LIBRARY, 311 n., 330
London Magazine, The, 165
London Review, The, New Radical review under John Mill's direction, 191; Mills agreed upon need of, 193; Molesworth provides money, 194; **195–208**; distinguished writers, 196; first number, James Mill "State of the Nation", John Mill on Sedgewick, 197; second number, James Mill on Church of England, John Mill on Tennyson, 199; third number, John Mill on de Tocqueville, 199–203; John Mill in 1836, "Civilization" and "Definition of Political Economy", 207; *London* buys *Westminster*, continues as *London and Westminster Review* [q.v.], 209, 224, 228, 255, 370
LONDON SCHOOL BOARD, 413
LONDON, UNIVERSITY OF, 102, 105; John Mill attends, 127; 208, 222, 260, 434
London and Westminster Review, The, 58, 105 n.; Mill's efforts to broaden, 209; Carlyle's contributions, 210; Robertson sub-editor, 211; 212; effect of James Mill's death, 213; differences with old Radicals, 214; praise of *French Revolution*, 215; 216; finances, 217–8; Mill's articles on Carrell and de Vigny, 218; 219; Sterling on Montaigne, 220; break with Radicals, 221; Mill on Bentham, 221–3; Molesworth gives up, 221; 225; Mill's support for Durham, 230; and defence of, 233; failure of Mill's hopes for Liberal Party with *Review* as organ, 234; Harriet as "Armida" of *Review*, 236; Harriet Martineau's contributions, 236; 241; Sterling on Carlyle, 242, 243; final number, Mill on Coleridge, Monckton Milnes on Emerson, 244–6; Hickson and Cole take over as *Westminster Review*, 247; 264, 271, 284, 320, 321, 325, 326, 370, 478
LONGMAN, WILLIAM, 448, 448 n., 450, 486
LONGMANS (Publishers), 168, 299 n.; new cheap editions of Mill's works, 448; 448 n., 478, 490
LORD MAYOR (OF LONDON), Mill appears before, 57
LORD'S DAY OBSERVANCE SOCIETY, 473
LORDS, HOUSE OF, 229, 478; Mill considers obsolete, 481
Lotus-Eaters, Mill's review of, 199
LOUIS NAPOLEON (NAPOLEON III), Mill's hatred of, 280; Austins' friendship with, 323; 387, 390 n., 419, 456, 504
LOUIS PHILIPPE (Citizen King), 100, 323
LOWE, ROBERT, 451, 454, 455
LUBBOCK, JOHN, 434
LUCAS, FREDERIC, 375
LUDDITES, 60
LUNARDI (gas-balloonist), 24, 43
LYELL, CHARLES, 270, 430
LYONS, Harriet ill at, 393

MACAULAY, THOMAS BABINGTON, 20, 52, 70; attacks James Mill and Utilitarians in *Edinburgh*, **87–90**; effect on John Mill, 90; 101, 102, 106, 107 n., 187 n., 209, 216
MACAULAY, ZACHARY, 87
Macbeth, Helen's favourite book, learns role of Lady Macbeth, 330; 385
M'CAFFERTY (Irish rebel), 463
M'CULLOCH, S. R., 38, 39 n., 70, 101, 296
Mackintosh, Fragment on, 197, 440
MCLAREN, DUNCAN, 457
MACLEAN, DONALD, 71 n.
Macmillan's Magazine, 449
MADEIRA, 239, 261, 334; George Mill in, 348; 360
MAINE, SIR HENRY JAMES SUMNER, 73; Mill's review of "Village Communities", 478

MALLESON, W. T., 449
MALTA, Austins in, 208; 213, 214; Malta Commission, 214 n., 238
MALTHUS, REV. T. R., 37, 38, 52, 270, 300, 301; Mill's continued belief in Malthus' population theory, 302; 437
MANCHESTER, 417; Women's Suffrage Society, 493
MANSEL, HENRY LONGUEVILLE, 441; Mill's opinion of the *Limits of Religious Thought*, 443; 444, 445
MANTLE, G. J., 461
MARBLE ARCH, 458; freedom of speech, 462
MARLOW, Mill family spend summer at, 46
MARMONTEL. *See* MÉMOIRES
MARRIAGE, James Mill's attitude to, 32; Harriet Mill on her parents, 33 n., 124; Harriet's early opinion of, 125, 126; John Mill and Harriet on, **137–8**; 194; Comte's views on, 275, 276; 301, 327; opinions of Harriet and Mill, 344; Mill's formal protest against marriage laws, 348; George Mill's confusion over, 353; and *see* Women, Position of
MARSEILLES, 238; Harriet and Mill sail from, 239, 361, 411
MARSHALL, MR. (Leeds manufacturer), 74
MARTIAL LAW IN JAMAICA, 467; not repealed for month, 468; 469, 471, 472
MARTINEAU, HARRIET, 121, 124, 126, 128, 131, 140, 149, 174, 216, 218; contribution to *L. and W. Review*, 236; 237; 284; Mill's dislike of, 321; 350; translated Comte's *Système de Philosophie positive*, 370
MARTINEAU, JAMES, 121, 196, 359
MASKELYNE AND DEVANT, 413
MASSON, DAVID, J. S. Mill offers to read manuscripts, 291; on Mill family, 291; description of George Mill, 352
MAURICE, FREDERICK DENISON, 83; Mill's opinion of, 85, 109, 183, 444
MAURICE, MRS. FREDERICK DENISON, 285
MAYOR OF AVIGNON, 397, 398, 485, 488
MAZZINI, 205, 236, 358
Medical Times, 438
MELBOURNE, LORD, 193, 213, 227; Durham sent to Russia, 227; 228, 229, 230; sacrifices Durham, 231; 233, 234
MELBOURNE BOTANICAL MUSEUM, 486
MÉMOIRES (OF MARMONTEL), Effect on John Mill, 78–9; 80
MELCOMBE REGIS (near Weymouth), 349; wedding of Mill and Harriet, 350
Mermaid's Song, Harriet's poem, 126
METAPHYSICS, GERMAN, 93, **163–4**; 169, 177, 183, 253, 440
Michelet's History of France, Mill's article on, 293, 294
MICKLEHAM. *See* DORKING
MIDDLE AGES, Mill's views on, 294–5
MILAN, 208, 381
MILL, CLARA ESTHER (Sister of J. S. Mill), 20; education of, 32; 34, 35, 36, 46, 260, 262, 265, 334, 349; attempts call on Harriet, 351; 354, 356
MILL FAMILY, Place describes at Ford Abbey, 32–4; Bain writes of, 76; Henry Solly at Dorking, 76; and again, 105; Carlyle at Dorking, 206; Caroline Fox at Kensington, 265; Masson at Kensington, 291; Kensington, 349; Mill's break with family, **351–6**; 505
MILL, GEORGE (Brother of J. S. Mill), 204, 207, 263, 287; friend of Harriet's family, 329; 334, 348, 351; dying of consumption in Madeira, 352; blunders in letter on Mill's marriage, 353; Harriet and Mill break with, 354; ends life, 354
MILL, HARRIET (Wife of John Stuart Mill). *See* TAYLOR, HARRIET
MILL, HARRIET ISABELLA (Sister of J. S. Mill), 22, 25 n.; defends her mother, 33 n.; 35, 46; on teaching by father and John, 47; 260; 263, 267, 265, 349, 356, 507
MILL, HENRY (Brother of J. S. Mill), 51; Mill writes about Father's health, 205; 207; 208, 240; description of, 260; 262; death, 263; bond between Sterling and Mill, 264; 265, 285
MILL, JAMES, birth of, 4; education of, 5–6; tutors daughter of Sir John Stuart, 5–6; licensed as a preacher, 7; goes to London, 8; edits journals, 8–10; marries, 9; calls eldest son John Stuart, 9; begins *History of India*, 10; joins Volunteers, 10; meets Jeremy Bentham, 11; theory of education, 14–16; visits Bentham at Barrow Green, 18–19; teaches John Greek, 20; lives in Milton's house, 21; further education of John, 22–4; criticized in *Autobiography*, 24–6; at Ford Abbey, 27–36; scorns his wife, 32–3; teaches his children, 32–4; enters East India Company, 36; friendship with Ricardo, 37–9; his *Elements of Political Economy*, 39; fatherly advice to John, 40; 41, 45; daughter's opinion of, 47; his plans for John's future, 47–9; 51; writes *Analysis of the Human Mind*, 53; 55, 58; decides to form new Party, 59; launches *Westminster Review*, 61–2; his attack on the *Edinburgh Review*, 62; 63, 64, 68, 69, 70; John's attitude to, 76; John's growing independence of, 80; 81; his *Essay on Government*, 87; Macaulay's attack on, 88–9; his attitude to Reform, 101; his part in passing the Reform Bill, 102; Chief Examiner, 104; 106, 107; 109; on the Council of University College, 127; 129, 138; comparison with Carlyle, 158–9; 163, 192; John in agreement with, 193; 196; writes for *London Review*, 197; collapses, 197; 198; an invalid, 204; on John's affair with Harriet, 204; death, 205; his work

devolves on John, 208; John's respect for, 213; effect of his death on the *Review*, 213–4; 254, 268, 281, 296; dislike of railways, 300; 329, 360, 387; defends East India Company, 388; 400, 446; his *Analysis of the Human Mind* revised by John Mill, 476

MILL, MRS. JAMES (*née* BURROW, Mother of J. S. Mill), 9, 21, 25, **32–3**, 35, 76; complete omission in *Autobiography*, 129, 260, 291, 349; opinion of Mill's marriage, 349; attempts family reconciliation, 355–6; illness, 355; death, 356

MILL, JAMES BENTHAM (Brother of J. S. Mill), 28, 35, 46, 105, 127, 204, 260, 348, 365, 449

MILL, JANE (Sister of J. S. Mill), 35, 348, 349

MILL, JOHN STUART, parentage, 3–9; birth, 9; education, 19–26, 36–41; at Ford Abbey, 26–36; visits Sir Samuel Bentham in France, 41–6; studies Jeremy Bentham's works, 49; studies law with John Austin, 50; loses his watch, 51; forms Utilitarian Society, 53; first publications, 53; enters India House, 55; distributes pamphlets on birth-control, 56–9; first articles in *Westminster Review*, 63; friendship with Roebuck and Graham, 66–8; forms a second society, 68–9; forms London Debating Society, 69–72; edits Bentham's *Rationale of Judicial Evidence*, 72–4; mental crisis of his youth, 74–82; meets John Sterling, 82, 85–6; influenced by Macaulay, 89–90; dealings with the Saint-Simonians, 91–7; *The Spirit of the Age*, 98; revolutionary symptoms of, 99–104; enters society, 106–7; looks for a wife, 108–10; meets Harriet Taylor, 110, 127–8; his affair with her, 129–44; follows her to Paris, 145; his dissatisfaction after their return, 149–50; *modus vivendi* established, 151; ridiculed at the Bullers' 152; breach with Roebuck, 153; comparison of his mental crisis with Carlyle's, 160–1; meets Carlyle, 168–70; correspondence with Carlyle, 171–8; accidentally destroys first volume of Carlyle's *French Revolution*, 185–7; edits *London Review*, 191, 194, 196–7; his contributions, 197–204; overwork and illness, 204–8; his father's death, 205; edits *London and Westminster Review*, 209–16; becomes sole proprietor, 217; widens its scope, 218–21; on Bentham, 222–3; tries to form new party, 226; champions Durham, 233–4; goes to Italy with Harriet, 237–40; publishes Sterling's review of Carlyle, 242–3; on Coleridge, 244–6; parts with the *Review*, 247; writes *System of Logic*, 251–60, 266–72; with his family and Caroline Fox at Falmouth, 262–3; and in London, 264–5; his relations with Auguste Comte, 273–84; and with Sterling, 284–7; his life in the India House, 289–90; at home, 291; more journeys with Harriet, 292; incidental writings 1842–1844, 293–5; writes his *Principles of Political Economy*, 295–306; adds Harriet's chapter on the working classes, 307–8; dedicates the work to her, 309–10; reverses his thesis at her demand, 312–15; his personal relationship with Harriet, 317–21; withdraws from society, 321–7; injures himself, 332; accompanies Harriet to Pau, 333; attends her at her husband's death, 336–9; his predicament afterwards, 344–7; prepares to marry her, 348; breaks news to his family, 348–9; marries her, 350; insults his family, 351–7; settles at Blackheath, 357–9; gives her consumption; 360; takes her to Hyères and returns, 361; lives alone at Blackheath, 361–4; is very ill with consumption, 365–7; plans his remaining works with Harriet, 368–71; his subordinance to Harriet, 370–1; he thinks of retiring, 371–2; goes alone to Brittany, 373; tours Italy, Sicily, Corfu, and Greece, 374–82; assists in Harriet's family quarrels, 383; defends East India Co. as Chief Examiner, 387–91; retires and sets out with Harriet for Continent, 392; death of Harriet at Avignon, 394; Mill buys house at Avignon, 398–9; publishes *On Liberty*, 399; writes epitaph, 407–9; erects tomb, 411–12; publishes *Thoughts on Parliamentary Reform*, 414; adopts proportional representation, 415–19; publishes *Utilitarianism*, 420; praises England, 422–3; disgusted with England over American Civil War, 423–7; visits Greece with Helen Taylor, 427–8; his life at Avignon, 428; makes new friendships, 429–39; his relationship with Herbert Spencer, 431–434; and with the Amberleys, 434–9; his *Examination of Sir William Hamilton's Philosophy*, 440–4; invited to stand for Westminster, 446; his terms, 447; his election, 449–51; his bearing in Parliament, 451–7; secures freedom of speech in Hyde Park, 457–62; gains reprieve for Irish rebels, 462–4; prosecutes Governor Eyre, 464–72; loses his election, 473–5; returns to Avignon, 476; brings *Autobiography* up to date, 477; helps John Morley, 478; his correspondence, 479–84; is assisted by Helen Taylor, 480–1; his gifts to charity, 484; life in Avignon, 485–6; friendship with Fabre, 486–8; his views on Socialism, 488–91; his efforts for women's votes and education, 492–501; publishes *Subjection of Women*, 494; defends prostitutes, 501–3; last years, 504–6; his death, 507

—WALKING TOURS, 67, 74; Berkshire,

Buckinghamshire, Surrey in 1828, 82; Lake country in 1831, 131; South of England, New Forest in 1832, 107, 139; Cornwall in 1832, 139, 141; Wales in 1837, 212; Axminster in 1838, 238; Brittany in 1854, 373–4; Sicily and Greece in 1855, 376–80; French Jura in 1855, 383; 384; Lake District in 1857, 387; Derbyshire Peaks in 1858, 387; Cevennes in 1859, 411; Pyrenees in 1860, 412; Alps in 1869, 481; Mont Ventoux when living in Avignon, 485; throughout England and Scotland botanizing, 486

WORKS, COMPLETE EDITION OF, German, 429 n., 448 n.

MILL, MARY (Sister of J. S. Mill), 204, 348, 351, 355, 356; Mill's assistance, 505; 507

MILL, MAY (Sister of James Mill), 4, 5, 7, 8

MILL, WILHELMINA FORBES, 12, 19, 20, 24; education of, 32, 34, 35, 36, 46; 205, 348, 349

MILL, WILLIAM (Brother of James Mill), 4, 5, 7

MILLER, BETTY, 320 n.

MILMAN, DEAN, 83

MILNE, name becomes Mill, 4

MILNE, JAMES (Father of James Mill), 3, 5

MILNES, RICHARD MONCKTON (LORD HOUGHTON), 70, 99, 106, 216; article on Emerson, 244; 493

MILTON, JOHN, 17; house in Jeremy Bentham's garden, 21; 25, 124

MINEKA, F. E., 71 n., 121 n.

Mirabeau, 210, 214

Miscellaneous and Posthumous Works of H. T. Buckle, edited by Helen Taylor, 478; 505

MISSIONARIES, 225, 464; Baptists in Jamaica, 466, 467

"MISS TREVOR" (Helen Taylor's stage name). *See* TAYLOR, HELEN

MISTRAL, FRÉDÉRIC, 496

MITFORD'S *Greece*, 24

Modern Humanists Reconsidered, 184 n.

MOLESWORTH, SIR WILLIAM, 191, 193, **194–5**; 197, 205, 207, 212; founds Reform Club, 213; 215, 216; gives up *Review*, 217; 221; interest in colonization, 224; 228; assists Durham mission, 230, 232, 233, 234, 235; contribution for Comte, 282; 283

MONOPOLY in Industry, 299; Mill's opinion on public utilities, natural properties as state monopolies, 300, 306; 308

MONTAIGNE, MICHEL DE, John Sterling's article on, 220

MONTAUBAN, 42, 43

MONTESQUIEU, CHARLES DE SECONDAT, 485

MONTPELLIER, 45; Mill attends University, 46; 47, 47 n., 66; Mill visits again, 374, 375; 382, 392, 394

MONTROSE ACADEMY, 5, 6

Monthly Repository, Development of, under W. J. Fox, 121–3; 124, 128; Harriet's contributions, 132; Mill's article on "Genius", 133; Mill's "What is Poetry?", 134; and "Dialogues of Plato", 136; 137, 145, 148, 149, 173, 177, 193, 348

MOORE, THOMAS (Poet), 58, 131

MORGAN, AUGUSTUS DE, 445; Mill's letter on pure cones, 487; women on voting register, 493, 494; disagrees with Mill on Women's suffrage, 495

MORLEY, JOHN, 315, 429, 430, 431, 438 n., 443, 470; despair over Mill's defeat, 475; Mill's help for, 478; willed copyright Mill's works, 478; description of Mill, 505–6

MORLEY, MRS. JOHN (ROSE), 505

Morning Advertiser, 444

Morning Chronicle, **53**, 54, 59, 101, 102, 193, 204, 211, 284; Mill's leaders on Irish famine, 296; 299 n.; Mill offered joint control, 309

MOTLEY, JOHN LOTHROP, 424

MUNICH, Harriet and Mill visit, 240

MURRAY, JOHN (Publishers), 167, 271

MUSÉE CALVET (Avignon), Mill's botanical specimens from Vaucluse, 486

MUSIC, Jeremy Bentham on organ, 32; 44, 78, 255; Harriet encourages children in, 330; Mill's playing of piano, 334; Mill plays for Harriet, 358; 375

MUSKAU, PRINCE PUCKLER, 179

MUSSET, ALFRED DE, 153 n.

NAPIER, MACVEY, 30, 176, 218

NAPLES, 116, 238, 239, 241, 376

NAPLES, KING OF, 376

NAPOLEON BUONAPARTE, 48, 63, 91, 163, 165

NAPOLEON III. *See* LOUIS NAPOLEON

National, The, 147

NATIONAL COLONIZATION SOCIETY, 224, 225, 228, 229

NAVY, THE ROYAL, 16, 42, 43, 224, 420; Mill on Navy as natural weapon for Britain, 456; 470, 501, 502

Nearer My God to Thee, 122

NEAVES, LORD, 445, 446

NEFF, PROFESSOR EMERY, 316

NELSON, COLONEL (later Brigadier), 467, 471

NESBITT, G. L., 63 n.

NEW FOREST, 107, 139, 491

NEW LANARK, 26, 29

New Letters of Thomas Carlyle, 326 n.

New Quarterly Review, 96 n.

NEW ZEALAND ASSOCIATION, 225; Durham President, 228;

NEWINGTON GREEN, 21, 22, 26, 127

NEWMAN, FRANCIS, 285, 493

NEWMAN-PUSEYITES, THE, 272

NICE, 207, 361, 365, 393, 398, 420, 507

NICHOL, PROFESSOR JOHN PRINGLE, 136, 194, **194** n., 196, 208, 218, 221; Mill's

letter on Durham in Glasgow, 226; 228, 285
NIGHTINGALE, FLORENCE, 497, 501
NISARD, DÉSIRÉ, 202
NON-CONFORMISTS, schools for, 29; 62, 102; families of Harriet and John Taylor, 116, 117, 118; various sects, **119–23**; 127, 148–9, 164; permission to marry, 192; 261, 264; Baptists in Jamaica, 464; 466, 467
NORMANDY, 202; Mill and Harriet on holiday, 292
North American Review(er), 168; on *Political Economy*, 311
NORTHAMPTON, Bradlaugh stands for, 473, 474
NORTON, CHARLES ELIOT, 151 n., 154 n., 315, 324, 326, 326 n.; description of Mill as host, 430; blames Helen for Mill's interest in Women's suffrage, 497; 508
NORTON, SARAH, 151 n., 154 n.
NORWICH, 51, 119, 121, 420
Not Paul but Jesus, 29–30
Nouveau Christianisme, Le, 92, 96 n.

Occasional Discourse on the Nigger Question, 346, 464, 465
O'CONNELL, DANIEL, 192
Ode to Liberty, 505
ODGER, GEORGE, 450, 473
OLD BAILEY, 57, 471
On Liberty, 137, 246, 315, 325, 368, 368 n.; first conception of book, 376; **399–406**; Harriet's ideas, 399; published, 402; whole intellectual climate opposed to, 403; widely read, 403; Russian edition in 2 years, 403; dedication to Harriet, 407; 414, 435; cheap edition, 448; 478
On the Margin, 75 n.
ONTARIO, 228
OPIE, MRS., 321
ORANGE LODGES, 224
ORDINANCE (Durham's), 230, 231, 233
Origin of Species, Mill on, 270; 270 n., 402
D'ORLÉANS, DUC, 41
ORSINI, FÉLIX, 390 n., 504
OWEN, ROBERT, 26, 95, 97, 138, 266
OWENITES, 69, 92, 297
OXFORD, 43, 70
OXFORD MYSTICISM, 84
OXFORD ORATOR, 71 n.
OXFORD UNION, 70
OXFORD UNIVERSITY, 19, 272, 441, 478
OXTED, 18

PAKINGTON, SIR JOHN, 454, **502–3**
PALAIS ROYAL, 41, 100
PALERMO, Mill visits, 376
PALEY, WILLIAM, 198
Pall Mall Gazette, 443, 491 n.
PALMERSTON, LORD, 225, 388, 390, 390 n.; Mill's objections to, 422; 451
Pamphlets for the People, 152
PANOPTICON, THE, 26, 50
PANKHURST, DR. RICHARD MARSDEN, on meaning of "man", 493; 493 n.
PANKHURST, EMILY (Wife of Dr. R. M. Pankhurst), 493 n.
PARIS, John Mill in, 41; 47 n., 56, 93, 94; after Revolution John Mill, Graham and Roebuck visit, 100; 110, 110 n., 132 n.; Harriet and John Mill in, 142–7; 171, 172, 174, 175, 176, 201; Harriet and Mill in, 207, 208; 218; Harriet and Mill in, 238, 239; 273; Sarah Austin meets Comte, 278; Grote meets Comte, 282; 312; 322, 324, 325, 331; Mill accompanies Harriet to, 333; Mill and Harriet in, 336, 361, 366, 367, 374; Harriet meeting Mill in, 381, 382; 383; the Mills' last days in, 392; 429; Declaration of, 456
PARKER, J. W. (Publisher), accepts *System of Logic*, 271; *Political Economy*, 308; 309; Mill offers *On Liberty*, 399; 403; Mill guarantees loss on Bain's books, 410; 448
PARKES, JOSEPH, 213
PARLIAMENT, 38, 39, 59–52, 70, 71 n., 102, 152; Reformed Parliament, 191–3; 195, 213, 215, 225, 226, 229; Mill's hopes for Durham as Radical Prime Minister, 229; 232, 233; end of Philosophical Radical party, 235; Mill offered Irish seat, 325; 370, 375; Mill's petition for East India Company, 389; 435, 446; Mill stands for Westminster, 449; and elected, 451; Mill's unpopularity in first days, 452; Roebuck's advice to Mill, 452; and success, 453; Mill on Conservatives, 454; influence, 455; Mill's advanced proposals and small advanced group, 456–7; 458; Mill prevents closing of Hyde Park, 462; Mill denounces Eyre, 470; Mill's defeat, 473; 474, 475, 476, 479, 488, 492, 493, 500
Parliamentary History and Review, 74
PARTHENON, THE, 378, 428
PASCAL (Avignon Architect), 411
Past and Present, 307
PAU, 333; Harriet describes, **334–5**;
Pauline, 123, 135
PEACOCK, THOMAS LOVE, 66, 196, 208, 276; retired as Chief Examiner, 387
"PEDANTOCRACY," 276, 284
PEEL, SIR ROBERT, 39, 235
PELOPONNESE, 427
PENTELICUS, MOUNT, Mill climbs, 378, 379
PENTONVILLE, 12 Rodney Terrace, 9, 21
PENZANCE, 107
PEOPLE'S EDITIONS (of Mill's Works), 448, 448 n.
Perils of the Press, The, 13
PETERLOO, 60, 459
PETERS, MR., Minister of Logie Pert, 5, 7, 8
PETRARCH, 375, 428

"PHILOSOPHES", 160, 174, 175
PHILOSOPHICAL RADICALS. *See* RADICALS
Physiology of the Épicier, 210
Phytologist, Mill's botanical notes, 368; Mill's articles, 412
PIC DU MIDI DE BIGORRE, LE, John Mill climbs, 45
Pickwick Papers, Reviewed by Charles Buller, 218
Pippa Passes, 123
PISA, Harriet and Mill visit, 237, 239
PITT, WILLIAM, 8, 20, 60
PLACE CRILLON (Avignon), Rey proposes Mill statue for, 485
PLACE, FRANCIS, 14; pays James Mill's debts, 28; 29, 30, **31**; visits Ford Abbey, 32–4; on John Mill, 34; 48, 55; birth-control pamphlets, 56–8; 67; Reform Bill, 102; 124, 193; break with Radicals, 235
PLACIDIA (Cat), 504
Plan of Parliamentary Reform, 14
PLANTERS (In West Indies), Sterling's opinions on, 183; compensation for loss of slaves, 192; in Jamaica, 464
PLATO, 6, 223, 262, 368, 369 n., 401, 435; Mill's review of Grote on, 476; 477
POLIGNAC, JULES ARMAND, 100
Political Economy. See *Principals of Political Economy, The*
POLITICAL ECONOMY CLUB, 52, 53, 358; Mill attends again, 410; 450
PONT DU GARD, Mill's first visit to, 375; 428
POPE, MR. (Mill's travelling companion in Brittany), 373
POPE, ALEXANDER, 23, 25
POPE PIUS IX, Mill's description of, 375; 375 n., 376
PORTIA, Helen learns role of, 330
Portrait of Robert Browning, 320
PORTRAITS OF MILL, Cunningham's at Falmouth, 263, 263 n., 485; Watt's in 1873, 505, 505 n.
PORTSMOUTH, John Mill visits, 43
POSITIVISM, 274–80; Mill's first enthusiasm for, 274–6; differences with, 276–7; Harriet on, 277, 278; political creed of, 278–80; Mill's horror of, 280; 283; Church of Humanity, Conduit Street, London, 284; distinguished devotees of, 284; 403, 478
Post, The, 375
POSTE RESTANTE, Harriet and Mill employ for correspondence, 237
POSTMASTER GENERAL, 419
POTEMKIN, 42
POWELL, MR. (Neighbour at Blackheath), the rat problem, 364; 449
PRESCOTT (Grote's Partner), 68, 99, 192, 365
PRIESTLEY, JOSEPH, 120, 127
PRIME MINISTER, Mill on Durham as, 229–30
Principles of Geology, 270 n.
Principles of the Penal Code, The, 12
Principles of Political Economy, The, 154 n., 290; first draft, 295–306; Harriet's criticisms, additions and chapter on working classes, 307–8; Harriet's business acumen, 308; Dedication to Harriet, 309–310; published 1848, immediate success, 310; attacked by Dickens and Ruskin, supported by Holyoake and Christian Socialists, 311; Harriet's chapter reprinted by Christian Socialists, 311; Harriet insists all objections to Socialism and Communism removed in second edition, 313; and again in third, 314; additions on women's position in third edition, 315; Mill's statement on "joint production", 316; Austin's dislike of, 323; 325, 331, 334, 359, 368, 370; continued sale, 372; 399, 411; Fawcett's admiration of, 418; 425; cheap edition, 448; seventh edition, 477
PROCLAMATION, Durham's to Canada, 232, 233
Producteur, Le, First Saint-Simonian journal, 94
PROPERTY, RIGHTS OF, Saint-Simonian views on, 92; John Mill's early attitude to, 95; 97; James Mill's views on, 101; Comte's system, 279; Mill in Political Economy, 297, 298, 299, 300; taxes on inheritance, 303; taxes, 305; Mill thought conservative, 312; 314; Mill's election platform, 449; graduated income tax, 455; single Tax, 479; national expediency sole test of, 489; limitation of inheritance, 490; land to be nationalized, 490; special taxes on land income, 491 n. And *see*, LAND, OWNERSHIP OF.
PROPORTIONAL REPRESENTATION, Hare's treatise on, 415–17; Mill's enthusiasm for, 416; Mill supports throughout life, 417; Fawcett's pamphlet on, 418; 436, 457, 478
PROTESTANT CHURCH (Avignon), 398, 485
PROVENCE, 397, 476; the Provençaux, 485
PROVISIONAL GOVERNMENT (IN PARIS), 322, 323
PRUSSIA, PRINCESS ROYAL OF, 481
PRUSSIANS, 504, 505
Punch, 435
PUNISHMENT, CORPORAL, 13, 23, 449, 482, 483
PYRENEES, 45, 81; Harriet at Pau, 334; 336; 411, 412

QUAKERS, 29, 119; at Falmouth, 261; 264
Quarterly Review, The, 29, **16**; attacked by James Mill, 63; attacked by John Mill, 199; 218 n., 243, 285, 336
QUEEN SQUARE, WESTMINSTER, 16; Milton's house in, 21; 26, 36, 39, 46; Bentham's garden, 50; 68, 87, 104, 106, 178

Radical Club, Formed by Fawcett, 419; Mill a member, 419
"Radical Jack", *See* Durham, Earl of
Radical Party. *See* Radicals
Radicals, 14, 18; and the Burdett Riots, 31; 54; new political party, 59–61; *Westminster Review*, new party organ, attacks *Edinburgh*, 62; and *Quarterly*, 63; 83, 84; *Edinburgh* replies to *Westminster*, 87–9; 99, 101; Philosophical Radicals, 102, 194, 221; rapprochement with non-conformists, 127; 133, 152, 168; new *Review* proposed, 177; Radicals in Reformed Parliament, 191–3; dissensions of, 192–3; 195; Mill's wish to resolve their discords, 212; Reform Club, 213; election defeat, 215; 217, 218; Mill's quarrel with, 221; lasting achievement of, 224; Durham as possible leader, 226–7; 229; chances of success, 230–2; 231; against Durham's Ordinance, 233; 234; decline of party, 235; 247, 446, 461, 470
Ragged Schools, 351
Raikes-Currie (Banker), Contribution to Comte, 282; 283
Railways, Mill advocates state ownership, 300, 479
Rajon, P. A., 505 n.
Ramadge, Dr. Francis Hopkins, book on consumption, 366; Mill goes to, 366; offers hope for Mill, 367; 374, Helen sent for cure, 383
Ramsay, Provost Marshal, 467, 468
Raphael, 28, 430, 482
Rationale of Judicial Evidence, 30, 72, 106, 470
Ravenscroft, 437, 504
Reader, The, 433
Reasoner, The, Holyoake's Weekly, 311
Rebels (Canadian), 228, 230, 231, 233
Rebels (Irish), 462–4
Rebels (Jamaican), clash at Morant Bay, 467; immediate suppression, 467–8
Record, on John Sterling, 219; on Mill, 444
Reform Bill of 1832, 6, 98, **100–3**; John Mill's opinion of, 102–3; 191, 194, 212, 222, 224, 226, 230, 269, 414, 446
Reform Bill of 1866, unsuccessful, 449; Mill's attitude to, 454; 457
Reform Bill of 1867 (Disraeli's), 200, 417; "leap in the dark", 454; Mill turns it to account, 457; 463, 488, 492
Reform Club, 211, 213
Reform League, **458–62**; Mill temporizes with, 459–60; his differences with, 460; he speaks at mass meeting on free speech in Parks, 460–61
Reformed Parliament, 152, **191–3**; 195, 213, 226
Refugees, Spanish, 99; 118, 128, 140; Italian, 236; French, 323, 430
Regent's Park, Taylor home at Kent Terrace, 141; 180; Mill and Harriet walk in, 237; 321
Reid, Thomas. *See* Common Sense, Scottish School of, 6, 329, 440, 441, 445
Reminiscences of T. Carlyle, 217, 243
Rent, Doctrine of, 38, 298
Representative Government, 368, 369 n., 370, 389; defends Proportional Representation, 417; cheap edition, 448; 454, 489
Republican, The, 54, 58
Republican Club in Cambridge, 419
Repudiation of 1842, American, J. S. Mill's losses, 281; 291
Requien Collection (Avignon), 486
Revolution
—John Mill's views on, 98, 99, 103–4, 168, 460; "not English", 489
—James Mill's views on, 101–2
—Frederick Engels on, 267
—Prospects of, 100–1, 457; Fenian, 462
Revolution, French, 44; John Mill's knowledge of, 48; 91; John Mill intends to write about, 98; encourages Carlyle to do so, 174–5; 299, 301, 398
Revolution of 1830, John Mill assists at, 100; results of, 132; 147
Revolution of 1848, effect of, on Harriet and Mill, 312; Austins caught in, 322; Mill's defence of, 323; Harriet travels through aftermath of, 333; her opinion of, 335
Rey, Pastor Louis, intimate friend of Mill and Helen, 485; continued devotion to Mill, 485, 507–8
Rhine, River, 330–1
Rhone, River, 239, 361, 411, 476
Ricardian Society, 38, 52
Ricardo, David, 37–8; James Mill's best friend, 39; 41, 48, 51, 52, 53, 68, 101, 296, 298, 300; fallacy of his Wage Fund theory, 302
Rifle Volunteers, 420
Rise of the Dutch Republic, 424
Robertson, Croom, 498
Robertson, John, 58, 59 n., **211–12**, 216, 217, 218, 220, 230, 236, 237; difficulties with Carlyle, 242; article on Cromwell, 243; 247, 271, 289, 321
Robertson, J. M., 184 n.
Robinson Crusoe, 22
Rochdale Pioneers (Co-operative Wholesale Society), 308, 311
Roebuck, John Arthur, 62; friendship with John Mill, 66–8, 69; in London Debating Society, 70, 71, 72; 74, 76, 81; quarrels with Mill over poetry, 82; 100, 108, 110, 128, 152; breaks with Mill, 153; 174, 191, 192; fights duel, 193; 194, 196, 212, 213, 214; loses election, 215; 218, 221; radical standpoint on Canada, 228; 230, 231; attacks Durham, 232; 233, 235, 240, 323; advice to Mill on speaking in Parliament, **452–3**; 453 n., 454 n., 475
Rogers, Samuel, 106

ROME, 239; Mill and Sterling at Baths of Caracalla, 240; 241, 330, **375–6**, 381, 437
ROMILLY, SIR J. (Later Lord), 52, 70, 192, 338, 447, 493
ROMILLY, SIR SAMUEL, 13, 30
RUSKIN, Attacks *Political Economy*, 310; 403; Eyre Defence Committee, 471
RUSSELL, BERTRAND, 59 n.; Helen and Mill godparents of, 439
RUSSELL, LORD JOHN, 192, 193, 229, 234, 353; father of Amberley, 434; 436, 447, 450, 451
RUSSIA, 28, 42, 91, 478, 496
RYDE (Isle of Wight), 117, 241

ST. ANDREWS, UNIVERSITY OF, Mill elected Rector, 448; Mill's address on Higher Education, 476; 500 n.
ST. GOTHARD PASS, Mill crosses on sledge, 381
ST. JAMES' HALL, Mill addresses meeting, 463
ST. PETER'S (ROME), Mill attends mass, 375
"SAINT OF RATIONALISM", 455
SAINT-SIMON, COMTE DE, John Mill sees in Paris, 41; contrast with Comte, 91; 92
SAINT-SIMONIANS, Origin and philosophy of, 91–7; d'Eichthal's efforts to convert Mill and Tooke, 93, 94, 95; influence upon Mill, 97, 98; Mill meets Enfantin and Bazard in Paris, 100; 103, 104, 147, 168, 174, 273, 297, 400
ST. VÉRAN (Avignon), Harriet buried at, 397; Mill buys house nearby, 398; 399; 411; Amberleys' visit, 437; Fabre's visits to Mill, 486; 487
SAND, GEORGE, 153 n., 277, 344
SANDOWN BAY, 132, 331
SAONE RIVER, 239, 361
Sartor Resartus, **167–8**, 176, 182, 210; Sterling proposes to review, 220; Mill reads aloud, 265
Saturday Review, 473
SAY, M. JEAN BAPTISTE, John Mill visits in Paris, 41
SCHELLING, 183, 330
SCHILLER, 165, 330
SCHUYLER (American Ambassador), 430, 496
SCOTT, SIR WALTER, 6, 25, 61; John Mill's review of *Life of Napoleon*, 63; 216
SEDGWICK, PROFESSOR, John Mill's article on, 197–8
SENIOR, NASSAU WILLIAM, 214
Senses and the Intellect, The, 410
SHAKESPEARE, 211, 330; Helen's absorption in, 384
SHEE, SERGEANT, 72
SHEFFIELD, Roebuck loses seat held for twenty years, 475
SHELLEY, PERCY BYSSHE, 19, 25, 61, 122; Harriet's favourite, 134; Mill visits tomb, 375; Mill reads *Ode to Liberty* to Amberleys, 505
SHEPLEY, 115, 116
SICILY, Mill's mule trip over, 376–8
SIDGWICK, HENRY, 478
Simonides, 220
SINGLE TAX LEAGUE, 491 n.
SIRENA, LA (Inn at Sorrento), Mill and Harriet stay at, 239; Mill revisits, 239 n., 317
SISTINE CHAPEL, Mill and Sterling visit, 239
Slave Power, The, 425
SLAVERY, 87; Carlyle and Sterling differ on, 183; recompense to owner, 192; de Tocqueville's predictions on, 201; 312; American Civil War, 423–7; freed slaves in Jamaica, 464; 493
SMITH, ADAM, 37, 296
SMITH, GOLDWIN, 408, 470
SMITH, DR. SOUTHWOOD, 127; dissection of Jeremy Bentham's corpse, 222
SMITH, SYDNEY, 61, 68, 102, 106, 107 n., 255
SMITH, W. H., 449, 449 n., 451, 473
SMYRNA, Helen and Mill visit, 428
SOCIALISM, James Mill on, 101; 102; Comte's Socialist Dictatorship, 278–80, 283; Mill's first views on Socialism, **297–8**, 307, 308, 311; Harriet's conversion to, 312; her radical effect on Mill, **313–14**, **319**; Mill's eventual views on, **488–91**, 500
SOCIETY FOR THE PREVENTION OF CRUELTY TO ANIMALS, Mill refuses to become Vice-President, 484; wills Society £500, 484
Society of the Rights of Man, 147
SOCRATES, 133, 410, 421
SOLLY, HENRY, Describes James Mill's attitude to his wife, 76; description of Mills at Dorking and John Mill in India House, 105
Songs of the Months, 122; John Mill's praise of, 136
Songs and Verses, Social and Scientific (Lord Neaves'), 445 n.
Sordello, 236
SORRENTO. *See* SIRENA, LA
SOUTHERN, HENRY, 64, 127
SOUTHEY, ROBERT, 29, 61, 63, 96, 107, 170, 215
SOUTH AUSTRALIA ASSOCIATION, 225
SOUTH PLACE CHAPEL (Finsbury), Built for W. T. Fox, 116; 118, 120, 121, 122, 145, 148, 430
SPAIN, 91, 99
SPARTA, Mill's essay on, 293; Mill's journey through, 379–80
Spectator, The, 122; Roebuck attacks Durham, 232; Mill's first article in defence of Durham, 233; 322
SPENCER, HERBERT, 410, 430, **431–4**; contrast with Mill in temperament and philosophy, 431–3; Mill's assistance,

433; 470, 477, 478, 486; objects to votes for women, 495
SPENCER, LADY, 23
Spirit of the Age, The, John Mill's articles, 98; 133; attracts Carlyle, 168, 169
STAËL, MME. DE, 330
STANLEY, DEAN, 437
STANLEY, LORD (of Alderley, Kate Amberley's Father), 434
STANLEY, LOUISA, 424, 499
STANSFIELD, MRS., 493
State of the Nation, The, 197
STEPHEN, SIR JAMES FITZJAMES, attacks *On Liberty*, 404–5; 443, 470; attacks *Subjection of Women*, 495; on Mill's personal charm, 503
STEPHEN, LESLIE, 18, 79, 316; on Mill's feminine traits, 318; 404; on Fawcett's admiration of Mill, 418; 478; 489 n.
STEPHENS, "HEAD CENTRE", 462
STERLING, CAPTAIN ANTHONY, 100; collects John Sterling's letters, 287; requests permission to print Sterling–Carlyle letters on Mill, 337, 338
STERLING CLUB, THE, John Sterling's friends, 219, 219 n., scandals over Club, 287
STERLING, JOHN, Attends Debating Society, 82, 83; disciple of Coleridge, 83; growth of friendship with Mill, 85, 86; an Apostle, 99, 100; Mill's letter on coming Revolution, 103; Mill on his loneliness, 108; 109, 129, 131, 133; Mill's first impressions of Carlyle, 169; 174; friendship with Carlyle, 183–4; 207, 209, 210; the "Sterling Club", 219; articles for *Review*, 220; 221; in Rome with Mill, 239, 240; reply to Carlyle on Mill and Harriet, 241; full appreciation of Carlyle's works in *Review*, 242; 243; advises Mill on Coleridge article, 244; 246, 247; in Falmouth with Mills, Foxes, and Calvert, **261–4**; dying of consumption, 263; description of Mill, 261; renewed friendship with Mill, 264; induces Mill to read German logic, 271; enthusiasm for *Logic*, 272; **284–7**; poetry a failure, 284; loses wife and mother, 285; proposes to Caroline Fox, 286; Mill's love for, 286; death, 287; disputes over Life of, 287; 316, 320, 325, 337, 337 n.; Harriet's opinion of, 338; 360
STERLING, MRS. JOHN (*née* BARTON), 99, 131, 183, death, 285
STEWART, DUGALD, 6, 440, 445
STIRLING, FANNY, helps Helen to become actress, **384–5**; in the *Red Vial*, 392; on Harriet's exceptional qualities, 409; 428
STRUTT, EDWARD, 52, 106, 192, 197
STUART, LADY JANE, 5
STUART, SIR JOHN, 5; daughter of, 5–6; 8; John Stuart Mill called after, 9; 49
Subjection of Women, 125, 134, 315, 369 n., 370; written in 1861, 420; published in 1869, 494; of all Mill's works caused most antagonism, 495; translated into German, French, Polish, 496; 498; discretion on divorce, 499
SUEZ CANAL, 422
Sun, The, 168
SWING, CAPTAIN, 100
SWITZERLAND, Harriet and Mill in, 207, 208; Mills and Helen visit, 383, 384; 428; Mill and Helen holiday in Alps, 485; 505
SYRACUSE, Mill visits, 377
System of Logic, 105 n., 246, **251–60**; Mill's definition of logic, 253; **266–72**; first draft completed 1840, 271; published 1843, 271; work of Mill alone, 272; success, 272; debt to Comte, 273; 275, 276; in later editions Mill cuts praise of Comte, 280; 285, 289, 290, 291, 296, 306, 308, 309, 317; Mill considers mere prologue to later work, 368; continued sale, 372; 378; Spencer attacks, 410; 422, 433, 440, 441, 443 n., 448 n.; definitive eighth edition, 1870, 477
Système de Politique positive, 93, 278–80; translated by Harriet Martineau, 370

Table of the Springs of Action, 223
TAINE, HIPPOLYTE, Enthusiastic review of Mill's *Hamilton*, 444; Mill's article on, 478
Tait's Magazine, 135, 148, 177, 193, 194 n.
Tale of a Tub, 167
TAXES. *See* PROPERTY, RIGHTS OF
TAYLOR, ALGERNON (Haji, son of Harriet Taylor), birth, 126; 207, 240, 292, 328; disappointment to his family, 329; 330, 333, 349, 351, 352, 353, 354; lives at Blackheath, 358; 359, 362, 363; becomes temporary inmate of a monastery, 383; 384; accompanies "Miss Trevor", 385; 386, 392, 398, 408; to attend erection of Harriet's tomb, 412; 419; marriage, 420
TAYLOR, MRS. ALGERNON (ELLEN GURNEY), 420
TAYLOR, CYPRIAN (Son of Algernon Taylor), 420
TAYLOR, DAVID (Uncle of John Taylor), 116, 238
TAYLOR, MISS ELIZA (Sister of John Taylor), 338, 348
TAYLOR, HARRIET (*née* HARDY), first meets John Mill, 110; passport description, 110 n.; appearance, **110–11**; birth, family, early life, **115–16**; marriage, 116–18; 119, 120, 121; friendship with Eliza Flower, 123–4; early writings, 124–6; birth of her three children, 117, 126; 127, 128; John Mill's growing interest, 129–30; her attraction to him, 130–1; her work in *Monthly Repository*, 132; her immediate effect upon Mill's work,

134; 135, 136; on marriage and divorce, 137–8; tries to "renounce sight" of Mill, 139; fails, 140; their meetings, 141; decides to go to Paris, 142; combats Mill's uncertainties, 143–4; is followed by Mill, 145; 146; returns to London, 147; defines affection, 148; 149; defends her compromise solution, 150, 153–4; acquires country residence, 151; insulted at the Bullers', 152; 170, 171, 172, 173, 175; meets the Carlyles, 179; their interest and growing hatred, 180–2; 185, 186, 187, 199, 203; state of her affair with Mill, 204–5; escorts Mill to Continent for his health, 207–8; 212, 219 n.; blamed for Mill's retirement from society, 221, 321–4; little share in the *Review*, 236; her dislike of Harriet Martineau, 236; feminine influence on Mill, 237; goes with Mill on winter holiday to Italy, 238–40; happiest time of her life, 241; visits her Hardy relatives at Birksgate, 241; her love of travelling, 241; 246, 264; attends Carlyle lectures with Mill, 264–5; no influence on *Logic*, 272; her opinion of Comte, 277–8, 278 n., 280; 281; family troubles, 288; health deteriorates, 289, 291; health improves during 1844, and she goes to Normandy, 292; keen interest in *Political Economy*, 306; adds chapter to it, 307–8; conducts business of its publication, 308–9; pleasure at its dedication to her, 309–10; anger with Holyoake, 311; and with Hume, 312; induces Mill to remove objections to Socialism from subsequent editions, **313–14**; ascendancy over Mill's mind, **315**; reluctance of critics to allow her due share in Mill's work, 315–17; degree of her intimacy with Mill, 317–18; reasons for it, 319–20; fear of gossip, 320–1; 323, 324; Jane Carlyle's description of, 325; Harriet very spoilt, 327; her care for her children, and their emotional development, 328–30; lover of sacred music, 330; tours the Rhine with Helen and Mill, 330; return of ill-health, 331; distaste for her Hardy relatives, 331; search for a new country house, 331; everybody ill, 332; decides to go to Pau, 332–3; Mill escorts her, 333; at Pau, 334–5; sound advice to John Taylor, 335; returns home with Mill, 336; death of John Taylor, 336–9; scorns Mill's friends, 338; her love for John Taylor, 343; reasons for marrying Mill, 344–5; her *Enfranchisement of Women* printed, 347; marries Mill, 348–50; not to blame for Mill's break with his family, 351; 352; anger with George Mill, 353–4; 355, 356; her home in Blackheath Park, 357–9; contracts consumption from Mill, 360; dangerously ill at Nice, 361; winters at Hyères, 361; her correspondence with Mill, 362–4; Mill keeps his own grave illness secret, 365–7; she returns to Blackheath, 367; whole of Mill's future work drafted under her direction, **367–70**; her enormous share, **371**; their finances, 371–2; Mill tours Brittany alone, looking for a home, 372–3; returns cured, 374; Mill takes Harriet to Torquay, 374; he goes to Greece, 374–82; 376; they reject offer in Ionian islands, 378; 379, 381; they meet in Paris, 382; Hardy family quarrels, 382–3; holiday in Geneva, 383; Harriet's doubts over Helen's stage career, 384–5; Fanny Stirling's adoration, 384; Harriet's concern for Helen's success, 385–6; joins her in Glasgow, 386; Mill brings her home, 387; 391; Mill retires, and they set out for the Continent, 392; death of Harriet, 393–4; buried at Avignon, 397; 398; the ideas in *On Liberty* mostly hers, 399; Mill's struggle to express grief, **407–8**; her epitaph, 408; her extraordinary power and charm, 408–9; her grave, 411–12; 413, 414; her continued influence on Mill's work, 422; 428, 442; her loss makes Mill hope for future life, 443; 446; 450; 452; 485, 489, 497, 499, 507; Mill buried in her tomb, 508

TAYLOR, HELEN (Lily, Daughter of Harriet Taylor), birth, 126; 131, 151, 207, 238, 240, 291, 292; no mention of Mill in her Diary, 321; 326; Harriet's handmaiden, 327; her devotion to Harriet, 328; continental tours, 329; her reading, taste for poetry, drama, cathedrals, 330; 331, 332, 333; with Harriet at Pau, 334; nurses her father, 336; 349, 351; lives at Blackheath, 358; 361, 366, 370; shows symptoms of consumption, 383; becomes an actress, 384–6; known as "Miss Trevor", 385; as Jane Shore, 386; 392; in Aberdeen, 393; 394; with Mill in Avignon after Harriet's death, 398, 399; her misery, 409; 410; keeps house at Avignon, and gardens in the cemetery, 411; trip to the Pyrenees with Mill, 412; devotes herself to Mill, 413; her subsequent history, **413**; 419, 420; visits Greece with Mill, **427–8**; Thornton's opinion of, 428; Theodor Gomperz falls in love with, 429; as hostess at Blackheath, 430; friendship with the Amberleys, 435–9; godmother to Bertrand Russell, 439; 443; 449, 453 n.; rebukes Mill, 474–5; Mill's admiration of her improvements at Avignon, 476; edits *Works of H. T. Buckle*, 477–8; invited to take over the *Examiner*, 479; writes many of Mill's letters, 480; Mill's confidence in her, 480–7; inherits all his papers, 480; good housewife, 484; 485, 486, 489; on General Committee of Women's

Suffrage Society, 493; her large part in its foundation, 497; writes *The Claims of Englishwomen*, 497; 498; Women's Rights, 499; 500 n., 504, 505, 505 n., 506, 507, 508
TAYLOR, SIR HENRY, 70, 71, 106, 107; describes John Mill, 109; 170, 216
TAYLOR, HERBERT (Son of Harriet Taylor), 117, 207, 240, 321; unsympathetic to Harriet, 329; joins father's business, 329; trips to America, 329, 330; 332, 333, 338, 339; marries, lives in City, 358; 372; in charge of family business, 383; 392
TAYLOR, JEREMY, 330
TAYLOR, JOHN (Father of Sarah Austin), family of, 50; 119, 121
TAYLOR, JOHN (Husband of Harriet), 110, 111; marries Harriet Hardy, **116–17**; character and appearance of, **118**; 119, 124; fondness for Harriet, 126; 127, 128, 138; told of Harriet's love for Mill, **139–40**; 141; trial separation from Harriet, 142–3, 145–7; compromises, 147–8; 149, 150; capitulates, 151–2; Carlyle's description of, 180; 204, 213, 236, 237, 238, 240, 241; drawn into Hardy family quarrels, 288; asks Carlyle to act as his children's trustee, 288; 289, 292; his interests neglected, 309; disapproves of Mill's dedication of *Political Economy* to Harriet, 309–10; 318; his reputation injured, 320; 321; his tolerance, 327; 328, 329, 330, 331; his fondness for good living, 332; objects to Harriet's visit to France, 332–3; Harriet's sound advice to, 335; death of, **336–8**; gratitude for Harriet's nursing, 337; funeral of, 338–9; Harriet's love for, 343; his steadying influence, 343–4; wills fortune to Harriet, 345; 348, 349; his fondness for Mill's brother George, 352; 450
TAYLOR, MARY (Daughter of Algernon), 412 n., cares for Helen Taylor, 413, 420
TAYLOR, P. A., 457, 470
TAYLOR, MRS. P. A., 493, 497, 498
TENNYSON, ALFRED, 20, 99, 134; J. S. Mill's article, **199**; 469
TERRY, ELLEN, 505 n.
TEUFELSDROCKH, PROFESSOR, 158; his existence doubted, 168; 184
THACKERAY, W. M., 194, 215
THEOCRITUS, 376
Theodor Gomperz, Briefe und Aufzeichnungen, 429 n.
THERMOPYLAE, 379
THIRLWALL, CONNOP (later Bishop), 69, 219, 287
THOMPSON, COLONEL PERRONET, 64, 96, 102, **194**, 217
THOMPSON, WILLIAM. *See* OWENITES
THOMSON, THOMAS, 6, 28–9, 32, 55
THORNTON, WILLIAM, 382; Mill undertakes his work, 387; 390; presents inkstand to Mill, 391; 398, 420, 425; describes Mill's life in Avignon, 428; 429, 430, 476; discredits Wage Fund theory, 488
Thoughts on Parliamentary Reform, a political corollary to the *Liberty*, 414; educational qualifications for voting, **414–15**; open voting, 415; 450
THREADNEEDLE STREET, 68, 74, 106
Three Essays on Religion, 368 n., **442–3**; 477
"THUNDERER" of *The Times* (Father of John Sterling), 85, 272
Times, The, chilly obituary of Mill, 58; 72 n.; 62; "Thunderer" of, 85; 215 n.; Mill's poor opinion of, 322; 335; notice of Mill's marriage, 350; 375; notice of Harriet's death, 398; 424, 425, 435, 473; 499
TOCQUEVILLE, ALEXIS DE, **199–204**; Harriet's opinion of, 338; influence on the *Liberty*, 401
TOLERATION, Harriet's article on, 134, 203, 400
TOLPUDDLE MARTYRS, 224
To Married Working People, 56
TOMB (of Harriet, at Avignon), **407–8**, **411–12**; Mill visits daily, 428; Amberley admires, 434; 476, 507; Mill buried in it, 508
TOM THUMB, GENERAL, 370
TOOKE, THOMAS, 52
TOOKE, WILLIAM EYTON, 52, 62, 76, 90, 93, **95**, 108
TORIES, THE, 38, 60–3, 71; Coleridge best representative of, 84; 191, 192, 193, 212; Tory gain on accession of young Queen, 215; 221, 226; attitude to Durham, 229–32; 235, 246, 309, 323, 389, 403, 414; machinations against United States, 425; 449; afraid of Mill, 452; "the stupid party", 454–5; appeal to Mill to prevent revolution, 457, 459; their ingratitude, 461; 471, 472; defeat Mill at election, 473; 502
TORQUAY, 284, 374, 382, 412 n., 413
TORRENS, COLONEL ROBERT, 53
TORRENS, W. T. M., 457
TORRIJOS, GENERAL, 99, 131
TOULOUSE, 42, 43, 44, 336
TOWNSHEND, PROFESSOR, 49
TRADE UNIONS, Grand National Consolidated, 224; 235, 403, 478, 489–90
TRAFALGAR SQUARE, 370, 458
Traité de Législation. *See* DUMONT
Translators of Faust, 209 n.
TRANSPORTATION, 101, 224; Committee's report on, 225
TRANT, WILLIAM, 448 n.
Traveller, The, 53
TRAVERS, JOHN INGRAM, appointed trustee for Harriet Taylor's children, 289
TRAVERS, JOSEPH (Brother-in-law of John Taylor), 288, 289
TRENCH, R. C., 99

TRENT AFFAIR, 424
TREVELYAN, G. M., 56 n.
TREVELYAN, G. O., Mill's support, 368
TRINITY COLLEGE, CAMBRIDGE, 19, 49, 255, 458
True Sun, The, 209
TUSSAUD, MME., 222
TYNDALL, JOHN, 434
TYRANNY (by Majority Rule), **202–3**, 401–2

UNDERHILL, DR., 466
UNDERWOOD, MR., SCHOOL OF, Taylor boys attend, 329; Mill takes German, 329
UNITARIANS, 62, Harriet and John Taylor, 116; 118, 119, **120–3**; influence of W. J. Fox, 120–1; Harriet's intimacy with *Repository* contributors, 123–6; **127**, 148–9
UNITED STATES, 180; de Tocqueville on, **200–1**, 202, 203; 228; 229, 231, 233, 299, 329, 358, 384, 417, 418; Mill's opinion on the Civil War, **423–7**; 438, 462; 464; Chinese coolie labour, 479; 480; Mill on American education, 482; 496, 499
UNIVERSITY COLLEGE. *See* LONDON, UNIVERSITY OF
Unto this Last, 310
USIGLIO, Italian Patriot, 236
UTILITARIANS(–ISM), BENTHAMITES(–ISM), 31, 49, 51, 52; origin of word, **53** n.; James Mill defines creed, 62; 69; Macaulay's attack on, 88–90; 98, **101–2**, 120; their relation to Unitarians, **127**; 131; Carlyle on, 168, 169; 173; their mistrust of Carlyle, 177; John Mill revises creed, **197–8**, **420–2**; narrowness of, 212–14, 223; end of their political importance, 235; Mill's comparison with Coleridge, **244–6**; 261, 267; their logic, **268–9**; their political economy, **296–7**; 401, 432
Utilitarianism, 368, 369 n., **401**; ethical doctrine and publication of, **420–2**
Utilitarianism Unmasked, 18
UTILITARIAN SOCIETY, formation of, 53; meeting described, 67; end of, 68, 74; 102

VAUCLUSE (Department of), 485; Mill's botanical specimens, 486; Flora of, 488
—(Valley of), 375, 428
VAUX, CLOTHILDE DE, 138, 279
VENICE, 240, 507
VENTNOR (Isle of Wight), 285
VENTOUX, MONT, 475, 485
VENUS CALLIPYGE, 376
—DE MEDICI, 376; Mill's opinion, of, 381
VÉRAN, JULES, 485
VERONA, 381
Vestiges of Creation, 270 n.
VICTORIA, QUEEN, 215, 227, message to Durham, 230; 236, 365, 388, 407, 458, 463, 464, 466, 468, 481
VICTORIA AND ALBERT MUSEUM, 136 n.
VICTORIA STREET (10 Albert Mansions), 454 n., 505
VIENNA, 428, 429
VIGNY, ALFRED DE, Mill's article, 218
VILLARI, PASQUALE, 358, 381, 390 n., 407, 491; Mill on growth of women's suffrage, 494
VILLIERS, CHARLES AND HYDE, 52, 70, 106; Charles' wit, 109
VIRGIL, 477
Vivia Perpetua, 122
VOLTAIRE, 6, 43, 80, 160, 174, 274

WADE, JOHN, 61
WAKEFIELD, EDWARD GIBBON, **224**, 225, 228; Durham's Canadian mission, 229; assists with Durham's report on Canada, 232, 238
WAGE FUND THEORY, 38, 300; Mill later admits error on, 302; Thornton's book discredits, 488
WAKLEY, DR., 192
WALLAS, GRAHAM, 56
WALPOLE, SPENCER, 459, 460, 462
WALWORTH, Home of Hardy family, 115, 116, 149, 151
WAR, 303; Crimean, 387; Mill on American Civil War, 423–7; National Conscript Army, 437; Amberley's League, 438 n.; Mill against disarmament, flogging and purchase of commissions, 449; Mill on need of British Navy, 456; Mill's article against war with Russia, 478; Mill's views on Peace societies, 483; Mill on Prussians, 504
WARBURTON, HENRY, 192
Watchman, What of the Night? 127
WATTS, GEORGE FREDERICK, 505, 505 n.
WALTON-ON-THAMES, Harriet's second country cottage, 151; 151 n.; moves to in 1839, 241; Carlyle visits, 288; Harriet lives as an invalid at, 289; Helen's love for, 292; 306; Harriet on relationship with Mill, 317, 318; no mention of Mill in Helen's diary, 321; Austins and Guizots settle near, 323; George Mill visits, 329; 330; spoiled by new cottages and Austins nearby, 331, 334, 335
WELLINGTON, DUKE OF, 54, 101, 102
WELSH, JANE BAILLIE. *See* CARLYLE, JANE WELSH
WELSH, MRS. (Mother of Jane Welsh Carlyle), 162, 165
WESLEYAN MISSION, 119
WEST INDIES, 100, 108, 131, 183, 469
WEST, JULIUS, 489 n.
WESTMINSTER, mob, 12; Jeremy Bentham's home, Queen Square Place, 16; Mills move to 1 Queen Square, 26; 36, 46; James Mill moves from, 104; 460, 461

WESTMINSTER ABBEY, 56, 72 n., 330, 437, Grote's burial, 505
WESTMINSTER, BOROUGH OF, Election of 1810, 31; James Mill in control of, 102; 193, 213, 436, 438; Mill asked to stand for, 446; his terms, 447; his policies, 449; his speech to working people, 450; his election, 451; 454, 470; Mill stands again, 473; his defeat, 473; 475
WESTMINSTER CITY HALL, 505 n.
WESTMINSTER ELECTION COMMITTEE (of Mill), 447, 449, 450, 458 n., 474
Westminster Review, The (1824–1836), 54; Jeremy Bentham finances, 62; first number James Mill on *Edinburgh*, 62; John Mill heavy contributor, 63; James Mill on *Quarterly*, 83; dissension with Bowring, 64; 74, 82, 89; 102, 127, 177; Perronet Thompson's difficulties with, 194; bought by the *London Review*, 209; 214, 217, 446
Westminster Review, The (1840–), 272; Mill on Comte, 280; 284, 293; Mill's defence of Revolution of 1848, 323; Harriet's *Enfranchisement of Women*, 347; Mill's last article on Whewell, 359; 370, 422; Mill on the *Slave Power*, 425; 445, 478
WESTMINSTER SCHOOL, 19, 23, 194
WEYBRIDGE, 323
WHATELY, DR., 65, 69
What is Love? 58
What is Poetry? Mill's article in *Monthly Repository*, 134
WHEWELL, DR. WILLIAM, Mill's dissensions from, in *Logic*, 255, 256; 260, 264, 270, 272, 346; Mill's estimate of, 359; 425, 445
WHIGS, THE, 12, 29, 38, 53, **59–62**, 88, 102; Reformed Parliament, 191, 192, 193, 195, 212, 213, 215, 224, 226, 229, 230, 231, 232; against Durham, 233; 234, 235, 388, 389
WHITE, JOSEPH BLANCO, 217
WILBERFORCE, SAMUEL, 70, 219, 264
WILSON, DAVID ALEC, 315, 318, 325, 326 n.; on Harriet Taylor, 328
WILTON PLACE (London), 240
WOMEN'S POSITION, John Mill's first statements on, 63; 80, 80 n.; Macaulay on one half of human race, 89; John Mill adopts Macaulay's ideas, 90; St. Simonian views on, 93–4; "la femme libre", 97; 109, 121, 124; Harriet on, 125; Harriet and John Mill on, 137, 138; Carlyle's attitude to, 181; 202; female authors, 218; Comte and Mill dispute over, 276–7; 295, 311 n., 312, 318, 319; Harriet's article, 347; 415; Married Women's Property Act, 455; 481; in United States, 493; publication of *Subjection of Women*, 494; **495–9**; Mill's immense influence on, 500; Contagious Diseases Act, 501–3
WOMEN'S SUFFRAGE, early proposal of vote, 80 n., 152; Women's Rights Convention, 347; Harriet's *Enfranchisement*, 347; 413, 448, 457, 460, 478, 480; Mill in Parliament, 492; Society activities, 497–9; women admitted to local elections, 500; Women's Suffrage Act, carried first reading in 1870, 500; later readings, 501
WOMEN'S SUFFRAGE SOCIETY, principal recipients of Mill's charitable donations, 484; formed, **492–3**; General and Executive Committees organized by Mill and Helen, 493; whole existence of Society due to Helen, 497; meeting at Stoke-on-Trent, 497; meeting in Hanover Square, 498; Kate Amberley's meetings at Stroud and Bristol, 499
WOOLER, THOMAS JONATHAN, 58
WORDSWORTH, DR. (Brother of William Wordsworth), 255
WORDSWORTH, WILLIAM, 25; Mill's discovery of, 81–2; Mill meets, 107; 108; Mill calls on, 131; 152, 170, 255, 261
WORKMEN, BRITISH, 31, 224; Mill's opinions on, 298; Rochdale Pioneers, 308; and again, 311; 417, 424, 448 n.; Mill's speech to voteless workers of Westminster, 450, 451; demonstration over Reform and closing Hyde Park, **458–9**; Reform League Council meeting, 460; mass meeting Islington, **460–1**; meeting at St. James' Hall, 463; Mill's support for Parliament seats, 473, 476; 484, 488, 489, 491
WORTHING, Harriet Taylor's stay at, 332
WRIGHT, CHAUNCEY, 497
WRITER'S SOCIETY, NEOPHYTE, Mill's opinion on writers and writing, 483, 484
Written at Daybreak, 124
WYATT, DIGBY, 391
WYSE, SIR THOMAS, 379

XENOPHON, 20

YORKSHIRE, 115, 116, 241, 333
YOUNG, ARTHUR, on property, 299

ZANTE, 378
ZOO (LONDON), 237